Communications
in Computer and Information Science 722

Commenced Publication in 2007
Founding and Former Series Editors:
Alfredo Cuzzocrea, Dominik Ślęzak, and Xiaokang Yang

More information about this series at http://www.springer.com/series/7899

Javier Bajo · Zita Vale
Kasper Hallenborg · Ana Paula Rocha
Philippe Mathieu · Pawel Pawlewski
Elena Del Val · Paulo Novais
Fernando Lopes · Nestor D. Duque Méndez
Vicente Julián · Johan Holmgren (Eds.)

Highlights of Practical Applications of Cyber-Physical Multi-Agent Systems

International Workshops of PAAMS 2017
Porto, Portugal, June 21–23, 2017
Proceedings

 Springer

Editors

Javier Bajo
Departamento de Inteligencia Artificial
Universidad Politécnica de Madrid
Madrid, Spain

Zita Vale
Polytechnic Institute of Porto
Porto, Portugal

Kasper Hallenborg
University of Southern Denmark
Odense, Denmark

Ana Paula Rocha
University of Porto
Porto, Portugal

Philippe Mathieu
Lille University of Science and Technology
Lille, France

Pawel Pawlewski
Poznan University of Technology
Poznan, Poland

Elena Del Val
Polytechnic University of Valencia
Valencia, Spain

Paulo Novais
University of Minho
Braga, Portugal

Fernando Lopes
National Laboratory of Energy and Geology
Lisbon, Portugal

Nestor D. Duque Méndez
National University of Colombia
Manizales, Caldas
Colombia

Vicente Julián
Polytechnic University of Valencia
Valencia, Spain

Johan Holmgren
Malmö University
Malmo, Sweden

ISSN 1865-0929   ISSN 1865-0937   (electronic)
Communications in Computer and Information Science
ISBN 978-3-319-60284-4   ISBN 978-3-319-60285-1   (eBook)
DOI 10.1007/978-3-319-60285-1

Library of Congress Control Number: 2017943000

Printed on acid-free paper

This Springer imprint is published by Springer Nature
The registered company is Springer International Publishing AG
The registered company address is: Gewerbestrasse 11, 6330 Cham, Switzerland

Preface

The PAAMS Workshops complement the regular program with new or emerging trends of particular interest connected to multi-agent systems.

PAAMS, the International Conference on Practical Applications of Agents and Multi-Agent Systems, is an evolution of the International Workshop on Practical Applications of Agents and Multi-Agent Systems. PAAMS is an international yearly event in which to present, to discuss, and to disseminate the latest developments and the most important outcomes related to real-world applications. It provides a unique opportunity to bring multi-disciplinary experts, academics, and practitioners together to exchange their experience in the development of agents and multi-agent systems.

This volume presents the papers that were accepted in the workshops during the 2017 edition of PAAMS: Workshop on Agent-Based Applications for Air Transport and Application of Agents to Passenger Transport; Workshop on Agent-based Artificial Markets Computational Economics; Workshop on Agents and Multi-agent Systems for AAL and e-HEALTH; Workshop on Agent-Based Solutions for Manufacturing and Supply Chain; Workshop on MAS for Complex Networks and Social Computation; Workshop on Decision Making in Dynamic Information Environments; Workshop on Multi-agent-Based Applications for Smart Grids and Sustainable Energy Systems; Workshop on Multi-agent System-Based Learning Environments; Workshop on Smart Cities and Intelligent Agents. Each paper submitted to the PAAMS workshops went through a stringent peer review by three members of the international committee of each workshop. From the 80 submissions received, 41 were selected for presentation at the conference.

We would like to thank all the contributing authors, the members of the Program Committee, the sponsors (IEEE SMC Spain, IBM, AEPIA, AFIA, APPIA, Universidad Politécnica de Madrid, Polytechnic Institute of Porto, and CNRS), and the Organizing Committee for their hard and highly valuable work. Their work contributed to the success of the PAAMS 2017 event. Thanks for your help – PAAMS 2017 would not exist without your contribution.

This work was supported by the Spanish Ministry of Economy, Industry and Competitiveness (I+D+i Project Ref. TIN2015-65515-C4-3-R – SURF: Self-organizing sensors and biometrics architecture for dynamic vehicle control in smart cities).

May 2017   Javier Bajo
                                                                      Zita Vale

Organization

Workshops

W1 – Workshop on Agent-Based Applications for Air Transport and Application of Agents to Passenger Transport

W2 – Workshop on Agent-Based Artificial Markets Computational Economics

W3 – Workshop on Agents and Multi-agent Systems for AAL and e-HEALTH

W4 – Workshop on Agent-Based Solutions for Manufacturing and Supply Chain

W5 – Workshop on MAS for Complex Networks and Social Computation

W6 – Workshop on Decision-Making in Dynamic Information Environments

W7 – Workshop on Multi-agent-Based Applications for Smart Grids and Sustainable Energy Systems

W8 – Workshop on Multi-agent System-Based Learning Environments

W9 – Workshop on Smart Cities and Intelligent Agents

Workshop on Agent Based Applications for Air Transport and Application of Agents to Passenger Transport

Program Committee Chairs

Ana Paula Rocha	LIACC, University of Porto, Portugal
António Castro	University of Porto and TAP Portugal, Portugal
Jan A. Persson	Malmö University, Sweden
Johan Holmgren	Malmö University, Sweden
Kai Nagel	TU Berlin Sekr. SG 12, Germany

Program Committee

Alexei Sharpanskykh	Delft University of Technology, The Netherlands
Andrew Cook	University of Westminster, UK
Daniel Silva	University of Porto, Portugal
Elisabete Arsenio	LNEC, Portugal
Henk Blom	Delft University of Technology, The Netherlands
Jorge Silva	University of Beira Interior, Portugal
Lorenzo Castelli	University of Trieste, Italy
Pernilla Ulfvengren	KTH, The Netherlands
Ricardo Hoar	Mont Royal University, Canada
Rodrigo Ventura	IST, Portugal
Rosaldo Rossetti	University of Porto, Portugal
Yang Gao	University of Surrey, UK
Ana Bazzan	Federal University of Rio Grande do Sul, Brazil
Armando Bazzani	University of Bologna, Italy
Gunnar Flötteröd	KTH Royal Institute of Technology, Sweden

Jan A. Persson   Malmö University, Sweden
Johan Holmgren   Malmö University, Sweden
John Polak   Imperial College London, UK
Kai Nagel   Technische Universität Berlin, Germany
Kay W. Axhausen   ETH Zürich, Switzerland
Luk Knapen   Hasselt University, Belgium
Martin Kagerbauer   Karlsruhe Institute of Technology, Germany
Oded Cats   Delft University of Technology, The Netherlands
Peter Vortisch   Karlsruhe Institute of Technology, Germany
Peter Vovsha   WSP|Parsons Brinckerhoff, USA
Rolf Moeckel   Technische Universität München, Germany
Stephane Galland   Université de Technologie de Belfort-Montbéliard,
                             France

Workshop on Agent-Based Artificial Markets Computational Economics

Program Committee Chairs

Philippe Mathieu (Co-chair) Université des Sciences et Technologies de Lille,
                             France
Shu-Heng Chen (Co-chair)   National Chengchi University, Taiwan

Program Committee

Jasmina Arifovic   Simon Fraser University, Canada
Javier Arroyo   University Complutense of Madrid, Spain
Yuji Aruka   Chou University, Japan
Bruno Beaufils   University of Lille1, France
Hugues Bersini   Université libre de Bruxelles, Belgium
Olivier Brandouy   University of Bordeaux IV, France
Shu-Heng Chen   National Chengchi University, Taipei
Siew Ann Cheong   Nanyang Technological University, Singapore
Florian Hauser   University of Innsbruck, Austria
Duk Hee Lee   Korea Advanced Institute of Science and Technology,
                             South Korea
Philippe Mathieu   University of Lille1, France
Adolfo López Paredes   University of Valladolid, Spain
Paolo Pellizzari   Ca'Foscari University of Venice, Italy
Ragu Pathy   Goldsmiths, University of London, UK
Marco Raberto   University of Genoa, Italy
Roger Waldeck   Telecom Bretagne, France
Murat Yildizoglu   University of Bordeaux IV, France
Freiderike Wall   Alpen-Adria Universität, Klagenfurt Austria
Ling Xue   Peking University, China

Workshop on Agents and Multi-agent Systems for AAL and e-Health

Program Committee Chairs

Kasper Hallenborg (Co-chair)	University of Southern Denmark, Denmark
Sylvain Giroux (Co-chair)	University of Sherbrooke, Canada

Program Committee

Juan M. Corchado	University of Salamanca, Spain
Javier Bajo	Technical University of Madrid, Spain
Juan F. De Paz	University of Salamanca, Spain
Sara Rodríguez	University of Salamanca, Spain
Valerie Camps	Paul Sabatier University of Toulouse, France
Cristian I. Pinzón	Technical University of Panama, Panama
Sigeru Omatu	Osaka Institute of Technology, Japan
Paulo Novais	University of Minho, Portugal
Luis F. Castillo	University of Caldas, Colombia
Florentino Fernandez	University of Vigo, Spain
Belén Pérez Lancho	University of Salamanca, Spain
Jesús García Herrero	Carlos III University of Madrid, Spain
Helena Lindgren	University of Umea, Sweden
Goretti Marreiros	Instituto Superior de Engenharia do Porto, Portugal
Gaetano Carmelo La Delfa	University of Catania, Italy
Tiancheng Li	Northwestern Polytechnical University, China

Workshop on Agent-Based Solutions for Manufacturing and Supply Chain

Program Committee Chairs

Pawel Pawlewski	Poznan University of Technology, Poland
Patrycja Hoffa	Poznan University of Technology, Poland

Program Committee

Zbigniew J. Pasek	IMSE/University of Windsor, Canada
Paul-Eric Dossou	ICAM Vendee, France
Grzegorz Bocewicz	Koszalin University of Technology, Poland
Paweł Sitek	Kielce University of Technology, Poland
Izabela E. Nielsen	Aalborg University, Denmark
Peter Nielsen	Aalborg University, Denmark
Allen Greenwood	Mississippi State University, USA

Workshop on MAS for Complex Networks and Social Computation

Program Committee Chairs

Vicente Botti	Universitat Politècnica de València, Spain
Miguel Rebollo	Universitat Politècnica de València, Spain
Elena Del Val	Universitat Politècnica de València, Spain

Program Committee

Angelo Costa	Universidade do Minho, Portugal
Daniel Villatoro	Vodafone, UK
Carlos Carrascosa	Universidad Politécnica de Valencia (UPV), Spain
Francisco Grimaldo	Universitat de València, Spain
Katarzyna Musial-Gabrys	Bournemouth University, UK
Vicente Julián	Universidad Politécnica de Valencia (UPV), Spain
Guillem Martínez	Universitat de València, Spain
Alberto Palomares	Universidad Politécnica de Valencia (UPV), Spain
Victor Sanchez Anguix	Coventry University, UK

Workshop on Decision-Making in Dynamic Information Environments

Program Committee Chairs

Tiago Oliveira	Universidade do Minho, Portugal
Jose Carlos Montoya	Universidad Carlos III, Spain
Paulo Novais	Universidade do Minho, Portugal
Ken Satoh	National Institute of Informatics, Japan

Program Committee

Ângelo Costa	University of Minho, Portugal
Claudia Schulz	Imperial College London, UK
Davide Carneiro	University of Minho, Portugal
Goreti Marreiros	Polytechnic of Porto, Portugal
Hiroshi Hosobe	Hosei University, Japan
José Neves	University of Minho, Portugal
Jason J. Jung	Chung-Ang University, South Korea
Javier Bajo	Technical University of Madrid, Spain
Kristijonas Cyras	Imperial College London, UK
Paulo Moura Oliveira	University of Trás-os-Montes e Alto Douro, Portugal
Pedro Henriques	University of Minho, Portugal
Randy Goebel	University of Alberta, Canada
Tony Ribeiro	Ecole Centrale de Nantes IRCCyN, France
Vicente Julián	Valencia University of Technology, Spain
Fábio Silva	University of Minho, Spain
Igor Kotenko	Laboratory of Computer Security Problems, Russia

Brahim Ouhbi	Ensam-Meknès University, Morocco
Nuno Silva	Polytechnic of Porto, Portugal
Vali Derhami	Yazd University, Iran
Antonio Fernández Caballero	Universidad de Castilla-La Mancha, Spain
Ryuta Arisaka	National Institute of Informatics, Japan

Workshop on Multi-agent-Based Applications for Smart Grids and Sustainable Energy Systems Committee

Program Committee Chairs

Fernando Lopes	LNEG National Research Institute, Portugal
Roozbeh Morsali	Swinburne University - Melbourne, Australia
Rainer Unland	University of Duisburg-Essen, Germany

Program Committee

Anke Weidlich	Offenburg University, Germany
Christian Derksen	Universität Duisburg-Essen, Germany
Costin Badica	University of Craiova, Romania
David Sislak	CTU in Prague, Czech Republic
Fernando Lopes	LNEG National Research Institute, Portugal
Georg Frey	Saarland University, Germany
Giancarlo Fortino	Università della Calabria, Italy
Helder Coelho	University of Lisbon, Portugal
Hugo Morais	Denmark Technical University, Denmark
Jan Treur	Vrije Universiteit Amsterdam, The Netherlands
Lars Braubach	University of Hamburg, Germany
Lars Monch	University of Hagen, Germany
Marcin Paprzycki	Polish Academy of Sciences, Poland
Matthias Klusch	Research Center for AI (DFKI), Germany
Nir Oren	University of Aberdeen, UK
Olivier Boissier	ENS Mines Saint-Etienne, France
Peter Palensky	TU Delft, The Netherlands
Rainer Unland	University of Duisburg-Essen, Germany
Ryszard Kowalczyk	Swinburne University of Technology, Australia
Sascha Ossowski	University Rey Juan Carlos, Spain
Zita Vale	Polytechnic Institute of Porto, Portugal
Bo Norregaard Jorgensen	University of Southern Denmark, Denmark
Hugo Algarvio	Technical University of Lisbon, Portugal
Nick Bassiliades	Aristotle University of Thessaloniki, Greece
Tiago Pinto	University of Salamanca, Spain

Workshop on Multi-agent System-Based Learning Environments

Program Committee Chairs

Ricardo Azambuja Silveira   Universidade Federal de Santa Catarina, Brazil
Rosa Vicari   Universidade Federal do Rio Grande do Sul – UFRGS,
    Brazil
Néstor Darío Duque   Universidad Nacional de Colombia, Colombia
Méndez

Program Committee

Néstor Darío Duque   Universidad Nacional de Colombia, Colombia
Méndez
Ricardo Silveira   UFSC, Brazil
Ana Belén Gil González   University of Salamanca, Spain
Jose Cascalho   Universidade dos Azores, Portugal
Rosa Vicari   UFRGS, Brazil
Demetrio Arturo Ovalle   Universidad Nacional de Colombia - Sede Medellín,
Carranza   Colombia
Marta Rosecler Bez   UFRGS, Brazil
Ramon Fabregat   Universitat de Girona, Spain
Silvia Margarita Baldiris   Universitat de Girona, Spain
Navarro
Tiago Primo   Samsung Research Institute, Brazil
Martin Llamas-Nistal   University of Vigo, Spain
Fernando De La Prieta   University of Salamanca, Spain
María N. Moreno García   University of Salamanca, Spain
Patricia Jaques   UNISINOS, Brazil
Júlia M.C. Silva   Instituto Federal do Rio Grande do Sul, Brazil
Rosangela Bez   SAMSUNG Research Institute, Brazil
Fernando Koch   SAMSUNG Research Institute, Brazil
Vicente Julian Inglada   Universidad Politecnica de Valencia, Spain
Fernando Moreira   Universidad PortoCalense, Portugal
Juan Pavón   Universidad Complutense Madrid, Spain
Angela Cristina Carrillo   Universidad Javeriana, Colombia
Ramos

Workshop on Smart Cities and Intelligent Agents Committee

Program Committee Chairs

Vicente Julián   Universitat Politècnica de València, Spain
Adriana Giret   Universitat Politècnica de València, Spain
Juan Manuel Corchado   Universidad de Salamanca, Spain
Alberto Fernández   Universidad Rey Juan Carlos, Spain
Holger Billhardt   Universidad Rey Juan Carlos, Spain
Javier Bajo   Universidad Politécnica de Madrid, Spain

Program Committee

Adriana Giret	Universidad Politécnica de Valencia, Spain
Alberto Fernández	Rey Juan Carlos University, Spain
Fabio Carrera	Worcester Polytechnic Institute, UK
Holger Billhardt	Rey Juan Carlos University, Spain
Javier Bajo	Universidad Politécnica de Madrid, Spain
Juan Manuel Corchado	Universidad de Salamanca, Spain
Jürgen Dunkel	Hannover University of Applied Sciences and Arts, Germany
Kuldar Taveter	Tallinn University of Technology, Estonia
Michael Batty	University College London, UK
Paul Davidsson	Malmö University, Sweden
Ryszard Kowalczyk	Swinburne University of Technology, Australia
Rosaldo Rossetti	Universidade do Porto, Portugal
Sascha Ossowski	Rey Juan Carlos, University, Spain
Stéphane Galland	IRTES-SET
Vincent Corruble	Université Pierre et Marie Curie, France
Vicente Julián	Universidad Politécnica de Valencia, France
Ramón Hermoso	University of Zaragoza, Spain
Roberto Centeno	National Distance Education University (UNED)
Marin Lujak	Rey Juan Carlos University, Spain
Angelo Costa	Universidade do Minho, Portugal
Carlos Carrascosa	Universidad Politécnica de Valencia, Spain
Michael Weiss	Carleton University, Canada
Julian Padget	University of Bath, UK
Victor Sanchez-Anguix	Coventry University, UK
Vincent Hilaire	UTBM/IRTES-SET, France

Organizing Committee

Javier Bajo (Chair)	Universidad Politécnica de Madrid, Spain
Zita Vale (Co-chair)	Polytechnic of Porto, Portugal
Brigida Teixeira	Polytechnic of Porto, Portugal
Filipe Sousa	Polytechnic of Porto, Portugal
João Soares	Polytechnic of Porto, Portugal
Luís Conceição	Polytechnic of Porto, Portugal
Luís Gomes	Polytechnic of Porto, Portugal
Nuno Borges	Polytechnic of Porto, Portugal
Sérgio Ramos	Polytechnic of Porto, Portugal
Tiago Sousa	Polytechnic of Porto, Portugal

PAAMS 2017 Sponsors

Contents

CNSC

DeMaDIE

MASGES

MASLE

SCIA

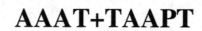

AAAT+TAAPT

Agent Based Model for Hub Operations Cost Reduction

Luis Delgado[1]([⊠]), Jorge Martín[2], Alberto Blanch[2], and Samuel Cristóbal[2]

[1] Department of Planning and Transport, University of Westminster, London, UK
l.delgado@westminster.ac.uk
[2] The Innaxis Foundation and Research Institute, Madrid, Spain
{jm,ab,sc}@innaxis.org

Abstract. Hub operations are complex as not only flight delay but also passengers' connections need to be managed to minimise airlines' operating costs. When facing delayed aircraft, the aircraft operator can speed up incoming flights to the hub to reduce the delay and/or actively delay outbound flights to wait for passengers that would miss their connection, these outbound flights can be speeded up on their turn. This optimisation cannot be carried out in isolation as the system has limited resources that need to be allocated in concurrence with other flights. For this reason, a negotiation process is required. In this context, the use of agent based modelling techniques allows us to describe the behaviour of the different stakeholders in a smooth manner and to analyse complex interactions and the impact of local decisions at network level.

Keywords: Collaborative decision making · Airline delay recovery · Dynamic cost index · Wait for passenger

1 Introduction

Airlines' operations at hubs require maintaining flights on schedule while managing passengers' connections and delay. This paper presents the agent based model (ABM) framework developed for DCI-4HD2D project [14], where a reduction of the total operating cost at a hub is obtained by combining the recovery of delay by modifying the flights' cost index (CI), i.e., increasing the operating speed, which will have an impact on the fuel usage, and by applying wait-for-passengers (WFP) rules on outbound flights, i.e., deciding to actively delay outbound flights at the hub to ensure that connecting passengers do not miss their connections. These strategies have been applied on 2010 traffic environment, on a scenario where ground operations have been improved, which leads to a reduction on the turn-around times, and on a futuristic scenario that combines the ground improvements with SESAR enhancements on the airborne phase. DCI-4HD2D is an extension of one of the cases of study analysed in CASSIOPEIA (Complex Adaptive Systems for Optimisation of Performance in Air Traffic Management) project that was presented in [11].

© Springer International Publishing AG 2017
J. Bajo et al. (Eds.): PAAMS 2017 Workshops, CCIS 722, pp. 3–15, 2017.
DOI: 10.1007/978-3-319-60285-1_1

Current low levels of fuel cost might incentive airlines to use higher cost indexes to recover delay. However, when minimising the total operating cost, other parameters should also be considered, such as, passengers compensation and provision costs (Regulation 261), soft-costs due to negative airline perception, maintenance and crew costs [8,10].

An ABM approach is suitable for this type of modelling due to the high heterogeneity of data required, the diversity of agents and interactions and the negotiations required to deal with limited resources such as arrival slots, which can be handled with an extended arrival manager (E-AMAN) [2]. In this problem there is a smooth alignment of stakeholders to agents and processes.

Our model can be seen as a disruption management problem as it adapts the operations to disturbances experienced in the system [15]. These type of problems have previously been addressed. For example, in [6] the effects of disturbances in all an airline's flights is explored and focus on the coordination between agents when dealing with these disturbances is given in [5]. These studies consider operational and delay costs in a simplified approach (e.g., without passenger compensation). Our model considers more than one airline in the same hub and the allocation of limited resources but is simpler from an agent perspective due to the simulation complexity.

This paper describes the ABM architecture, data management and the processing of the results. The problem modelled is presented in Sect. 2, followed by the cases of study and data sets used (Sect. 3). The ABM is presented in Sect. 4. Section 5 summarises some of the implementation issues. Finally the methodology to process and analyse the results is described in Sect. 6.

2   Problem Description

Cost index represents the relationship between cost of time and cost of fuel used for a given flight. A low cost index instructs the aircraft to follow a trajectory that minimises fuel consumption; while higher values, reduce time at expenses of using more fuel [4]. The concept of dynamic cost indexing (DCI) entails modifying the value of this parameter during the flight considering the current situation [8].

As presented in Fig. 1, when an inbound flight is delayed different CI can be selected. Each possibility recovers different amounts of delays, i.e., the Estimated

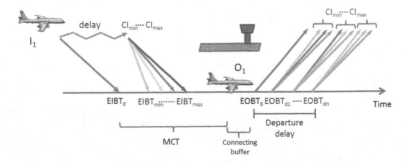

Fig. 1. Diagram of DCI usage

In Block Time (EIBT) of the flight would be modified. Each option involves different costs in terms of fuel and delay. Passengers connections and the minimum connecting time at the hub (MCT) should be considered during this decision. For each outbound flight, different options are also possible. In some cases, the most economical one might involve delaying one or several outbound flights to wait for connecting passengers, i.e., modifying their Estimated Off Block Time (EOBT), and to apply, in their turn, an increment on their CI.

Each inbound flight has a set of outbound flights to which passengers connect (in our dataset, of one day of operations in a hub, each inbound flight has on average connections to 12 outbound flights). Each outbound flight, in its turn, has a set of inbound flights feeding it (13 inbound flights on average in our dataset). From a computational point of view, deciding for each flight the optimal strategy in terms of delay recovery and wait-for-passenger rules is a very complex task. As an example, if 10 possible CI are considered per flight, the number of combinations to be estimated in the order of $\sim 10^{18}$. Moreover, the system has uncertainties and limits on the resources available. Therefore, an ABM architecture is more suitable than an analytical optimal solution.

In the concept of operations modelled in this paper, the Airline Operating Centre (AOC) centralises the decisions for all flights of its airline. It communicates the CI that the flights should use at the different stages and if outbound flights should wait for delayed inbound passengers and for how long. These decisions might change over time.

In general, an E-AMAN leads to reductions on fuel and emissions along with improved en-route capacity [2]. Previous studies have considered the mathematical optimisation of arrivals [12], in this work, a collaborative decision making process to assign slots taking into consideration airlines' preferences is modelled.

Finally, the behaviour of the outbound flights, minutes of waiting and cost index selected, is recomputed each time new information is provided to the AOC. When the outbound flight reaches its top of climb (TOC) a final estimation of its delay and an optimisation of the cost index is carried out.

3   Cases of Study and Datasets

One day of operations in a hub is modelled, this accounts for 676 flights (336 inbound and 340 outbound) and 61,446 individual passengers' itineraries from which 11,570 are connecting at the hub (18.9%), i.e., 73,016 passengers' legs.

Considering four different variables to generate the scenarios, see Table 1, a total of 54 different scenarios are tested. The scenarios are run in a stochastic manner with Monte-Carlo simulations. Each one is executed 50 times requiring a total of 2,700 executions. Kolmogorov-Smirnov tests have been carried out to analyse the similarities between scenarios and Chi^2 tests to test the normality of the results. Confidence intervals of the metrics are used to analyse the relative error and the convergence of the solutions.

As shown in Table 2, there are seven data categories that are required to generate the input for the model: traffic and passengers data to generate the

Table 1. Variables considered to generate scenarios

Variable	Values
Flight database	– 2010 operations
	– Ground improvement: reduction on the minimum turnaround time and on the subsequent flight schedules
	– Ground improvement and SESAR en-route benefits, i.e., direct route from origin to destination
Fuel costs	– Medium
	– High
Optimisation strategies	– Current operations: for 10% of the flights, if estimated delay is greater than 15 min, the flight tries to recover it up to a remaining of 5 min. An outbound flight only waits for connecting passengers if total required waiting time is lower than 20 min and inbound flight with connecting passengers is already speeding up to recover delay
	– Cost optimised strategy: the decision to speed up is based on the estimated total cost. DCI is considered for all delayed flights at top of climb. Costs are assessed for each of the different DCI options and the minimum cost decision taken. The outbound flights wait for connecting passengers based on the overall total costs
	– Cost optimised strategy but with higher uptake of passengers' claims
Initial system delay	– Low
	– Medium
	– High

flight plans and passengers' itineraries; aircraft performances for the estimation of delay recovered with DCI and fuel consumption; regulatory data to model the cost of passengers' compensations and the claim uptake; uncertainty in the system to model stochastic realistic operations; the costs of delay and fuel; and the delay in the system for the flights.

Some data has also been estimated, see Table 3. The reader is referred to [9] for a more detailed description of the different datasets used and the data pre-processing to generate the input for the model.

4   Agent Based Modelling

Figure 2 presents the different agents that are modelled and their interactions. These agents are implemented using Jadex [3,13]. There is a direct mapping

Table 2. Data sources

Category	Data	Source
Traffic data	Flight schedules	PRISME
	Flight trajectories and phases	so6 data file
	Taxi times	Central Flow Management Unit (CFMU) Post-operational data
Passengers data	Passenger itineraries	Anonymised airport data
	Minimum connecting time	Airport data
Aircraft performances	Fuel performances	BADA
	Nominal speeds	BADA
	Effect of CI on trajectory	Airbus Performance Engineering Program (PEP)
Regulation	Passengers' compensation	Regulation 261 Consultation
Uncertainty	Climb and cruise uncertainty	AIRAC 1313-1413 DDR2 data (m1, m3)
	Taxi in and out uncertainty	
Costs	Cost of delay	Consultation
	Cost of fuel	Historical values consultation
Delay	Input delay	Central Office for Delay Analysis (CODA) data Post-operational data

between physical entities and their processes and the agents and roles modelled. The different roles played by the agents are defined as follows:

- Aircraft operator centre (AOC): centralises airlines' decisions.
- Inbound flight (IF): implements the DCI strategy defined by the AOC.
- Outbound flight (OF): implements the WFP and DCI.
- Arrival manager (AMAN): manages arrival traffic to meet the airport arrival capacity by assigning flights to slots based on airlines' requests and priorities.
- Departure manager (DMAN): assigns slots to departing traffic to meet the airport's capacity on a first come first served basis.

Each inbound flight updates its EIBT at different stages during the flight: when reaching the TOC and when entering the action radius of the E-AMAN. At the TOC, the flight communicates its current delay to the AOC (d_i). The AOC assesses the situation and computes the CI that the inbound flight should select (dci_i). For each outbound flight that has connecting passengers with this delayed inbound flight, the AOC reassesses if wait-for-passenger should be implemented (w_j) and the subsequent optimal CI for that outbound flight (dci_j).

When the flight enters the scope of the AMAN, 60 min before the passing time over the initial approach fix, there is a request of arrival slots available to

Table 3. Data estimation

Category	Data	Estimation based on
Traffic data	Taxi times	CFMU taxi times modified Taxi out: flight plan departure with respect to EOBT Taxi in: corrected CFMU with average error considering post-operational data analysis
	Arrival buffers	Schedule with respect to gate-to-gate times
	Minimum turn around time	Based on airline type, wake turbulence of the aircraft and if hub airline
	Turn around buffers	Minimum turn around and flights' registration
	Airport capacity	Arrival and departure planned demand
Aircraft performances	Average cruise wind	Cruise duration and average cruise speed
	Effect of CI on trajectory	Airbus performance engineering program
	Flight level	Analysis of AIRAC 1313-1413 DDR2 data
	Reference average cruise weight	BADA performance analysis at different FL and cruise speeds
	Reference speed	BADA adjusted to be in aircraft envelope
	Minimum and maximum speed	BADA
Regulation	Claim uptake	Consultation
Uncertainty	Climb and cruise uncertainty	Analysis of AIRAC 1313-1413 DDR2 data (m1, m3)
	Taxi uncertainty	CODA delay data and post-operational data
Delay	Departure delay	CODA delay data and post-operational data
Ground improvements	Minimum turnaround time (MTT) reduction	Literature review
	SOBT modifications	Based on MTT reduction
SESAR improvements	FP reduction	Literature review, great circle distance origin to destination

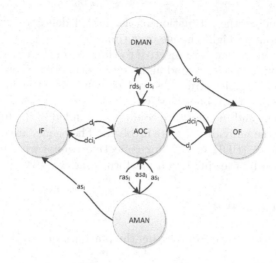

Fig. 2. Diagram of agents and their interactions

the AMAN (asa_i). The AOC prioritises the slots considering the total cost, i.e., analysing the fuel, connections and possible outbound cost index updates, and sends this prioritisation to the AMAN (ras_i). Then the AMAN solves the slot assignment taking into account the requests from all the different flights/aircraft operators within the AMAN scope without slot yet allocated. This allocation is done following a deferred acceptance collaborative decision making model as the one described in [1], and a slot is assigned to the flight (as_i). At this time, the AOC updates the wait-for-passengers and the CI for the outbound flights connected to that inbound flight.

For each outbound flight, the WFP and DCI strategy is updated each time an inbound flight with connecting passenger modifies its EIBT, which might lead to new w_j and dci_j values. However, the outbound flight might be delayed for independent reasons of the WFP strategy (d_j). Each time there is an update on the delay of the outbound flight, the AOC is notified so it can take this information into consideration when following inbound flights are delayed, e.g., there is no need to increase CI for the inbound flight is connections are already ensured because the outbound flight is delayed for other reasons. When the outbound flight is ready for departure, a request of departure slot is submitted to the DMAN (rds_j) which will provide a departure slot (ds_j); and when the outbound flight reaches the TOC, a final update on its CI is carried out by the AOC (d_j and dci_j). With this approach, outbound flights adjust their strategy each time an inbound flight connected to them update their EIBT; and the state of the outbound flights is taken into consideration on the optimisation of subsequent inbound flights. The combination of DCI and WFP selected is the one which provides the minimum expected cost at the time of the assessment.

Finally, in order to model the acquisition of information from the agents in a more realistic manner, adding some uncertainty on the belief of the AOC on the actual departing delay, the estimation of the initial delay for the flights, both inbound and outbound, might change over time.

As described, some agents are reactive to changes in the environment and to requests, e.g., inbound and outbound flight, while others are proactive, analysing the situation, updating the strategies and coordinating the limited resources allocation, e.g., AOC, AMAN and DMAN. The use of ABM allow us to capture complex interactions and the platform could be extended in the future to expand the capabilities of the individual agents involved. The agents are developed using belief-desire-intention (BDI) models for collective agents with implementation methodology driven by the simulation platform (Jadex) [13].

5   Implementation

Different challenges arise when developing the platform due to the characteristics of the agent model.

Heterogeneous Data Sources. As shown in Sect. 3, datasets are heterogeneous and there is a significant effort on parameters' estimation. Consequently, the time required to merge all the sources of data into a single input dataset is high. For this reason, the initial dataset is created, before the run of the simulations, storing the data into a MySQL database. The database keeps the data structured reducing complexity when mapping the tables with simulation objects and reducing the storage requirements by using the right encoding for the different data types. Some of the required pre-processing is human assisted.

High Model Complexity. Several features of the model difficult its implementation. When slots are negotiated within the E-AMAN feedback loops appear, as the decision of one agent affects the resources available for the others, impacting the optimisation of the delay recovery and the waiting-for-passengers. Moreover, the decisions performed when an inbound flight changes its EIBT affect all the other inbound flights that are connected to it through shared outbound flights. Any change experienced by a flight, such as a delay or speed change is publicly available for all the agents involved in the simulation. Finally, agents schedule the time when interactions takes place as a function of the experience delay by the flights. These challenges have been addressed by delegating some responsibilities to the agent simulation platform (Jadex). Jadex simplifies the definition of agents' knowledge (both learnt and perceived) and the triggering of events to simulate agents' behaviour whenever there are interactions or changes in their knowledge. Jadex also provides a discrete event simulation scheduler, used to perform fast time simulations with dynamic scheduling, and an agent awareness module, which supports the agents' communications.

Randomness. Some elements in the agent environment change dynamically during the simulation as they are stochastically modelled, e.g., the amount of slots available, the EIBT of inbound fights, the estimation of delay for outbound flights. The simulation tool delegates on Apache Commons Math library the responsibility of reproducing the required degree of randomness by using pre-implemented probability distributions.

Post-process of Simulation Results. Two different types of results are generated from the model: microscopic results (for model validation and verification) and performance indicators (for quantification of scenarios), see Sect. 6 for more details on the analysis of the results.

Microscopic results, besides the indicators described in Sect. 6, include the options of cost index and waiting for passengers, with their estimated costs, that the AOC evaluated before each decision. These data are stored in a relational database minimising the storage requirements.

Performance indicators include the metrics reported in Sect. 6. Platform performance indicators are generated so they can be aggregated into meaningful metrics. Global indicators are computed, e.g., departure delay, and aggregated, e.g., per airline type. A descriptive analysis is performed using Commons Math library and these performance indicators are stored in CSV files, supported by most data analysis tools such as R, Excel and Matlab.

Reusability and Scalability. The simulation platform aims to be a template for the development of other simulation tools that reproduce air traffic management (ATM) scenarios. The platform design is flexible enough to fit in different project schedules because of its reusability and scalability.

The platform proposes a modular architecture with loosely coupled open source components that can be easily extended or interchanged. Each component can be improved iteratively due to their internal design. For example, the tables used to store performance indicators can be used in different simulation scenarios out-of-the-box, as they are general enough to store different types of metric's values. There is also a decoupling between the pre-processing of the input data in the model, the simulations and the analysis of the results. The model has been tested in different hardware platforms to quantify its performance and scalability. The execution time varies between 4 to 7 min on an Intel Xeon E5 2509 with 16 GB RAM and about the same time in a comparable cloud instance Amazon Web Services (AWS) instance. The platform implementation uses separated threads for storing data in the database and for the agent simulation, so it is possible to run several simulations at the same time with additional threads.

6   Results

For each flight in the model a total of 140 indicators are estimated, e.g., selected speed, actual time when reaching TOC. To facilitate the analysis of the results, a total of 22 performance indicators are computed, e.g., flight departure delay, passenger delay, aircraft operator costs; with different aggregators, e.g., average, percentile 90; applying different restrictors, e.g., all flights, only full service carriers. All these combinations provide us a total of 381 metrics including passengers specific, e.g., gate-to-gate time [7].

The 22 performance indicators are divided into three categories: delay, costs and efficiency. Delay performance indicators are in their turn divided between flight and passenger performance. Costs are considered for the different carriers in the model and for hub and non-hub operators. Finally, to understand the complexity of the scenarios and other parameters, efficiency factors are computed: passenger performance (missed connections), complexity (number of changes on the decisions), emissions and holding times at the AMAN.

6.1 Validation

The model produces micro-level results that are used to generate the macro-level results. From both types of results there are expected values and behaviours that can be a priori defined. The analysis of the discrepancies between the observed results and these expected values are used to improve the model in an iterative process. This incremental process validates the optimisation mechanism and each of the different sub-models: fuel, cost and delay. In some cases, this validation can be done with just the pre-computed input data, e.g., estimated maximum delay recovered and fuel consumption by analysing flight plans and aircraft fuel performance models.

6.2 Statistical Analysis

Relying on average values is not desirable, e.g., the optimisation process might change the distribution of delay experienced by passengers but not significantly the average delay. This could be the case if the number of missed connections decreases, as the number of passengers connecting might not be high enough in comparison with single-leg passengers and hence the average delay might not decrease by much. However, in that case, the values of high passengers' delay (e.g., 90th percentile of passenger delay) might be reduced.

The outputs of the simulation are considered samples of random variables with unknown distribution. Therefore the system needs to be simulated a number of times and a statistical analysis performed in order to consolidate the results. Statistical tests are carried out to consolidate the results and understand the distributions of values that lay underneath, e.g., Chi2 tests to check normality. Confidence interval are computed for the parameters that follow a normal distribution to analyse in which interval a parameter is more likely to be and to estimate if more simulations are required for the convergence of the solutions. Finally, boxplots are generated as they allow us to analyse in which interval the metrics are found and compare in this manner different scenarios.

6.3   Methodology

Due to the high number of metrics computed and the scenario driven approach, a standard methodology of hypothesis testing is used to analyse the results. The methodology consists on setting hypotheses, test them with the metrics obtained from the model, analyse the results and obtain conclusions to learn about the model.

The hypotheses are defined based on team expertise, common knowledge or just formalizing research questions. Only qualitative hypotheses are defined, not needing to make numerical estimates. These hypotheses are divided into three categories: delay, costs and efficiency. An example of the hypothesis is: *Higher claims on passenger compensation might lead to less connections missed and a reduced gate-to-gate time.*

For each of the hypotheses a set of representative metrics are selected along with the scenarios that need to be compared in order to test them. Then ad-hoc reports are generated to compare those metrics and those scenarios. As an example, the metrics and scenarios to be compared for testing the hypothesis previously presented are: *number of missed connections and passengers gate-to-gate time for scenarios where the number of passenger claim in increased with respect to the scenario where the system is optimised but claims are not increased.*

After performing the hypothesis testing, it will be either corroborated (justifying an a priori knowledge), non-corroborated (generating new knowledge which can be unintuitive), or non conclusive where the data can not support nor reject the hypothesis.

Finally, a conclusion is reached with final statements made of confirmed or quantified hypothesis, in some cases reformulated to make more clear remarks.

6.4   Example of Results Obtained

An example of a hypothesis that was able to be validated with the model is that the optimisation strategy reduces operating costs by a small percentage and that an increase on passenger claims increases airline costs. The data analysed shows that there is an average improvement on the operating cost of 0.7% on nominal delay situations and an increase on passenger claiming compensation reduces this benefit. An unintuitive results obtained is that fuel costs affect the number of flights recovering delay but do not modify significantly the passengers' gate-to-gate time. Part of the reason is another unexpected result: when the optimisation is implemented, airlines decide to trade delay for fuel at the AMAN if the delay in the system is not very high. See [9,14] for a complete description of the hypothesis tested and their results in order to expand on results of the project from an air traffic management point of view.

7   Conclusions and Further Work

An ABM model has been designed and implemented to represent operations at a hub where DCI and WFP rules are used with a collaborative E-AMAN. The modelling matches the stakeholders and entities. The optimisation carried out by the aircraft operator centre considers the status of the flights of its airline in the system to select the option that provides a lower estimated cost. The platform is implemented following ABM standards and open source technologies. The high heterogeneity of data the pre-computation required to generate the input for the model represents a significant part of the process. As the output of the simulations are samples of random variables with unknown distribution statistical analysis are required to consolidate the results of the simulations. Moreover, a methodology has been followed based on the definition of hypotheses and tests to extract knowledge from the platform.

Automatic learning techniques could be applied so that the agents can select options that might provide an expected better outcome. This learning process will lead to more distinguished agents and behaviours seeing emergence in terms of strategies to deal with disruptions and delay.

Results show the importance of coordination of decisions, in particular to avoid extra fuel consumption due to speed variations when not required. Waiting for passengers in the hub might be a competitive strategy in some cases. This justify further research on collaborative decision making and on the integration in functional airspace blocks (FAB) which might facilitate the increment of scope of action of E-AMAN systems.

Acknowledgement. This work is co-financed by EUROCONTROL acting on behalf of the SESAR Joint Undertaking (SJU) and the European Union as part of the SESAR Exploratory Research programme. Opinions expressed in this work reflect the authors' views only. EUROCONTROL and/or the SJU shall not be considered liable for them or for any use that may be made of the information contained herein.

References

1. de Arruda Junior, A.C., Weigang, L., Nogueira, K.B.: Enhancement of airport collaborative decision making through applying agent system with matching theory. In: 8th International Workshop on Agents in Traffic and Transportation (2014)
2. Bagieu, S.: SESAR solution development, unpacking SESAR solutions, extended AMAN. In: SESAR Solutions Workshop (2015)
3. Bellifemine, F., Rimassa, G., Poggi, A.: JADE a FIPA-compliant agent framework. In: 4th International Conference on the Practical Applications of Agents and Multi-agent Systems (PAAM 1999), December 1999
4. Boeing: Fuel conservation strategies: cost index explained. Technical report, p. 26 (2007)
5. Bouarfa, S., Blom, H.A., Curran, R.: Agent-based modeling and simulation of coordination by airline operations control. IEEE Trans. Emerg. Topics Comput. **4**(1), 9–20 (2016)
6. Castro, A.: A distributed approach to integrated and dynamic disruption management in airline operations control. Ph.D. thesis, University of Porto, Porto, Portugal (2013)
7. Cook, A., Tanner, G., Cristóbal, S., Zanin, M.: Passenger-oriented enhanced metrics. In: 2nd SESAR Innovation Days, November 2012

8. Cook, A., Tanner, G., Williams, V., Meise, G.: Dynamic cost indexing: managing airline delay cost. J. Air Transp. Manag. **15**(1), 26–35 (2009)
9. Delgado, L., Martín, J., Blanch, A., Cristóbal, S.: Hub operations delay recovery based on cost optimisation. In: 6th SESAR Innovation Days, November 2016
10. European Commission: Regulation (EC) No. 261/2004 of the European Parliament and of the Council of 11 February 2004 establishing common rules on compensation and assistance to passengers in the event of denied boarding and of cancellation or long delay of flights, and repealing Regulation (EEC) No. 295/91 (2004)
11. Molina, M., Carrasco, S., Martin, J.: Agent-based modeling and simulation for the design of the future European air traffic management system: the experience of CASSIOPEIA. In: Corchado, J.M., et al. (eds.) PAAMS 2014. CCIS, vol. 430, pp. 22–33. Springer, Cham (2014). doi:10.1007/978-3-319-07767-3_3
12. Montlaur, A., Delgado, L.: Delay assigment optimization strategies at pre-tactical and tactical levels. In: 6th SESAR Innovation Days, December 2015
13. Pokahr, A., Braubach, L., Lamersdorf, W.: Jadex: implementing a BDI-infrastructure for JADE agents. In: EXP - in Search of Innovation, vol. 3, pp. 76–85 (2003)
14. SESAR Join Undertaking: DCI-4HD2D - D3.2 Final technical report. Technical report (2016)
15. Yu, G., Qi, X.: Disruption Management: Framework, Models and Applications. World Scientific, Singapore (2004)

Argumentation in the Re-accommodation of Airline Passengers Using Mobile Devices

Jorge Lima[1], Ana Paula Rocha[1,2], and Antonio J.M. Castro[2(✉)]

[1] DEI, Faculty of Engineering, University of Porto, Porto, Portugal
[2] LIACC, University of Porto, Porto, Portugal
ajmc@fe.up.pt

Abstract. In an airline company, one of the most important tasks is to control the operational plan, i.e., making sure that flights are executed according to the scheduled plan. When the normal functioning is affected by an unexpected event, disruption management appears in order to solve all possible issues. From aircraft to passenger, operation control centers have to effectively fix all the disrupted parts in the fastest time possible minimizing at the same time further costs. In this paper a mobile application that uses argumentation-based negotiation is introduced, allowing disrupted passengers to actively participate in the re-accommodation process, by interacting with the airline computerized system and without having to contact the airline customer service. This results in higher passenger satisfaction and less operational costs for the airlines.

Keywords: Argumentation · Multi-agent systems · Transportation

1 Introduction

In an airline company, the planning and subsequent monitoring of flights is a complex problem because it involves the consideration of multiple and costly resources and their dependencies. Unexpected events force a change in the previously envisaged plans, making it necessary for some entity to be responsible for the resolution of possible problems that occasional irregularities might cause.

The Operational Control Center (OCC) is the entity that manages the operations of an airline company and its primary objective is to recover from flights delays, minimizing as much as possible their impact in cost. Three major consequences of these irregularities are the delays and cancellation of flights and the loss of transfers of passengers in transit to other destinations.

The resolution of an irregularity usually has three major dimensions: the aircraft and flight schedule, the passengers itinerary and the crew schedule. If one of the affected parts is the passenger, currently he is only informed by the company of an alternative route. If eventually he disagrees with the given solution he must head for the irregularities desk or call the company in order to find another solution.

© Springer International Publishing AG 2017
J. Bajo et al. (Eds.): PAAMS 2017 Workshops, CCIS 722, pp. 16–27, 2017.
DOI: 10.1007/978-3-319-60285-1_2

A balance between the need of minimizing the costs and the importance of increasing the passenger satisfaction, is very important. In the work of Bratu and Barnhart [1] two models were developed that optimize the balance between airline operating costs and passenger costs by identifying flight departure times and cancellation decisions. The first model, named Disrupted Passenger Metric, minimized the sum of operating and disrupted passenger costs. The second model, named Passenger Delay Metric, the delay costs are more accurately computed by explicitly modeling passenger disruptions, recovery options, and delay costs.

Another work on the passenger recovery problem was made by Zhang and Hansen [5]. The authors introduce ground transportation modes as an alternative to the passenger recovery by air during disruptions in hub-and-spoke networks. An integer model with a nonlinear objective function allows to substitute flight legs with other forms of transportation, respecting the ground transportation times. The objectives of the model are aimed at minimizing passenger costs due to delay, cancellation or substitution, as well as minimizing the operating cost of the transportation.

The MASDIMA system (Multi-Agent System for Disruption Management) [2] aims to manage the operation of airlines, monitoring unexpected events that may affect and cause flight delays. It uses software agents where each agent represents a part of the problem including its preference and goals: aircraft, crew and passenger. Another software agent (supervisor) represents the global view of the airline company. Through an automated negotiation process, called Generic Q-Negotiation (GQN), the best integrated solution is chosen according to the global interest of the airline and complying with the time available for arriving to a solution.

These models however do not take into account the passengers personal interests. When offered a proposal the passenger might agree or disagree with it. In case of disagreement the disrupted passenger is obliged to go to the company's irregularities desk in order to see his problems solved in another way. The lack of a personalized solution might decrease the customer satisfaction and therefore the loyalty to the airline company.

As stated by Maher [4] the passenger recovery is generally considered as the final stage in the resolution process, and hence passengers experience unnecessarily large impacts resulting from the referred disruptions making this approaches far from optimal in the disrupted passenger point-of-view.

This paper proposes an approach where it is possible for an active participation of the passenger in the resolution of the problem through a mobile device, arguing with the airline system (e.g. MASDIMA), thereby trying to increase both the satisfaction and the commodity of the customer, minimizing the inherently existing drawbacks, by obtaining a more personalized solution. This approach uses argument-based negotiation [3] as a mechanism for achieving cooperation and agreement between the airline (represented by the computerized system) and the passenger.

On Sect. 2 the passenger problem and resolution is described, including the argumentation algorithm used. On Sect. 3 the experimentation performed using a prototype of the mobile application and results obtained are presented and, finally, in Sect. 4 the conclusions and future work are presented.

2   The Passenger Problem and Resolution

In order to solve the passenger disruption, we propose for an active participation of the passenger in the resolution process through an argumentative process with the airline company. In face of a disruption, the airline disruption management system calculates several possible solutions for the disrupted passenger, each one with possible different costs for the airline. The airline will try to use the solution that minimizes its cost, but at the same time that maximizes the passenger satisfaction. For that, an argumentative process occurs between the two parts, airline company and passenger. Moreover, the passenger can participate in this process using a mobile device, what makes it possible to carry out it remotely and avoids the stress and waste of time of look for the irregularities desk. In order to ensure proper communication between the human passenger (hereinafter referred to simply as Passenger) and the company without the need of human supervision, a software agent representing the airline point of view (hereinafter APA - Airline Passenger Agent) was defined and implemented.

Figure 1 presents the system architecture. In this proposal, we use MASDIMA [2] as the airline disruption management system. It is important to mention that our proposed approach can be integrated with current OCC practices with or without a computerized system.

The passenger uses a *mobile application* to interact with the system (Fig. 2), that enables him to start a discussion with the company regarding its problem without the need of dislocations or any kind of effort besides some clicks on his smartphone. This application will present the passenger with a simple yet intuitive interface allowing this interaction.

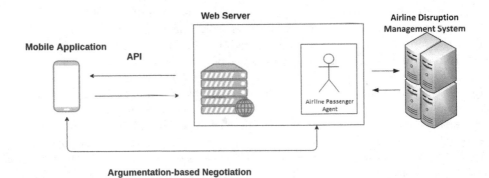

Fig. 1. System architecture.

Fig. 2. Mobile application GUI example.

To ensure proper communication channels between the passenger mobile application and the APA, a *web server* was developed. The web server wraps an agent container which contains the APA. This way it will be able to exchange messages through the exposure of an API (Application Programming Interface). After deciding which message to send, it will be converted to an API request according to its characteristics, providing an adequate communication environment.

The *APA* is the software agent that represents the airline point of view in the resolution process. It will be assigned to each disrupted passenger in order to try to solve his particular problem.

The passenger will exchange messages with APA through a *negotiation protocol based on arguments* such that the resulting solution is according to his preferences. Through the use of argumentation and based on the information the APA has according both to the passenger and the environment he is inserted, it is allowed, in addition to justify more verbally and clearly the choice of a specific proposed solution, find the closest possible solution to the needs and criteria of each affected passenger with minimal cost to the airline. APA will continuously offer new alternatives in case of disagreement with the passenger if the latter presents valid arguments. The passenger will also communicate with APA, agreeing or disagreeing with it through the use of argumentation techniques. Next subsections will describe in more detail each one of these components.

2.1   Airline Passenger Agent

The Airline Passenger Agent is a critical piece of the system since it is the one who will represent the airline company while communicating with the disrupted passenger.

Interaction with the Gateway Agent

The proposed system contains two types of software agents: a Gateway Agent and an Airline Passenger Agent. A diagram showing the interaction between these two agents is depicted in Fig. 3.

The gateway agent is a simple mediator agent, that allows the communication between the airline disruption management system and the server where the APA is located. Its only function is to wait for messages from the passenger and send them to the correct APA. When the gateway agent receives a message from the server, it translates it into an ACL (Agent Communication Language) message defining each performative according to the message received, that is then sent to the specific APA. Table 1 refers to the connection between the received messages from the server and the correspondent ACL message.

Table 1. Correspondence between received messages from API and ACLMessage.

From server (gateway agent)	ACLMessage (airline passenger agent)	
	Performative	Content
Connection intent	INFORM	Connection message
Request alternatives intent	CFP	Request message
Reject alternatives inten	REJECT-PROPOSAL	Arguments message
Accept alternative intent	ACCEPT-PROPOSAL	Selected alternative
Revert claims intent	REQUEST	Claims to remove

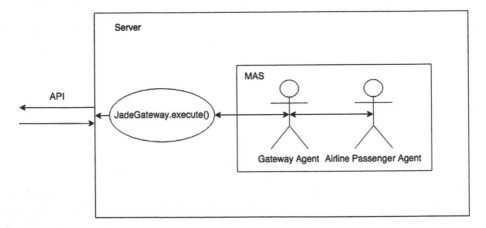

Fig. 3. Gateway agent and airline passenger agent interaction.

Airline Passenger Agent Behaviours

The Airline Passenger Agent is implemented using the JADE framework, that uses a **behaviour** abstraction that allows the developer to personalize the agent to suit his needs. Taking advantage of this, the APA was equipped with four main behaviours: ConnectionBehaviour, ProposeBehaviour, ArgumentBehaviour and RevertClaimBehaviour.

The APA also makes use of a single cyclic behaviour to wait for messages from the Gateway Agent. After evaluating the received message the APA decides which of the main behaviours it should launch to achieve the desired effect. These are described in next paragraphs.

Connection Behaviour. The APA will launch this behaviour when an intent of connection is sent by the passenger (*Connection Intent* in Table 1). It then verifies if there is any disruption affecting that passenger and in a positive case sends him the disruption details finishing afterwards.

Propose Behaviour. This behaviour is triggered when the passenger intends to start the negotiation process (*Request Alternatives Intent* in Table 1). APA sends to the passenger the first four alternatives with the least cost for the airline company. No reasoning is made while obtaining these first alternatives since the passenger has not yet argued.

Argument Behaviour. This behaviour is triggered when APA receives an argument from the passenger justifying his rejection of previous alternatives (*Reject Alternatives Intent* in Table 1). APA analyses the passenger arguments and decides whether or not to send new alternatives. A proper algorithm was developed for that purpose, and it is described in next section.

Revert Claim Behaviour. This behaviour is triggered when the passenger intends to void an already sent claim (*Revert Claims Intent* in Table 1). APA sends to the passenger the best proposals that match the desired claims.

2.2 Argumentation Based Resolution

As stated previously, the use of argumentation will allow a verbose justification for each proposal and counter-proposal made by each participant, either the passenger or the APA. A claim and a reason will compose an argument that will be exchanged along with the rejection of alternatives, allowing the passenger to engage on an argumentation with the APA.

It is through argumentation that the APA and the passenger will negotiate and stand by their point of view until a mutually acceptable conclusion is reached. The APA will start by presenting the passenger with four initial alternatives to his disrupted flight.

After analyzing those alternatives the passenger should decide whether or not to start an argumentation process with the APA by rejecting the presented proposals. In case of acceptance of any of the four initial proposed alternatives, the negotiation process terminates successfully. If not, an iterative argumentative process occurs between the passenger and the APA, until a mutually acceptable conclusion is reached. This last step will be detailed in the remaining of this section. It is important to point out that this process can end up unsuccessfully meaning that no agreement was achieved and the disrupted passenger will have to use the traditional methods to change the final outcome, if he so wishes. A representative diagram of the overall interaction between the passenger and the APA is presented in Fig. 4.

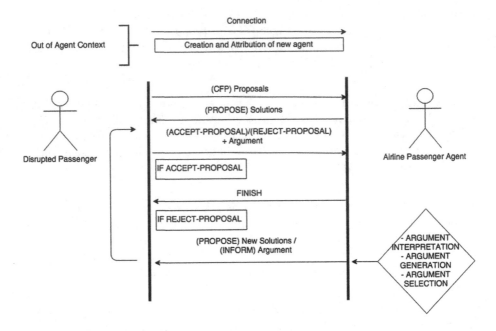

Fig. 4. Argumentation resolution process.

Before starting the description of the argumentation process itself, the argument structure should be defined. The argument is composed by two elements, a claim and a reason, and is represented as a pair $\mathbf{A} = <Claim, Reason>$.

In this scope, the *Claim* represents how and what the disrupted passenger wishes to improve in the previously analyzed alternatives. For instance, the time of arrival being before some date, or the number of transfers being inferior to some number. The *Reason* element represents why the passenger thinks his claims should be approved. It is this reason that should be convincing or persuading enough to change others mental state. The claims and reasons the disrupted passenger can use are limited, since natural language processing is not part of this system at the moment. The defined Claims and Reasons are the following:

- Claims: Time of Arrival, Waiting Time on Transfers, Transfer Location, Number of Transfers.
- Reasons: Personal, Professional, Health.

In this particular scenario, the disrupted passenger will argument about parameters such as those referred above, and the APA will argument on the rejection of the latter. Now that the argument was defined, it is necessary to develop an algorithm that analyzes the arguments received and decides what to do.

The argumentation reasoning by the disrupted passenger will be made solely by himself so the focus in the argumentation process will be on the APA reasoning.

When the disrupted passenger decides to start a negotiation process, a message containing his argument is sent to the server, redirecting this message to the APA assigned to that passenger. This APA will trigger an argument behaviour as referred above and start reasoning about the presented situation. This will not only contain the arguments the disrupted passenger has sent, but also knowledge the APA might have about the latter. The argumentation algorithm is described in listing Algorithm 1.

At first, the APA verifies the arguments veracity by calculating how many times the passenger has sent that argument in that context. If that value is higher than a minimum limit, it then proceeds with the negotiation, rejecting otherwise. Next the APA will check for previous alternatives that match the claims sent so far and add them, if available, to the output array (attack by rebut). Next it will verify if any argument that attacks the received one can be found, returning it if found (attack by undercut). If none of the latter steps is triggered the APA can now move on and find new alternatives that match the desired claims before sending them back to the passenger. An explanation about other methods in the Argument Algorithm follows.

Check Previously Sent Alternatives. This method will verify from all the already sent alternatives all that still match the passenger requirements. The designed algorithm is presented in listing Algorithm 2.

Finding Attacking Arguments. This method will verify if the APA can refute the passenger argument by attacking it. The APA will search in available data for elements that could verify the passenger argument. For instance, searching in the passengers special requests for health and/or professional related requests. The passenger importance is a relevant variable since it will define the range of acceptability of the argument as the APA will soften its aggressiveness based on that importance. The algorithm is presented in listing Algorithm 3.

Algorithm 1. Argumentation Algorithm

Input: Argument
Output: Response

```
1  best = null;
2  if argumentVeracity >= veracityLimit then
3  │   previousAlternatives = checkPreviousAlternatives();
4  │   if previousAlternatives not empty then
5  │   │   best += previousAlternatives;
6  │   end
7  │   args = findAttackingArguments();
8  │   if args is empty then
9  │   │   for Round in roundsSoFar do
10 │   │   │   currentClaims = getCurrentClaims();
11 │   │   │   bAlternatives = findBestAlternatives(currentClaims);
12 │   │   │   best += bAlternatives;
13 │   │   │   Response = best;
14 │   │   end
15 │   else
16 │   │   Response = args;
17 │   end
18 else
19 │   Response = error message;
20 end
```

Algorithm 2. Check Previously Sent Alternatives Algorithm

Input: Argument
Output: Response

```
1  matches = [];
2  if numberOfRounds > 1 then
3  │   for Round in roundsSoFar do
4  │   │   for Alternative in AlternativesSentInRound do
5  │   │   │   for Argument in ArgumentsToClaim do
6  │   │   │   │   if alternativeMatchClaim then
7  │   │   │   │   │   matches += true;
8  │   │   │   │   else
9  │   │   │   │   │   matches += false;
10 │   │   │   │   end
11 │   │   │   end
12 │   │   │   if matches not contains false then
13 │   │   │   │   Response += Alternative;
14 │   │   │   end
15 │   │   end
16 │   end
17 end
```

Algorithm 3. Find Attacking Arguments Algorithm

Input: Argument
Output: Response

```
1  paxIntel = retrievePaxHistory();
2  args = verifyIntel(paxIntel);
3  if args not null then
4  │   Response = null;
5  else
6  │   paxImportance = paxIntel.importance;
7  │   if paxImportance greaterThan importanceLimit then
8  │   │   Result = null;
9  │   else
10 │   │   Result = args;
11 │   end
12 end
```

Find Best Alternatives. The APA will find all the possible alternatives that match the current claims, and add them to the output array in order to send them to the passenger. The alternatives are increasingly ordered by cost for the company, so the first ones are the least cost, and so minimizing the loss of the company at each step. After finishing its reasoning, APA will whether send to the disrupted passenger new alternatives, or a message containing the rejection message and a new round will start.

Reverting Claims. During the negotiation process the disrupted passenger might have the need to rollback some claim in order to see his preferences matched. In this case he could use the revert claim feature that would remove the selected claim from the claims used so far, allowing the disrupted passenger to review his selections in each round of the negotiation.

3   Experiments and Results

To validate our approach, we asked ten passengers to use the mobile application developed during our work and test three different scenarios designed based on real examples provided by an European airline. The idea was to see how many interactions (rounds) were necessary to achieve a solution that suits better the disruptive passenger interest, finishing with the acceptance (or not) of an alternative flight. The scenarios were as follows:

- **Scenario 1**: Passenger with flights AMS-LIS-OPO. Flight AMS-LIS delayed 80 min making the passenger to miss the LIS-OPO flight. In other two previous disruptions the passenger has used personal reasons as an argument to achieve better alternative flights.

- **Scenario 2**: Passenger with flights FRA-LIS-FNC. Flight FRA-LIS delayed 42 min making the passenger miss the LIS-FNC flight. During the check-in the passenger declared health related issues and in previous disruptions the passenger has argued with professional reasons.
- **Scenario 3**: Passenger with flights FCO-LIS-GIG. Flight FCO-LIS delayed 35 min making the passenger to miss the LIS-GIG flight. The passenger is a frequent flyer to Rio de Janeiro (GIG) and in previous disruptions has argued with professional reasons to achieve better alternative flights.

At the end, we asked them to fill a three questions form, evaluating from 1 (Very Bad) to 5 (Very Good) their satisfaction about the solution (alternative flight) and the use of the application. The questions were:

- **Q1**: How good was the final solution proposed?
- **Q2**: How do you classify the use of the application in a daily basis?
- **Q3**: How was the flow of the argumentation process?

Regarding the argument acceptance and number of rounds, Fig. 5 shows the results. As it is possible to see 30% of the proposed solutions were accepted at the first round, without the need for the passenger to argue for a different solution and 63.3% accepted after the second round, having the passengers used professional reason argument in 20% times, personal reasons on 26.7% and health reasons on 16.7% of the times. Only 6.3% required a third round to reach a better alternative flight. Also, the fact that in all experiments the passenger accepted the solution in, at most, the third round, reflects the good performance of the system.

Fig. 5. Argument acceptance vs number of rounds.

Regarding the passenger satisfaction level, Fig. 6 shows the results. As it is possible to see, regarding the quality of the final solution (Q1) they classified as Very Good (80%) and Good (20%). Regarding the use of the application (Q2) most of them classified as Very Good (60%) and Good (30%) and a small percentage as Average (10%). Finally, regarding the flow of the argumentation process, 40% classified as Very Good and 60% as Good.

Although no one classified the application as Bad or Very Bad, there are improvements to be made as we state on the conclusion section.

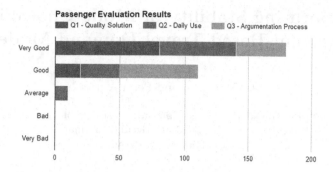

Fig. 6. Evaluation results.

4 Conclusion

The contribution of this paper is twofold. From a more scientific point of view, the proposed argumentation algorithm includes a way of find attacking arguments. Although simple, it includes interesting features such as the verification of argument's veracity, passenger importance and claims reversion.

From the air transport point of view, the application of automated argument based negotiation between a disrupted passenger and a computerized multi-agent system as well as the use of a mobile application by the disrupted passenger to participate in the passenger re-accommodation process, without having to contact the airline company passenger services, contribute to increase the passenger satisfaction and allows the airline to reduce their fixed operational costs.

Regarding future work, the argumentation process could be improved by using machine learning (namely, case based reasoning) and natural language processing, in order to open the range of possible arguments to be used. On the one hand to generate brand new arguments and on the other hand to parse any input the disrupted passenger might use.

References

1. Bratu, S., Barnhart, C.: Flight operations recovery: new approaches considering passenger recovery. J. Sched. **9**(3), 279–298 (2006)
2. Castro, A.J.M., Rocha, A.P., Oliveira, E.: A New Approach for Disruption Management in Airline Operations Control. Studies in Computational Intelligence, vol. 562. Springer, Heidelberg (2014)
3. Kraus, S., Sycara, K., Evenchik, A.: Reaching agreements through argumentation: a logical model and implementation. J. Artif. Intell. **104**(1–2), 1–69 (1998)
4. Maher, S.J.: A novel passenger recovery approach for the integrated airline recovery problem. Comput. Oper. Res. **57**, 123–137 (2015)
5. Zhang, Y., Hansen, M.: Real-time intermodal substitution: strategy for airline recovery from schedule perturbation and for mitigation of airport congestion. Transp. Res. Rec.: J. Transp. Res. Board **2052**, 90–99 (2008)

Incorporating Stability of Mode Choice into an Agent-Based Travel Demand Model

Nicolai Mallig$^{(\boxtimes)}$ and Peter Vortisch

Institute for Transport Studies, Karlsruhe Institute of Technology,
Kaiserstrasse 12, 76131 Karlsruhe, Germany
nicolai.mallig@kit.edu

Abstract. Agent-based modelling is a promising technique, which allows to combine the advantages of different approaches to travel demand modelling. Agent-based modelling provides a framework that allows to easily substitute individual submodels. This paper shows, using the example of mobiTopp, how stability of mode choice can be integrated into an agent-based travel demand model. This has been achieved by replacing the submodel for mode choice by an extended variant, which takes stability of mode choice into account. The improved model reproduces this stability, as measured by two indicators based on mode usage and mobility styles, quite well.

1 Introduction

Traditional approaches to activity-based travel demand modelling are classified as either *utility-maximizing*, *constraint-based*, or *computational process* models [16]. Utility-maximizing models build on the economic concept of a rational decision maker who is confronted with a finite set of alternatives and choose the alternative with the highest utility [17]. Constraint-based models are based on the idea that activities take place in the continuum of space and time. The actual locations where activities can take place are restricted by different constraints [7], especially space-time constraints. Space-time constraints restrict a person's activity space to the locations that are reachable during the available time with the travel-speed of the currently used mode. Computational process models, also known as *rule-based* models, describe a class of models that use heuristics and situation-dependent rules to model the behaviour of the persons. However, in many cases a hybrid approach is used [9].

Agent-based modelling provides an opportunity to integrate different approaches to travel demand modelling. As an agent is defined as a "autonomous decision-making entity" that "individually assesses its situation and makes decisions on the basis of a set of rules" [4], it is possible to use the most appropriate decision model for each situation. This might be a utility-maximization model in case of a mode choice decision or a constraint-based model in case of a destination choice decision.

Another important advantage of agent-based simulation is the handling of time. In a purely utility-based approach, time is often modelled only at a broad

J. Bajo et al. (Eds.): PAAMS 2017 Workshops, CCIS 722, pp. 28–39, 2017.
DOI: 10.1007/978-3-319-60285-1_3

scale, for example using four [5] or five [15] broad time periods. Whereas, in an agent-based approach quasi-continuous time is an integral part of the model. With time as an integral part of the model, it is a minor step to consider not only a simulation period of one day, but a longer period, for example one week. Modelling travel demand over a week implies a longitudinal perspective, where stability of travel behaviour is relevant.

Here, we understand stability of mode choice as repeatedly using the same modes instead of arbitrarily switching between different modes. Different forms of stability can be distinguished based on frequency, number of changes between different modes, or the visibility of a repeated pattern [13]. Other authors have used the terms *habit* [1], *inertia* [19] or *latent modal preference* [18] to describe this effect of repeatedly choosing the same mode.

There exist some approaches to integrate stability into models of activity choice [6], destination choice [1], or mode choice [19], but these models have been primary used for analysis and have not been incorporated into a full-scale travel demand model.

The present work integrates stability of mode choice behaviour into the agent-based travel demand model mobiTopp. For this purpose, two mode choice models have been estimated: a cross-sectional model, which ignores stability, and a longitudinal model, which takes the mode used for the previous trip into account. Two indicators have been defined to measure stability of mode choice behaviour. The results show that the cross-sectional model is not able to reproduce the stability found in the survey data. The longitudinal model can be calibrated to reproduce the stability quite well.

2   The MobiTopp Model

mobiTopp [12] is an agent-based travel demand model, able to simulate travel demand over a period of one week. mobiTopp consists of two parts; one models the aspects that are stable in the long run, the other models the short-term travel behaviour (see Fig. 1). The long-term model consists of population synthesis, assignment of home zone and zone of workplace, and transit pass ownership. These long-term aspects define the framework conditions for the travel demand simulation. The short-term, agent-based, travel demand simulation models the activities, trips, destination choices, and mode choices over the course of the simulation period.

2.1   Long-Term Model

The long-term model consists of modules for population synthesis, activity schedule generation, assignment of fixed destinations for work and school, car ownership, and transit pass ownership. It serves as setup for the short-term model.

The population synthesis module is based on an iterative proportional fitting procedure [3] similar to the procedure described in [14]. In the first stage, an initially equally distributed weight is assigned to each household. These weights

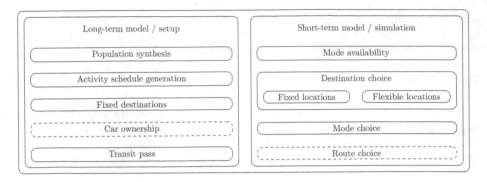

Fig. 1. mobiTopp's overall structure

are iteratively adjusted until the weighted distribution of the households matches the given distribution of the household types and the distribution of the persons, weighted by the corresponding household weights, matches the given marginal distributions of the persons. In the second stage, the corresponding number of household for each household type is randomly drawn with replacement from the survey data, weighted by the weights calculated in the first step. Drawing a household comprises all its attributes including number of cars owned and all members of the household.

In mobiTopp, an activity schedule consists of a sequence of activities. Each activity has the attributes activity type, duration, and planned start. For activity schedule generation, two implementations exist. One of these implementations is very basic; it copies the activity schedules of the corresponding person of the survey. The other implementation is a prototypical implementation of the *actiTopp* approach [10], which generates activity schedules synthetically. For the results presented here, we have use the basic implementation.

For the assignment of workplaces only one implementation exists. This implementation is based on external matrices representing the distribution of workplaces and school places for the inhabitants of each zone. For the current work, the matrices have been taken from an existing VISUM model. Alternatively, results from a land use model could be used. In this implementation, workplaces and school places are assigned to the agents based on these matrices. Agents whose prototypes in the survey have reported long commuting distances are assigned workplaces with long distances from their home zones, while agents whose prototypes reported short commuting distances are assigned workplaces close to their home zones. This ensures that the commuting distance is consistent with the activity program, which is taken from the survey data.

The number of cars a household owns is an attribute of the household. The car ownership model determines the segment and the engine type. A basic implementation always assigns a midsized car and the engine type at random with a given probability for an electric engine.

The transit pass model decides which agent owns a transit pass. The implementation is based on a binary logit model.

2.2   Short-Term Model

During the simulation stage, the travel behaviour of all agents is simulated chronologically and simultaneously for a simulation period of one week. During the simulation period, the agents execute their activity programs. Each agent typically starts the simulation at home. When an agent has finished his current activity, he inspects his activity schedule and identifies the next activity. For this activity, he makes a destination choice followed by a mode choice, taking into account the available modes. Then he makes the trip to the chosen destination using the selected mode. When he reaches the destination, he starts performing the next activity.

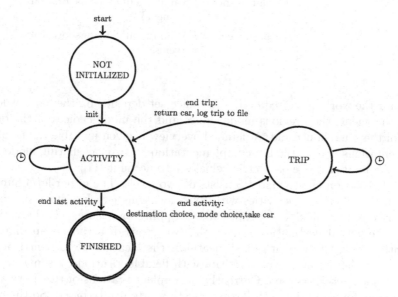

Fig. 2. State diagram describing the behaviour of an agent during mobiTopp's short-term model.

An agent's behaviour can be described as a state diagram (see Fig. 2). The circles denote states and the arrows denote transitions between states. The clocks at the arrows indicate that the agent remains in these states until some specific time has elapsed, i.e. until the trip is finished or the activity is finished.

mobiTopp aims at modelling the available choice set realistically. For example, an agent who is not at home and has arrived to his current location by public transport should not have available the modes cycling and car driver for his next trip. Or, if an agent is at home and all cars of his household are currently in use by other agents, then the agent should not be able to choose the mode car driver. This functionality is encapsulated in the *mode availability model*. This model is used by the destination choice model and by the mode choice model. Currently, there are three implementations. In the basic implementation, which

Table 1. Choice set for mode choice in different situations.

At home	Car available	Mode before	Choice set
Yes	Yes	–	{Walking, cycling, public transport, car passenger, car driver}
Yes	No	–	{Walking, cycling, public transport, car passenger}
No	–	Car driver	{Car driver}
No	–	Cycling	{Cycling}
No	–	Walking	{Walking, public transport, car passenger}
No	–	Public transport	{Walking, public transport, car passenger}
No	–	Car passenger	{Walking, public transport, car passenger}

is used for the work described here, the choice set depends on the current location of the agent, the previous mode choice and the mode choices of the other agents of the same household. A detailed overview is given in Table 1. The other implementations extend the basic implementation by two car-sharing modes [8], or take the limited range of electric vehicles into account [11].

The destination choice model consists of two levels. The upper level handles the distinction between activities with fixed locations (work, school, at home) and activities with flexible locations like shopping or leisure. The lower level handles the actual destination choice; the two types of activities are handled differently. For activities with fixed locations, the locations determined by the long-term model are used. For activities with flexible locations, a separate destination choice model is used. Currently, all implementations of the destination choice model for activities with flexible locations are utility-based. So the overall destination choice model is a combination of a rule-based and a utility-based approach.

The model, which is used for the results presented here, is based on the following variables: purpose, attractivity of the potential destination zone, travel time and travel cost. Travel time and travel cost are not only based on the current zone and the potential destination zone, but also on the next zone where an activity with fixed location takes place [2]. So agents take into account the next location they know they will visit. This is basically a soft variant of time-space constraints [7].

A Multinomial Logit model with the following utility function is used:

$$
\begin{aligned}
V_{ij} = {} & \beta_{time \times purpose} \cdot (t_{ij} + t_{jn}) \cdot x_{purpose} \\
& + \beta_{time \times employment} \cdot (t_{ij} + t_{jn}) \cdot x_{employment} \\
& + \beta_{cost \times purpose} \cdot (c_{ij} + c_{jn}) \cdot x_{purpose} \\
& + \beta_{opportunities \times purpose} \cdot \log(1 + A_{j,purpose}) \cdot x_{purpose}
\end{aligned}
$$

V_{ij} is the utility for a trip from the current zone i to the zone j. $A_{j,purpose}$ is the attractivity of zone j for an activity of type $purpose$. t_{ij} and c_{ij} are travel time and travel cost from the current zone i to zone j. t_{jn} and c_{jn} are travel time and travel cost from zone j to the next zone n of an activity with fixed location. The variables $x_{purpose}$, $x_{employment}$ are dummy variables describing the purpose of the trip and the employment status of the person, respectively, with the corresponding coefficients $\beta_{time \times purpose}$ and $\beta_{time \times purpose}$, $\beta_{cost \times purpose}$, and $\beta_{opportunities \times purpose}$.

For calibration an additional scaling parameter $\gamma = \gamma_{purpose} \cdot \gamma_{employment}$ has been introduced, initially set to 1. The parameters $\gamma_{purpose}$ and $\gamma_{employment}$ have been manually adjusted during calibration against the observed trip length distributions. So the resulting selection probability for each zone is given by

$$P_{ij} = \exp(\gamma_{purpose} \cdot \gamma_{employment} \cdot V_{ij}) / \sum_k \exp(\gamma_{purpose} \cdot \gamma_{employment} \cdot V_{ik}).$$

mobiTopp models only the main transportation mode for each trip, from the location of one activity to the location of the next activity. So each trip has exactly one mode. mobiTopp distinguishes between five modes: walking, cycling, public transport, car driver, and car passenger. The actual available choice set is calculated by the *mode availability model*.

The actual model used for mode choice is configurable. Currently, all implementations are utility-based. For the results presented in this paper, two different mode choice models based on Multinomial Logit models have been used. The first is a cross-sectional mode choice model, which ignores stability of mode choice, the second is a longitudinal mode choice model, which takes the mode of the previous trip into account.

The cross-sectional mode choice model is a Multinomial Logit Model with the following utility function:

$$\begin{aligned}
V_m = {}& \beta_{m,0} + \beta_{m,dist} \cdot x_{dist} + \beta_{time} \cdot x_{m,time\_km} + \beta_{cost} \cdot x_{m,cost\_km} \\
& + \beta_{m,intra} \cdot x_{intra} \\
& + \beta_{m,female} \cdot x_{female} + \beta_{m,employment} \cdot x_{employment} + \beta_{m,age} \cdot x_{age} \\
& + \beta_{m,ticket} \cdot x_{ticket} + \beta_{m,licence} \cdot x_{licence} \\
& + \beta_{m,purpose} \cdot x_{purpose} + \beta_{m,day} \cdot x_{day},
\end{aligned}$$

where x_{dist} is the road-based distance between zone centroids, $x_{m,time\_km}$ and $x_{m,cost\_km}$ are travel time per kilometre and travel cost per kilometre for the mode m based on the distance x_{dist}. The binary variable x_{intra} denotes, whether the trip is an intrazonal trip or a short trip with a distance $x_{dist} < 1$. The variables x_{female}, $x_{employment}$, x_{age}, x_{ticket} und $x_{licence}$ are person specific variables for sex, employment status, age group, season ticket ownership, and holding of a driving licence. The variables $x_{purpose}$ and x_{day} denote the purpose of the trip and the day of the week. The coefficients β_{time} and β_{cost} are generic. The constants $\beta_{m,0}$ and the other coefficients are alternative-specific, which means they are different for each mode m. With the inclusion of travel time and travel cost, the mode choice model is sensitive to transport policy changes. The inclusion of the sociodemographic variables accounts for heterogeneity in the population.

The longitudinal mode choice model is a Multinomial Logit Model with the following utility function:

$$V_m = \beta_{m,0} + \beta_{m,dist} \cdot x_{dist} + \beta_{time} \cdot x_{m,time\_km} + \beta_{cost} \cdot x_{m,cost\_km}$$
$$+ \beta_{m,intra} \cdot x_{intra}$$
$$+ \beta_{m,female} \cdot x_{female} + \beta_{m,employment} \cdot x_{employment} + \beta_{m,age} \cdot x_{age}$$
$$+ \beta_{m,ticket} \cdot x_{ticket} + \beta_{m,licence} \cdot x_{licence}$$
$$+ \beta_{m,purpose} \cdot x_{purpose} + \beta_{m,day} \cdot x_{day}$$
$$+ \beta_{m,mode\_same\_as\_previous} \cdot x_{mode\_same\_as\_previous}$$

The only difference to the utility function of the cross-sectional mode choice model is the binary variable $x_{mode\_same\_as\_previous}$. This variable denotes whether the mode is the same as the mode used for the previous trip. It has the effect that the utility for this mode gets a bonus.

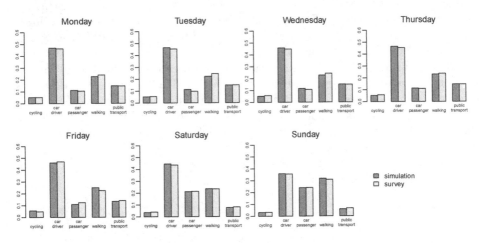

Fig. 3. Modal split by day of the week for the cross-sectional mode choice model.

3   Results and Discussion

The model has been applied to the Greater Stuttgart Area, consisting of the city of Stuttgart and the surrounding administrative districts, which has a population of approximately 2.7 million. The study area comprises 1 012 traffic analysis zones and 152 external zones.

Parameters of the destination choice model and the mode choice models have been calibrated iteratively. Parameter values estimated with *GNU R*'s *mlogit* package have been used as starting values. Trip length distributions differentiated by purpose and employment type have been used for calibrating the destination choice model; modal split differentiated by day of week, purpose, and employment type has been used for calibrating the mode choice models. In addition, two stability indicators, described in the following section, have been used to calibrate the longitudinal mode choice model. The modal split differentiated by day of the week for the calibrated cross-sectional mode choice model is shown in Fig. 3; the results for the longitudinal mode choice model look similar.

3.1 Indicators for Measuring Stability of Mode Choice

In order to assess the match between simulated data and survey data in the longitudinal perspective two indicators, *mode usage* and *mobility style*, have been defined. *mode usage* is a quite simple indicator, defined for each mode as share of persons having used this mode as main transportation mode for a trip at least once during the analysis period of one week.

The indicator *mobility style* measures the shares of different mobility styles in the population. A mobility style is defined here based on the set of modes used during the analysis period of one week, where the mode *walking*, which is used by most of the persons, is only considered to distinguish the style *walking only* from the other styles and is ignored for the definition of the other styles. We distinguish 11 mobility styles: five unimodal styles (*walking only, cycling, public transport, car passenger*, and *car driver*); three bimodal styles (*car driver/car passenger, car driver/public transport*, and *car passenger/public transport*); the style *cycling/other* consisting of the persons having used the mode *cycling* and one or two of the modes *car driver, car passenger*, and *public transport*; and two multimodal styles (*public transport/car driver/car passenger* and *all modes*).

3.2 Cross-Sectional Mode Choice Model

As expected for the cross-sectional mode choice model, both indicators show noticeable differences between the simulation results and the survey data (Fig. 4). In the *mode usage* plot in Fig. 4(a) the values for the simulation results are decisively greater than for the survey data for all modes. This observation indicates a greater variability of mode choice in the cross-sectional mode choice model than in reality. Or, put another way, mode choice in reality shows some stability, meaning that people do not switch arbitrarily between modes but rather stick to a mode already chosen, which is not adequately captured in this model.

The results of the *mobility style* plot shown in Fig. 4(b) support this hypothesis. The share of persons with a unimodal mobility style (*public transport, car passenger, car driver*) or some bimodal mobility style (*car driver/car passenger, car driver/public transport*) is heavily underestimated in the simulated data, while the share of persons with a multimodal mobility style is grossly overestimated. In other words, the model underestimates the share of persons with a more stable mobility style and overestimates the share of persons with a more variable mobility style. So this indicator confirms that the cross-sectional mode choice model does not capture adequately the stability in the mode choice behaviour that exists in reality.

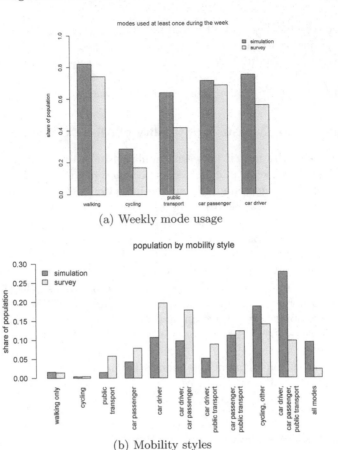

(a) Weekly mode usage

(b) Mobility styles

Fig. 4. Weekly mode usage (share of population having used this mode at least once during the week) and mobility styles (population classified by their mobility style defined as the set of modes used during the week) based on the cross-sectional mode choice model.

Based on these results we draw the conclusion that the proposed indicators are suitable to detect differences between simulated data and survey data in the longitudinal perspective. In addition, the results show clearly the need for a mode choice model that takes the longitudinal perspective into account.

3.3 Longitudinal Mode Choice Model

The longitudinal mode choice model has been calibrated with the aim of a good match for the indicators *mode usage* and *mobility style*, while at the same time providing a good match for the modal split for different aggregations. The results for the modal split are comparable to the results of the cross-sectional mode choice model.

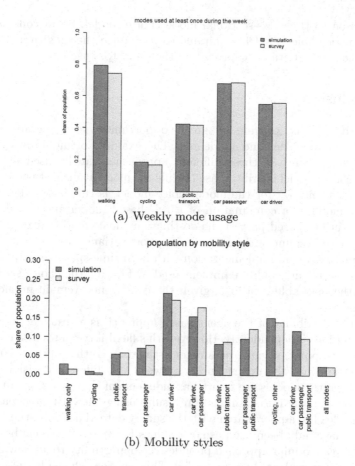

(a) Weekly mode usage

(b) Mobility styles

Fig. 5. Weekly mode usage (share of population having used this mode at least once during the week) and mobility styles (population classified by their mobility style defined as the set of modes used during the week) based on the longitudinal mode choice model.

In addition, the stability indicators show a good match in the longitudinal perspective (Fig. 5). For the indicator *mode usage* (a) the simulation results match the survey results almost perfectly for all modes except *walking*. We were not able to improve the match for *walking* in the weekly mode usage without sacrificing the good match of the modal split or worsening the match of the *mobility styles*. So we accepted this small deviation in favor of better matches for the other indicators. The indicator *mobility style* (b) also shows a good match between simulated data and survey data. The mobility styles *walking only, car driver, cycling/other,* and *car driver/car passenger/public transport* are slightly overestimated in the simulation result; the mobility styles *car passenger, car driver/car passenger,* and *car passenger/public transport* are slightly underestimated. Overall, the indicators show that the results improved considerably in comparison to the cross-sectional mode choice model. So in conclusion the extended mode choice model is suitable to reproduce the longitudinal aspects found in the survey data, as captured by the indicators used.

4   Conclusions

Agent-based models provide a great opportunity to integrate different approaches to travel demand modelling. The example of mobiTopp has been used to demonstrate how these different approaches can be used in practice. The mode choice model is utility-based, while the mode availability model, which generates the choice set for the mode choice model, is rule-based. The destination choice model is a combination of a rule-based model and a utility-based model. The utility-based part of the destination choice model takes time-space constraints into account, although only in a soft variant. However, it would be easy to replace it by an implementation with hard time-space constraints. Hard time-space constraints could be implemented by filtering the choice set in a way that only the reachable locations, given the constraints, remain in the filtered choice set.

This great flexibility of the agent-based approach is a result of treating the different decisions independently. However, this flexibility comes at a cost. From an econometric point of view, parameter estimation of the different submodels is problematic, since the dependencies between the different decisions are not captured when the models are treated as independent. For practice, this has the consequence that the initial simulation results using the estimated parameters directly may lead to a poor match with the survey data. Therefore, the estimated parameters have only been used as start values for an extensive calibration.

mobiTopp's modular approach provides the opportunity to start with simple submodels and to replace them as needed. This has been shown here for the case of the mode choice model. The basic implementation of this model was sufficient for a simulation period of one day. Extending the simulation period to one week showed that the basic implementation cannot reproduce the stability of mode choice behaviour found in the survey data. In order to describe this stability, two indicators, *mode usage* and *mobility style* have been defined. In order to reproduce stability, the utility function of the mode choice model has been extended by a variable that takes into account the mode used for the previous trip. With this simple longitudinal extension, we were able to successfully calibrate the model to reproduce the stability of the mode choice behaviour characterized by the two indicators. More complex extensions of the mode choice model are possible, however the simple extension presented here has led to satisfying results, at least for the indicators considered.

Acknowledgement. This work has been supported by Deutsche Forschungsgemeinschaft (DFG) under grant No. VO 1791/4-1.

References

1. Adamowicz, W.L.: Habit formation and variety seeking in a discrete choice model of recreation demand. J. Agric. Resour. Econ. **19**(1), 19–31 (1994)
2. Arentze, T.A., Ettema, D., Timmermans, H.J.: Location choice in the context of multi-day activity-travel patterns: model development and empirical results. Transp. A: Transp. Sci. **9**(2), 107–123 (2013)
3. Beckman, R.J., Baggerly, K.A., McKay, M.D.: Creating synthetic baseline populations. Transp. Res. Part A: Policy Pract. **30**(6), 415–429 (1996)
4. Bonabeau, E.: Agent-based modeling: methods and techniques for simulating human systems. Proc. Nat. Acad. Sci. U.S.A. **99**(10, Suppl. 3), 7280–7287 (2002)
5. Bowman, J.L., Ben-Akiva, M.E.: Activity-based disaggregate travel demand model system with activity schedules. Transp. Res. Part A: Policy Pract. **35**(1), 1–28 (2001)
6. Cirillo, C., Axhausen, K.W.: Dynamic model of activity-type choice and scheduling. Transportation **37**(1), 15–38 (2010)
7. Hägerstraand, T.: What about people in regional science? Pap. Reg. Sci. **24**(1), 7–24 (1970)
8. Heilig, M., Mallig, N., Schröder, O., Kagerbauer, M., Vortisch, P.: Implementation of free-floating and station-based carsharing in an agent-based travel demand model. Travel Behav. Soc. (2017). doi:http://dx.doi.org/10.1016/j.tbs.2017.02.002
9. Henson, K., Goulias, K., Golledge, R.: An assessment of activity-based modeling and simulation for applications in operational studies, disaster preparedness, and homeland security. Transp. Lett. **1**(1), 19–39 (2009)
10. Hilgert, T., Heilig, M., Kagerbauer, M., Vortisch, P.: Modeling week activity schedules for travel demand models. In: 96th Annual Meeting of the Transportation Research Board. Washington, DC, January 2017
11. Mallig, N., Heilig, M., Weiss, C., Chlond, B., Vortisch, P.: Modelling the weekly electricity demand caused by electric cars. Future Gen. Comput. Syst. **64**, 140–150 (2016)
12. Mallig, N., Kagerbauer, M., Vortisch, P.: mobiTopp - a modular agent-based travel demand modelling framework. Procedia Comput. Sci. **19**, 854–859 (2013)
13. Mallig, N., Vortisch, P.: Measuring stability of mode choice behavior. In: TRB 96th Annual Meeting Compendium of Papers. Transportation Research Board of the National Academies, Washington, DC, No. 17–01942, Accepted for Publication in Transportation Research Record, January 2017
14. Mueller, K., Axhausen, K.: Hierarchical IPF: generating a synthetic population for Switzerland. In: ERSA Conference Papers. European Regional Science Association (2011)
15. Outwater, M., Charlton, B.: The San Francisco model in practice: validation, testing, and application. In: Paper and Presentation for the Transportation Research Board (TRB) Innovations in Travel Demand Modeling Conference (2006)
16. Timmermans, H., Arentze, T., Joh, C.H.: Analysing space-time behaviour: new approaches to old problems. Prog. Hum. Geogr. **26**(2), 175–190 (2002)
17. Train, K.E.: Discrete Choice Methods with Simulation. Cambridge University Press, Cambridge (2009)
18. Vij, A., Carrel, A., Walker, J.L.: Incorporating the influence of latent modal preferences on travel mode choice behavior. Transp. Res. Part A: Policy Pract. **54**, 164–178 (2013)
19. Yáñez, M.F., Cherchi, E., Ortúzar, J.D.D., Heydecker, B.G.: Inertia and shock effects on mode choice panel data: implications of the transantiago implementation. In: The 12th International Conference on Travel Behaviour Research, Jaipur, India, 13–18 December 2009

A Cost-Optimization Model in Multi-agent System Routing for Drone Delivery

Miae Kim and Eric T. Matson$^{(\boxtimes)}$

M2M Lab, Purdue University, West Lafayette, IN 47906, USA
{miae,ematson}@purdue.edu

Abstract. Unmanned Aerial Vehicles (UAVs) have received attention in the last decade because of their low cost, small size, and programmable features. Drone delivery is one of the most promising applications to deliver packages efficiently. However, there are still doubts like "How to overcome the drone's limited capacity and battery life?". This paper will show a proposal to solve this problem by collaborating a drone delivery system with existing public transportation. A delivery system composed by UAVs and buses is a heterogeneous multi-agent system. This study will allocate the tasks to the UAVs and buses in the context of the multi-agent delivery system. Also, this work finds a path for each package by solving the vehicle routing problem (VRP) to find the cost-optimized path given the heterogeneous multi-agent system and minimize the number of UAVs needed for deliver. The experimental results show that the routing algorithm will reduce the total mileage and the number of UAVs given the same set of orders.

Keywords: Multi agent system · Vehicle routing problem · Unmanned aerial vehicle

1 Introduction

This section presents the motivation by introducing the importance of the cost of shipping, reviewing the related works about VRP and describing a research problem on top of VRP by adapting public transportation systems.

1.1 Motivation

More and more mobile vehicles are expected to connect to the cloud as companies like Amazon and FedEx try to launch drone delivery systems. Drone delivery intends to reduce a huge amount of costs by replacing delivery drivers and expensive trucks. However, there are still many obstacles, such as distance limit and limited capacity, to adapt drones to the real delivery task environment. This paper focuses on the cost-optimization model in multi-agent routing system for drone delivery where the cost of the system will be the total weighted mileage of UAVs and distance limits.

© Springer International Publishing AG 2017
J. Bajo et al. (Eds.): PAAMS 2017 Workshops, CCIS 722, pp. 40–51, 2017.
DOI: 10.1007/978-3-319-60285-1_4

When it comes to multi-agent routing systems, time is the one of most important factors to optimize. In some cases, however, time is not the only factor for optimization. There are huge demands of much mid-sized low-cost shipping. Free shipping in e-commerce is a good example of low-cost shipping. A ComScore survey stated that "free shipping orders produce an average of 15–20% higher order values than orders without the promotion." and 75% of consumers replied that they would switch to another retailer at checkout when shipping was not free [1]. A more recent ComScore survey in 2014 showed that free shipping continues to grow in importance, hitting an all-time non-Q4 high in Q3 at 68%, suggesting there is still a need for retailer deals [2].

The cost reduction in a drone delivery system would encourage more e-commerce retailers to adapt free or low cost shipping. In this study, UAVs are the only vehicles which require investment because this study will exploit the public transportation which already exists. The cost of public transport is assumed to be fixed.

1.2   Related Works

The UAV route planning algorithm is very similar to the solution of the traveling salesman problem (TSP) but it is challenging where there are limited constraints such as limited flying time and capacities. There are several approaches to solve the VRP problem with optimization methods like the multi variable integer programming.

Eksioglu et al. [3] classified the VRP by creating taxonomy in order to wrap up existing models and its objectives. Based on their taxonomy, this paper is classified as below.

- Number of stops on route: known
  Customer service demand: quantity deterministic
- Heterogeneous vehicles
- Travel time: function dependent
- Travel cost: vehicle dependent
- and so on

Researchers in the United States Air Force formulated VRP with time windows (VRPTW) for the military scenarios focused for precise intelligence, surveillance and reconnaissance. [4] VRPTW is a type of vehicle routing problem variant and it finds a route given destinations with time windows. The first focus was to cluster targets then implements the clustered information into mixed integer linear program (MILP).

All of these previous works are known as NP-hard problem, that is the size of the solution and thus the computational cost increases exponentially. Therefore, researchers in Air Force [4] used a clustering method before applying MILP.

Heuristic methods were applied to the routing problem to reduce the search space. The A* algorithm is a popular algorithm for finding a path [5]. The A* algorithm cut down or pre-computing the graph results for better performance in practical travel-routing systems [6] and in road networks [7]. Both researches precompute and contract the graph to predict the cost by using a heuristic function. Pisinger and Ropke [8] introduced a heuristic graph search method for the pickup and delivery problem within a certain time frame. Sundar and Rathinam [9] also suggested heuristics to solve VRP problem for UAVs with fuel constraints with 6 depots and 25 targets for UAVs. They used covering algorithm with the LinKernighan-Helgaun (LKH) heuristic which is an effective implementation for traveling salesman problem [10].

1.3   Problem Description

For many decades, the Vehicle Routing Problem (VRP), including its variants, have been studied to optimize the route to minimize the total cost of providing service. The objective of VRP is to minimize the total cost such as monetary cost, Euclidian distance, a weighted sum of some vehicles or estimated time of arrival.

This study is an application of a VRP variant, a single-depot VRP. The depot is fixed where all delivery starts from the warehouse. This study assumes there are two groups of UAVs; UAVs reside in the warehouse and UAVs deliver the packages. The UAVs in the warehouse load the packages to the bus and the other UAVs deliver the packages on the bus and return to the warehouse. This study optimize the total weighted mileage of UAVs to deliver the packages and minimize the delivery UAVs' battery consumption.

When the delivery system adopts public transportation to its system, the integrated system does not guarantee time optimization, but it saves cost. This study adopts a bus as the public transportation option, and this results in time delay when UAVs wait for the bus and the bus delay because of heavy traffic. However, the system saves the cost by maximizing the number of the packages available per UAV. UAVs recharge their battery when they ride the bus. The bus can transfer multiple packages from one point to another point. The bus is used because it is the most common transportation in cities and the bus stop is located within walking distance in the city; the average distance from a bus stop to a residence or office is 400 m. [11,12] the average speed of a bus is 27 to 48 km/h [13], which is similar to the speed of the UAV, but buses have no given limitation as they can charge fuel. The study will simulate the algorithm in a controlled environment using small class 1 UAVs instead of fixed-wing VTOL UAV and UGVs (unmanned ground vehicles) instead of the bus.

2   Conceptual Design

Section focuses on answering the question: "What is the effect of using the public transportation system on the drone delivery system?" by showing how to integrate the public transport system with UAVs. The scattered path should be merged first then each bus assign UAVs they need so that the UAVs reach the destination in a timely manner.

1. Find path to every destination
2. Build optimal path by merging bus routes
3. Assign UAVs for each bus route

   This paper assumes that

- There is a single warehouse, called as depot D. Therefore, every UAV will start from the depot and deliver their assigned packages and return to the depot.
- Each UAV can deliver only one package at one time.
- There are UAVs to deliver packages and the UAVs reside in the warehouses. This paper assumes that there are enough UAVs in the warehouses.
- The UAVs which reside in the warehouse load the packages to the buses departing from the warehouses.
- This algorithm will minimize the total mileage of UAVs when they deliver packages.
- UAVs are fast enough to return to the bus after delivering the package to the destination.
- the UAV will distribute the packages directly for near points or take buses to get to the far way destinations.

2.1 Finding the Path

As mentioned in the introduction section, UAVs does not have enough battery power to deliver the packages for long journeys. Algorithm 1 shows how to find a path combined with buses and UAVs. With the list of bus routes, the algorithm will first build a graph with bus routes, then match the node to the bus stops.

When Algorithm 1 adds a node to the other node, the weight is haversine distance, published by James Andrew [14], between the nodes. Haversine distance is the shortest distance between two points on the surface of a sphere given their longitudes and latitudes. Then, the algorithm finds k-nearest bus stops from the starting point, so called "starts", and k-nearest bus stops from the destinations point, so called "ends". Among all combination of "starts" and "ends", the algorithm will choose the best combination with the shortest distance. For each bus stop combination (the pair of i-th nearest bus stop from starting point and j-th nearest bus stop from the destination $[start_i, end_j]$), the algorithm will calculate the total distance by adding the haversine distance from starting point to $[start_i, end_j]$ to the destination and the path between $[start_i, end_j]$ (See Eq. 1). In order to get the path between $[start_i, end_j]$, the algorithm used Dijkstra's algorithm [15], which searches the shortest path between two points on the graph.

2.2 Merging the Bus Routes

Without the cooperation between UAVs and the bus, assuming there are n demanding points, each UAV can deliver one package at a time, so the problem

---

Algorithm 1. Path one to other point

Data: List of bus stops, bus routes,
coordination of a starting point(starting_point),
coordination of a ending point(ending_point)
Result: route from starting point to the destination
graph = build_graph(bus_routes)
                          `// Build symmetric directed Graph based on bus routes`
starts = nearest(starting point, bus stops)
                          `// Find k-nearest bus stop from starting point`
ends = nearest(destinations, bus stops)
                          `// Find k-nearest bus stop from the destination`
min_val = ∞
for $start \in starts$ **do**
    for $end \in ends$ **do**

$$
\begin{aligned}
total\_path = &\, haversine(starting\_point, start) \\
&+ path(graph, start, end) \\
&+ haversine(end, ending\_point)
\end{aligned} \tag{1}
$$

        if $total\_path.val < min\_val$ **then**
            min_val = total_path.val
            min_path = total_path
        end
    end
end
return min_val, min_path

---

will require n UAVs and deliver one UAV to each one of the destinations. The capacity limits, not only the delivery range, but also the chance to optimize the delivery routes.

This problem can save the cost of delivery by cooperation between agents, solving single-depot VRP [16]. Consider the depot D and n destinations. Then, the total mileage of the delivery will be $\sum_n^{i=1} 2d(D, i)$, where $d(D, i)$ is a sum of flight from the starting point to the bus stop, riding the bus, flight from the bus stop to the destination, see Eq. 2.

$$d(D, i) = f(D, b_i) + g(b_D, b_i) + f(b_i, D) \tag{2}$$

With Clarke and Wright's "savings" algorithm (Algorithm 2), we can optimize the route by merging two routes. If we choose a UAV to deliver for the two points i and j, we can save the amount of mileage by a difference between the original cost and merged cost, known as "savings" $s(i, j)$.

$$
\begin{aligned}
s(i, j) &= 2d(D, i) + 2d(D, j) - [d(D, i) + d(i, j) + d(D, j)] \\
&= d(D, i) + d(D, j) - d(i, j)
\end{aligned} \tag{3}
$$

After calculating all paths from i to j (n^2 paths), the algorithm could be n^2 savings. The savings will be saved in a priority queue "savings", with descending order so that the highest saving will "pop" at first.

Algorithm 2 chooses the largest savings $s(i, j)$ from the priority queue and links i, j to the route based on following rules.

Algorithm 2. Build a single-depot VRP (CW Algorithm) [17]

Data: Priority queue of savings queue($s(i, j)$)
Result: The merged route
Start from empty routes;
while *True* **do**
    Choose route $r(i, j)$ with the largest savings.
    If adding $r(i, j)$ violates the constraints, ignore.
    switch X **do**
        case *both i and j are not in routes* **do**
            build and include node i, j as route.
        end
        case *either i xor j is on any route, and the point is in the middle of the route* **do**
            merge i, j to the existing route.
        end
        case *both i and j included in different routes and neither point is NOT in the middle of the route* **do**
            two routes are merged
        end
    end
end

The merged route R is a set of list of nodes, $R = \{r_1, r_2, \cdots, r_k\}$, where k is the number of routes. Each route r_i is a set of bus stops like $r_4 = \{n_0, n_3, n_9, n_8, n_0\}$ where the UAVs should follow the order of nodes. Every route r_i starts with depot node n_0 and ends with n_0, by assumption.

2.3   Assign UAVs for Each Bus Route

In the previous section, Algorithm 2 built the set of routes $R = \{r_1, r_2, \cdots, r_k\}$ from n destinations, each route will require how many UAVs they need. There is an algorithm that calculates the number of UAVs we needed from routes R.

There is a lower bound and upper bound of the number of UAVs. At worst case, each route can deliver as many as number of UAVs assigned to the routes(n). The best case will be the number of UAVs needed is the same as the number of routes(k). Therefore, the number of delivery UAVs is in range $[n, k]$, note that it does not count the UAVs in the warehouse.

3   Experiment

In this section, we will compare the total mileage of UAVs when they deliver 10 packages to 10 destinations. In the control group, each UAV will deliver the packages to each destination. On the other hand, the treatment group merges the destinations so that the total mileages are optimized.

3.1 Data Preparation

This paper uses the bus route data and bus stop data in Citybus [18] and Fig. 1 and Table 1 shows 10 random destination points around West Lafayette, Indiana, USA. The city bus center (node 0) is the depot where all delivery starts, while there are multiple destinations which lie along same bus track.

Table 1. List depot and destinations

Node	Sign	Name	Full name	Latitude	Longitude
0	D	CITY	City Bus Center	40.420681	−86.894445
1	n_1	KNOY	Knoy Hall	40.427711	−86.911190
2	n_2	KSQC	K-SW Square	40.426067	−86.909755
3	n_3	IUAH	IU Health Arnett Hospital	40.401298	−86.806595
4	n_4	MAMA	Mama Ines Mexican Bakery	40.422548	−86.858854
5	n_5	STNS	Steak 'n Shake	40.417822	−86.858552
6	n_6	DRFR	Division of Family Resources	40.415367	−86.834892
7	n_7	EAST	Goodrich Eastside 9	40.420538	−86.852039
8	n_8	ICHI	Ichiban Sichuan	40.417157	−86.893233
9	n_9	SAMS	Sams' Club	40.413342	−86.837559

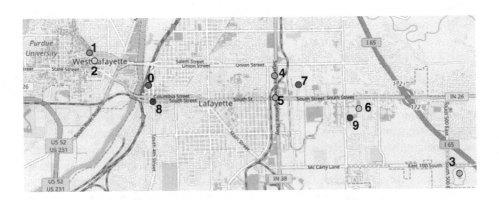

Fig. 1. Figure of the depot and destinations

3.2 Control Group - Using only UAVs

If there is no cooperation between agents, each UAV will dispatch to the n destinations, resulting in the worst case. The total distance will be the sum of the round-trip to each destination, Table 2 shows the distance between depot n_0 to each destination and its sum, where the total mileage of UAVs will be $35887.87057 \times 2 = 71775.74114$ (Table 3).

Table 2. From depot D to destination n_i

Dest node	Mileage	Dest node	Mileage
1	1567.41385	6	6320.24940
2	1567.53242	7	4508.24506
3	7947.14107	8	1211.73436
4	3062.99572	9	6964.16097
5	2738.39768	TOTAL*2	71775.74114

Table 3. Savings (below diagonal) and distances (above diagonal)

D	n_1	n_2	n_3	n_4	n_5	n_6	n_7	n_8	n_9
D		1567	1567	7947	3062	2738	6320	4508	1211	6964
n_1	-		134	11251	6259	5934	9516	7704	3792	9801
n_2	-	3000		11252	6259	5934	9516	7704	3792	9801
n_3	-	−1737	−1737		3637	3956	2021	3452	7367	1717
n_4	-	−1628	−1628	7372		325	1396	185	4040	1556
n_5	-	−1628	−1628	6728	5476		3582	1738	3412	3257
n_6	-	−1628	−1628	12245	7986	5476		1212	7338	160
n_7	-	−1628	−1628	9002	7385	5508	9616		5412	1372
n_8		−1013	−1013	1791	234	537	193	307		6932
n_9	-	−1269	−1269	13194	8470	6444	13123	10100	1243	

3.3   Treatment Group - UAVs with Bus

With Algorithm 2, Table 4 builds the final routes in Fig. 2. Algorithm 2 starts with "popping" the largest saving $s(9,3)$ from Table 4, as both 9 and 3 are not in routes, so it builds a new route r_1, initiated as $r_1 = [9,3]$. In this example, there are no other constraints, so constraints are not checked. Then, pop the next one $s(9,6)$. Since 9 is already in r_1, new saving is merged to the existing route. $r_1 = [6,9,3]$. The next saving is $s(6,3)$, which both 6 and 3 included in same route, although this the saving does not affect the existing route. The next saving $s(9,7)$ is rejected because 9 is already included in the route. The $s(7,6)$ is merged to r_1, so $r_1 = [7,6,9,3]$. Then, $s(7,3)$ is ignored where the route already had both nodes. If we follow the procedure in Algorithm 2, the final routes are $r_1 = [4,7,6,9,3,5,8]$ and $r_2 = [1,2]$, but we are assuming the starting point and the destination is n_0, so the routes become $r_1 = [0,4,7,6,9,3,5,8,0]$ and $r_2 = [0,1,2,0]$, shown in Fig. 2.

Table 4. The list of savings

Savings	(i, j)	Savings	(i, j)	Savings	(i, j)	Savings	(i, j)
13194	(9, 3)	8470	(9, 4)	5508	(7, 5)	537	(8, 5)
13123	(9, 6)	7986	(6, 4)	5476	(5, 4)	307	(8, 7)
12245	(6, 3)	7385	(7, 4)	5476	(6, 5)	234	(8, 4)
10100	(9, 7)	7372	(4, 3)	3000	(2, 1)	193	(8, 6)
9616	(7, 6)	6728	(5, 3)	1791	(8, 3)		
9002	(7, 3)	6444	(9, 5)	1243	(9, 8)		

Fig. 2. Solution of grouping destinations using Algorithm 2

Therefore, the total mileage of the final route is $\sum_k \sum_{i,j \in r_k} d(i,j)$. Table 5 shows the distance between nodes and the total mileage. Unlike the current VRP problem, the capacity is not allocated for each route because a UAV can carry one item at a time. For example, if the two different packages are far enough, the UAV can deliver both packages by returning to the bus. However, it is not possible for the UAV to deliver adjacent packages.

Table 5. From depot D to destination n_i

r_1		r_2		Total
$d(0,4)$	3062.99572	$d(0,1)$	1567.41385	18188.87058
$d(4,7)$	185.58617	$d(1,2)$	134.40979	
$d(7,6)$	1212.20674	$d(2,0)$	1567.53242	
$d(6,9)$	160.51234			
$d(9,3)$	1717.17613			
$d(3,5)$	3956.79301			
$d(5,8)$	3412.50999			
$d(8,0)$	1211.73436			

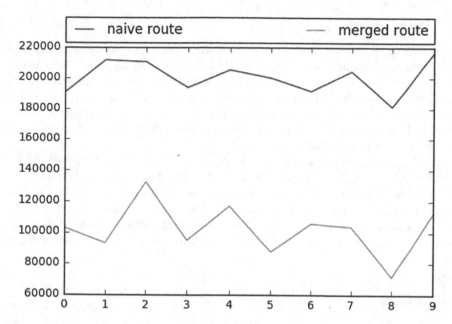

Fig. 3. Comparison of total mileages for 10 different datasets, each dataset is composed of 20 random destinations.

3.4   Results

In the experiment section, there are 10 packages to deliver. Table 2 compares the total mileage of UAVs and buses. Without any collaboration between drone and bus, each UAV should carry the package by itself. Therefore, there are 10 routes and mileage for each routes is a round-trip distance. After Algorithm 2, there are two routes to travel $r_1 = [0, 4, 7, 6, 9, 3, 5, 8, 0]$ and $r_2 = [0, 1, 2, 0]$, and the total mileage of UAVs and buses is 35290 which is half of the total mileages before merging, 71775. Figure 3 shows the cost reduction for ten different experiments, each experiment compares the cost for 20 random destinations.

4   Conclusions and Future Work

4.1   Conclusion

This paper has proposed a delivery system with heterogeneous UAV agents and public transportation which will reduce the total cost of the system by rebuilding its route. The routing algorithm assumes that all agents are cooperative, and this routing optimization seeks to maximize the amount of savings when the algorithm merges two distinct destinations. Figure 3 show that joining similar destinations reduces the total mileage of UAVs by 50%. Therefore, we can conclude that the cost of the delivery system through cooperation between agents is reduced.

4.2 Future Work

This application aims to work a at more flexible environment by adapting two VRP variants; Dynamic Vehicle Routing Problem (DVRP) and the Vehicle Routing Problem with Pickups and Deliveries (VRPD). To be specific, this study takes into account dynamic costs in real-time due to the bus schedules, traffic, the capacity of the current bus and battery level of UAVs, for example. Also, UAVs will load multiple packages on the bus then pick up and deliver the packages on the bus to the destination.

In this paper, we assume that the UAV is fast enough to return to the bus, so the number of UAVs needed is same as the number of routes. However, we need to consider the case of destination density. UAVs cannot return to the bus before arriving in the next destination. If we estimate the number of UAVs needed for each route, we can assign more UAVs to the route. Besides, this paper assumes a single depot, but it needs to extend the case where there are multiple warehouses.

References

1. Fulgoni, G.: State of the U.S. Online Retail Economy in Q4 2009 (2010). Accessed 13 April 2016
2. Lipsman, A., Fulgoni, G.: State of the U.S. Online Retail Economy in Q3 2014 (2014). Accessed 13 April 2016
3. Eksioglu, B., Vural, A.V., Reisman, A.: The vehicle routing problem: a taxonomic review. Comput. Ind. Eng. **57**(4), 1472–1483 (2009)
4. Weinstein, A., Schumacher, C.: UAV scheduling via the vehicle routing problem with time windows. In: AIAA Infotech@ Aerospace 2007 Conference and Exhibit, p. 2839 (2007)
5. Hart, P.E., Nilsson, N.J., Raphael, B.: A formal basis for the heuristic determination of minimum cost paths. IEEE Trans. Syst. Sci. Cybern. **4**(2), 100–107 (1968)
6. Delling, D., Sanders, P., Schultes, D., Wagner, D.: Engineering route planning algorithms. In: Lerner, J., Wagner, D., Zweig, K.A. (eds.) Algorithmics of Large and Complex Networks. LNCS, vol. 5515, pp. 117–139. Springer, Heidelberg (2009). doi:10.1007/978-3-642-02094-0_7
7. Zeng, W., Church, R.: Finding shortest paths on real road networks: the case for A*. Int. J. Geogr. Inf. Sci. **23**(4), 531–543 (2009)
8. Pisinger, D., Ropke, S.: A general heuristic for vehicle routing problems. Comput. Oper. Res. **34**(8), 2403–2435 (2007)
9. Sundar, K., Rathinam, S.: Algorithms for routing an unmanned aerial vehicle in the presence of refueling depots. IEEE Trans. Autom. Sci. Eng. **11**(1), 287–294 (2014)
10. Lin, S.-H.: Finding optimal refueling policies in transportation networks. In: Fleischer, R., Xu, J. (eds.) AAIM 2008. LNCS, vol. 5034, pp. 280–291. Springer, Heidelberg (2008). doi:10.1007/978-3-540-68880-8_27
11. Committee, F., et al.: Walking Distance Research (2013)
12. Daniels, R., Mulley, C.: Explaining walking distance to public transport: the dominance of public transport supply. World **28**, 30 (2011)

13. Hinebaugh, D.: Characteristics of bus rapid transit for decision-making. Technical report (2009)
14. Van Brummelen, G.: Heavenly Mathematics: The Forgotten Art of Spherical Trigonometry. Princeton University Press, Princeton (2013)
15. Dijkstra, E.W.: A note on two problems in connexion with graphs. Numer. Math. **1**(1), 269–271 (1959)
16. Larson, R.C., Odoni, A.R.: Urban Operations Research. Number Monograph (1981)
17. Golden, B.L., Magnanti, T.L., Nguyen, H.Q.: Implementing vehicle routing algorithms. Networks **7**(2), 113–148 (1977)
18. Citybus: City Bus Routes. http://citybus.doublemap.com/map/v2/routes. Accessed 05 Feb 2017

Microsimulation Travel Models in Practice in the US and Prospects for Agent-Based Approach

Peter Vovsha[✉]

WSP|Parsons Brinckerhoff,
1 Penn Plaza, 2nd Floor, New York, NY 10119, USA
vovsha@PBworld.com

Abstract. The paper summaries author's view on the Agent-Based Modeling (AgBM) and what it brings to travel modeling in addition to the existing microsimulation techniques already in practice. It provides practical examples where AgBM proved to be useful and looks as a promising way to improve the model structures. The new AgBM features include: (1) making individual agents (households and persons) "intelligent" by having individual memory and dynamic state dependence mechanisms with referencing, (2) ability of individual agents to adapt to the changing environment, when they can change parameters such as Value of Time (VOT), (3) direct interactions between the individual agents and not only with the aggregate environment, (4) learning from others through social and spatial networks, in particular, in the context of "modality", (5) distinguishing between the planning layer and real-time implementation layer (simulation) in the model system, and (6) explicit competition for a constraint supply of activities, for example, in the context of workplace location choice.

Keywords: Agent-Based Modeling · Learning · Adaptation · Intra-household interactions · Inter-household interactions

1 Microsimulation Activity-Based Travel Model (ABM) vs. Agent-Based Model (AgBM)

The paper summaries author's view on "Agency" and what it brings to travel modeling in addition to the existing microsimulation techniques already in practice. It provides practical examples where "Agency" proved to be useful and looks as a promising way to improve the model structures. "Ordinary" micro simulation models of travel demand in practice have become the dominant travel model paradigm in the US in the period 2000–2017 for the large urban areas. These models are frequently referred to as Activity-Based Models (ABMs) and their success in practice relates to such well-discussed advantages over aggregate (so-called 4-step) models as 1 = better representation of user heterogeneity (unlimited segmentation), 2 = computationally efficient format of the database, especially when spatial details come into play (rosters

© Springer International Publishing AG 2017
J. Bajo et al. (Eds.): PAAMS 2017 Workshops, CCIS 722, pp. 52–68, 2017.
DOI: 10.1007/978-3-319-60285-1_5

of trips instead of trip matrices), and 3 = deeper conditional decision making trees with many additional sub-models that 4-step models cannot incorporate [20].

Agent-Based Modeling (AgBM) paradigm introduces additional important facets of microsimulation. AgBMs are useful when the physics of interaction between the particles become easier to describe than transition rules of the entire system [4]. ABMs in practice provide first examples of AgBM components and demonstrate what "Agency" can add on top of microsimulation:

- Making individual agents (households and persons) "intelligent" by having individual memory, and dynamically updated information coming with learning from individual experience. It can be said that in AgBM, information becomes an explicit part of simulation (i.e. we model not only what people *do* but also what they *know*).
- Ability of individual agents to adapt to the changing environment, when they can change parameters such as Value of Time (VOT) as a function of situational time pressure. This is important for long-term forecasting.
- Direct interactions between the individual agents and not only with the aggregate environment. This includes intra-household interactions and also inter-household interactions such as bids, negotiations, cooperation and different forms of group decision-making.
- Learning from others through social and spatial networks (so-called "contagion") in particularly in the context of "modality" (long-term mode preferences).

In addition to these general features, there are several other emerging AgBM features of advanced ABMs in practice that are less typical for AgBMs elsewhere:

- Distinguishing between the planning layer and real-time implementation layer (simulation) in the model system. Planning layer relates to generation and scheduling of activities and trips for the next day while the real-time implementation layer relates to activity and trip rescheduling within the simulated day.
- Explicit competition for constraint supply of activities, for example, in the context of workplace location choice with a predetermined number of jobs for each occupation in each zone.

These AgBM features and corresponding practical examples are discussed in the subsequent sections.

2 Limited Knowledge and Learning from Individual Experience

2.1 Behavioral Interpretation of Large Choice Sets

One of the major conceptual challenges of the existing ABMs in practice relates to a fundamental behavioral question of how people make complex multidimensional choices out of billions of alternatives such as joint choice of trip mode, destination, and departure time with the necessary level of spatial and temporal resolution, and how they could be effectively modeled. Significant progress has been made in handling choice models with thousands of alternatives. ABMs in practice incorporated such complex joint choices as daily activity pattern, destination choice, and time-of-day choice. However, these big joint choice models are questioned and probably represent a "dead end" of these particular modeling structures since they are not appealing behaviorally and also computation burdensome.

Attempts to replace a one-step choice model with a large number of alternatives are routed back to the seminal work of Mansky where a two-step decision model was introduced [11] with the following steps: (1) Formation of choice set out of the universal set of all alternatives, and (2) Ultimate choice of a single alternative out of the formed choice set of considered alternatives. Mansky's two-step model is appealing for long-term strategic decisions like residential choice. However, this attractive concept proved to be problematic for travel choices such as destination choice. It is doubtful that travelers do such an intensive "homework" on the given day for each trip. It is also doubtful that travelers process all alternatives in the first step and have full information about them. For this reason, the prevailing practice in the ABMs in practice is to consider all possible alternatives with sometimes random sampling of them. The crux of the problem is that people manage to make complex travel choices of "horrendous" dimensionality in reality through an iterative trial-and-error process with incremental adjustments. This process is inherently dynamic and cannot be compressed to a static 2-step procedure. The AgBM concept fully recognizes that and employs a learning mechanism that is built upon the fact that ABMs already incorporate iterative equilibration and sampling of alternatives. AgBM capitalizes on that but replaces the random sampling with a more intelligent analysis and selection of alternatives.

In the destination choice context, the AgBM concept is presented in Fig. 1. It assumes that at each iteration the individual updates the destination choice set ("mental map" [3]) by evaluating the chosen alternative and either dropping it or retaining it, as well as processing information about some other (non-chosen) alternative and dropping some of them or adding some new ones to the choice set.

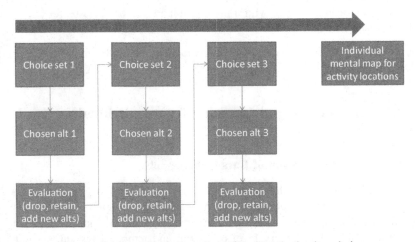

Fig. 1. Conceptual representation of AgBM destination choice

In the time-of-day choice context, the AgBM concept is presented in Fig. 2. It is an iterative process similar to the destination choice set described above. However, there are two different layers of learning. The upper one relates to the sequence of activities in the individual Daily Activity Pattern (DAP). A good example of a decision in this layer is to have a discretionary activity like visiting a gym either before or after work. The lower layer relates to the details of activity start and end time. If the decision has been made to undertake the discretionary activity after work, the individual may proceed with the detailed alternatives such as starting this activity at 6 pm or 7 pm or 8 pm.

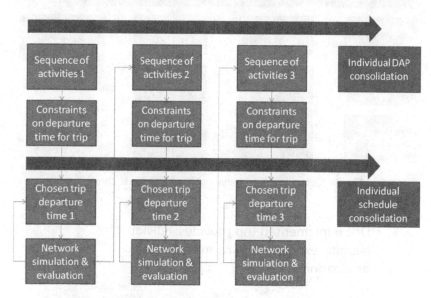

Fig. 2. Conceptual representation of AgBM time-of day choice

In the mode choice context, the AgBM concept is presented in Fig. 3. Again, it is an iterative process at two layers. The upper layer relates to the individual modality and specifically to the consideration of available modes. For example, for many trips in the US metropolitan regions, travelers may not even consider such modes as transit or bike. In the lower layer, the actual mode choice is made within the same modality. For example, a transit-oriented person still may need to decide between rail and bus, and try both of them before making the decision.

2.2 Dynamic Choice Set Formation in the Context of ABM-DTA Integration

The approach described above was successfully applied in practice in the microsimulation models where ABM was integrated with Dynamic Traffic Assignment (DTA) developed for Columbus, OH and Atlanta, GA. These models followed a so-called "deep" integration schema with learning about space (travel time and cost to different destinations) from individual trajectories (see [18]) in combination with dynamic choice sets [14] (Fig. 4).

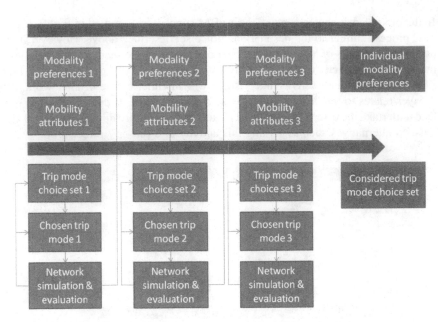

Fig. 3. Conceptual representation of AgBM mode choice

- One implemented trip provides individual learning experience w.r.t multiple destinations

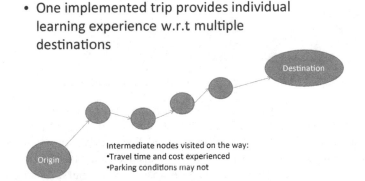

Fig. 4. Learning space from individual trajectories generated by DTA

One of the major revisions of the ABM structure relates to the way how destination choice alternatives are sampled at each iteration. In the standard ABM implementation, 30 alternatives are sampled out of thousands of zones for each individual choice. This sampling is implemented randomly with importance weights. With this implementation, a convergence in terms of aggregate Origin-Destination (OD) patterns and trip-lengths distribution is quite good. However, due to a substantial random variation in the sampling of 30 alternatives out of thousands of zones, this method has a substantial random variation of destinations at the individual level. This results in a very low probability for individual DTA trajectories to be reused between the iterations. The revised method for sampling destination choice alternatives allows for an efficient accumulation of individual trajectories. It is also behaviorally appealing since it mimics a real-world process of how individuals learn about the activity supply and adapt to it through systematic trials. This method makes the model closer to the realm of AgBM where individual "agents have memories and experiences based on the simulation results at previous iterations. Two following sets of activity locations are maintained and updated from iteration to iteration:

- Sets of first type are formed for each household and each non-mandatory activity. This set of potential locations (for example, preferred shopping destinations) is assumed shared across the household members.
- Sets of second type are formed for each worker and student and non-mandatory activity and they are used to generate stops on mandatory (work or school) tours.

For workers and students, usual workplace or school location represents an important second spatial anchor in addition to the residential location. For non-mandatory home-based tours, the home location represents a natural spatial anchor around which most of the non-mandatory activities are centered. For work and school commuters, preferred locations for non-mandatory activities can be close to the usual mandatory activity location, especially if it is in a dense central area with a variety of opportunities. Alternatively, commuters can choose a location between the home and workplace if it does not require a substantial detour.

The choice set formation procedure is based on the classification of potential locations for each individual and activity as shown in Table 1. Sets 1, 2, and 3 are explicitly tracked and updated at each iteration. Set 4 represents a residual stock of destinations. Set 1 represents destinations that are transitioned from one iteration to the next and that have been already visited (as the chosen destination or on the way to some other destinations). For destinations from Set 1 the most detailed travel time and cost estimates from the individual trajectories are available. Set 2 includes newly added destinations or destinations that were kept from the previous iteration but have not been visited yet. Set 3 includes potential destination with the known travel time and cost that have not been yet included in the choice set or were dropped because of the negative experience. Set 3 represents a potential for Set 1 for the next iteration. Set 4 represents a potential for Set 2 for the next iteration. Sets 1 and 2 form the actual sample of destinations for the ABM at the current iteration.

Table 1. Classification of activity locations for dynamically updated individual destination choice sets

Inclusion in activity set	Visited with recorded trajectory (travel experience)	Not yet visited
Included	Set 1: Visited and considered destinations (stayed in the choice set)	Set 2: Exploratory destinations (known to individual via media or social networks)
Not included	Set 3: Visited (on the way) but not yet considered (or dropped at previous iterations)	Set 4: Not visited and not considered (all other)

Based, on this classification, formation of an individual activity location set at each iteration of the model system equilibration can be summarized as shown in Fig. 5. The algorithm starts with current choice set used for the previous iteration. The set is broken into Set 1 of visited destinations and Set 2 of not yet visited destinations. These choice subsets are retained with probabilities P1 and P2 applied for each individual destination from the respective subsets. If the destination is chosen to be replaced with a new location, the decision is modeled from which subset to choose a new destination that is governed by probability P3. If the decision was made to search amongst the already visited locations of Set 3, each of these locations is evaluated using a probability function P4. If the decision was made to search amongst new destinations of Set 4 that have never been visited yet each of these locations is evaluated with a probability function P5.

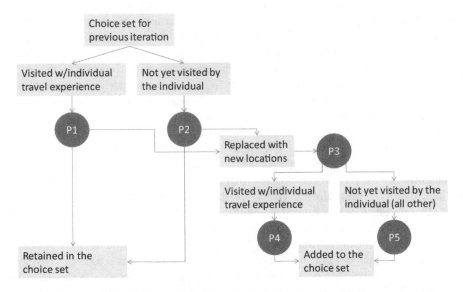

Fig. 5. Formation of individual destination choice set

Interesting further generalization of the iterative choice formation through learning is the concept of dynamically updated daily plans where the entire daily pattern is evaluated for each individual and either retained or replaced for the next global iteration [21].

3   Adaptation to Changing Environment by Adjustment of Model Coefficients

A traveler's willingness to pay for travel time savings depends on his/her socio-economic characteristics, travel purpose, and situational factors such as time pressure under which the travel is undertaken. Earlier literature on Value of Time (VOT) analysis focused mostly on the first two factors but did not examine the last factor thoroughly. However, in the real world a worker would be willing to pay more during the before-work period than during the after-work period since most of the workers should reach his/her work place by a certain time while the post-work schedule in general should be more relaxed.

The additional time pressure during the before-work period makes time more valuable, thus increasing VOT. In some cases, where a worker with a flexible schedule has a high-priority post-work activity with a fixed schedule (for example tickets to a concert) the situation can be reversed. Recent studies aimed to capture such impacts of daily activity patterns on a person's VOT using a comprehensive trip segmentation framework that is comprised of several integrated mode and trip departure TOD choice models applied as part of the ABM developed for Jerusalem, Israel [13]. Each of these integrated models was estimated using both Revealed Preference (RP) and Stated Preference (SP) data from a large-scale GPS-assisted Household Travel Survey undertaken in Jerusalem, Israel. The results shed a light on the variation of VOT with daily travel patterns. This AgBM feature was incorporated through iterative equilibration of the ABM where VOT becomes endogenous outcome. An important practical implication of this approach is that VOT would in general grow with growing congestion that ensures that the model is realistically sensitive to future scenarios. With conventional ABMs, VOT as well as all other model coefficients remain the same until they are changed exogenously for future scenarios.

4 Direct Interactions Between the Agents

Most of the ABMs in practice in the US include some forms of intra-household interactions with respect to individual mobility attributes (such as car ownership and transit pass holding), joint activities and travel, schedule synchronization between different household members, escorting arrangements, etc. In most cases, these interactions when modeled explicitly are reduced to combinatorial household-level choices where the choice dimensions are combined across persons in a Cartesian way. The utility function normally includes individual components and added utility of joint participation and synchronization [4, 10].

While this method can be considered as a (simplified) AgBM component, there were recently attempts to extend the modeling techniques to include explicit group preference consolidation mechanisms such as cooperative behavior [8]. One particular example of an innovative approach that is close to the AgBM concept relates to inter-household interactions for participation in special events in the Phoenix, AZ ABM [14]. In this model, a synthetic population of participants in a special event such as a football game or large-scale exhibition is generated first. Then, the participants are allocated to residential zones. Finally, participants from the same or neighboring zones are allowed to form a travel party (either intra-household or inter-household). Travel party formation is implemented as a rule-based algorithm that was trained to replicate the observed distribution of travel parties by size and composition. This AgBM component proved to be very useful in practice since special events in Phoenix, AZ are characterized by very different mode choice and car occupancy compared to other discretionary trips.

5   Learning Through Social and Spatial Networks

There is a growing recognition that individual travel choices are strongly subject to the examples from the spatial and social networks. For example, person's modality and mode preferences, and specifically consideration of bike as an alternative mode in the US, are very much correlated with the general bike acceptance in the neighborhood. The corresponding general techniques were suggested in AgBMs long ago in the context of residential population clusters and culture dissemination by adoption of features from the neighbors [2].

Examples of others (family, neighborhood, friends, social networks, or information channeled through Internet or media) can strongly stimulate travel choices and change long-term individual preferences (i.e. underlying model parameters). One of the suggested techniques in this regard is to include aggregate "neighborhood" mode shares in disaggregate mode choice model [4]. This technique was tested in the ABMs developed for New York, NY and Chicago, IL. It was particularly useful to explain differences in the bike modal shares across different sub-areas. This technique like many other AgBM methods capitalizes on the overall model equilibration – see Fig. 6.

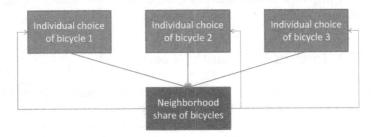

Fig. 6. Iterative application of individual mode choice model with aggregate modal shares

Addition of aggregate shares to the individual choice utility affected the results quite strongly. When compared with the conventional model it created more extreme and diverse aggregate outcomes (very low and very high shares of bikes) that were closer to the reality. A conventional model would require a proliferation of geography-specific constants to achieve the same result. Another observation is that it helped explain some observed "irrational" individual choices, i.e. choices made with very low probability assigned by the conventional choice model (for example, elderly people biking).

6   Planning Layer and Real-Time Implementation Layer

6.1   "Deep" Integration of ABM and DTA

Several recent large-scale projects in the US included development of a complete microsimulation travel model where the demand side was handled by an ABM while the network simulation side was handled by DTA. These projects were undertaken in parallel for Columbus, OH and Atlanta, GA. The concept of "deep" integration is based on the following principles that quite resonate with the AgBM paradigm:

- Avoid aggregation biases such as using averaged time and cost skims instead of individual trajectories.
- Ensure that the persons experience individual time and cost for each trips that is based on their VOT and mode or route preferences, and make travel decisions based on this individual experience.

Even with this advanced research agenda the very concept of ABM and DTA integration is somewhat conceptually limited. It largely a legacy from 4-step modeling paradigm that travel demand model and network simulation model should be separated and only iteratively equilibrated between them – see [18]. While the travel choices that correspond to the first three steps of 4-step were integrated in the ABM structure in a new way, the route choice and network loading procedures (last assignment step of 4-step) remain separate (Fig. 7).

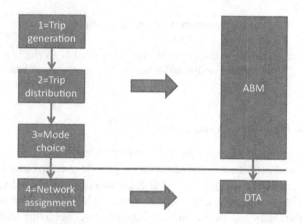

Fig. 7. Separation of demand and network models as legacy from 4-step

Further analysis of the ABM and DTA structure reveals quite a fundamental difference between these two models. DTA has two distinct layers – planning layer (route choice) and real-time implementation layer (vehicle movement simulation). These layers use quite different models and rules although the difference might be somewhat blurred, for example, when drivers are allowed to dynamically change their routes during the simulation. Contrary to that, a standard ABM has only a planning layer (activity frequency, location, scheduling, trip chaining, mode choice, etc.) while a real-time implementation layer is missing. The reason for that is historical since in the 4-step structure that operates exclusively with trips, the only possible real-time simulation component is trip simulation in the network. The ABM structure operates with activities and tours where real-time effects of trip travel times and activity durations for the same individual are appealing. In this regard a concept of "loading trip chains" as an extension of trip-based DTA represents a step towards a deeper ABM-DTA integration with inclusion of activity durations in the real-time simulation context [1].

In the recent projects, several gaps were filled to bring ABM and DTA closer to each other. However, in addition to filling the obvious gaps, a fundamental change in the model system structure is envisioned where the ABM and DTA entities could be replaced with planning and real-time implementation entities of AgBM [18]. Rather than separate activities and trips, the system would completely integrate activity-travel decisions but distinguish day-to-day planning from real-time implementation – see Table 2. The planning module would generate and schedule activities and trips based on the best approximation of travel times. The real-time implementation module would track individuals in time and space during the simulated day with the corresponding time-space constraints and real-time adjustments to the planned schedule. This distinction between the planning layer and physical layer is very close to the AgBM concept described in [22] where the term "mental layer" is used instead of "planning layer".

Table 2. ABM-DTA: from software coupling to deeper conceptual Integration

Emergent new AgBM sub-models	Historic ABM	Historic DTA
Planning and scheduling	Activity generation, tour formation, trip scheduling	Routing
Real-time implementation and response	Missing in classic ABM, the gap is filled by dynamic individual schedule adjustment	Vehicle movement simulation and en-route decisions

6.2　Individual Time-Space Constraints

Individual schedule consistency means that for each person, the daily schedule (i.e. a sequence of trips and activities) is formed without gaps or overlaps as shown in Fig. 8. This way, any change in travel time would affect activity durations and vice versa. The concept of individual schedule consistency closely relate to a general principle of time-space constraints as one of the cornerstones of travel behavior analysis [15].

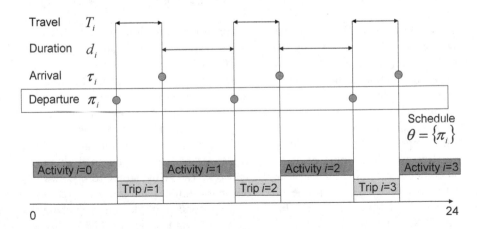

Fig. 8. Individual schedule consistency

Individual schedule consistency is one of the central concepts for a new generation of ABMs and new ways of ABM-DTA integration in practice. It is important for a practical realism of the model outcome since it imposes important constraints on the transportation system state through millions of individual constraints. This concept can also be thought of as a dynamic "tracking" of each individual throughout the day in the real-time implementation layer without illogical gaps or overlaps between activities and trips; that brings it closer to the AgBM realm. It has also strong implications in the planning layer, for example for constraining sets of possible destinations by the available time window (in addition to learning approach that by itself constrains the destination choice sets).

7 Explicit Consideration of a Constrained Supply of Activities

7.1 Workplace Location Choice

Choice of workplace for each worker is one of the most important sub-models of any travel model that largely defines the commuting patterns and flows that contribute the most to the congestion in major metropolitan regions. This model falls into the category of choices with a constrained supply since the number of jobs available in each zone is normally fixed in a travel model. The corresponding techniques have a long history routed back to the aggregate 4-step models. The most frequently used aggregate method in 4-step models is a segmented doubly constrained gravity model that is equivalent to a destination choice model with shadow pricing. The segmentation is normally implemented by income groups or by employment type (occupation or industry). The aggregate model generates fractional probabilities referred to as "true probabilities" in the numerical experiment described below.

Essentially the same technique of shadow pricing was inherited by many ABMs in practice where individual destination choice is followed by a calculation of shadow pricing for each destination zone and then all individuals are re-simulated iteratively with shadow prices added to the individual destination choice utilities until the constraints are met. This technique normally requires 5–10 multiple iterations with a full re-simulation of all individuals that can be computationally quite intensive. Also, due to a microsimulation variability the constraints can only be matched approximately. This technique is referred to as "shadow pricing" in the numerical experiment below. The principal difference and advantage of micro simulation is that the destination choice utility can include any number of individual variables such as income, age, gender, occupation, education level, presence of children while the aggregate segmentation is limited [19].

ABMs implemented in a disaggregate microsimulation fashion also provide examples of alternative techniques that are closer to the AgBM paradigm. One of them is an individual destination choice model with gradual removing of chosen jobs from the zone size variables with each individual choice as was implemented in the New York, NY, and Columbus, OH, ABMs [16]. In terms of behavioral richness of the utility function, this model is identical to the microsimulation model with shadow pricing. However, this model is more appealing behaviorally. It has a property appreciated by practitioners that all zonal constraints by number of jobs by type are matched exactly. This model is also more efficient computationally since it does not require multiple iterations. In the numerical example discussed below, two versions of this model are presented. The first version referred to as "size adjustment sequential" is based on simulating individuals in the sequential order of zones numbered from the central area outward. The second version referred to as "size adjustment random" is based on a completely random processing of individuals.

All four models were compared using a sample of 100,000 individuals with the same utility functions. The corresponding trip-length distributions as a compact measure of the model performance are shown in Fig. 9.

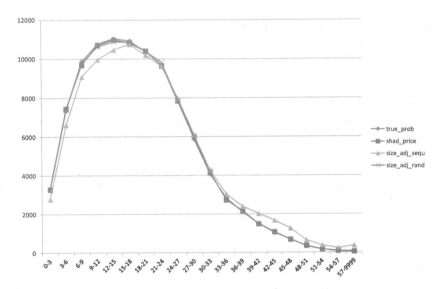

Fig. 9. Comparison of constrained destination choice models

The results proved to be virtually identical across three models where the spatial correlation was avoided. The only problematic formulation was the model with an adjustment of the zonal size terms by removing the taken jobs where the processing of individuals was done according to the sequence of zones. In this case, a path dependence associated with the order of processing individuals had a systematic impact on the results. The model with an adjustment of size variables where individuals are processed in a completely random order, simply replicated the results of the two first models. In this case "agency" only brought some computational gain but did not change the underlying model since there was no real direct interaction between the agents. Further refinement of the competition process outlined in the 3rd and 4th models is possible that could potentially lead to a meaningfully different model.

In this direction, consideration of a so-called "bid-choice" model looks like a promising next step. A Bid-Choice AgBM is principally different from conventional choice model [12]. In the context of destination choice, it is illustrated in Fig. 10. In the conventional choice model every decision-making unit (individual) chooses a "passive" alternative although with a limited supply. The only feedback that individual workers have from the alternative job locations is a diminishing supply with each job taken. In the bid-choice model, the alternatives themselves are "active" and can reject an individual "bid" even if supply is still available that is much more behaviorally realistic for workplace location choice.

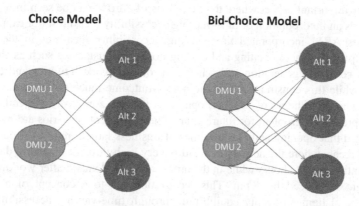

Fig. 10. Bid-choice vs. choice

The principal algorithm of a bid-choice can be outlined as the following 3-step iterative procedure:

1. Every worker from each residential zone who does not have a job yet, chooses the best job from the correspondent segment (type of job) from destination zone (employer) based on individual job preferences and accessibility. The choice may have a random error.
2. Every employer ranks bids by preferences and compare to the size variable (jobs available). Evaluation may have a random error. Top bids are accepted until the size has been exhausted. Bottom bids are rejected.
3. Size variable are adjusted by removing the accepted bids. Rejected bids go to step 1.

7.2   Long-Term Dynamics and Evolution with a Constrained Supply

Consideration of long-term dynamics has been an inherent component of land-use models from which some of the techniques were transferred to travel models in the context of integrated land-use and transportation systems [15]. One specific "gray area" between land-use and transportation models where long-term dynamics proved to be essential is a population synthesis for future years. In most microsimulation ABMs in practice, population synthesis is implemented independently for each year. Only the control variables and exogenously defined trends represent the dynamic effects. However, there are first promising examples of the "true" household evolution models such as one applied for the Los-Angeles, CA and Baltimore, MD ABMs where the future synthetic population evolves from the base year population [7]. The household evolution model is principally different from a standard population synthesis although both models operate with individual lists of households and persons. In a standard population synthesis, the created households and persons do not exhibit any individual memory, learning, adaptation, or other aspect of intelligence. In the household evolution process, the created households and persons act as adaptable and interacting "agents" that evolve through years (age, die, give birth, marry, divorce, split, etc.).

Another important aspect where the first signs of AgBM can be seen in the ABMs in practice, is an incorporation of time-varying accessibility measures. For example, the Los-Angeles ABM incorporated time-varying accessibility measures in the activity generation process where opening and closing hours for businesses such as shops and restaurants constrain generation and scheduling of non-work activities and trips [9]. However, while this constraint makes the model outcome much more realistic for the base year where the hours of business operation in each zone can be specified as an input, it represents a problem for future years where different scenarios are possible. It is recognized that opening and closing times of business largely reflect the demand. In the central areas, where the activity demand is very high through the entire day, shops are open until very late hours while in the areas with low demand after working hours, shops might be closed by 5 pm. This recognition led to a concept of a regional spatio-temporal demand-supply equilibrium through time-varying accessibility measures shown in Fig. 11. In this equilibrium, three types of agents interact dynamically: (1) individuals making decisions regarding time-of-day and destination choice for non-work activities based on the accessibility of activity supply, (2) owners of retail establishments making decisions about opening and closing hours of their business based on the demand, and (3) retail employees making commuting time-of-day choices based on the demand for labor from the retail industry.

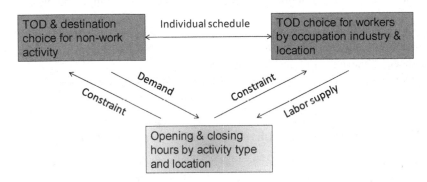

Fig. 11. Spatio-temporal equilibration of activity demand and supply.

8 Important Future Directions

It can be concluded from the examples above that AgBM represents a promising and quite natural extension of the ABM techniques already established in practice in the US. These first examples will arguably evolve over time into a more complete and coherent approach where such elements of "agency" as individual memory, learning, adaptation, direct interactions between the agents, planning and real-time adjustments, as well as competition for a constrained activity supply, would become standard techniques. However, we should also expect some other principal transformations of the model structures in view of new tendencies that may have a strong impact on the mobility patterns and also on information available for their analysis and modeling. Two important factors should be mentioned at this point of time.

The first one relates to an inevitable advent of autonomous vehicles that would result in extended mobility options compared to the travel and activity patterns known today. However, it can be mentioned that an explicit separation of activities and trips in advanced ABMs with AgBM components already proved beneficial for modeling impacts of autonomous vehicles as the recent experience with the Phoenix, AZ ABM demonstrated. In particular, it was found reasonable how the AgBM responded to the introduction of autonomous vehicles with respect to the tour formation and combination of trips modes on the tour with the same number of activity episodes.

The second possible principal change in model structures relates to the so-called "big" data. Big data has many advantages over conventional travel surveys but the main question is how it could be used beyond a model validation. Big data is not "behavioral" compared to household surveys in a sense that many important characteristics of the individual such as income and car ownership as well as of the trip such as trip purpose and mode are not known. However, the recent research and first attempts to use big data for travel model development showed possible ways of either processing the big data itself or restructuring of the travel model that can resolve most of the issues. For example, trip purpose can be imputed based on the detailed parcel-level land use and temporal profile of the activity over multiple days. More interestingly, the travel model can be reformulated in terms of activity profiles and establishment types rather than in terms of the traditional trip purpose labels. Instead of the "shopping" trip purpose the model could operate with a "recurrent weekly activity of 2 h or less at a shopping center". Trip mode can be imputed reliably based on the speed profile and comparison of the itinerary to the detailed road and transit networks. Household income can be replaced with the average residential zone income as an explanatory variable that in several ABMs performed statistically better than the individual household income.

References

1. Abdelghany, A.F., Mahmassani, H.S.: Temporal-spatial microassignment and sequencing of travel demand with activity-trip chains. Transp. Res. Rec. **1831**, 89–97 (2003)
2. Axelrod, R.: The dissemination of culture: a model with local convergence and global polarization. J. Conflict Resolut. **41**(2), 203–226 (1997)
3. Arentze, T.A., Timmermans, H.J.P.: Representing mental maps and cognitive learning in micro-simulation models of activity-travel choice dynamics. Transportation **32**, 321–340 (2005)
4. Bonabeau, E.: Agent-based modeling: methods and techniques for simulating human systems. PNAS **99**(Suppl. 3), 7280–7287 (2002)

5. Bradley, M., Vovsha, P.: A model for joint choice of daily activity pattern types of household members. Transportation **32**(5), 545–571 (2005)
6. Dugundji, E.R., Walker, J.L.: Discrete choice with social and spatial network interdependencies. Transp. Res. Rec. **1921**, 70–78 (2005)
7. Eluru, N., Pinjari, A.R., Guo, J.Y., Sener, I.N., Srinivasan, S., Copperman, R.B., Bhat, C.R.: Population Updating System Structures and Models Embedded Within the Comprehensive Econometric Microsimulator for Urban Systems (CEMUS), Center for Transportation Research, The University of Texas at Austin. Report 167260-1 (2007)
8. Goldstone, R.L., Janssen, M.A.: Computational models of collective behavior. TRENDS Cogn. Sci. **9**(9), 424–430 (2005)
9. Goulias, K.G., Chen, Y., Bhat, C.R., Eluru, N.: Activity-based microsimulation model system in southern california: design, implementation, preliminary findings, and future plans. In: Proceedings of the 3rd Conference on Innovations in Travel Modeling (ITM), TRB, Tempe, AZ (2010)
10. Gupta, S., Vovsha, P.: A model for work activity schedules with synchronization for multiple-worker households. Transportation **40**, 827–845 (2013)
11. Manski, C.F.: The structure of random utility models. Theor. Decis. **8**(3), 229–254 (1977)
12. Martinez, F.J.: The bid-choice land-use model: an integrated economic framework. Environ. Plan. A **24**, 871–885 (1992)
13. Paleti, R., Vovsha, P., Givon, D., Birotker, Y.: Impact of individual daily travel pattern on value of time. Transportation **42**(6), 1003–1017 (2015)
14. Paul, B., Vovsha, P., Hicks, J., Livshits, V., Pendyala, R.: Extension of the activity-based modeling approach to incorporate supply side of activities: examples for major universities and special events. Transp. Res. Rec. **2429**, 138–147 (2014)
15. Pendyala, R.M., Kitamura, R.: Phased implementation of a multimodal activity-based travel demand modeling system in Florida. Final report. Vol. II: FAMOS Users Guide. Florida Department of Transportation. Report BA496 (2004)
16. Petersen, E., Vovsha, P., Donnelly, R.: Managing "competition" in micro-simulation: implications for destination choice and non-motorized modeling. Presented at the 81st TRB Meeting, Washington D.C. (2002)
17. Salvini, P., Miller, E.J.: ILUTE: an operational prototype of a comprehensive microsimulation model of urban systems. Netw. Spat. Econ. **5**(2), 217–234 (2005)
18. Vovsha, P., Hicks, J.E., Anderson, R., Giaimo, G., Rousseau, G.: Integrated model of travel demand and network simulation. In: Proceedings of the 6th Conference on Innovations in Travel Modeling (ITM), TRB, Denver, CO (2016)
19. Vovsha, P., Gupta, S., Freedman, J., Sun, W., Livshits, V.: Workplace choice model: comparison of spatial patterns of commuting in four metropolitan regions. Presented at the 91st TRB Meeting, Washington D.C. (2012)
20. Vovsha, P., Petersen, E., Donnelly, R.: Micro-simulation in travel demand modeling: lessons learned from the New York best practice model. Transp. Res. Rec. **1805**, 68–77 (2002)
21. Nagel, K., Flötteröd, G.: Agent-based traffic assignment: going from trips to behavioural travelers. In: Pendyala, R., Bhat, C. (eds.) Travel Behaviour Research in an Evolving World – Selected Papers from the 12th International Conference on Travel Behaviour Research, pp. 261–294. International Association for Travel Behaviour Research (2012)
22. Balmer, M., Cetin, N., Nagel, K., Raney, B.: Towards truly agent-based traffic and mobility simulations. In: Autonomous Agents and Multiagent Systems (AAMAS 2004) (2004)

Towards a Testbed for Dynamic Vehicle Routing Algorithms

Michal Maciejewski[1,2]([⊠]), Joschka Bischoff[1], Sebastian Hörl[3], and Kai Nagel[1]

[1] Transport Systems and Transport Telematics, Technische Universität Berlin,
SG12, Salzufer 17–19, 10587 Berlin, Germany
[2] Division of Transport Systems, Poznan University of Technology, Piotrowo 3,
60-965 Poznan, Poland
michal.maciejewski@put.poznan.pl
[3] IVT, ETH Zürich, 8093 Zürich, Switzerland

Abstract. Since modern transport services are becoming more flexible, demand-responsive, and energy/cost efficient, there is a growing demand for large-scale microscopic simulation platforms in order to test sophisticated routing algorithms. Such platforms have to simulate in detail, not only the dynamically changing demand and supply of the relevant service, but also traffic flow and other relevant transport services. This paper presents the DVRP extension to the open-source MATSim simulator. The extension is designed to be highly general and customizable to simulate a wide range of dynamic rich vehicle routing problems. The extension allows plugging in of various algorithms that are responsible for continuous re-optimisation of routes in response to changes in the system. The DVRP extension has been used in many research and commercial projects dealing with simulation of electric and autonomous taxis, demand-responsive transport, personal rapid transport, free-floating car sharing and parking search.

Keywords: Dynamic vehicle routing · DVRP · Multi-agent · Traffic flow · MATSim · Autonomous taxis · Shared taxis · Demand-responsive transport · DRT · Testbed · Benchmark

1 Introduction

The recent technological advancements in ICT provide novel, on-line fleet management tools, opening up a broad range of possibilities for more intelligent transport services: flexible, demand-responsive, safe and energy/cost efficient. Significant enhancements can aid in both traditional transport operations, like regular public transport or taxis and introduction of novel solutions, such as demand-responsive transport (DRT) or personal rapid transport (PRT). However, the growing complexity of modern transport systems, despite all benefits, increases the risk of poor performance, or even failure, due to the lack of precise design, implementation and testing.

© Springer International Publishing AG 2017
J. Bajo et al. (Eds.): PAAMS 2017 Workshops, CCIS 722, pp. 69–79, 2017.
DOI: 10.1007/978-3-319-60285-1_6

A traditional approach to test algorithms are benchmark instances (e.g. [11, 26]). A number of instances are made available, often on the web, and algorithms to solve these problems are collected, together with performance numbers. To make performances comparable, all algorithms should be run on the same computers, maybe provided by the team that is providing the benchmark. And ideally there would be a "blind" part of the testing, where the submitted algorithms are run on benchmark instances that were not published beforehand.

Benchmark instances have been successfully applied to analyse and compare performances of algorithms solving different kinds of static Vehicle Routing Problems (VRP) [10, 31], where, in the most basic version of the problem, one wants to determine minimal-cost vehicle routes, which begin at the depot, visit a subset of the customers, and return to the depot.

The *Dynamic* VRP (DVRP, [2, 23, 24]) is different from the static problem in that not all information relevant to the planning of the routes is known when the routing process begins, and some information, such as expected travel times, may be imprecise and stochastic. In the dynamic case, like in other online problems, where algorithms need to run *while* the controlled system is evolving [8], the use of static benchmark datasets is problematic. For example, with a static benchmark dataset one needs to be really diligent not to make the algorithm look into the future when the future (e.g. future requests) is already available in the input data. Also, with a pre-computed benchmark, it is impossible to have the system react to the control – for example cancelling requests when pick-ups take too long. Moreover, even simple pre-planned event sequences may lead into inconsistencies: for example, serving a request between its scheduled submission and cancellation. Finally, the controlled system may be stochastic, in which case there needs to be either an analytic description of the stochastic properties of the system, or some way to generate random draws from the system. Consequently, there has been no reference benchmarks for DVRP so far [23].

These above problems could potentially be addressed by theoretical approaches to the analysis of online optimisation algorithms, such as competitive analysis [8]. However, their use is mostly limited to simplified cases, and for large and complex real-life problems the simulation approach is often the only viable way to evaluate, compare and refine dynamic algorithms [12]. For example, for dynamic vehicle routing problems, one could have a simulation tool that generates requests and travel times randomly. A to-be-evaluated dispatch algorithm then needs to direct a fleet of vehicles to serve these requests.

In order to be realistic, such tools have to model, in detail, not only the dynamically changing demand and supply of the relevant service, but also traffic flow and other existing transport services, including mutual interactions/relations between all these components. Although several approaches have been proposed [1, 9, 17, 25], as far the authors know, no existing solutions provide large-scale microscopic simulation that include all the components above. [28] provides a recent review of existing agent-based simulators for DRT.

2   MATSim and DVRP

One possible solution to simulation-based benchmarking of online algorithms is to use an existing transport/traffic simulator instead of creating one from scratch. Such a tool should allow for detailed modelling of complex interdependencies between the three main components, that is customer demand, traffic flow, and vehicle fleet, and be able to run large-scale simulation. MATSim (Multi-Agent Transport Simulation) [15] offers a comprehensive set of features that renders it suitable for benchmarking purposes. First of all, it is a multi-agent activity-based microsimulation system for daily transport demand analysis. Secondly, due to a fast and efficient traffic simulation, it is able to conduct analyses for large scenarios, even concerning a whole country. Last but not least, MATSim modularity and openness (open-source software) allow for extending and adjusting its functionality to one's needs.

To enable simulation of vehicle routing in MATSim, the DVRP (*Dynamic Vehicle Routing Problem*) extension [19] has been developed. The extension is designed to be highly general and customizable to model a wide range of dynamic vehicle routing problems, including the so-called *Rich DVRPs*. Compared to the classic VRP, the major model enhancements are: (a) one-to-many (many-to-one) and many-to-many topologies, (b) multiple depots, (c) dynamic requests, (d) request and vehicle types, (e) time windows for requests and vehicles, (f) time-dependent stochastic travel times and costs, and (g) network-based routing (including route planning, vehicle monitoring and diversion). The DVRP extension is in direct interaction with the simulation during the execution of the traffic flow simulation. Figure 1 shows the interaction of the main MATSim modules and the DVRP extension. One can easily extend the existing model even further to cover other specific cases (see Sect. 5), which then require at least a specific optimizer (see Sect. 4).

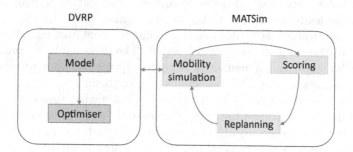

Fig. 1. Integration of the DVRP module in the MATSim multi-iterative simulation process [14].

3 DVRP Model and Simulation

3.1 Basic Model

The DVRP extension is responsible for modelling both demand and supply of the transport service in question, while MATSim simulates them together with other components of the overall transport system.

In the most basic setup, the DVRP problem is defined by a fleet of `Vehicles` that serves submitted `Requests`. Requests come in over time, and not all requests need to be known when the first request is served. In addition, the traffic state is not fully known ahead of time, although travel time and cost estimates are available.

The way a vehicle serves assigned requests is defined by its schedule that consists of a sequence of `Tasks`, such as driving from one location to another, or staying at a given location. Schedules are computed and managed by the optimiser algorithm (Sect. 4). In order to build a valid schedule, the optimiser needs to take into account all constraints. Among them are network constraints, such as turning or vehicle restrictions, and time constraints, such as time windows or travel times. Therefore, when planning a drive from one place to another, the optimiser uses one of the least cost path calculators available in MATSim. It finds a minimum-cost path through the network, given the departure time, vehicle type and cost function.

3.2 Dynamic Agents

The standard day-to-day re-planning approach in MATSim [14] assumes that agents can make complete daily activity plans only between simulation runs. During simulation, plans are executed without any change. This renders MATSim's standard implementation of agents not suitable for simulating Dynamic Vehicle Routing Problems, where each driver agent (either human or robot) behaves dynamically and follows tasks coming continuously from the dispatcher. In order to overcome this limitation, the dynamic agent was introduced as an alternative to the standard pre-planned agent. The dynamic agent provides the foundation for simulating dynamically behaving agents in a wide range of different simulation scenarios, DVRP being only one of them.

In general, the dynamic agent can actively decide what to do at each simulation step instead of using a pre-computed plan. It is up to the agent whether decisions are made spontaneously or (re-)planned in advance. In some applications, the agent is fully autonomous and acts according to his/her desires, beliefs and intentions, whereas in other ones, it may just follow orders systematically issued from the outside, which is the case of dynamic vehicle routing.

Contrary to the standard MATSim agent executing a fixed plan of static activities and legs, the dynamic agent performs dynamic activities and legs, which are usually created on the fly, and can be modified at any time. Moreover, dynamic activities and legs are simulated. For instance, when driving a car, the agent can change the route, destination or even decide about picking up or dropping off somebody on the way.

In the present paper, the dynamic agent will be used to represent the taxicab driver. In general, however, it can be used to represent arbitrary agent types.

3.3 Simulation

Realistic simulation of DVRP requires a proper behavioural model of the taxicab driver agent. At a higher level, this agent follows its dynamically changing schedule. After completing one task, it switches to the next one. The new task is then translated into a dynamic action, which is performed by the agent. For instance, a pickup task is translated into a dynamic pickup activity, where the driver agent first waits for the passenger agent (if not yet there), and then lets it board the vehicle. In this specific case, simulation of the task includes a direct interaction between agents. In other cases, the interaction may be indirect, e.g. an agent moving through the network contributes together with other drivers to the overall traffic.

While executing scheduled tasks, the driver can be continuously monitored with task trackers that offer functionality similar to GPS navigation, such as tracking its movement or predicting task completion time. Moreover, the communication can be two-way. For instance, while executing a drive task, the agent can be ordered to divert from its current destination.

The current implementation of the driver agent logic assumes that drivers strictly follow the schedules which are managed centrally by the optimiser. However, the logic can be modified in order to give more autonomy to drivers (e.g. planning routes, accepting/rejecting requests, specifying their availability). In the most extreme case, drivers could fully decide for themselves, while the optimiser would act as a middleman, only establishing contact between customers and drivers.

4 Optimiser

As in real-life online fleet management systems, the central element in the DVRP extension is the optimisation algorithm. The optimiser reacts to events generated during simulation, which could be: request submissions, vehicle departures or arrivals, etc. Additionally, it can monitor the movement of individual vehicles, as well as query other sources of online information, e.g. current traffic conditions. In response to changes in the system, the optimiser may update vehicles' schedules, either by applying smaller modifications or re-optimizing them from scratch. Vehicles are notified about changes in their schedules and adjust to them as soon as possible, including immediate diversion from their current destinations.

The extension's architecture allows the plugging in of various on-line vehicle routing algorithms (optimisers). In order to plug an optimiser into the simulator, it has to implement the base `VrpOptimizer` interface or one of its more specialised subinterfaces. The base interface contains the following two methods:

- `requestSubmitted(Request request)`—called on submitting `request`; in response, the optimiser either adapts vehicles' schedules so that `request` can be served, or rejects it.
- `nextTask(Vehicle vehicle)`—called whenever `vehicles`'s current task has been completed and the vehicle will switch to the next planned task; this is the last moment to make or revise the decision on what to do next.

This basic functionality can be freely extended. References to more complex optimisers used for such services like taxi, shared taxi or demand-responsive transport can be found in Sects. 5 and 6.

In general, there are two ways of responding to the incoming events. They can be handled either *immediately (synchronously)* or *between simulation time steps (asynchronously)*. In the former case, schedules are re-calculated (updated or re-optimised) directly, in response to the calling of the optimiser's methods. This simplifies accepting/rejecting new requests, since the answer is immediately passed back to the caller. In the latter case, all events observed within a simulation period are buffered and then processed collectively just before the next simulation period begins. Mixing both approaches by answering immediately to some events, and buffering other ones is also possible. Regardless of the approach taken, special care must be given to thread safety when running multi-threaded simulation and/or optimisation.

5 Example

This section discusses creating a DVRP optimiser and running a MATSim simulation for autonomous taxi (AT) service, which dispatches ATs in response to continuously incoming taxi calls. The central part is the `ATOptimizer` class (Listing 1). As stated above, by implementing the standard `VrpOptimizer` interface, the optimiser can react to two types of events: submission of a new request, and switching to the next tasks. The former is handled in the `requestSubmitted(Request)` method, where the optimiser schedules the newly submitted `request`. The latter, in turn, is handled in the `nextTask(Vehicle)` method, which is called when `vehicle` finishes its current task. In this case, the optimiser updates this vehicle's schedule, and then switches `vehicle`'s current task to the next one.

Listing 1. ATOptimizer.java

```
public class ATOptimizer implements VrpOptimizer {
    public void requestSubmitted(Request request) {
        scheduleRequest(request);
    }

    public void nextTask(Vehicle vehicle) {
        updateScheduleAndSwitchToNextTask(vehicle);
    }
    ...
}
```

The standard procedure of running a MATSim simulation consists of the following four steps:

1. load a config file (containing all simulation parameters)
2. load scenario data (i.e. read data and initialise all object structures)
3. create and configure a simulation controller
4. run simulation.

Because simulating ATs requires the DVRP extension to be added, the base scheme has to be extended with loading the fleet data and then adding the implemented optimiser to the controller (between steps 3 and 4). Listing 2 presents a code that configures and runs AT simulation. In this example, all *taxi* trips will be served by `fleet` of ATs according to the optimisation algorithm defined in the `ATOptimizer` class.

Listing 2. AT simulation

```
Config config = loadConfig(); // (step 1)
Scenario scenario = loadScenario(config); // (step 2)
Controler controller = new Controler(scenario); // (step 3)

Fleet fleet = loadFleet();
addVrpOptimizer(controller,"taxi", fleet, ATOptimizer.class);

controller.run(); // (step 4)
```

Complete, executable examples presenting the use of the DVRP extension to simulate different on-demand transport services can be found in the following places in the MATSim project:

- `RunOneTaxiExample` (see http://matsim.org/javadoc → `dvrp`) – the most basic example on dispatching a single taxi to serve incoming requests
- `RunRobotaxiExample` (see http://matsim.org/javadoc → `av`) – a robotaxi (AV taxi) fleet is used to replace all private car trips of a random population in the city of Cottbus, Germany
- `RunTaxiExample` (see http://matsim.org/javadoc → `taxi`) – used to benchmark the taxi optimisers available in the taxi extension; a fleet of taxis in dispatched to serve taxi calls in the city of Mielec, Poland
- `RunSharedTaxiExample` (see http://matsim.org/javadoc → `taxi`) – a simple shared taxi algorithm for up to two passengers with different origins and destinations set in Braunschweig, Germany.
- `RunTaxibusExample` (see http://matsim.org/javadoc → `taxi`) – an example for a DRT shuttle system where passengers want to reach a train station in Braunschweig, Germany.

6   Existing Applications

The development of the DVRP testbed originated in the simulation of taxi fleets and was more recently extended to larger fleets of AVs and demand-responsive transport. One first use case was the simulation of taxi demand in the Polish city of Mielec. For this scenario, different dispatch algorithms have been developed and tested. The model has been used for comparison of off-line and on-line taxi dispatching optimization algorithms [18,22] and simulation of electric taxicab fleets [3].

Based on the actual demand for taxi trips in Berlin [6] and Barcelona [30], several different taxi dispatch algorithms were measured in their performance under different demand levels. The results suggest that First-In-First-Out algorithms are capable of handling typical taxi demand levels reasonably well. In sudden demand peaks, however, strategies focusing on minimizing idle mileage for vehicles (thus maximising throughput) rather than customer waiting times perform far better in terms of waiting time for the majority of passengers. Also approaches based on solving a linear assignment problem were experimented [20]. The strategy produced better results for both drivers (less idle driving) and passengers (less waiting) than rule-based approaches, but is more demanding in terms of computational requirements.

Another field of usage of the DVRP testbed is the investigation of demand-responsive transport (DRT) systems, which generally incorporate the transportation of several passengers with different destinations at the same time. The conceptual use cases for them are wide ranged and can possibly include one-to-many or many-to-many relations with different kinds of operational schemes in terms of spatial limitation or usage of stops and pre-bookings.

In one case study, a pre-booked dial-a-ride DRT service for commuter transit of a car production plant was developed and assessed for the Wolfsburg region in central Germany. With car traffic to and from the production plant causing considerable congestion during peak hours, a high-quality DRT service picking up passengers at home and dropping them off at their workplace could possibly help to reduce congestion around arterials. To achieve this, while keeping the commuting times of DRT users at an acceptable level, a compromise between vehicle capacity, waiting times and in-vehicle travel times was found [7]. Using 8-seat vehicles, travel times of DRT passengers were simulated to be only slightly higher than using private cars.

Further DRT applications include an application to evaluate several DRT schemes for a thinly populated area in Australia [27]. Based on the same infrastructure, a DRT service that includes both passenger and parcel distribution has also been simulated [29]. A possible DRT system using public transport stops and allowing passengers with common trip patterns to share rides was evaluated on a pseudo-realistic scenario of the Cottbus region (Germany) [16].

More recently, the ability to simulate very large fleets of (automated) taxis have been assessed. The largest scenario calculated so far is based on the inner-city car trips in Berlin. These accumulate to roughly 2.5 million trips per day and are usually handled by a fleet of roughly 1.2 million privately owned cars. In [4,5] these trips were shifted from car mode to shared autonomous vehicle (SAV). While this resembles an extreme scenario (no more private cars), it demonstrates the overall potential of SAVs and opens up further branches of research. In order to cope with a fleet size of hundreds of thousands of vehicles, vehicle dispatch is based on rule-based heuristics that either assign the vehicle closest to a request (in times when there is an oversupply of vehicles) or assign a vehicle to the closest request. Zonal registers were used to pre-filter vehicles and requests close to each other. Results suggest that a fleet of 100 000 to 110 000 vehicles is sufficient to replace all car trips, leading to a possible fleet reduction of 90%. Waiting times for passengers can be kept in a range between 3 to 5 min for the majority of customers even during peak times. On average, vehicles spend more than 80% of the driven mileage with a customer on board. Pick-up trips are generally longer in the outskirts of the city [4], leading to the question whether offering such a service in less-densely populated areas is of commercial or communal interest. During further research, the possible positive impact of an improved traffic flow of automated vehicles has been assessed, concluding that a minor increase in traffic flow capabilities of SAVs would be enough to (over)-compensate the negative congestion impact of the additional empty trips of SAV fleets [21].

The interplay of multiple dynamic AV taxi services has been tested in combination with a responsive demand in [13]. A coherent framework of utility scoring for traditional modes of transport, as well as for autonomous vehicles has been set up, such that the artificial simulation population is able to choose between conventional means of transport and the new services. On the supply side, single-passenger SAVs have been offered in competition to multi-passenger ("pooled") AVs. Both services used a dispatching heuristic by Maciejewski and Bischoff [5], while the latter one aggregated up to four yet unserved requests with origin and destination locations not being farther apart than 400 m. The study showed that with MATSim and DVRP it is possible to model coherent demand reactions to new forms of dynamic transportation. While both AV offers were used at peak-hours, customers favoured the pooled AVs at off-peak hours, where they were able to weigh the slightly increased travel times but low prices of the pooled service against considerably higher prices (but shorter travel times) of the AV taxi service.

7 Conclusions

This paper presents the current functionality and typical use cases of the DVRP extension. By providing an abstraction layer for modelling of fleet management operations, the extension allows for simulation of dynamic vehicle routing in MATSim. Since 2011, the extension has been actively developed and continuously new features are being added. Currently, our efforts are focused on: (a) simplifying the process of plugging in custom-made VRP optimisers and models by means of dependency injection, (b) speedup and parallelisation of large-scale simulations, and (c) standardisation of the DVRP interfaces. By being able to simulate large and complex transport systems at the microscopic level of detail, and offering code modularity and openness, MATSim and DVRP can serve as a testbed platform for dynamic vehicle routing problems.

References

1. Barcelo, J., Grzybowska, H., Pardo, S.: Vehicle routing and scheduling models, simulation and city logistics. In: Zeimpekis, V., Tarantilis, C.D., Giaglis, G.M., Minis, I. (eds.) Dynamic Fleet Management, pp. 163–195. Springer, New York (2007)
2. Bektas, T., Repoussis, P.P., Tarantilis, C.D.: Dynamic vehicle routing problems, chap. 11, pp. 299–347. http://epubs.siam.org/doi/abs/10.1137/1.9781611973594. ch11
3. Bischoff, J., Maciejewski, M.: Agent-based simulation of electric taxi-cab fleets. Transp. Res. Procedia **4**, 191–198 (2014). (VSP WP 14-10. http://www.vsp.tu-berlin.de/publications)
4. Bischoff, J., Maciejewski, M.: Autonomous taxicabs in Berlin - a spatiotemporal analysis of service performance. Transp. Res. Procedia **19**, 176–186 (2016)
5. Bischoff, J., Maciejewski, M.: Simulation of city-wide replacement of private cars with autonomous taxis in Berlin. Procedia Comput. Sci. **83**, 237–244 (2016). http://www.sciencedirect.com/science/article/pii/S1877050916301442
6. Bischoff, J., Maciejewski, M., Sohr, A.: Analysis of Berlin's taxi services by exploring GPS traces. In: 2015 International Conference on Models and Technologies for Intelligent Transportation Systems (MT-ITS), pp. 209–215, June 2015
7. Bischoff, J., Soeffker, N., Maciejewski, M.: A framework for agent based simulation of demand responsive transport systems. Technical report, presented at OR 2016 (2016)
8. Borodin, A., El-Yaniv, R.: Online Computation and Competitive Analysis. Cambridge University Press, Cambridge (2005)
9. Certicky, M., Jakob, M., Pibil, R., Moler, Z.: Agent-based simulation testbed for on-demand transport services. In: Proceedings of the 2014 International Conference on Autonomous Agents and Multi-agent Systems, AAMAS 2014, pp. 1671–1672. International Foundation for Autonomous Agents and Multiagent Systems, Richland, May 2014. http://dl.acm.org/citation.cfm?id=2615731.2616118
10. Dantzig, G.B., Ramser, J.H.: The truck dispatching problem. Manag. Sci. **6**(1), 80–91 (1959)
11. Geiger, A., Lenz, P., Stiller, C., Urtasun, R.: The KITTI vision benchmark suite. Accessed 16 Feb 2017
12. Grötschel, M., Krumke, S.O., Rambau, J., Winter, T., Zimmermann, U.T.: Combinatorial online optimization in real time. In: Grötschel, M., Krumke, S.O., Rambau, J. (eds.) Online Optimization of Large Scale Systems, pp. 679–704. Springer, Heidelberg (2001)
13. Hörl, S.: Agent-based simulation of autonomous taxi services with dynamic demand responses. Technical report, Arbeitsberichte Verkehrs-und Raumplanung 1229 (2017)
14. Horni, A., Nagel, K., Axhausen, K.W.: Introducing MATSim. In: Horni, A., Nagel, K., Axhausen, K.W. (eds.) The Multi-agent Transport Simulation MATSim. Ubiquity, London (2016). http://matsim.org/the-book
15. Horni, A., Nagel, K., Axhausen, K.W. (eds.): The Multi-Agent Transport Simulation MATSim, chap. 1. Ubiquity, London (2016). http://matsim.org/the-book
16. Hosse, D., Neumann, A.: Modelling of operational variants for the use of personal rapid transit in public transit (2015). https://www.innoz.de/sites/default/files/heart_2015_submission_88_final.pdf

17. Liao, T.Y., Hu, T.Y., Chen, D.J.: Object-oriented evaluation framework for dynamic vehicle routing problems under real-time information. In: Annual Meeting Preprint 08-2222, Transportation Research Board, Washington, D.C., January 2008
18. Maciejewski, M.: Benchmarking minimum passenger waiting time in online taxi dispatching with exact offline optimization methods. Arch. Transp. **30**(2), 67–75 (2014)
19. Maciejewski, M.: Dynamic transport services. In: Horni, A., Nagel, K., Axhausen, K.W. (eds.) The Multi-agent Transport Simulation MATSim, chap. 23. Ubiquity, London (2016). http://matsim.org/the-book
20. Maciejewski, M., Bischoff, J., Nagel, K.: An assignment-based approach to efficient real-time city-scale taxi dispatching. IEEE Intell. Syst. **31**(1), 68–77 (2016)
21. Maciejewski, M., Bischoff, J., Nagel, K.: Congestion effects of autonomous taxi fleets. Transport (2017, in preparation)
22. Maciejewski, M.: Online taxi dispatching via exact offline optimization. Logistyka **3**, 2133–2142 (2014)
23. Pillac, V., Gendreau, M., Guéret, C., Medaglia, A.L.: A review of dynamic vehicle routing problems. Eur. J. Oper. Res. **225**(1), 1–11 (2013). http://www.sciencedirect.com/science/article/pii/S0377221712006388
24. Psaraftis, H.N., Wen, M., Kontovas, C.A.: Dynamic vehicle routing problems: three decades and counting. Networks **67**(1), 3–31 (2016)
25. Regan, A., Mahmassani, H., Jaillet, P.: Evaluation of dynamic fleet management systems: simulation framework. Transp. Res. Rec. **1645**, 176–184 (1998)
26. Reinelt, G.: TSPLIB95. https://www.iwr.uni-heidelberg.de/groups/comopt/software/TSPLIB95/. Accessed 16 Feb 2017
27. Ronald, N.: Yarrawonga and Mulwala: demand-responsive transportation in regional Victoria, Australia. In: Horni, A., Nagel, K., Axhausen, K.W. (eds.) The Multi-Agent Transport Simulation MATSim, chap. 95. Ubiquity, London (2016). http://matsim.org/the-book
28. Ronald, N., Thompson, R., Winter, S.: Simulating demand-responsive transportation: a review of agent-based approaches. Transp. Rev. **35**(4), 404–421 (2015)
29. Ronald, N., Yang, J., Thompson, R.G.: Exploring co-modality using on-demand transport systems. Transp. Res. Procedia **12**, 203–212 (2016). http://www.sciencedirect.com/science/article/pii/S2352146516000600
30. Salanova, J.M., Romeu, M.E., Amat, C.: Aggregated modeling of urban taxi services. Procedia Soc. Behav. Sci. **160**, 352–361 (2014). http://www.sciencedirect.com/science/article/pii/S187704281406248X
31. Toth, P., Vigo, D.: Vehicle Routing. Society for Industrial and Applied Mathematics, Philadelphia (2014). http://epubs.siam.org/doi/abs/10.1137/1.9781611973594

ABAM

On Simulating the Adoption of New Products in Markets with Rational Users and Companies

Juan Manuel Sanchez-Cartas$^{(\boxtimes)}$ and Gonzalo Leon

Universidad Politecnica de Madrid, Campus de Montegancedo, Madrid, Spain
{juanmanuel.sanchez,gonzalo.leon}@upm.es

Abstract. We simulate the diffusion of products and technologies using an agent-based model that considers rational users and companies. We simulate two theoretical markets that represent the launching of a digital device and the launching of a digital platform. We find that consumers' heterogeneity and information spread are key in determining prices and the adoption of technologies/products. We find highly differentiated markets reach lower adoption levels. Also, when companies cooperate in spreading information, markets reach higher adoption levels. Lastly, we find that highly differentiated markets are prone to failure.

Keywords: Diffusion of technology · Agent-based models · Price competition · Digital markets

1 Introduction

Prices and information play a major role in the launching processes of new products and understanding when and why they accelerate or slow down adoption is key for both predicting the penetration of a new technology (or product) and for developing business strategies. However, the role of companies' decisions tends to be neglected in the diffusion of innovations literature.

We adopt the agent-based methodology to simulate the adoption of technologies and products in two different markets. The novelty of our approach is that we consider endogenous companies' decisions. We simulate optimal ways of fixing prices and we address the role of prices and information in the launching of new products.

We simulate two theoretical economic models, which imitate the launching of new digital devices (like fitness trackers) and the launching of digital platforms (like IoT platforms). We assume all consumers are connected by a random network through which they know about the products. Initially, all consumers (except a small percentage of innovators) have no willingness to consume the products, and only when other consumers adopt the product, are they willing to buy it.

G. Leon—This work has been supported by the Project H2020 FI-WARE, particularly by the Joint Research Unit between the Technical University of Madrid (UPM) and Telefonica R&D.

© Springer International Publishing AG 2017
J. Bajo et al. (Eds.): PAAMS 2017 Workshops, CCIS 722, pp. 83–94, 2017.
DOI: 10.1007/978-3-319-60285-1_7

We consider three different cases of heterogeneity in the consumers population, and three other different patterns of how information spreads in the market. We find that consumers' heterogeneity and how consumers know about the products are the key variables in boosting and slowing down adoption instead of prices. Very differentiated populations will lead to higher prices, and companies that spread information about their own products and not about the common technology will reach lower adoption levels. We also find that failures in launching are more likely in these cases.

Although we make predictions about adoption in theoretical markets, these models allow for a first impression of the potential outcome of launching new products. To the best of our knowledge, this is the first work in the diffusion of innovation literature that considers endogenous prices.

2   The Launching of New Products and Its Prediction

The launching of a new product is a critical phase for all companies and a lot has been written about the diffusion of new technologies and products. One of the most interesting developments in literature is the introduction of agent-based modeling.

However, companies tend to be omitted in literature and only a few works consider the relevance of companies in the launching process such as [12,16]. But, if we consider the launching of digital platforms, we find only a single work that addresses the launching of a platform [3], and this work is from industrial organization literature in which platforms have been extensively addressed when the market is mature. There is no work in diffusion of innovation literature that considers them. Thus, we are making the first contribution to the relevant literature by adapting and simulating a theoretical model proposed by [6] in which two digital platforms compete for users and developers.

The implementation of theoretical models from industrial organization literature is scarce. Models from diffusion of innovation literature tend to rely on considering only the consumers' behavior, exogenous prices, monopoly frameworks or no competition between companies. Those features are incompatible with the vast majority of models from industrial organization literature and they have to be taken loosely if we want to consider models from that literature.

With regard to prices, [2] states: *"research on the price, the most important attribute of a product, are very rare."* And, to the best of our knowledge, no work has considered endogenous or optimal pricing behavior despite being recognized as a key variable by other authors, such as [10].

This absence of research on prices can be related to the omission of the "supply side". However, despite the importance of its role, only a few works have considered companies' behavior, such as [12,16]. The first one considers that companies' decisions are not based on what others are doing, and there is no relationship between prices and quantities, with the result that no optimal prices are found in this model.

The second one considers a Cournot model, but they solve it before simulating it and therefore the authors are constrained by the theoretical assumptions of the Cournot model. Also, they consider that there is a correlation between two variables that, theoretically, have to be uncorrelated. This correlation creates a contradiction between the simulated model and the Cournot model. Another work that considers a Cournot model is [7], but they also rely on solving the model before simulating it. By contrast, in our work it is not necessary to solve the theoretical model in advance, it will be solved by the algorithms that simulate the agents' interaction in the artificial market.

On the other hand, the industrial organization literature does not address what happens between the launching of a platform and the creation of mature platform markets. Only in [3] is this issue considered, but they focus on the role of the critical mass to sustain the platform and not on how a platform is launched.

Other works assume that "everyone wants to consume", which simplifies the problem but is not realistic. Another common assumption is that "everyone is connected to everyone once they are on the platform", i.e. it is assumed that networks are fully connected, which is unrealistic. These two assumptions are present in a lot of models such as [6, 13] or [1]. Lastly, another common characteristic is that no work considers agent-based modeling.

As a summary, no empirical or theoretical literature is available regarding the diffusion of innovation literature to simulate the launching of platforms, optimal prices, or competition. Our work contributes to the literature by incorporating an algorithm that simulates endogenous pricing by companies and by simulating the launching of two-sided platforms that compete with each other. Also, we consider the role of both the degree of differentiation and the spread of information among customers when launching a product.

3   Agents-Based Modeling

3.1   Theoretical Frameworks

We consider two theoretical sources to simulate the diffusion of innovations. First, we consider the diffusion of innovation literature from which we adopt three of the most common assumptions in this literature:

1. Agents are related by a random network, as in [5, 10, 11].
2. The diffusion process depends on an infection process (word-of-mouth).
3. Agents will have a propensity to adopt the product that is normally distributed to simulate the existence of innovators, early-adopters, laggards, etc.

Second, we consider two theoretical models from industrial organization literature that provide us with a framework to simulate the market. The first one is the classical Hotelling model, in which there are two price-competing companies and horizontally differentiated consumers. That implies that, at the same price and with the same features, some consumers prefer one product over the competitors'. We also consider the Hagiu and Halaburda's model, in which platforms compete for horizontally differentiated users and developers in a two-sided market. We consider only the case in which users and developers adopt one and only one platform and they have rational expectations[1].

3.2 Hotelling's and Hagiu and Halaburda's Framework. A Brief Introduction to Consumers' Behavior and the Market

In the simulated market, users (and developers in the two-sided case) want to buy the product which provides them with the largest non-negative utility. The utility that each agent obtains from products depends on the following parameters.

A reservation value (or a propensity-to-buy) c_u that is drawn from a normal distribution with negative mean to reproduce the existence of innovators, laggards, etc. The consumers' subjective tastes for the ideal product (x_i), which are distributed uniformly on the interval [0,1]. In this case, the distance between products and users in that interval can be interpreted as a "cost" because users have to go from their position (that represents their ideal product) to companies' positions (l_j, that represents the position of the real product) that we assume are at the extremes of that interval. This cost is called "transportation cost" or "nuisance cost" (tc) and we consider three different transportation costs to show how market differentiation affects the overall adoption.

Each consumer pays a price p_j for consuming the product j. Prices will start at zero in the case of the platform market because it is the normal pricing scheme in all digital platforms like Spotify, LinkedIn, etc. However, prices will start at 1 in the Hotelling's case because it represents the pricing scheme of the launching of devices like fitness trackers or smart TVs that tend to be expensive at the beginning. Other prices can be considered without loss of generality. Given that all consumers pay the same price, the utility of a consumer i buying the device j in the Hotelling's model can be written as:

$$U_{i,j} = c_i^u + q_j - tc * |l_j - x_i| - p_j \tag{1}$$

And the utility of a consumer i on the platform j in the Hagiu and Halaburda's model can be written as:

$$U_{i,j} = c_i^u + q_j - tc * |l_j - x_i| - p_j + \delta n_{-j} \tag{2}$$

Without loss of generality, we introduce an exogenous variable to control the quality (q) that is equal to 1 and will guarantee symmetric platforms. Nonetheless, other values can be considered and are available upon request. In the Hagiu and Halaburda's case, there are indirect network effects (n_{-j}), which implies that users (developers) value the presence of all developers (users) in that platform. Following Hagiu and Halaburda, δ is constant for all users (developers) and, for simplicity and without loss of generality, it is equal to 0.2. However, this assumption does not change the main conclusions of this work.

---

[1] Agents know that their actions will change the decisions of other agents, and the decisions of those agents will affect them and so on. Agents can perfectly forecast the consequences of their decisions.

This slight difference between both utilities is key. In the Hotelling's case, users are not influenced by the number of consumers buying the product, but in the Hagiu and Habalurda's case, they are. When competing in prices, platforms have to take into account that changes in prices also lead to changes in participation on one side which also lead to changes in participation on the other side that, at the same time, influence the participation. This infinite loop is the key challenge of this model.

Companies try to maximize their profits by competing in prices. To reproduce the pricing behavior, we consider two algorithms that rely on giving instructions to all agents to do what is more beneficial to them: agents choose the best available product that provides them with the largest non-negative utility; and companies choose to raise (decrease) prices if that change (in combination with the change in demand) is more profitable than maintaining actual prices (and demands)[2] (Fig. 1).

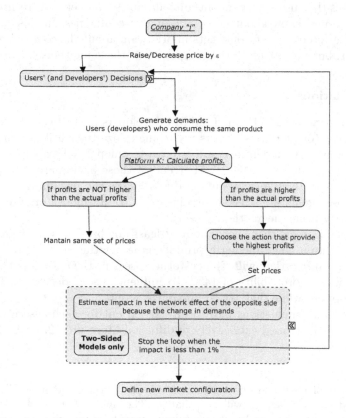

Fig. 1. Price algorithm. Dashed lines applied only to the Hagiu and Halaburda case

---

[2] The code can be downloaded at: https://goo.gl/abKujU

3.3   Word-of-Mouth. Algorithms of Diffusion of Information About Products

Although all agents try to maximize the utilities defined in the previous section, initially, the vast majority of them do not know about the existence of the products/platforms. We assume agents know about technology or the products by "infection" through other agents in their network. We consider that the process of adoption follows an infection process as in [5,8]. Once one user has knowledge of the product or technology, there is a probability of "infecting" other users in his/her network. On one hand, infection can be independent of consumption and agents can spread their information even when they do not consume the products. This is the most common case in the literature. On the other hand, if the spread of information depends on consuming the products, agents have to consume to infect other agents with their knowledge about products. Additionally, in this case, two cases can be addressed: when agents know about technologies, which implies that users know about all companies that sell that technology; or when agents only know about none, one or two companies. In this case, when an user is "infected", he/she only gets information about the company that sells the product, but not about all the companies at the same time.

3.4   Simulations

We create a world with 314 users (and 314 developers in the two-sided case) and two companies (or platforms). Users try to maximize their utilities and companies their profits. A random network is created among each category of agents with a link-probability of 1%. Five percent of those agents are categorized as "innovators" and they know about products before the beginning of the simulations. Those agents are selected by clustering so, all innovators are less than one node away from one another.

At each step, users that know about at least one product will evaluate if the utility they obtain when buying a product is larger than not buying at all. If they are consuming, they will "infect" other users in their networks with that knowledge with a probability of 14%. To influence users' decisions, companies can change prices while they try to maximize profits.

One thousand simulations have been carried out for each case in NetLogo, [14], which has been used extensively in diffusion literature, [2,4,8,9,12,15].[3]

---

[3] The number of users and developers is arbitrarily selected, other numbers can be considered and conclusions will not change. The link-probabiliy of 1% is chosen because it is small enough to avoid a full-connected network and to guarantee the presence of no-connected nodes. We choose 5% of innovators because it is a common assumption throughout the diffusion of innovation literature. Lastly, we chose 14% of probability of infection arbitrarily, other probabilities can be considered too, but the main conclusions of this work will not change because it only affects the speed of diffusion.

4   Results

4.1   Hotelling's Model

Let's consider first that information about the technology spreads in the network independently of its consumption. In this environment, the first interesting question to ask is what happens with prices. The lefthand graph of Fig. 2 depicts the convergence to an equilibrium price in three cases that represents low $(tc = 0.2)$, intermediate $(tc = 0.5)$, and high $(tc = 0.7)$ differentiation levels. The simulations show prices will be higher in more differentiated markets. The intuition of this behavior is the following: if users have "n" options but they prefer one of them because of their tastes, they will be willing to pay more for that option. Companies recognize that their products are not easily substitutable by competitors' and they fix higher prices.

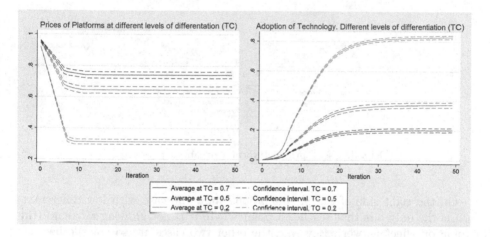

Fig. 2. Information about technology

On the right side of Fig. 2, we observe how prices affect the adoption of technology. In the case with the lowest differentiation, the adoption is almost 80%, while in the case with the highest differentiation, the adoption is almost 20%. The reasoning is the following: in the differentiated market, companies are aware that users are loyal and it will be difficult to reach users in other segments, so they prefer a low adoption and higher prices to a high adoption and lower prices. The opposite is true when markets are not differentiated. Those results highlight the relevance of knowing the market where the product is launched. If we consider that information about the technology spreads in the network dependently of its consumption, there will be no big differences with respect to the previous case in terms of prices and adoption, so this slightly change is not critical when considering diffusion.

Lastly, let's consider that companies spread information about their own products but not about the common technology. On the left side of Fig. 3, simulations show that prices are more volatile. This behavior is normal because new users are entering the market at each moment, then companies try to adjust prices because of the expansion of the market, but companies are also competing so they try to reduce prices. Prices only reach a stable position in the case with low differentiation because the competition is stronger than the expansion effect.

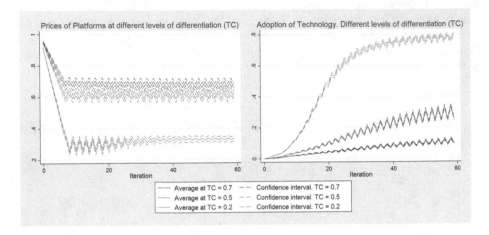

Fig. 3. Users' prices. Information about products

On the right side of Fig. 3, simulations show the case with low differentiation is the only one that reaches a point where it is not growing anymore (the expansion effect is over). However, the other two cases are so volatile because the spread of information is less regular and slower than before.

High prices are a barrier that block other users from becoming a node of infection, which limits the adoption. On the other hand, users only know about the individual products, so there are cases where users are only aware of one product and, because information initially spreads from clusters, there will be clusters that will never know about the existence of other companies. In this situation, volatility in prices and adoption appear because there is a trade-off between rising prices (because of the differentiation levels and the market expansion) and reducing prices (because of the competition between platforms and the boosting effect that it has on the demands).

4.2 Hagiu and Halaburda's Model

Intuitively, this case is close related to the launching of a digital platform like a social network, or a digital market like Apple Store or Play Store where there are two sides (users and developers) that need each other in some way. Given the symmetry of the model, for simplicity's sake and without loss of generality, we address only the users' side. Let's consider that information about the technology (and products) only spreads if users consume a platform.[4]

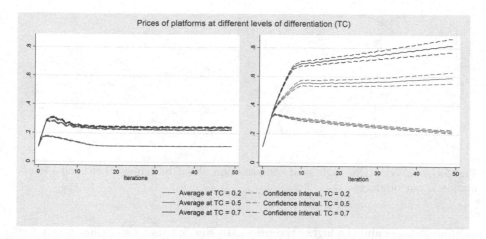

Fig. 4. Users' prices. Righthand - information about technology. Lefthand - information about products

In Fig. 4, simulations show a similar result to that of the Hotellings' case, the more differentiation, the higher the price. On the left side, there is the case in which platforms spread information about the technology and we observe that prices increase at the beginning but then they reach a maximum and they start to slowly converge to a lower price. The higher the differentiation, the slower the convergence. The intuition is the following: the initial increase in prices is consequence of recognizing users are willing to pay more because of the differentiation levels and/or because users value the growing number of developers on the other side and they will continue buying the platform even with high prices. But after a few iterations, platforms realize they have to compete for users, and they reduce prices. This reduction will be faster in less differentiated market because a price reduction attracts more users than in other cases. However, when platforms spread information about their products (right side), prices increase quickly at the beginning and then continue to increase, but more slowly. The continuous increase in prices in this case is due to the following: information about platforms spreads so slowly that the set of users that is indifferent between buying one platform or the other one is so small that platforms can focus on the users who are loyal and will buy the platform anyway, so platforms fix higher prices. Note that, the higher the differentiation, the smaller the set of

---

[4] We will not consider the case in which information about the technology spreads in the network independently of consumption because it does not provide additional insights.

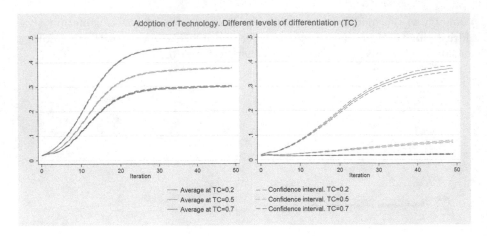

Fig. 5. Users' adoption. Righthand - information about technology. Lefthand - information about products

indifferent users and the higher the prices. In Fig. 5, simulations show how price dynamics translate to the diffusion of technology. Just as before, the higher the differentiation, the lower the adoption.

To summarize, one interesting point about those two models is the role of how information spreads. If companies focus on spreading information about their own products, the adoption is lower. Although price seems to be relevant, it is the differentiation levels and the role of information that are most relevant because they define the price levels.

4.3   Failures in Launching

One of the most terrifying scenarios for entrepreneurs or managers is failure in the launching of their products. The literature focuses on diffusion and analyzing successes, however failures are the other side of the coin and they are neglected in many works. Nonetheless, we can address the cases in which at least one platform has failed to enter the market. To do that, we create a variable that takes value 1 when the demand of at least one platform is null and 0 otherwise. In Table 1, simulations show that cases with high differentiation are more prone to failure. The intuition is the following: highly differentiated market tend to have higher prices, which is by itself a barrier to adoption, but if the information does not spread properly, high prices and the lack of information will lead to a failure in launching. On the other hand, Hagiu and Halaburda's model is less prone to failure due to three reasons: prices start at a low level, so there is always more willingness to buy the platform; network effects increase as new users or developers adopt the platform; and lastly, we consider only 50 iterations in each simulation. In some cases the death of a platform may occur later in the Hagiu and Halaburda's case than in Hotelling's.

Table 1. Failures in launching

Failures. Information/models		Hotelling			Hagiu and Halaburda		
Independent	Differentiation	Low	Intermediate	High	Low	Intermediate	High
	Failures	24	219	334	0	0	0
By technology	Differentiation	Low	Intermediate	High	Low	Intermediate	High
	Failures	272	700	802	0	0	0
By products	Differentiation	Low	Intermediate	High	Low	Intermediate	High
	Failures	245	716	796	0	3	45

5 Discussion

Prices play a key role in launching a new product, however, its role is poorly addressed in the literature, only works with exogenous prices are considered and they are a minority. We propose a novel way to introduce endogenous prices in agent-based models. The analysis of real cases can benefit from this contribution in two ways: first, it allows us to incorporate endogenous prices in simulated markets, but also, given that our approach is based on industrial organization theory, we can use real data to calibrate the parameters, in that way, real cases can be addressed with our framework. Although our work contributes in the understanding of launching new products by addressing not only the companies' decisions about prices, but also by linking diffusion literature with industrial organization theory, it will be necessary to study if the key role of prices is also motivated by other market characteristics. Our results need to be tested in other environments, other features of digital markets have to be introduced and external shocks have to be considered. We have only scratched the surface of what can be made with agent-based modeling applied to the diffusion of technologies/devices, but we feel we contribute in opening a new field in literature that links industrial organization theory with diffusion of innovation literature.

6 Conclusions

We propose a new way of dealing with the simulation of diffusion of products and technologies that considers endogenous pricing decisions. Companies fix prices by trying to maximize profits and consumers choose their most preferred option when trying to maximize their utility. The novelty of this work is not only that prices are endogenously determined, but also that we can explain the key role of prices in the launching process. We consider two theoretical frameworks in which three ways of spreading information and three levels of differentiation are considered. We prove differentiation is the key variable leading to high prices, and partly responsible for different market shares. Information, and how it spreads in the market, is the other variable responsible for different market shares. Both variables explain the evolution of prices, and such evolution also shows when prices are influenced by differentiation or by how the information spreads. When considering failures in launching, the failure is more likely in those cases with high differentiation, and when companies only spread knowledge about their products.

References

1. Armstrong, M.: Competition in two-sided markets. RAND J. Econ. **37**(3), 668–691 (2006)
2. Diao, J., Zhu, K., Gao, Y.: Agent-based simulation of durables dynamic pricing. Syst. Eng. Procedia **2**, 205–212 (2011)
3. Evans, D.S., Schmalensee, R.: Failure to launch: critical mass in platform businesses. Rev. Netw. Econ. **9**(4), 1–26 (2010)
4. Fuks, K., Kawa, A.: Simulation of resource acquisition by e-sourcing clusters using netlogo environment. In: Håkansson, A., Nguyen, N.T., Hartung, R.L., Howlett, R.J., Jain, L.C. (eds.) KES-AMSTA 2009. LNCS, vol. 5559, pp. 687–696. Springer, Heidelberg (2009). doi:10.1007/978-3-642-01665-3_69
5. Günther, M., Stummer, C., Wakolbinger, L.M., Wildpaner, M.: An agent-based simulation approach for the new product diffusion of a novel biomass fuel. J. Oper. Res. Soc. **62**(1), 12–20 (2011)
6. Hagiu, A., Hałaburda, H.: Information and two-sided platform profits. Int. J. Ind. Organ. **34**, 25–35 (2014)
7. Hamill, L., Gilbert, N.: Agent-Based Modelling in Economics. Wiley, New York (2016)
8. Kim, J., Hur, W.: Diffusion of competing innovations in influence networks. J. Econ. Interact. Coord. **8**(1), 109–124 (2013)
9. Kim, S., Lee, K., Cho, J.K., Kim, C.O.: Agent-based diffusion model for an automobile market with fuzzy topsis-based product adoption process. Expert Syst. Appl. **38**(6), 7270–7276 (2011)
10. Leite, R., Teixeira, A.A.C.: Innovation diffusion with heterogeneous networked agents: a computational model. J. Econ. Interact. Coord. **7**(2), 125–144 (2012)
11. Pegoretti, G., Rentocchini, F., Marzetti, G.V.: An agent-based model of innovation diffusion: network structure and coexistence under different information regimes. J. Econ. Interact. Coord. **7**(2), 145–165 (2012)
12. Rixen, M., Weigand, J.: Agent-based simulation of policy induced diffusion of smart meters. Technol. Forecast. Soc. Change **85**, 153–167 (2014)
13. Salim, C.: Platform standards, collusion and quality incentives. Discussion Paper no. 257, Governance and the Efficiency of Economics Systems, Free University of Berlin (2009)
14. Wilensky, U.: NetLogo (1999). https://ccl.northwestern.edu/netlogo/
15. Zhang, T., Zhang, D.: Agent-based simulation of consumer purchase decision-making and the decoy effect. J. Bus. Res. **60**(8), 912–922 (2007)
16. Zhang, T., Wade Brorsen, B.: Oligopoly firms with quantity-price strategic decisions. J. Econ. Interact. Coord. **6**(2), 157–170 (2011)

Optimality of a Two-Tier Rate Structure for a Transaction Tax in an Artificial Market

Danilo Liuzzi[1], Paolo Pellizzari[2], and Marco Tolotti[1(✉)]

[1] Department of Management, Ca' Foscari University of Venice,
Cannaregio 873, 30121 Venice, Italy
{danilo.liuzzi,tolotti}@unive.it
[2] Department of Economics, Ca' Foscari University of Venice,
Cannaregio 873, 30121 Venice, Italy
paolop@unive.it

Abstract. In this paper we discuss the effects of a Transaction Tax on an artificial market with varying liquidity where a large number of agents can trade a share of a risky asset. A market maker is in charge to optimally set the level of taxation in order to obtain a desired mixture of activity and volatility. We show that, depending on the liquidity of the market, two possible regimes of optimal taxation emerge: a non-negligible level of taxation for highly liquid markets and low (close to zero) levels of taxation for low liquidity markets. This outcome resembles the two-tier rate structure discussed by Spahn in his famous contributions (see [1]).

Keywords: Artificial markets · Tobin Tax · Market Games

1 Introduction

Since the collapse of Lehman brothers, that marks the conventional beginning of the recent financial crisis, we have witnessed extraordinary actions, known under the umbrella-term of 'quantitative easing', put in place by various central banks and the whole banking sector was reformed with the Basel III rules, approved by the Basel Committee on Bank Supervision between January 2008 and September 2010. On the other hand, the debate about ways to curb excessive financial exuberance dates back at least to the early seventies,[1] when James Tobin proposed the introduction of a Transaction Tax (TT) to "throw some sand in the wheels of speculation". After decades of fierce clashes, there is still no consensus on the benefits of the introduction of a TT: a useful friction to limit speculative high frequency trading, [2,3]; or a dangerous instrument, whose scope may be offset by a reduction in liquidity and other adverse effects (see [4] or [5] for a recent overview of the gargantuan literature on the Tobin Tax).

Following this debate, the main goal of this paper is to examine the effects of the introduction of suitable TT on a artificial market. In particular, we address

---

[1] The idea was, however, clearly present in some texts written by Keynes.

© Springer International Publishing AG 2017
J. Bajo et al. (Eds.): PAAMS 2017 Workshops, CCIS 722, pp. 95–106, 2017.
DOI: 10.1007/978-3-319-60285-1_8

the problem of a market maker in charge to optimally design taxation policies to control for volatility and market activity.

In the face of the intuitive belief that a transaction tax could be a workable way to control markets, a vast body of empirical works show that a TT has no or negative practical effects: [6], say, uses a quasi-natural experiment based on Paris Bourse data to find evidence that "higher transaction costs in general, and security transaction taxes in particular, should be considered as volatility increasing", which is exactly the opposite of what TT advocates hope for. The seminal paper [7] has similar results and reports that an early TT introduced in Sweden in 1986 derailed the market (as most of the traders migrated to London to dodge the imposition).

Given the huge problems in assessing the effects of the introduction of a TT in practice, Artificial Markets (AMs) have been increasingly recognized as useful computational testbed to investigate the repercussions of regulatory shifts in the trading rules. AMs, such as [8,9,13], typically have many heterogenous and boundedly rational agents, who trade based on limited information and heuristic rules. In [10], authors argue that the effects depend, in particular, on the level of (endogenous) liquidity of the specific markets under consideration.

One of the most interesting discussion of the Tobin's idea is due to Spahn, see [1], who argued that the Tobin Tax in its basic form is "not viable" and proposed a two-tier system with a low tax rate in ordinary times and a substantial rate in exceptional circumstances. This faceted version of the TT, known as Spahn Tax, acknowledges that different rates may be appropriate depending on the situation of the market.

Taking inspiration from and building on this body of ideas, we develop a framework in which the rate is set by a market maker who cares about volatility, as well as about activity, and crucially depends on (a proxy of) the liquidity available in the market. In principle, any market model where volatility and activity in broad sense can be measured or quantified could be used to investigate the effects of a TT. We build on the artificial market developed in [11], where many agents can buy and sell one unit of a risky asset under a variety of environments as far as liquidity and tax rate are concerned. The model allows to describe in a semi-analytical form some market aggregates characterizing the Nash equilibrium emerging by the strategic interactions among traders. Indeed, we compute the levels of volatility and activity at the equilibrium in the asymptotic model where the number of agents tends to infinity; moreover, implications on the finite dimensional model with a large number of agents will be addressed using numerical simulations.

The paper is organized as follows. In Sect. 2, we describe the market model, the trading rules and the role of the market maker. Section 3 is devoted to the analysis of the outcomes of the model. In Sect. 4 we conclude by stressing some policy implications.

2   A Simple Artificial Market

In this section we present a simple artificial market where a risky asset is traded. We set up a trading mechanism where investors buy and sell based on the forecast of future returns and a market maker (or another external authority) is in charge to determine a transaction tax. The rest of this section is divided into two parts. In the first one, we characterize the demand side of the market formed by a large number of (small) investors; the second part is devoted to the supply side which is represented by a market maker in charge to settle the price and set the level of taxation.

2.1   The Demand Side: A Large Population of Small Investors

We use the setting described in [11] to model demand and consider N agents who can trade one share of the asset at discrete dates. To keep the mechanism as simple as possible, we assume that at each trading date the agents may own at most one share of the asset. We denote by $\omega_i(t) \in \{0,1\}$, for $i = 1, \ldots, N$, the *ownership* state variable: $\omega_i(t) = 1$ means that agent i does own the share for the investment period $(t, t+1]$; if not, $\omega_i(t) = 0$ means that agent i does not own any asset. The aggregate quantity

$$q_N(t) = \frac{1}{N} \sum_{j=1}^{N} \omega_j(t) \tag{1}$$

defines the proportion of agents owning the asset on $[t, t+1)$. Note that q_N is also a proxy for the demand of the asset: if $q_N(t)$ increases in time, it means that the demand for the asset is increasing.[2] In particular $\Delta q_N(t) = q_N(t) - q_N(t-1)$ is a measure of variation of the demand for the asset.

The agents decide to invest/disinvest on the market (i.e., to alter their strategy profile $\omega_i(t)$, $i = 1, \ldots, N$) depending on their forecast about the future one-period return $R(t)$. We assume that the return depends linearly on the variation on the demand for the asset

$$R(t) = k(q_N(t) - q_N(t-1)), \tag{2}$$

where $k > 0$ is a measure of market depth: the lower is k, the higher is the ability of the market to absorb oscillations in demand. Put differently, k represents the inverse of liquidity.[3]

Agents' decision to invest in the market depends also on the imposition by the market maker of a transaction tax. We assume that this is done deducting

---

[2] We assume that the demand is always fulfilled. The market maker acts as a lender of last resort. We will see that the market maker can tune taxation in order to limit the activity on the market.

[3] Although aware of the fact that in real markets liquidity is not constant and, possibly, endogenously influenced by the taxation, in this paper we stick to the simplifying assumption that liquidity is constant in time.

a constant term $\mu \geq 0$ from the realized returns. Observe that is equivalent to a transaction tax proportional to the asset price that is exchanged.

We introduce heterogeneity in actions by adding a idiosyncratic term ϵ_i drawn from a common probability distribution η which summarizes any kind of distortion in the perception of the returns the single agents may have.

Agent i, owning the asset, decides to exit the market if and only if her perception of tomorrow's return is smaller than the exit cost μ, i.e., if and only if

$$R(t) + \epsilon_i < -\mu.$$

Put differently, agents exit the market when the perceived returns of keeping the share are negative and lower than the cost to be paid to the market maker.

Conversely, an agent j who's not holding the share buys one unit if and only if the perceived return net of the cost of entering the market is higher than the stay-out option (which yields null return in the considered period):

$$R(t) + \epsilon_j - \mu > 0.$$

Table 1. Decision scheme for the agents.

Original status	(State variable)	Activation threshold
Owner	$(\omega_i(t-1) = 1)$	$\epsilon_i < -R(t) - \mu$
Not owner	$(\omega_j(t-1) = 0)$	$\epsilon_j > -R(t) + \mu$

Note that this decision scheme is far from trivial: first, $R(t)$ is a function of $q_N(t)$ and it implicitly depends on tomorrow's actions of all the agents on the market. This features introduces a *strategic interaction mechanism*: in order to take a decision about her choice $\omega_i(t)$, agent i needs to forecast the entire vector $\underline{\omega}(t) = (\omega_1(t), \ldots, \omega_N(t))$ in order to form an expectation of the market return $R(t)$; second, perceived profits depend on individual noise terms reflecting the heterogeneity of opinions in the market. This decision mechanism can be summarized in the thresholds model described in Table 1. Whenever the threshold condition is met, the agent activates and her status changes.

We are interested in monitoring two significant aggregate statistics describing the market, namely the activity (A_N) describing the proportion of agents trading at a certain date and the volatility (σ_N) of the returns. Both these quantities can be related to the variation of the demand q_N on the market. In particular,

$$A_N(t) = \frac{1}{N} \sum_{i=1}^{N} \omega_i(t)(1 - \omega_i(t-1)) + \frac{1}{N} \sum_{i=1}^{N} \omega_i(t-1)(1 - \omega_i(t))$$

$$= q_N(t) + q_N(t-1) - \frac{2}{N} \sum_{i=1}^{N} \omega_i(t)\omega_i(t-1); \tag{3}$$

and

$$\sigma_N(t) = k|\Delta q_N(t)| = |R(t)|. \tag{4}$$

Notice that A_N is the normalized sum of the number of agents buying/selling the asset. The absolute value of the return is natural measure of dispersion and we use it as a proxy for volatility in our setting.

In the three panels of Fig. 1 we show three representative time series depicting the returns as emerging from the system with $N = 1000$ agents, for different values of the parameters. Panel A is obtained for $k = 0.25$ and $\mu = 0.10$; here excursions of returns stay within $\pm 3\%$. Panel B, with $k = 35$ and $\mu = 0.10$, shows a situation in which returns exhibit "volatility bursts" and fluctuate in a range of $\pm 20\%$; moreover, we recognize to different regimes: for some periods, returns are more volatile with picks close to 20%, whereas for other periods they are close to zero. Panel C, with $k = 0.25$ and $\mu = 0.01$, depicts returns which are large and almost regular. It is worth to mention that those trajectories are typical, as revealed by the formal analysis in [11]. In that paper, the asymptotic model where the number of agents tends to infinity is studied in closed form.

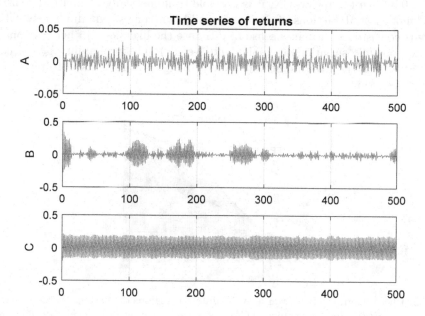

Fig. 1. Time series of returns for different values of the parameters. In panel A, $k = 0.25$ and $\mu = 0.10$; in B, $k = 0.35$ and $\mu = 0.10$ and in C, $k = 0.25$ and $\mu = 0.01$.

Indeed, it turns out that the behavior of $q(t)$, in the limit for $N \to \infty$, is characterized by the following closed form (implicit) equation:

$$q(t) = q(t-1)\,\eta(k(q(t)-q(t-1))+\mu) + (1-q(t-1))\,\eta(k(q(t)-q(t-1))-\mu). \tag{5}$$

The attractors of this equation result to be of two kinds:

(i) the fixed point $\bar{q} = 1/2$; (ii) a periodic trajectory of period 2 such that, for large t, $q(t)$ solving (5), oscillates between two values q^u and q^l, where $0 < q^l < 1/2 < q^h < 1$. Moreover, there are values of the parameters where the two attractors coexist meaning that, depending on the initial conditions on the market, the system may converge to one of the two long run attractors described above (we will refer to this situation as (iii)).

Figure 2 depicts the phase diagram of the system in k and μ and represents the situation. Here, we have chosen a logistic distribution[4] for the noise terms ϵ_i, i.e., $\mu(x) = 1/(1 + e^{-\beta x})$, with $\beta = 10$. In particular, the region labelled as FP pertains to the fixed point attractor; in the second region, denoted by TC, a two-cycle develops; finally, region CX is where the coexistence of the two regimes (i) and (ii) is detected.

The picture shows that, for large values of μ, the price "collapses" to a constant fixed point where the returns are freezed to zero. Conversely, for low levels of μ, the market almost always converges to a very volatile situation where the two-cycle prevails. In the intermediate regime (iii), the two coexist. We call k_{bif} the level of market depth at which the diagram bifurcates (in our simulations, $k_{bif} \approx 0.33$). In the region CX, it is possible to numerically estimate the size of the domains of attractions of the two possible outcomes; put differently, when there is coexistence, it makes sense to estimate the likelihood of being in one of the two possible situations (fixpoint and 2-cycle). The probability $p_{k\mu}$ of converging toward the fixed point is depicted in Fig. 2 using shades of gray in the coexistence region.

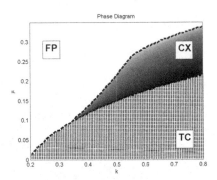

Fig. 2. Phase diagram of the market with different regions depending on the values of k and μ: in FP there is a fixpoint; TC denotes the region where 2-cycles develop; TX signals the coexistence of the two.

Moreover, relying on (5), it is possible to derive the dynamics of the two statistics we want to monitor, namely activity $A(t)$ and volatility $\sigma(t)$:

$$A(t) = q(t) - q(t-1)[2\eta(k(q(t) - q(t-1)) + \mu) - 1] \qquad (6)$$

---

[4] The use of a logistic distribution is rather standard for discrete choice models. See [11] for a more detailed discussion about this issue.

and

$$\sigma(t) = k|q(t) - q(t-1)|. \tag{7}$$

Therefore, when referring to the asymptotic ($N \to \infty$) model, the long-run values for A and σ can be computed accordingly. Indeed, $\bar{\sigma} = k\Delta$, where $\Delta = 0$ in the case of a fixed point or $\Delta = q^u - q^l$ in the case of a two-cycle. Similarly,

$$\bar{A} = q^u - q^l \left[2\eta(k\Delta + \mu) - 1\right]$$

where $q^u = q^l = 1/2$ in the case of a fixed point.

We remark that the typical behavior of the time series for returns in the three regions, when the number of agents is large but finite, is captured by trajectories as in Fig. 1. Evidently, when N is finite, the trajectories are noisy and fluctuate around the equilibrium values. In particular, panel A of Fig. 1 corresponds to the FP region (returns fluctuate around zero); panel C corresponds to the two-cycle region (returns are more pronounced) and, finally, panel B corresponds to region CX where the fixed point and the two-cycle coexist. In this region, the finite dimensional system spends some time close to one attractor to suddenly move towards the other one.

2.2   The Supply Side: The Role of the Market Maker

As seen in the previous section, once the parameters have been determined and a distribution η is chosen for the individual shocks, the dynamics of demand, returns, activity and volatility are easily computed. The market maker is in charge to *optimally* set the level of taxation to reach a desired blend of (high) activity and (low) volatility. In the one hand, sustained activity is needed to keep the market alive; on the other hand, too high levels of liveliness makes the returns too volatile and it is likely that the market maker is going to strike a balance between these two conflicting goals.[5]

The market maker's preference about the relevance of the aforementioned objectives is shaped by the parameter λ weighting the two of them in a simple (linear) way. In particular, we choose the following form which has the advantage of keeping the target limited in the compact $[0, 1]$:

$$\pi(\mu, k, \lambda) = \lambda\bar{A}(\mu, k) + (1 - \lambda)e^{-\bar{\sigma}(\mu,k)} \tag{8}$$

where $\lambda \in [0, 1]$ is a preference weight. Some remarks on the functional form of π are needed. First of all, note that we are weighting the two goals through a convex combination. The exponential transformation for the volatility is used to make this figure (and, hence, the target) to lie in the unit interval. Indeed, since $0 \leq \Delta \leq 2$, necessarily $\sigma \in [0, 2k]$, therefore, $e^{-\sigma} \in [e^{-2k}, 1]$. Finally,

---

[5] *Market quality* is a complex and multidimensional object involving, among other factors, spreads, price stability, high execution rates and low volatility (see for instance, [12]). Consequently, in this model where information is not taken into account, it is reasonable to consider two of the main dimensions involved: volatility and activity.

since $q^u > q^l > q^l$ and $2\eta(k\Delta + \mu) - 1 > 0$, we have that $\bar{A} \in [0, 1]$. Therefore, $\pi \in [0, 1]$.

The market maker aims at maximizing π given the values of k and λ. In this paper, k is an intrinsic characteristic of the market, whereas λ is a fixed preference parameter. The optimization problem is thus

$$\max_{\mu \geq 0} \pi(\mu, k, \lambda). \tag{9}$$

3   Simulations and Results

In the previous section we have described the market maker's preferences via the objective function $\pi(k, \mu, \lambda)$. For low values of λ the market maker puts more attention on curbing the volatility than on the level of market activity. Conversely, high levels of λ mean that the market maker preferences lean toward the level of activity, somewhat disregarding the risks connected to high volatility.

In the remainder of this section, we discuss and compare the optimal behavior of the market maker under three different scenarios characterized by a increasing weight λ (i.e., a decreasing level of volatility risk aversion). In particular, we assume that $\lambda_1 = 0.18$, $\lambda_2 = 0.42$ and $\lambda_3 = 0.61$.[6] Figures 3, 4 and 5 depict both the objective function $\pi(k, \mu, \lambda)$ (left panels) and, more crucially, the corresponding optimal policy $\mu^*(k, \lambda)$ (right panels) for the values of the parameters corresponding to the three situations. For clarity sake, we superimpose the curve $\mu^*(k, \lambda)$ on the phase diagram proposed in Fig. 2.

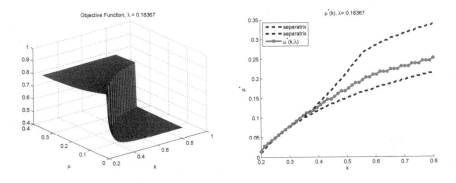

Fig. 3. The left panel shows the levels of $\pi(\mu, k.\lambda)$ for $\lambda_1 = 0.18$. In the right panel we plot the optimal taxation $\mu^*(k, \lambda)$ for $\lambda = \lambda_1$ (green line), showing that it lies in the coexistence region CX (where it exists). (Color figure online)

In Fig. 3 we consider the scenario with $\lambda = \lambda_1 = 0.18$. The two panels show the objective function and the optimal rate $\mu^*(k, \lambda_1)$ in this case. Notice

---

[6] The three values of λ have been selected with the only purpose of showing the variety of possible behaviors arising from the model. Similar values would produce essentially the same results.

from the left panel that the optimum is reached along the "cliff" formed at the level of points lying at the middle of the domain. Concerning the optimal taxation, the right panel shows that $\mu^*(k, \lambda_1)$ is monotonically increasing along the considered range of the market depth. This monotonicity can be explained taking into account that the market maker avoids too volatile situations (region TC) or freezed markets (region FP). Therefore, when $k \leq k_{bif}$, i.e., when non coexistence is possible the market maker sets μ^* in order to lie on the common boundary of the regions FP and TC. As soon as $k > k_{bif}$, she chooses μ^* to let the market end up in the coexistence region (CX).

As a matter of fact, for a wide range of k, the market maker finds it optimal to choose a taxation level in such a way that the long run evolution of the market results to be on the verge of two opposite regimes, trying somehow to strike a balance between activity and volatility.

In Fig. 4 we consider a scenario with $\lambda = \lambda_2 = 0.42$, which makes the objective function less sensitive to high volatility regimes, as it is easily seen by comparing the left panels of Figs. 3 and 4. The behavior of the optimal taxation deserves more attention, though. In contrast to the previous scenario, there is a level k_{th} of market depth, such that, for $k < k_{th}$, the optimal taxation μ^* is increasing in k. At the level k_{th}, the optimal μ abruptly falls to a level close to zero. In the market maker's perspective, it is optimal to slash the taxation if the market depth goes above a certain threshold. In other words, the optimal taxation is significant only if the liquidity of the market becomes too high (i.e., if the inverse of liquidity, k, is smaller than the value k_{th}). It is important to stress that sooner or later, for large enough values of k, any market maker would ultimately set the taxation rate to a value close to zero. Put differently, the existence of k_{th} does not depend on λ, although its value does.[7] Simulations show that the greater is λ the lower is k_{th}: the less volatility averse the market maker is, or the more focused on the volume she is, the higher the threshold in liquidity required to switch on a significant taxation. Put differently, the dependence of this threshold on the parameter λ tells us that the moment in which market makers are willing to take action is influenced by their preferences, but not the action itself. Note that the taxation, for $k \geq k_{th}$, although sensibly smaller, does not drop to zero.

Finally, in the shoes of a market maker whose $\lambda = \lambda_3 = 0.61$, the level of activity is of paramount importance and the high level of volatility that could result matters less. Figure 5 is almost the photographic negative of Fig. 3. The priorities are reversed: the optimal taxation is everywhere low but for very small levels of k (i.e., $k_{th} \approx 0.24$ is very small). In other words, in order to optimally decide to rise the taxation, the level of liquidity in the market has to reach a considerable level.

We now briefly address how the trajectories of returns under "optimal taxation" look like. To this aim, given λ and k, we consider the optimal $\mu^*(\lambda, k)$. Typical trajectories are of three kinds: in case where $k < k_{bif}$, $\mu^*(k, \lambda)$ lies on the

---

[7] The reason why we did not see a threshold like k_{th} in Fig. 2 is that it lies out of the range of values of k used in our simulations.

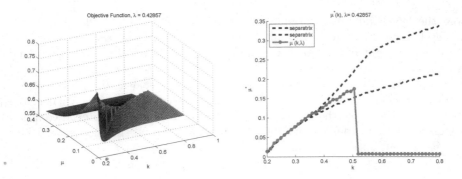

Fig. 4. The left panel shows the levels of $\pi(\mu, k.\lambda)$ for $\lambda_2 = 0.42$. In the right panel we plot the optimal taxation $\mu^*(k, \lambda)$ for $\lambda = \lambda_2$ (green line). It is evident the threshold level $k_{th} \approx 0.5$ at which $\mu^*(k, \lambda)$ collapses to values close to zero. (Color figure online)

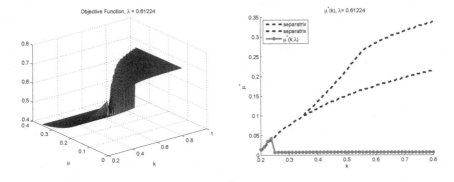

Fig. 5. The left panel shows the levels of $\pi(\mu, k.\lambda)$ for $\lambda_2 = 0.61$. In the right panel we plot the optimal taxation $\mu^*(k, \lambda)$ for $\lambda = \lambda_3$ (green line). Here $k_{th} \approx 0.23$ is lower compared to the case of MM2. (Color figure online)

frontier between region FP and TC. This situation is depicted in Fig. 6. We see that returns fluctuate without any regularity. This is due to the fact that, being the parameters on the boundary, there is no clear predominance between the fixed point and the two-cycle attractor. In case $\lambda = \lambda_1$ and $k > k_{bif}$, $\mu^*(k, \lambda_1)$ belongs to the CX region. The corresponding returns are depicted in panel B of Fig. 1. Finally, in panel C of Fig. 1, we see the situation in which $\mu^* \approx 0$, i.e., $k > k_{th}$. In this case, the returns are clearly in the domain of attraction of the two-cycle.

A few implications may be drawn from the previous simulations of the model: it's clear that some policy maker, based on the preferences captured by λ, would pick (optimal) taxation rates that indefinitely steer the market in a situation where stable periods can be seen jointly with short volatility bursts. While our analysis is eminently static, as k is exogenous and kept constant, the argument is related to and confirms Spahn's observation that the market maker should adjust the rate to avoid both unwanted exuberance as well as too dull periods. Indeed,

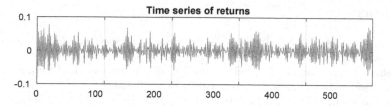

Fig. 6. Time series of returns in case of $k = 0.25$, $\mu = \mu^*(0.25) = 0.05$. In this case, the parameters lie exactly on the boundary region separating the regions FP and TC.

by extending our setting to allow for ripples in liquidity k, the two-tier proposal by Spahn would be nearly optimal in view of what we have demonstrated for any given value of k.

4   Conclusion

In this paper we present an artificial market where a market maker sets the optimal level of taxation, given the level of liquidity of the market, in order to balance opposite objectives.

In our model the microfoundation of the demand side brings about three different asymptotic regimes for the relevant quantities, namely activity and volatility: depending on the values of liquidity and taxation, a first regime witnesses a collapse in the market activity, a second regime allows for high activity at the expense of significantly high volatility, and a third regime actually embraces the two previous regimes in a coexistence scenario. The preferences of the market maker take into account both the activity and the volatility as decision criteria. The exact weight attached to the single criterion depends on the market maker's volatility risk aversion. We show that, no matter how volatility averse the market maker is, it is always optimal to stick to a two-tier rate structure: there is threshold in liquidity beyond which the market maker abruptly raises the rate from a low (close to zero) to a (high) non-negligible level. In realistic setups, where liquidity fluctuates in real time and may dynamically change, this suggests that the Spahn modification of Tobin's idea may reach good, if not optimal, results. The level of liquidity that triggers the transition depends on the preferences of the market maker and the measure could be implemented, similarly to what is done for circuit breakers, by increasing the tax rate as soon as the volatility exceeds a predefined level.

In either situation, the optimal level of taxation is still chosen in such a way that a balance between activity and volatility is met: the taxation rate keeps the market either "inside" the coexistence regime, or on the verge between the two asymptotic regimes of the activity and the volatility. Sensibly, this means that "controlled" volatility bursts are the norm in markets, even when optimally managed by a realistic market maker as he will invariably keep away from both the situations of too large and too stable returns.

References

1. Spahn, P.B.: International financial flows and transactions taxes: survey and options (1995)
2. Hasbrouck, J., Saar, G.: Technology and liquidity provision: the blurring of traditional definitions. J. Financ. Mark. **12**(2), 143–172 (2009)
3. Hasbrouck, J., Saar, G.: Low-latency trading. J. Financ. Mark. **16**(4), 646–679 (2013)
4. European Parliament: The feasibility of an international "tobin tax". Economic Affairs Series (1999)
5. Burman, L.E., Gale, W.G., Gault, S., Kim, B., Nunns, J., Rosenthal, S.: Financial transaction taxes in theory and practice. Natl. Tax J. **69**(1), 171 (2016)
6. Hau, H.: The role of transaction costs for financial volatility: evidence from the Paris Bourse. J. Eur. Econ. Assoc. **4**(4), 862–890 (2006)
7. Umlauf, S.R.: Transaction taxes and the behavior of the Swedish stock market. J. Financ. Econ. **33**(2), 227–240 (1993)
8. Arthur, W., Holland, J., LeBaron, B., Taylor, P.: Asset pricing under endogenous expectations in an artificial stock market. In: Arthur, W., Lane, D., Durlauf, S. (eds.) The Economy as an Evolving Complex System II. Addison-Wesley, Boston (1997)
9. Ghoulmie, F., Cont, R., Nadal, J.: Heterogeneity and feedback in an agent-based market model. J. Phys. Condens. Matter **17**, 1259–1268 (2005)
10. Pellizzari, P., Westerhoff, F.: Some effects of transaction taxes under different microstructures. J. Econ. Behav. Organ. **72**(3), 850–863 (2009)
11. Fontini, F., Sartori, E., Tolotti, M.: Are transaction taxes a cause of financial instability? Phys. A Stat. Mech. Appl. **450**, 57–70 (2016)
12. Madhavan, A.: Market microstructure: a survey. J. Financ. Mark. **3**(3), 205–258 (2000)
13. Mathieu, P., Beaufils, B., Brandouy, O. (eds.): Artificial Economics: Agent-Based Methods in Finance, Game Theory and Their Applications, vol. 564. Springer Science & Business Media, Heidelberg (2005)

Evolving Trading Signals at Foreign Exchange Market

Svitlana Galeshchuk[1,2(✉)] and Sumitra Mukherjee[3]

[1] Faculty of Accounting and Audit, Ternopil National Economic University,
Ternopil, Ukraine
`svitlana.galeshchuk@univ-grenoble-alpes.fr`
[2] Laboratoire d'Informatique de Grenoble,
Université Grenoble Alpes, Grenoble, France
[3] Nova Southeastern University, Fort Lauderdale, USA
`sumitra@nova.edu`

Abstract. Paper examines the merit of evolutionary algorithms to generate trading signals for trading decisions at financial markets. We focus on foreign-exchange market. It is among the largest financial markets. "Technical" traders base their decisions on a set of technical rules evolved from past market activity. We employ a genetic algorithm to learn a set of profitable trading rules considering transaction costs; each rule generates a 'buy', 'hold', or 'sell' signal using moving average technical rule. We empirically evaluate our approach using exchange rates of four major currency pairs over the period 2000 to 2015. Performance evaluation on out-of-sample data indicates that our approach is able to provide acceptably high returns on investment. Comparison with exhaustive search proves convincing performance of our approach.

Keywords: Trading rules · Forex market · Excess returns · Evolutionary algorithms

1 Introduction

Financial markets bring together buyers and sellers of economic assets. Depending on the type of the market, different participants create market demand and supply. Classical definition of the pricing mechanism for financial markets incorporates the balance between demand and supply of the trading asset. The foreign exchange (forex) market is one of the most liquid financial markets in the world. Forex rates are quoted in terms of a base-quote currency pair; the rate represents the number of units of quote currency to be exchanged for each unit of the base currency. Basic trading strategy implies the following rule: the base currency should be sold (exchanged to obtain quote currency) as the rate decreases and bought as the rate increases. Thus it is essential to forecast movements in foreign exchange rates accurately [1].

Rules for foreign exchange trading selected through back-testing on past data suffer from some limitations: No single rule consistently results in satisfactory profit levels

---

S. Galeshchuk—Fulbright Scholar at Nova Southeastern University, 2015–2016

J. Bajo et al. (Eds.): PAAMS 2017 Workshops, CCIS 722, pp. 107–116, 2017.
DOI: 10.1007/978-3-319-60285-1_9

over subsequent periods [2]. It explains why the traders rely on the set of rules to create profitable strategy rather than on one particular rule. However, the major shortcoming of such ad hoc combinations of rules is their poor performance on out-of-sample data (i.e., it often suffers from failures while testing on empirical data). The changeability of underlying data generation process over time is one of the major impediments for developing robust trading rules for forex trading. Hence, it remains a challenging task for market participants.

We address this problem by developing an approach for evolving trading strategies based on a 'buy', 'hold', or 'sell' signals generated from trading rules at foreign-exchange market. Our method foresees two following steps: First, we generate a diverse set of moving average trading rules that yield good results on back-testing. The rules' diversity means that they have different strengths and weaknesses and function well under different levels of instability in the underlying data generation processes. We evolve a set of profitable rules using a genetic algorithm. Secondly, we create an ensemble that merges the trading signals generated by the evolved rules to achieve a combined trading signal. We consider transaction costs as a parameter for evolving trading rules.

The paper is organized as follows: Sect. 2 provides a brief review of the related literature. Section 3 describes the methodology. Section 4 presents results from our experiments. Section 5 concludes with some observations on our findings and identifies directions of future research.

2 Literature Review

In this section we briefly review the role of technical analysis in foreign exchange trading and methods for evolving trading strategies.

2.1 Technical Analysis for Foreign Exchange Trading

The conceptual idea behind the currency market lies in facilitating the collaboration among the companies that accomplish their payments in the foreign currencies. Meanwhile, nowadays the essential part of market participants does not conduct any international trade of goods and services but leverages exchange rate movements to get profits. These facts, combined with the immense trading volume, and plethora of influencing factors of economic, political, and psychological nature, has made exchange rate prediction one of the most difficult and demanding applications of financial forecasting [3].

Technical analysis attempts to predict future assets prices based on the patterns detected in past prices. These patterns make foundation for creating trading rules important for generating trading signals (i.e. buy, sell, hold). Neely and Weller [4] argue about the philosophy of technical analysis that implies three main principles: (1) assets price history uses all relevant information so any research assets fundamentals is pointless; (2) assets prices are moving with trends; (3) history tends to be repeated itself. Lissandrin et al. [5] evaluate prediction performance of technical indicators for future markets.

A number of researchers prove profitability of the technical trading rules in currency exchange market [6–10]. Study of Owen and Palmer [11] shows that momentum trading strategies are more profitable with greater exchange rate volatility. Schulmeister's [12] results suggest that most of technical trading rules would have resulted in profitable trading strategies even after adjusting for interest expense and transaction costs. [13] focuses on extracting simple trading decisions when faced with multiple technical trading signals. Researcher assumes that it is necessary to determine the optimal number of trading rules for the decision-making mechanism using a more complex methodology. We refer to the findings of [14] that among the trading rules moving averages have been most intensively employed in the foreign-exchange market. Hence, it motivates us to employ these methods for signal generation.

We assume that the relationship between trading rules and trading strategy can be explained as follows: trader uses a number of trading rules to maximize the returns of trading strategy.

2.2 Evolutionary Approaches for Developing Trading Strategies

Genetic algorithms have already been employed to a number of financial problems [14, 15]. A number of researches [16, 17] argue that the genetic programming approach of [18] is the most applicable and promising because of its flexibility for adjusting the trading rules to the current environment. Experiments with genetic programing with application at the foreign exchange markets are observed in economic literature [19, 20]. The findings of [10] show strong evidence of economically significant out-of-sample excess returns of technical trading rule over the period 1981–1995 using genetic programming techniques. Their testing results indicate that the trading rules detect patterns in the data that are not captured by standard statistical models. In [21] with application of evolutionary computation techniques to rule discovery in stock algorithmic trading authors find that a significant bias toward the applications of genetic algorithm-based and genetic programming-based techniques in technical trading rule discovery is observed in recent economic literature. [22] focus on how to accelerate the speed of computation with evolutionary approach for developing trading strategies, enabling the generation of more results in the same time and making it more feasible to analyze larger problems. [23] suggest another application of evolutionary approaches for trading. Their paper considers the multi-objective evolutionary optimization of technical trading strategies, which involves the development of trading rules that are able to yield high returns at minimal risk. [15] explore possibility of employing genetic programming to stock exchange markets. However, instead of using market indices such as Dow Jones, S&P 500, they concentrated on individual companies and their market performance. However, majority of researchers do not take into account the transaction costs although they may lead rules do not earn consistent excess returns with test data.

3 Methodology

We first describe the data used to evaluate our proposed method. We describe and formalize the trading rules used. Next, we focus on the genetic algorithm developed to generate ensemble trading signals. Finally, we detail our experimental set up to evaluate performance of proposed method with brute-force search.

3.1 Data Used

We use the daily closing rates between four pairs of currencies – Euro and US Dollar (EUR/USD), British Pound and US Dollar (GBP/USD), US Dollar and Japanese Yen (USD/JPY), US Dollar and Swiss Franc (USD/CHF) – to develop and evaluate our method. These are among the most widely traded reserve currency pairs. This data is freely available and obtained from: http://www.global-view.com/foreign exchange-trading-tools/foreign exchange-history/. Each time series contains rates for sixteen years (2000–2015) with a total of 4174 observations. The moving averages track the significant upward and downward moves of the rates with a lag while smoothing brief market corrections.

3.2 Trading Rules

Recall that a profitable trading strategy is based on the principle that the base currency should be sold (exchanged to obtain quote currency) as the rate decreases and bought as the rate increases. The random fluctuations in the rates due to noise should be ignored in determining trends. A moving average smoothen the rate curves while preserving the approximate turning points in rates use simple moving average and exponential moving average as two competitive methods in technical analysis. In both cases the signals 'buy', 'sell' are issued when there is a change of moving average slope: negative to positive or vice versa respectively. Simple moving average of order p at time t is computed as:

$$ma(x,p,t) = p^{-1}\sum\nolimits_{k=t-p+1}^{t} x_k \tag{1}$$

Define the sign of the slope of a moving average of order p at time t as:

$$\delta(x,p,t) = sign(ma(x,p,t) - ma(x,p,t-1)) \tag{2}$$

The signal is generated as follows:

$$s(x,p,t) = \begin{cases} -1 & \text{if } \delta(x,p,t-1) > 0 \text{ and } \delta(x,p,t) < 0 \\ +1 & \text{if } \delta(x,p,t-1) < 0 \text{ and } \delta(x,p,t) > 0 \\ 0 & \text{otherwise} \end{cases} \tag{3}$$

The lower the order of the moving averages, the lower is the proportion of hold signals and the higher is the proportion of executed trades (buy or sell). Since the transaction costs increase with the number of trades, transaction costs are lower when using higher order moving averages. However, higher order moving averages may lead to excessive smoothing and loss of opportunities to execute profitable trades based on short term trends. This problem may be addressed by using relatively lower order moving averages and explicitly setting limits on the frequency of trades. We model this by defining a function ρ with a holding time parameter h that specifies the minimum number of periods between consecutive trades. Let $prev(t)$ denote the last time period before t when a trade has been executed and signal $s_t = s(x, p, t)$. Then:

$$\rho(s_t, h) = s_t \text{ if } t - prev(t) \geq h; \quad \rho(s_t, h) = 0 \text{ otherwise} \qquad (4)$$

We put attention to the concern motivated by transaction costs. The transaction is not profitable unless the absolute value of the percentage change in rates between consecutive trades exceeds a minimum threshold value. We model this using a function τ with a minimum change parameter β. Since transaction cost of c is expressed as a percentage of the trade value, we set $\beta > 0.01c$ and define the function as follows:

$$\tau(s_t, \beta) = s_t \text{ if } |x_t - x_{prev(t)}|/x_{prev(t)} \geq \beta; \quad \tau(s_t, \beta) = 0 \text{ otherwise} \qquad (5)$$

A signal generated at time t for a time series x using a moving average of order p, holding time parameter h, and minimum change parameter β is given by:

$$signal(x, p, t, h, \beta) = \tau(\rho(s(x, p, t), h), \beta) \qquad (6)$$

Overview of Genetic Algorithm
We use Eq. (6) to generate trading signals at time t given parameters p, h and β. Thus a rule is characterized by a parameter vector $\langle p, h, \beta \rangle$. We conduct the evaluation of the GA performance by calculating the return on investment given formula 2. An exhaustive search (ES) is performed over parameter space $p \in P$, $h \in H$ and $\beta \in B$ by back-testing on available data. The criterion for the use of the ES is the size of the parameter space, than the best rules may be identified. Our experimental findings demonstrate that the best solutions tend to be clustered around a few points in the $\langle P, H, B \rangle$ parameter space and lack diversity.

Recall that we have mentioned that ensemble signals work better on out-of-sample data when the constituent signals are diverse. It motivates us to use a genetic algorithm (GA) as one of the best available solutions to evolve a set of rules that result in sufficiently high returns. Design of our GA tends to prevent premature convergence on local optima (i.e., a population for an optimization problem converged too early), but to guarantee the diversification of the obtained rules in the sense that they represent a widely distributed set of points in the parameter pace. We outline our GA:

Step 1: Generation of the initial population of candidate solutions.
Step 2: Selection of the candidate solution as parents. They are paired randomly.

We use a 2-tournament selection strategy that repeats the following process n_P times, selecting one individual at each iteration. The choice of 2-tournament selection is motivated by diversity considerations. A stochastic approach, rather than a deterministic one further promotes diversification.

Step 3: Recombination by generating a pair of offsprings from each pair with probability p_r.

Step 4: Offsprings mutation with probability p_m. The mutation rate is maintained relatively high to maintain diversity and prevent premature convergence to local optima. However, it is low enough to prevent the evolution from degenerating into a random search process.

Step 5: Replacement of the current population with the n_P mutated offspring.

Step 6: Return population.

Given that the algorithm mixes the population of signals coming from a diversified set of predictors, developed ensemble signal generator combines the signals with linear weighting: At each period t, assign a weight w_t^i to each of the K constituent rules in the ensemble such that $\sum_{i=1}^{K} w_t^i = 1$, and compute a weighted average of the signals s_t^i produced by the rules:

$$\bar{s}_t = \sum_{i=1}^{K} w_t^i . s_t^i \tag{7}$$

$\bar{s}_t$ may range from -1 to $+1$, we define our ensemble signal in terms of a threshold λ (where $-1 < \lambda < +1$) as:

$$s_t = \begin{cases} -1 & if\ \bar{s}_t < -\lambda \\ +1 & if\ \bar{s}_t > +\lambda \\ 0 & otherwise \end{cases} \tag{8}$$

In our experiments we choose $\lambda = 0.1$ based on the following considerations: In a situation where the K rules carry equal weight, the ensemble generates a trade signal (-1 or $+1$) if and only if the absolute value of the difference between the number of buy signal and number of sell signals exceed $\lceil \lambda K \rceil$. If the signals are non-informative and p is the proportion of trade (non-zero) signals generated by the rules, then the probability that the ensemble generates a trade signal may be modeled as the probability that the absolute difference between the number of successes and number of failures exceed $\lceil \lambda K \rceil$ in $\lceil pK \rceil$ Bernoulli trials with probability of success 0.5. In our experiments K = 100. On the average, approximately 20% of the signals are trade signals and thus p = 0.2. The probability that the absolute difference between the number of successes and number of failures exceed 10 in 20 Bernoulli trials is approximately 0.01. This probability corresponds to the event that our ensemble generates a trade signal merely due to random noise. Our experimental results corroborate this threshold choice of $\lambda = 0.1$. At higher values of λ very few trades are executed, leading to returns that are similar to those obtained using a buy and hold strategy. At significantly lower values of

λ too many trades are executed resulting in transaction costs offsetting relatively minor gains.

Experimental Set-Up for Evaluation

Foreign exchange rate data from each of the four currency pairs is yearly clustered, thus we obtain $4 \times 16 = 64$ data sets. We identify $K = 100$ trading rules separately for each data set based on back-testing. The rules identified are then tested using data from the subsequent year for the same currency pair. Hence, out-of-sample testing is performed on the 60 data sets for the years 2001 to 2015.

4 Results

We present findings on comparison of rules identified by exhaustive search and GA. The trading rules are implemented at forex market with the data for four currency pairs over the 16 years from 2000 to 2015. We conclude with two important observations from in-sample results: First, that the sample of rules employed in this study yield satisfactory returns on training data; annual returns obtained using the best 100 SMA rules range from 4.9% to 13.1%, with a mean return of 8.4%. Secondly, that the returns produced using rules identified by the GA are only marginally lower than those produced by rules identified through exhaustive search; on the average the difference in the annual returns is less than 0.5%. We make a conclusion that presented GA can identifying profitable rules efficiently. Each GA run took less than 20 s on a Windows desktop with 24 GB of RAM and an i7-4790 processor running at 3.6 GHz. However, in-sample results do not necessarily illustrate the real performance of evolved rules. Hence we next test the performance of these rules on out-of-sample data.

The best $K = 100$ rules obtained using back-testing in a year are applied to data for the subsequent year to obtain out-of-sample results. Figure 1 compares the average out-of-sample returns produced by rules identified through exhaustive search and our GA for simple moving average rules and exponential moving average for the four currency pairs over the 15 years from 2001 to 2015. On the average, the rules obtained using presented GA with simple moving average yield significantly higher returns than those produced by rules identified through exhaustive search with out-of-sample data. Apart from two tests out of the sixty (USD/CHF in the years 2004 and 2010) the rules identified by the GA outperformed ES. Moreover, in 14 of the 60 tests, the rules identified using exhaustive search resulted in negative returns on investment. One of the reasons that may explain poor performance of ES on out-of-sample data is lack diversity and its flexibility with back-testing with in-sample data. However, the rules identified by the GA do not lack diversity and on the average result in positive returns on test data.

114   S. Galeshchuk and S. Mukherjee

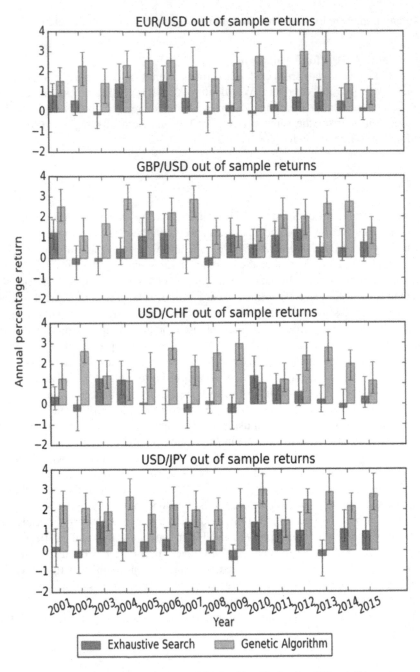

Fig. 1. Average test-returns of rules identified using ES and GA

5 Conclusion

Results show the mean returns for the three currency pairs from 2000 to 2015 produced by rules identified through exhaustive search (ES) and our GA. In-sample data shows slightly better performance of ES. However, out-of-sample experiments prove GA is more efficient trading signal generator than ES. Future research foresees experiment to combine evolved set of trading rules (ensemble signal generator) using particle filters to get better resulting returns on testing examples.

References

1. Galeshchuk, S.: Neural networks performance in exchange rate prediction. Neurocomputing **172**, 446–452 (2016)
2. Menkhoff, L., Taylor, M.P.: The obstinate passion of foreign exchange professionals: technical analysis. J. Econ. Lit. **45**(4), 936–972 (2007)
3. Beran, J., Ocker, D.: Volatility of stock-market indexes—an analysis based on SEMIFAR models. J. Bus. Econ. Stat. **19**(1), 103–116 (2001)
4. Neely, C.J., Weller, P.A.: Intraday technical trading in the foreign exchange market. J. Int. Money Financ. **22**(2), 223–237 (2003)
5. Lissandring, M., Daly, D., Sornette, D.: Statistical testing of DeMark Technical Indicators on Commodity Futures (2016). Early review paper
6. LeBaron, B.: Technical trading rule profitability and foreign exchange intervention. J. Int. Econ. **49**(1), 125–143 (1999)
7. Menkhoff, L., Schlumberger, M.: Persistent profitability of technical analysis on foreign exchange markets? PSL Q. Rev. **48**(193), 189–215 (2013)
8. Hoffmann, A.O., Shefrin, H.: Technical analysis and individual investors. J. Econ. Behav. Organ. **107**, 487–511 (2014)
9. Prat, G., Uctum, R.: Expectation formation in the foreign exchange market: a time-varying heterogeneity approach using survey data. Appl. Econ. **47**(34–35), 3673–3695 (2015)
10. Taylor, N.: The rise and fall of technical trading rule success. J. Bank. Financ. **40**, 286–302 (2014)
11. Owen, A.L., Palmer, B.: Macroeconomic conditions and technical trading profitability in foreign exchange markets. Appl. Econ. Lett. **19**(12), 1107–1110 (2012)
12. Schulmeister, S.: Components of the profitability of technical currency trading. Appl. Finan. Econ. **18**(11), 917–930 (2008)
13. Lento, C.: Combined signal approach: evidence from the Asian-Pacific equity markets. Appl. Econ. Lett. **16**(7), 749–753 (2009)
14. Bauer, R., Cosemans, M., Eichholtz, P.: Option trading and individual investor performance. J. Bank. Finance **33**(4), 731–746 (2009)
15. Gallo, C.: The Forex market in practice: a computing approach for automated trading strategies. Int. J. Econ. Manag. Sci. **3**(169), 1–9 (2014)
16. Potvin, J.Y., Soriano, P., Vallée, M.: Generating trading rules on the stock markets with genetic programming. Comput. Oper. Res. **31**(7), 1033–1047 (2004)
17. Kattan, A., Fatima, S., Arif, M.: Time-series event-based prediction: an unsupervised learning framework based on genetic programming. Inf. Sci. **301**, 99–123 (2015)
18. Koza, J.R.: Introduction to genetic programming. Adv. Genet. Program. **1**, 21–45 (1994)

19. Vasilakis, G.A., Theofilatos, K.A., Georgopoulos, E.F., Karathanasopoulos, A., Likothanassis, S.D.: A genetic programming approach for EUR/USD exchange rate forecasting and trading. Comput. Econ. **42**(4), 415–431 (2013)
20. Pelusi, D., Tivegna, M., Ippoliti, P.: Intelligent algorithms for trading the euro-dollar in the foreign exchange market. In: Corazza, M., Pizzi, C. (eds.) Mathematical and Statistical Methods for Actuarial Sciences and Finance, pp. 243–252. Springer, Cham (2014). doi:10. 1007/978-3-319-02499-8_22
21. Hu, Y., Liu, K., Zhang, X., Su, L., Ngai, E.W.T., Liu, M.: Application of evolutionary computation for rule discovery in stock algorithmic trading: a literature review. Appl. Soft Comput. **36**, 534–551 (2015)
22. Straßburg, J., Alexandrov, V.N.: Facilitating analysis of Monte Carlo dense matrix inversion algorithm scaling behaviour through simulation. J. Comput. Sci. **4**(6), 473–479 (2013)
23. Chiam, S.C., Tan, K.C., Al Mamun, A.: Dynamic index tracking via multi-objective evolutionary algorithm. Appl. Soft Comput. **13**(7), 3392–3408 (2013)

ResMAS - A Conceptual MAS Model for Resource-Based Integrated Markets

Thiago R.P.M. Rúbio[⊠], Zafeiris Kokkinogenis, Henrique Lopes Cardoso,
Eugénio Oliveira, and Rosaldo J.F. Rossetti

LIACC/DEI, Faculdade de Engenharia, Universidade do Porto,
Rua Dr. Roberto Frias, 4200-465 Porto, Portugal
{reis.thiago,kokkinogenis,hlc,eco,rossetti}@fe.up.pt

Abstract. Contemporary information systems provide extended capabilities to support both system and market operations and favour the emergence of dynamic marketplaces to complement traditional market organisations. An integrated market-based approach considers the coexistence of different market types and their interaction. We discuss ResMAS, a conceptual model for resource-based integrated markets where the entities are modelled as a Multi-Agent System (MAS). In this paper we exemplify the application of ResMAS in a plausible scenario: electricity markets. The main contributions of the ResMAS model comprise the capability to model complex agent decisions, the possibility to analyse the interaction among markets, and the possibility to create new regulation mechanisms to achieve the expected outcomes.

Keywords: Market-based model · Multi-Agent Systems · Resource-based market

1 Introduction

Markets are economic systems where two or more parties engage in resource exchange, whether related to goods or services. Their main role is to coordinate the flow of a given demand in respect to a given supply of resources. Contemporary information systems provide extended capabilities to support both system and market operation as well as improve the observability and controllability of the system. The proliferation of Cyber-Physical Systems (CPS) and other technological paradigms has allowed market-oriented approaches to be implemented, achieving more efficient control on resource allocation and supply [7,8]. This possibility has fostered the emergence of new "side-market" structures, operating in parallel with traditional markets within a given system. These new structures are characterised by: (a) the possibility of consumers (typically resource users) to act as providers (or even producers), and (b) their volatility.

It is very important to understand how these different market structures interact and what are the impacts on the whole system. That is, market failures can emerge due to externalities, such as possible imbalances, self-interest

© Springer International Publishing AG 2017
J. Bajo et al. (Eds.): PAAMS 2017 Workshops, CCIS 722, pp. 117–129, 2017.
DOI: 10.1007/978-3-319-60285-1_10

demand, poor prediction on resource production, or failure in the production itself. Moreover, the aforementioned integration becomes more important when decentralised and de-regulated emerging markets are considered, such as peer-to-peer and virtual markets. A holistic view is still not well documented.

The main contribution from this work is the design and formalisation of ResMAS (Resource-based Market Agents Systems), a conceptual model of multi-markets environments. We present an overview of the potential market structures that can exist in contemporary systems, exemplified in a particular instance: the electricity market. Our objective is to define the elements that compose the system in a formal way and characterize their interactions. We use the Business Process Modelling Notation (BPMN) to describe the orchestration of the activities in two market flows. Finally, we present a preliminary simulation model that instantiates the specification of ResMAS on the electricity market to serve as an example of how different set-ups in one of the markets lead in different behaviours of others.

The rest of the paper is organised as follows: Sect. 2 overviews market organisation aspects. Section 3 presents the ResMAS model, complemented by the definition of market processes in Sect. 4. Section 5 describes a preliminary simulation analysis, and Sect. 6 discusses some conclusions and future work.

2   Overview on Market Organisations

For the concept of market organisation we consider the mechanisms and the participants involved in the trading of goods. Figure 1 depicts an idealisation of a market ecosystem composed of five markets, each having its own organisation:

Wholesale market (M.1). The principal actors that participate in this market are: the *suppliers* (E.1) and the *providers* (E.2). Considering the case of electricity market, suppliers are the producer companies that own power plants, while providers are the retail distributor utilities. Wholesale markets are characterised by the trade of big volumes, and by the pricing mechanisms (usually auction-based [9]). These markets are built on the aggregate demand and supply curves. Depending on the domain, consider we might find different wholesale markets operating in parallel.

Retail market (M.2) is composed of a group of providers and a group of *customers* (E.3). Characteristics of the market are: (a) the low volumes of products traded between a provider and the end-user (customer), and (b) the tariff mechanism with which the price of the goods is set. Providers design and publish tariffs in order to respond to an aggregate demand (customers' portfolio) in a way that will allow to maximize their profits and match the supply they purchase in the wholesale market [1,3].

Bilateral contracts market (M.5) are characterized by the establishment of bilateral financial or physical relations between suppliers, on one side, and eligible customers or providers on the other [6]. These contracts involve separated negotiations for several aspects, such as the price and a large volume of goods/services to be supplied and consumed over a specified period of time, in order to satisfy a demand not applicable on the other markets.

Virtual markets (M.3) are emerging organizations and can receive different interpretations based on the application domain that is considered, differently from wholesale, retail and bilateral market organizations, which reflect the traditional trading contexts. Characterized by a dynamic aggregate demand that forms short-term coalitions of customers to achieve a particular goal, virtual markets can operate similarly to a retail market. However, a representative acts as a buyer on the other markets, while switching role as provider for the others in the coalition. Examples of such economic structures are the virtual power plants (VPPs) concept in smart grids [5,10].

Peer-to-peer Markets (M.4) are organizations where customers can exchange resources (goods or services) between themselves, without the existence of a provider. It is a market that emerges within the context of *sharing economy*, where participants grant collaborative access to products or services [4]. Peer-to-peer markets are often characterized by high degree of heterogeneity [2].

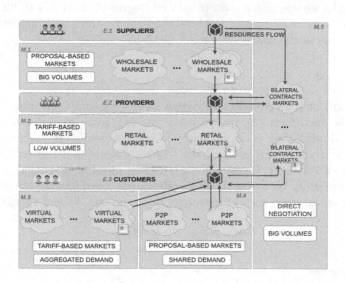

Fig. 1. An integrated architecture for multi-market MAS

Market Regulation (represented by the "R" in Fig. 1) is twofold: one with a systemic scope and the other with agent-scope. The first is usually referred to as governmental regulation and in real-life is provided by regulation agencies. It comprises the norms established in order to guarantee the correct operation of the system. On the other side, agent-scoped regulation comprises the mechanisms participating agents (usually providers) provide to some groups of customers in order to influence their behaviour, such as incentives or discounts. If some compliance rate is achieved, the provider benefits from this policy by manifesting more competitive participation.

Usually, managers use economic tools such as market-based policies to guide their decisions and drive their system towards the desired outcome. Indeed, current decisions focus on a single market in order to apply a regulatory policy, which often leads to a short-sighted decision in such integrated markets environment where policies might have impact on the whole system.

Thus, the ResMAS environment described below is put forward as a first step towards this complex scenario of multi-market applications, where regulation plays a central role regarding policy-making processes.

3   A Conceptual Architecture for Market-Based MAS

Given the growing relevance of market-based environments in different scenarios, novel approaches including autonomous and automatic decision-taking systems will be needed. In this sense, Multi-Agent Systems are presented as the right direction towards representing human preferences and decisions. In the following paragraphs we describe a conceptual architecture that comes to fill the gaps between the broad spectrum of market-based applications and impacts of individual decisions in the whole system.

3.1   ResMAS

Resources are common elements in market-based systems, appearing under different names and kinds. Agents play the market game in order to exchange resources and fulfill their needs for required resources while providing their own available resources. In this context, the requiring agent is called *buyer* and the providing is called *seller*. Resources can describe physical or virtual goods, services or information. We define ResMAS (Resource-based Market Agent System) as an environment with a set of resources Res, markets $\mathcal{M}$ and agents $\mathcal{A}$.

$$ResMAS = \langle Res, \mathcal{M}, \mathcal{A} \rangle$$

3.2   Resources

In the ResMAS world, there can be a limited or unlimited quantity of resources, given their nature (type). We define a resource as follows.

Definition 1 (Resource). *A resource comprehends two main concepts: the resource type τ, defined in an ontology, representing its name (or nature); and the information about its application domain σ. The domain σ is the dimension where the resource is located and can be seen as the applicable unit. $r = \langle \tau, \sigma \rangle$. In practice, agents deal with resource instances, which are samples of that resource, defined in the domain expressed by r.*

For instance, let r_{elec} be a resource instance of electricity: $r_{elec} = \langle \text{SOLAR\_ENERGY}, 50\,\text{Kw} \rangle$ means that r_{elec} is 50 Kw of solar energy, an instance of the resource electricity. Two basic operations are provided for managing resource instances: $addition(r_1, r_2)$ and $subtraction(r_1, r_2)$. These operations are valid only for resources of the same type: the result is a new resource instance. Thus, different resource instances can be aggregated in a set $Res = \{r_1, ..., r_q\}$ representing a collection of resources. Here, two basic operations are provided: $add(r, Res)$ and $subtract(r, Res)$. The first allows adding new resources to the set and the second allows removing resources from the set. Agents use these operations in order to manage and exchange resources in the markets.

3.3   Markets

Definition 2 (Markets). *Different markets can be found in a single ResMAS system:* $\mathcal{M} = \{m_1, ..., m_k\}$. *They comprise the negotiation environment where agents can exchange resources. Each market* m_i *have a group of allowed participants Part* $\subseteq \mathcal{A}$, *a set of artefacts Art, a regulation mechanism Reg and, finally, a set of processes Proc that describe resource allocation mechanisms.*

$$m_i = \langle Part, Art, Reg, Proc \rangle$$

The *participants Part* represent the set of agents that are allowed to participate in the market. It means that different markets can filter which agents can participate. *Artefacts* are market objects that carry information over the negotiated resources: $Art \subseteq \{tariff, proposal, transaction, contract\}$.

A *tariff* can be seen as a plan with multiple associations between quantities (or specific resource instances) and the price to pay for each of them, called rates, and a set of fees (sign-up fee, periodic fee, withdraw-fee, etc.), so $tariff^r = \langle Rates, Fees \rangle$ with $Rates = \{\langle r, price \rangle, ...\}$ where $price \in Res$ is the price to pay for the resource r. In a tariff-based process, the tariffs are published in the market and the customers can subscribe to that plan. Actually, tariffs act as templates for the contract applicable rules. On the other hand, a *proposal* is an exchange proposition between two individuals. Differently from tariffs, there is no subscription plan here, just a direct negotiation for a resource instance. $prop^r = \langle price, a_i, a_j \rangle$, where r is the resource, the desired price $price \in Res$, and the seller agent $a_i \in Part$, and the buyer agent $a_j \in Part$.

Tariffs and proposals are subject to a *contract*, which contains the rules of the deal and determines the services and the obligations the agents shall comply in order to assure the agreement. $Contract = \langle Parties, Service, Obligations \rangle$. Finally, a *transaction* represents the resource exchange between the agents, from the agent a_i to the agent a_j, following the corresponding payment. Multiples transactions might occur under a contract.

Still in the market elements, the *regulation policies Reg* represent the mechanisms used to provide control over the system and reduce negative externalities such as market failures. In this paper, we consider regulation policies as simple authorizations, but we intend to explore this area in the future using more complex mechanisms, such as incentives, norms and trust. Section 4 is fully dedicated to better explain how market processes are conceptualized in ResMAS. Basically, we considered two types of market processes: tariff-based and proposal-based. Although one can design different processes, we believe that these two types can characterize most of the markets, even with different requirements in terms of the flows and agent activities, the basic operations are usually either tariff-based (pool) or proposal-based (direct). Note the distinction from the term *proto-col* in the way that the processes are much more generic, describing the agents' responsibilities and activities in the whole allocation mechanism flow (that might include some negotiation protocols in the task to match buyers and sellers).

3.4   Agents

Definition 3 (Agent). *The set of agents $\mathcal{A}$ is composed by the agents that participate in the ResMAS world. A simple agent $a \in \mathcal{A}$ is an entity that has a role, which specifies its behaviours, two dynamic sets of resources, the available and the required ones and goals Γ. We consider that this simple agent represents the providers, since they just deal with resources, but never uses (consume or produce) it.*

$$a = \langle role, Avail, Req, \Gamma \rangle, \ a \in P$$

So, let's call a' the agents that can manipulate the resources. In addition to the simple agent definition, customers and suppliers can have a group of appli-ances App that represent the actual devices that can use the resources and a Π set of preferences for using this appliances. Thus,

$$a' = \langle role, Avail, Req, \Gamma, Apps, \Pi \rangle, \ a' \in C \cup S$$

We will write $Avail_a^t(r)$ or $Req_a^t(r)$ to denote the available or required quan-tities of resources r that agent a has at the time t.

Definition 4 (Group). *A group is an aggregation of agents that play the same role, which can be supplier, provider, customer. Three main groups can be defined: S, P and C:*

$$S = \{a \in \mathcal{A} \mid role_a = supplier\}$$
$$P = \{a \in \mathcal{A} \mid role_a = provider\}$$
$$C = \{a \in \mathcal{A} \mid role_a = customer\}$$

Definition 5 (Appliances). *For the sake of simplicity, we consider supplier agents as only capable of producing, never requiring resources ($Req = \varnothing$). Providers, in turn, do not produce or consume, just negotiate resources, act-ing as intermediary agents (brokers). On the other hand, customers can have both production and consumption capabilities. The set of appliances of an agent a, $Apps_a$ is defined:*

$$Apps_a = \{app_1^r, \ldots, app_z^r\}, \quad iff \ a \in C$$

To represent the actual resources usage, a load function $\mathcal{L}$ is defined. Given a appliance app^r in an instant of time t (where $T = \{t_0, \ldots t_n\}$, is the time horizon), the load function $\mathcal{L}$ represents the instantaneous consumption/production.

$$\mathcal{L} : Apps \times T \to \mathbb{R}$$

Definition 6 (Appliances Preferences). *An utilization occurrence of the appliance U_{app}^r is described by the appliance activation in a given time t with the duration δ. So $U_{app} = \langle t, \delta \rangle$.*

Each agent a has a set of possible utilizations for the appliance app^r that can be used to create an actual schedule. So, for each appliance, the agent has a totally ordered set π_{app} corresponding to the preferences of the agent a_i over the possible utilizations of the appliance: $\pi_{app} = \{U_1 \succeq U_2 \cdots \succeq U_w\}$. Given that the agent might have different appliances, the partially ordered set resulting from the union of all of an agent's preferences is $\Pi_{a_i} = \pi_{app_1} \cup \pi_{app_2} \cdots \cup \pi_{app_z}$.

Definition 7 (Scheduling mechanism). *In order to use the appliances, the customer agent creates a schedule function to organize the activation of appliances. The scheduling mechanism Ψ corresponds to the actual plan of executing some of the utilization occurrences.*

Due to space limitations, the scheduler modelling is out of the scope of this work. We only refer to the scheduled tasks in order to know what are the actual appliances activated in a given time t. The results of the scheduler Ψ are represented as:

$$\Psi_a^t(app) = \begin{cases} 1, & \text{iff } app \text{ is activated in } t \\ 0, & \text{otherwise} \end{cases}$$

The *list of active appliances* at time t is $Lapp_a^t = \{app \in Apps \mid \Psi_a^t(app) = 1\}$.

Definition 8 (Required resources). *The required resources $Req_a^t(r)$ are the resources agent a will need in a given time t. In ResMAS, agents can negotiate resources through all the markets they are allowed to participate in order to acquire the required resources from other agents. As seen previously, suppliers present an empty required set. A provider's tariff subscription mechanism makes its required set an aggregation of its subscribed customers' required resources $(C' \subseteq C)$. The resources amount required by a provider is called demand and represented by Dem. Thus, a customer's required resources comprise the sum of the load $\mathcal{L}$ of all appliances that are activated in the given time t.*

$$Req_a^t(r) = \begin{cases} 0, & \text{iff } a \in S \\ Dem_a^t(r) - Avail_a^t(r), & \text{iff } a \in P \\ \sum_{j=1}^{z}[\mathcal{L}(app_j, t) \cdot \Psi_a(app_j, t)], & \text{iff } (a \in C) \wedge (app \in Apps_a) \end{cases}$$

$$Dem_a^t(r) = \sum_{i=1}^{n} Req_{a_i}^t(r), \quad a_i \in C'$$

Definition 9 (Available resources). *The available resources $Avail_a^t(r)$ are the resources the agent a can provide in market in a given time t. Similarly to required resources, agents' available resources are computed differently according to the agent group. Suppliers and Customers have different available resources in each time t. It means that either they have production capabilities, so $v \in \mathbb{R}^+$. Or they do not and $v = 0$. Providers, in turn, depend on the subscriber's customers available resources. The available amount is called* Supply *and represented by* Sup.

$$Avail_a^t(r) = \begin{cases} v \in \mathbb{R}, & \text{iff } a \in S \cup C \\ Sup_a^t(r) & \text{iff } a \in P \end{cases}$$

$$Sup_a^t(r) = \sum_{i=1}^{n} Avail_{a_i}^t(r), \quad \text{iff } a_i \in C'$$

Let the *market actions buy* and *sell* be the high level results of the market activities. $\mathcal{X}_m^t(r)$ is the set of possible actions in the market m:

$$\mathcal{X}_m^t(r) \ni \text{buy}_m[Req_a^t(r)] \iff a \in C \cup P$$
$$\mathcal{X}_m^t(r) \ni \text{sell}_m[Avail_a^t(r)], \quad \text{iff } a \in C \cup S \cup P$$

The resulting values of the aforementioned market actions are: V_{buy} the value paid on the action of buying $buy_a \implies V_{buy} \in \mathbb{R}$; and V_{sell} the value received for selling $sell_a \implies V_{sell} \in \mathbb{R}$. The agents seek to participate in the markets buying and selling accordingly to their goals.

Definition 10 (Agent goals). *The agent goals Γ represent the satisfying conditions the agents intend to pursue in order to maintain a correct participation in the system.*

Γ_{a_i} depends on the role of the agent a_i. Let γ_{sup} be the supplier's goals, γ_{prov} be the provider's goals and γ_{cust} be the customer's goals. Since the suppliers are only intended to sell the maximum amount of resources available, the supplier's goal is to maximize the value obtained from selling the resources (V_{sell}). So $\gamma_{sup} = max(V_{sell})$. In turn, the provider's goals comprise a reduction on the imbalance from supply (Sup) and Demand (Dem) in order to require less from suppliers. It means the provider's seek autonomy from suppliers, at the same time looking for a profitable participation, i.e. to maximize the profit ϕ when performing the market actions of buying and selling $\gamma_{prov} = Req \to 0 \quad \wedge \quad max(\Phi)$ subject to $\Phi = V_{sell} - V_{buy}$.

Finally, the customer's seek to achieve the greater value on selling V_{sell} when there are production capabilities meanwhile minimizing the buying value V_{buy}, constrained also by a budget value β that represents a threshold for the maximum value on buying. Moreover, the customer wants also to maximize the utility of the scheduling mechanism, i.e. the number of appliances scheduled for a given instant. Then: $\gamma_{cust} = max(V_{sell}) \quad \wedge \quad (min(V_{buy}) \mid V_{buy} \leq \beta) \quad \wedge \quad max(\|List_{app}\|)$.

4   Modelling Market Protocols as Processes

In Sect. 3.3 we said that processes are an important element of markets. They represent the logical flow lead by the market operator in order to coordinate agent activities and allocate the resources by using a *negotiation protocol*. Negotiation protocols are sub-processes that try to find a match between possible buyers and sellers, according to specific rules. Examples of negotiation protocols are auctions, direct negotiation, etc. As a part of the process, we do not intend to further detail the negotiation protocols in this paper. Instead we assume that even if the negotiation changes, it will not affect the essence of the process.

The process, in turn, seems to define the whole market. In our model, two processes are considered: tariff-based and proposal-based. Tariff-based processes, as seen in Fig. 2, occur in two main flows. The tariff publication (left) starts with the intention of providing a tariff for a group of customers and if the market operator authorizes, the customers can see it in a tariff pool and possibly subscribe to it (right). Again, if the market operator authorizes this subscribe operation, a contract is established (a sub-process to be described later). The process ends when the contract is finished.

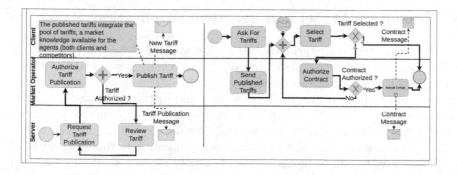

Fig. 2. Tariff-based market process

Markets operated in a proposal-based fashion follow a different process. Instead of having a pool, the proposals comprise a direct way of establishing a transaction. The agent (customer or provider) creates a proposal requesting a service or good. The market finds the agent that will provide the resource either by selecting a specific agent or initiating a negotiation protocol (sub-process). If a match is established, a contract is consolidated. Figure 3 represents proposal-based processes.

Finally, the process of establishing and executing a contract is defined according to Fig. 4. The service terms (rules) are registered and three main flows might follow in parallel: the client reports provider violations, i.e., the provider does not comply with the contract terms; the converse (client violates the contract); or the service is correctly executed. Occurring the applicable transactions.

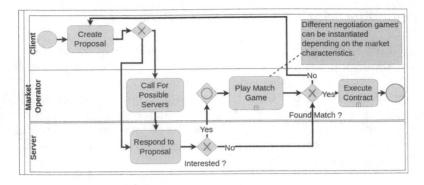

Fig. 3. Proposal-based market process

To the best of our knowledge, there are still no works in modelling market processes. We have used Business Process Modelling (BPM) to describe the processes; for lack of space, we do not include details on how the processes modelled are implemented by the agents.

5   Simulation Model and Practical Application

The evolution of electricity grid towards a self-organized Cyber-Physical System, known as Smart Grid, has introduced significant challenges not only from the technological, but also from economic perspective. The analysis of smart grid markets need to be performed in a integrated and distributed fashion, allowing better comprehension of how suppliers, providers and customers interact and share electricity as a resource. Considering ResMAS specification, we are able to map the role and behaviours of each smart grid entity. In this section we will instantiate ResMAS meta-model on the electricity market simulating two common structures of it: wholesale (proposal-based) and retail (tariff-based) markets. Thus, we show the relevance of our integrated approach in order to evaluate ResMAS expressiveness in modelling such a real-world application. The purpose

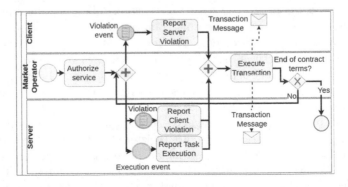

Fig. 4. Contract process

of the simulation is to show how different set-ups in one of the markets lead in different behaviours of other. ResMAS can be considered for designing both simulation models and deployable applications for already developed markets.

Suppliers represent the generator companies (GenCO), providers are the retailers (distributors) and customers are *prosumers*, with production and consumption capabilities. In all the cases we consider that customers can change their contracts at any time. Three scenarios are defined:

- Scenario 1: 1 Supplier, 0 Providers, 100 Customers
- Scenario 2: 1 Supplier, 1 Provider, 100 Customers
- Scenario 3: 5 Suppliers, 10 Providers, 100 Customers

Scenario 1 assumes that there are no intermediaries: customers buy energy directly from the suppliers. Besides the supplier, in Scenario 2 customers can subscribe to a provider's tariff. Finally, Scenario 3 includes multiple supplier options and multiple providers for the customers. We assume that providers are allowed to have only one tariff published and each simulation run through 3 months (2160 ticks, time resolution for a tick is one hour). Tariffs can change each day (24 ticks) and contracts are valid for 30 days (720 ticks). Each experiment averages the data of 10 runs.

The goal of the experiments is to observe the evolution of the system when multiple entities can negotiate in different markets. Some metrics are defined to evaluate the simulation results: average produced and required resources (customers); average imbalance between supply and demand (providers); number of system failures (required resources exceeding availability, peaks) and number of individuals without contracts.

Table 1 reports the results regarding the aforementioned metrics. The average values corroborates the ideas of our conceptual model. In fact, we can clearly see that in scenario 1, there are no system failures, since the customers negotiate directly with the supplier. The supplier should have enough production capabilities to endure all required resources. When a provider is introduced (Scenario 2), the imbalance represents the quantity of energy negotiated in the wholesale market; the demand exceeded a threshold 26 times, meaning a peak (failure) in the grid. Moreover, for 11 times (average) customers did not want to subscribe to the available tariff, meaning that it was not interesting for all the customers. Finally, in Scenario 3, the high number of available tariffs helped reducing the

Table 1. Average metrics results

	Available	Required	Imbalance	Failures	Individuals without contract
Scenario (1)	2360 Kw	7680 Kw	-	0	-
Scenario (2)	2690 Kw	8520 Kw	5830 Kw	26	11
Scenario (3)	2470 Kw	7930 Kw	5460 Kw	17	3

peaks and improved the susceptibility of customers finding a suitable tariff. In all experiments the quantities of available and required energy are similar because the number of customers did not change.

Table 2 shows average results of the simulations regarding the market artefacts. To the tariffs number we included also the number of tariff updates. Here, we can observe that in Scenario 1 all the customers' proposals were effective, creating the same number of transactions. No tariffs were present. On the other hand, between Scenario 2 and 3 the introduction of multiple tariff alternatives made possible for customers to change tariffs more frequently, looking for better opportunities. In fact, the proposals number is directly related to the number of auctions in the wholesale market.

Table 2. Average number of market artefacts

	Proposals	Tariffs	Contracts	Transactions
Scenario (1)	2160	0	2160	2160
Scenario (2)	4	91	93	2236
Scenario (3)	15	417	1498	9321

6   Conclusions and Further Work

This work describes an integrated conceptual architecture for market-based scenarios where traditional market organizations are complemented by emerging marketplaces. A model that discusses how different markets of the same domain interact and analyses the impact of participation in multiple markets, has not been previously fully considered. This paper formalizes the ResMAS conceptual architecture using the Multi-Agent Systems metaphor. We describe the market processes, modelled using BPMN, to show the orchestration of the activities in two market flows: tariff-based markets and proposal-based markets. Furthermore, we devised a preliminary simulation model of the electricity markets, based on ResMAS, to show how interaction in different set-ups change the system behaviour. Although ResMAS is presented with emphasis to electricity markets, it finds application to various other domains. As future work, we intend to explore ResMAS in the context of regulation-aware agents, creating new market and agent decision processes that consider regulation mechanisms, such as norms and incentives to achieve better coordination and avoiding system failures.

Acknowledgements. This work is partially funded through IBRASIL, a Full Doctorate programme under Erasmus Mundus, Action 2 – STRAND 1, Lot 16, and FCT, the Portuguese Agency for R&D, under PhD Scholarship grant SFRH/BD/67202/2009.

References

1. Bojei, J., Julian, C.C., Wel, C.A.B.C., Ahmed, Z.U.: The empirical link between relationship marketing tools and consumer retention in retail marketing. J. Consum. Behav. **12**(3), 171–181 (2013)
2. Einav, L., Farronato, C., Levin, J.: Peer-to-peer markets. Annu. Rev. Econ. **8**, 615–635 (2016)
3. Gottwalt, S., Ketter, W., Block, C., Collins, J., Weinhardt, C.: Demand side management – a simulation of household behavior under variable prices. Energy Policy **39**(12), 8163–8174 (2011)
4. Heinrichs, H.: Sharing economy: a potential new pathway to sustainability. Gaia **22**(4), 228 (2013)
5. Kahlen, M., Ketter, W.: Aggregating electric cars to sustainable virtual power plants: the value of flexibility in future electricity markets. In: AAAI, pp. 665–671 (2015)
6. Niu, H., Baldick, R., Zhu, G.: Supply function equilibrium bidding strategies with fixed forward contracts. IEEE Trans. Power Syst. **20**(4), 1859–1867 (2005)
7. Rajkumar, R.R., Lee, I., Sha, L., Stankovic, J.: Cyber-physical systems: the next computing revolution. In: Proceedings of the 47th Design Automation Conference, pp. 731–736. ACM (2010)
8. Ramos, C., Liu, C.C.: AI in power systems and energy markets. IEEE Intell. Syst. **26**(2), 5–8 (2011)
9. Tesfatsion, L.: Auction basics for wholesale power markets: objectives and pricing rules. In: IEEE Power and Energy Society General Meeting, PES 2009, pp. 1–8. IEEE (2009)
10. You, S., Træholt, C., Poulsen, B.: A market-based virtual power plant. In: 2009 International Conference on Clean Electrical Power, pp. 460–465. IEEE (2009)

Initial Solution Heuristic for Portfolio Optimization of Electricity Markets Participation

Ricardo Faia[1(⊠)], Tiago Pinto[1,2], and Zita Vale[1]

[1] GECAD – Research Group on Intelligent Engineering
and Computing for Advanced Innovation and Development,
Institute of Engineering, Polytechnic of Porto (ISEP/IPP), Porto, Portugal
{rfmfa, tmcfp, zav}@isep.ipp.pt, tpinto@usal.es
[2] BISITE Research Centre, University of Salamanca (US), Salamanca, Spain

Abstract. Meta-heuristic search methods are used to find near optimal global solutions for difficult optimization problems. These meta-heuristic processes usually require some kind of knowledge to overcome the local optimum locations. One way to achieve diversification is to start the search procedure from a solution already obtained through another method. Since this solution is already validated the algorithm will converge easily to a greater global solution. In this work, several well-known meta-heuristics are used to solve the problem of electricity markets participation portfolio optimization. Their search performance is compared to the performance of a proposed hybrid method (ad-hoc heuristic to generate the initial solution, which is combined with the search method). The addressed problem is the portfolio optimization for energy markets participation, where there are different markets where it is possible to negotiate. In this way the result will be the optimal allocation of electricity in the different markets in order to obtain the maximum return quantified through the objective function.

Keywords: Electricity markets · Heuristic search · Meta-heuristic optimization · Portfolio optimization

1 Introduction

Metaheuristics can be defined as a set of search methods, such as construction heuristics, local search and more general orientation criteria to solve a specific problem. These have attracted the attention of many users due to their simplicity of implementation. In turn, the metaheuristics do not always reach an optimal solution, even for long computing times, but they manage to arrive at a near-optimal solution in a short time, which a deterministic resolution cannot obtain [1].

This work has received funding from the European Union's Horizon 2020 research and innovation programme under the Marie Sklodowska-Curie grant agreement No 641794 (project DREAM-GO) and grant agreement No 703689 (project ADAPT); and from FEDER Funds through COMPETE program and from National Funds through FCT under the project UID/EEA/00760/2013.

© Springer International Publishing AG 2017
J. Bajo et al. (Eds.): PAAMS 2017 Workshops, CCIS 722, pp. 130–142, 2017.
DOI: 10.1007/978-3-319-60285-1_11

The performance measures, such as the value of the target solution and the execution time can be seen as random variables, because with an algorithm of this nature it is never known beforehand what the final result will be. Support for research on metaheuristics can be provided by statistics. With statistics, it is possible to construct a systematic framework for the collection and evaluation of data, maximizing the objectivity and the reproducibility of the experiences. It is possible to construct a mathematical foundation that provides a probabilistic measure of events based on inference from the empirical data. In [2], it is possible to analyze the use of statistical tools in the study of algorithms and heuristics.

The work presented in [3] analyzes and compares the use of this type of algorithms, where the analysis is executed considering two models defined by the author:

- The univariate model, which considers the cost of the solution or the execution time;
- The multivariate model, in which both the cost of the solution and the execution time are of interest.

In the first case, the user is concerned with the cost of the solution (e.g., maximization/minimization problem) or the execution time as a measure of algorithm performance. When the interest is the cost of the solution, it is assumed that the computational resources are used in the same way by the different algorithms under study, it is called the principle of fairness. On the other hand, if the execution time is the parameter to be analyzed, it will have to be taken into account the number of times that a solution is obtained with the same characteristics in all the algorithms [3].

In the second case, the performance analysis of the algorithm includes the cost of solution and the execution time. In this case, the analysis falls within the scope of multivariate statistics, the authors [3] distinguish two specific scenarios about the multivariate model that may be of interest to the user, both are based on the cost of the solution and the time of execution, although they are distinguished by: In the first scenario the user only registers the final value (cost function x run time), and in the second scenario the user must save a set of values from the beginning of the search to the end, at each iteration it will save the value (cost function x run time).

In order to be able to return a solution to the problems described above, the case of the final value of the cost function can be a random value, the following methodology is proposed, as expressed in the pseudo-code of Fig. 1.

Figure 1 shows the pseudo-code of a multi start procedure. The solution x_i is constructed in Step 1 at iteration i. This is a typically performed with an iterative algorithm. Step 2 is devoted to improving this solution, obtaining solution x_i'. A simple improvement method can be applied. However, this second phase has recently become more elaborate and, in some cases, is performed with a complex metaheuristic that may or may not improve the initial solution x_i (in this latter case we set $x_i' = x_i$) [4].

This type of procedure is called multi-start methods, considering the pseudo-code of the Fig. 1, in the first step the construction of the initial solution can be developed through a simpler search method (Local Search (LS), Tabu Search (TS)), and in step 2, a more elaborate method (Particle Swarm Optimization (PSO), Genetic Algorithm (GA), or Simulated Annealing (SA)), which will require more complexity in implementation.

$Initialise\ i = 1$
while $(Stopping\ condition\ is\ not\ satisfied)$
{

      Setp 1. $(Generation)$
          $Construct\ solution\ x_i$
      Step 2. $(Search)$
          $Apply\ a\ search\ method\ to\ improve\ x_i$
          $Let\ x_i'\ be\ the\ solution\ obtained$
    if $(s_i'\ improves\ the\ best)$
          $Update\ the\ best$
    $i = i + 1$

}

Fig. 1. Multi-start procedure [4]

More search time should be given to the second step, because a more powerful algorithm is used to obtain better values in its performance.

The presented pseudo-code can be applied to any type of problem as long as it has a type of objective function to solve. In the case addressed by this paper, the problem in hands is the optimization of portfolios in electricity markets. This paper proposes a heuristic methodology to determine an initial solution in the portfolio optimization problem. The objective of this heuristic is to provide a good initial point for the search process, so that the meta-heuristics can achieve solutions nearer to the global optimum, and in faster execution times (without the need for long search processes). According to the pseudo-code presented above, in the first step a solution is generated through the use of the heuristic created for this purpose. In the second step, the optimization with different algorithms, PSO, GA and SA, is performed. In the end, a comparison is made on the performance of the algorithms with the use of the proposed initial solution heuristic and without its use. This comparison takes into account the multivariate analysis model, where it considers the value of the function cost, execution time and also the number of iterations.

After this introductory section, Sect. 2 presents the mathematical formulation of the electricity markets participation portfolio optimization problem that is addressed. The proposed heuristic for generating the initial solution is also presented in this section. Section 3 presents the description of the case study used to validate the proposed method, and Sect. 4 presents the achieved results. Finally, Sect. 5 presents the most relevant conclusions of this work.

2 Portfolio Optimization

The portfolio optimization problem was firstly introduced by Markowitz [5], with application in the field of finance and economics. This problem addressed by Markowitz considers a model which efficiently allocates a number of assets so that the future will bring positive return with a certain level of risk. In energy markets this problem is also relevant, especially concerning the support of market negotiating player's decisions. Given the available market opportunities, players need to decide whether to and how to participate in each market type, in order to obtain as much gain as possible from their negotiations.

The problem of portfolio optimization has been applied in different areas, but more important than that is the techniques that have been applied to try to solve it. In 1956, the author who presented the methodology presented in [6] a discussion about the application of a computational technique to solve the model using the formulation of quadratic problems. But three years later Wolfe in [7], proposes the resolution of the problem using the simplex method.

Years later, with the development of science and technology, the artificial intelligence (AI) was born, and it would bring with it the intelligent research algorithms. Nowadays many types of meta-heuristics have been applied to solve the problem, for example, local search techniques were applied in [8], the SA optimization technique was implemented to the problem in [9], the PSO [10], neural networks (NN) [11] and GA [12] were also already used to solve the problem of portfolio optimization in different fields of application. The application of the portfolio optimization model in the electric sector has, however, been a rather absent subject of research. Among the few exceptions are a model of risk management in the short term, by applying the Markowitz model to optimize the portfolio and minimize risk in energy markets [13].

A methodology for participation in electricity markets for the following day is presented in [14] using portfolio optimization. IA techniques are used in this work, namely the PSO. In this publication, the author's main objective is to provide support to the participants' participation in electricity markets. For this reason, the methodology proposed by the author is part of a decision support system called Multi-Agent Simulator for Competitive Electricity Markets (MASCEM) [15].

In this work, as previously mentioned, a heuristic is presented, which allows the construction of a valid initial solution, which serves as input data for the portfolio optimization problem. This heuristic thus aims at improving the initial search point from different AI algorithms. The final results are used to provide decision support to electricity market participants in order to aid them in taking the most profitable negotiation decisions.

2.1   Mathematical Formulation

In this section the presentation of the proposed model for the optimization is made. It should be emphasized that the considered model does not follow mathematically the model proposed by Markowitz, but the basis concept is the same. The proposed model, tries to allocate electricity in the different electricity markets in an optimal way, generating a maximum level of profit, while respecting the imposed rules.

Equation (1) represented the objective function, which models the optimization of players' market participation portfolio. This function considers the expected production of a market player for each period of each day, and the amount of power to be negotiated in each market is optimized to get the maximum income that can be achieved [14].

$$
(Spow_{M...NumS}, Bpow_{S1...NumS}) = Max \left[\begin{array}{c} \sum_{M=M1}^{NumM} (Spow_{M,d,p} \times ps_{M,d,p} \times Asell_M) - \\ \sum_{S=S1}^{NumS} (Bpow_S \times ps_{S,d,p} \times Abuy_S) \end{array} \right] \quad (1)
$$
$$
\forall d \in Nday, \forall p \in Nper, Asell_M \in \{0,1\}, Abuy \in \{0,1\}
$$

In Eq. (1) d represents the weekday, $Nday$ represent the number of days, p represents the negotiation period, $Nper$ represent the number of negotiation periods, $Asell_M$ and $Abuy_S$ are boolean variables, indicating if this player can enter negotiations in each market type, M represents the referred market, $NumM$ represents the number of markets, S represents a session of the balancing market, and $NumS$ represents the number of sessions. Variables $ps_{M,d,p}$ and $ps_{S,d,p}$ represent the expected (forecasted) prices of selling and buying electricity in each session of each market type, in each period of each day. The outputs are $Spow_M$ representing the amount of power to sell in market M, and $Bpow_S$ representing the amount of power to buy in session S.

In Eq. (2) is expressed the way in which the negotiation prices are obtained. As one can see, sale prices $ps_{M,d,p}$ and purchase prices $ps_{S,d,p}$ are considered.

$$
ps_{M,d,p} = Value(d, p, Spow_M, M)
$$
$$
ps_{S,d,p} = Value(d, p, Bpow_S, S) \quad (2)
$$

The $Value$ is obtained by Eq. (3), and is calculated from the application of the clustering and fuzzy approach.

$$
Value(day, per, Pow, Market) = Data(fuzzy(pow), day, per, Market) \quad (3)
$$

With the implementation of this model, it is possible to obtain market prices based on the traded amount. In order to achieve this, for the modeling of the prices are considered the expected production of a market player for each period of each day. The results of the application of this methodology can be observed in [16]. Equation (3) defines this condition, where Data refers to the historical data that correlates the amount of transacted power, the day, period of the day and the particular market session.

Equation (4) represents the main constraint of this problem. The constraint imposes that the total power that can be sold in the set of all markets is never higher than the total expect production (TEP) of the player, plus the total of purchased power.

$$
\sum_{M=M1}^{NumM} Spow_M \leq TEP + \sum_{S=S1}^{NumS} Bpow_S \quad (4)
$$

Equations (5), (6) and (7) represent other constraints that can be applied to the problem. This depends on the nature of the problem itself, e.g. type of each market, negotiation amount, type of supported player (renewable based generation, cogeneration, etc.).

$$TEP = \sum Energy_{prod}, Energy_{prod} \in \{Renew_{prod}, Therm_{prod}\} \tag{5}$$

$$0 \leq Renew_{prod} \leq Max_{prod} \tag{6}$$

$$Min_{prod} \leq Therm_{prod} \leq Max_{prod}, if\ Therm_{prod} > 0 \tag{7}$$

By (5) it can be seen that the energy production may come from renewable sources and thermoelectric sources. If the player is a producer of thermoelectric power, the production must be set at a minimum since it is not feasible to completely turn off the production plant, as can be observed by Eq. (7). If the producer is based on renewable energy, the only restriction is the maximum production capacity, as in (6).

2.2   Proposed Initial Solution Heuristic

The proposed heuristic for initial solutions generation aims at providing an adequate initial point for metaheuristics search process. Thus, the goal is to use ad-hoc knowledge on the problem to create a set of generic rules that allow initial solutions to be generated automatically in order to feed the metaheuristic methods. The proposed heuristic is composed by the following steps:

- 1st - In the Spot market, since it is impossible to buy energy, when the player participates to sell, the value of this variable is automatically zero (8);

$$if\ M = Spot\ Market, Bpow_M = 0 \tag{8}$$

- 2nd - The spot market price is compared with the prices of the intraday and balancing market sessions, and the higher price is saved (9);

$$search(\max ps_{M,d,p}), save\ ps_{M,d,p} \tag{9}$$

- 3rd - The sale or purchase price is calculated for bilateral contracts and local markets (considered in this model as Smart Grid (SG) level markets), considering the maximum amount of power available for purchase. If the maximum selling price is greater than these, the maximum purchase quantity in the two previous markets is allocated (10). This enables players to purchase power at lower prices in order to sell it in market opportunities with higher expected price;

$$\begin{aligned} if\ saved\ price \geq ps_{M,d,p}(\max Bpow) \\ Bpow_M = \max quantity, for\ M = Bilateral\ and\ SG \end{aligned} \tag{10}$$

where:

- max *quantity* is the maximum purchase quantity
- 4th - Since in the various sessions of the balancing and intraday market it is only possible to perform one of the shares in each negotiation period (buy or sell), the maximum price verified in all market sessions is compared with the purchase price

of the maximum quantity in each of the balancing market sessions. If the maximum price is higher, the maximum amount of purchase will be automatically allocated in the balancing or intraday market sessions (11), following the same logic as in step 3;

$$if\ ps_{M,d,p}(\max Bpow)\ for\ balancing\ sections \leq price\ saved$$
$$Bpow_M = \max\ quantity,\ for\ balancing\ session \quad (11)$$

- 5th - The sum of the power amount allocated to be bought with the available quantity resulting from own production is obtained, thus obtaining the total quantity available to sell (12);

$$\max\ quantity\ for\ sale = \max\ quantity\ buy + TEP \quad (12)$$

- 6th - Since there are markets where the expected price is highly dependent on the negotiated quantity (e.g. bilateral contracts), the sale price in those markets is calculated for several intervals of quantities (e.g. from 10 in 10 MW) up to the maximum available for sale (13);

$$if\ Bpow,\ Spow\ dependent\ the\ quantity,\ search\ the\ best\ option$$
$$best\ option = best\ value\ in\ all\ intervals \quad (13)$$

- 7th - A search is made iteratively to search if there is an amount of electricity in which the price in the market is higher than the maximum found price. This search is done only for markets where the expected price is highly dependent on the negotiated quantity. If any is found, the correspondent quantity is allocated to that market (14).

$$if\ M = Bilateral\ and\ SG,$$
$$search\ quantity\ where\ price > saved\ price \quad (14)$$

- 8th - The quantity available for sale is updated based on the amount allocated in the two previous markets (15);

$$sale\ quanty = \max\ quanty\ for\ sale - Spow_M;\ M = (Bilateral, SG) \quad (15)$$

- 9th - To allocate the electricity that is lacking, look for the market where the remaining amount can be more profitable and, respecting the impossibility of buying and selling in the same market, this quantity is allocated (16).

$$Bpow = \max\ price\ for\ sale\ quantity,\ for\ Spot\ or\ Balancing \quad (16)$$

After all the steps have been completed, the constraints of the problem must be applied in order to guarantee that the solution is valid and that the research is started without creating a random solution.

3   Case Study

This case study considers seven different metaheuristic algorithms to perform the optimization of the presented portfolio optimization formulation, being them: PSO [17], EPSO [18], QPSO [19], NPSO-LRS [20], MPSO-TVAC [21], AG [22] and SA [23]. The proposed heuristic is used to find an initial solution for the algorithms. A comparison is made between the performances of the algorithms when using the proposed initial solution heuristic and when using a random initial solution.

In order to define a realistic scenario, five different market types have been considered, thereby enabling the supported market player to sell and buy in all of them. The considered markets are the day-ahead spot market, negotiations by means of bilateral contracts, the balancing (or intra-day) market, and a local market, at the Smart-Grid (SG) level. The balancing market is divided into different sessions. In the day-ahead spot market the player (acting as seller) is only allowed to sell electricity, while in the other market types the player can either buy or sell depending on the expected prices. Limits have also been imposed on the possible amount of negotiation in each market. In this case, it is only possible to buy up to 10 MW in each market in each period of negotiation, which makes a total of 40 MW purchased. It is possible to sell power on any market, and it can be transacted as a whole or in installments. The player has 10 MW of own production for sale.

In this problem, it has also been imposed that in each session of the balancing market, the player can only either sell or buy in each period. In bilateral contracts and in SG negotiation, it is possible to both sell and purchase in the same period (by negotiating with different players). Since the optimization requires real market data, so that it can be used to support players' decisions in a realistic environment, it is necessary that the electricity prices are provided. The real electricity market prices data, concerning the day-ahead spot market, the intraday market, and bilateral contracts have been extracted from website of the Iberian electricity market operator – MIBEL [24]. Local SG market prices are based on the results of previous studies [14].

4   Results

Table 1 presents the results for the first period of the considered simulation day, of the various methods when using a random initial solution, and when using the initial solution generated by the heuristic proposed in Sect. 2.2 (methods with the suffix - ST). When using the proposed heuristic, all the presented algorithms start their search from a solution already defined by the set of rules expressed by the heuristic. It should be noted that the algorithms were all applied in the same conditions (same machine, same input data, etc.) so that there are no variations due to external factors. A total of 1000 executions have been run for each simulation.

As can be seen from Table 1, when the algorithms are executed using the initial solution generated by the proposed heuristic, the observed values for the objective function undergo changes. The algorithms that use the initial solution, as expected, present a minimal solution larger than those that do not use it. In terms of maximum reached value, most of the algorithms can reach very close maxima, with or without initial solution. The algorithms using the initial solution have a higher average than others, as well as a lower standard deviation, which means that the variability of results when using an initial solution is lower. In terms of execution time and required number of iterations, the values generally decrease when using the proposed heuristic.

Figure 2 presents the box plots for all applied methods. The box plots are constructed based on the observed results obtained in the simulations, namely the maximum and minimum, and from three calculated parameters: the median, the value of the first quartile and the third quartile. This representation is very useful because it allows a representation of how the results data is distributed as to the greater or lesser concentration, symmetry or existence of values outside the context of the results. It is also very useful in comparing groups of results.

Table 1. Optimization results for the different methods

Algorithms	Value of objective function (€)				Execution time (s)		Iteration number	
	Min	Max	Mean	STD	Mean	STD	Mean	STD
PSO	571,5	1998,6	1483,8	270	0,184	0,035	64	10,9
PSO - ST	1805,7	2000,6	1981,1	47,4	1,046	0,277	384	101
EPSO	482,8	2000,6	1579,4	307	27,93	54,814	1621	3173,9
EPSO - ST	1875,1	2000,6	1972,7	28,4	13,168	30,568	783	1808,2
QPSO	320,7	1998,9	1232	305	0,292	0,116	61	35,2
QPSO - ST	1730,2	2000,6	1939,2	56,4	0,282	0,09	63	26
NPSO-LRS	1416,4	2000,6	1762,4	144	1,5	0,466	363	112
NPSO-LRS - ST	1889,1	2000,6	1992,1	20,9	1,806	0,499	448	122
MPSO-TVAC	1416,6	2000,6	1947,2	133	6,841	0,871	492	60,2
MPSO-TVAC - ST	1816,7	2000,6	1873,7	85,1	4,059	0,232	298	11,4
AG	1545,5	2000,6	1971,2	76,4	7,478	0,679	2625	218
AG - ST	1730,2	2000,6	1993	40,3	4,728	0,743	1663	255
SA	1781,5	1927,2	1884	55,5	0,551	0,021	1831	26,1
SA - ST	1945	2000,6	1988,3	11,7	0,51	0,02	1730	6,4

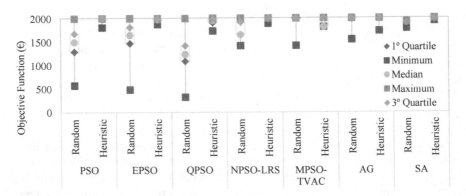

Fig. 2. Box plot for the applied methods

As can be seen from Fig. 2, it is visible that the minimum values undergo considerable changes when using the proposed heuristic for generation of the initial solution. It is noteworthy that the QPSO, which was the algorithm that suffered the greatest change of minimum value, went from 1232.7 € to 1956 €. Another of the characteristics to be considered is the value between 1st quartile and 3rd quartile, since this distance represents 50% of the observations; the less the distance the more reliable the method will be. All methods using the proposed heuristic have significantly decreased the distance between these two quartiles. In terms of maximum values, although the algorithms with the initial solution reached the best maximums, the previous versions with random initial solutions also managed to reach very close values (at the cost of higher execution times and variability); except the SA, as it was the method that obtained a greater improvement.

Table 2 presents the results of upper bound, lower bound and error values for the 95% confidence intervals of all the executed simulations (1000 simulations).

Table 2. Error of confidence interval 95%

Type solution		PSO	EPSO	QPSO	NPSO-LRS	MPSO-TVAC	AG	SA
Random	Upper bound	1500,58	1598,41	1250,89	1771,31	1955,41	1975,91	1887,48
	Lower bound	1467,09	1560,38	1213,03	1753,42	1938,90	1966,44	1880,61
	Error	16,74	19,01	18,93	8,94	8,25	4,73	3,43
Heuristic	Upper bound	1984,01	1974,49	1942,69	1993,35	1879,00	1995,46	1988,99
	Lower bound	1978,13	1970,97	1935,70	1990,76	1868,46	1990,47	1987,54
	Error	2,90	1,75	3,49	1,29	5,27	2,49	0,72

From Table 2 it can be verified that there is a great difference of values between the results when using the random solution and the heuristic for the majority of the presented methods. The PSO, EPSO and QPSO methods are the ones that benefit most with the proposed method, because as it is possible to observe, both the upper and lower limits have risen considerably to near the maximum value. On the other hand, the error value has decreased considerably. From the analysis of the results of the 95% confidence intervals, the proposed heuristic for the determination of the initial solution shows clear advantages over the random solution.

In Fig. 3 is presented the performance of NPSO-LRS with random solution and heuristic solution. This algorithm is chosen because it showed a great difference in terms of objetive funtion STD when comparing the random and heuristic solution.

From Fig. 3 it can be seen that both algorithms converge to very close maximum solutions. The big difference is in the STD, which decreases considerably when using the proposed initial solution heuristic (from 144 to 20.9 when using the random initial solution). It should also be noted that the results of the heuristic solution have a scale on the y-axis different from the random solution, this is due to the initial solution of the heuristic solution being 1730 €. Figure 4 shows the energy purchased and sold in each market for the SA whne using the random solution and heuristic solution, this algorithm was chosen because it is possible to observe the large differences in the two algorithms.

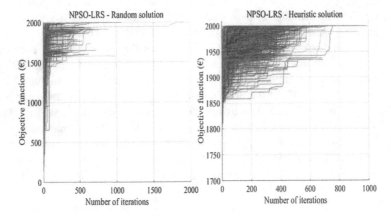

Fig. 3. NPSO-LRS performance

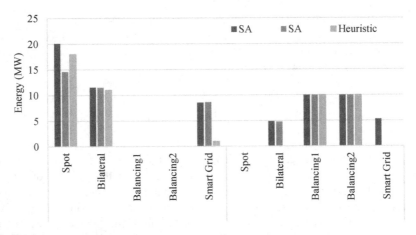

Fig. 4. Purchase and the sale in different markets

Figure 4 shows the results of the SA algorithm when using the random solution, when using the proposed heuristic for initial solution and also the values generated by the proposed heuristic by itself. By analyzing the objective function values, the SA Random registered 1927 €, SA heuristic 2000, 6 € and heuristic 1730 €. It is possible to verify that the heuristic presents a solution that is already close to the maximum vale achieved by the meta-heuristic search process, and then it is up to the algorithms to refine that solution to obtain a better result. The SA heuristic was the one that registered the best value of objective function and one can see that it defined to buy the maximum quantity of electricity in the balancing markets (10 MW), and to purchase of 4.7 MW in bilateral contracts. The sale is set to the Smart Grid in 8.6 MW, 13.3 MW in Bilateral Contracts and 13.8 MW in the Spot market.

A curiosity is that SA random has a higher volume of transacted electricity (40 MW), but does not represent a greater profit because it was necessary to buy more electricity. The SA heuristic traded 34.7 MW and made a better profit.

5 Conclusions

This paper presented a heuristic to generate a good initial solution for meta-heuristic methods. The proposed heuristic proved to be advantageous since the results present considerable advantages in relation to the previous results, using random initial solutions. By defining this starting point for the algorithms they can obtain better values in their general search process. This is visible by the analysis of the STD, because the lower value means that the solutions are closer to the average. The average with this modification also gets closer to the maximum value which, coupled with the small STD, makes the set of solutions very strong.

As future work, authors intend create a multiobjective a model of that considers the risk in calculation of the return, as well as to develop a heuristic that allows the same association between profit and risk.

References

1. Barr, R.S., Golden, B.L., Kelly, J.P., et al.: Designing and reporting on computational experiments with heuristic methods. J. Heuristics **1**, 9–32 (1995). doi:10.1007/BF02430363
2. Coffin, M., Saltzman, M.J.: Statistical analysis of computational tests of algorithms and heuristics. INFORMS J. Comput. **12**, 24–44 (2000)
3. Chiarandini, M., Paquete, L., Preuss, M., Ridge, E.: Experiments on Metaheuristics: Methodological Overview and Open Issues. Technical report, DMF-2007-03-003, University of Copenhagen, Denmark (2007). ISSN: 0903-3920
4. Martínez, R.: Multi-start methods. In: Glover, F., Kochenberger, G.A. (eds.) Handbook of Metaheuristics, pp. 355–368. Springer, Boston (2003)
5. Markowitz, H.: Portfolio selection. J. Finan. **7**, 77 (1952). doi:10.2307/2975974
6. Markowitz, H.: The optimization of a quadratic function subject to linear constraints. Nav. Res. Logist. Q. **3**, 111–133 (1956). doi:10.1002/nav.3800030110
7. Wolfe, P.: The simplex method for quadratic programming. Econometrica **27**, 382–398 (1959)
8. Schaerf, A.: Local search techniques for constrained portfolio selection problems. Comput. Econ. **20**, 177–190 (2002)
9. Crama, Y., Schyns, M.: Simulated annealing for complex portfolio selection problems. Eur. J. Oper. Res. **150**, 546–571 (2003). doi:10.1016/S0377-2217(02)00784-1
10. Xu, F., Chen, W., Yang, L.: Improved particle swarm optimization for realistic portfolio selection. In: Eighth ACIS International Conference on Software Engineering, Artificial Intelligence Networking, Parallel/Distributed Computing (SNPD 2007), vol. 1, pp. 185–190 (2007). doi:10.1109/SNPD.2007.375
11. Fernández, A., Gómez, S.: Portfolio selection using neural networks. Comput. Oper. Res. **34**, 1177–1191 (2007). doi:10.1016/j.cor.2005.06.017
12. Chang, T.-J., Yang, S.-C., Chang, K.-J.: Portfolio optimization problems in different risk measures using genetic algorithm. Expert Syst. Appl. **36**, 10529–10537 (2009)

13. Yu, Z.: A spatial mean-variance MIP model for energy market risk analysis. Energy Econ. **25**, 255–268 (2003)
14. Pinto, T., Morais, H., Sousa, T.M., et al.: Adaptive portfolio optimization for multiple electricity markets participation. IEEE Trans. Neural Netw. Learn. Syst. **PP**, 1 (2015)
15. Vale, Z., Pinto, T., Praça, I., Morais, H.: MASCEM: electricity markets simulation with strategic agents. IEEE Intell. Syst. **26**, 9–17 (2011)
16. Faia, R., Pinto, T., Vale, Z.: Dynamic fuzzy estimation of contracts historic information using an automatic clustering methodology. In: Bajo, J. (ed.) PAAMS 2015. CCIS, vol. 524, pp. 270–282. Springer, Cham (2015). doi:10.1007/978-3-319-19033-4_23
17. Kennedy, J., Eberhart, R.: Particle swarm optimization. In: IEEE International Conference on Neural Networks, Proceedings, vol. 4, pp. 1942–1948 (1995)
18. Miranda, V., Miranda, V., Fonseca, N.: New evolutionary particle swarm algorithm (EPSO) applied to voltage/VAR control. In: Proceedings of 14th Power Systems Computation Conference (2002)
19. Sun, J., Fang, W., Palade, V., et al.: Quantum-behaved particle swarm optimization with Gaussian distributed local attractor point. Appl. Math. Comput. **218**, 3763–3775 (2011)
20. Selvakumar, A.I., Thanushkodi, K.: A new particle swarm optimization solution to nonconvex economic dispatch problems. IEEE Trans. Power Syst. **22**, 42–51 (2007)
21. Gang, M., Wei, Z., Xiaolin, C.: A novel particle swarm optimization algorithm based on particle migration. Appl. Math. Comput. **218**, 6620–6626 (2012)
22. Goldberg, D.E.: Genetic Algorithms in Search, Optimization and Machine Learning, 1st edn. Addison-Wesley Longman Publishing Co., Inc., Boston (1989)
23. van Laarhoven, P.J.M., Aarts, E.H.L.: Simulated Annealing: Theory and Applications. Springer, Dordrecht (1987). doi:10.1007/978-94-015-7744-1
24. MIBEL. Mercado Iberico de Eletrecidade (2007). http://www.mibel.com/index.php?lang=pt. Accessed 27 Feb 2016

Autonomous Safety System for a Smart Stove for Cognitively Impaired People

Nicola Kuijpers[1,2](✉), Sylvain Giroux[1], Florent de Lamotte[2], and Jean-Luc Philippe[2]

[1] Université de Sherbrooke,
2500 boul. Université, Sherbrooke, QC J1K 2R1, Canada
{nicola.kuijpers,sylvain.giroux}@Usherbrooke.ca
[2] Lab-STICC, Université de Bretagne-Sud,
Rue de Saint Maudé, 56321 Lorient, France
{florent.lamotte,jean-luc.philippe}@univ-ubs.fr

Abstract. This paper presents an autonomous system which increases safety for cognitively impaired people living in smart homes during cooking activities. Smart homes are alternative solutions in order to keep elderly and cognitively impaired people at home as long as possible, allowing them to benefit longer from their home comfort. The user's cooking activity is analyzed and according to predefined safety rules the system reacts when danger appears. Experiments are carried out to validate our solution.

Keywords: Smart homes · Autonomic computing · Safety · Alzheimer · Activities of daily living

1 Introduction

The population in developed countries such as France or Canada is ageing. Studies foresee a raise up to one third of the population which will be aged over 60 years by 2050 [1, 2]. An ageing population is often synonym of cognitive and motor impairments. Those impairments have huge human, social and economic costs. Since the population is ageing and caregiver's resources remain scarce, alternative solutions must be found to keep people suffering from cognitive disabilities independent as long as possible. A way to reduce these costs is to keep these people at their home as long as possible. Therefore, homes must be adapted. Smart Homes (SH), can assist people in their Activities of Daily Living (ADL), such as meal preparation. Meal preparation is a key ADL for cognitively impaired people to gain autonomy. For this purpose, our work is aimed to guide people with cognitive impairments as Alzheimer in meal preparation. Since impairments are experienced differently by each person, it is vital to be sure that the assistance given to these people suits their individual needs.

This paper will present an autonomous system integrated in a smart stove. Our system analyzes cooking related activities and situations and enhances the safety of related kitchen appliances according to predefined safety rules.

Section two will develop a background study in the fields of intelligent kitchen appliances. Then, we present some of the safety rules that were defined. The next section will show the equipment we use for our work. Section five presents the

J. Bajo et al. (Eds.): PAAMS 2017 Workshops, CCIS 722, pp. 145–156, 2017.
DOI: 10.1007/978-3-319-60285-1_12

implementation of our system. Section six presents the experimentation and the validation of our system. Finally, we conclude our work and present some perspectives.

2 Background

Assisting impaired people in SH and assuring their safety is a huge challenge. Some work is oriented to assist elderly suffering from cognitive impairments for meal preparation. Cook's Collage [3] is a memory aid for elderly so they can remember the progress of their meal preparation. This helps the person remember the order in which every task has to be executed, but doesn't prevent from any risks.

Today, intelligent kitchen appliances are developed. For example, [4, 5] are intelligent pans that help people during meal preparation. The pans tell them when to flip food in the pan and when to serve. Since these smart pans control the cooking temperature, they can prevent fire in the kitchen. Other smart devices such as fridges help people manage their food and expiry dates. Smart washing machines can be controlled from a mobile device and inform about the remaining time of the current cycle. Services such as [6, 7] can automatically order new consumables for smart devices when they run low. Smart stoves today allow people to control their stove from their mobile phone [8] and propose recipes. Other work are more specific for elderly and cognitively impaired people [9] that shuts down the stove when nobody is detected in the near environment or on a timer to decrease fire risks. If a situation arises and the system is connected to the Internet, iGuardFire sends an alert message to people in a contact list to get help quickly. Moreover, [10] proposes a cooking assistant for people suffering from TBI based on a smart stove increasing their autonomy.

All these devices and services make it easier for the inhabitants to manage their ADL. However, they do not really increase inhabitants' safety (except fort iGuardFire). iGuardFire increases the safety during meal preparation only by checking if the stove is active and shutting it down if needed. It is unable to obtain more detailed information about what the person is preparing and what parts of the stove he is using.

Preparing dinner represents a challenging activity for cognitive impaired people, with a multitude of subtasks that can present danger and burning injuries [11]. Our work aims to reduce those risks and enhance user safety.

3 Objectives

Our work is aimed to be deployed in any household kitchen. Since no technician will be available, the system has to be autonomous. Autonomic computing is a vision of a computer system that configures, optimizes, heals and protects itself autonomously [12]. Autonomic computing is composed of four concepts:

1. Self-configuration makes the system able to integrate and configure new parts to make a homogeneous whole. In SH the environment is continually evolving, this concept makes it possible to integrate new devices and sensors automatically.
2. Self-Optimization is capable of optimizing every parameter for optimal performance. In our work, optimization can be seen in two parts: (1) Optimization of use

of sensors, we will explain how we see sensor optimization later in this paper. (2) Optimization of safety rules according to user profiles.

3. Self-Healing: redundancy makes it possible for the system to detect sensor failure and find alternative solutions in order to maintain system operation and reliability.
4. Self-Protection makes the system aware of external malware. In SH, self-protection is a difficult issue since a wide variety of different devices connect to networks [13].

Moreover, the system will be deployed on existing appliances which must not be modified and user safetyduring use of the appliances has to be enhanced through the elaboration of safety rules.

4 Safety Rules

In order to improve user safety while using cooking appliances, several safety rules have been defined by occupational therapists [14]:

1. If a person uses the oven and leaves the environment. This rule presents four cases: (1) If the oven is at a temperature above 400 °F, (2) between 300 °F and 400 °F, (3) under 300 °F and (4) if broil mode is activated. The user can leave the stove for X minutes (where X is configurable according to the user's abilities).
2. If a person leaves the environment for X minutes while one of the kitchen appliances connected to our system is still active, it has to be switched off and locked. For example, hobs cannot be kept activated without any human surveillance for a given time.
3. If a person uses the oven but the oven door stays open for more than X seconds.
4. If the oven is active but empty for more than X minutes.
5. If an electric burner is active but empty for more than X seconds.

If one or more of these cases are violated, users will receive warnings, in form of visual or sound alerts informing about the forgotten task. If these warnings are ignored, the power of the appliance is switched off and the system locked. In which case, a professional caregiver or an authorized person (which can be a family member) must take note of the problem and unlock the appliance. Since we don't want to make any modifications on existing appliances, shutting down a device is done by shutting down its electric supply by connecting an extension cord with relays.

5 Equipment

To apply those safety rules, we have at our disposal of a multitude of different kitchen appliances. This work is carried out in two different laboratories; The DOMUS laboratory is equipped with an all-in-one electric stove. It contains an oven and a top hob with four electric burners. The oven has a grill and a broil function. An embedded industrial computer, running on a Windows operating system, and an ADAM acquisition module (for sensor data collecting) are found in the lower drawer of the stove.

The solution adopted by the Lab-STICC laboratory is made of an individual multi-function micro-wave and a ceramic hob with two electric burners. The micro-wave oven has a grill mode, a convection mode and classic micro-wave mode.

The intelligence is placed on a low-cost solution which is composed of a Raspberry Pi 3 model B+ (running on a Linux based Raspbian Jessie) and analog to digital converters (ADC) for sensor data collection. The communication between those two components is provided by a SPI bus (Serial Peripheral Interface).

The aim of these different solutions is to show the flexibility of our system to work on different platforms and devices. We want our system to be used and easy to install on existing appliances that are already at people's homes. The sensors we use to collect data are therefore sensors that can be placed in/on the appliances without any modification, except for, opening the appliance itself. The sensors we use are the following: (1) Force sensors are placed underneath the appliances to detect if they are loaded. (2) Current sensors in form of current clamps placed inside the devices, measure the electric activity of the appliances. (3) Temperature sensors tell the system if the appliances are hot. (4) Presence detectors are used to check if the person remains near the appliances when preparing dinner. These sensors are also used to detect if utensils are present on the hobs. (5) Contact sensors are used to check if the door of the stove is correctly closed. (6) A RFID (Radio Frequency Identification) antenna is used for the system to have knowledge about which user is currently using the appliance. (7) A touch pad is used as mobile device for the system to discover and integrate new devices.

Our system is aimed to be flexible and able to accept other types of sensors that can connect at any time. Mobile devices such as tablets and smartphones are devices with a multitude of embedded sensors that enlarge the systems environmental knowledge [15].

6 Implementation

Our system, called StoveMAS, is based on a Multi-Agent System (MAS). Each agent in our MAS has a specific role. Agents can interact using high level communication protocols such as FIPA-ACL [16]. Those communications make agents able to cooperate, coordinate and negotiate together [17].

Our architecture is divided into two parts (Fig. 1); on the left, sensor data is gathered by previously discussed methods. Device activity is analyzed independently of lower level data acquisition methods. On the right, user activity is analyzed through presence sensors and user profiles. User profiles are developed according to multiple user classes. Our work is aimed to impaired people, but we also consider their family members, caregivers and technicians. All those persons are able to use StoveMAS. In this model, the agents we use in our MAS are represented in green:

- *DeviceAgents(DA)* which each monitor the activity of a device. These agents will track information about the activity of each component at a high level. These agents gather the sensor data they need through several platform dependent agents (regrouped in *GPIO* in Fig. 1):
  - *SPIAgent* is used on the Raspberry Pi to retrieve sensor data from ADCs.
  - *WirelessAgent* manages the wireless sensors or devices that can connect to the stove. For example, the use of a wireless presence detector is more appropriate than a wired one in certain kitchen layouts. This agent will update the system's environmental knowledge. Mobile devices such as tablets or smartphones can connect to the system via this agent, allowing the system to have an additional interface. Sensor data is also collected to strengthen the system's knowledge.

- *ADAMAgent* has the same role as *SPIAgent* but is used at the DOMUS laboratory and gathers sensor data from the ADAM acquisition module.
- *UserAgent* (*UA*) manages user profiles. Every user profile is represented by a structured file with a unique configuration. User profiles customize the way the system behaves on how the person can use the appliance and adapts safety rules according to the abilities of the person. The configuration within this file is elaborated by occupational therapists that have monitored the abilities of the person. To obtain user data, *UserAgent* uses an RFID interface:
  - *RFIDAgent* is used for listening events on the RFID antenna. If a tag is detected, this agent communicates the tag's code with the *UserAgent*. The latter checks if the tag can unlock the appliances and transmits information to the *UserAgent* to identify the user related to the tag. To do so, the tag code is compared with known authorized tag codes.
- Several *RiskAgents* which represent and apply a specific safety rule to our system. The number of these agents depends on the number of rules we want to apply to our system.
- The *SecurityAgent* checks the state of each agent in our MAS and carries out self-protection and self-healing functions of autonomous systems. The *SecurityAgent* periodically sends a message to the *WatchdogAgent* in order to keep the appliances powered. In fact, if the *SecurityAgent* freezes for some reason, we don't want the users to be in danger. The *WatchdogAgent* will lock the appliances if he hasn't received any messages from the *SecurityAgent* for a certain time.
- *InterfaceAgent* is used to give notifications and warnings to the user. It is also used for debugging. If no interface is available for the system, the interface of the mobile device will be used by default. If no interface at all is available, the system will work properly, but the users will not be informed about any warning or lockdown.

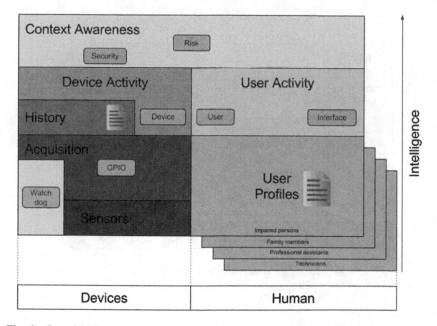

Fig. 1. StoveMAS architecture with agents (represented in green). (Color figure online)

6.1   The Flexibility of Our Solution

As mentioned before, we want our system to be as flexible as possible, running on different operating systems, we use the JADE platform for running our MAS. JADE (Java Agent DEvelopment framework) is based on Java that can run on any platform where a JVM (Java Virtual Machine) exists. With JADE, agents evolve in containers. Multiple containers can exist in a JADE platform and multiple JADE platforms can represent a single MAS. For our agents, a single JADE platform and container are needed. Agents can be arranged into high level organizations [18] which all have they advantages and drawbacks. Since our MAS has to dynamically integrate new devices or new safety rules have been defined, new agents can dynamically appear in our MAS. We choose to represent our MAS with a congregation organization. Congregations are groups of agents in which every agent has its own goals. They can appear dynamically and disappear when their goal is achieved. This behavior is perfectly according to the goals of our MAS.

Sensor data is logged into files, and in the same time, device activity is analyzed with *DeviceAgents*. For each device, an instance of a *DeviceAgent* is created. Thus, devices can easily be added to our system. Parallel to devices activity recognition, user activity is analyzed. User activity is defined by the user's profile, and how the users use the devices. Device and user activity have to correspond one to another, otherwise, safety risks may arise. This way, we obtain an intelligent system between Device, User and Risk agents analyzing high level cooking activities (Fig. 2). Each *DA* gathers sensor data concerning the device it is monitoring and deduces an activity for that device. In the same way, *UA* gather user preferences and medical information from his profile which is stored in a configuration file. Changes in device activity and user profile are sent to every *RA*, which each check if the user correctly uses the devices.

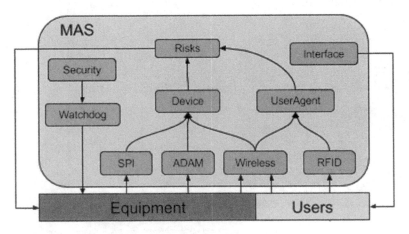

Fig. 2. Agent communications and interactions.

6.2 User Profiles

Since multiple users can use the appliances at the same time. Multiple people can connect to our system at the same time as well. When multiple people are connected, we choose to generate a resulting user profile which is the combination of the profiles of the connected users. This is an efficient solution while the users are from the same class. If an impaired person wants to prepare dinner with a healthy family member, we don't want the member to suffer from the restrictive profile of the impaired person. In which case, we have defined a coaching ability in user profiles allowing family members to "coach" impaired people. Its numerical value indicates the number of impaired persons the member can coach. Figure 3 illustrates three situations where the resulting profile changes according to the connected users. On the left, two impaired people are connected (both coaching abilities are strictly negative). In this case, we consider best to take into account the worst case of both profiles. This means that every restriction of users are added. The center case represents a situation where the family member cannot coach the impaired person, therefore, the resulting profile equals the impaired persons' profile. This is a usual case when the family member is unable to coach an impaired person, such as a child. The last case considers the family member as coaching the impaired person, therefore, the resulting profile equals the family members' profile. This case only occurs when the resulting coaching ability is null or positive.

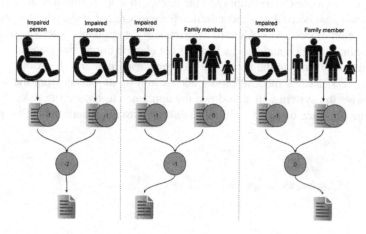

Fig. 3. Coaching ability variants according to users.

7 Experiments

Experiments have been carried out to validate our system and the safety rules. For the experiments, we create two personas: (1) René is an old man suffering from Alzheimer (stage 4 on the Reisberg scale) [19]. At this stage of Alzheimer illness, René is suffering from increasing memory losses, becomes disoriented and has concentration difficulties. His medical profile allows him to use only one device at a time (hobs or micro-wave/oven) between 5 pm. and 9 pm. (2) Jeanne, is René's healthy wife. She may use the appliances as needed. Since Jeanne is a person close to René, she is allowed to unlock the appliances with her RFID tag after a problem has occurred. René also has a RFID tag to adapt the system to his profile, but unlike Jeanne, he cannot unlock the appliances with it because of his medical situation. The following scenarios are carried out in both locations to test both system configurations. We asked local students to embody each persona.

7.1   Scenario 1: Preparing Dinner

The appliances are off, locked and StoveMAS is running. René wants to boil some water to prepare pasta. He unlocks the appliance with his RFID tag and places the pan filled with water on the hob and turns the button at highest level. StoveMAS detects the use of the hob through current sensors, but does not detect any weight on the hob through the force sensors. The system analyses presence of the pan through presence detectors and notes the pan is placed on the wrong electric burner. Instantly René will be notified of his mistake and is encouraged to place the pan on the right electric burner. His medical profile allows René to correct his error within 30 s; otherwise the system will lock the appliance to prevent fire risks. This warning is shown until René corrects his error or until the system locks the appliance.

Since the hob's activity is binary (Fig. 4). Once the electric burner is at its temperature, it shuts down the electric supply to the burner to stop it from heating too much. Once the burner has cooled down under the defined temperature, it starts heating again for temperature regulation. StoveMAS must keep track of the appliance's activity over time; else, the warning will pop and leave whenever the electric burner has stopped heating.

René must stay close to the hob while he is preparing dinner to keep an eye on the cooking progress. René's medical profile allows him to stay away from the hobs for 20 s; otherwise the system will shut down the appliance to reduce fire risks. Figure 5 illustrates the presence of René during his cooking activity, where the higher parts of

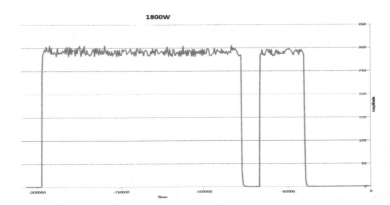

Fig. 4. Sensor data from the current sensor placed on the rear burner of the electric hob (1800 W).

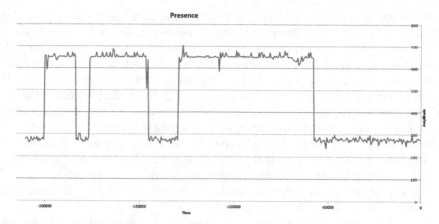

Fig. 5. René's presence during cooking scenario. Data collected from the presence detector placed near the hobs.

the signal represent user presence. StoveMAS sees that René has been away twice for a couple of seconds and sends a warning message. A minute later, René is away for a longer period than his medical profile allows him to, StoveMAS shuts down the power of the hobs (Fig. 4) and the electric activity is suddenly stopped. The hobs are now locked and René can't continue preparing dinner. Jeanne has to witness René's mistakes and give feedback. She eventually unlocks the appliances with her RFID tag so René can continue preparing dinner.

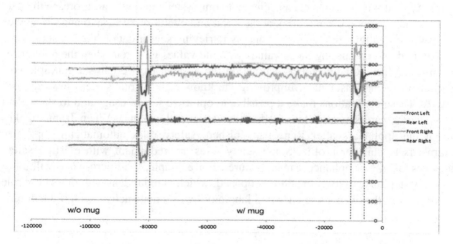

Fig. 6. Force sensors data while heating a mug of milk in the micro wave.

7.2 Scenario 2: Warming up a Mug of Milk

The appliances are off, locked and StoveMAS is running. René wants to prepare a hot mug of milk. He unlocks the appliances with his RFID and selects the micro-wave power on 900 W, the time on 1 min and presses the start button. Since no weight evolution has been detected, StoveMAS directly notifies René that he is trying to use the appliance while empty. For this appliance, René has ten seconds to stop the micro-wave and correct his error, otherwise it will be locked. Running an empty micro-wave can damage the appliance itself and can be harmful for the inhabitants. He corrects his error and relaunches the device. StoveMAS detects the presence of the mug in the micro-wave via force sensors placed under each device's foot. Figure 6 represents the collected data of all four force sensors during the scenario. The two major peaks - between dotted lines - occur respectively when René opens the micro-wave's door to place the mug, and opening it again to retrieve the hot mug. The difference in amplitude between the sensor readings represents the distance between the sensor's position and the mug. For instance, the sensors on the left of the device are closer to the mug, hence, the amplitudes between w/ and w/o mug are greater.

As for the previous scenario, René cannot leave the environment for too long. The micro-wave is a closed environment, risks are lower and thus, René's medical profile allows him to leave the environment longer than in the case of the hobs. Hobs are devices where the heat is spread out and can easily harm somebody. These safety parameters appear in the user profile of René and have to be adapted by professional caregivers for each appliance.

8   Results

The graphs shown in the previous section show the gathered sensor data during scenarios. Since unknown sensors can connect to our system, and we can't foresee the data send by such sensors, we only look at the trend and evolution of data to analyze device activity (self-configuration). This is done by retrieving sensor data while the appliances are not used and comparing those values with the values gathered when the appliances are in use. When René performs actions on the appliances, we can see multiple correlations between sensor data, improving the knowledge of our system towards user activity. These correlations make it possible to optimize sensor usage and to strengthen the system toward sensor failure (self-optimization and healing). When Jeanne makes use of the appliances after René has finished, safety rules automatically optimize parameters to suit her profile. Some safety rules are redundant with existing safety measures taken by appliances' manufacturer. For example, the micro-wave will automatically stop its activity if the door is opened, which is redundant with our safety rule n°3. However, the oven at the DOMUS laboratory will remain active even if the door is open.

9   Conclusion and Perspectives

Elderly and impaired people can see some ADL as difficult challenges. SH allow them to stay longer at home and assist them to successfully accomplish their tasks. Stove-MAS helps impaired people to correctly accomplish their cooking activity with maximum safety. The use of MAS makes it possible for StoveMAS to be flexible for every kitchen layout, adaptable for every type of sensor and each user profile. The flexibility makes the system easy to put in place on commercial appliances. An experimental model has been developed and experiments show the viability of our solution for real life situations. Several more experiments have to be carried out in order to improve sensor failure, dynamic sensor configuration and the use of the mobile interface. The mobile device will also improve safety of our system with an additional authentication through the users' mobile account.

Future work can consist of integrating and configuring new sensors through learning the sensors behavior according to device activity. We also aim to replace the RFID user identification with NFC (Near Field Communication) identification available on mobile devices. Future work can also consist of adapting this system to other household appliances and other impairments.

Acknowledgements. This work takes place within the Lab-STICC laboratory in Lorient, France and the DOMUS laboratory in Sherbrooke, Canada. We thank the rehabilitation center of Kerpape for the collaboration with the Lab-STICC laboratory. We also thank S. Pinard, C. Bottari, F. Le Morellec, C. Fecteau-Mathieu, M. Olivares and C. Laliberté for elaborating the safety risks used in this work.

References

1. ISQ. Données sociales du Québec (2009)
2. INSEE. Population par âge Population par âge. In: TEF, pp. 34–35 (2010)
3. Tran, Q.T., Calcaterra, G.: Cook's Collage. Access 2005
4. Baxi, P.B.R.: Smartypans (2016). https://smartypans.io/
5. Pantelligent (2016). https://www.pantelligent.com/
6. Amazon Dash Replenishment (2016). https://www.amazon.com/oc/dash-replenishment-service
7. Whirlpool 6e sens (2016). http://www.whirlpool.fr/innovation/innovation.content.html
8. Dacor smart stove (2016). http://www.dacor.com/Products/Ranges/Discovery-36-Dual-Fuel-Range
9. iGuardFire (2016). http://iguardfire.com/
10. Giroux, S., et al.: Cognitive assistance to meal preparation: design, implementation, and assessment in a living lab. In: 2015 AAAI Spring Symposium Series, pp. 01–25 (2015)
11. Ahrens, M.: Home fires involving cooking equipment, November 2015
12. Kephart, J.O., Chess, D.M.: The vision of autonomic computing. Computer (Long. Beach. Calif.) **36**, 41–50 (2003)
13. Arabo, A., Brown, I., El-Moussa, F.: Privacy in the age of mobility and smart devices in smart homes. In: Proceedings of 2012 ASE/IEEE International Conference on Privacy, Security, Risk and Trust 2012, ASE/IEEE International Conference on Social Computing Society 2012, pp. 819–826 (2012)
14. Pinard, S., et al.: Maximizing safety during meal preparation in persons with TBI. In: Canadian Association of Occupational Therapists (2016)
15. Android Sensor Overview (2016). https://developer.android.com/guide/topics/sensors/sensors_overview.html
16. Poslad, S.: Specifying protocols for multi-agent systems interaction. ACM Trans. Auton. Adapt. Syst. **2**(4), 15 (2007)

17. Wooldridge, M.: An Introduction to Multi-agent Systems (2009)
18. Horling, B., Lesser, V.: A survey of multi-agent organizational paradigms. Knowl. Eng. Rev. **19**(4), 281 (2005)
19. Reisberg, B., Ferris, S.H., De Leon, M.J., Crook, T.: The global deterioration scale for assessment of primary degenerative dementia. Am. J. Psychiatry **139**(9), 1136–1139 (1982)

Multi-agent Systems for Epidemiology: Example of an Agent-Based Simulation Platform for Schistosomiasis

Papa Alioune Cisse[1,2(✉)], Jean Marie Dembele[1,2], Moussa Lo[1,2,3], and Christophe Cambier[2]

[1] LANI, UFR SAT, Université Gaston Berger, BP 234, Saint-Louis, Senegal
papaaliounecisse@yahoo.fr, {jean-marie.dembele,
moussa.lo}@ugb.edu.sn
[2] UMI 209 UMMISCO, Bondy Cedex, France
christophe.cambier@ird.fr
[3] LIRIMA, M2EIPS, Saint-Louis, Senegal

Abstract. In this paper, we show the convenience of multi-agent systems to help computational epidemiology come to the rescue of mathematical epidemiology for its practical limits on modeling and simulation of complex epidemiological phenomena. Herein, we propose as an example, an agent-based simulation platform for schistosomiasis (commonly known as Bilharzia, which is a parasitic disease found in tropical and subtropical areas and caused by a tapeworm called schistosome or bilharzias) that we have experimented with actual data of schistosomiasis in Niamey (Niger).

Keywords: Complex systems · Mathematical modeling · Multi-agents system · Agent-based modeling and simulation · Schistosomiasis · Computational epidemiology

1 Introduction

Epidemiological phenomena often involve a large number of entities - host, vector, pathogen, environment, etc. - that can interact and give rise to complex dynamics ranging over several spatiotemporal scales. These dynamics can have serious health consequences like the spread over large geographical areas and the contamination of a large number of persons. Epidemiological phenomena, because of their evolution that results from the elements interactions, can be described as complex systems. To efficiently study them, it is necessary to go through a process of modeling and simulation in order to produce prediction tools and define prevention and control policies.

For many infectious diseases including schistosomiasis, mathematical modeling has proved to be a valuable tool for predicting epidemic trends and designing control strategies. But, still, they suffer from some conceptual limitations.

In this paper we thus present multi-agent systems as a complementary approach to push the limits of mathematical approaches in modeling the spread of epidemics, offering an agent-based simulation platform for schistosomiasis. Schistosomiasis is a

© Springer International Publishing AG 2017
J. Bajo et al. (Eds.): PAAMS 2017 Workshops, CCIS 722, pp. 157–168, 2017.
DOI: 10.1007/978-3-319-60285-1_13

disease vector for which fresh water (pond, river, canal, etc.) constitutes a transfer medium of the pathogen, from the final host (individual) to the vector (mollusk) and vice-versa. It is a parasitic disease found in tropical and subtropical areas, the spread of which is closely related to the nature of water activity of populations in potentially infectious water points.

After presenting in Sect. 2 computational epidemiology by confronting it with mathematical epidemiology, we expose, in Sect. 3, the agent-based approach for modeling the spread of infectious diseases. Section 4 presents the platform we propose for Schistosomiasis, experimentations, and simulations.

2   Computational Epidemiology

2.1   From New Epidemiological Challenges on the Spread of Diseases

Traditional mathematical epidemiology has always been an essential discipline for epidemiological problems and continues to be so. It focuses on the use of models based on differential equations to represent disease. These models, when combined with appropriate methods of analysis, may be appropriate tools for predicting future epidemics, comparing alternatives and methods, and can even help prepare effective intervention strategies of combatting the evolution of diseases [1, 2]. In these models, the population represented in the study of a disease is partitioned into subgroups according to various criteria (e.g.: the demographic characteristics and pathological states), and differential equations allow to describe the dynamics of the disease through these subgroups [3, 4]. However, it should be noted that most of mathematical epidemiology models to study the dynamics of disease, are based on ordinary differential equations (ODE). These models, neglecting the spatial aspect in the spread of disease, are based on the assumption that the population in question, with its various sub-groups (e.g.: Susceptible, Infected and Recovered) is distributed homogeneously on the space [4]. In the literature, this approach for modeling the spread of infectious diseases is sometimes highly criticized when the role of space is considered [1]. [5], through several examples, provides clear evidence that some infectious diseases spread geographically.

To overcome the problem of space in the ODEs models, other mathematical models, based on partial differential equations (PDE), are used to reject the homogeneous mixture of the population and represent the geographical spread of disease [6]. Yet, these models based on PDE, as well as those based on ODE, deal with subgroups of the population, represented in the equations, as *"continuous entities, and neglect the fact that populations are composed of individuals in interaction"* [4, 7]. This is problematic when we observe the social and interactional aspects of populations in the spread of disease. Indeed, these models do not take into account the complexity of human interactions which serve as a mechanism for the transmission of diseases [8].

Through different epidemiological concerns such as roles of geo-spatial, social and interactional aspects in the spread of disease, new epidemiological challenges of modeling and simulation are to examine to better understand and fight against the spread of infectious disease [1, 3, 9].

The Challenge to Make Complex Models of Infectious Diseases. It should be noted with [3], that the potential weakness of mathematical models is their inability to grasp the complexity inherent in the propagation of infectious diseases. Yet, this complexity is, in part, involved in human interactions and behavior which are apprehended through the networks of social and spatial (or geographical) interactions [8, 10]. It is for these reasons, for instance, that most recent surveys in epidemiology [1, 8, 10, 11], announce an urgent need for using computer science to develop models, for explaining the spatial, social, and interactional aspects to better understand the spread dynamics of infectious diseases.

The Challenge of Data Integration in Models. Data used in modeling and simulation are more and more stored in newer formats like Geographic Information System (GIS) [1]. Thus, as emphasized in [11], there is an urgent need to develop computational tools to take into account these data because, *"the integration of these data in simple compartmentalized epidemiological models is often difficult, requiring the use of computer models which are more complex, but also more effective"*.

Ultimately, computer epidemiology is a discipline the main objective of which is the application of computer concepts and resources (including technical, approaches and tools for modeling and simulation), and geographical tools (including tools for the representation and visualization of complex geospatial data) to provide epidemiologists with friendly tools which enable them to better understand the fundamental problems of epidemiology, such as the spread of disease.

2.2   …To Computer Solutions for Modeling and Simulation

Considering the various considerations in the previous section, other computing paradigms of modeling and simulation can now be used in epidemiology: cellular automata and multi-agent systems [1, 10]. We focus here on the multi-agent systems because it is the most commonly used computer modeling approach in the literature.

3   The Agent-Based Models of Infectious Diseases

There are, in the literature, several perceptions, and thus definitions, of the concepts of agents, multi-agent system, environments, etc. In this section, we propose some which we judge helpful in modeling the spread of infectious diseases in general and the spread of schistosomiasis in particular. A multi-agent system is a dynamic system, and its dynamism usually comes from two factors: the behavior of agents and the dynamics of the environment [12]. We consider the environment here as composed of the physical (or spatial) and social milieu. The dynamics of the physical environment specifies the principles, processes and all the rules that govern and support the actions and inter-actions of agents [13]. The dynamics of the social environment, often determined as an organization (a set of roles, groups, etc.), specifies constraints that tell agents how they should behave [13, 14]. The agent behavior is usually specified by a perception-decision-action loop [15] (see Fig. 1). With this behavioral loop, agents are often seen

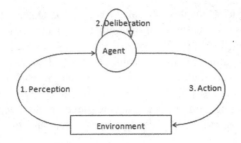

Fig. 1. Behavior of an agent (perception-decision-action loop) (source: [12])

as consisting of two parts: the body and the mind. The body serves as an interface to an agent, allowing them to perceive and act in the physical environment [16]; the spirit of an agent allows them to make decisions based on their perceptions of their internal state (representation of the world, memory, constraints of the social environment, …) [12].

In the description of the dynamic behavior of the agents, we deliberately distinguished two processes performed by agents: a behavioral process (perception, reaction) that occurs in the physical environment and a decision-making process (deliberation, communication, etc.) involving the social environment. These are the two types of representations that exist in multi-agent systems: Reactive Architecture and cognitive architecture. There is an intermediate representation that combines the two architectures: it is the hybrid architecture [17–19]. In our work, we are more interested in hybrid architectures, especially those based on the principle of separation between the body and the mind of an agent [14, 20, 21]. The idea, as stated in [12], is to separate the decision-making mechanisms of the agent (internal dynamics): their mind, their action and perception mechanisms of the environment: their body. Thus, agents are present in two environments in which they perform different but complementary processes. The multi-agent system is seen as a two-level design system [17].

Generally, modeling the spread of an infectious disease in a population with the agent-based approach is doubly beneficial. On the one hand, it allows to individualize populations (representing each individual as agent) in order to take into account their individual actions and interactions between them that are essential in the transmission of an infectious disease from one person to another. On the other hand, it helps integrate spatial and social dimensions which are specific to the spread of epidemics. In this regard, an agent-based model of the spread of an infectious disease is generally composed of [10, 22, 23]:

- A population of agents where each agent is described by two components: a set of identifiers attributes (including their health) and a set of behaviors that include their individual actions (e.g., moving from one place to another) and the actions they perform in relation with other agents (e.g., buy a product in direct contact with a seller).
- A space environment, which generally describes the objects in the environment used by agents (e.g., schools, markets, businesses, roads, water points, …) and rules for using these objects (e.g., moving on a road in a very precise direction, undressing to swim in a pool, etc.).

- A social environment, which generally describes groups of agents (e.g., co-workers, classmates, members of a household, ...) and behavioral rules within these groups (for example, in a traditional village, boys are charged with fetching water from the river, by turn, for the needs of the household; women are responsible for doing the laundry and washing in the river, etc.).

In the literature, many recent studies use the agent-based approach to model the spread of infectious diseases. Here are, without details, few references on malaria [24, 25]; on tuberculosis [1]; on Rubella [10]; on influenza [22]; on Dengue [26]; on Fever Rift Valley [27].

4 Our Agent-Based Simulation Platform for Schistosomiasis

4.1 The Platform Backgrounds

In the study of social and natural complex phenomena, it is sometimes necessary to combine several dynamics or more views of a system to properly understand its operation and development [28, 29]. Thus, modelers of these systems are increasingly confronted with difficulties of representing them with a single model. Moreover, they are usually based on multi-disciplinary theories and use different modeling approaches to represent these systems. This often results, firstly, in the fact of having several models for a system, and secondly, in the need to properly integrate these different models to better understand the systems. It is in this context that our platform intervenes.

Indeed, in previous works [30, 31], we made separate studies of spatial and social dynamics of schistosomiasis, offering, respectively, two multi-agent models of these dynamics. However, these two models based on agents were established in two opposite directions for Multi-Agent Systems (cognitive and behavioral approach or reactive approach). In the study of social dynamics of schistosomiasis, the model based on agents that we have proposed, is based on cognitive architecture called BDI (Belief, Desire, Intention) to represent the mental processes of agents [30]. This model, without considering the behavior of the agents, deals exclusively with their decision and deliberative aspects. A platform dedicated to this type of representation was implemented and simulated in JASON [32]. In the study of the spatial dynamics, the established model focuses on behavioral aspects and reactive agents [31]. It is implemented with the GAMA platform [33].

From a global point of view, this system must be seen as a multi-agent model in which each agent, to decide how to behave in their environment (behavioral model), questioned their mental state, which is represented in a cognitive model as a separate decision engine: it is the separation principle of mind/body we dealt with above.

4.2 Basic Assumptions of the Platform

General Case. Our platform fits in the context of the study of human-water contact activities (individuals' activities in potentially infectious water points). Specifically, it is interested in the following question: why do people continue to contaminate water during their excretory activities and contacting potentially infectious water sources? To answer this question, we consider water activities as part of a dynamic social process instead of a series of discrete activities performed by individuals [34].

Thus, water activities appear as a set of tasks that can be located in time and in space; and dependent on well-determined socio-economic conditions. Considering human activities as taking place only at specific locations and limited time periods, we make the distinction between the activities of an individual based on their degree of flexibility in time and space: the fixed activities (such as the fact of going to school) are those that cannot easily be reprogrammed or postponed; while flexible activities (such as swimming) can be so without difficulties [35, 36].

Let us consider the activity of "going to school" for a schoolboy. This activity, which is fixed, in so far as it is programmed a priori and constitutes an obligation for the student, takes place only in a specific location and within a period time well-defined. One can easily identify constraints linked to the execution of this activity: it only suffices that the current day be a school day, and the current time a school hour as well. On the other hand, an activity such as "swimming" in a pool or a canal is a flexible activity. Indeed, for a schoolboy, this activity may depend on several parameters: enough free time outside mandatory activities, availability and accessibility of a water site for this activity, a favorable temperature for practice, etc. In addition, unlike the fixed activities where, for a given period of time, only one activity is feasible; several flexible concurrent activities can be realized in the same period of time. The choice of either of them will depend on real-time constraints.

Indeed, on an off-day (e.g. Sunday), the schoolboy may want to carry out these activities in the day: "staying at home", "fetching water," "swimming with friends "etc. We cannot define a priori any order in the realization of these activities, or whether they actually will be realized. Nevertheless, we can define a set of constraints or criteria relating to the realization of each activity. We call these criteria "determining factors".

Case Study. The specific case that is modeled and simulated with our platform is that of schoolboy in the city of Niamey. The data are expressed as variables that can provide vital information at multiple levels on the schoolboy's behavior:

- Local level: data are relative to some districts of Niamey city. They cover 23 districts which are socioeconomically and geographically characterized [37, 38]:
  - Socio-economically, there are three types of districts: Modern districts (modern housing, home water supply, low population density, upper social class); Renovated districts (modern or traditional housing, public standpipes, middle social class); Traditional districts (traditional housing, lack of water supply, high population density, disfavored social classes and migrants).
  - Geographically, there are three types of areas according to their location relative to the Niger River: waterside districts (the river is one of the boundaries of districts), central districts (which are limited by other districts) and peripheral districts (those with an open limit outside Niamey).

- Domestic level: data are relative to domestic household environments. They cover 900 households in the 23 districts, and relate to the type of habitat (precarious housing or villas), household water supply, household income, etc. [37].
- Individual level: data are relative to schoolboys themselves [37, 38]. They involve 1000 students belonging to the 900 households in the domestic level and are on their age, gender, houses (households, districts, and schools).

4.3   The Architecture of the Platform

From a conceptual point of view, we must see the architecture of the platform, as described in Fig. 2(left), as being composed of two levels of abstraction: a cognitive level and a behavioral level. It is a hybrid architecture in the sense of [17]. Each level of conception is managed by a platform dedicated to its type of representation: the cognitive level in JASON and the behavioral level in GAMA. Our platform therefore couples GAMA and JASON. In the interactions, the behavioral model (GAMA) transmits environmental characteristics to the decisional model (JASON) which, in turn, selects and transmits to the behavioral model the behavior that agents should take in the environment.

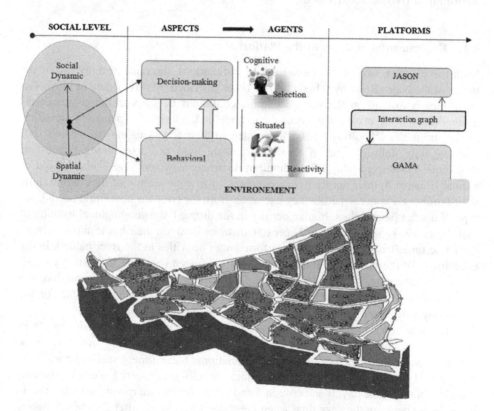

Fig. 2. (Above): Architecture of the platform. (Below): Visualization of the Niamey's GIS in GAMA with only districts (in gray), schools (in yellow), the Niger's River (blue) that affect our simulations; green elements represent schoolchildren. (Color figure online)

From a semantic and syntactic point of view, we must see that both models represent the same agents (and therefore have the same number of agents), but with different processes, according to different formalisms as well. The decisional model represents the agents' decision-making behavior (selection, deliberation, etc.) and social behavior (communication, negotiation, influence, etc.), while the behavioral model represents active and interactional behavior in the physical environment.

The decisional model defines a library of plans (representing all the activities that schoolboy can perform in the day) and a selection function, based on a process of multi-criteria decision, intended to select the appropriate action plans, under the real-time conditions of environment. For its part, the behavioral model implements the agents' activities on the physical environment. It also incorporates Niamey's geographic (housing, water environments, roads and their specific characteristics) and social configurations of populations. The latter aspect is specified in specific elements: districts and households (see previous section). All of these elements (houses, aquatic environments, roads, districts, schools, households and their specific characteristics) are incorporated into a Geographic Information System (GIS). The set of files that makes up GIS is presented as initial parameter to the model, and constitute the overall environment (physical and social).

4.4   Experimental Settings of the Platform

With the platform, we aim to reproduce, by simulations, the rates of daily use of the banks of the Niger River by schoolchildren (rates provided by survey data in [38]). The basic idea is to lean on the socio-economic conditions of schoolchildren (the determining factors), expressed in the decisional model in the form of explanatory variables, to determine the schoolboys' behavior related to their access to the river banks. For this, we have defined a set of variables that are used as "determining factors" to determine the susceptibility of a schoolboy to frequent waters: age, gender, type of habitat (relative to their family living standards), the water supply of their home (how their family gets water: whether they use water from the river for household needs), the type of district (social class, human density in the district), the geographical location of their home vis-à-vis the River of Niger (the distance between their home and the river), their free time (leisure time spent to perform water activities in the river banks). In the experiment of the platform, all these variables are frozen (because from survey data), except the free time. It is the only model parameter to be calibrated to reproduce the "schoolboy-river" contact rate expected. It represents the free time available for the schoolboy when they can perform their water activities for a whole day.

The execution step of the platform is 5 min (the time a schoolboy needs to walk to school, for example). Thus, "free times" of schoolchildren to carry out their water activities are precisely determined in the simulations: break time: usually, between 10 a.m. and 11 a.m., on working days; rest time: ordinarily, between 1 o'clock p.m. and 3 o'clock p.m. for the day, then between 5 and 7 p.m. for the afternoon. Actually, this is the moment between the very time when the student gets home after the end of classes (which is relative to the walked distance to get home) and the next school time (3 or 7 p.m.); all the morning and all the evening, on off-days (Saturday and Sunday). In all these situations, the only flexible activities (apart from the other fixed activities) that we take into account in our simulations for each schoolboy are: (@P1) going to the water during free time; or (@P2) staying at home (for resting time) or at school (during the break). For each of these two flexible activities (@P1 and @P2), all the factors (or explanatory variables) that determine their choice are to be specified in the model. These variables are then used by the selection function to determine the eligibility of each activity (by calculating an eligibility value that can be positive, zero or negative) and choose the activity that has the greatest value of eligibility. For (@P2), no factor has been defined in the model, to determine its choice: its eligibility is therefore always zero for all schoolboys. For (@P1), the determining factors are: (during rest): distance between the schoolboy's school and the river; and duration of break time; (during break and off-days): in short all the factors defined above. Thus, (@P2) is chosen only when the eligibility of (@P1) is negative.

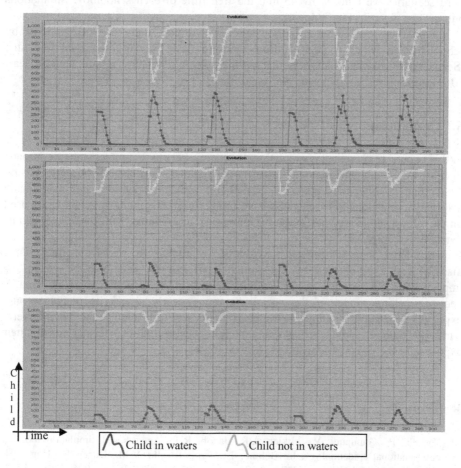

Fig. 3. (Up) "school-river" contact rate with default unoccupied time: ~45%. (Middle) "school-river" contact rate with default unoccupied time – 30 min: ~20%. (Down) "school-river" contact rate with default unoccupied time – 45 min: ~17%.

4.5   Simulations of the Platform

The objective of the simulations is to see how the free time of schoolchildren, added to other influencing factors, influences their susceptibility to go to water during days of class. For this, we choose as an indicator, the daily rate of "schoolboy-river" contact provided by survey data in [38]; and reproduced in [31]: This contact rate turns around 20.5%, on working days. In the first scenario, each schoolboy uses their default free time that is: 60 min (during breaks); and 60 to 115 min, the time of the following class (i.e., 3 p.m. or 7 p.m.) - the time to come home after the end of class (i.e., 1 p.m or 5 p.m.). Simulations of outputs are given in Fig. 3(up).

In other scenarios, we try the experiment which consists in finding the ideal free time to meet the expected contact rate ($\sim 20.5\%$). For this, we gradually diminish the schoolboys' free time. In the second scenario, we have decreased by 30 min the free time of each schoolboy. Simulations outputs are given in Fig. 3(Middle). Finally, in a third scenario, we reduced by 45 min the free time of each schoolboy. Simulations outputs are given in Fig. 3(down).

Comparing these three scenarios (Fig. 3) with the daily use of the river by schoolchildren which is 20.5% during working days [31, 38], the ideal free time (Scenario 3 - Fig. 3(Middle)) is that during which schoolboy is still busy at least 30 min during resting moments and break times.

5   Conclusion

In this paper, we presented computational epidemiology as a complementary approach to deal with some epidemiological aspects (spatial and social aspects in particular) on the spread of infectious diseases, aspects for which epidemiological mathematic (especially Equations-based models) have limits. From this point of view, we focused on the relevance of agent-based approach to model and simulate schistosomiasis and its dynamics of spread.

The model presented (which is a coupling of spatial and social dynamics of the disease) and experimented by co-simulation of GAMA and JASON, where are implemented respectively a behavioral model of the spatial dynamic and a decision-making model of the social dynamic, clearly shows its predictive and explicative capacities. It allows reproducing the rate of utilization of the Niger River's banks by Niamey's child and explaining the influence of children's leisure time on their exposure to the risk of contracting schistosomiasis.

References

1. Patlolla, P., Gunupudi, V., Mikler, A.R., Jacob, R.T.: Agent-based simulation tools in computational epidemiology. In: Böhme, T., Larios Rosillo, V.M., Unger, H., Unger, H. (eds.) IICS 2004. LNCS, vol. 3473, pp. 212–223. Springer, Heidelberg (2006). doi:10.1007/11553762_21

2. Bonabeau, E., Toubiana, L., Flahault, A.: Evidence for global mixing in real influenza epidemics. J. Phys. Math. Gen. **31**(9), L361 (1998)
3. Marathe, M., Ramakrishnan, N.: Recent advances in computational epidemiology. IEEE Intell. Syst. **28**(4), 96–101 (2013)
4. Fuks, H., Lawniczak, A.T.: Individual-based lattice model for spatial spread of epidemics. Discret. Dyn. Nat. Soc. **6**(3), 191–200 (2001)
5. Fukś, H., Duchesne, R., Lawniczak, A.T.: Spatial correlations in SIR epidemic models, Mai 2005. arXiv:nlin/0505044
6. Murray, J.D., Stanley, E.A., Brown, D.L.: On the spatial spread of rabies among foxes. Proc. R. Soc. Lond. B Biol. Sci. **229**(1255), 111–150 (1986)
7. Fu, S.C., Milne, G.: A flexible automata model for disease simulation. In: Sloot, P.M.A., Chopard, B., Hoekstra, A.G. (eds.) ACRI 2004. LNCS, vol. 3305, pp. 642–649. Springer, Heidelberg (2004). doi:10.1007/978-3-540-30479-1_66
8. Barrett, C.L., Eubank, S., Marathe, M.V.: An interaction-based approach to computational epidemiology. In: AAAI, pp. 1590–1593 (2008)
9. Gorder, P.F.: Computational epidemiology. Comput. Sci. Eng. **12**(1), 4–6 (2010)
10. Perez, L., Dragicevic, S.: An agent-based approach for modeling dynamics of contagious disease spread. Int. J. Health Geogr. **8**, 50 (2009)
11. O'Hare, A., Lycett, S.J., Doherty, T., Salvador, L.C.M., Kao, R.R.: Broadwick: a framework for computational epidemiology. BMC Bioinform. **17**, 65 (2016)
12. Siebert, J.: Approche multi-agent pour la multi-modélisation et le couplage de simulations. Application à l'étude des influences entre le fonctionnement des réseaux ambiants et le comportement de leurs utilisateurs. Ph.D. thesis, Université Henri Poincaré - Nancy I (2011)
13. Weyns, D., Omicini, A., Odell, J.: Environment as a first class abstraction in multiagent systems. Auton. Agents Multi-Agent Syst. **14**(1), 5–30 (2007)
14. Stratulat, T., Ferber, J., Tranier, J.: MASQ: towards an integral approach to interaction. In: Proceedings of the 8th International Conference on Autonomous Agents and Multiagent Systems-Volume 2, pp. 813–820 (2009)
15. Ferber, J.: Les systèmes multi-agents: un aperçu général. Tech. Sci. Inform. **16**(8) (1997)
16. Demange, J.: Un modèle d'environnement pour la simulation multiniveau - Application à la simulation de foules. Ph.D. thesis, Université de Technologie de Belfort-Montbeliard (2012)
17. Muller, J.P.: Des systemes autonomes aux systemes multi-agents: Interaction, emergence et systemes complexes. HDR, Habilitation a diriger des recherches – Informatique (2002)
18. Jennings, N.R., Sycara, K., Wooldridge, M.: A roadmap of agent research and development. Auton. Agents Multi-Agent Syst. **1**(1), 7–38 (1998)
19. Chaib-Draa, B., Jarras, I., Moulin, B.: Systèmes multi-agents: principes généraux et applications, pp. 1030–1044. Ed. Hermès (2001)
20. Payet, D., Courdier, R., Sebastien, N., Ralambondrainy, T.: Environment as support for simplification, reuse and integration of processes in spatial MAS. In: 2006 IEEE International Conference on Information Reuse and Integration, pp. 127–131 (2006)
21. Boissier, O., Bordini, R.H., Hübner, J.F., Ricci, A., Santi, A.: Multi-agent oriented programming with JaCaMo. Sci. Comput. Program. **78**(6), 747–761 (2013)
22. Khalil, K.M., Abdel-Aziz, M., Nazmy, T.T., Salem, A.-B.M.: An agent-based modeling for pandemic influenza in Egypt. In: Lu, J., Jain, L.C., Zhang, G. (eds.) Handbook on Decision Making, pp. 205–218. Springer, Heidelberg p (2012)
23. Shi, Z.Z., Wu, C.-H., Ben-Arieh, D.: Agent-based model: a surging tool to simulate infectious diseases in the immune system. Open J. Model. Simul. **2014** (2014)
24. Reyes, A.M., Diaz, H., Olarte, A.: An agent-based model for the control of malaria using genetically modified vectors. In: ECMS, pp. 31–36 (2012)

25. Ferrer, J., Albuquerque, J., Prats, C., López, D., Valls, J.: Agent-based models in malaria elimination strategy design. In: EMCSR 2012 (2012)
26. Daudé, É., Vaguet, A., Paul, R.: La dengue, maladie complexe. Nat. Sci. Sociétés **23**(4), 331–342 (2015)
27. Paul, P.N.T., Bah, A., Ndiaye, P.I., Ndione, J.A.: An agent-based model for studying the impact of herd mobility on the spread of vector-borne diseases: the case of rift valley fever (Ferlo Senegal). Open J. Model. Simul. **2014** (2014)
28. Fianyo, Y.E.: Couplage de modèles à l'aide d'agents: le système OSIRIS. Paris 9 (2001)
29. Gaud, N.A.: Systèmes multi–agents holoniques: de l'analyse à l'implantation : méta-modèle, méthodologie, et simulation multi-niveaux. Besançon (2007)
30. Cisse, P.A., Dembele, J.M., Lo, M., Cambier, C.: Assessing the spatial impact on an agent-based modeling of epidemic control: case of schistosomiasis. In: Glass, K., Colbaugh, R., Ormerod, P., Tsao, J. (eds.) Complex 2012. LNICSSITE, vol. 126, pp. 58–69. Springer, Cham (2013). doi:10.1007/978-3-319-03473-7_6
31. Cisse, P.A., Dembele, J.M., Cambier, C., Lo, M.: Multi-agent simulation of water contact's patterns in relation to schistosomiasis: a BDI architecture using kernel functions. In: 2014 Second World Conference on Complex Systems (WCCS), pp. 536–541 (2014)
32. Bordini, R.H., Hübner, J.F., Wooldridge, M.: Programming Multi-Agent Systems in AgentSpeak Using Jason (Wiley Series in Agent Technology). Wiley, Hoboken (2007)
33. Drogoul, A., et al.: GAMA: a spatially explicit, multi-level, agent-based modeling and simulation platform. In: Demazeau, Y., Ishida, T., Corchado, J.M., Bajo, J. (eds.) PAAMS 2013. LNCS, vol. 7879, pp. 271–274. Springer, Heidelberg (2013). doi:10.1007/978-3-642-38073-0_25
34. Watts, S., Khallaayoune, K., Bensefia, R., Laamrani, H., Gryseels, B.: The study of human behavior and schistosomiasis transmission in an irrigated area in Morocco. Soc. Sci. Med. 1982 **46**(6), 755–765 (1998)
35. Hägerstrand, T.: What about people in regional science? Pap. Reg. Sci. Assoc. **24**(1), 6–21 (1970)
36. Miller, H.J.: A measurement theory for time geography. Geogr. Anal. **37**(1), 17–45 (2005)
37. Ernould, J.-C., Labbo, R., Chippaux, J.-P.: Evolution de la schistosomose urinaire à Niamey. Niger. Bull. Société Pathol. Exot. **96**(3), 173–177 (2003)
38. Ernould, J.C., Kaman Kaman, A., Labbo, R., Couret, D., Chippaux, J.P.: Recent urban growth and urinary schistosomiasis in Niamey. Niger. Trop. Med. Int. Health **5**(6), 431–437 (2000)

Transforming Medical Advice into Clinical Activities for Patient Follow-Up

António Silva[1]([✉]), Tiago Oliveira[2], José Neves[1], and Paulo Novais[1]

[1] Algoritmi Centre/Department of Informatics, University of Minho, Braga, Portugal
id6783@alunos.uminho.pt, {pjon,jneves}@di.uminho.pt
[2] National Institute of Informatics, Tokyo, Japan
toliveira@nii.ac.jp

Abstract. The delivery of Computer-Interpretable Guidelines occurs mainly in the form of tools following a Q&A strategy for the interaction with users. Despite the interactivity conferred by this style of communication, currently available tools do not possess control mechanisms to ensure the fulfilment of clinical recommendations. With the CompGuide personal assistant web application for scheduling clinical tasks, besides the normal input of information and the production of recommendations by an execution engine, there is a mapping of these recommendations to an agenda of activities for the health care professional. These activities are also monitored and notifications are produced to ensure their delivery times.

1 Introduction

Clinical Practice Guidelines (CPGs) are systematically developed statements that provide clinical advice for specific circumstances. Their representation and deployment in Clinical Decision Support Systems (CDSSs) confers them the designation of Computer-Interpretable Guidelines (CIGs) [10]. Existing tools specialized in CIG-based advice follow a style of communication that resembles a digital Q&A, in which a recommendation is produced, followed by a question to obtain information about the state of the patient, then followed by another recommendation. They possess no mechanisms to incentivize users to put recommendations in practice and do not monitor their execution [3]. As is known, monitoring patients is a laborious task due to the number of patients that a health care professional has to take care of and the complexity of procedures to be applied. Although CDSSs for patient-specific advice may help to ease this burden, the simple provision of recommendations may prove to be insufficient to generate a positive impact in the outcomes of care [6].

There is a growing need for CDSSs that, along with their patient-specific advice, also provide functionalities that would allow them to become more prominent in daily clinical practice, specially when it comes to patient tracking, patient follow-up, scheduling of procedures, and monitoring of procedure constraints.

© Springer International Publishing AG 2017
J. Bajo et al. (Eds.): PAAMS 2017 Workshops, CCIS 722, pp. 169–176, 2017.
DOI: 10.1007/978-3-319-60285-1_14

At the same time, it is important for these functionalities to be available in any setting, at any time, so that clinical advice can reach the health care professional in the most diverse situations.

The CompGuide framework is based on digital versions of clinical protocols for automatic interpretation. The application performs the role of a personal assistant for health care professionals that provides decision support and treatment recommendations.

Thus, the present work based on the CompGuide framework, proposes a new method for the integration of the advice of CPGs in the daily life of health personnel, such as physicians and nurses. The underlying principle is mapping clinical recommendations, with their respective temporal constraints, to an agenda of activities for a health care professional to perform.

The present paper is organized as follows. Section 2 describes related work regarding tools for CIG execution, along with a description of their current drawbacks and aspects to improve. Section 3 presents the CompGuide architecture for the deployment of CIGs and how its services are used as a basis for the health care assistant tool developed to accompany health care professionals. Section 4 describes the main elements of the personal assistant web application and its main functionalities. Finally, Sect. 7 presents the conclusions drawn so far with the development of the health care assistant and future directions for the work.

2   Related Work

Following the existence of numerous approaches to CIG modelling, there is an equal number of tools to operationalize CIGs and make them executable against patient data. This is the case of CIG execution engines such as GLEE [14], the Spock Engine [15], the GLARE Execution Engine [13], or SAGEDesktop [1], which were specifically developed for the application of guidelines to patients in health care settings. Their objective is to run CIG instructions against data from patients and produce tailored recommendations, according to the observed state. In these systems, the role of the execution engine is straightforward, in the sense that it is merely concerned with following the constraints of the clinical careflow, comparing items of the patient state with conditions stated in rules dictating whether a recommendation should be provided or not. Most tools for CIG execution, including the above-given examples, exist in the form of client-server applications, with the intelligence engine placed on the client side. Furthermore, these applications are mostly available as desktop applications, which is an obstacle to their potential for reaching health care professionals and their ease of deployment.

The idea of enhancing CDSSs with additional features that allow them to achieve a higher level of integration of clinical recommendations in clinical practice comes from the ever-increasing role of Ambient Assisted Living (AAL) in enabling new information and communication services which transparently support people in their everyday lives [5,7]. In fact, a similar idea has been explored in [2], where a personal memory assistant, capable of intelligent scheduling and deployed over a platform called iGenda. The assistant acts as the support for a centralized manager system that can manage several services and is responsible for the scheduling of multiple agendas, taking into account the availability of resources or the health conditions of the users. However, here the agenda manager is directed towards patients, which are, predominantly elderly people. Although different, the work proposed herein can be related to this project and to others such as the Collaborative Memory Aids [11] and Hermes [4], but with the focus placed on the health care professional.

3 CompGuide Architecture for CIG Execution

The CompGuide architecture, shown in Fig. 1 is service-oriented and provides the functionalities of an execution engine. The *Core Server* is the central component of the architecture and was developed as a RESTful service application. The usage of web services as the means to access the *Core Server* offers expandability and the possibility to improve selected services without compromising others. This grants greater flexibility when integrating CIG execution functionalities in third party applications [8].

The *Core Server* has four modules. The first is the *Authentication Agent* which provides authentication and authorization to the different types of users of the system, namely administrators, health care professionals, or patients. The *Guideline Handler* is responsible for managing updates to the *Guideline Repository*, keeping different CIGs represented according to the CompGuide ontology [9], organized by authorship and by date. In order to use a guideline for execution, the *Guideline Handler* accesses the selected CIG in the *Guideline Repository* and pulls the corresponding careflow, delivering it to the *Guideline Execution Engine*, which, in turn, uses information about the patient state provided by the *Database Handler* to fill in the data entry points of the careflow and produce recommendations. The *Guideline Execution Engine* interprets all the scheduling constraints on the tasks and controls enactment times, which means that starting and ending times are verified and delivered to other applications. These mechanisms to follow the application of procedures over time and to verify the execution of tasks are absent from most CIG frameworks [12], but they are essential to have a decision support that is truly capable of following up on the application of a CPG.

These features are made available by the Core Server as RESTful web services in order to ensure they can be easily integrated into any type of application. The Core Server is implemented in Java, using the RESTEasy API over a WildFly Application Server. The personal assistant, which uses the web services available in the CoreServer, was developed as a web application following the Model-View-Control(MVC) paradigm using Java Server Faces (JSF). The purpose of the *Core Server* is to make available CIG services that anyone can integrate in their own applications, with a special focus on AAL applications.

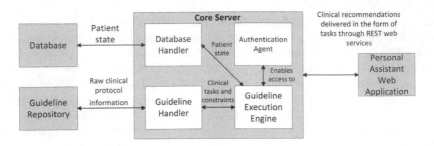

Fig. 1. Architecture of CompGuide server application.

4 Health Care Personal Assistant Web Application

The overall objective of the introduction of CPGs in decision support systems is to lead to a better acceptance and application of these good medical practices, since these systems are able to monitor the actions and observations of health care professionals. By using information and communication technology, it is possible to provide CIGs with a dynamism, presence, and interactivity that may bring them closer to the concept of living guidelines, which conveys a greater impact of good practices in health care, while still allowing the adaptation of these good practices to particular settings and situations.

In order to achieve this, it is necessary to develop a tool that not only allows the management of patients and the search for a CPG to apply, but also to control a number of circumstances of CIG execution, namely their execution times. That is the purpose of the CompGuide personal assistant web application.

5 Main Elements of the Application

In the application, it is possible for health care professionals to visualize the clinical tasks provided by the execution engine. This visualization can take one of two forms. The first is a timeline in which all the clinical tasks are displayed over a chronogram. A timeline of activities has the ability to compress multiple tasks into a single continuity that makes the succession of clinical procedures easy to understand. The benefits from such a representation include the ability to sequence events and reduce the potential for overburdening the health care professional. Additionally, by visualizing all of the pieces of a guideline treatment, care providers can make more focused, effective decisions about resources and timetables. This view is shown in Fig. 2. In it, it is possible to observe clinical tasks for the management of colon cancer, namely sequential workup actions to ascertain the state of the patient.

The other available view is a calendar in which the health care professional can visualize the tasks according to the temporal granularity he sees fit, namely week, day, and month. While with the timeline it is easier to detect the starting and ending points of tasks, with the calendar view it is easier to grasp the

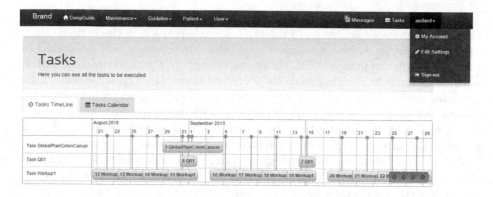

Fig. 2. Timeline view of clinical procedures in the CompGuide personal assistant web application.

temporal constraints that bind clinical tasks such as durations, waiting times and periodicities. Figure 3 shows the same tasks as in the timeline, but displayed over a week, where it is possible to verify, for instance, how long a clinical task should be applied.

Fig. 3. Calendar view of clinical procedures in the CompGuide personal assistant web application.

6   Functionalities Supporting Care

The CompGuide personal assistant web application makes it possible to manage information about CPGs, health care professionals that are users in the system, and patients to which CPGs are applied. As such, one can create, edit and delete all this information, according to the type of authorization in the system.

The *Execution Engine* from the CompGuide architecture was integrated in the tool in order to interpret CIGs in the repository and produce inferences that ultimately result in recommendations of clinical tasks. Once these recommendations are retrieved, their constraints (in this case, their temporal constraints) are interpreted by the tool and mapped onto the different views mentioned earlier. As an example, considering that the *Execution Engine* recommends a clinical action to perform a complete physical exam on the patient every 6 months, for 2 years, the application will interpret these restrictions and unfold the recommendation in multiple events and register them in the timeline. As such, the result would be four new events scheduled 6 months apart. Then, the user can consult on the timeline and calendar widgets the scheduling of these events in order to execute the clinical task and so manage better his time.

In order to ensure the execution of tasks at the designated time, it was necessary to implement a notification system and a message box. These elements are both shown in Fig. 4. The message box features messages such as indications about the tasks that should be performed or should have already been performed, offering the possibility to mark them as executed. As for the notification system, it is used to periodically alert the user about task enactment times, according to their respective temporal restrictions. The notifications are shown as a pop-up message.

Fig. 4. Message box and notification in the CompGuide personal assistant web application.

7   Conclusions and Future Work

The personal assistant presented herein aims to stretch the reach of CIGs far beyond the medical office. Its purpose as a reminder tool is to ensure the timely enactment of clinical procedures over the course of patient management, removing the possibility of inadvertently skipping steps that may prove to be crucial later on for his recovery. In addition to decision support functionalities, common to other CIG systems, the tool provides additional scheduling and alert features to assist the health care professional in keeping track of their patients. Therefore, its main contribution is a new method to integrate CPG advice in a clinical setting and make it easily available. With the development of the CompGuide personal assistant web application, new questions arose. The first is: how should the delays in task execution be handled? In this case, there are several alternatives, but all of them have drawbacks. Re-scheduling the task may imply verifying if the state of the patient allows the enactment of the procedure at a later time. Not performing the task may be equally damaging to the patient. Another issue is: how should parallel clinical tasks be shown to the health care professional in order to avoid confusion? These are issues we plan to address in future work.

Acknowledgements. This work has been supported by COMPETE: POCI-01-0145-FEDER-0070 43 and FCT – Fundação para a Ciência e Tecnologia within the Project Scope UID/CEC/ 00319/2013.

References

1. Berg, D., Ram, P., Glasgow, J., Castro, J.: SAGEDesktop: an environment for testing clinical practice guidelines. The 26th Annual International Conference of the IEEE Engineering in Medicine and Biology Society, vol. 4, pp. 3217–3220 (2004)
2. Costa, A., Novais, P., Corchado, J.M., Neves, J.: Increased performance and better patient attendance in an hospital with the use of smart agendas*. Log. J. IGPL **20**(4), 689–698 (2012). doi:10.1093/jigpal/jzr021
3. Isern, D., Moreno, A.: Computer-based execution of clinical guidelines: a review. Int. J. Med. Inf. **77**(12), 787–808 (2008)
4. Jiang, J., Khelifi, F., Trundle, P., Geven, A.: HERMES: a FP7 funded project towards the development of a computer-aided memory management system via intelligent computations. J. Assist. Technol. **3**(3), 27–35 (2009). http://dx.doi.org/10.1108/17549450200900022
5. Lima, L., Novais, P., Neves, J., Bulas, C.J., Costa, R.: Group decision making and quality-of-information in e-health systems. Log. J. IGPL **19**(2), 315–332 (2011)
6. Musen, M.A., Shahar, Y., Shortliffe, E.H.: Clinical decision-support systems. In: Shortliffe, E.H., Cimino, J.J. (eds.) Biomedical Informatics. Health Informatics, pp. 698–736. Springer, New York (2006). doi:10.1007/0-387-36278-9_20
7. Novais, P., Costa, R., Carneiro, D., Neves, J.: Inter-organization cooperation for ambient assisted living. J. Ambient Intell. Smart Environ. **2**(2), 179–195 (2010)
8. Oliveira, T., Leão, P., Novais, P., Neves, J.: Webifying the computerized execution of clinical practice guidelines. In: Bajo Perez, J., et al. (eds.) Trends in Practical Applications of Heterogeneous Multi-Agent Systems. The PAAMS Collection. AISC, vol. 293, pp. 149–156. Springer, Cham (2014). doi:10.1007/978-3-319-07476-4_18

9. Oliveira, T., Novais, P., Neves, J.: Representation of clinical practice guideline components in OWL. In: Pérez, J., et al. (eds.) Trends in Practical Applications of Agents and Multiagent Systems. Advances in Intelligent Systems and Computing, pp. 77–85. Springer, Cham (2013). doi:10.1007/978-3-319-00563-8_10

10. Peleg, M.: Computer-interpretable clinical guidelines: a methodological review. J. Biomed. Inform. **46**(4), 744–763 (2013)

11. Picking, R., Robinet, A., Grout, V., McGinn, J., Roy, A., Ellis, S., Oram, D.: A case study using a methodological approach to developing user interfaces for elderly and disabled people. Comput. J. **53**(6), 842 (2010). http://dx.doi.org/10.1093/comjnl/bxp089

12. Shalom, E., Shahar, Y., Lunenfeld, E.: An architecture for a continuous, user-driven, and data-driven application of clinical guidelines and its evaluation. J. Biomed. Inform. **59**, 130–148 (2015)

13. Terenziani, P., Montani, S., Bottrighi, A., Torchio, M., Molino, G., Correndo, G.: The GLARE approach to clinical guidelines: main features. Stud. Health Technol. Inform. **101**(3), 162–166 (2004)

14. Wang, D., Peleg, M., Tu, S.W., Boxwala, A.A., Ogunyemi, O., Zeng, Q., Greenes, R.A., Patel, V.L., Shortliffe, E.H.: Design and implementation of the GLIF3 guideline execution engine. J. Biomed. Inform. **37**(5), 305–318 (2004)

15. Young, O., Shahar, Y.: The spock system: developing a runtime application engine for hybrid-asbru guidelines. Artif. Intell. Rev. **3581**(1), 166–170 (2005)

A Multi-agent Architecture for Labeling Data and Generating Prediction Models in the Field of Social Services

Emilio Serrano, Pedro del Pozo-Jiménez, Mari Carmen Suárez-Figueroa,
Jacinto González-Pachón, Javier Bajo(✉), and Asunción Gómez-Pérez

Ontology Engineering Group, Universidad Politécnica de Madrid, Madrid, Spain
{emilioserra,jbajo}@fi.upm.es

Abstract. Prediction models are widely used in insurance companies and health services. Even when 120 million people are at risk of suffering poverty or social exclusion in the EU, this kind of models are surprisingly unusual in the field of social services. A fundamental reason for this gap is the difficulty in labeling and annotating social services data. Conditions such as social exclusion require a case-by-case debate. This paper presents a multi-agent architecture that combines semantic web technologies, exploratory data analysis techniques, and supervised machine learning methods. The architecture offers a holistic view of the main challenges involved in labeling data and generating prediction models for social services. Moreover, the proposal discusses to what extent these tasks may be automated by intelligent agents.

Keywords: Multi-agent systems · Human-agent societies · Social services · Machine learning

1 Introduction

Building artificial intelligence and machine learning based systems has never been easier than today thanks to: (1) open-source tools such as TensorFlow or Spark; and, (2) massive amounts of computation power through cloud providers such as Amazon Web Services and Google Cloud [4]. Machine learning prediction models are widely employed, among others, in health services. These systems have a deep impact because there is strong evidence supporting that early detection of medical conditions results in less severe outcomes. For instance, the reader may calculate the risk of suffering a heart disease at different webs [3].

Social services, also called welfare services or social work, include publicly or privately provided services intended to aid disadvantaged, distressed, or vulnerable persons or groups. The economic crisis is undermining the sustainability of social protection systems in the EU [1]: 24% of all the EU population (over 120 million people) are at risk of poverty or social exclusion. The fight against poverty and social exclusion is at the heart of the Europe 2020 strategy for smart, sustainable and inclusive growth. Social services deal with a number of

J. Bajo et al. (Eds.): PAAMS 2017 Workshops, CCIS 722, pp. 177–184, 2017.
DOI: 10.1007/978-3-319-60285-1_15

undesirable conditions that affect not only the quality of life of individuals, but also the equity and cohesion of society as a whole [10].

Why not producing prediction models for the field of social services as in health services? Machine learning could answer a number of questions such as: will this individual suffer chronic social exclusion?; will generational transmission of poverty occurs in this family?; how much economic aid is needed to integrate this person into society?; how long does it take aid to have an impact on a case? Something that may go unnoticed by outsiders to the field of data science is that all these questions are forms of *supervised learning*. Therefore, these questions fall into two broad categories: (1) *classification* ("is this A or B?", or "is this A or B, or C. . . ?"); and (2) *regression* (questions answered with a number: "how much", "how many", "how long").

Unsupervised learning and reinforcement learning achieve outstanding results when applicable, but they are not adequate to answer these questions. On the other hand, supervised learning is based on the premise that lots and lots of labeled and annotated data is available. There are a number of challenges in gathering this labeled data in social services. (1) There is not public and accepted datasets in the field, typically because of privacy reasons. (2) Even if there were such data, the labels to predict would not correspond to the needs of all social services because there is a strong coupling between the predictive tool and the data it is fed with. (3) Moreover, the conditions social services are concerned about depend on the society they deal with, not allowing prediction results to be extrapolated from a country or even a city to another one. (4) Finally, the complex and multi-dimensional nature of processes such as social exclusion may require a case-by-case debate and deciding a label is complicated even for social workers experts.

For the reasons explained above, the hardest part of building new artificial intelligence solutions for social services is not the machine learning algorithms, but the data collection and labeling. This paper copes with this problem by a multi-agent architecture that combines semantic web technologies, exploratory data analysis techniques, and supervised machine learning methods. The architecture is composed of a number of cooperating intelligent agents that assist social workers and data scientists in the labeling of sensitive data and in the subsequent generation of prediction services.

The rest of the paper is organized as follows: Sect. 2 revises the related work. Section 3 presents the proposed architecture. Finally, the preliminary conclusions obtained are presented in Sect. 4.

2   Related Works

Predictions models are widely used in insurance companies to allow customers to estimate their policies cost. Manulife Philippines [2] offers a number of online tools to calculate the likelihood of disability, critical illness, or death before the age of 65; based on age, gender, and smoking status. Health is another application field where risk estimations are undertaken for preventive purposes.

More specifically, the risk of heart disease can be estimated at different websites such as at the Mayo clinic web [3]. The labeling of these cases is relatively simple a posteriori: roughly speaking there is no doubt when someone has suffered one of these conditions. There are also a few online tools that social services may use for early detection. In this manner, Rank and Hirschl [14] give an online calculator that evaluates the probability of experiencing poverty in the next 5, 10 or 15 years. Labeling poverty cases is something automatic when defined as falling below a certain annual income[1].

The multi-dimensional nature of conditions such as social exclusion makes considerably more challenging to analyze, detect, treat, and predict it than poverty. There are a number of data analysis works in social exclusion that are detailed enough to learn from their labeling methods for the presented work. Ramos and Valera [13] use the *logistic regression* (LR) model to study social exclusion in 384 cases labeled by social workers through a manual heuristic procedure. According to this procedure, an individual is considered at a consolidated phase of exclusion if: (1) he or she is living for at least 3 years in unstable accommodation; (2) has very weak links, or none at all, with family or friends; (3) is almost permanently unoccupied; and, (4) presents a substantial or total loss of working habits, self-care or motivation for inclusion. Similar conditions are defined for the initial phase of exclusion. This example of rule of thump used by the social workers illustrates the complexity and ambiguity of deciding if someone is suffering social exclusion. Moreover, the heuristic has to be define before starting gathering data so the social workers can use it. Finally, the fully manual approach only allows a very limited number of cases: less than 400. Lafuente-Lechuga and Faura-Martínez [9] undertake an analysis of 31 predictors based on segmentation methods and LR. The authors consider the aggregation of scores in different fields related to social exclusion to decide if a person is under this condition. After a cluster analysis, this score is used to rank and analyze the most important variables to decide whether there is vulnerability to social exclusion. In a similar style, Haron [6] studies the social exclusion in Israel labeling data by various indicators that are aggregated in a single weighted average score. The author proposes the *linear regression* as a better alternative to the LR. The problem with this approach is that, besides the difficulty in defining these aggregations functions and weights, the machine learning techniques will tend to calculate precisely the aggregation formula since it is defined based exclusively on the training data. Suh et al. [16] analyze over 35K cases of 34 European countries using LR. The particular objective of this work is a subjective study and not an objective measure of the social exclusion, for which the researchers use LR over responses to a survey of direct questions about whether people feel excluded from society. Therefore, as the authors point out, there is a subjectivity aspect that is the responsibility of the interviewee

---

[1] In this vein, the adult dataset [8] is a well known public labeled dataset that allows predicting whether an adult income exceeds $50K a year based on a 1994 census database. It can be used to train prediction models as a proof of concept before collecting and labeling the own proprietary data.

instead of the social worker expert. These inspiring works support the hypothesis that machine learning can greatly benefit social services. Also, that the most interesting questions to assist social services belong to the supervised learning. However, there are no general methods and tools proposed for labeling the data before building a predictive model.

A number of approaches study interesting synergies between agent theory and machine learning [15]. Ponni and Shunmuganathan [12] propose multi-agent system for classification in multi-relational databases with, among others, Support Vector Machines (SVM). Kiselev and Alhajj [7] describe an efficient adaptive multi-agent approach to continuous online clustering of streaming data in complex uncertain environments. Giannella et al. [5] propose an implementation of distributed clustering algorithms with multi-agent systems. Park and Oh [11] introduce a multi-agent system to filter data that automatically selects and tunes a clustering or dimensionality reduction method. These significant contributions improve machine learning paradigms in a number of aspects by rethinking them from the perspective of multi-agent systems. More importantly for the work presented here, several of these references deal with exploratory data analysis techniques such as clustering and dimensionality reduction. These are natural solutions to summarize, simplify, condense, and distill a collection of data before labeling it. However, the revised multi-agent systems do not offer specific guidelines to go from the clusters or the principal components to the wanted labels. Clusters are in the eye of the beholder, and the architecture presented in this paper instead of focusing on implementing faster clustering techniques, is meant to adapt to the beholder and to recommend actions to label data intuitively.

3   Multi-agent Architecture Segmentation and Prediction

This section describes the proposed architecture, see Fig. 1.

In the lower layer of the architecture, there is an interface that allows accessing the databases that are used for the different applications and records in social services and linking them with the rest of the architecture. The agents of this layer, besides controlling the protocols of access to the databases, will ensure that the information that the upper layers obtain is anonymous. Users with special privileges may require this layer, through services in upper layers and with the purpose of labeling a case, to link an anonymous identifier with an identity.

The data handled by the interface are also accessed by a layer of persistence transverse to the architecture. This persistence layer has capacities of semantic technologies as dealing with ontologies in languages such as RDFS and OWL. To favor the tagging service, the architecture offers functionality for the formal representation of the knowledge treated by social services through a network of ontologies. In addition to these ontologies, the layer stores intermediate data such as: data tables obtained from pre-processing the databases accessed by the interface, unsupervised learning models, supervised learning models, and users' preferences and history of decisions for recommendation and decision support.

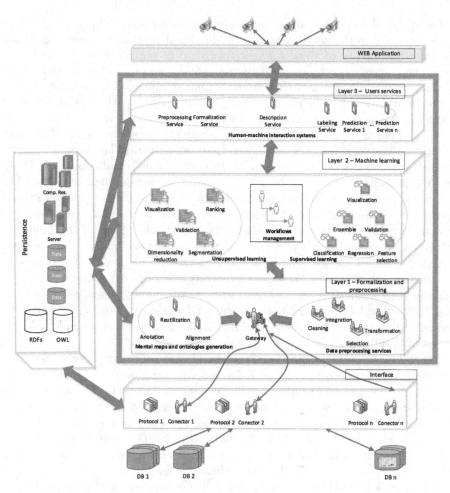

Fig. 1. A multi-agent architecture for labeling data and generating prediction models.

Layer 1 of the architecture is devoted to the formalization and preprocessing of social services data, on the one hand, to have a powerful query model based on semantic technologies and, on the other hand, to allow the machine learning methods to learn from this data. These two differentiated services are connected through a gateway: data processing services and ontology construction. The first service includes agents specialized in: (1) data selection; (2) its integration from various sources accessed by the interface; (3) cleaning the data by detecting noise and inconsistencies; (4) and, transforming the data into forms suitable for mining. The agents in charge of assisting the process of generating mental maps and ontologies are specialized in tasks such as: (1) data annotation; (2) reuse of already built ontologies; and, (3) ontology alignment, i.e. determining corre- spondences between concepts in ontologies.

Layer 2 of the architecture is the machine learning layer. This layer provides unsupervised learning services to obtain simplified representations of data for labeling. The agents of these services specialize in segmentation through different algorithms, dimensionality reduction, validation methods of unsupervised learning (as the silhouette method to determine an adequate number of clusters or the information loss in principal component analysis), the visualization of clusters and data in n-dimensions (with methods as star diagrams or Chernoff faces), and the calculation of rankings by similarity to a given case. The layer also offers supervised learning services so that, once the first labels are available, interpretable models of these data are built such as rule-based classifiers. These machine learning models can be used by social workers as heuristics to label new cases. In addition, learning paradigms of higher predictive power will also be generated requiring little or no parameter tuning by social services, such as random forest or AdaBoost with decision trees (considered one of the best out-of-the-box classifier). Quality metrics for these supervised models can be used as a stop criterion in the process of labeling cases. The agents of this service specialize in: classification, regression, feature selection, ensemble methods to combine the results of several models, validation (among others: leave-one-out cross-validation, fold cross-validation, and with a test set), and visualization of models and evaluation metrics. A workflow manager allows combining this layer processes in different workflows.

Layer 3 offers distinguished user services: (1) pre-processing services for data scientists; (2) formalization services for ontology engineers; and (3) concept description services and (4) labeling services for social workers. The agents these services are composed of are the only ones that interact with the agents of lower layers and the transverse layer of persistence. For each user service, there is a *decision support system* (DSS) that provide users with explicit decision suggestions. For the labeling service, an example of decision suggestion could come after the first input of labels. If an underfitting situation is detected with a few tagged examples, labeling new examples will not improve the future prediction model. In this case, some suggestions include: (1) revising the labels that might be inconsistent; (2) collecting more fields for the cases; (3) or, considering changing the purpose of the prediction model. On the other hand, if a high accuracy is achieved with the currently labeled data (or it does not improve in many iterations), stopping the labeling process could also be suggested. Finally, these services agents have to learn from the users' preferences and recommend actions and alternatives through techniques as *collaborative filtering*. Once again, clusters are in the eye and there are no inherently better cluster analysis methods than others.

In the top layer, user services are accessed through responsive web applications. In this way, users can use these services through a variety of devices: smartphones, tablets, laptops, etcetera. The ultimate goal is to provide social workers with intelligent prediction models in the palm of the hand, which allow them to anticipate events for the sake of their "social patients". But as discussed, the hardest part to get there is labeling the data.

4   Conclusion and Future Works

This paper presents a multi-agent architecture for labeling data and generating social services prediction models. The proposal responds to the enormous importance of social services in today's Europe and to the difficulty of generating predictive models that help social workers in their day-to-day work. To improve this situation, the architecture supports an iterative and incremental data labeling until a predictive model that attends a specific social service is obtained.

The core of the proposal is based on offering services and assistance to social workers in cluster analysis and dimensionality reduction as a means to summarize, simplify, condense, and distill a collection of data before labeling it. Intelligent agents not only automate this analysis as much as possible, but also learn from workers' preferences since there is a lack of objectivity in the generation of useful summaries and visualizations of unlabeled data. Furthermore, the architecture includes agents for supervised learning that, in each iteration in which new labels are added, contribute with: explanatory models of the data; selections of the most important predictors; and, stopping conditions to the labeling process automatically checked. Finally, it provides a service for the consultation of ontology networks that facilitates the unambiguous description of the concepts included in the cases to be tagged and their relations.

Although the architecture has not been implemented, many of the ideas and proposals have been put into practice for the generation of an online social exclusion prediction service in the Spanish region of Castilla y León (http:// webpact.oeg-upm.net/).

Future work includes: implementing the architecture in a multi-agent platform; extending the decision support system for the labeling service; and, a better exploitation of the ontologies and semantic resources to include forms of advanced learning such as case-based reasoning, transfer learning, and graph mining.

Acknowledgments. This publication would not have been possible without the inputs and collaboration of the Social Services of Castilla y León. This research work is supported by the "Junta de Castilla y León" under the public contract: "Servicios de elaboración de modelos matemáticos para realizar segmentación poblacional" (A2016/000271); by the EU Programme for Employment and Social Innovation (EaSI) under the project PACT ("people-oriented case management for social inclusion proactive model"); and, by the Spanish Ministry of Economy, Industry and Competitiveness under the R&D project Datos 4.0: Retos y soluciones (TIN2016-78011-C4-4-R, AEI/FEDER, UE).

References

1. European Commission's DG for Employment, Social Affairs & Inclusion. http:// ec.europa.eu/social/main.jsp?catId=751. Accessed Feb 2017
2. Manulife Philippines. Calculate your risk, your partner's risk or both. http://www. insureright.ca/what-is-your-risk. Accessed Feb 2017

3. Mayo Clinic. Heart Disease Risk Calculator. http://www.mayoclinic.org/ diseases-conditions/heart-disease/in-depth/heart-disease-risk/itt-20084942. Accessed Feb 2017
4. de Oliveira, L.: Fueling the Gold Rush: The Greatest Public Datasets for AI. https://goo.gl/mJO8nf. Accessed Feb 2017
5. Giannella, C., Bhargava, R., Kargupta, H.: Multi-agent systems and distributed data mining. In: Klusch, M., Ossowski, S., Kashyap, V., Unland, R. (eds.) CIA 2004. LNCS, vol. 3191, pp. 1–15. Springer, Heidelberg (2004). doi:10.1007/ 978-3-540-30104-2_1
6. Haron, N.: On social exclusion and income poverty in israel: findings from the european social survey. In: Berenger, V., Bresson, F. (eds.) Poverty and Social Exclusion Around the Mediterranean Sea. Economic Studies in Inequality, Social Exclusion and Well-Being, pp. 247–269. Springer, Boston (2013). doi:10.1007/ 978-1-4614-5263-8_9
7. Kiselev, I., Alhajj, R.: A self-organizing multi-agent system for adaptive continuous unsupervised learning in complex uncertain environments. In: Fox, D., Gomes, C.P. (eds.) AAAI 2008, pp. 1808–1809. AAAI Press, Chicago (2008)
8. Kohavi, R., Becker, B.: Adult Data Set. https://archive.ics.uci.edu/ml/datasets/ Adult. Accessed Feb 2017
9. Lafuente-Lechuga, M., Faura-Martínez, U.: Análisis de los individuos vulnerables a la exclusión social en españa en 2009. An. de ASEPUMA, (21) 2013
10. Levitas, R., Pantazis, C., Fahmy, E., Gordon, D., Lloyd, E., Patsios, D.: The Multidimensional Analysis of Social Exclusion. Social Exclusion Task Force, Cabinet Office, London (2007)
11. Park, J.-E., Oh, K.-W.: Multi-agent systems for intelligent clustering. Int. J. Comput. Electr. Autom. Control Inf. Eng. 1(11), 275–280 (2007)
12. Ponni, J., Shunmuganathan, K.L: Multi-agent system for data classification from data mining using SVM. In: 2013 International Conference on Green Computing, Communication and Conservation of Energy (ICGCE), pp. 828–832, December 2013
13. Ramos, J., Varela, A.: Beyond the margins: analyzing social exclusion with a homeless client dataset. Soc. Work & Soc. 14(2), 104–120 (2016)
14. Rank, M.R., Hirschl, T.A.: Calculate Your Economic Risk. New York Times (2016)
15. Serrano, E., Rovatsos, M., Botia, J.: A qualitative reputation system for multiagent systems with protocol-based communication. In: Proceedings of the 11th International Conference on Autonomous Agents and Multiagent Systems - Volume 1, AAMAS 2012, Richland, pp. 307–314 (2012)
16. Suh, E., Tiffany, T., Vizard, P., Asghar, Z., Burchardt, T.: Quality of life in Europe: social inequalities. In: 3rd European Quality of Life Survey (2013)

AMSC

Multiagent Managerial Model of Technical Infrastructure Used at Ore Mining

Arkadiusz Kowalski[1](✉) and Tomasz Chlebus[2]

[1] Faculty of Mechanical Engineering, Wrocław University of Technology,
27 Wybrzeże Wyspiańskiego St, 50-370 Wrocław, Poland
arkadiusz.kowalski@pwr.edu.pl
[2] Faculty of Computer Science and Management,
Wrocław University of Technology,
27 Wybrzeże Wyspiańskiego St, 50-370 Wrocław, Poland
tomasz.chlebus@pwr.edu.pl

Abstract. Nature of mining processes realised in the room-and-pillar system, utilising many types of machines and appliances, as well as their multi-stage structure and dispersion on a large area, make these processes suitable to be modelled by multiagent systems. In the paper, these processes are described for the needs of a managerial model of technical infrastructure used during mining an ore deposit. For this purpose, the BPMN notation was used. Complex relationships between the environment describing the mining field and the agents representing individual types of machines and appliances are specified. A schematic multiagent model of ore extraction in an underground mine is suggested, with the goal to increase productivity at unchanged ore production level.

Keywords: Multiagent system · Building concept · Operation management · Ore deposit extraction

1 Introduction

Undoubtedly, the starting point for deliberations about the concept of a multiagent management system for technical infrastructure used during mining an ore bed should be presentation of the processes to be modelled. The examined mining processes are executed in an underground mine operating in the room-and-pillar system.

1.1 Mining a Deposit in the Room-and-Pillar System

Mining works on ore deposits in underground mines are generally carried-out in variable room-and-pillar systems using rock bolting. This system consists of two main stages: cross-cutting and retreating with use of various self-propelled machines. During cross-cutting stage, a network of crossing (most often perpendicularly) galleries is made, leaving some pillars that secure the ceiling against uncontrolled collapse. The ceiling is additionally stabilised by roof bolting. At the retreating phase, the pillars are most often cut-in to the widths similar to that of the galleries, which reduces their

© Springer International Publishing AG 2017
J. Bajo et al. (Eds.): PAAMS 2017 Workshops, CCIS 722, pp. 187–196, 2017.
DOI: 10.1007/978-3-319-60285-1_16

volume and thus reduces mining losses. Next, controlled collapse of the roof is performed in a few ways. Typical dimensions of a pillar at the cross-cutting stage are 18 × 12 m and the gallery width is 5.5 to 6 m [3]. The room-and-pillar systems differ from each other in many technical details, adapting this excavation system to local geological-mining conditions, e.g. bed thickness or geotechnical parameters of rocks.

Course of mining works on an extraction field, carried-out in the room-and-pillar system, is shown in Fig. 1, with the following designations: 1 – heavy-equipment chamber (HEC) where machines and equipment are prepared for the daily work; 2 – loading the winning on a haulage truck with a loader (when the face is significantly distant from the reloading point over the belt conveyer); 3 – loading the winning that will be conveyed by the loader directly to the nearby reloading point; 4 – reloading point over the belt conveyer and 5 – discharging the winning "on stock".

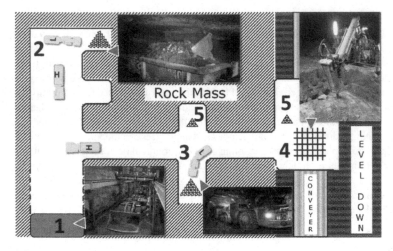

Fig. 1. Fragment of a panel in a room-and-pillar mine, schematic presentation of mining works [9]

Before extraction starts, the field is contoured by a group of galleries in that belt conveyers with discharge points are located. A bunch of galleries controlling the field ensures proper ventilation of the faces and include main transport roads. The complex, multistage and widely spread process requires strategic and operational support by variable IT tools.

1.2   Stages of Works at Faces – Extraction Process

Extraction is the main process taking place in ore mines. The primary goal of this process is to guarantee proper – depending on demand of the ore enrichment plant – quantity and quality of ore. Volume of the extracted winning is planned at the level of the mine managing board.

As the main mining process, extraction does not happen independently, but is accompanied by a significant number of sub-processes and ancillary processes, without that the output could not be acquired. Correct run of the main process depends on effective preparation, execution and monitoring of preparatory and ancillary processes [8].

The main preceding processes are opening-out and preparation of mining, and the ancillary processes required for extraction are such ones like delivery of mining machines, ventilation and water management. Because of high dampness of copper ore deposits and high temperature (ca. 28 °C, depending on depth and kind of rocks), excavation of ore would not be possible without the a.m. ancillary processes. Mining production requires means and material resources that are each time delivered to the opened-out and prepared deposit. The process itself shown in Fig. 2 is realised by means of specialised machines like face-drilling rigs (FDR), blasting vehicles (BV), wheeled loaders (WL), haulage trucks (HT), roof bolters (RB) and ancillary machines. Before each shift, each of these machines is delivered to the planned face and performs a specific work during one shift.

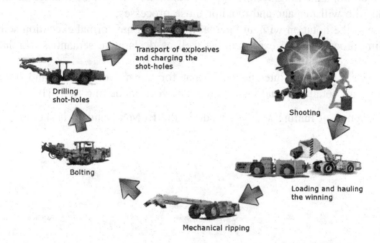

Fig. 2. Sequence of mining works at gallery faces [9]

Mining works at a gallery face run in the following way:

- a FDR machine drills shot-holes in a previously prepared face. Number of the shot-holes is strictly determined in the shooting instruction and can be different for each face.
- A blasting vehicle BV provided with explosive charges fills the drilled holes with mining explosives, primes the charges and prepares the face for shooting in order to tear-off a determined layer of the rocks.
- Sets WL + HT transport the blasted material to the winning reception point, from that it will be later transported to the processing plant.

In the extracted face, as well as in the tunnel left after explosion, it happens that some loose but not detached rocks are left, so it is necessary that such rocks are removed to secure the tunnel. The last step is bolting and holding the roof that is much enlarged after winning.

1.3 Recording the Realised Processes for Analysis of the Possibility to Apply A Multiagent System

The first step towards building a multiagent model of infrastructure management was recognising and describing the mining processes in the BPMN notation (Business Process Modelling Notation). BPMN is a graphical standard of modelling descriptions directed at business processes and a standard describing Web services. Primary purposes of BPMN are threefold:

- to provide a notation that is readily understandable by all business users, from business analysts creating initial drafts of the processes, to those performing processes or implementing technology to automate them and, finally, to business people who will manage and monitor those processes;
- to support the notation with an internal model that has formal execution semantics enabling process model execution, as well as declarative semantics to relate processes and interactions;
- to provide a standard interchange format for transfer of process and interaction models, and detailed visual information, between modelling tools [10].

A description of mining at a face made in the BPMN standard is shown in Fig. 3.

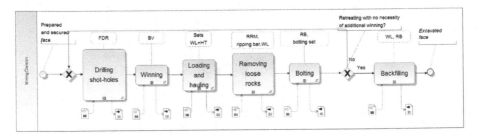

Fig. 3. Description of mining at a face in BPMN standard

The next parameter necessary for such description is condition of transport roads and in particular their silting, irregularities and breaches, gradient and waterlogging. It significantly affects the way of operation of loaders and haulage trucks. The worse condition of roads, the higher failure frequency of the machines and the lower mean velocity.

Condition of roads is the parameters difficult to describe, so this can be done by fuzzy logic that helps to manage effectively with many ambiguities and seems to be the best tool considering and interpreting this type parameters in industrial practice [4, 5].

1.4   Logistic Chain of the Winning Transport (Face, Loader, Conveyer, Output Shaft)

Examples of multi-agent systems used for modeling logistic chains are found in available publications [2], but little information is available about logistic processes in deep-sea mines.

Loading and hauling make a sub-process of the mining process. This sub-process is nested at two levels. The first level is the mining division in that planning and allocation of mining and haulage machines take place. At the division level, the main goal is haulage of ore from the faces to the discharge point or to stock. The preceding process is winning (shooting) the faces and the following one is bolting (securing) the faces. The machines – loaders and haulage trucks – are distributed to the blasted faces. Usually, there is more than one blasted face, so a decision must be taken, to which face a set L+HT is to be sent and to which a loader alone is enough. Such a decision can be taken with regard to variety of sizes and capacities of the loaders present in the given mining division. The machines and appliances are serviced and repaired in the heavy-equipment chamber.

The second decisive level on that loading and hauling take place is the face area. On the input to the process, winning at a strictly determined face is located, and on the output – ore hauled to the discharge point or to stock. In the case of a specific face, selection of the machines for loading is not arbitrary, since that decision was already taken at the level above, at the briefing conducted even before the process begins. The process of loading and hauling the winning is shown in Fig. 4. In a similar way, all stages of the bed mining, e.g. bolting or drilling shot-holes, are described. These diagrams are not shown here because of limited space of the paper.

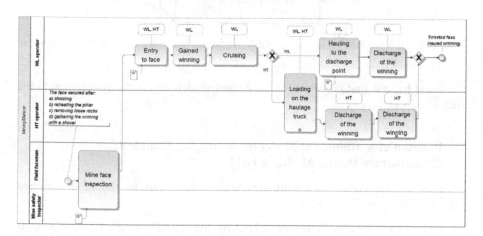

Fig. 4. Loading and haulage of winning

Both in the first and in the second case, the measure of the process effectiveness is volume of hauled ore in Mg per shift to the discharge point and machine-hours of the mining equipment.

The next stages of the logistic chain of the winning transport are as follows: winning is transported by belt conveyers joining together in main lines leading to the shaft station where the winning is stored and mixed with that from other mining fields and is often preliminarily broken-up. The next step is loading skips in the output shaft, transporting them up and unloading on the surface.

2   Design and Assumptions to the Multiagent Model of Ore Mining

The most important elements at designing agent models include: goals of the agents, their adaptive behaviour, decisive processes and interaction mechanisms. Behaviour of the agents is indirectly controlled by the environment; the agents perceive signals from their surrounding environment, process them and on that ground take decisions about their own behaviour. The agents react according to their internal principles, thus adapting their behaviour to the surrounding environment, see Fig. 5.

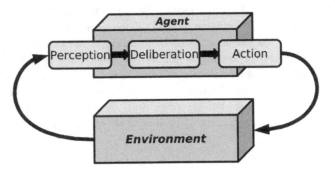

Fig. 5. Cyclical way of the agents' action – three-stage reaction to signals from the environment [1]

It could be said that properties of multiagent models are perfectly matched to the nature of mining processes.

2.1   Diagram of a Multiagent Model for Managing Technical Infrastructure During Mining a Field

Before starting construction of a multiagent model, a few questions should be answered to facilitate designing the model:

1. What specific problem should be solved by the model? What specific questions should the model answer? What value-added would agent-based modelling bring to the problem that other modelling approaches can not bring?
2. What should the agents be in the model? Who are the decision makers in the system? What are the entities that have behaviours? What data on agents are simply descriptive (static attributes)? What agent attributes would be calculated endogenously by the model and updated in the agents (dynamic attributes)?

3. What is the agents' environment? How do the agents interact with the environment? Is an agent's mobility through space an important consideration?
4. What agent behaviours are of interest? What decisions do the agents make? What behaviours are being acted upon? What actions are being taken by the agents?
5. How do the agents interact with each other? With the environment? How expansive or focused are agent interactions?
6. Where might the data come from, especially on agent behaviours, for such a model?
7. How might you validate the model, especially the agent behaviours? [6]

The answers for the a.m. questions should facilitate construction of multiagent models of variable systems.

2.2   General Description of the Model Idea

The main goals of a mining division to be considered in the suggested model can be defined as follows:

- to reach higher productivity of mining processes in individual mining divisions, maintaining the so-far existing output level (increase of production would require building new output shafts, which is not economically justified when the beds are depleting); the output shaft should be treated as a bottle-neck and efforts should be made to reach its highest utilisation degree (e.g. by utilising water storage reservoirs at the shaft station);
- to reach reduction of production costs in the entire production chain (previous attempts of reorganisation resulted most often in reduced costs in the rationalised area, but global costs increased);
- to guarantee continuous supply of the winning to the ore processing plant with respect to continuous nature of the enrichment process – discrete nature of the mining processes hinders realisation of this goal. Moreover, the winning should have possibly stable and high concentration of the acquired element (to increase effectiveness of the enrichment process);
- to rationalise reactions of mining divisions to disturbances of the processes realised in variable conditions of ground, dispersed on a large area, difficult to be directly controlled in the circumstances of a widespread underground network of galleries.

If a specific production level is maintained, higher productivity can be obtained only by better utilisation of the available technical infrastructure of the mine. The main components of technical microstructure of mining divisions include variable self-propelled trucks. It can be accepted in an intuitive way that each type truck will establish a separate agent. Mining works at a face are carried-out according to a technical project determining conditions for individual stages: drilling shot-holes (with use of face-drilling rigs FDR), winning (blasting vehicles BV), loading and hauling the winning (several types of wheeled loaders WL; for longer distances and larger loads – a set of a loader plus suitable number of haulage trucks HT), removing loose rocks (rock-ripping machines RRM) and bolting (bolting trucks BT). Smooth transition between the mentioned stages during cross-cutting and efficient retreating is essential for management of a mining field in the room-and-pillar system. It should be remembered that this is only a basic level of management and only a beginning of the logistic chain of transporting the gained winning.

An example showing how the environment changes behaviour of the agents can be the processes realised at the stages of cross-cutting and retreating. The same set of machines and appliances realises mining processes in a completely different way, according to the art of mining (e.g. a driller makes shot-holes acc. to various schemes), depending whether this is the cross-cutting stage or the retreating stage. The diagram demonstrating influences of the identified environments on the agents and relationships between them is shown in Fig. 6.

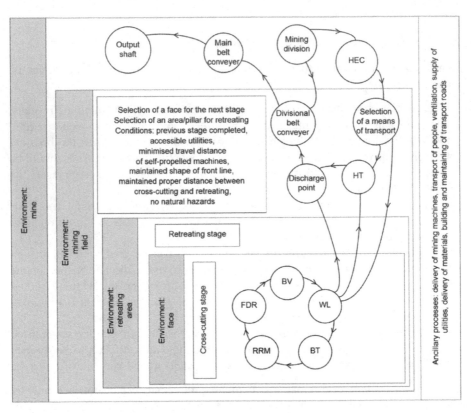

Fig. 6. Diagram of a multiagent model of ore gaining processes in the room-and-pillar system

The most important relations between the environment and the agents include: selection of a face for the next stage (similarly: selection of a pillar for the next stage at retreating), checking availability of utilities (required e.g. for drilling) or ensuring minimisation of the distance covered by the machines between the faces with maintained C-shape of the exploitation front. An important issue is also selection of a means of transport for the specific task and fulfilling the requirement of transporting a determined quantity of the winning at the determined distance (between faces and the discharge point) within the determined time of one working shift.

Selection of a tool for building a multiagent management model of technical infra-structure is not easy, even because of a large number of possibilities and differences between features of individual systems and simulation languages. A list of possible tools to be used for building a model is presented in Fig. 7; the available number of these tools causes that the task is not trivial. In addition, it should be noted that the list of modelling languages does not correspond with that of simulation packages.

List of Modelling languages		List of Simulation Software
ADELE-TEMPO, ALFA, AMBER, APPEL, APPL/A, ARIS, Articulator, BAM, BPEL4WS, BPML, Chou-UML. CIMOSA, Conversation Builder, CSP, CSPL, E3, EAI, ebXML, EDOC, EEML, ENVI12204, EPC, EPOS, EVPL, FUNSOFT, GEM, GREI, GRAPPLE, Hakoniwa, HFSP, IDES, IEM, ITM, JIL, LATIN, LOTOS, LSPI, MARVEL, Melmac, Merlin, M-VPL, OIKOS, OORAM, PADM, PEACE+, Petri Net, PMDB+, Process Weaver, Promenada, PSL, RAD, REA, Rosetta Net, SDL,SLANG, Socca, SPADE. SPELL. SPM, STATEMENT, System Dynamics, TEMPO, UEML, UML, UML2, UPM, Woflan, WPDL, XPDL, YAWL	$\neq$	@RISK, AgenRisk, Analytica 4.0, AnyLogic, Arena, Arena Contact Center, AutoMod, AutoShed AP, BusinessSimulationSoftware, Certified Distributions for use with Monte Carlo simulation, Crew Station Design Tool (CSDT), Crystal Ball Professional, Crystal Ball Standard, CSIM 19, CSIM for Java, eM-Planet, Emergency Department Simulator, Enterprise Dynamics. ExpertFit, ExtendSim AT, ExtendSim OR, ExtendSim, Suite, Flexsim CT (Container Terminals), Flexsim Simulation Software, Flexsim Warehouse Analyzer, ForeTell-DSS, GoldSim, GPSS/H, Integrated Performance Modelling Environment (IPME), L-SIM, Lean-Modeler, MAST, MedModel Optimization Suite, Micro Saint Sharp, mystrategy, NAG C Library, NeuralTools, Plant Simulation (=eM-Plant; =SiMPLE++), Portfolio Simulator, ProcessSimulator, ProcessModel Professional, Profimax, TechnoThermPlus, TechnicalAudit, TechnoMaint, TechnoPlan, TechnoCorr, TechnoBlend, Process Model for HPI, ProjectSimulator, ProMode Optimization Suite, Proof Animation, Quantitative Methods Software (QMS), Renque, SAIL, ServiceModel, Optimization Suite, ShowFlow 2, ShowFlow Simulation Software, Sigma, SimCad Pro, SIMPROCESS, SIMUL8 Professional, SIMUL8 Standard, SLIM, SLX. Stat::Fit, The DecisionsToolSuite, Vanguard System, VISIO Simulation Solution, WebGPSS, WITNESS Simulation, XLSim

Fig. 7. List of modelling languages and list of simulation software [7]

Final selection of a tool for building a multiagent model is a resultant of the agents' features and their usefulness for the specific case, but it often depends also on the degree in that these tools are known by the persons building the simulation model.

3 Summary

The processes of mining non-ferrous metal ore in an underground mine are multistage processes. During their execution, numerous interdependences exist between the stages, operated machines or appliances and natural conditions resulting from geotechnical parameters of the rocks. Complex nature of mining works can be best modelled by multiagent models. In natural way, self-propelled mining machines are suitable for modelling in form of agents performing determined tasks in the environment of a mining field. Before starting construction of the presented model, it appeared necessary to write shapes of the processes with the BPMN notation.

The task set to the multiagent model was formulated in a specific way: to increase productivity with unchanged level of ore output. Reaching the so defined goal is only possible with better utilisation of the machines and appliances designed for gaining the winning and of the remaining technical infrastructure.

References

1. Drogoul, A., et al.: Multi-agent systems and simulation: a survey from the agent community's perspective. In: Weyns, D., Uhrmacher, A. (eds.) Multi-Agent Systems. pp. 3–51 CRC Press (2009)
2. Hoffa, P., Pawlewski, P.: Agent based approach for modeling disturbances in supply chain. In: Corchado, Juan M., Bajo, J., Kozlak, J., Pawlewski, P., Molina, Jose M., Gaudou, B., Julian, V., Unland, R., Lopes, F., Hallenborg, K., García Teodoro, P. (eds.) PAAMS 2014. CCIS, vol. 430, pp. 144–155. Springer, Cham (2014). doi:10.1007/978-3-319-07767-3_14
3. Hustrulid, W., Bullock, R. (eds.): Underground Mining Methods. Engineering Fundamentals and International Case Studies. Society for Mining Metallurgy and Exploration Inc. (SME), Littleton (2001)
4. Kłosowski, G., et al.: Application of fuzzy logic controller for machine load balancing in discrete manufacturing system. Found. Manag. **4**, 1 (2012)
5. Kłosowski, G., et al.: Application of fuzzy logic in assigning workers to production tasks. In: Omatu, S., et al. (eds.) Distributed Computing and Artificial Intelligence, pp. 505–513. Springer International Publishing, Cham (2016)
6. Macal, C.M., North, M.J.: Tutorial on agent-based modelling and simulation. J. Simul. **4**(3), 151–162 (2010)
7. Pawlewski, P.: Multimodal approach to modeling of manufacturing processes. Procedia CIRP. **17**, 716–720 (2014)
8. Saniuk, A., et al.: Environmental favourable foundries through maintenance activities. Metalurgija. **54**(4), 725–728 (2015)
9. Stefaniak, P., et al.: Idea syntezy informacji z systemu monitoringu samojezdnych maszyn górniczych na potrzeby oceny efektywności pracy operatorów. Presented at the Szkoła Eksploatacji Podziemnej, Kraków September 15 (2015)
10. White, S.A., Bock, C.: BPMN 2.0 Handbook Second Edition: Methods, Concepts, Case Studies and Standards in Business Process Management Notation. Future Strategies Inc., Lighthouse Point (2011)

Analysis of the Survival of Complex Systems with an Actions Coordination Mechanism

Katarzyna Grzybowska and Patrycja Hoffa-Dabrowska[✉]

Chair of Production Engineering and Logistics, Faculty of Engineering
Management, Poznan University of Technology, Strzelecka 11,
60-965 Poznan, Poland
{katarzyna.grzybowska,
patrycja.hoffa-dabrowska}@put.poznan.pl

Abstract. A complex system, as is the supply chain, should be characterized by durability, denoting the ability to resist rapid change and the ability to survive. It was hypothesized: if a complex system survives one month, with a quantity of 2 Business Relations it is to be presumed that the system was built relatively strong and durable. The paper presents results of the simulation of the Supply Chains with the mechanism of coordination of actions as well as the results of the survival analysis of the simulated objects, with appropriate comments.

Keywords: Coordination activity · Supply chain · Complex systems · Survival analysis · Multimodal networks · Simulation

1 Introduction

A feature of the contemporary complex systems is the continuous expansion of economic impact in space. Not only the structure and the configuration of complex systems undergo constant change, but also their activity and scope of action. Therefore, they require modeling and problem solving as well as optimization [1, 2]. The publication is focused on the issue of cooperation and learning of complex systems (supply chains). In the supply chains there are a number of economic organizations that wish to cooperate in order to make a profit. They join the cooperation as others have done before (coordination occurs). If the cooperation in the supply chain has not been interrupted and is followed by cooperation in the subsequent orders, then such a system can be determined as relatively strong and durable. This also means that the system learns and gains experience. Two hypotheses can be drawn from combining the fact: if the complex system survives 1 month period it must be assumed that the constructed system is relatively strong and durable.

The aim of the publication is to present the results of a simulation experiment using the program FlexSim and to convey an empirical analysis of the survival of the simulated supply chains. The structure of work is as follows: the second part presents the necessary information concerning the analysis of survival. The areas of application of survival analysis were identified as well as its potential. The third part discusses the simulation model. It was indicated which mechanism of action coordination was applied in the simulation experiments and showed their results. The next part was

© Springer International Publishing AG 2017
J. Bajo et al. (Eds.): PAAMS 2017 Workshops, CCIS 722, pp. 197–208, 2017.
DOI: 10.1007/978-3-319-60285-1_17

devoted to the survival analysis performed on the basis of the conducted experiments. The paper concludes with a summary and conclusions.

2 Survival Analysis – Basic Information

Survival analysis covers various statistical techniques of analyzing random variables concerning time from a well defined starting point to an occurrence of a specific event, which is regarded as the end point [3, 4]. A well defined end point is definite and certain if at the time of conclusion of the analysis it is known that the object does not change its state. The survival analysis allows for constructing models of survival, studying their features and characteristics. The scope of application of the survival analysis is broad, e.g. reliability analysis [5, 6], duration analysis [7, 8]. This applies both to multiple disciplines and research areas. For the purpose of the work the authors have attempted to analyze the interaction of complex systems with a mechanism of action coordination.

2.1 General Model of Survival

The survival model is the probability distribution of a positive random variable. It takes the time elapsed since the initial moment into account, which is "the appearance of the object", until the occurrence of an event. This time is a random variable. The event, which occurs during the test, is valid for the object and associated with the phenomenon observed [10]. It is assumed that the observed object can experience an event ending only once in an observation. This event is the end point determining the "death". The event should be understood as a transition from one state to another (e.g. the death of the patient, equipment failure, interruption of cooperation).

On the basis of the initial and end point (event-free survival) survival time of the object examined can be determined. The survival time of the tested object is not identical with the duration of the study. Therefore, the time of observation of each object is individual. Consequently, the individual survival time is calculated from the moment of its incorporation to the test until the occurrence of the end point or interruption of the observation due to the termination of the study.

The study may incorporate cut observations (Fig. 1). These are observations that do not specify the exact survival time. This is closely connected with the analysis of survival. One reason for the lack of endpoint information is the non-occurrence of the end point to the end of the study. Figure 1 is an example of the observation of a number of individual objects, three out of which are considered as cut off.

Figure 1 shows exemplary individual times of inclusion in the study. Objects C, E and F were included in the study at the moments when the test was already taking place. The cut observations of objects were also shown - they are: A, C and F. Here end point was not observed during the study (termination of cooperation). This prevents the accurate measurement of time to the occurrence of the end point, because it is beyond the scope of time for the completion of the study. Hence the data on the objects of the study are "cut from the right side." The observations of objects B, D and E resulted in the end point.

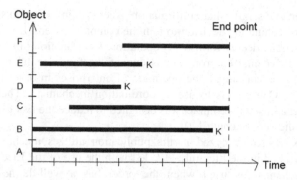

Fig. 1. Individual survival time of exemplary objects including different time inclusion in the study – data censored due to the date of completion of the study; own study based on [10]

The survival analysis allows comparing the probability of survival/hazard between the different groups of objects. The survival function can be estimated using the estimator proposed by Kaplan and Meyer according to the formula [9]:

$$S(t) = \prod_{t_j \le t} \left(1 - \frac{m_t}{n_t}\right) \tag{1}$$

where:

$S(t)$ – estimated survival function,

Π – symbol of the product,

m_t – number of objects in which end point occurred in the t period,

n_t – number of all objects exposed to occurrence of end point in the t period.

S(t) signifies unconditional probability that the event occurs after t moment, and hence that the cooperation will last at least until t moment. This function expresses the pattern of survival in the examined population.

The method uses a logical assumption: a complex system such as the supply chain, in order to maintain cooperation for e.g. 10 units of time in the study, must survive all the previous units of time and the end point cannot occur in the 10th unit of time of an individual observation. The unit of time determines any accepted measure of time. Product-Limit Estimator specifies the survival probability of t periods, where t takes on the value of *1, 2, ..., k* and *k-th* period is the last subject of observation. To determine the probability of survival, e.g. in 10 units of time, the survival probability of further, previous months, provided the event-free survival [11].

3   Simulation Model

3.1   Complex System with a Coordination Mechanism

Each complex system, such as a supply chain, [12, 13], a production system [14–18], a transport system is composed of several subsystems with interactions [19]. So as to effectively cooperate it should share information. Access to information seems to be the main driving force behind the decision to join the complex system. It is also a gateway to undertake closer and deeper forms of cooperation. Coordination of enterprises in the supply chain in a dynamic environment is one of the fundamental problems in the supply chains: how to coordinate the operation of enterprises in order to successfully complete the task? One way is to use a coordination mechanism. There is a known coordination mechanism with contract was designed to reduce the risk of ordering from every partner in the supply chain [20].

The complex system analyzed in the publication utilizes mechanism of action coordination discussed in the literature [12, 13] with the use of the Electronic Bulletin Board. This mechanism is used when the order has a well-defined structure of sub-contracts or sub-tasks. In order to create a reference model (Fig. 2), the modified methodology IDEF0.

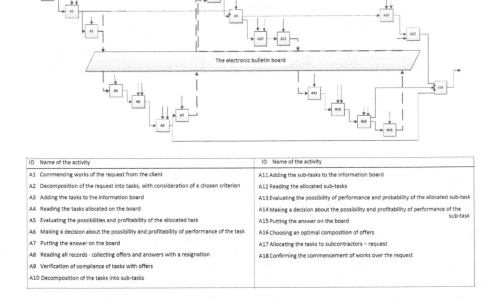

ID	Name of the activity	ID	Name of the activity
A1	Commencing works of the request from the client	A11	Adding the sub-tasks to the information board
A2	Decomposition of the request into tasks, with consideration of a chosen criterion	A12	Reading the allocated sub-tasks
A3	Adding the tasks to the information board	A13	Evaluating the possibility of performance and probability of the allocated sub-task
A4	Reading the tasks allocated on the board	A14	Making a decision about the possibility and profitability of performance of the sub-task
A5	Evaluating the possibilities and profitability of the allocated task	A15	Putting the answer on the board
A6	Making a decision about the possibility and profitability of performance of the task	A16	Choosing an optimal composition of offers
A7	Putting the answer on the board	A17	Allocating the tasks to subcontractors – request
A8	Reading all records - collecting offers and answers with a resignation	A18	Confirming the commencement of works over the request
A9	Verification of compliance of tasks with offers		
A10	Decomposition of the tasks into sub-tasks		

Fig. 2. Reference model: the Electronic Bulletin Board [13]

3.2 Simulation Model – General Information and Experiments

For the purposes of this article was using the simulation model with using the Electronic Bulletin Board. This model is detailed described in [12, 13]. But some assumptions and changes were made. Firstly, on this simulation only one size of order was considered: the small order. On the size of order depend: the time of each activity, number of tasks and subtask for one order. These information stay unchanged. In the first step of research it was decided to research the time of survival for the one size of orders. The reason of not mixing the different orders (of various sizes) was following: (1) the complexity of process – many operations, (2) using a random distribution for description each processes time and (3) possibility of clear analysis the results for one type or order.

Second change is: a share of positive decisions (expressed in %) in the two decision-making points (A5 and A13) defined as 80%. Third, and the biggest change is adding the transportation part in the simulation model. Figure 2 present only decision process, which consist of 18 operations. In this case authors decided to added a transport activity in the analysis. Authors divided new version of model with using the Electronic Bulletin Board into two parts: first is decision part and second – transportation part. The transportation part consists of three operation:

- T1 – the operation of transport realization.
- T2 – the operation of determination the satisfaction level of the implemented service.
- T3 – the operation of checking the service's satisfaction and making the decision of reject the object or re-admission to the circulation (the decision on further cooperation).

The algorithm of transportation part with all details is presented at Fig. 3.

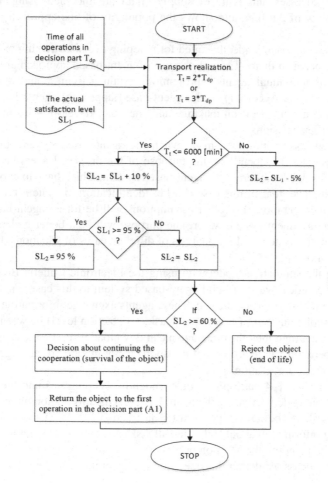

Fig. 3. The algorithm of transportation part; own study

For the described model the experiments were performed. The goal of these research was the analysis of the survival of complex systems with an actions coordination mechanism. The observed values in experiments were:

(1) the survival time for object – it consists of decision and transportation operation time for each cycle.
(2) the satisfaction level of the implemented service – using for verification the proper operation of the model.
(3) number of cycle for each object (organizations) – it shows how many times was undertaken the cooperation with this object. It depends on satisfaction level.

In the next part of this article, according to the theme of this paper, authors focus only at the analysis of the survival time for object.

3.3   Agent Based Approach in Logistics

The logistics processes and issue of supply chain are modeled using agent-based approach. Review of the literature shows the popularity of this approach in analyzed area [21–27].

Agent-based approach is ideally suited for mapping decision-making processes and the interaction between them. Through the use of agent-based approach are simulated: the behavior of individual agents representing certain activities, and also relations between these agents. According to the agent-based approach, agents have a certain freedom of action – in decision-making, and they can develop – learning through making the earlier decisions.

The different assumptions are made when the agent-based system for a specific system are designed. It depends on the purpose of the proposed agent-based system. The assumptions will be different for agent-based system, which have to cooperate with existing system. The goal in this case can be: identification of system properties, the improvement the operation. The other assumptions will be for an agent-based system for a virtual environment system, where the purpose will be a better understanding of the processes in the system and the analysis of different cases of situations, for example in critical situations [27].

Analyzing the simulation model with using the Electronic Bulletin Board, authors noticed two theoretical ways of build agent-based system to this case. First, presented at Fig. 4, in which 6 agents are created. These agents exchange information about each order (for example: number of task and subtask, satisfaction level) between each other or they can write it (and then the other agent can download it) to the Electronic Bulletin Board. The operation T1 (realization of transport) is not in range of any agent, because this is not a decision operation.

While the agents 1–4 can operate independently, keeping in mind the transfer of information about ended activities, the agent No. 5 needs information on the number of tasks and subtasks to be able to perform the last action for the analyzed order. Only after gathering information about end of the all tasks and subtasks, agent no 5 can make the decision about ending the decision process for this order. After that will be done the transportation process. And after this operation the agent no 6 will be active. This agent

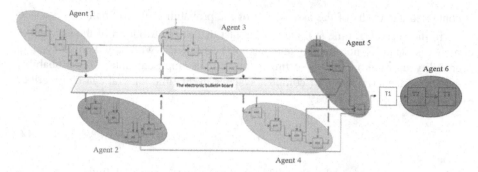

Fig. 4. The electronic bulletin board – proposition of agents number; own study

needs information about whole decision process and satisfaction level for this order, so he have to contact with other agents (or download this information from Electronic Bulletin Board).

Another solution is to replace the 6 described agents through one, which collects the necessary information at each stage of the process and then makes a proper decision. The work of agent can be supported by informatics system – the Electronic Bulletin Board, in which partial and final information can be stored.

Referring the proposed solutions to the real conditions – in the case of a small company (which realizes several orders in one time) the solution with a single agent will imitate the work of one person, who is responsible for analyzed process. In the case of company which takes many orders in the same time, it would be impossible for one person to remember all the information – so the variant with 6 agents – 6 employees will be more appropriate. In this case it is possible use a version with 1 agent, but it is necessary to have appropriate information system which will support the work. Basic property of this system has to be possibility of saving information at every stage of realization the decision process for each orders. Of course, the way of mapping the decision-making process in real case and the number of agents must be adapted to each analyzed case.

4 Results of the Survival Analysis

The analysis of survival of a simulated complex system takes the following assumptions into account: (1) the objects of observation are simulated complex systems; (2) were analysed 200 objects; (3) the survival time of the examined objects is the total operating time; (4) The data covers the period 6 months; (5) the initial event is the starting point of observation of a simulated process; (6) the final event for the object is the end point or the end of the study.

The overall survival analysis distinguishes the following models: parametric, semi-parametric and non-parametric. For the purpose of the work, the non-parametric, tabular model will be adopted, because unlike parametric models, non-parametric models make no assumptions about the probability distributions of the variables being assessed. A cohort table of the simulated complex systems was developed (Table 1).

It contained the results of the assessment of the probability of termination of cooperation in the interval of time ($\hat{f_t}$). Due to the fact that the distribution of the survival of complex systems is not known and cannot be assigned with any known type of probability distribution, it was estimated based on empirical data. The probability estimator on the termination of complex systems in the time interval can be described by the formula $\hat{f_t}$:

$$\hat{f_t} = \frac{m_t}{n_t} \tag{2}$$

Another parameter is the S(t). This is the estimated survival function and was presented earlier. It determines the probability that a complex system cannot survive after time $t + 1$. Evaluated survival function decreases with time. The speed with which it decreases, known as the intensity function (hazard) ($\hat{h_t}$) depends on the duration of the complex system. It can be described by the formula:

$$\hat{h_t} = \frac{\hat{f_t}}{(S_t + S_{t+1})/2} \tag{3}$$

Table 1. The cohort table of survival of simulated complex systems; own work

Intervals of duration time	Number of objects that survived	Number of objects, which have not survived	Number of objects, which have censored	Probability estimator on the termination of complex systems f(t)	Estimated survival function S(t)	Intensity function (hazard) Ht
					1	
0	200	113	0	0.565	0.435	0.788
1. month	87	1	0	0.011	0.430	0.027
2. month	86	1	0	0.012	0.425	0.027
3. month	85	1	0	0.012	0.420	0.028
4. month	84	1	0	0.012	0.415	0.029
5. month	83	69	0	0.831	0.070	3.428
6. month	14	9	5	0.643	0.070	9.183

The cohort table of survival of simulated complex systems is presented in Table 1. In the cohort survival table (Table 1), the first column contains intervals of duration time of the simulated complex systems (objects). Monthly periods of time were established. The column shows the beginning of the interval, which is also the moment of observation. The second column indicates the number of simulated objects that survived to the designated point of observation. The output population of the analyzed cohort amounted to 200 subjects. With time, this number is reduced by the number of objects, which have not survived (third column) and the censored (fourth column).

A total of 113 objects did not survive in the first period from the start of the study until the end of the first month. In the subsequent time intervals the number of objects that did not survive is considerably lower. It is rising again in the penultimate time interval with a number of 69 objects. Throughout the study, 195 of the simulated complex systems did not last. Termination of the cooperation was associated with a lack of satisfaction with the implemented service. The level of satisfaction with the cooperation could not be lower than 60%.

Five of the simulated objects were censored in the study. This means that these objects have survived until the last moment of observation, which is the end of the study. They represent 3% of the study cohort. It is also worth noting that after the first month of the cooperation 87 objects have survived, which accounts for 44% of the study sample. At the end of the fifth month the number of objects that have survived is 83 (42%).

Table 1 provides an assessment of the probability objects, which have not survived (column 5). The probability of termination of cooperation (not surviving of the simulated complex systems) in the first period of time is the highest. The analysis of the circulation of orders indicates that the probability relates to objects with one or two circuits. It constitutes the value of 0.565 and then drops to a level of 0.012, in order to increase again in the final interval to a value of 0.831. Preliminary assessment and verification of the conditions of cooperation may last from a few to several business relations. The study draws attention to the fact that after exceeding five business relations the stabilization of the cooperation occurs, increasing involvement in business relations.

The table also presents the estimated function of the simulated objects. The survival function for all objects (Fig. 5) confirms the great psychological significance of the early stages of cooperation, which determine the continuance of the complex system. The estimated survival function decreases with time, only to increase rapidly once again to a value of 0.831.

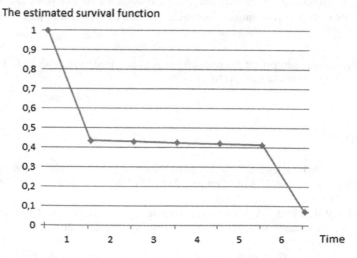

Fig. 5. The estimated survival function; own work

The final column of the table presents an assessment of the hazard function. This is a function of the intensity, which denotes the risk of termination of cooperation provided that it did not occur until the end of the study. The results of this function indicate that after the first time interval the probability of not surviving within the next time interval is much lower. The intensity function for the tested cohort of objects takes the shape of the letter U, with a minimum in the time interval of 2–5 months. Therefore, after exceeding these time intervals the risk of termination of cooperation increases again.

5 Conclusion

For the purpose of the article a simulation of 200 objects was performed, which were subsequently subjected to survival analysis. The results of the analysis indicate that the probability of the termination of the cooperation in the first time interval is the highest. Survival analysis is highly useful in assessing the risk of losing a business partner in a supply chain. Allows you to specify time periods for which the probability of losing a business partner is greatest. It also indicates the time intervals of the least probability. The study confirms that if the conditions of the cooperation are satisfactory in the first business contacts (the lower limit is two business relations) there is a large chance to build a relatively stable and strong system. Further positive business relationships lead to the integration of companies in the system by reducing the level of uncertainty and risk. The analysis conducted confirmed the hypothesis: if the complex system survives one month having a number of two business relations, it should be assumed that the constructed system is relatively strong and durable.

Presented model has plenty of possibilities for its development, because of assumptions and simplifications which were made during built this model. First proposition of developing is analyzing the survival time for medium and big task also, not only small tasks. Thanks to this it will be possible to defined time of cooperation in case of more complexity cases. An interesting direction for further work is also analyze the possibility of hiring few entities for realization the transportation part, not only one entity.

Acknowledgements. Support for this research has been provided by the Faculty of Engineering Management 503217/11/140/DSPB/4150.

References

1. Sitek, P.: A hybrid approach to the two-echelon capacitated vehicle routing problem (2E-CVRP). Adv. Intell. Syst. Comput. **267**, 251–263 (2014). doi:10.1007/978-3-319-05353-0_25
2. Sitek, P., Wikarek, J.: A hybrid programming framework for modeling and solving con-straint satisfaction and optimization problems. Sci. Program. **2016** (2016). doi:10.1155/2016/5102616
3. Miller, R.G., Gong, G., Munoz, A.: Survival Analysis. Wiley, New York (1981)

4. Collett, D.: Modelling Survival Data in Medical Research. Chapman & Hall, London (1994)
5. Chakraborty, S., Chowdhury, R.: A semi-analytical framework for structural reliability analysis. Comput. Methods Appl. Mech. Eng. **289**, 475–497 (2015)
6. Wrachien, N., Cester, A., et al.: Reliability study of organic complementary logic inverters using constant voltage stress. Solid-State Electron. **113**, 151–156 (2015)
7. Castro, V.: The duration of economic expansions and recessions: more than duration dependence. J. Macroecon. **32**(1), 347–365 (2010)
8. Relich, M.: Portfolio selection of new product projects: a product reliability perspective. Eksploatacja i Niezawodnosc-Maint. Reliab. **18**(4), 613–620 (2016)
9. Kaplan, E., Meier, P.: Nonparametric estimator from incomplete observations. J. Am. Stat. Assoc. **53**(282), 457–481 (1958)
10. Balicki, A.: Analiza przeżycia i tablice wymieralności. PWE, Warszawa (2006)
11. Bland, J.M., Altman, D.G.: Survival probabilities the Kaplan-Meier method. BMJ **317**, 1572 (1998)
12. Grzybowska, K., Kovács, G.: Logistics process modelling in supply chain – algorithm of coordination in the supply chain – contracting. Adv. Intell. Syst. Comput. **299**, 311–320 (2014)
13. Grzybowska, K., Hoffa, P.: Approving with application of an electronic bulletin board, as a mechanism of coordination of actions in complex systems. In: Omatu, S., Malluhi, Q.M., Gonzalez, S.R., Bocewicz, G., Bucciarelli, E., Giulioni, G., Iqba, F. (eds.) 12th International Conference Distributed Computing and Artificial Intelligence, AISC, vol. 373, pp. 357–365. Springer, Cham (2015). doi:10.1007/978-3-319-19638-1_41
14. Burduk, A.: An attempt to adapt serial reliability structures for the needs of analyses and assessments of the risk in production systems. Eksploatacja i Niezawodność – Maint. Reliab. (3) 85–96 (2010)
15. Majdzik, P., Akielaszek-Witczak, A., Seybold, L., Stetter, R., Mrugalska, B.: A fault-tolerant approach to the control of a battery assembly system. Control Eng. Pract. **55**, 139–148 (2016)
16. Burduk, A., Jagodziński, M.: Assessment of production system stability with the use of the FMEA analysis and simulation lmodels. In: Jackowski, K., Burduk, R., Walkowiak, K., Woźniak, M., Yin, H. (eds.) IDEAL 2015. LNCS, vol. 9375, pp. 216–223. Springer, Cham (2015). doi:10.1007/978-3-319-24834-9_26
17. Jasiulewicz-Kaczmarek, M.: Participatory Ergonomics as a Method of Quality Improvement in Maintenance. In: Karsh, B.-T. (ed.) Ergonomics and Health Aspects. EHAWC 2009. LNCS, vol. 5624, pp. 153–161. Springer-Verlag, Heidelberg (2009). doi:10.1007/978-3-642-02731-4_18
18. Butlewski, M., Slawinska, M.: Ergonomic method for the implementation of occupational safety systems. In: Occupational Safety and Hygiene Ii, pp. 621–626 (2014)
19. Relich, M.: Identifying project alternatives with the use of constraint programming. In: Borzemski, L., Grzech, A., Świątek, J., Wilimowska, Z. (eds.) Information Systems Architecture and Technology: Proceedings of 37th International Conference on Information Systems Architecture and Technology – ISAT 2016 – Part I. AISC, vol. 521, pp. 3–13. Springer, Cham (2017). doi:10.1007/978-3-319-46583-8_1
20. Fu, X., Dong, M., Han, G.: Coordinating a trust-embedded two-tier supply chain by options with multiple transaction periods. Int. J. Product. Res. **55**, 1–15 (2017)
21. Allwood, J.M., Lee, J.H.: The design of an agent for modelling supply chain network dynamics. Int. J. Prod. Res. **43**(22), 4875–4898 (2005)
22. Baykasoglu, A., Kaplanoglu, V.: A multi-agent approach to load consolidation in transpor-tation. Adv. Eng. Softw. **42**, 477–490 (2011)

23. Janssen, M.: The architecture and business value of a semi-cooperative, agent-based supply chain management system. Electron. Commer. Res. Appl. **4**(4), 315–328 (2005)
24. Krejci, C.C., Beamon, B.M.: Modeling food supply using Multi-Agent Simulation. In: Winter Simulation Conference, pp. 1167–1178 (2012)
25. Lau, J.S.K., Huang, G.Q., and Mak, K.L.: Impacts of sharing production information on supply chain dynamics: a multi-agent simulation study. In: Proceedings of the 30th International Conference of Computers & Industrial engineering, 29 June–2 July, Tinos Island, Greece, pp. 527–532 (2002)
26. Mangina, E., Vlachos, I.P.: The changing role of information technology in food and beverage logistics management: beverage network optimization using intelligent agent technology. J. Food Eng. **70**(3), 403–420 (2005)
27. Nawarecki, E., Koźlak, J.: Agentowy model systemu logistycznego. Automatyka **13**(2), 494–500 (2009)

A Multi-level Framework for Simulating Milk-Run, In-plant Logistics Operations

Allen G. Greenwood$^{(\boxtimes)}$, Kamila Kluska, and Pawel Pawlewski

Poznan University of Technology, ul.Strzelecka 11, 60-965 Poznań, Poland
{allen.greenwood, pawel.pawlewski}@put.poznan.pl,
kamila.kluska@student.put.poznan.pl

Abstract. This paper proposes a framework that provides the basis for simulating in-plant logistics systems that use the milk-run concept. Simulation is a major tool used to design and improve system operations and performance. The multi-level framework defines the major components that are needed to represent the operation of such systems, including the physical actions of vehicles and operators, logistics activities, and strategic-level planning and decision variables. Based on the framework, a hybrid modeling approach that includes both discrete-event and agent-based simulation modeling is recommended.

Keywords: Agents · Logistics systems · Milk run · Simulation

1 Introduction

The handling of materials is a key activity in any production system; and in many industries, it contributes a significant portion of total manufacturing cost. Material handling activities are generally referred to as in-plant logistics and involve: (1) supplying raw materials to production areas, (2) collecting finished goods from production areas and transporting to a warehouse, (3) supplying work-in-progress materials from production areas to other production areas for further processing, and (4) returning empty containers that are used to transport materials to their storage areas. The first three activities are considered primary transport activities and the return of empty containers is considered secondary.

Of course, in-plant logistics involves more than just physically moving material between locations. It involves deciding what and when to move the material and by what means. This is done by considering the availability of materials at their source areas and the need requirements for materials where they are used.

Since in-plant logistics processes have a significant effect on overall system performance, it is the focus of many studies and improvement projects. In many cases, discrete-event simulation (DES) modeling and analysis is used to assist with, and enhance, the design, assessment, and analysis of alternative approaches in order to identify the best option in terms of cost and service [3].

There are many approaches for operating in-plant logistics systems, but one that is of increasing interest, especially for lean production systems with small lot sizes, is referred to as a milk-run system.

© Springer International Publishing AG 2017
J. Bajo et al. (Eds.): PAAMS 2017 Workshops, CCIS 722, pp. 209–220, 2017.
DOI: 10.1007/978-3-319-60285-1_18

While a milk-run approach provides operational benefits, it is more challenging to design and to model. Rather than just responding to primarily single requests for material from production areas, a milk-run system is more proactive and involves handling multiple material requests in one transport. The single multi-material transport may be made either based on a fixed schedule or a fixed route. The planning of routes adds considerable complexity to material-handling process design and thus to its modeling and simulation.

The main reasons for using a simulation model is to understand the dynamics of a system, i.e. how its behavior changes over time, and to predict its performance, especially in comparison to alternatives. How a system behaves over time is determined by the many, and typically complex, interactions among its components and by variability inherent in its components. Variability is introduced through nondeterministic process times, random downtimes, changing production plans that cause uneven demand for materials, etc.

The objective of this paper is to provide a framework for representing the operation of in-plant logistics systems that use the milk-run concept. The framework provides the foundation for simulating such systems so that alternative designs and policies can be considered and performance assessed.

This paper is organized as follows. Section 2 defines in-plant logistics systems in general and Sect. 3 defines those that use the milk-run concept. Section 4 defines and describes a modeling framework for simulating milk-run systems. Section 5 identifies some modeling approaches using the proposed framework. Section 6 provides conclusions and plans for further research.

2   In-plant Logistics Systems

As mentioned earlier, in-plant logistics systems involve a series of flows, including:

1. supplying production areas with materials that are needed for production; i.e., picking up raw materials from storage areas and delivering them to production areas,
2. collecting finished goods from production areas; i.e., picking up materials from production areas and delivering them to finished product storage areas,
3. supplying work-in-progress materials from production areas to other production areas for further processing, and
4. returning empty containers that are used to transport materials to their storage areas.

The basic flows defined above are illustrated in Fig. 1. The solid flow lines in Fig. 1a are the primary objective of an in-plant logistics system, to deliver: (1) raw material from various storage areas (denoted as R) to production areas (denoted as P), (2) in-process items between production areas, (3) production items to finished product storage areas (denoted as F), or any combination of these. In addition, counter flows to these are also possible, as indicated by the dashed flow lines in the figure. These secondary flows in an in-plant logistics system represent the possible return of empty, reusable containers that hold the delivered materials. While the diagram on the left side of the figure defines the flow relationships between the areas (e.g., from R1 to P1), the diagram/layout in Fig. 1b displays the locations of the areas and their spatial relationships. Both must be considered in the design of an in-plant logistics system.

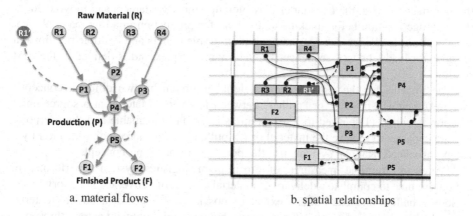

a. material flows   b. spatial relationships

Fig. 1. Example material flows and spatial relationships in an in-plant logistics system.

Material is either loaded or unloaded at each of the areas shown in Fig. 1. The places where materials are loaded/unloaded in each area are indicated in Fig. 1b by dark circles. These are referred to as either source-points, e.g. R1, or use-points, e.g. P1; they may also denote stop locations for logistics trains. For the primary flows, a material is either: (1) loaded at a R and unloaded at a P (e.g., R1 to P1), (2) loaded at a P and unloaded at a F (e.g., P5 to F1), or (3) loaded at a P and unloaded at another P (e.g., P2 to P4). The opposite is true for the secondary flows. Since empty containers are oftentimes physically stored in a different location from the material, different areas are designated in the diagram. For example, the secondary flow from P1 to R1 in the diagram involves a different location at R and thus is denoted as R1'. Similarly, multiple intermediate products may move between production areas and thus must be differentiated. For example, P1 may produce two different components needed by P4; therefore, they may be denoted as P1.1 and P1.2.

Therefore, the basic operation performed by an in-plant logistics system is to move a quantity q of material m between two points, from a source location to a use location, i.e., from a to b. The move operation is denoted as $m[a, b, q]$ and involves three tasks, load q units of m at a, travel from a to b, and unload q units of m at b. Thus:

$$m[a, b, q] \rightarrow \{load(m, a, q) + travel(a, b) + unload(m, b, q)\} \qquad (1)$$

Each location has a name and a position that is defined in terms of x and y coordinates relative to a reference point. Therefore, a and b are actually defined as $a(x, y)$ and $b(x, y)$. However, for simplicity, we drop the spatial notation. Locations may also be positioned in the z direction, but this is ignored here, again for simplicity.

This notation is appropriate for a material handling system that processes one load at a time, such as with a fork truck, pallet jack, etc. The single load approach uses a simple repetitive task sequence: travel to source point, load, travel to use point, unload, and repeat. The task sequence might involve a shorter segment prior to returning to a source in order to minimize traveling empty. For example, the basic transport activity might be from a raw material storage area to a production line, but before returning to the raw material area, the transporter may pick up empty containers and move them to their storage location before picking a new load for production in a raw material area.

The multi-load approach uses a train with multiple trailers and multiple positions in a trailer for loads. Its task sequence is much more complex and is defined in the next section.

The impetus for the movement of material is driven by two different concepts; material is either "pushed" or "pulled" between locations. Material at a source-point location is either: (1) pushed to a use-point as it becomes available and the use point has the capacity to receive the material or (2) pulled from a source-point location by a use-point's need. Kanban systems use the pull type of handling concept.

There are multiple measures of an in-plant logistics system's performance, including: time to complete a delivery of material or a set of deliveries, inventory levels at source buffers and use buffers, extent of possible shortages at a buffer (material outage), the amount of time buffers operate below a minimum inventory threshold, utilization of resources, such as operators, transport equipment, etc. These measures are typically summarized as averages and percentiles.

3   In-plant Logistics Systems Using a Milk-Run Approach

This section first defines in-plant logistics systems and then describes its basic components and operations.

3.1   Definition of Milk-Run Systems

The concept of logistics milk-run systems is derived from the dairy industry where a tanker truck collects milk every day from several farmers and delivers a full truckload to a processing plant [1]. This basically involves mixed loads from different suppliers. Another derivation of the term is from the former practice of delivering milk to homes, where a milkman's daily route involves both delivering full bottles of milk to customers and picking up their empty bottles.

In terms of manufacturing, milk-run systems were first used outside of the plant, as a means to connect suppliers. For example, instead of five suppliers each sending a truck once a week to a customer in order to meet its weekly demand, one truck visits each supplier daily. While five vehicle loads are still shipped each week, each vehicle load delivers the customer's full daily requirements from each supplier [1].

As defined by Klenk and Galka [4], an in-plant milk-run system is a transport concept to supply various goods to various points of end use in one run. Typically, the milk run uses a fixed route. In some cases, it operates on a fixed schedule ([5] references [4]).

3.2   General System Description

Figure 2 provides a sample of views of in-plant milk-run systems. These views are used to identify and define the key components of such a system, such as a material mover or logistics train (a), interactions at the use- and source-points, (b) and (c) respectively, and loading/unloading operations (d).

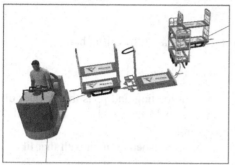

a. material mover, logistics train
Source: own study

b. interaction at a use-point, work cell
Source: www.aberle-automation.asia

c. interaction at a source-point, storage area
Source: www.konekesko.com

d. material loading/unloading
Source: jungheinrich.com

Fig. 2. Various views of in-plant material-handling systems.

Since the focus of the system is on materials, materials are a key component. They have a range of sizes and shapes and are of four main types: raw material, work in process, finished products, and reusable devices that contain the materials (e.g. totes, bins, and fixtures).

Milk-run systems use a multi-load approach, rather than the single-load approach defined in Sect. 2; therefore, the general notation needs to be modified. As described further below, a milk-run system uses a train with multiple trailers that has a route composed of stops at various points between a beginning point a and a concluding point b, either to load/unload different materials or the same material.

If a material is unloaded at several positions, q then depends on multiple bs. Thus, a more general expression for (1) is:

$$m[a,\ b,\ q] \rightarrow \{load(m,\ a, \Sigma q_i) + travel(a,\ b_i) + unload(m,\ b_i,\ q_i)\} \quad (2)$$

The material may need to be loaded onto specific trailers and in specific locations on the trailers. Similarly, the material may need to be unloaded from multiple trailer locations and multiple trailers. In both cases, when multiple trailers are involved, the operator needs to interrupt a load/unload activity in order to move the train to into position for a subsequent trailer. Therefore, a more general formulation of the tasks associated with a material move is:

$$m[a,\ b,\ q] \rightarrow \{load(m,\ a, \Sigma q_i) + p_l * pos(a) + travel(a,\ b_i)$$

$$+ unload(m,\ b_i,\ q_i) + p_u * pos(m,\ b)\} \quad (3)$$

where p_l is the number of positioning tasks, pos($\bullet$), at loading and p_u is the number of positioning tasks at unloading, (p_l, $p_u \geq 1$) since each load/unload task requires the proper positioning of a trailer and a source/use point.

The travel activity for material from a to b is accomplished along a path that likely involves stops between a and b for loading and unloading other materials.

Logistics Train

A key component in any logistics system is the material mover. In a milk-run system, materials are transported via a logistics train that is composed of: (1) a number of trailers that actually carry the materials, (2) a tugger or lead vehicle, and (3) an operator that loads and unloads the materials.

As shown in Figs. 2 and 3, trailers vary in size, shape, and capacity depending on the materials they carry. Trailers are composed of multiple storage zones. For example, as illustrated below, the three example trailers have four, one, and two zones, respectively. Each zone has different storage dimensions and the capacity of a zone depends on the sizes of the materials being transported. Zone capacity can be defined in terms of number or size. If size is used, then a zone may be specified by: dimension (x, y, z), planar area (x*y), volume (x*y*z), or a hybrid (e.g. x*y and z). In terms of modeling, the simplest case is to assume one zone per trailer with a capacity expressed only in terms of units. The most complex situation is to consider zone size, material size, and the amount of space available in the zone at the time of material pickup.

Fig. 3. Example types of trailers.

A tugger is the lead vehicle of the train. Other than its size, speed is a key characteristic. The tugger may control the train, but normally an operator does this.

In addition to driving the train, the operator positions the trailers at each stop and loads and unloads materials to a buffer area associated with a stop. The operator also sets or follows a work plan that defines the sequence of stops.

Stops and Paths

Another key component shown in Fig. 2 is the stops where the logistics train either picks up or deposits materials, i.e. the source-points and use-points, respectively. Each of these points has a location, i.e., it is defined by an x-y coordinate in the production facility. (A z-coordinate may be specified if the train travels on something other than a single plane.)

Associated with each source- and use-point is a mechanism that provides or consumes materials. Some operations are required at each source-point to prepare materials for transport, e.g. filling containers with parts. Similarly, operations at each use-point consume the delivered materials, e.g., using a material in an assembly operation. As a result, source- and use-points are usually associated with storage or buffer areas where material is stored until it is picked up by a train or consumed by an operation. Thus, buffers are directly associated with source- and use-points.

Trains travel on paths that are connections between stops. Paths may be in a straight line or curved. For curved paths trains must respond to the shape of the path in order capture its turn radius, as shown in Fig. 4. Therefore, each trailer and the tugger act independently as they traverse the path. This presents a modeling challenge in that many simulation modeling software would consider the entire train as a single object and thus would move it as such. From a modeling perspective this is primarily a visual issue and may not significantly affect the system's performance measures, but in many contexts the train needs to appear to behave as in the real system to instill confidence in the model. Much like a road system, paths are directional (one- or two-way), have speed limits, and may have action zones where trains must interact with other trains or other objects, e.g., intersections or crossways.

Travel along any path involves a speed, or multiple speeds (e.g. slowing down at busy intersections and turns), and accelerating from a stop and decelerating to a

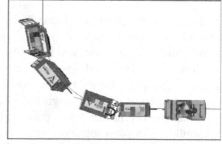

a. response in real system   b. response in simulation model
Source: www.handling-network.com   Source: own study

Fig. 4. Example of a logistics train (tugger and each trailer) responding to path characteristics.

stop. That is, trains must have situational awareness as to its location relative to curves and intersections as well as to other trains on its path (collision detection and avoidance). The actual speed at any time is actually the combination of a: (1) train's maximum speed, which may depend on the number, size, and loading of trailers, (2) train's rates of acceleration and decelerations, and (3) path's speed limit within a zone, e.g. straight travel in an uncongested area, congested area with a lot of potential ancillary activity, intersection, and radius of curve.

Another key operational consideration related to trailers, and not the overall train, is that they must be positioned at each source/use point in order to be loaded or unloaded. As a result, the train must be positioned or repositioned, by the operator, so that the correct trailer is in the correct position. For example, if multiple materials at a source point must be loaded onto several trailers on the train, then the operator's load operation must be interrupted in order to move the train each time a different trailer is needed.

Work Plan

A major component that is not visible in any of the pictures in Fig. 2 is a work plan. It is not visible since it is an information resource, and not a physical resource. The plan is comprised of a sequence of stops and activities (load/unload) performed at each stop. In order to develop a work plan for an in-plant logistics system that uses the milk-run concept, the "what, when, and how" of the move must be specified. The what aspect includes not just what material, but also where (from/to) and how much of the material to move. The when aspect includes at what time and in what sequence the material is moved. The how aspect includes in which zone, on which trailer, attached to which train (tugger and operator) the material is moved.

Thus the following must be specified: What {material, where (from/to), how much), When {time, sequence}, How {zone, trailer, train (tugger/operator)}, which answers the following question for each material move:

How much of what material is moved from where to where at what time and in what *sequence* in which *zone* on which *trailer* attached to which *train (tugger* and *operator)*.

4   A Modeling Framework for Simulating Milk-Run Systems

Based on the operational description in the previous section, a modeling framework is proposed that captures the: (1) primary physical elements that comprise the system, including their key attributes and the relationships among physical elements, (2) salient operational activities that define the work that the system accomplishes, and (3) principal decisions that drive its performance. The framework sets the requirements for the features of a milk-run in-plant logistics system that must be incorporated into amodel's representation. The framework is presented in Table 1.

A milk-run in-plant logistics system has three main classes of physical elements: the materials that are moved, logistics trains that move materials, and logistics networks on which trains travel. As shown in the framework the elements are defined in terms of attributes related to size, location, capacity, speed, reliability, availability, etc.

Table 1. Framework for simulation modeling of in-plant, milk-run logistics systems.

	Physical elements

1	a. **Material** to be transported; attributes: size, location of source and use points
	b. **Logistics train**
	    i. Trailer containing material to be transported; different types
	       1. trailer type attributes: shape, size, configuration (storage arragement), capacity; numer of each type available
	       2. train composition: numer of each type of trailer and arragement of trailers on a train
	    ii. Tugger, lead vehicle, guides train; attributes: size, speed, reliability
	    iii. Operator attributes: speed, shift and break schedules
	c. **Logistics network**
	    i. Source/use points where material is available or used; a nodes in a network; attribute: location
	    ii. Paths, routes between nodes on which logistics train move; attributes: distance, shape (straight, curved, combination), speed limit
	    iii. Source/use storage- area where material is actually stored; attributes: location, capacity
	d. **Relationships** among physical elements
	    i. Material has both a source point and use point
	    ii. Source and use points are connected through paths
	    iii. Source and use points each have an associated storage area
	    iv. Each storage area has a means to provide material to be moved (at source) or material that has been delivered to be consumed (at use)
	    v. Material is transported on a trailer
	    vi. Operator drives the train by means of the tugger; trailers follow the tugger

	Operational activities

2	Operational activities – interactions among physical elements creating system dynamics
	a. **Path Travel**
	    i. horizontal movement between points considering speed, shape, distance
	    ii. trailers and tugger independently conform to path shape
	    iii. handling of disturbances – intersections, other trains, etc.
	b. **Train Positioning** – placing the trailer associated with a material at a source/use point
	c. **Load/Unload** material between trailers and storage areas by an operator
	d. **Source/use mechanism** – means to either produce materials to be moved or consume material once moved (create demand for material)
	e. **Reliability/Availability** – breakdowns and recharging on tuggers; lunch and personal breaks for operators

	Decision variables
3	Decision variables – drive the bahavior and performance of the system; defines the work plan for a specified period of time through the 4Ws (what, where, when, who) and 2Hs (How much and How) a. **What** – set of tasks in m[a, b, q] b. **Where** – location of activities, a(x, y). A travel path is formed between locations c. **How much** – quantity of material handled d. **When** – time a material is handled in an use area; expressed as an absolute time or position in a sequence of route activities e. **How** material is moved – specific transport and possibly location on trailer f. **Who** – which train (tugger and operator) material and trailer are connected

Of course these physical elements are related and must interact; the relationships among the elements are defined in Sect. 1 of the framework.

As shown in Table 1, the framework defines five primary operational activities that are conducted with the physical elements; i.e., they involve interactions among physical elements. The activities include: path travel, train positioning, loading/unloading, availability and use of material at source/use points, and reliability/availability. The path travel activity involves not only traversing between points but also conforming to the shape of the path and interactions with other logistics trains, high traffic areas, etc.

Decision variables drive the operational activities and the use of the physical elements. The interactions result in system behavior and performance. Some of the decisions are tactical and related to facility design, such as vehicle sizes, vehicle and operator speeds, and locations of source and use points. Oftentimes, most of these are considered fixed due to facility and other resource constraints, but they may be a design variable. Other decisions are more strategic, or at least considered a decision variable that can be manipulated to search for system improvement. Examples of such decisions include the quantity and frequency of material movements, number of trailers on a logistics train, etc. Most often the decision variables form the foundation of a work plan – the operational scheme for moving a set of materials over a specified time span.

The framework in Table 1 defines the decision variables in terms of six operational questions about the system: what, where, when, who, how and how much – the 4Ws and 2Hs.

What happens is defined by flows, e.g. move material m from source location R1 to production area P1. Based on the notation defined earlier, this is denoted as m[R1, P1, q] and includes the set of tasks associated with the move, e.g. load, travel, position.

Where activities occur is defined by the object location, or spatial aspects, defined in terms of an x, y coordinate system. For example, R1(x, y) is the physical location of where a load activity occurs. A travel path is formed between a source location from where a material is moved and a use location to where the material is moved.

How much refers to the quantity of a material moved, loaded, and unloaded.

When refers to the time a material is loaded at a source and unloaded at its use area. It may be expressed as an absolute time or as a position in a sequence of activities performed in a route.

How a material is moved refers to the specific trailer used for transport and possibly the location on the trailer.

Who refers to which train, tugger and operator, the material and trailer are associated.

The proposed framework identifies three levels of modeling. The first level relates to the physical elements and their relationships; this level is considered static. The second layer involves the operational activities and creates the system dynamics. The third, and highest level in terms of sophistication and complexity, includes decision making – the setting, and use, of the values of the decision variables. The decision variables drive the system's behavior and performance.

5 Simulation Modeling of Milk-Run Systems

The levels in the proposed framework indicate a need for different modeling approaches. Of course, the final, overall model needs to encapsulate all of the approaches.

The first level of the framework, involving the physical elements of the system, is static and mostly involves spatial information and spatial relationships. Therefore, it can be represented by a facility layout and set of drawings, which might be represented in a CAD (Computer-Aided Design) model. Of course, the train operator and any movements of the train would require dynamics, but they are addressed in the second level. In terms of simulation, the first level provides the foundation, such as the scaled background on which discrete-event simulation (DES) objects in the model are placed to ensure spatial conformity with the real system.

The second modeling level adds operational activities that interact with and use the physical elements. The activities add the time dimension to the modeling effort and their interactions result in system dynamics. The system dynamics involving activities and processes are typically modeled using DES software. Many of the activity times are driven by locations and distances, as well as speeds; these are derived from the physical layer.

The third level provides the opportunity to apply agent-based simulation (ABS) since the modeling involves decision making, some intelligence, and extensive communication and coordination among objects. Examples of combining the ABS and DES modeling approaches in material-handling operations include Greenwood [2] and Pawlewski [6].

6 Conclusions and Future Research

This paper provides a framework for modeling in-plant logistics systems that use the milk-run concept. Milk-run systems, with their multi-load transports, are much more complex to operate than traditional single-load material handling. Therefore, due to the complexity, analysis and improvement of such systems benefit from the use of simulation modeling. Since the systems are complex, simulation modeling becomes more challenging. The proposed framework facilitates modeling by identifying and defining the salient components and requirement of such a system. The framework involves the physical elements of the system, its key activities, and the decisions that drive behavior and performance.

The framework suggests that multiple types of models need to be used to represent the static and dynamic aspects of the system. Based on the framework, the authors suggest a hybrid discrete-event and agent-based simulation approach to modeling milk-run logistics systems.

A natural extension of this work is the use of framework to develop and validate, simulation models in order to analyze in-plant milk-run logistics systems. Work is underway to do just this, but it is the subject of another paper.

Acknowledgements. Support for this research has been provided by the Faculty of Engineering Management 503217/11/140/DSPB/4150 Poznan University of Technology and Atres Intralogistics Sp.z.o.o.

References

1. BusinessDisctionary.com WebFinance, Inc., 31 January 2017 www.businessdictionary.com/definitions/milk-run.html
2. Greenwood, A.G.: An approach to represent material handlers as agents in discrete-event simulation models. In: Bajo, J., Escalona, M.J., Giroux, S., Hoffa-Dąbrowska, P., Julián, V., Novais, P., Sánchez-Pi, N., Unland, R., Azambuja-Silveira, R. (eds.) PAAMS 2016. CCIS, vol. 616, pp. 98–109. Springer, Cham (2016). doi:10.1007/978-3-319-39387-2_9
3. Jasiulewicz-Kaczmarek, M.: Improving performance of a filling line based on simulation. In: ModTech International Conference – Modern Technologies in Industrial Engineering IV, IOP Conference Series: Materials Science and Engineering, vol. 145 (2016)
4. Klenk, E., Galka, S.: Analysis of parameters influencing in-plant milkrun design for production supply. In: 12th International Material Handling Research Colloquium, Technische Universität München (2012)
5. Knez, M., Gajsek, B.: Implementation of in-plant milk-run systems for material supply in lean automotive parts manufacturing. In: International Conference on Logistics and Sustainable Transport (2015)
6. Pawlewski, P.: DES/ABS approach to simulate warehouse operations. In: Bajo, J., Hallenborg, K., Pawlewski, P., Botti, V., Sánchez-Pi, N., Duque Méndez, N.D., Lopes, F., Julian, V. (eds.) PAAMS 2015. CCIS, vol. 524, pp. 115–125. Springer, Cham (2015). doi:10.1007/978-3-319-19033-4_10

A Hybrid Modeling Approach for Simulating Milk-Run In-plant Logistics Operations

Allen G. Greenwood[✉], Kamila Kluska, and Pawel Pawlewski

Poznan University of Technology, ul.Strzelecka 11, 60-965 Poznań, Poland
{allen.greenwood, pawel.pawlewski}@put.poznan.pl,
kamila.kluska@student.put.poznan.pl

Abstract. This paper describes a hybrid modeling approach, using discrete-event and agent-based simulations, for analyzing the operation of milk-run logistics systems. The approach considers the physical actions of the vehicles and the operator as well as strategic-level systems planning and design. The approach leverages constructs currently available in simulation software and is implemented in *FlexSim*. In addition to the approach, an example is provided that illustrates the implementation of the first phase of the approach.

Keywords: Agents · Logistics systems · Milk run · Simulation

1 Introduction

In-plant logistics, the handling and movement of materials, is a key activity in most production systems; and, in many industries, it is a significant contributor to total manufacturing cost. In-plant logistics involves supplying raw materials to production areas, collecting finished goods from production areas and transporting them to a warehouse, and supplying work-in-progress materials from production areas to other production areas for further processing. It also includes returning empty containers that are used to transport materials to their storage areas.

Since in-plant logistics processes significantly affect overall system performance, it is the focus of many studies and improvement projects to identify the best option in terms of cost and service. In-plant logistics involves more than just moving material – performance is significantly affected by decisions regarding what, when, and how to move, considering the availability of materials at their source areas and the need requirements for materials where they are used.

One approach for operating in-plant logistics systems that is quite popular, especially for lean production systems and those with small lot sizes, is referred to as a milk-run system. A milk-run approach is more challenging to design and to model since it involves handling multiple material requests in one transport.

Simulation modeling and analysis is commonly used in such studies and projects in order to evaluate and analyze alternative logistics system design. Simulation enables understanding the dynamics inherent in most production systems, i.e. how system behavior changes over time. The behavior is determined by the many, and typically complex, interactions among a system's components and by the variability inherent in

© Springer International Publishing AG 2017
J. Bajo et al. (Eds.): PAAMS 2017 Workshops, CCIS 722, pp. 221–231, 2017.
DOI: 10.1007/978-3-319-60285-1_19

its components, such as nondeterministic process times, random downtimes, changing production plans, etc.

The first step towards building a useful and valid simulation model, or even deciding what type of modeling approach best represents a system, is to have a solid understanding of the system and its operation [7]. For in-plant logistics systems using a milk-run approach, Greenwood et al. [1] provide that foundation – they provide a framework for modeling milk-run systems and suggest the use of both discrete-event (DES) and agent-based simulation (ABS) modeling.

The objective of this paper is to provide a mixed-model approach for simulating the operation of in-plant logistics systems that use the milk-run concept based on the Greenwood et al. framework. The approach combines DES and ABS modeling and leverages capabilities that are currently available in DES modeling and analysis software.

This paper is organized as follows. Section 2 briefly describes milk-run systems and the framework proposed by Greenwood et al. [1]. Section 3 defines an approach for simulating milk-run systems based on the framework. Section 4 discusses the use of agent-based simulation for in-plant logistics. Section 5 describes an initial implementation of the proposed approach in DES software (*FlexSim*). Section 6 provides conclusions and plans for further research.

2   Modeling In-plant Milk-Run Logistics Systems

In general, in-plant logistics systems involve the following activities:

1. supplying production areas with materials that are needed for production; i.e., picking up raw materials from storage areas and delivering them to production areas,
2. collecting finished goods from production areas; i.e., picking up materials from production areas and delivering them to finished product storage areas,
3. supplying work-in-progress materials from production areas to other production areas for further processing, and
4. returning empty containers that are used to transport materials to their storage areas.

In many systems, each of the above activities is handled as a single load using equipment such as a fork truck, pallet jack, etc. However, a milk-run system uses a multi-load approach that involves a train composed of multiple trailers and multiple positions in a trailer for loads. As defined by Klenk and Galka [3], an in-plant milk-run system is a transport concept to supply various goods to various points of end use in one run. The operation of the system, and the modeling of such a system, is much more complex that the more traditional, single-load concept.

A key component in any material handling system is the material mover. As shown in the figure, in a milk-run system the material mover is a logistics train. The train consists of (1) a tugger, or lead vehicle, (2) an operator to drive the tugger and load and unload the material, and (3) a number of trailers that carry materials. However, the train is just one component, albeit a major one, in an in-plant, milk-run system (Fig. 1).

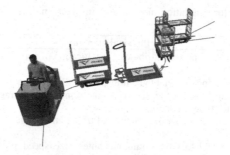

Fig. 1. Logistics train for moving material in a milk-run in-plant logistics system.

Greenwood et al. [1] propose a comprehensive framework for modeling in-plant logistics systems, with the focus on milk-run systems. It sets the requirements for the system features that must be incorporated into a model's representation. The framework captures the:

1. primary **physical elements** of the system, including their key attributes and the relationships among physical elements,
2. salient **operational activities** that define the work that the system accomplishes, and
3. principal **decision variables** that drive its performance.

Each of these aspects of the framework are defined in Table 1 and briefly discussed below.

The framework considers three main classes of physical elements in a milk-run system: the materials that are moved, logistics trains that move materials, and logistics networks on which trains travel. The elements are defined in terms of attributes related to size, location, capacity, speed, reliability, availability, etc. The physical elements are related and must interact and the framework defines those relationships.

The framework in Table 1 also defines five primary operational activities that are conducted with the physical elements. The activities involve train travel on paths, train positioning, material loading/unloading, resource availability, and the supply of, and demand for, materials in the system. The path travel activity involves not only traversing between points but also conforming to the shape of the path and interactions with other logistics trains, high traffic areas, etc.

The third major aspect of the framework in Table 1 is the definition of the key decision variables that drive the operational activities and the use of the physical elements. Some of the decisions are tactical and related to facility design, such as vehicle sizes, vehicle and operator speeds, and locations of source and use points. Oftentimes, most of these are considered fixed due to facility and other resource constraints, but they may be a design variable. Other decisions are more strategic, or at least considered a decision variable that can be manipulated to search for system improvement. Examples of such decisions include the quantity and frequency of material movements, number of trailers on a logistics train, etc. Most often the decision

Table 1. Framework for simulation modeling of in-plant, milk-run logistics systems [1].

	Physical elements

1	a. **Material** to be transported; attributes: size, location of source and use points
	b. **Logistics train**
	   a. **Trailer** containing material to be transported; different types
	     i. trailer type attributes: shape, size, configuration (storage arragement), capacity; numer of each type available
	     ii. train composition: numer of each type of trailer and arragement of trailers on a train
	   b. **Tugger,** lead vehicle, guides train; attributes: size, speed, reliability
	   c. **Operator** attributes: speed, shift and break schedules
	c. **Logistics network**
	   a. Source/use points where material is available or used; a nodes in a network; attribute: location
	   b. Paths, routes between nodes on which logistics train move; attributes: distance, shape (straight, curved, combination), speed limit
	   c. Source/use storage- area where material is actually stored; attributes: location, capacity
	d. **Relationships** among physical elements
	   a. Material has both a source point and use point
	   b. Source and use points are connected through paths
	   c. Source and use points each have an associated storage area
	   d. Each storage area has a means to provide material to be moved (at source) or material that has been delivered to be consumed (at use)
	   e. Material is transported on a trailer
	   f. Operator drives the train by means of the tugger; trailers follow the tugger

	Operational activities

2	Operational activities – interactions among physical elements creating system dynamics
	a. **Path Travel**
	     i. horizontal movement between points considering speed, shape, distance
	     ii. trailers and tugger independently conform to path shape
	     iii. handling of disturbances – intersections, other trains, etc.
	b. **Train Positioning** – placing the trailer associated with a material at a source/use point
	c. **Load/Unload** material between trailers and storage areas by an operator
	d. **Source/use mechanism** – means to either produce materials to be moved or consume material once moved (create demand for material)
	e. **Reliability/Availability** – breakdowns and recharging on tuggers; lunch and personal breaks for operators

	Decision variables
3	Decision variables – drive the bahavior and performance of the system; defines the work plan for a specified period of time through the 4Ws (what, where, when, who) and 2Hs (How much and How) a. **What** – set of tasks in m[a, b, q] b. **Where** – location of activities, a(x, y). A travel path is formed between locations c. **How much** – quantity of material handled d. **When** – time a material is handled in an use area; expressed as an absolute time or position in a sequence of route activities e. **How** material is moved – specific transport and possibly location on trailer f. **Who** – which train (tugger and operator) material and trailer are connected

variables form the foundation of a work plan – the operational scheme for moving a set of materials over a specified time span.

The three levels of the framework relate to three levels of modeling. The first, or physical, level is considered static. The second layer, related to the operational activities, creates the system dynamics. The third, and highest level in terms of sophistication and complexity, includes decision making – the setting, and use, of the values of the decision variables. The decision variables drive the system's behavior and performance.

3 Simulation Modeling of Milk-Run Systems

Defining relationships and interactions among entities is an important aspect of modeling. The framework in Table 1 provides the basis for defining the relationships. The physical elements in a milk-run system are defined in the upper right portion of Fig. 2 (the cells above the diagonal line). The chart is read from left to right in each row. For example, in row one, Material "is on" Trailer, Material "is loaded/unloaded by" Operator, Material "has" Source/Use Points, etc.

The interactions among entities lead to operational activities. They are also denoted in Fig. 2 – in the lower-left portion of figure (the cells below the diagonal line). The operational activities are combinations of the physical interaction cells. In the figure, the physical interaction cells from the upper-right portion of the chart are reflected to the lower-left portion. For example, the Material-Trailer relationship "is-on" is reflected to the Trailer-Material cell as "contains". The cells are grouped to form operational activities. For example, the Load/Unload activity is the combination of six physical interactions: Trailer-Material, Operator-Material, Source/Use Storage-Material, Trailer-Operator, Operator-Source/Use Storage, and Source/Use Points-Source/Use Storage; these cells are denoted with solid borders. Similarly, the Path Travel activity is the combination of the physical-interaction cells with large-dashed borders and the Train Positioning interactions have small-dashed cell borders. There is only one interaction between Material and Source/Use Mechanism and it is denoted with a mixed-dashed border. The downtime activity only involves the physical elements themselves – in the figure, this includes the Tugger, Operator, and Source/Use Mechanism.

The elements of an in-plant logistics system and their interactions are illustrated in Fig. 3. The representation includes the three framework levels – physical, operational activities, and decisions. The basic operations include forming a train from the available tuggers, operators, and trailers. Based on the material to be moved, the appropriate trailer is positioned at the applicable source or use point. The material is loaded/unloaded by the train operator to/from a source/use point buffer. The train travels between source/use points on a path. The sequence of stops and the type and amount of material moved is driven by the work plan. The tugger and operator are subject to downtime events. Consumption mechanisms use materials at the use-point buffers; similarly, production mechanisms generate materials at the source-point buffers.

The three levels in the framework, and their corresponding levels of modeling, indicate a need for different modeling approaches. Of course, the final, overall model needs to encapsulate all of the approaches.

		Material	Logistics Train			Logistics Network			
			Trailer	Tugger	Operator	Source/Use Points	Paths	Source/Use Storage	Source/Use Mechanisms
	Material		is on		is loaded / unloaded by	has		is in	is provided by
Logistics Train	Trailer	contains		follows	is loaded / unloaded by	stops at	follows		
	Tugger		leads		operated by	travels to	follows		
	Operator	loads / unloads	loads / unloads	operates		travels to	follows	picks up from, delivers to	
Logistics Netwotk	Source/Use Points	have	stops at	destination for	destination for		are on	connected to	
	Paths		direct	direct	direct	connect			
	Source/Use Storage	contains			load / unload location	connected to			connected to
	Source/Use Mechanisms	provide							

Key	Activities	Load/Unload	Path Travel	Train Positioning	Downtime	Supply / Demand

Fig. 2. Relationships among physical elements and operational activities.

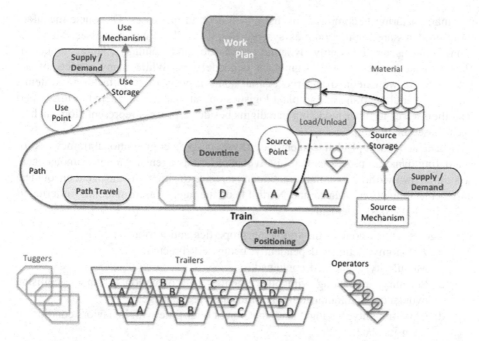

Fig. 3. Representation of the structure of a milk-run in-plant logistics system.

Since the first level mostly involves spatial information and relationships, it can be represented by a CAD (Computer-Aided Design) model. Of course, the train operator and any movements of the train would require dynamics. The first level provides the spatial foundation for a discrete-event simulation (DES) model.

The second modeling level adds operational activities that interact with, and use, the physical elements. The activities add the time dimension to the modeling effort and their interactions result in system dynamics. The system dynamics involving activities and processes are typically modeled using discrete-event simulation. Locations and distances derived from the physical layer, as well as speeds, drive many of the activity times.

The third level provides the opportunity to apply agent-based simulation (ABS) since the modeling involves decision making, some intelligence, and extensive communication and coordination among objects. Examples of combining the ABS and DES modeling approaches in material-handling operations include Greenwood [2] and Pawlewski [6].

4   Agent-Based Simulation in In-plant Logistics

Modeling and analyzing manufacturing systems using agent technologies have a long history as noted in Monostori et al. [5] and Shen et al. [8], to name a few. However, the major focus is primarily on manufacturing control systems. Greenwood [2] posits that one reason agent-based modeling is not as widely applied in manufacturing systems is that manufacturing is composed of many well-defined processes. Of course manufacturing systems are highly complex systems despite well-defined processes. Manufacturing systems are inherently dynamic, stochastic, and contain a large number of elements and processes with significant dependencies. While many aspects of the processes are well defined and procedural, some aspects of manufacturing systems, such as material handling and in-plant logistics operations, as considered in this paper, lend themselves to other modeling paradigms besides a process representation, such as agent-based modeling.

Macal and North [4] define agent-based systems as "a computational framework for simulating dynamic processes that involve autonomous agents. An autonomous agent acts on its own without external direction in response to situations the agent encounters during the simulation." Macal and North [4] define agent-based modeling in terms of following three basic elements.

(1) Agents, which contain the following properties and attributes:
   a. Autonomy, acting independently, being self directed.
   b. Modularity, being self contained.
   c. Sociality, interacting with other agents, e.g. contention for space, collision avoidance, communication and information exchange.
   d. Conditionality, having a state that varies over time with behaviors conditional upon its state.
(2) Agent Relationships, methods of interaction; networks are a common topology for interaction among agents.
(3) Agents' Environment, functioning and interacting with their surroundings.

Agent technology is applicable in modeling the behavior of milk-run systems due to the complexity of the coordination activities among multiple objects. While it may be possible to model such interactions with DES technology, taking an agent-based approach is more intuitive and straightforward. In this application, agent-based concepts are applied to the basic task-executer objects (in *FlexSim*).

The three components of a logistics train are the trailer, tugger, and operator and are modeled as task-executer objects with agent-based characteristics added. For example, the Path Travel operational activity involves coordination among all three of train components and each is considered an agent object. The solid directed lines in Fig. 4 show some of the dynamic communications that must be made between the train objects in order travel between source and use points. For example, the operator cannot load/unload material until the trailer is in position, the tugger cannot move until all material on all trailers at the present location have been handled (loaded or unloaded), a trailer cannot move until the preceding object (tugger or trailer) is moving, etc.

5   Illustrative Example – Initial Implementation

Using an example, this section describes implementation of the proposed approach in the simulation software *FlexSim*. *FlexSim* provides a powerful, open, object-oriented simulation environment that contains all of the basic constructs needed to represent material handling as an agent-based system in a discrete-event simulation model.

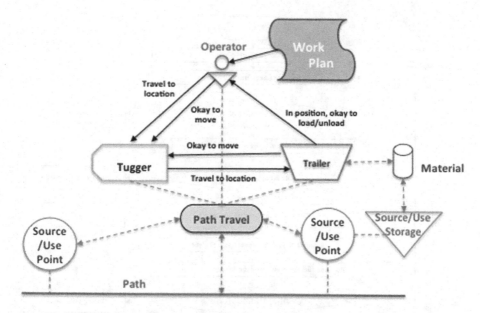

Fig. 4. Example interactions among modeling elements in a milk-run in-plant logistics system.

The initial implementation of the use of agents for modeling milk-run systems is shown in Fig. 5. Both the overall system and a close-up of a load activity are shown. The overall system includes the travel paths, train formation area, and source/use points with their associated buffers. The overall view shows trains operating on a single

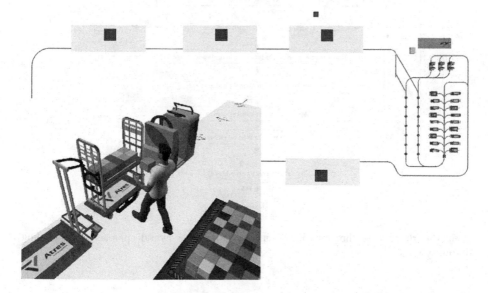

Fig. 5. Initial implementation of a hybrid approach for modeling milk-run systems.

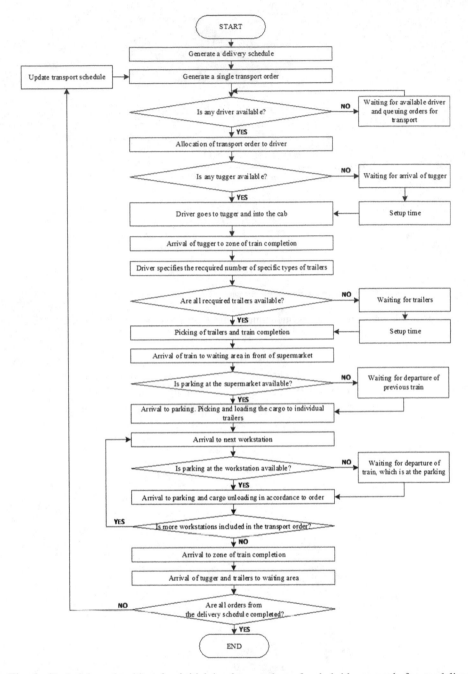

Fig. 6. Underlying algorithm for initial implementation of a hybrid approach for modeling milk-run systems.

milk-run path as well as the train-forming and trailer/tugger storage areas (in the right-hand side of the figure. The close-up view in Fig. 5 shows an operator loading material to a trailer on the logistics train. In the initial implementation material is loaded based on total capacity of the trailer and not by size and zones on the trailer.

Figure 6 provides a flowchart view of part of the implementation of the hybrid DES and ABS approaches. It is a more specific representation of Fig. 4 and includes formation of the logistics train.

6 Conclusion and Future Research

This paper presents an approach for simulating the operation of milk-run, in-plant logistics systems. The hybrid approach – using discrete-event and agent-based modeling – is based on the framework proposed by Greenwood et al. [1]. The initial implementation of the approach is in *FlexSim* simulation software. It leverages the existing modeling capability in *FlexSim* and thus does not require special agent-focused software to be linked with, or integrated into, the DES software, nor does it require links to sophisticated algorithms written in other languages, such as C++.

Since this paper provides initial results, future work will further develop and expand the functionalities of the agents.

Acknowledgements. Support for this research has been provided by the Faculty of Engineering Management DS 503217/11/140/DSPB/4150 2016 Poznan University of Technology and Atres Intralogistics Sp.z.o.o.

References

1. Greenwood, A.G., Kluska, K., Pawlewski, P.: A multi-level framework for simulating milk-run, in-plant logistics operations. In: Bajo, J., et al. (eds.) PAAMS 2017 Workshops. CCIS, vol. 722, pp. 209–220. Springer, Cham (2017)
2. Greenwood, A.G.: An approach to represent material handlers as agents in discrete-event simulation models. In: Bajo, J., et al. (eds.) PAAMS 2016. CCIS, vol. 616, pp. 98–109. Springer, Cham (2016). doi:10.1007/978-3-319-39387-2_9
3. Klenk, E., Galka, S.: Analysis of parameters influencing in-plant milkrun design for production supply. In: 12th International Material Handling Research Colloquium, Technische Universität München (2012)
4. Macal, C.M., North, M.J.: Introductory tutorial: Agent-based modeling and simulation. In: Winter Simulation Conference, pp. 6–20 (2014)
5. Monostori, L., Váncza, J., Kumara, S.: Agent-based systems for manufacturing. Ann. CIRP **55**, 697–720 (2006)
6. Pawlewski, P.: DES/ABS approach to simulate warehouse operations. In: Bajo, J., Hallenborg, K., Pawlewski, P., Botti, V., Sánchez-Pi, N., Duque Méndez, N.D., Lopes, F., Julian, V. (eds.) PAAMS 2015. CCIS, vol. 524, pp. 115–125. Springer, Cham (2015). doi:10. 1007/978-3-319-19033-4_10
7. Pawlewski, P., Jasiulewicz-Kaczmarek, M., Bartkowiak, T., Hoffa-Dąbrowska, P.: Validation of simulation model of the filling line failures. J. KONBiN **2**(38), 179–200 (2016)
8. Shen, W., Hao, Q., Yoon, H.J., Norrie, D.H.: Applications of agent-based systems in intelligent manufacturing: an updated review. Adv. Eng. Inform. **20**, 415–431 (2006)

CNSC

Multi-agent System for Privacy Protection Through User Emotions in Social Networks

G. Aguado$^{(\boxtimes)}$, V. Julian, and A. Garcia-Fornes

Departamento de Sistemas Informáticos y Computación (DSIC),
Universitat Politècnica de València, Camino de Vera s/n, Valencia, Spain
{guiagsar,vinglada,agarcia}@dsic.upv.es

Abstract. In this research privacy and decision making in social networks are addressed through a multi-agent system, using a model of the temperament of users, taking into account their emotions through the messages they put on the social media and the visual information obtained from them. We use opinion mining from a social network and images from users to get the data and calculate a model of temperament based on the PAD model generated from images and in the polarity of the messages they write. For this reason we propose a method to calculate a temperament state based on the history of PAD values of the user and the history of text polarities. We use also a method that analyzes the sentiment expressed in a message and helps the user to make the decision of posting it or not.

Keywords: Agents · Multi-agent system · Social networks · Privacy · Sentiment analysis · Pleasure · Arousal · Dominance · Advice · Users

1 Introduction

Social networks have become an important aspect of the daily life for a huge partition of world population, including people from all different ages. Today you can find easily teenagers that are users of social networks. This is a challenging step for the developers of such content, since those can have risks at the media. Vanderhoven et al. [1] cited the risks that teenagers face at social networks, and the characteristics that make them more vulnerable to those risks, like that an study predicts that they are less likely to recognize the risks and the future consequences of their decisions [2]. Additionally, people in general that use the social media frequently should bear in mind that there are risks, and they usually involve privacy [3]. Even those who are spontaneous users are affected by the problems that a lack of privacy can generate. Privacy on SNSs have been addressed before, in [25], privacy improving in social networking sites (SNS) has been discussed in the way of designing the interface of the system for that purpose, e.g. having the core features of privacy visible and having privacy "reminders", and customized privacy settings.

Additionally, emotional states are an important factor to take into account when managing decision making. When a person has an emotional state in which

© Springer International Publishing AG 2017
J. Bajo et al. (Eds.): PAAMS 2017 Workshops, CCIS 722, pp. 235–245, 2017.
DOI: 10.1007/978-3-319-60285-1_20

one cannot feel secure, for example, it is easier to make a decision that you will regret. Christofides et al. [4] explained the consequences that posting a message can have, and the possibilities that lead to a regret on posting. It is advisable then that a social network system might be able to help users in their decision making process by means of analyzing their emotional state. Moreover, this information about emotional state will lead to a safer behavior in SNSs through improving decision making, avoiding situations where we make posts that we don't want to be seen by someone that could be dangerous, for example, since his or her emotional state can lead to an unwanted behavior upon us when our post has been published. In this way, not only our own emotional information may help us, but the information about emotional states from other people can help the system guide us to make the right decision. Additionally, avoiding to post a message that we don't really like to be published may lead to further safer situations in general, and protect us from future problems with other users. A person can be in a variety of emotional states, for this reason researchers try to address the state using a concrete set of states. More concretely, we use the set of temperament states derived from the PAD (Pleasure, Arousal, Dominance) three-dimensional state model, proposed by Mehrabian [5].

Aiming to address these issues, we propose a model of the temperament state of users in a social network, that is updated through time, using as instruments both opinion mining from their posted messages and PAD model inference from the visual information of the users. We then use this model to detect changes in the temperament and give an advice to the users, in order to protect their privacy and help them to make better decisions. We also propose a method to help users in their decision making process, analyzing the emotional state of their messages with opinion mining, using the information of their temperament model and using a rule based system that suggests an action based on its adequacy.

Multi-agent systems (MAS) are systems with multiple autonomous entities on them working together or being potentially affected by each other, at least. Taking into account that each agent performs its actions and the sum of the actions of all the agents composes the full system, they can be used to model a system where we can find different activities performed, which could each be done by an agent.

As the architecture of our application, we propose a multi-agent system that uses an agent to perform each task. We then have several agents on the system operating together as part of it and as users. The user agents just log in to the system and perform actions to interact with the system and other users, whereas the system agents perform the operations for calculating PAD models, opinion mining and temperament states and to give advices to the users.

The rest of the paper is organized as follows. Section 2 introduces previous works on opinion mining and sentiment state modeling. Section 3 describes our proposed system, including the method that extracts the sentiment of a message in real time and analyzes it to give an advice about posting it. Section 4 explains the results of a theoretical execution of the process of the method that gives advices about posting messages to users. Finally, Sect. 5 gives an overview of the contribution and possible future work.

2 Related Work

In this section we are going to discuss the previous approaches in the areas of sentiment analysis, user modeling and emotional state modeling, topics that are worked in our contribution in order to improve privacy in social networks.

The field of research, labeled as opinion mining, sentiment analysis, or subjectivity analysis, studies the phenomena of opinion, sentiment, evaluation, appraisal, attitude, and emotion [6]. This could be studied from sources like written text, for example, but also on other media such as images. Four cases that are usually addressed in previous works regarding the field of sentiment analysis are document-level sentiment analysis, sentence-level sentiment analysis, aspect-based sentiment analysis and comparative sentiment analysis [7]. Moreover, a topic that appears in several recent works and its worked in this paper is aspect-based sentiment analysis, because we want to extract the sentiment from the individual aspects of the posts, in order to obtain a more fine grained sentiment analysis.

According to the literature, there are two main issues to address when dealing with aspect-based sentiment analysis, aspect extraction and sentiment classification, but sometimes we can find also hybrid approaches, and there are several techniques aiming to solve those aforementioned topics, which also have various techniques for solving them [8]. Some of these techniques are, for aspect detection, frequency based methods, that use the frequency in which the word appear to create the aspects [9]; syntax based methods, that use syntax trees to extract aspects [10]; generative models like CRF (Conditional Random Fields) to detect aspects, using a diverse set of features, such as whether a direct dependency relation exists between this word and a sentiment expression or whether this word is in the noun phrase that is closest to a sentiment expression [11]; non supervised machine learning methods that generate aspects like LDA (Linear Discriminant Analysis) [12]; hybrid methods that work at the same time (e.g. a supervised model detect frequent aspects while a non supervised detects the less frequent aspects) [13], or one producing the input of the other [14].

For sentiment classification, we can distinguish dictionary based methods and machine learning methods (supervised and not). The former use a base set of terms with a polarity assigned, and an additional method to get the polarity of the text [8], and the latter use Support Vector Regression and several techniques for obtaining the features to train the model from the data. Non supervised methods are less frequent [8]. There is a work that use techniques to extract sentences that are likely to have sentiment, and assigns a sentiment to them using relaxation labeling [14], an unsupervised technique from the computer vision area.

Finally, hybrid approaches intend to detect aspects and assign a polarity to them simultaneously [8]. There are syntax based methods, which get the words associated to a sentiment and then extract aspects based on grammatical relations [15]. CRF that relate sentiments to aspects by exploiting relations between words [16]. Hybrid methods that use a MaxEnt classifier to help an LDA model to detect which words are related to aspects, sentiments or just noise [17].

To the best of our knowledge, sentiment analysis have not been used for improving privacy on Social networks, or even in the net. Our work aims to use it in order to categorize posts and people, to latter use this information for helping the user to avoid negative situations, in which he could post something he would regret for example. This can lead to avoiding future privacy issues, since people would be more aware of the repercussions of their posts.

Recently, there are works that try to introduce the information of characteristics from the user to their model by means of creating a model with this information. Seroussi et al. [18] proposed a nearest-neighbor collaborative approach, that was used to train user-specific classifiers. The outputs of those were then combined with user similarity measurement in a task of sentiment analysis at text. Tang et al. [19, 20] introduced user, product and review information on a neural network built for the occasion, allowing them to learn a distributed representation of users and products.

Li et al. [21] created a three dimension tensor with user, product and review features. Gao et al. [22] created a model that computes user or product specific sentiment inclination for sentiment classification. Diao et al. [23] introduced a probabilistic model that used collaborative filtering and topic modeling, which was used to compute user and product features.

Rincon et al. [24] proposed a social emotional model which allows to extract the social emotion of a group of intelligent entities. The model presented, uses the PAD three-dimensional emotional space to represent the individual emotions of each one of the entities. They used an artificial neural network to learn the emotion of the group after some event happened.

Another contribution from our work is that we also use the information about PAD states for improving privacy, and we create a novel method to generate a model of the state of the users using both sentiment analysis and PAD models generated from information about the users.

Having into account that researchers have made several works in the field of sentiment analysis on SNSs, and some used user model to enrich their system, we can say that our prototype can be successfully created and tested over real data.

3   Multi-agent System for Privacy Protection Through User Emotions

Our proposal is to create a MAS in which there is a series of user agents and non-user agents, the former are just data structures that have a temperament model associated and represent an user on the system, and the latter are components of the system that are associated with different functionalities. The user temperament model will be calculated for all the users on a social network, using the information retrieved from images taken by a camera and the text messages written by users, focusing to build a PAD model of the emotional state of the user and supporting it with information from text polarity.

This model of the user is updated through time due to an on-line method, that re-calculates the temperament value of the user based on the new input received. Moreover, we use the built model to make predictions of consequences about posting messages, combining it with sentiment analysis on the post and using a rule-based system. We give advices and warnings to the users to protect their privacy, and mark the messages as private according to the privacy policy.

3.1   MAS Architecture

First of all, our application is structured into diverse agents. It also has different layers, and every agent belong to one layer. Those agents are both user related agents and agents non-associated to users on the system, that interact with them and calculate their temperament models, PAD models, polarities, give them feedback as advices and warnings and collect their input. Regarding the system agents, we can find different agent types (e.g. Persistence agent type), and the final system may implement several instances of each type. In the next subsection we will explain the different layers of the application and its agent types. Figure 1 shows the architecture of the system and all the agent types working at different layers.

3.2   Main Components (Agents) of the System

In this subsection we will discuss the design of the different kinds of agents that compose the system (organized by layers), and the methods and tools they use.

Presentation Layer. The presentation layer is structured with only one agent type that gets the information retrieved from the user at the moment of posting a message or taking a photo of him, and supplies this information to the agents on the logic layer. This agent also gets the information from the logic layer to give an advice or warning to the user interacting with the presentation layer.

The way this agent works out its tasks is as follows: There are several widgets that control the input given by the users and can retrieve it as text. Moreover, there is a camera that can retrieve images of the users in real time. In a similar way, this agent can give information to the user agents via text using widgets.

Logic Layer. This layer has several agents of different types that operate together to transform the information retrieved from the users at the presentation layer into user model, PAD model of the users and polarities from written messages.

1. PAD calculator agent type: This type of agent takes as input the image from an user and using the visual information about the face of the user, extracts

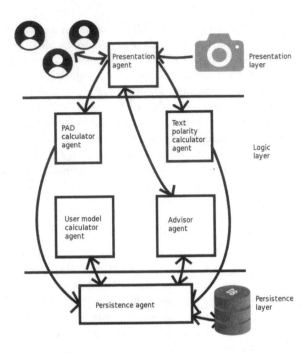

Fig. 1. Arquitecture of the multi-agent system

the emotional features on the gestures of the face. After this is done, it calculates his PAD three-dimensional model based on those facial features and sends this model to the persistence layer, for storing it on the database. The PAD model calculated for the user is a 3 dimension vector representing his levels of Pleasure, Arousal and Dominance.

2. Sentiment analysis agent type: For being able to perform sentiment analysis on the text messages, we choose to use a variant of aspect-based sentiment analysis that uses a frequency based method for aspect detection and an artificial neural network for polarity detection.

   We get the information of text messages from the application when the users post them, so the presentation layer retrieves it, and this agent type works performing a classification using the information about polarity from the terms of the text that are associated with a polarity.

   First of all, we use the frequency based method for creating a set of aspects to classify with the neural network. We perform a search on the set of data and calculate the most frequent terms that are associated with an emotion. Next, we train the neural network with features associated with the terms, such as usage on positive evaluations on a commentary system about products. Finally, we classify the terms extracted previously and assign a polarity to them for further classification of post messages.

   The features selected for the neural network are an important step on the construction of this sentiment analysis system. We select the features in order to maximize the probability of detecting the correct polarity for the terms.

When we have the system ready, the agent or agents search the post or message for the terms that has stored on the set of terms that we decided to have a relation to sentiments in social networks, and use the polarity calculated to infer the final polarity of the post as a function of all the polarities found on it. This function is the sum of the polarities found, latter normalized to be in the interval chosen for polarity strength (the same as the individual polarities).

3. User model calculator agent type: This agent type searches at the database the information related to user agents and update their model, using an algorithm designed for that purpose.

The way this agent deals with the dynamics of emotional states is by using only the most recent information about the user stored in the database, in a way that we only keep track of the recent state fluctuations (We only use the recent PAD models and polarity information for the calculation). If we used the old data for the calculation instead, there may appear errors in the state modeling since a person may change its emotional state eventually and old data may not correspond to his actual emotions or emotional state. We chose the moment of time from which we start retrieving data for the calculation as a parameter of this agent, and may be useful to try different values for it.

It calculates the temperament state and stores it as the user agent model. Those states extracted from the PAD model are: Exuberant, Bored, Dependent, Disdainful, Relaxed, Anxious, Docile and Hostile [5].

The proposed algorithm works as we detailed in Algorithm 1. It performs the method proposed in a high level way, which means that the further implementation should be a reflex of this pseudo-code.

4. Advisor agent type: This agent type works at the moment of posting a message, by performing sentiment analysis on it and using this information and the information about the user agent temperament model to give an advice about posting or not. Given the current model of the user agent (temperament), and the polarity of the message (positive or negative) we determine if it could be dangerous to post in this way:

If the polarity is negative, it gets a negative point.

If the polarity is positive, it gets a positive point.

Depending on the current temperament associated to the user agent, the system adds another point, positive or negative, and those are explained on Table 1.

Finally, if the result as a sum of the two points is negative, it shows a warning for avoiding publishing the message and establish a policy of "private" to that post. This means that if the message has a negative polarity associated and also the user is known to have at the current moment a negative temperament, we show him an alert and mark the post as private, according to the privacy policy (which also means that the post should only be shared with family or close friends, we explain it to the user), in order to protect his or her privacy by means of avoiding a difficult or bad situation that could trigger safety and privacy issues. Additionally, other forms of privacy aid are

---

Algorithm 1. User Model update algorithm

1: **procedure** USER MODEL UPDATE
2:     Extract a list of PAD models from database associated with user agent
3:     Extract a list of polarities from database associated with user agent
4:     **for** each value $i \in$ {Pleasure, Arousal, Dominance} **do**
5:         Calculate i from the polarity list
6:         **for** each model $j \in$ list of PAD models of user agent **do**
7:             agregate ponderated i value from model j to total accumulated i value
8:         **end for**
9:         agregate ponderated i value calculated with polarities to total i value
10:     **end for**
11:     Calculate temperament of user agent with the total aggregated PAD values calculated previously and assign it as the user agent model
12:     Retain this information in database via the persistence layer
13: **end procedure**

Table 1. Assessment of PAD states

Exuberant	Gets a positive point
Bored	Gets a positive point
Dependent	Gets a positive point
Disdainful	Gets a negative point
Relaxed	Gets a positive point
Anxious	Gets a negative point
Docile	Gets a positive point
Hostile	Gets a negative point

likely to be implemented using the information extracted from text polarities and user temperament models.

Persistence Layer. This layer contains a single agent type that retrieve information and store it at the database, like user models, PAD models from user agents and polarities. It has various functions that act as an interface between the persistence layer and the database of the application, such as one for storing user model, another for retrieving a list of PAD models from a given user agent calculated over time, etc. And it also acts as an interface for the agents of the logic layer, to make them able to access and store information from the database.

4   Execution Example

In this section, we will expose a theoretical step by step trace of the system execution, allowing us to explain the functionality of the system that we propose.

Initially, we turn on the server where the MAS and the social network are located, and those get initialized and ready to host users. The data about polarities and models is empty because the system is just starting to run, therefore, the database don't have any of this data to retrieve. In a moment of time, the users log in to the server and the system automatically creates agents that represent them on it. Still no information about their emotions is stored or calculated.

At certain times, people start posting messages and taking photos, and the system automatically sends them to the agents in the MAS that will calculate the polarity of the text (Sentiment analysis agent), and the PAD model from the images (PAD calculator). Moreover, the user model calculator agent gets triggered because there is new data available and recalculates the model of the user, taking into account the data from recent PAD models and text polarities, and assigns this model as the user agent model.

We are going to expose a theoretical execution of the system, where we find an user that is going to post a message, and the system interacts with him. This will allow us to demonstrate the functionality of the system that we propose.

In a moment of time, an user is about to make a new post, so as an on-line feature, the system automatically calculates the polarity of the post and retrieves his temperament model, finally calculates the danger of posting the message as follows on the next paragraph.

The sentiment analysis on the post shows a negative valence or polarity on the text written, but his temperament model shows a "relaxed" temperament state, so the advisor agent or agents conclude that a negative valence isn't enough while having that "relaxed" temperament to infer that there is danger, because he could have written something with negative connotations but still not make any damage on the community or on himself (e.g. a message talking about people dying is not enough evidence for concluding that there is a danger in talking about it). If his temperament had dangerous connotations, the system would have warned him because there are two signals that indicate danger at the same time (temperament and analysis of the post). In this scenario, assuming that the user understands that there could be a danger in making that post, because some people could start harassing the user or thinking that he or she is not a good person anymore, he don't send the post and nothing more happens. If he still decided to send the post, according to his privacy configuration we could still mark it as private and send it only to some close friends or family to avoid difficult situations and privacy issues.

The system continues gathering data from users and calculating their user models using data from polarities and PAD models (only recent data), and giving advices to the users until the server shuts down.

5   Conclusions

In the present work we have addressed privacy in social networks by means of analyzing the sentiment that is latent on the posts users make performing sentiment analysis and in the images from them, creating the PAD models.

We latter built an on-line model of every user that keeps a track of the user actual temperament state, and it's influenced by both information sources: the PAD models through time and the polarity of the posts he or she write on the social network. Based on this information, we designed a method for giving advices to the users about posting or not a message on the network, and to mark it as private or not, according to the privacy policy. This may help to avoid future possible privacy problems and from other kinds. At the moment, we are developing a prototype of the proposed system.

There are several possible future works, including the testing of the system over a large amount of real data from a social network and test users, creating new functions for privacy protection and introducing them to the system, and improving one of the agents, to perform for example a more sophisticated kind of sentiment analysis or user model creation. Moreover, the method for advising an action at the moment of posting could be improved by introducing various new factors to take into account for performing the calculation, such as, context information. Additionally, we could introduce more sophisticated policies, such as taking into account the emotional state from friends for assigning a public for a post, and not only the emotional state from the user that is going to post it and the sentiment analysis on the text itself.

Acknowledgements. This work was supported by the project TIN2014-55206-R of the Spanish government.

References

1. Vanderhoven, E., Schellens, T., Valcke, M.: Educating teens about the risks on social network sites. An intervention study in secondary education. Comunicar **XXII**(43), 123 (2014)
2. Lewis, C.C.: How adolescents approach decisions: changes over grades seven to twelve and policy implications. Child Dev. **52**(2), 538 (1981). http://dx.doi.org/10.2307/1129-172
3. Vanderhoven, E., Schellens, T., Vanderlinde, R., Valcke, M.: Developing educational materials about risks on social network sites: a design based research approach. Educ. Tech. Res. Dev. **64**, 459–480 (2016)
4. Christofides, E., Muise, A., Desmarais, S.: Disclosures on Facebook: the effect of having a bad experience on online behavior. J. Adolesc. Res. **27**, 714–731 (2012)
5. Mehrabian, A.: Outline of a general emotion-based theory of temperament. In: Strelau, J., Angleitner, A. (eds.) Explorations in Temperament: International Perspectives on Theory and Measurement, pp. 75–86. Plenum Press, New York (1991)
6. Liu, B.: Sentiment Analysis and Opinion Mining, series Synthesis Lectures on Human Language Technologies, vol. 16. Morgan, San Mateo (2012)
7. Feldman, R.: Techniques and applications for sentiment analysis. Commun. ACM **56**(4), 82–89 (2013)
8. Schouten, K., Frasincar, F.: Survey on aspect-level sentiment analysis. IEEE Trans. Knowl. Data Eng. **28**(3), 813–830 (2016)
9. Hu, M., Liu, B.: Mining opinion features in customer reviews. In: Proceedings of the 19th National Conference on Artifical Intelligence, pp. 755–760 (2004)

10. Zhao, Y., Qin, B., Hu, S., Liu, T.: Generalizing syntactic structures for product attribute candidate extraction. In: Proceedings of Conference of the North American Chapter of the Association for Computational Linguistics: Human Language Technologies, pp. 377–380 (2010)
11. Jakob, N., Gurevych, I.: Extracting opinion targets in a single and cross-domain setting with conditional random fields. In: Proceedings of the 2010 Conference on Empirical Methods in Natural Language Processing, pp. 1035–1045 (2010)
12. Blei, D.M., Ng, A.Y., Jordan, M.I.: Latent Dirichlet allocation. J. Mach. Learn. Res. **3**, 993–1022 (2003)
13. Blair-Goldensohn, S., Neylon, T., Hannan, K., Reis, G.A., Mcdonald, R., Reynar, J.: Building a sentiment summarizer for local service reviews. In: Proceedings of Workshop NLP Information Explosion (2008)
14. Popescu, A.-M., Etzioni, O.: Extracting product features and opinions from reviews. In: Proceedings of the conference on Human Language Technology and Empirical Methods in Natural Language Processing, pp. 339–346 (2005)
15. Nasukawa, T., Yi, J.: Sentiment analysis: capturing favorability using natural language processing. In: Proceedings of 2nd International Conference Knowledge Capture, pp. 70–77 (2003)
16. Li, F., Han, C., Huang, M., Zhu, X., Xia, Y.-J., Zhang, S., Yu, H.: Structure-aware review mining and summarization. In: Proceedings of 23rd International Conference on Computational Linguistics, pp. 653–661 (2010)
17. Zhao, W.X., Jiang, J., Yan, H., Li, X.: Jointly modeling aspects and opinions with a MaxEnt-LDA hybrid. In: Proceedings of Conference Empirical Methods Natural Language Processing, pp. 56–65 (2010)
18. Seroussi, Y., Zukerman, I., Bohnert, F.: Collaborative inference of sentiments from texts. In: Bra, P., Kobsa, A., Chin, D. (eds.) UMAP 2010. LNCS, vol. 6075, pp. 195–206. Springer, Heidelberg (2010). doi:10.1007/978-3-642-13470-8_19
19. Tang, D., Qin, B., Liu, T.: Learning semantic representations of users and products for document level sentiment classification. In: Proceedings of 53rd Annual Meeting of the Association for Computational Linguistics (2015)
20. Tang, D., Qin, B., Liu, T., Yang, Y.: User modeling with neural network for review rating prediction. In: Proceedings of 24th International Joint Conference Artifical Intelligence, pp. 1340–1346 (2015)
21. Li, F., Liu, N., Jin, H., Zhao, K., Yang, Q., Zhu, X.: Incorporating reviewer and product information for review rating prediction. In: Proceedings of 22th International Joint Conference Artifical Intelligence, vol. 11, pp. 1820–1825 (2011)
22. Gao, W., Yoshinaga, N., Kaji, N., Kitsuregawa, M.: Modeling user leniency and product popularity for sentiment classification. In: Proceedings of IJCNLP, Nagoya, Japan (2013)
23. Diao, Q., Qiu, M., Wu, C.-Y., Smola, A.J., Jiang, J., Wang, C.: Jointly modeling aspects, ratings and sentiments for movie recommendation (JMARS). In: Proceedings of 20th ACM SIGKDD International Conference Knowledge Discovery and Data Mining, pp. 193–202 (2014)
24. Rincon, J.A., de la Prieta, F., Zanardini, D., Julian, V., Carrascosa, C.: Influencing over people with a social emotional model. In: International Conference on Practical Applications of Agents and Multiagent Systems (2016)
25. Xie, W., Kang, C.: See you, see me: teenagers self-disclosure and regret of posting on social network site. Comput. Hum. Behav. **52**, 398–407 (2015)

Simulating the Impacts of Information Diffusion on Meningitis Outbreak in West-Africa Using Agent-Based Model

Eric Youl[1,3], Mahamadou Belem[2,3(✉)], Sadouanouan Malo[2],
and Issouf Traoré[4]

[1] Université Ouaga 1 Pr Joseph Ki Zerbo, Ouagadougou, Burkina Faso
`eric_youl@yahoo.fr`
[2] Université Polytechnique de Bobo-Dioulasso, Bobo-Dioulasso, Burkina Faso
`mahamadou.belem@gmail.com`, `sadouanouan@yahoo.fr`
[3] Complex System Modeling, West African Science Service Center on Climate
Change and Adapted Land Use; Competence Center,
Ouagadougou, Burkina Faso
[4] Centre National de Recherche en Santé de Nouna, Nouna, Burkina Faso

Abstract. This paper describes a model for the simulation of the information diffusion impacts on the spread of meningitis in West-Africa. The approach is based on agent-based modeling to represent explicitly (1) the relationships and interactions among individuals through their social networks and (2) the spread of the disease at individual and system level. The model is applied to explore the impacts of the structure of social networks and the trust distribution on the information diffusion and the spread of the meningitis disease.

Keywords: Meningitis · Information diffusion · Social networks · Agent-based model · West-Africa

1 Introduction

The meningitis is a major health problem in Sahelian Africa [1, 2]. Meningitis disease is an infection of the meninges. Under certain circumstances the bacteria becomes pathogenic with a significant risk of death. Mental retardation, deafness, epilepsy are the major aftermaths of the meningitis in 10% to 20% of survivors (OMS). The bacteria are transmitted from person-to-person by aerosols through droplets of respiratory or throat secretions from carriers. Close and prolonged contact facilitates the spread of the disease. The average incubation period ranges between 2 and 10 days (OMS).

Different measures are currently used by the public health agencies to control the spread of meningitis disease. These measures include the early detection of an epidemic, deployment of polysaccharide vaccines [3] and awareness-raising. The objective of awareness-raising is to spread information on the meningitis disease to make easier the access to the information and to reduce the spread of the disease. It involves the use of interpersonal, social networks, organizational and media communication strategies aimed at informing and influencing individual and collective decisions to prevent the spread of the disease.

© Springer International Publishing AG 2017
J. Bajo et al. (Eds.): PAAMS 2017 Workshops, CCIS 722, pp. 246–256, 2017.
DOI: 10.1007/978-3-319-60285-1_21

In the framework of meningitis spread control, the social networks are characterized by a range of individuals and organizations (families, associations, neighborhood relationships, confessional groups, etc.). The individuals are different by their perceptions on the disease, their behaviors and their relationships in various social networks. Then, they do not answer to the same way to different strategies of information diffusion. The individuals share information on the disease between them through the organizations that are multiples and dynamics. The information sharing in the social networks impacts the individual behaviors (change of the perception, reduction of risk of contamination) and the global properties of the system (spread of the disease, access to the information, innovation). The main challenges for the policy makers is how to determine the best strategies of awareness-raising through the social networks that are complex to control the spread of the meningitis disease.

Modeling is a relevant tool to understand how the flows of information in the social networks impact the spread of the disease. The system approach can be used to assess the effect of interactions between individuals on their behaviors and the spread of the disease at the system level. Agent-based model is the most relevant system modeling approach. Agent-based model allows to take into account the heterogeneity of actors' decision making, the multiplicity of their points of view [4], the effect of social network on individuals' behavior [5, 6], and finally the impacts of policy interventions on individual behavior [7, 8].

In this research, we used the agent-based modeling approach to assess the impact of information diffusion on the spread of meningitis. The resulting model names MeningSim is generic, meaning that is designed for the Sahelian Africa. The model is applied to explore the impacts of the structure of social networks and the trust distribution on the information diffusion and the spread of the meningitis disease. The results showed the effectiveness of the MeningSim to support the assessment of information diffusion measures for the meningitis.

2   Material and Method

Selection of Tools and Models

Agent-based model is based on understanding of global phenomena making assumption on individual behaviors of agents. Agent has its own decision model and can perceive its environment that it can modify through its actions [9]. Agent interacts with other agents to share resources and information. Such interactions take place in organizational contexts that can be the social organization of agents [10]. Then, using agent-based model allows to take into account the heterogeneity of actors and the explicit representation of social organization of a system. [5] used agent-based model to simulate the effect of social networks on flood risk communication. [11] used agent-based models to simulate the product diffusion in a market. Agent-based model is used in epidemiology modeling to assess the spread of disease [12] and to assess the impact of information diffusion on diseases control [13].

In this current research we used the agent-based modeling approach to represent the information spread through the social networks, the impact of information spread on the individual behavior and the meningitis disease spread. We used the innovation diffusion theory to represent the meningitis information spread through the social networks. The innovation diffusion theory distinguishes five categories of adopters: innovators, early adopters, early majority, late majority, and laggards. In the MeningSim model, the adoption concerns the appropriation (acceptation) of information received from the social networks. To represent how an individual accepts an information and changes its behavior, we used the threshold models approach. Then, we assumed that an individual adopts an information if the trust to the information received from the social networks reaches some threshold. The trust to an information depends on the quality of the relationships between individuals. The quality of relationships is specified by a weight quantifying the social relationship between two agents based on the notion of trust [14] as defined in [13].

To represent the meningitis spread among individuals, the MeningSim model uses the SIER model [15]. SIER model is a variant of SIR [16] model currently used in epidemiology simulation. In the SIER model, an individual can be susceptible, infectious, infected or Removed. Susceptible are individuals who are not infected but may become infectious when they gain contact with an infectious or infected individual. Infectious are individuals who carry the parasite and are in the period of incubation. They can spread the disease. Infected are individuals who are carrying pathogenic parasites and have the potential to spread it. Removed are individuals who have either recovered from the disease or died, and cannot spread the disease.

2.1   Modeling Procedure

The first step of the modeling procedure concerned the definition of the study scope. The objective was to understand the target problem and to delimit the problem from the scientists points of view. Then, discussion has been organized with scientists from different domains: geography, social science, epidemiology, climatology, modeler and computer scientists.

Based on the points of view from these various scientists, a conceptual model has been developed using the Unified Modeling Language (UML). In this study, the conceptual model is used as a support of communication between scientists and a support for the model implementation.

At the thirst step, the data is collected from different sources and integrated for the model simulation. After, Netlogo [17] is used to develop the MeningSim model. Finally various scenarios are simulated to assess different scenarios.

In this paper, we used the ODD protocol [18] to describe the MeningSim model.

2.2   Description of MeningSim Model

Purpose

The model is developed to provide decision support tool to assess the impacts of information spread on the spread of meningitis disease. The objective of information spread is to impact the behavior of individuals by making them adopting behavior that prevents or limits the spread of meningitis disease.

Variables

The structure of the MeningSim model is composed of different entities: (1) Persons representing the individuals in the system and (2) Organization. The individuals are linked and interact between them through their organizations that represent their social networks (Fig. 1).

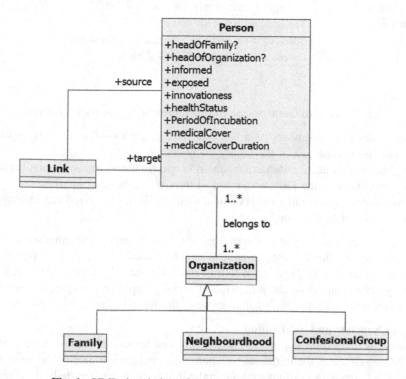

Fig. 1. UML description of the agents and their social groups

The Agents

One type of agent is represented in the model: the Person. A Person is characterized by its social networks, the healthy status, the innovative behavior, the attitude and the medical cover status (Table 1). According to their attitude, we have exposed and not-exposed agents. The contamination rate of the exposed agent is higher than the one of the not-exposed agent. Not-exposed are agents which are informed and have adopted appropriate behavior to prevent the spread of the disease. Exposed agents are agents which have not adopted appropriate behavior to prevent the spread of the disease. In the model, the objective is to spread information in order to reduce the number of exposed agents and consequently to control the meningitis outbreak.

Table 1. Attributes and status of the agents

Attributes	Status
headOfFamily?	Head of the family or not
headOforganization?	Head of organization or member
Informed	Has received or not the information
Exposed	Exposed or not-exposed
Innovation	Innovators, early adopters, early majority, late majority, and laggards.
HealthyStatus	Susceptible, infectious, infected, removed
PeriodOfincubation	The incubation period
MedicalCover	Specifies if the agent beneficiates of medical cover
MedicalCoverDuration	Specifies the duration of medical cover

Organization

In the model, we have different social groups representing the social networks:

- Family: links the members of a same family. In the model, the decision of the Family Head is the one of the family members.
- Neighborhood: links families among them to specify the relations of neighborhood. For simplification, the families are linked through the head of families.
- Confessional group: links member of a same religion. They receive information from the Head of the group.

A Person can belong to several social groups. Only person in the same social group can interact among them. A Person accepts an information from another depending on the weight of their link. Then, each link is characterized by a weight. The weight is randomly defined and depends of the type of social group. For example, the weight of the families relationship is higher than those of the Neighborhood relationships.

Process Overview and Scheduling

The model is daily time step base. The dynamics of the model follows several steps. The first step concerns the initialization where the population of agents and their social networks are created according to the initial parameters. After, the daily dynamics of the agents are defined: information diffusion, movement, and evolution of the disease. At each step, when an agent receives an information, he informs the other agents in the same social networks following some rules (cf. sub module: Information diffusion). The information diffusion impacts the behavior of the agents. If agents receive and accept information on the disease, they change their behavior and the exposed agent becomes a not-exposed agent and consequently the contamination rate of the agent decreases.

Agent moves from one place (market, church, etc.) to another. At each step, an agent can visit a maximum of 5 places. Agents are contaminated during their movement. The evolution of the disease in an individual depends on the attitude of the agent. Because, the meningitis is a seasonal disease, the duration of the simulation concerns the period from January to May (120 days).

Design Concepts
Interactions
In the model, the agents share the information on meningitis disease through their social networks.

As other form of interactions, we have the physical contact that occur when the agent moves in the environment. During their movement, the agents gain physical contact and can become contaminated.

Stochasticity
Stochasticity is used to specify the behaviors of the agents. The agents move from cell to cell randomly. And they gain physical contact randomly. And agent is contaminated randomly. The evolution of the disease in an agent is defined in stochastic way and depends on the attitude of the agent. In addition, an agent selects randomly the agents from their neighborhood to share information. Finally, the weights of the links between agents are randomly defined.

Observation
The models allows to observe the movement of the agents. In addition, different charts are proposed to observe the evolution of the disease and the information spread.

Sub Models
Information Diffusion
Different steps of decision is used to represent the information adoption by the agents as defined in the innovation diffusion theory [19]:

Step 1. Reception of information: the agent receives information from another agents from the same networks

Step 2. Persuasion: Several cases may arise:
- case (a): the receiver is an innovator, it takes a favorable attitude (it is willing to share the information) to the information
- case (b): the receiver is an imitator (early adopters, early majority, late majority), it takes a favorable attitude to the information
- case (c): the receptor is a conservative: it rejects the information

Step 3. Decision: Several cases may arise:
- case (a) it is innovative: it accepts the information and informs other agents in the same social networks (appropriation of the information).
- case (b): it is imitator: if the trust to the information reaches some threshold, thus it accepts the information and informs other agents in the same social networks. The trust to the information is the sum of the weight of the received information. The weight of an information corresponds to the weight of the link relating the target and the source agent.
- case (c): it is conservative: it simply rejects the information.

Step 4. Implementation: if an agent accepts the information, he changes his attitude. Then, an exposed agent becomes a not-exposed agent.

Movement and Contamination
At each step, each agent selects randomly the places to visit. To move from a place to another, the agent moves randomly from a cell to another. During the movement, agent

gain physical contact with an agent selects randomly among closest agents. Depending on the healthy status of the two agents, their exposure (exposed and not-exposed) to the disease, one of them can be contaminated. But, the contamination is stochastically determined. When, a susceptible gain contact with an infectious or infected agent, the contamination rate of the susceptible is the product of the contamination rate of the two agents.

Disease Evolution in a Person
The disease evolves in a person depending on the healthy status and the interactions with other persons. The changes of an person healthy status are determined based on transition rates as probabilities. The transition rates depend on the exposure of the individual and the medical cover. When an not-exposed agent is infected, he goes to the hospital and beneficiates of a medical cover. The exposed agent never goes to the hospital and does not beneficiate of a medical cover.

Initialization
Depending on the size of the population the agents are created. After, the confessional group is created and an agent is randomly selected to be the head of the confessional group. Then, families are created as follows:

1. a family is created
2. the size of the family is randomly defined based on the minimum and the maximum size of a family
3. depending on the size of the family, agents are randomly selected to be members of the family
4. one agent among the members of the family is randomly selected to be the head of the family and linked to the family
5. the head of the family is linked to the confessional group
6. the other selected agents are linked among them and to the head of the family
7. the process continues until each agents is linked to a family

After the creation of families, the heads of families are linked between them to form the neighborhood network depending on the size of neighborhood (a parameter). Based on the innovation population sharing, the innovation status of the agents is randomly determined. Finally, the healthy status of the agent is randomly determined.

Simulations
Several scenarios have been simulated to assess how the information diffusion can contribute to the control of the disease evolution. For that, we simulated the diffusion of information in two different configurations of the social networks. In the first, we consider that each family has 4 family neighbors while in the second each family has 8 family neighbors. Considering that the agents interact among them depending on the trust, the two social networks configurations have been simulated in two contexts of trust distribution: the context of high trust and a context of low trust. Consequently, 4 scenarios were simulated (Table 2).

Table 2. The simulated scenarios

	Scenario 1	Scenario 2	Scenario 3	Scenario 4
Number of agents	1000	1000	1000	1000
Number of neighborhood links	4	4	8	8
Trust	Low	High	Low	High

3   Results and Discussion

The results showed that the configuration of social networks and the trust distribution impact the information spread and the meningitis outbreak. We observed that the information spread is higher in scenarios with higher trust distribution than in scenarios with lower trust distribution. However, with the same trust distribution, the information spread is higher in scenarios with 8 family neighbors (Fig. 2).

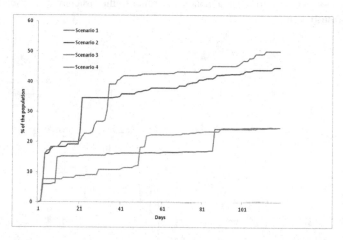

Fig. 2. The evolution of information spread according to the structure of the social networks and the trust distribution

The spread of information impacts the information adoption. Higher is the information spread higher is the information adoption by the individuals (Fig. 3). When the agents receive many messages from their networks, the threshold for the information adoption is rapidly reached leading to the rapid information adoption by the agents. That explains why the information adoption is higher in scenarios 3 and 4 than in scenarios 1 and 2. The number of neighborhood relationships between agents in the scenarios 3 and 4 is higher than in scenarios 1 and 2.

When the agents adopt the information, they adopt behavior preventing the spread of the disease. Consequently, higher is the adoption of information, lower is the spread of disease (Fig. 4). In addition, lower is the information adoption, higher is the mortality (Fig. 5).

From what precede, the results showed that the information diffusion is a relevant tool to control the spread of disease. The strategies of information diffusion should take

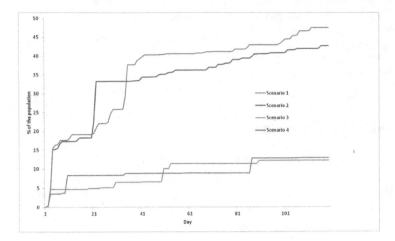

Fig. 3. The evolution of information adoption according to the structure of the social networks and the trust distribution

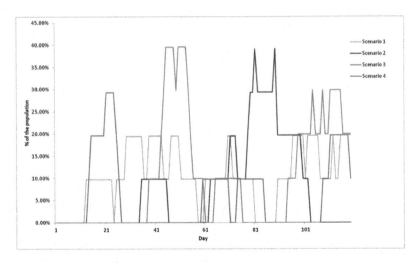

Fig. 4. The evolution of the disease spread according to the structure of the social networks and the trust distribution

account the structure of the social network particularly the number of relationships between individuals. To increase the number of relationships between individuals, the public health agencies should rely on the existing social groups but also create several groups of information diffusion. Since the trust to the information plays an important role, the use of media (radio, television) could play an important role in meningitis outbreak control.

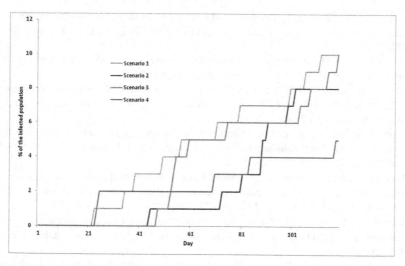

Fig. 5. The evolution of the death in the infected population according to the structure of the social networks and the trust distribution

4   Conclusion

This study aimed to develop an agent-based model to simulate the impacts of information diffusion on the meningitis spread. The resulting model is generic so that it can represent the meningitis system of the West-Africa.

The resulting model takes account the information diffusion through the social network, the adoption of information by the individuals and the spread of the disease. Several simulations have been achieved to assess the impacts of the structures of social networks on the disease control. The simulations showed that the number of relationships and the trust among the individuals impact the adoption of information and the spread of the disease.

The further works would concern the simulation of information diffusion and the spread of the disease at regional scale. In addition, the impacts of climate would be taken account.

Acknowledgement. This work was funded by "Centre d'excellence africain en Mathématiques, Informatique et Technologies de l'Information et de la Communication (CEA-MITIC)". The author wish to appreciate the efforts put in by the anonymous reviewers whose comments and criticisms have assisted in improving the quality of this manuscript to make it worthy of publication.

References

1. Yaka, P.: Rôles des facteurs climatiques et environnementaux dans l'apparition et la prédiction des épidémies de méningite cérébro-spinale en zone sahélo-soudanienne de l'Afrique de l'Ouest; cas du Burkina Faso et du Niger (2008)
2. Mohammed, I., Iliyasu, G., Habib, A.G.: Emergence and control of epidemic meningococcal meningitis in sub-Saharan Africa. Pathogens Glob. Health **111**(1), 1–6 (2017)

3. Thomson, M.C., Jeanne, I., Djingarey, M.: Dust and epidemic meningitis in the Sahel: a public health and operational research perspective. IOP Conf. Ser. Earth Environ. Sci. **7**(1), 012017 (2009)
4. Papazian, H., et al.: A stakeholder-oriented framework to consider the plurality of land policy integration in Sahel. Ecol. Econ. **132**, 155–168 (2017)
5. Haer, T., Botzen, W.J.W., Aerts, J.C.J.H.: The effectiveness of flood risk communication strategies and the influence of social networks—Insights from an agent-based model. Environ. Sci. Policy **60**, 44–52 (2016)
6. Lakon, C.M., et al.: Simulating dynamic network models and adolescent smoking: the impact of varying peer influence and peer selection. Am. J. Public Health **105**(12), 2438–2448 (2015)
7. d'Aquino, P., Bah, A., Turner, B.L.: Multi-level participatory design of land use policies in African drylands: a method to embed adaptability skills of drylands societies in a policy framework. J. Environ. Manag. **132**, 207–219 (2014)
8. Drogoul, A., Huynh, N.Q., Truong, Q.C.: Coupling environmental, social and economic models to understand land-use change dynamics in the Mekong Delta. Front. Environ. Sci. **4**, 19 (2016)
9. Ferber, J.: Multi-agent Systems: An Introduction to Distributed Artificial intelligence. Addison Wesley Longman, London (1999)
10. Belem, M., Müller, J.P.: An organizational model for multi-scale and multi-formalism simulation: application in representation of carbon dynamics in West-Africa Savanna. Simul. Model. Practice Theory **32**, 83–98 (2013)
11. Stummer, C., et al.: Innovation diffusion of repeat purchase products in a competitive market: an agent-based simulation approach. Eur. J. Oper. Res. **245**(1), 157–167 (2015)
12. Cissé, A., et al.: Un modèle à base d'agents sur la transmission et la diffusion de la fièvre de la Vallée du Rift à Barkédji (Ferlo, Sénégal). Stud. Inform. Univ. **10**(1), 77–97 (2012)
13. Cindy, H., et al.: Simulating the diffusion of information: an agent-based modeling approach. Int. J. Agent Technol. Syst. (IJATS) **2**(3), 31–46 (2010)
14. Kelton, K., Fleischmann, K.R., Wallace, W.A.: Trust in digital information. J. Am. Soc. Inf. Sci. Technol. **59**(3), 363–374 (2008)
15. Artalejo, J.R., Economou, A., Lopez-Herrero, M.J.: The stochastic SEIR model before extinction: computational approaches. Appl. Math. Comput. **265**, 1026–1043 (2015)
16. Kai, Z., Lei, Y.: Information source detection in the SIR model: a sample-path-based approach. IEEE/ACM Trans. Netw. **24**(1), 408–421 (2016)
17. Wilenky, U.: NetLogo (1999). http://ccl.northwestern.edu/netlogo/. Center for Connected Learning and Computer-Based Modeling, Northwestern University. Evanston, IL
18. Grimm, V., et al.: The ODD protocol: a review and first update. Ecol. Model. **221**(23), 2760–2768 (2010)
19. Roger, E.: Diffusion of Innovations. Free Press, New York (1995)

An Adaptive Temporal-Causal Network Model for Enabling Learning of Social Interaction

Charlotte Commu, Mathilde Theelen, and Jan Treur[✉]

Behavioural Informatics Group,
Vrije Universiteit Amsterdam, Amsterdam, The Netherlands
{c.a.commu, m.a.h.theelen}@student.vu.nl,
j.treur@vu.nl

Abstract. In this study, an adaptive temporal-causal network model is presented for learning of basic skills for social interaction. It focuses on greeting a known person and how that relates to learning how to recognize a person from seeing his or her face. The model involves a Hebbian learning process. The model also addresses avoidance behavior related to enhanced sensory processing sensitivity. In scenarios persons without and with enhanced sensory processing sensitivity are compared. Mathematical analysis was performed to verify correctness of the model.

1 Introduction

Faces play a crucial role as one of the most information-rich types of stimuli used in social interaction, and thus of the greatest interests for researchers. Darwin was one of the first researchers who looked at the importance of face recognition [8]. The importance of faces for social interaction is also emphasized by the fact that children have a strong preference for looking at faces, even in the first hours after the child is born [33]. A network in the brain has been found that is specialised in recognizing and interpreting the faces of others [24]. Recognizing a person from a face is in general something humans are very good at [10], although there are some situations in which it is harder to recognize a person. One of those situations is when encountering someone in a context that is different than the usual context [1], for example when seeing a colleague when being on a holiday. Moreover, some persons find more difficulties when trying to recognize persons from faces. Especially for persons with enhanced sensory processing sensitivity (an element of the Autism Spectrum Disorder, ASD), this can be hard [3, 33]. Such problems in recognition are at the basis of social dysfunction for persons with ASD [9, 27]. Training methods have been developed to help this group [30].

In this paper, an adaptive temporal-causal network model is presented addressing the learning of social interaction and in particular the role of recognizing persons by their faces. The model has been designed according to the Network-Oriented Modeling approach described in [32]. The paper has the following structure: at first, the neurological background for the model is briefly discussed. After this, the adaptive temporal-causal network model is described, followed by the simulations and the mathematical analysis.

© Springer International Publishing AG 2017
J. Bajo et al. (Eds.): PAAMS 2017 Workshops, CCIS 722, pp. 257–270, 2017.
DOI: 10.1007/978-3-319-60285-1_22

2 Neurological Background

For social interaction, *mirror neurons* play a crucial role; e.g., [18]. For persons with ASD in particular, it has been found that they often show reduced mirror neuron activity when observing faces, as compared to typically developing persons [7]. These mirror neurons, which are important, for example, in identifying emotions in the faces of others, are said to be at the core of social deficits in persons with ASD [7]. There is also a significant correlation between the activity of the mirror neurons and empathic abilities of persons, which may also relate to face recognition [27]. Therefore, mirror neurons are an important aspect in the development of the model in this paper, since they can cause deficits in social interaction.

Self-other distinction means that persons can distinguish between their own feelings and mental representations and the feelings and mental representations of others [29]. For persons with ASD, it is known that they often have a reduced self-other distinction. This self-other distinction is often mentioned together with self-face recognition. This ability is important for social development and it is assumed that persons with ASD have specificities for this ability [21].

Another mechanism affecting social interaction is regulation to compensate for enhanced *sensory processing sensitivity*. For example, in [2], pp. 867–868, it is put forward that dysfunction in processing sensory information results in deviant behaviours to (down)regulate stimulation from the environment; see also [16]. This hypothesis has a long history, going back, for example, to [17, 31], who compared ASD-related behaviours to stereotyped and avoidance behaviours shown by animals when placed in stressful circumstances. In recent years the perspective of enhanced sensory processing sensitivity has become a quite active area of research; see for example, [2, 6, 11, 23, 26]. Using eye trackers that have become widely available, much work focuses on gaze fixation or gaze aversion behaviour in relation to over-arousal due to enhanced sensitivity for sensory processing of face expressions, in particular in the region of the eyes; e.g., [5, 20, 22, 25, 28]. To get rid of arousal which is experienced as too strong, the gaze can be taken away from the observed face or eyes.

Several tests were done, in which the face memory ability of persons with ASD was compared with typically developing persons. All of the six experiments that were found report a significant result for the reduced face memory ability in persons with ASD [35]. In one of the tests, the researchers made a comparison between the memory of houses, the perception of houses and the perception of faces. Where typical developing children score best on the test with faces as compared to the other tests, children with ASD had an equal score for all of the three tests [15]. This implies that persons with ASD have a reduced ability to remember a face.

3 The Adaptive Temporal-Causal Network Model

The adaptive temporal-causal network model for learning of social interaction is described in this section. The model describes how social interaction takes place, with a focus on greeting known persons involving learning to recognize them by their faces. It is hard to have a meaningful social interaction when a person is not recognized in the first place. In particular, the connection between the sensory representation of a face based on seeing this face and the interpretation or belief a person generates about who this person is, plays an important role in social interaction. By a learning process this connection is strengthened the more often the face representation and the belief about which person it is occur simultaneously. In the model the learning of this connection is based on a Hebbian learning principle as will be further explained below.

A conceptual representation of a temporal-causal network model in the first place involves representing in a declarative manner states and connections between them that represent (causal) impacts of states on each other, as assumed to hold for the application domain addressed. The states are assumed to have (activation) levels that vary over time. The following three notions are covered by elements in the Network-Oriented Modelling approach based on temporal-causal networks, and are part of a conceptual representation of a temporal-causal network model:

Connection weight $\omega_{X,Y}$. Each connection from a state X to a state Y has a *connection weight value* $\omega_{X,Y}$ representing the strength of the connection, often between 0 and 1, but sometimes also below 0 (negative effect) or above 1.

Combination function $c_Y(..)$. For each state a *combination function* $c_Y(..)$ is chosen to aggregate the causal impacts of other states on state Y.

Speed factor η_Y. For each state Y a *speed factor* η_Y is used to represent how fast a state is changing upon causal impact.

An *adaptive* temporal-causal network model occurs when some of the above elements, for example some of the connection weights, are also dynamic. The model presented here incorporates parts of the model described in [32], chap. 9. The conceptual and numerical representation of the model will be presented here.

The model was designed by integrating a number of theories some of which were discussed in Sect. 2: mirror neuron systems [7, 18], control neurons with self-other distinction function [4, 18], emotion integration [13, 14]. Furthermore, theories were incorporated addressing regulation in order to cope with enhanced sensory processing sensitivity [2, 5, 25, 28], and theories about face recognition and memory [35].

The developed model shows the difficulties persons with enhanced sensory processing sensitivity can have regarding social interaction. It addresses factors such as context, the avoiding behaviour due to enhanced sensory processing sensitivity, and the learning of connections between face representations and interpretations in the form of beliefs about who is the person. Figure 1 gives an overview of the conceptual representation of the model. The following notations are used for the states:

ws	world state	ss	sensor state	sr	sensory representation state
bs	belief state	ps	preparation state	cs	control state	es	execution state

Each state also has a label LPk that refers to the corresponding numerical representation described below. Parts the model that were introduced by [32], were adopted, but what is depicted as the upper part in Fig. 1 (indicated by LP16–LP23), and the learning process are new. This part of the model integrates the effect of seeing a face,

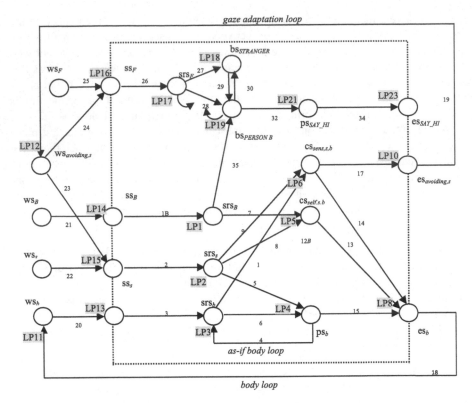

Fig. 1. Overview of the conceptual representation of the model

the recognition process, social actions that can follow from this, and the Hebbian learning process. An overview of the states, their connections and weights can be found in Table 1. States indicated by an F relate to the face of a person that is encountered, B indicates a known context in which this happens (e.g., at work), s is any stimulus that may cause disruption, b is used to refer to a body state which indicates emotion. For example, srs_b is considered as the feeling of the emotion.

Usually, connection weights have a value between 0 and 1, but they can also be negative when a suppressing effect is modeled. Negative weights in this model are chosen for ω_{14}, ω_{23}, ω_{24}, ω_{29}, and ω_{30}. For ω_{23} and ω_{24} a value of -1 has been chosen since they are the weights that express the negative influence of avoidance behaviour on the sensing ss_F of the face and the sensing ss_s of disturbances. For ω_{29} and ω_{30} a value of -0.2 has been chosen, since the states of the belief $bs_{STRANGER}$ that it is a stranger and the belief $bs_{PERSON B}$ that it is a known person B normally cannot both have a high activation level. Therefore, if one of the states is active, the other one is suppressed, and the other way around. It is assumed that the connection from the sensory representation srs_F of the face F to the belief $bs_{PERSON B}$ that it is a known person B can be learned. The adaptive connection weight involved in the learning process is ω_{28}; see Table 1, last row. The more often you see a certain face, while you

Table 1. Overview of the connections, their weights, and their explanations; see also Fig. 1

From state	To state	Weight	Connection	LP	Explanation
ss_B	srs_B	ω_{1B}	Representing B	LP1	Representing a person B from sensing B
ss_s	srs_s	ω_2	Representing s	LP2	Representing a stimulus s (e.g., another person B's smile or tears)
ss_b	srs_b	ω_3	Representing b	LP3	Representing a *body map* for
ps_b		ω_4	Predicting b		feeling b by sensing body state b, and via *as-if body loop* from preparation for body state b
srs_s	ps_b	ω_5	Responding	LP4	Preparing for *body state* b: emotional response b
srs_b		ω_6	Amplifying		
srs_B	$cs_{B,s,b}$	ω_{7B}	Monitoring B	LP5	*Control state* for *self-other distinction*
srs_s		ω_{8B}	Monitoring s		
srs_s	$cs_{sens,s,b}$	ω_9	Monitoring s	LP6	*Control state* for *enhanced sensitivity*
srs_b		ω_{10}	Monitoring b		
$cs_{self,s,b}$	es_b	ω_{13}	Controlling response	LP8	Expressing *body state b*
$cs_{sens,s,b}$		ω_{14}	Suppressing response		
ps_b		ω_{15}			
$cs_{sens,s,b}$	$es_{avoiding,s}$	ω_{17}	Executing avoidance	LP10	Directing *gaze, controlled* by *control state* for enhanced sensitivity
es_b	ws_b	ω_{18}	Effectuating b	LP11	Effectuating actual *body state*
$es_{avoiding,s}$	$ws_{avoiding,s}$	ω_{19}	Effectuating avoidance	LP12	Effectuating actual *gaze*
ws_b	ss_b	ω_{20}	Sensing b	LP13	Sensing body state b
ws_B	ss_B	ω_{21}	Sensing B	LP14	Sensing a person B
ws_s	ss_s	ω_{22}	Sensing s	LP15	Sensing stimulus s from world state s, *regulated*
$ws_{avoiding,s}$		ω_{23}	Suppressing sensing		by *gaze state* avoiding s
$ws_{avoiding,s}$	ss_F	ω_{24}	Sensing F	LP16	Sensing
ws_F		ω_{25}			
ss_F	srs_F	ω_{26}	Representing F	LP17	Representing the stimulus of a face
srs_F	$bs_{STRANGER}$	ω_{27}	Interpreting face F	LP18	Believing that there is a *stranger*
$bs_{PERSON\ B}$		ω_{30}	Suppressing belief stranger		
srs_F	$bs_{PERSON\ B}$	ω_{28}	Interpreting face F	LP19	Believing that there is a known person (*person B*)
srs_B		ω_{35}	Infer B from context		
$bs_{STRANGER}$		ω_{29}	suppress belief B		
$bs_{PERSON\ B}$	ps_{SAY_HI}	ω_{32}	Preparation to say hi	LP21	Preparing for *body state say hi*: greeting someone that you recognize
ps_{SAY_HI}	es_{SAY_HI}	ω_{34}	Executing saying hi	LP23	Expressing *body state for greeting*
srs_F	ω_{28}	1	Adapting by face		Hebbian learning of ω_{28}
$bs_{PERSON\ B}$		1	Adapting by context		

know from the context who it is, the more you will recognize the person from seeing the face. The Hebbian learning principle indicates that the more often these states are active simultaneously, the stronger this connection will become. At each time point t each state Y in the model has an activation level which is represented by a number $Y(t)$ between 0 and 1. A conceptual representation of temporal-causal network model can be transformed in a systematic manner into a numerical representation of the model [32]:

- at each time point t each state X connected to state Y has an *impact* on Y defined as $\textbf{impact}_{X,Y}(t) = \omega_{X,Y}\, X(t)$ where $\omega_{X,Y}$ is the weight of the connection from X to Y
- The *aggregated impact* of multiple states X_i on Y at t is:

$$\textbf{aggimpact}_Y(t) = \textbf{c}_Y(\textbf{impact}_{X_1,Y}(t), \ldots, \textbf{impact}_{X_k,Y}(t))$$
$$= \textbf{c}_Y(\omega_{X_1,Y}X_1(t), \ldots, \omega_{X_k,Y}X_k(t))$$

where X_i are the states with connections to state Y
- The effect of $\textbf{aggimpact}_Y(t)$ on Y is exerted *over time gradually*:

$$Y(t+\Delta t) = Y(t) + \eta_Y[\textbf{aggimpact}_Y(t) - Y(t)]\, \Delta t$$
or
$$dY(t)/dt = \eta_Y[\textbf{aggimpactY(t)} - Y(t)]$$

- Thus, the following *difference* and *differential equation* for Y are obtained:

$$Y(t+\Delta t) = Y(t) + \eta_Y\,[\textbf{c}_Y(\omega_{X_1,Y}X_1(t), \ldots, X_{k,Y}X_k(t)) - Y(t)]\Delta t$$
$$d_Y(t)/dt = \eta_Y[\textbf{c}_Y(X_{1,Y}X_1(t), \ldots, \omega_{X_k,Y}X_k(t)) - Y(t)]$$

Moreover, the adaptive weight ω for the connection from srs_F to $\text{bs}_{\text{PERSON } B}$ follows a Hebbian Learning rule [12]:

$$\omega(t+\Delta t) = \omega(t) + [\eta\, \text{srs}_F(t)\, \text{bs}_{\text{PERSON }B}(t)\, (1 - \omega(t)) - \zeta\, \omega(t)]\, \Delta t$$

Here η is a learning rate and ζ an extinction rate.

Different combination functions are used within the model. The states related to LP1, LP2, LP11, LP12, LP13, LP14, LP17, LP20, and LP21 make use of the identity combination function $c(V) = \textbf{id}(V) = V$. Those for LP3, LP4, LP5 and LP8 make use of the simple logistic sum combination function, which is represented numerically by:

$$c(V_1, \ldots, V_k) = \textbf{slogistic}(V_1, \ldots, V_k) = \frac{1}{1 + \textbf{e} - \sigma(V1 + .. + V_{k-\tau})}$$

Here σ is the steepness parameter and τ the threshold parameter. For the states related to LP6, LP8, LP10, LP15, LP16, LP18, LP19, LP22, and LP23 an advanced logistic sum function is used, which is represented numerically as follows:

$$c(V_1, \ldots, V_k) = \textbf{alogistic}(V_1, \ldots, V_k) = [\frac{1}{1 + \textbf{e} - \sigma(V_1 + .. + V_k - \tau)}$$
$$- \frac{1}{1+e^{\sigma\tau}}](1+e^{-\sigma\tau})$$

This combination function maps 0 impact levels to 0 aggregated impact; see also [32], chap. 2. The generation of a sensor state of a face F is not only affected by the corresponding world state of a face F, but also by the world state of avoiding behaviour representing gaze direction (which in turn is affected by the gaze adaptation loop). This means that because of the negative influence of this world state of avoiding behaviour the sensor state for a face may be not or less activated.

Based on the sensory representation state of a face, a belief can be generated on whether the face is from a person B that is known or from a stranger. Both beliefs influence each other, because the activation of one should exclude the other since a person cannot be a known person B and a stranger at the same time. The context B also has an effect on the belief that someone is a known person B [1]. The preparation states for greeting (saying hi to someone) is influenced by the beliefs that someone is a stranger or a known person B. If someone is a stranger, the preparation and execution states for saying hi will become less active. If someone is a known person B, the preparation and execution states for saying hi will become active.

4 Simulation Experiments

To analyse the designed adaptive temporal-causal network model, two scenarios were simulated in Matlab. The first scenario is the scenario for a persons with enhanced sensory processing sensitivity. In this scenario, it is expected that behaviour with a heavy fluctuating pattern will take place, as also reported in literature [19]. Furthermore, it is expected that it is harder to learn to connect the person to the face. The second scenario is for persons without enhanced sensory processing sensitivity. For those persons, the expectation is that it is easier to learn to connect the face to the person, and less fluctuation takes place [19]. The simulations of the first scenario have been performed with speed factor $\eta = 0.5$ for all states, $\Delta t = 0.5$, and the settings for threshold and steepness values as displayed in Table 2. On the resulting figures, time can be seen on the horizontal axis of the figures and the activation levels of the states are on the vertical axis.

Table 2. Settings for threshold and steepness values used

	LP3	LP4	LP5	LP6	LP8	LP10	LP15	LP16	LP18	LP19	LP23
τ	0.5	0.5	0.5	8	0.5	0.5	0.5	0.5	0.5	0.65	0.5
σ	40	40	40	1.1	40	8	8	8	8	15	8

For the Hebbian Learning rule, the learning rate was set at $\eta = 0.95$, and the extinction rate at $\zeta = 0.08$. The weights for the connection strengths ω_k were all set to 1, except a that have a different weight, as shown in Table 3. It can be noticed in Table 3 that two numbers are mentioned for the connection strength ω_{10}. This has been done because this weight differs for the two different scenarios.

Table 3. Settings for deviating connection weights

ω_{10}	ω_{14}	ω_{23}	ω_{24}	ω_{27}	ω_{28}	ω_{29}	ω_{30}	$\omega_{context}$
1/0.1	−1	−1	−1	0.7	0.1	−0.2	−0.2	0.9

The first scenario shows behaviour of persons with enhanced sensory processing sensitivity. For this scenario, the connection weight of ω_{10} has been set to 1 because persons with enhanced sensory processing sensitivity show longer periods of avoidance behaviour [19] and this high weight value will cause the control state to be highly active. Figure 2 displays the result of the simulation that has been performed. Note the monotonically decreasing (light green) line indicating that the context disappears. A closer look at the main states that cause the fluctuating behaviour is displayed in Fig. 3. Because of the longer periods of avoidance behaviour, the learning process to recognize persons from their faces in the time that the context ws_B is there will not take place. This means that the person does not learn to make a connection between a face and a person, and is not able to recognize the person as soon as the context is not there anymore. As can be seen, avoidance behaviour occurs and shows a fluctuating pattern ($ws_{avoiding,s}$ and $es_{avoiding,s}$). This causes disruption in the sensory state ss_F of a face which also fluctuates. At first, the context ws_B is highly activated; this causes that the reaction of the person at time $t = 18$ is to greet (es_{SAY_HI}) because he or she believes that it is B. But later, when the context is not there anymore this greeting does not take

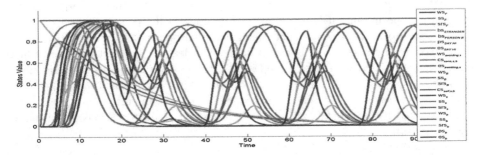

Fig. 2. Simulation of persons with enhanced sensory processing sensitivity (Color figure online)

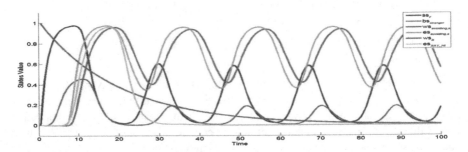

Fig. 3. Simulation of persons with enhanced sensory processing sensitivity: greeting (Color figure online)

place: the execution state es_{SAY_HI} to greet becomes low and almost inactive after $t = 40$. It can be noticed that after $t = 40$, in contrast the belief state $bs_{stranger}$ for believing that someone is a stranger becomes active and the person behaves accordingly.

Figure 4 displays the learning process: the values of the adaptive connection weight over time. It can be seen that the learning effect only partly takes place: the value never becomes higher than 0.5 and decreases when the context is disappearing. Thus, it is harder to learn a face in a particular context.

Figure 5 displays the results of the second scenario. This graph shows the behaviour of persons without enhanced sensory processing sensitivity when encountering faces. For this simulation the connection strength of ω_{10} has been set to 0.1 because such persons show shorter periods of avoidance behaviour. This weight will cause the control state to be partially active or active for shorter periods and causes the expected behaviour. Figure 6 explains a few of the states. In this figure it can be seen that because of the shorter and less active periods of avoidance behaviour, the learning process can take place and will lead to the recognition of a person from the face.

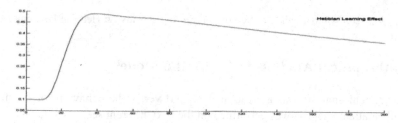

Fig. 4. A person with enhanced sensory processing sensitivity: Hebbian Learning Effect

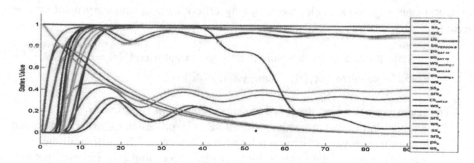

Fig. 5. Simulation of a person without enhanced sensory processing sensitivity

Figure 7 shows this learning effect. It can be seen that the learning effect takes place since its level becomes higher than 0.9. Therefore, it will be easier to recognise someone and have adequate social interaction.

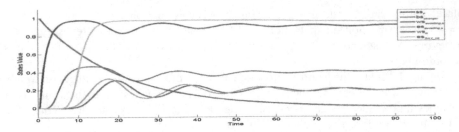

Fig. 6. Simulation of a person without enhanced sensory processing sensitivity: greeting

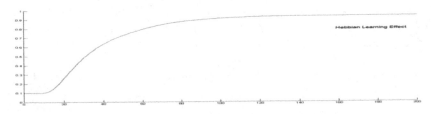

Fig. 7. A person without enhanced sensory processing sensitivity: Hebbian Learning Effect

5   Mathematical Analysis to Verify the Model

A mathematical analysis was used to analyse and verify the behaviour of the model. The mathematical analysis was performed on the two different scenarios that have been discussed in Sect. 4. More specifically, analysis of stationary points has been performed. Let Y be a state, then [32]: Y has a *stationary point* at t if $dY(t)/dt = 0$. An *equilibrium* occurs when for all states a stationary point at t occurs. For a temporal-causal network model the following criterion for a stationary point can be used [32], chap. 12:

$$\text{State } Y \text{ has a stationary point at } t \quad \Leftrightarrow \quad \mathbf{aggimpact}_Y(t) = Y(t)$$
$$\Leftrightarrow \mathbf{c}_Y(\omega_{X1,Y}X_1(t), \ldots, \omega_{Xk,Y}X_k(t)) = Y(t)$$

The latter expression is also called the *stationary point equation.*

The simulation of a person with enhanced sensory processing sensitivity does not end up in equilibrium values because a lot of the states keep fluctuating all the time. After some time most of the states seem to do this according to a repeated pattern. Therefore, this shows a limit cycle pattern. Within a limit cycle pattern, (temporary) stationary points of the states still can be found. The results of the simulation with enhanced sensory processing sensitivity can be found in the Table 4. As can be seen by the absolute deviations, all of the states except for one fulfil the stationary point equation with accuracy <0.1. The exception is the measured data at the maxima of es_b. Upon further investigation no error in the implemented model was found to explain this. This state has a very high steepness of 40 which makes that changes in value can occur very fast. Moreover the not very small step size $\Delta t = 0.5$ makes that the time point of a maximum or minimum may not fit well to a discrete time point of the simulation: this time point may deviate by 0.25, which would make that the maximum or minimum does not occur exactly at the indicated time point from the simulation. All in all, the outcomes give evidence that the model as implemented does what it is meant to do.

Table 4. Overview of the outcomes of the calculation of the stationary points

		ss_F	srs_F	$ws_{avoiding,s}$	ss_S	srs_S	$cs_{sens,s,b}$
Maxima	Time point	171	175	188	171	175	179
	State value	0.577	0.509	0.9311	0.575518179	0.5091	0.9309
	Aggregated impact	0.5756	0.4692	0.9146	0.5756	0.4692	0.9215
	Absolute deviation	0.0014	0.0398	0.0165	$-8.18\ 10^{-5}$	0.0399	0.0094
Minima	Time point	192	196	168	192	196	162
	State value	0.0234	0.0369	0.4133	0.023407501	0.03689	0.4049
	Aggregated impact	0.02808	0.04702	0.4219	0.02808	0.04702	0.4215
	Absolute deviation	-0.00468	-0.01012	-0.0086	-0.00467	-0.01013	-0.0166

		$es_{avoiding,s}$	ws_b	ss_b	es_b	$bs_{stranger}$
Maxima	Time point	184	168	171	166	178
	State value	0.9515	0.799028	0.699823	0.897906	0.1865
	Aggregated impact	0.9425	0.7093	0.6323	0.7154	0.1666
	Absolute deviation	0.009	0.08973	0.06752	0.18251	0.0199
Minima	Time point	165	193	195	189	162
	State value	0.3605	0.062296	0.103324	0.001891	0.007029
	Aggregated impact	0.3781	0.07432	0.06599	0.003124	0.007197
	Absolute deviation	-0.0176	-0.01202	0.03733	-0.00123	-0.00017

The simulated data of persons without enhanced sensory processing sensitivity shows a Hebbian adaptation process and this process ends up in an equilibrium. The equilibrium value for the adaptive connection weight ω can be determined using the following equation, when both $X_1 > 0$ and $X_2 > 0$; see [32], chap. 12:

$$\omega = \frac{1}{1 + \zeta/(\eta\, X_1 X_2)}$$

This equilibrium value can have its highest point when $X_1 = 1$ and $X_2 = 1$ and then results in a value of around 0.95. When analysing the Hebbian Learning Effect in Fig. 7, it can be noticed that this equilibrium value is almost reached. As the simulation is performed over a longer period of time it can be seen that an equilibrium happens in Fig. 8. After a certain time $t > 250$ the states do not change anymore and are all stationary points. Therefore, an equilibrium occurs.

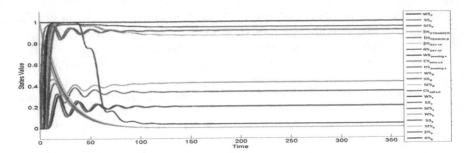

Fig. 8. Simulation of persons without enhanced sensory processing sensitivity: equilibrium

6 Discussion

This paper introduces a temporal-causal network model that describes some of the basic skills that enable social interaction and how they are learnt. Several simulations were done in order to test this model, showing behaviour in accordance with research of [19] which reported that persons with and without ASD both show fluctuating behaviour but both in varying degrees. A mathematical analysis was done of which the outcome gave evidence that the model as implemented does what it is meant to do. The model can be applied as the basis for human-like virtual agents, for example, to obtain a virtual patient model to study the way in which social interaction can deviate for certain types of persons. In further research real data can be used to test the model in more detail. Furthermore, more scenarios could be simulated to analyse more and different outcomes of the model. One example is the use of different intervals for the stimulus of a face. Currently, the world state for a face has been constantly one for all the simulations. It could be interesting to find out what happens when someone sees a face more often (multiple times in one simulation). Also scenarios can be explored in more depths for persons that have other aspects of the ASD spectrum, such as a reduced mirror system, reduced self-other distinction or reduced emotion integration.

References

1. Apps, M.A., Tsakiris, M.: Predictive codes of familiarity and context during the perceptual learning of facial identities. Nat. Commun. **4**, 2698 (2013)
2. Baker, A.E.Z., Lane, A.E., Angley, M.T., Young, R.L.: The relationship between sensory processing patterns and behavioural responsiveness in autistic disorder: a pilot study. J. Autism Dev. Disord. **38**, 867–875 (2008)
3. Blair, R., Frith, U., Smith, N., Abell, F., Cipolotti, L.: Fractionation of visual memory: agency detection and its impairment in autism. Neuropsychologia **40**(1), 108–118 (2002)
4. Brass, M., Spengler, S.: The inhibition of imitative behaviour and attribution of mental states. In: Striano, T., Reid, V. (eds.) Social Cognition: Development, Neuroscience, and Autism, pp. 52–66. Wiley-Blackwell, Oxford (2009)

5. Corden, B., Chilvers, R., Skuse, D.: Avoidance of emotionally arousing stimuli predicts social- perceptual impairment in asperger's syndrome. Neuropsychologia **46**, 137–147 (2008)
6. Crane, L., Goddard, L., Pring, L.: Sensory processing in adults with autism spectrum disorders. Autism **13**, 215–228 (2009)
7. Dapretto, M., Davies, M.S., Pfeifer, J.H., Scott, A.A., Sigman, M., Bookheimer, S.Y., Iacoboni, M.: Understanding emotions in others: mirror neuron dysfunction in children with autism spectrum disorders. Nat. Neurosci. **9**(1), 28–30 (2006)
8. Darwin, C.: The Expression of the Emotions in Man and Animals. John Marry, London (1872)
9. Dawson, G., Webb, S.J., Wijsman, E., Schellenberg, G., Estes, A., Munson, J., Faja, S.: Neurocognitive and electrophysiological evidence of altered face processing in parents of children with autism: implications for a model of abnormal development of social brain circuitry in autism. Dev. Psychopathol. **17**(03), 679–697 (2005)
10. Farah, M.J., Wilson, K.D., Drain, M., Tanaka, J.N.: What is "special" about face perception? Psychol. Rev. **105**(3), 482 (1998)
11. Gepner, B., Féron, F.: Autism: a world changing too fast for a mis-wired brain? Neurosci. Biobehav. Rev. **33**, 1227–1242 (2009)
12. Gerstner, W., Kistler, W.M.: Mathematical formulations of Hebbian learning. Biol. Cybern. **87**, 404–415 (2002)
13. Grèzes, J., de Gelder, B.: Social perception: understanding other people's intentions and emotions through their actions. In: Striano, T., Reid, V. (eds.) Social Cognition: Development, Neuroscience, and Autism, pp. 67–78. Wiley-Blackwell, Oxford (2009)
14. Grèzes, J., Wicker, B., Berthoz, S., de Gelder, B.: A failure to grasp the affective meaning of actions in autism spectrum disorder subjects. Neuropsychologica **47**, 1816–1825 (2009)
15. Hauck, M., Fein, D., Maltby, N., Waterhouse, L., Fein- stein, C.: Memory for faces in children with autism. Child Neuropsychol. **4**(3), 187–198 (1998)
16. Von Hofsten, C., Gredebäck, G.: The role of looking in social cognition: perspectives from development and autism. In: Striano, T., Reid, V. (eds.) Social Cognition: Development, Neuroscience, and Autism, pp. 237–253. Wiley-Blackwell, Oxford (2009)
17. Hutt, C., Hutt, S.J., Lee, D., Ousted, C.: Arousal and childhood autism. Nature **204**, 908–909 (1964)
18. Iacoboni, M.: Mirroring People: the New Science of How We Connect with Others. Farrar, Straus & Giroux, New York (2008)
19. Kajimura, S., Nomura, M.: When we cannot speak: eye contact disrupts resources available to cognitive control processes during verb generation. Cognition **157**, 352–357 (2016)
20. Kirchner, J.C., Hatri, A., Heekeren, H.R., Dziobek, I.: Autistic symptomatology, face processing abilities, and eye fixation patterns. J. Autism Dev. Disord. **41**, 158–167 (2011)
21. Kita, Y., Gunji, A., Inoue, Y., Goto, T., Sakihara, K., Kaga, M., Inagaki, M., Hosokawa, T.: Self-face recognition in children with autism spectrum disorders: a near- infrared spectroscopy study. Brain Dev. **33**(6), 494–503 (2011)
22. Kylliäinen, A., Hietanen, J.K.: Skin Conductance responses to another person's gaze in children with autism. J. Autism Dev. Disord. **36**, 517–525 (2006)
23. Lane, A.E., Young, R.L., Baker, A.E.Z., Angley, M.T.: Sensory processing subtypes in autism: association with adaptive behavior. J. Autism Dev. Disord. **40**, 112–122 (2010)
24. Leopold, D.A., Rhodes, G.: A comparative view of face perception. J. Comput. Psychol. **124**(3), 233 (2010)
25. Neumann, D., Spezio, M.L., Piven, J., Adolphs, R.: Looking you in the mouth: abnormal gaze in autism resulting from impaired top-down modulation of visual attention. Soc. Cogn. Affect. Neurosci. **1**, 194–202 (2006)

26. Smith, A.: The empathy imbalance hypothesis of autism: a theoretical approach to cognitive and emotional empathy in autistic development. Psychol. Rec. **59**, 489–510 (2009)
27. Schultz, R.T.: Developmental deficits in social perception in autism: the role of the amygdala and fusiform face area. Int. J. Dev. Neurosci. **23**(2), 125–141 (2005)
28. Spezio, M.L., Adolphs, R., Hurley, R.S.E., Piven, J.: Analysis of face gaze in autism using 'bubbles'. Neuropsychologia **45**, 144–151 (2007)
29. Steinbeis, N.: The role of self–other distinction in understanding others' mental and emotional states: neurocognitive mechanisms in children and adults. Phil. Trans. R. Soc. B **371**(1686), 20150074 (2016)
30. Tanaka, J.W., Wolf, J.M., Klaiman, C., Koenig, K., Cockburn, J., Herlihy, L., Brown, C., Stahl, S., Kaiser, M.D., Schultz, R.T.: Using computerized games to teach face recognition skills to children with autism spectrum disorder: the let's face it! program. J. Child Psychol. Psychiatry **51**(8), 944–952 (2010)
31. Tinbergen, E.A., Tinbergen, N.: Early Childhood Autism: An Ethological Approach. Advances in Ethology, vol. 10. Journal of Comparative Ethology Supplement. Paul Perry, Berlin (1972)
32. Treur, J.: Network-Oriented Modeling: Addressing Complexity of Cognitive, Affective and Social Interactions. Springer, Heidelberg (2016)
33. Valenza, E., Simion, F., Cassia, V.M., Umilta, C.: Face preference at birth. J. Exp. Psychol. Hum. Percept. Perform. **22**(4), 892 (1996)
34. Wallace, S., Coleman, M., Bailey, A.: Face and object processing in autism spectrum disorders. Autism Res. **1**(1), 43–51 (2008)
35. Weigelt, S., Koldewyn, K., Kanwisher, N.: Face identity recognition in autism spectrum disorders: a review of behavioral studies. Neurosci. Biobehav. Rev. **36**(3), 1060–1084 (2012)

Computing Aggregates on Autonomous, Self-organizing Multi-agent System: Application "Smart Grid"

Sai Manoj Marepalli[✉] and Andreas Christ

Offenburg University of Applied Sciences, Offenburg, Germany
{sai.marepalli,christ}@hs-offenburg.de

Abstract. Decentralized data aggregation plays an important role in estimating the state of the smart grid, allowing the determination of meaningful system-wide measures (such as the current power generation, consumption, etc.) to balance the power in the grid environment. Data aggregation is often practicable if the aggregation is performed effectively. However, many existing approaches are lacking in terms of fault-tolerance. We present an approach to construct a robust self-organizing overlay by exploiting the heterogeneous characteristics of the nodes and interlinking the most reliable nodes to form an stable unstructured overlay. The network structure can recover from random state perturbations in finite time and tolerates substantial message loss. Our approach is inspired from biological and sociological self-organizing mechanisms.

Keywords: Distributed computing · Self-organizing networks · Agent based systems · Reliability · Bio-inspired models

1 Introduction

An increasing demand for reliable energy and numerous technological advancements have motivated the development of a smart electric grid. Smart grids can be understood as complex networks of intelligent electronic devices (IEDs), consisting of wired and wireless sensors. The main distinction between the smart grid and the traditional electrical grid is that the smart grid has the ability to capture data of the sensor network, where each sensor node in the network is capable of measuring, communicating, and computing the information [1].

In the smart grid scenario sensor nodes are increasingly being used to monitor various parameters in a wide range of functional tasks including system monitoring (state estimation, security analysis, etc.) [2]. In many current instances, grid operators are interested in collecting raw data from sensor nodes and transport it to a centralized computing environment for analysis [1,2]. However, as time goes by, the number of devices added to the smart grid environment increases continuously providing powerful infrastructures that are not widely exploited due to current software limitations (scalability, real-time requirements, reliability etc.).

© Springer International Publishing AG 2017
J. Bajo et al. (Eds.): PAAMS 2017 Workshops, CCIS 722, pp. 271–283, 2017.
DOI: 10.1007/978-3-319-60285-1_23

As most of the smart grid applications are increasingly dependent on information systems [2]. Consequently, the reliability of these systems is utmost importance in the majority of the cases [2]. Different techniques are devised to develop reliable systems in decentralized environments. Typically, some kind of redundancy is employed in order to achieve high reliability [3]. If a hardware or software fail by crashing, a backup connection to another node would take over. The impact of fixing faults is reduced by using different software implementations in parallel [4]. In many approaches special fault tolerance management components are employed, to ensure continuous operation in spite of faults.

We propose an approach which does not require special fault tolerance management components or special fault tolerance algorithms. Instead, each software component, i.e. an agent exploits the heterogeneous capabilities of other participating agents using a social science-oriented *Tag* based coordination mechanism [5]. In our approach, each agent is assigned with a tag. Tags are observable markings. Agents receive these markings based on their characteristics (e.g. reliability, capacity, etc.). Agents can observe the tags of the other agents and take actions based on those observations altruistically. We assume in our model altruism as a basis for the evolution of groups of specialized heterogeneous agents. The mechanism involved in this model can therefore be interpreted as follows: the most reliable agents in the network are promoted as trusted or reliable nodes and the agents which are relatively less reliable tend to preferentially attach to the trusted/reliable agents. Reliable agents are interlinked to form an unstructured robust overlay structure. The strategies to bootstrap and maintain such a network with reliable and non-reliable agents is derived from biologically inspired protein to protein interaction networks (PPIN) [6]. The tag mechanism enables agents to promote or demote their roles between reliable to non-reliable agents based on a feedback mechanism which they receive from their environment. This process is evolutionary. As the agents coordinate their reconfiguration behavior indirectly through the environment, there is no centralized control structure or other single point of failure. Therefore, the fault-tolerant behavior is emergent.

As a motivation, the proposed approach can be applied to the data aggregation algorithms. Until now to the best of our knowledge there has been no aggregation protocol which has self-organizing mechanisms in a way we approach the problem. By adding self-organizing and emergent behavior to the data aggregation algorithms, it solves two purposes. It (1) contributes to the robustness of the aggregation network while reducing number of messages exchanged to maintain the structure of the aggregation protocol. (2) This system as a whole can easily be applied to smart grid's state estimation problem, as self-organizing networks would reduce the maintenance costs of the protocol.

In this work, our focus is on presenting an abstract model that represents our model and its requirements. We briefly describe the state of the art of distributed data aggregation algorithms and outline how our proposed model can be applied to the smart grid state estimation problem.

The reminder of this paper is organized as follows: In Sect. 2, we survey related distributed data aggregation algorithms. In Sect. 3, we describe the model of smart grid state estimation and data aggregation problem. The proposed self-organizing computing model from nature inspired design pattern is presented in Sect. 4. The aggregate tree construction algorithm is presented in Sect. 5. Section 6, gives concluding remarks and directions for future work.

2   Related Works

Aggregation is intended as a summarizing mechanism of the overall state within the network. The summary data is obtained through the use of set of a functions named aggregate functions. The basic aggregate functions: COUNT, SUM, AVERAGE, MIN, and MAX. Aggregation protocols are broadly classified into two perspectives (1) communication and (2) computation. In this section, we present few works related to the distributed aggregation, and explain how our approach is different from the existing protocols.

Communication Perspective: There are two categories/dimensions within the communication perspective, according to their characteristics and their communication topology (a) structured and (b) unstructured.

In the *Structured approach* protocols require a specific routing structure (for example spanning tree or cluster), and they estimate the aggregate with high accuracy given that network structure is stable. TAG [7] (The Tiny AGgregation), is a data-centric protocol based on a tree based structure. TAG processes aggregation in two phases, *distribution* and *collection*, but this protocol suffers huge waiting times to ensure the conclusion of the two phases. In the DAG [8] (Directed Acyclic Graph) for wireless sensor network the objective is to reduce the effect of message loss. This method takes advantage of path redundancy and improves the robustness. It offers better accuracy but at the cost of a higher message rate.

In the *Unstructured approach* algorithms operate independently from the network organization and structure, without establishing any predefined topology (e.g. Push-sum, push-pull, DRG etc.). The characteristics of this approach are simplicity, robustness and scalability. Nevertheless, the robustness of these protocols may not be directly attained by any algorithm. However, an algorithm correctness may depend on invariants that may not be straightforward [9].

Computational Perspective: In terms of computation, existing aggregation algorithms are based on the following categories:

Hierarchical are accurate and efficient (in terms of message and computational complexity), but not fault tolerant. TAG and DAG are algorithms belonging to this category.

Averaging algorithms perform iterative computation of partial aggregates (averages) by continuously averaging and exchanging data among all active nodes for the obtention of the final result. Push-Pull gossiping [10], DRG [11] (Distributed Random Grouping) are the algorithms that belong to this category. However, averaging protocols are reliable, and relatively accurate. But they are less efficient in terms of the required number of message exchanges.

Most of the previous work in related areas focus on either structured or random topologies. If nodes fail to participate in the structured tree-based topology, the entire sub-tree gets disconnected until a network maintenance algorithm repairs or reconstructs the tree. If the network protocol has to reconstruct the tree often, then the rendering tree aggregation gets unacceptably slow. In case of random topologies if a node fails, the other nodes will carry out the distributed computation without the failed node, but this approach is slower in terms of computing time. However, in our proposed approach the protocol is based on the self-organizing multi-agent paradigm. Agents with simple local rules collaborate to construct and reliably maintain the overlay continuously. Agents in our approach exploit the heterogeneity of agent reliabilities (availability, or capacity). Such that, agents which are most reliable are promoted to for the higher specialized roles in the network. The mechanisms to construct and maintain the overlay are inspired from sociological and biological phenomena.

3   Problem Statement

In this work we mainly consider a smart grid sensor network environment, whereby each sensor node in the network participates in the aggregate computation for estimating current consumption/generation of power at every Δt (e.g. $\Delta t = 5/10 \min$) in a decentralized fashion. These sensor nodes communicate via overlay network for the purpose of state estimation. We refer overlay network as a graph $G = (V, E)$ and consider the sensor nodes with heterogeneous computing capabilities and are not energy constrained.

The network graph $G(t) = (V(t), E(t))$ changes dynamically, where $i \in V(t)$ are sensor nodes and $e \in E(t)$ are edges/links. The nodes or edges/links may appear and disappear over time (t). Each node $i \in V$ holds an input value $w_i\,(1 \leq i \leq N)$. Based on the execution of the proposed tree based aggregation protocol (see Sect. 5) each network node compute a function $f(w(t))$, where $f(.) = f_1(.), f_2(.), f_3(.), ..., f_n(.)$ and $w(t) = w_1(t), w_2(t), w_3(t), ..., w_i(t)$. The former means that each node in the network computes its knowledge function f.

As the subset of nodes or links may appear or disappear in the network resulting in frequent disconnection of the overlay structure and also result in cascade effect. The goal to present the heuristic (in Sect. 4) is to address the problem of robustness of the overlay structure. This means, even in the case of catastrophic node failure events the overlay network recovers gracefully and carry out the aggregation process. The goal is to minimize the cascade effect and maximize the accuracy of aggregation result. The proposed heuristic is inspired from the work [12], they outlined a catalogue of bio-inspired self-organizing design patterns. Also they have shown interrelations among various self-organizing design patterns which facilitate for engineering a self-system. The classification has three layers which is depicted in Fig. 1. The basic layer mechanisms can be used individually or in composition. The composed layer are formed by the combinations of basic mechanisms, and the high level layer, shows different ways to exploit the basic and composed mechanisms. In our proposed model we intend to engineer the high-level design pattern (Tag) for which we have exploited the three basic patterns (Evaporation, Spreading, and Aggregation), and one composed pattern (Gossip). The detailed description of our model is presented in the next section.

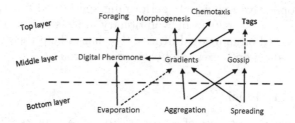

Fig. 1. Self-organizing design patterns and their relationships [12]

4   Self-organizing Data Aggregation Network

In this section, we propose our model which is called "Hub and Spoke". As decentralized systems requires high-level of self-management and resilience in the face of network churn, as central supervision is impossible. Through our approach we intend to enable decentralized systems with biological and sociological properties (namely resilience, emergent adaptation, and self-organization).

4.1   Model Description

The proposed *Hub and Spoke* model is inspired from biological and sociological mechanisms. The metaphoric inspiration for the construction of the overlay originates from the protein-to-protein interaction network (PPIN) [6]. This network has a number of properties that can be used to guide the self-organization of a overlay network topology. The mechanism to cooperate and optimize the nodes in the network is drawn from sociologically inspired Tag mechanism. In this section we briefly give a overview on both of these mechanisms.

Strategies Inspired from PPIN Mechanism. The interaction strategies of PPIN network are simple rules, but they are rich enough to provide emergent behaviors. In the PPIN network, protein nodes are divided into two types (1) hubs and (2) non-hubs. Hub proteins interact with many non-hub protein partners, whereas non-hub proteins only interact with their attached hub partners. The hubs in PPIN network are further classified into date and party hubs. Date hubs participate in a wide range of integrated connections required for a global organization in the whole protein network. In contrast, the party hubs interact with most of their partners (non-hub nodes) simultaneously.

Strategies Inspired from Tag Mechanism. The mechanism behind this social phenomenon promotes the altruistic, cooperative group behavior based on the concept of "tags" (tags are observable markings, cues or displays). Individuals observe the tags of others and take alternative actions based on those observations. The tag process can be understood as a form of evolution of groups composed of cooperative individuals performing specialized functions. Specialization and cooperation results from evolutionary process in which selection and reproduction is based on individual fitness. Specialists help their non-specialist group members, which optimizes the behavior as a group.

4.2 Conceptual Model

We identified multiple instances of self-organizing design patters in our design. This enabled us to conceptualize the following model as shown in Fig. 2, which has encompassed basic patterns such as (evaporation, aggregation, and spreading) with dynamic strategies of the PPIN model, and the Tag mechanism of social inspiration model. In this section we describe the conceptual model, and how it reflects the behavior of the system as a whole.

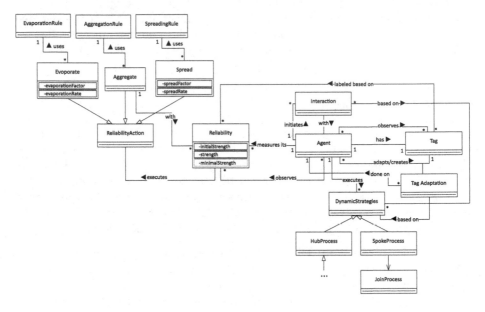

Fig. 2. Conceptual model of hub and spoke

Entities: the entities involved are (a) nodes/hosts (that provide sensors, communication capabilities, memory space, etc.) (b) software agents (that changes in behavior based on the environmental information) (c) environmental agents all that is external to the hosts (e.g. smart grid environment).

Approach: hub and spoke is relatively simple collection of rules and parameters to regulate the growth and maintenance of the overlay with agents continuously adjust their state and connections added. Inspired from PPIN metaphor the agents in the overlay network are divided into two types (1) hubs and (2) non-hubs (spoke). Hub agents are understood as reliable and capable agents, whereas spoke agents are relatively less reliable and less capable. Each agent in the hub and spoke model is characterized by a reliability value representing many characteristics (such as availability, capacity, computational power, etc.) of the agent. Hub agents are further classified into three different states/processes for response to the changing network conditions. The goal of these changing conditions is to push non-reliable (spoke) agent attachments towards the reliable (hub) agent and build interconnections into the overlay while maintaining resilience.

Dynamics: the dynamics of the hub and spoke is modelled using tag mechanism. Depending on the level of spoke agents concentration the hub agent switches between three different states. (1) dating/exploring state (2) Intermediate state and (3) party/satisfied state. The switching mechanism is inspired from a sociological design pattern namely Tag. The tag is a role/label given to each agent based on its current measure of capacity values. Hub agents are promoted to the higher states/roles when their threshold capacity of spoke concentration is increased. E.g., if a threshold capacity of spoke concentration is increased in exploring state, then the hub is promoted to next higher state (Intermediate state). If the hub agent due to dynamic network conditions reduce its spoke node concentration, then the hub agent is demoted to the lower roles/states. This sort of feedback mechanism makes the network evolving over time in response to changing conditions or parameters. The states are metaphorically interpreted as tags, where tags with higher roles altruistically contributes its resources to the non-hub spoke agents.

Feedback Mechanism: in the hub and spoke model, the overlay continuously exploits the heterogeneity of the system by promoting reliable and capable agents with specialized roles. The heterogeneity of the system is exploited by the tag mechanism. Tags are observable detectable attributes which are labelled to agents and are adjusted/added by the agents. The feedback mechanism keeps the problem of finding reliable and capable agent *open*. Thus, allowing agents to continuously sense their neighborhood for specialized/better performing neighbors, to preferentially attach to them in order to form a fitter group.

Implementation:

- *agent discovery mechanism:* each agent periodically selects a known agent and sends a copy of its entire neighbour list (which contains addresses, and time stamp) (*spreading*). Upon receiving such a message, the recipient combines that list with its own (*aggregation*), along with an entry for the sending peer timestamped with the current time. In order to prevent the lists from growing indefinitely, agents are removed from the list via a *evaporation* mechanism. Entries which are older are progressively discarded.

- *agent reliability mechanism:* each agent learns their respective reliability measure on its own, for instance an agent computational power is relatively constant whereas its *availability and capacity* measures varies during the time. An agent learns its availability measure by monitoring its past session length [13], in hub and spoke all the measures such as availability, computational power, and capacity are synthesized together and calculates a reliability measure. *ReliabilityAction* is the class which updates the calculated reliability measures at each agent shown in Fig. 2.
- *agent tag mechanism:* agent's tag represents its role/behavior/capability in the network. Agent may adapt to a new tag, based on the feedback it receives from the other agents. Agents can either be promoted/demoted based on their reliability or capacity measures. If a spoke agent has better reliability measure than its neighbouring hub agent, then spoke agent is promoted to hub agent, and hub agent is demoted to spoke agent. Hub agents switch between dating, intermediate, or party states to balance the spoke concentration and converge network with stable spoke and hub agents.
- the dynamics of roles/tags of agents are engineered in the classes (HubProcess, SpokeProces, etc.). These classes are presented as an algorithmic view in the next section.

4.3   Algorithmic Overview of Dynamic Agent Strategies

Initially all agents are in spoke state, and are initialized with the abstract reliability measure drawn from probability distribution (e.g. power law, or exponential) which represents the behavior of the network in general. This is measured based on statistical estimations [13].

As the network bootstrapping process initiates, the agents discover other spoke and hub agent and use a gossip mechanism to acquire tag information of other agents. The gossip mechanism is based on the Newscast protocol [14], which enables each node to pick randomly another node and exchange with it nodes lists and state/tag information. That is, whether the node is spoke, date/exploring, intermediate, or party/ satisfied.

Initialization Parameters:

$hubAgent\ h_a \leftarrow null$
$spokeAgent\ a_s \leftarrow null$
$dateHub\ h_d \leftarrow null$
$dateHub\ h'_d \leftarrow null$ ▷ A random dating hub
$intermediateHub\ h_i \leftarrow null$
$intermediateHub\ h'_i \leftarrow null$ ▷ A random intermediate hub
$partyHub\ h_p \leftarrow null$
$partyHub\ h'_p \leftarrow null$ ▷ A random party hub

All the agents work independently to construct the overlay network. Once the overlay network converges with stable hubs and spoke agents, the tree is

Algorithm 1. Agents behavior in Spoke state

```
1: function DODYNAMICS
2:     if as.isDisconnected() then
3:         Spoke agent searches for the hub agent from its neighbor list.
4:     else if connToHub.isDisconnected() || connToHub.isEmpty() then
5:         if ha == null then
6:             as.becomeDatingAgent();
7:         else
8:             spoke agent attempts to attach to only single hub agent;
9:             once it get attached to the hub agent, it takes no other action.
10:        end if
11:    end if
12: end function
```

Algorithm 2. Agents behavior in Dating/Exploring state

```
1: function DODYNAMICS
2:     if hd.isConnectedTo(hi) || hd.isConnectedTo(hp) then
3:         hd will attempt to form a link to one of those types randomly
4:     else if hd.isNotConnectedTo(hi) || hd.isNotConnectedTo(hp) then
5:         hd will search for another dating hub h'd
6:     end if
7:                                ▷ Search for a dating agent from hd neighbor list
8:     ▷ If two dating nodes are neighbors, then one neighbor get absorbed in another
9:     if hd.hasNeighbor(h'd) then
10:        if hd.spokeConnMeasure() > h'd.spokeConnMeasure() then
11:            h'd transfers all the spoke agents and hub links to hd
12:            h'd becomes a spoke agent and attaches to hi
13:        else
14:            hd becomes spoke agent, and attaches to h'd
15:            hd transfers its spoke agents and hub links to h'd
16:        end if
17:    end if
18:    if hd.spokeConncetionsExceedThresholdLimit() then
19:        hd promoted to intermediate agent;
20:    end if
21: end function
```

build on top of the hub network overlay. In the next section we present tree construction protocol executed on the unstructured hub agent network overlay.

5   Algorithm to Construct Aggregate Tree

The tree construction algorithm shown below is used to carry the operation of constructing a random forest tree structure, on top of the randomly generated hub overlay network. As each hub agent carries their reliability measure, we consider the maximum reliable hub agent to initiate the tree construction process.

Algorithm 3. Agents behavior in Intermediate state

1: **function** DODYNAMICS
2:     **if** $h_i.isUnderSpokeConnections()$ **then**
3:         h_i searches for dating hub h_d in its neighborhood
4:         **if** $h_i.isConnectedTo(h_d)$ **then**
5:             h_d transfers all its spoke agents to h_i and
6:             h_d becomes a spoke agent and attaches to h_i
7:         **end if**
8:     **end if**
9:     **if** $h_i.hasOverSpokeConnections()$ && $datingHub \neq null$ **then**
10:         push spoke connections to dating hub
11:     **end if**
12:     **if** $h_i.spokeConnMeasure() > h_i'.spokeConnMeasure()$ **then**
13:         h_i' transfers all the spoke agent connections and hub links to h_i
14:         h_i' becomes a spoke agent and attaches to h_i
15:     **else**
16:         h_i becomes spoke agent, and attaches to h_i'
17:         h_i transfers its spoke agents and hub links to h_i'
18:     **end if**
19:     **if** $h_i.spokeConncetionsExceedThresholdLimit()$ **then**
20:         h_i promoted to party/satisfied agent;
21:     **end if**
22: **end function**

Algorithm 4. Agents behavior in Party/Satisfied state

1: **function** DODYNAMICS
2:     **if** $h_p.isUnderSpokeConnections()$ **then**
3:         h_p searches for h_d or h_i in its neighborhood
4:         **if** $h_p.isConnectedTo(h_d)$ || $h_p.isConnectedTo(h_i)$ **then**
5:             h_d or h_i transfers all their spoke agents to h_p
6:             h_d or h_i becomes a spoke agent and attaches to h_p
7:         **end if**
8:     **else if** $h_p.hasOverSpokeConnections()$ **then**
9:         h_p will transfer the excess spoke connections to one of its hub neighbor
10:         **if** $h_p.unableToFindHubNeighbor()$ **then**
11:             h_p promotes one of its neighbor spoke agent to dating agent
12:             given the spoke agent posses maximum reliability measure
13:         **end if**
14:     **end if**
15:     **if** $h_p.cannotHandleEnoughSpokeConnections()$ **then**
16:         h_p demoted to intermediate agent;
17:     **end if**
18: **end function**

As the tree construction algorithm progresses it picks the maximum reliable node, then probes independently v vertices uniformly at random and compares it with its own reliability measure. If the probing node found the node with greater reliability than its own then it considers it as its parent. This process will continue until the degree reaches to $log\, n - 1$.

Algorithm 5. To construct reliable tree T on an unstructured hub and spoke overlay

---

```
1: function TREECONSTRUCTION
2:     Initialization parameters:
3:     Random overlay graph G(V, E)
4:     Each hub vertex (V) is initialized with minimum reliability measure re(x)
5:     max(re(x)) is initialized as a root, and
6:     it is a starting point C(s) to construct the tree
7:     for each node i ∈ V do
8:         Found ← FALSE
9:         parent(i) ← NULL
10:        k ← 0                              ▷ number of random nodes probed
11:        repeat
12:            probe independently the vertexes v uniformly at random
13:            from C(s) and compare its reliability measure;
14:            if re(u) > re(i) then
15:                parent(i) ← u
16:                Found ← TRUE
17:                k ← k + 1
18:            end if
19:        until Found == TRUE ∨ k < log n − 1
20:        if Found == TRUE then
21:            send a connection message including its identifier, i,
22:            to its parent node parent(i);
23:        else
24:            collect the connection messages and accordingly
25:            construct the set of its children nodes, Child(i);
26:        end if
27:        if Child(i) = ∅ then
28:            become a leaf node;
29:        else
30:            become an intermediate node;
31:        end if
32:    end for
33: end function
```

5.1 Algorithm for Aggregate Computation

The computation of aggregate result at the root is as follows: first, spoke agents push their estimates to the hub agents. Second, hub agents with its own estimate and the spoke estimates compute the partial aggregate. Third, the partial aggregates are forwarded to the intermediate hub agents. Fourth, the global sum is calculated at the root of the tree.

Algorithm 6. $con_{sum} = convergencecast(T, v)$

1: **function** TREECONVERGENCE
2:    **Input:** the reliability tree T and the value vector v over all agents in T
3:    **Output:** the global Ave aggregate vector con_{sum} over hub agents
4:    **Initialization parameters:**
5:    every node i stores a row vector $(v_i, w_i = 1)$, its value v_i and a size count w_i
6:    **for each** $leafHubAgent\ i \in T$ **do**
7:        send its parent a message containing the vector$(v_i, w_i = 1)$
8:        reset$(v_i, w_i) = (0, 0)$.
9:    **end for**
10:    **for each** $intermediateHubAgent\ j \in T$ **do**
11:        collect messages (vectors) from its children
12:        $v_j \leftarrow v_j + \sum_{k \in Child(j)} v_k$ ▷ where Child(j) = {j's children}
13:        $w_j \leftarrow w_j + \sum_{k \in Child(j)} w_k$
14:        send computed (v_j, w_j) to its parent
15:        reset its vector $(v_j, w_j) = (0, 0)$.
16:    **end for**
17:    **for each** $rootHubAgent\ z \in V$ **do**
18:        collect messages (vectors) from its children and compute the global sum
19:        $cov_{sum}(z, 1) \leftarrow v_z + \sum_{k \in Child(z)} v_k$ ▷ where Child(z) = {z's children}
20:        $cov_{sum}(z, 2) \leftarrow w_z + \sum_{k \in Child(z)} w_k$ ▷ the size count of the tree
21:    **end for**
22: **end function**

---

6   Conclusions and Future Work

In this work, we presented a hub and spoke model which is inspired from biological and sociological mechanisms. The aim of this model is to reliably estimate the state of the smart grid in a decentralized fashion. For this process we have studied the state-of-the art of existing decentralized aggregate computing architectures, and identified a trade-off between accuracy and computational time. By our proposed approach we are intend to balance the trade-off by devising a protocol that has self-organizing and emergent properties. Allowing nodes to emerge as most reliable nodes and build a robust overlay network. As part of the future work, we wish to simulate this algorithm on a simulation framework and test the performance, reliability and accuracy.

References

1. Yan, Y., Qian, Y., Sharif, H., Tipper, D.: A survey on smart grid communication infrastructures: motivations, requirements and challenges. IEEE Commun. Surv. Tutorials **15**, 5–20 (2013)
2. Moslehi, K., Kumar, R.: Smart grid - a reliability perspective. In: 2010 Innovative Smart Grid Technologies (ISGT), pp. 1–8 (2010)
3. Dell'Amico, M., Michiardi, P., Toka, L., Cataldi, P.: Adaptive redundancy management for durable P2P backup. Comput. Netw. **83**, 136–148 (2015)

4. Li, Z., Xie, G., Li, Z.: Efficient and scalable consistency maintenance for heterogeneous peer-to-peer systems. IEEE Trans. Parallel Distrib. Syst. **19**, 1695–1708 (2008)
5. Wolf, T.D., Holvoet, T.: A catalogue of decentralised coordination mechanisms for designing self-organising emergent applications. In: CW 458, Department of Computer Science, pp. 40–61 (2006)
6. Han, J.D.J., Bertin, N., Hao, T., Goldberg, D.S., Berriz, G.F., Zhang, L.V., Dupuy, D., Walhout, A.J., Cusick, M.E., Roth, F.P., et al.: Evidence for dynamically organized modularity in the yeast protein-protein interaction network. Nature **430**, 88–93 (2004)
7. Madden, S., Franklin, M.J., Hellerstein, J.M., Hong, W.: Tag: a tiny aggregation service for Ad-Hoc sensor networks. ACM SIGOPS Operating Syst. Rev. **36**, 131–146 (2002)
8. Motegi, S., Yoshihara, K., Horiuchi, H.: Dag based in-network aggregation for sensor network monitoring. In: International Symposium on Applications and the Internet, SAINT 2006, 8–pp. IEEE (2006)
9. Jesus, P., Baquero, C., Almeida, P.S.: Dependability in aggregation by averaging. arXiv preprint arXiv:1011.6596 (2010)
10. Kempe, D., Dobra, A., Gehrke, J.: Gossip-based computation of aggregate information. In: Proceedings of 44th Annual IEEE Symposium on Foundations of Computer Science, pp. 482–491. IEEE (2003)
11. Chen, J.Y., Pandurangan, G., Xu, D.: Robust computation of aggregates in wireless sensor networks: distributed randomized algorithms and analysis. IEEE Trans. Parallel Distrib. Syst. **17**, 987–1000 (2006)
12. Fernandez-Marquez, J.L., Serugendo, G.D.M., Montagna, S., Viroli, M., Arcos, J.L.: Description and composition of bio-inspired design patterns: a complete overview. Nat. Comput. **12**, 43–67 (2013)
13. Stutzbach, D., Rejaie, R.: Understanding churn in peer-to-peer networks. In: Proceedings of the 6th ACM SIGCOMM Conference on Internet measurement, pp. 189–202. ACM (2006)
14. Jelasity, M., Van Steen, M.: Large-scale newscast computing on the internet. Technical report, Citeseer (2002)

DeMaDIE

Evaluating the Perception of the Decision Quality in Web-Based Group Decision Support Systems: A Theory of Satisfaction

João Carneiro[1,3(✉)], Ricardo Santos[2], Goreti Marreiros[1],
and Paulo Novais[3]

[1] GECAD, Institute of Engineering, Polytechnic of Porto, Porto, Portugal
{jomrc,mgt}@isep.ipp.pt
[2] CIICESI, School of Technology and Management of Felgueiras,
Polytechnic of Porto, Felgueiras, Portugal
rjs@estgf.ipp.pt
[3] ALGORITMI Centre, University of Minho, Guimarães, Portugal
pjon@di.uminho.pt

Abstract. The future and success of organizations depend greatly on the quality of every decision made. It is known that most of the decisions in organizations are made in group. With the purpose to support the decision-makers anytime and anywhere, Web-based Group Decision Support Systems have been studied. The amount of Web-based Group Decision Support Systems incorporating automatic negotiation mechanisms such as argumentation is increasing nowadays. Usually, these systems/models are evaluated through mathematical proofs, number of rounds or seconds to propose (reach) a solution. However, those techniques do not say much in terms of decision quality. Here, we propose a model to predict the decision-makers' satisfaction (perception of the decision quality), specially designed to deal with multi-criteria problems. Our model considers aspects such as: alternatives comparison, style of behaviour, emotions, mood and expectations. The proposed formulation matches the assumptions previously defined in the literature.

Keywords: Group Decision Support Systems · Decision satisfaction · Decision quality · Outcomes · Affective computing

1 Introduction

It is known that many of the decisions in organizations are made in group [1]. Group Decision Support Systems (GDSS) have been widely studied throughout the last decades [2, 3] to support this type of decisions. However, in the last ten/twenty years, we have seen a remarkable change in the context where the decision-making process happens, especially in large organizations [4]. With the appearance of global markets, the growth of multinational organizations and a global vision of the planet, we easily find decision-makers (chief executive officers, managers and other members of global virtual teams) spread around the world, in countries with different time zones [5]. However, to support the group decision-making process in this context is especially

© Springer International Publishing AG 2017
J. Bajo et al. (Eds.): PAAMS 2017 Workshops, CCIS 722, pp. 287–298, 2017.
DOI: 10.1007/978-3-319-60285-1_24

complex, due to the decision-makers being geographically dispersed. To provide an answer and operate correctly in this type of scenarios, the traditional GDSS have evolved to what we identify today as Web-based GDSS [6, 7]. The idea behind the Web-based GDSS is to support the decision-making process "anytime" and "any-where" [4]. The automatic negotiation mechanisms can be used (in Web-based GDSS) to help overcome the lack of interaction caused in the context described before [8]. Usually, these systems/models are evaluated through mathematical proofs, number of rounds or seconds to propose (reach) a solution [9]. However, those techniques do not say much in terms of decision quality.

In fact, the decision quality is impossible to measure in the end of a group decision-making process. What is possible to measure, or what can be valuable to know in the end of a group decision-making process is the perception of the decision-quality of each of the decision-makers (or their satisfaction) [10]. Satisfaction is therefore a strong indicator, not only of the results, but also of the whole decision process [11]. When someone is questioned about the quality of a decision, the answer does not reflect only the assessment of outcomes, but also, even unconsciously; it includes the evaluation process necessary to reach the decision [11]. Satisfaction as a metric has been applied in the literature to many different issues: life satisfaction [12], job satis-faction [13], etc. Satisfaction has also been applied in the GDSS topic. However, the existent proposals are not concerned with the perception of the decision quality but are concerned with decision-maker's satisfaction regarding the GDSS performance, usability, etc. [14–16].

In this work, we study satisfaction as a metric to understand the decision-maker's perception of the decision quality. Our proposal is defined based in the assumptions and premises previously published in [10], which contemplate different approaches from researchers of a wide range of areas in this thematic (computer sciences, psy-chology, economy, etc.). It intends to allow automatic assessment of the participants' satisfaction in a meeting supported by a Web-based GDSS. To evaluate decision-maker's satisfaction, we consider the alternatives comparison, style of behaviour, emotions, mood and expectations.

The rest of the paper is organized as follows: in the next (Sect. 2) section our satisfaction model is presented and in Sect. 3 some conclusions are taken, along with the work to be done hereafter.

2 Methods

As we have seen in [10], when a decision-maker is questioned about the quality of a decision, the answer does not reflect only the assessment of the outcomes, but also, even unconsciously; it includes the evaluation process necessary to reach the decision. To understand how suitable a decision is, it is necessary to understand and analyse the means to reach that decision [17]. Thus, one should give prominence to the process, when drawing conclusions about the results. Besides, the researchers agree that there is a great variety of factors responsible for affecting the satisfaction of a decision-making element with the decision made in a meeting: emotional variables (affective compo-nents) [18], the process [19], the outcomes [11], the factors that affect the situation [20] and expectations [21]. Our proposal (follows the assumptions and premises proposed in [10]) deals with these factors making use of the typical data configured by the decision-makers in the Web-GDSS (in disperse meetings [22]).

2.1   Outcomes

The alternative chosen by the group has impact in the decision-maker's satisfaction. This is an inescapable fact, since achieving the outcomes is the reason why the decision-making process happens. The satisfaction or the perception of the decision quality is related to the outcomes [10]. However, to understand the outcomes impact it is necessary to see the big picture. Higgins [11] says that "psychologically, then, a decision is perceived as good when its expected value or utility of outcomes is judged to be more beneficial than the alternatives". Thus, whereas the preferred alternative is the best in the decision-maker's perspective, the distance between the preferred alternative and the chosen one means a loss of the decision-maker's satisfaction. The loss of satisfaction comprises the difference in the assessment made by the decision-maker for each of the alternatives, as well as what the participant did not achieve with the final decision. In this work, we consider the participant's assessment of each alternative varying in a [0; 1] range, where 0 means "I do not like at all" and 1 means "I like very much" (see our proposal of a practical implementation based on this in [23]). To understand the satisfaction considering alternatives comparison, we suggest the following formulas:

$$D_{Lost} = Alt_F - Alt_P \tag{1}$$

$$A_{Conversion} = 2Alt_F - 1 \tag{2}$$

$$D_{Outcomes} = (1 - |A_{Conversion}|) * D_{Lost} + A_{Conversion} \tag{3}$$

Where:

- D_{Lost} is the loss of decision maker's satisfaction based in the difference between the assessments made for the alternative chosen by the group (Alt_F) and for his preferred alternative (Alt_P). The loss is zero when the chosen alternative is the same as his preferred alternative;
- Alt_F is the assessment made by the participant for the final alternative, alternative chosen by the group;
- Alt_P is the assessment made by the participant for his preferred alternative;
- $A_{Conversion}$ is the conversion of the assessment made by the participant into our scale of dissatisfaction/satisfaction;
- $D_{Outcomes}$ is the participant's satisfaction concerning the outcomes. Intends to evaluate the satisfaction based in the assessment made by the participant to the alternatives, including the loss of satisfaction in the case where his preferred alternative is not chosen by the group.

We assume the $D_{Outcomes}$ is the purely analytical evaluation of the decision-maker's satisfaction. All other points (presented below) have impact in $D_{Outcomes}$. The other points will depend on the context.

2.2 Expectations

Consciously or not, people create expectations on (almost) everything [21]. The relationship between expectations and the satisfaction is clear. Considering what we have stated before and our previous work [10], it is easy to understand the following rules:

If Participant achieve goals = True
Then expectations impact = Positive or Neutral

If Participant achieve goals = False
Then expectations impact = Negative or Neutral

In this work, we consider the Web-based Group Decision Support System as the only existent mechanism for the decision-makers communicate. Thus, we consider relevant to know the decision-makers' expectations regarding the chances in attaining their objectives.

- Probability of the participant's preferred alternative to be chosen: Understanding the expectations regarding the probability of the participant's preferred alternative to be chosen. "How likely you think your preferred alternative will be chosen?".

In a real scenario, decision-makers are creating expectations all the time: "Is he going to accept my request?", "Will he help me supporting my idea?", etc. However, when automated negotiation techniques are used, the decision-makers only create expectations about issues that they can expect something and which they interact. That is why we only consider the expectations regarding the achievement of results (at this step). The expectations can influence satisfaction in three different ways:

- Positive impact: When the results exceed the expectations;
- Negative impact: When the expectations are not achieved;
- Without impact: When the expectations are achieved.

The expectation value will be within the range [0; 1]. To evaluate expectation in this context, approaches as the ones proposed in [23] can be used. The calculus of satisfaction including expectations is divided in 2 different conditions. Firstly, we address the situation where expectations are matched. This means, the expectations have a positive impact in satisfaction.

Positive Impact. This type of impact occurs when the chosen alternative is the one preferred by the participant. In this case, the impact of the expectation will be positive or neutral (in case the expectation is 1). The following formula is used to calculate the positive impact:

$$P_{Impact} = (1 - E) * Alt_P \tag{4}$$

Where:

- E is the participant's expectation regarding the possibility of his preferred alternative being chosen by the group.
  For a better understanding of the proposed formula, let us consider the scenarios where the impact should have the maximum and minimum values (extreme cases):

- The positive impact should be 1 (maximum impact) when the participant's expectation regarding the preferred alternative being chosen by the group is 0 and the value of alternative assessment is 1;
- The positive impact should be 0 (no impact) when the participant's expectation regarding the preferred alternative being chosen by the group is 1. This means that the decision-maker is taking it for granted. The maximum expectation on a positive situation does not bring any increased satisfaction as a form as impact.

We can include now the expectations in the satisfaction calculation. $D_{Outcomes}$ can be recalculated using the following formula:

$$D_{Outcomes} = D_{Outcomes} + (1 - |D_{Outcomes}|) * P_{Impact} \tag{5}$$

The most important point of this formulation is the possibility to recalculate the $D_{Outcomes}$ satisfaction using the impact in a form of a variable.

In our proposal, we first understand which impact the expectation has (according to the different situations) and use the correct impact next (calculated according to the context). The use of $(1 - E)$ in our formula intends to reflect the difference between the maximum expectation (which would be 1) and the participant's expectation.

Negative Impact. This type of impact occurs when the chosen alternative is not the one preferred by the participant. In this case the impact of the expectation will be negative or neutral (in case the expectation is 0). The following formula is used to calculate the negative impact:

$$N_{Impact} = (Alt_P - Alt_F) * E \tag{6}$$

In the case of a negative impact, we propose a different formula because in this situation the impact represents an expectation that has not been met, symbolizing a loss. Moreover, in this situation, to truly understand the expectation impact, we need to analyse the relation between this loss and the difference between the assessments of his preferred alternative and the one chosen by the group. As we have done before, let us consider the scenarios where the impact should have the maximum and minimum values (extreme cases):

- The negative impact should be 1 (total impact) when the participant's expectation regarding the preferred alternative being chosen by the group is 1, the assessment of the alternative chosen by the group is 0 and the assessment of his preferred alternative is 1;
- The negative impact should be 0 (no impact) when the expectation is 0.

We can include now the expectations in the satisfaction calculation. $D_{Outcomes}$ can be recalculated using the following formula:

$$D_{Outcomes} = D_{Outcomes} + ((1 - D_{Outcomes}) * (-1)) * N_{Impact} \tag{7}$$

2.3   Style of Behaviour

The number of works including affective aspects in the field of computer science is growing exponentially. Previously [24], we proposed a model to define styles of behaviour in agents to represent the decision-makers' intentions. We adopted the conflict styles proposed by Rahim and Magner [25], and redefined them to be more adequate to our context. We called them styles of behaviour and defined them as follows:

- Dominating: A dominating individual believes that he owns the key to solve the problem. He plays a very active role during the decision-making process and tries to force his opinion on other participants;
- Integrating: An integrating individual favours a collaborative style. He aims to achieve consensual decisions and greatly values his and others' opinion. He prefers to manage assiduously the entire decision-making process;
- Compromising: A compromising individual favours a collaborative style. He aims to achieve consensual decisions and values his and others' opinion. He plays a moderately active role during the decision-making process;
- Obliging: An obliging individual tends to give up on his opinion in favour of the group interests. He prefers to follow others' opinions rather than sharing his own;
- Avoiding: An avoiding individual prefers to be freed from responsibility. Fundamentally, he prefers to not be involved in the decision-making process and devalues both the process and the opinion of other participants.

In this proposal, we consider the styles of behaviour described before to formulate the satisfaction model. However, this proposal can be easily adapted to situations where aspects such as personality and conflict styles are used. In this satisfaction model, we aim to assess the decision-maker's satisfaction, so we use behaviour to understand the impact of the process in the decision-maker. The process impact will vary according to the decision-maker's intentions. For instance, let us consider a situation where the participant defined his conflict style as "Dominating". If he notices that the most of other decision-makers do not like his preferred alternative, we can associate to him emotions as distress and disappointment. On the other hand, if the participant defined his conflict style as "Obliging", he may not feel the same emotions because his main intention his not to achieve is preferred alternative but to please some other/s decision-maker/s. This is a simple example to demonstrate that the impact will vary according to how the decision-maker experiences the process.

We define a set of situations that decision-makers experience using a GDSS and correlate them with conflict styles, using the OCC model [26]. Ortony et al. [26] proposed a global structure of emotion types where they defined "valenced reaction to": consequences of events, actions of agents and aspects of objects. For our purpose, we only use the consequences of events. Into the consequences of events they distinguish between the consequences for other and consequences for self, what means a remarkable correlation with the classification of conflict styles proposed by Rahim and Magner [25] where they defined the conflict styles according to the concern for self and the concern for others (see Table 1).

We have considered that the integrating and compromising styles will be affected emotionally by the "consequences for other" and "consequences for self", the obliging

Table 1. Styles of behaviour

Style of behaviour	Concern for self	Concern for others
Dominating	High	Low
Integrating	High	High
Compromising	Moderate	Moderate
Obliging	Low	High
Avoiding	Low	Low

style will be affected emotionally by the "consequences for other", the dominating style will be affected by "consequences for self" and the avoiding will not be emotionally affected. The compromising style of behaviour will be affected with a half of the emotions intensities when compared with the integrating. The set of events that may occur are expressed in the Table 2. (CO is consequences for other and CS is consequences for self).

We have defined some rules to deal with hope and fear emotions (according to [26]).

Table 2. Considered events and respective definition

Event	CO	CS	Emotions
Participant's preferred alternative was chosen by the group	×	✓	Joy and (check rules below)
Participant's preferred alternative was not chosen by the group	×	✓	Distress and (check rules below)
Participant changed his preference to another alternative	×	✓	Hope
The majority prefers the participant's preferred alternative	×	✓	Joy and hope
A few or none decision-maker prefers the participant's preferred alternative	×	✓	Distress and fear
The preferred alternative of the decision-maker/s that the participant considers credible/important was chosen by the group	✓	×	Happy-for, joy and (check rules below)
The preferred alternative of the decision-maker/s that the participant considers credible/important was not chosen by the group	✓	×	Pity, distress and (check rules below)
The majority prefers the same alternative as some other decision-maker/s that the participant considers credible/important	✓	×	Happy-for, joy and hope
The majority do not prefer the same alternative as some other decision-maker/s that the participant considers credible/important	✓	×	Pity, distress and fear

If Participant experience hope and it is confirmed
Then Participant will experience satisfaction

If Participant experience hope and it is not confirmed
Then Participant will experience disappointment

If Participant experience fear and it is confirmed
Then Participant will experience fears — confirmed

If Participant experience fear and it is not confirmed
Then Participant will experience relief

2.4   Emotional Changes and Mood Variation

It is clear in the literature how important is to include in the analysis of satisfaction the affective and emotional components [18, 20, 21].

Due to the brilliant work proposed by Gebhard [27] where he correlates the PAD [28] and the OCC model, many works appeared using the triggered emotions in order to update the mood state (including ourselves). For this model, we propose a correlation between the events defined in Subsect. 2.3 with a set of triggered emotions for each of the situations (Table 2). We used the work proposed in [26] to define a set of emotions for each of situations and analyse the emotions triggered during the process to understand the emotional cost.

In Table 2, we presented the set of considered situations and the emotions associated to each situation. As we can see, all the situations are in some way related to the alternatives. These situations describe the scenarios the decision-makers face every time they interact with the system (GDSS). However, it is also important to define the impact of each situation. The impact of "Participant's preferred alternative was not chosen by the group", should be different if previously the participant face a situation of "A few or none decision-maker prefers the participant's preferred alternative" or a situation of "The majority prefers the participant's preferred alternative". Thus, we consider the process expectations:

$$P_{Expectations} = N_p/N_t \tag{8}$$

Where:

- N_p is the number of decision-makers supporting the participant's preferred alternative or some other decision-maker/s that the participant considers credible/important;
- N_a is the total number of decision-makers.

The $P_{Expectations}$ calculated in each situation will have impact in the emotions calculated in the next interaction because every time a decision-maker faces a new situation, he will be affected by the new information plus the expectations that he created based in previous information. Next, we will describe how to process the emotions created in each situation:

Let Emo_S be a set of emotions of one situation:

$$Emo_S = \{(P_1, A_1, D_1), \ldots, (P_n, A_n, D_n)\} \tag{9}$$

Where:

- n is the number of created emotions;
- P_i, A_i, D_i are the values of Pleasure, Arousal and Dominance for emotion i (based in [27]).

Let Emo_T be the sum of emotions in Emo_S:

$$Emo_T = \sum_{i=1}^{n} (P_i, A_i, D_i) \tag{10}$$

Where:

- n is the number of created emotions;
- $P_i, A_i, D_i \in Emo_S$.

Let Int_{Emo_T} be the intensity of Emo_T:

$$Int_{Emo_T} = \frac{\sqrt{(P)^2 + (A)^2 + (D)^2}}{\sqrt{3}} \tag{11}$$

Let $Exp_{Int_{Emo_T}}$ be the Int_{Emo_T} considering $P_{Expectations}$:

$$Exp_{Int_{Emo_T}} = Int_{Emo_T} * P_{Expectations} \tag{12}$$

Let $Pos_{Emotions}$ be the sum of intensities of all positive emotions (joy, hope, happy-for, satisfaction and relief) created in each situation along the process:

$$Pos_{Emotions} = \sum_{i=1}^{n} \left(Exp_{Int_{Emo_{T_i}}} \right), Emo_S \text{ is a set of positive emotions} \tag{13}$$

Let $Cons_{Emotions}$ be the sum of intensities of all negative emotions (distress, fear, pity, disappointment and fears-confirmed) created in each situation along the process:

$$Cons_{Emotions} = \sum_{i=1}^{n} \left(Exp_{Int_{Emo_{T_i}}} \right), Emo_S \text{ is a set of negative emotions} \tag{14}$$

After calculating $Pos_{Emotions}$ and $Cons_{Emotions}$, we compare the two intensities to understand the emotional cost. According to that, we propose the following simple rules:

If $Pos_{Emotions} = Cons_{Emotions}$
Then Cost = Neutral

If $Pos_{Emotions} > Cons_{Emotions}$
Then Cost = Positive

If $Pos_{Emotions} < Cons_{Emotions}$
Then Cost = Negative

Now, we normalize the $Pos_{Emotions}$ and $Cons_{Emotions}$, such that $Pos_{Emotions} + Cons_{Emotions} = 1$:

$$Norm_{PosEmotions} = Pos_{Emotions}/(Pos_{Emotions} + Cons_{Emotions}) \qquad (15)$$

$$Norm_{ConsEmotions} = Cons_{Emotions}/(Pos_{Emotions} + Cons_{Emotions}) \qquad (16)$$

The difference of intensities will then be considered as a gain or a loss (or neutral in case of no emotional cost). Let us assume this value as Dif_{Emo}:

$$Cost = Norm_{PosEmotions} - Norm_{ConsEmotions} \qquad (17)$$

2.5 Final Satisfaction Calculation

Considering the value of participant's satisfaction concerning the alternative chosen by the group and the value of his mood (both contemplating the expectations), now we are going to join them to do our final calculation of satisfaction:

$$Satisfaction = D_{Outcomes} + (1 - |D_{Outcomes}|) * Cost \qquad (18)$$

The interval for the result of satisfaction will be $[-1; 1]$. We propose an adaptation of a scale based in the work of Babin and Griffin [29] and represented in the Table 3.

Table 3. Scale of satisfaction

Designation	Interval
Extremely satisfied	[0,75; 1]
Much satisfaction	[0,5; 0,75[
Satisfaction	[0,25; 0,5[
Some satisfaction	[0; 0,25[
Some dissatisfaction	] −0,25; 0[
Dissatisfied	] −0,5; −0,25]
Very dissatisfied	] −0,75; −0,5]
Extremely dissatisfied	[−1; −0,75]

3 Conclusions and Future Work

In this article, we proposed a whole new model which allows the automatic assessment of the participants' satisfaction in a meeting supported by a Web-based Group Decision Support System. We believe that the proposed model allows the attainment of a large amount of useful and valuable information. The satisfaction can be used as a metric to compare different Web-based GDSS or automatic negotiation mechanisms. In addition, satisfaction can be used as a utility function to maximize the decision-makers' satisfaction or can be used by agents to predict the decision-maker's satisfaction. To evaluate satisfaction, we considered the alternatives comparison and evaluation, the expectations, emotions, mood and the process. The values obtained in the calculus of satisfaction respect the premises that were defined in a previous work.

As future work, we intend to conduct a case study with real people, in partnership with psychologists. With that work, we also intend to make the model more assertive by the possible improvements that might result after analysing and studying the collected data.

Acknowledgments. This work was supported by COMPETE Programme (operational programme for competitiveness) within Project POCI-01-0145-FEDER-007043, by National Funds through the FCT – Fundação para a Ciência e a Tecnologia (Portuguese Foundation for Science and Technology) within the Projects UID/CEC/00319/2013, UID/EEA/00760/2013, and the João Carneiro PhD Grant with the Reference SFRH/BD/89697/2012.

References

1. Lunenburg, F.C.: Decision making in organizations. Int. J. Manag. Bus. Adm. **15**, 1–9 (2011)
2. DeSanctis, G., Gallupe, B.: Group decision support systems: a new frontier. ACM SIGMIS Datab. **16**, 3–10 (1984)
3. DeSanctis, G., Gallupe, B.: A foundation for the study of group decision support systems. Manag. Sci. **33**, 589–609 (1987)
4. Grudin, J.: Group dynamics and ubiquitous computing. Commun. ACM **45**, 74–78 (2002)
5. Shum, S.B., Cannavacciuolo, L., De Liddo, A., Iandoli, L., Quinto, I.: Using social network analysis to support collective decision-making process. In: Engineering Effective Decision Support Technologies: New Models and Applications, pp. 87–103. IGI Global (2013)
6. Alonso, S., Herrera-Viedma, E., Chiclana, F., Herrera, F.: A web based consensus support system for group decision making problems and incomplete preferences. Inf. Sci. **180**, 4477–4495 (2010)
7. Kwon, O., Yoo, K., Suh, E.: UbiDSS: a proactive intelligent decision support system as an expert system deploying ubiquitous computing technologies. Expert Syst. Appl. **28**, 149–161 (2005)
8. Rahwan, I., Ramchurn, S.D., Jennings, N.R., Mcburney, P., Parsons, S., Sonenberg, L.: Argumentation-based negotiation. Knowl. Eng. Rev. **18**, 343–375 (2003)
9. Marreiros, G., Santos, R., Ramos, C., Neves, J.: Context-aware emotion-based model for group decision making. IEEE Intell. Syst. **25**, 31–39 (2010)
10. Carneiro, J., Marreiros, G., Novais, P.: Using satisfaction analysis to predict decision quality. Int. J. Artif. Intell. **13**, 45–57 (2015)
11. Higgins, E.T.: Making a good decision: value from fit. Am. Psychol. **55**, 1217 (2000)
12. Schimmack, U., Oishi, S., Furr, R.M., Funder, D.C.: Personality and life satisfaction: a facet-level analysis. Pers. Soc. Psychol. Bull. **30**, 1062–1075 (2004)
13. Judge, T.A., Heller, D., Mount, M.K.: Five-factor model of personality and job satisfaction: a meta-analysis. American Psychological Association (2002)
14. Briggs, R.O., de Vreede, G.-J., Reinig, B.A.: A theory and measurement of meeting satisfaction. In: Proceedings of the 36th Annual Hawaii International Conference on System Sciences, 8–pp. IEEE (2003)

15. Tian, X., Hou, W., Yuan, K.: A study on the method of satisfaction measurement based on emotion space. In: 9th International Conference on Computer-Aided Industrial Design and Conceptual Design, CAID/CD 2008, pp. 39–43. IEEE (2008)
16. Paul, S., Seetharaman, P., Ramamurthy, K.: User satisfaction with system, decision process, and outcome in GDSS based meeting: an experimental investigation. In: Proceedings of the 37th Annual Hawaii International Conference on System Sciences, pp. 37–46. IEEE (2004)
17. Beach, L.R.: Image theory: Decision making in personal and organizational contexts. Wiley, Chichester (1990)
18. Liljander, V., Strandvik, T.: Emotions in service satisfaction. Int. J. Serv. Ind. Manag. **8**, 148–169 (1997)
19. Simon, H.A.: A behavioral model of rational choice. Q. J. Econ. **69**, 99–118 (1955)
20. Bailey, J.E., Pearson, S.W.: Development of a tool for measuring and analyzing computer user satisfaction. Manag. Sci. **29**, 530–545 (1983)
21. Sherif, M., Hovland, C.I.: Social judgment: assimilation and contrast effects in communication and attitude change. (1961)
22. Bjørn, P., Esbensen, M., Jensen, R.E., Matthiesen, S.: Does distance still matter? Revisiting the CSCW fundamentals on distributed collaboration. ACM Trans. Comput.-Hum. Interact. (TOCHI) **21**, 27 (2014)
23. Carneiro, J., Martinho, D., Marreiros, G., Novais, P.: A general template to configure multi-criteria problems in ubiquitous GDSS. Int. J. Softw. Eng. Appl. **9**, 193–206 (2015)
24. Carneiro, J., Martinho, D., Marreiros, G., Novais, P.: Defining agents' behaviour for negotiation contexts. In: Pereira, F., Machado, P., Costa, E., Cardoso, A. (eds.) EPIA 2015. LNCS, vol. 9273, pp. 3–14. Springer, Cham (2015). doi:10.1007/978-3-319-23485-4_1
25. Rahim, M.A., Magner, N.R.: Confirmatory factor analysis of the styles of handling interpersonal conflict: first-order factor model and its invariance across groups. J. Appl. Psychol. **80**, 122 (1995)
26. Ortony, A., Clore, G.L., Collins, A.: The Cognitive Structure of Emotions. Cambridge University Press, Cambridge (1990)
27. Gebhard, P.: ALMA: a layered model of affect. In: Proceedings of the Fourth International Joint Conference on Autonomous Agents and Multiagent Systems, pp. 29–36. ACM (2005)
28. Mehrabian, A.: Pleasure-arousal-dominance: a general framework for describing and measuring individual differences in temperament. Curr. Psychol. **14**, 261–292 (1996)
29. Babin, B.J., Griffin, M.: The nature of satisfaction: an updated examination and analysis. J. Bus. Res. **41**, 127–136 (1998)

Decision Process to Manage Renewable Energy Production in Smart Grid Environment

João C. Ferreira[1,2(✉)], Vitor Monteiro[2], J.G. Pinto[2],
Ana Lúcia Martins[3], and João L. Afonso[2]

[1] Information Sciences, Technologies and Architecture Research Center
(ISTAR-IUL), Instituto Universitário de Lisboa (ISCTE-IUL), Lisbon, Portugal
joao.carlos.ferreira@iscte.pt
[2] Centro ALGORITMI, University of Minho, 4800-058 Guimarães, Portugal
{vmonteiro,gpinto,jla}@dei.uminho.pt
[3] Business Research Unit (BRU-IUL),
Instituto Universitário de Lisboa (ISCTE-IUL), Lisbon, Portugal
almartins@iscte.pt

Abstract. This research work is related to the Electric Vehicle (EV) integration in the electricity market, using the OpenADR open protocol for demand response. The proposed solution integrates a local developed EV charging system and a cloud management system, to coordinate the available energy produced from renewable energy sources, taking into account its intermittent production and the requirements of the EV charging process at home. Considering the smart mobility paradigm, all transactions processes are available at mobile devices in real-time, where users can define their usual behavior, configure the energy consumption profile at home, establish new profiles for specific days according to the EV charging process, and consult the historical transactions.

Keywords: Electric Vehicle · Renewable energy · OpenADR · EV charging · Decision system · Demand response · Smart grid

1 Introduction

Nowadays, the power grid operates under the hypothesis that the consumed energy is always available from the energy resources. This assumption requires a whole system with several layers synchronized in order to maintain stability from the production points until the final consumers. It is then mandatory to have energy production resources with low operation costs, full availability of energy production according to demand, and fast transaction between operating powers in full power operating range. Besides, it is expected to have reduced greenhouse gas emissions from the energy production resources.

In order to contribute to this scenario, renewable energy sources are introduced into the power grids in large scale, especially large solar photovoltaic and wind plants. However, these types of renewable energy sources have intermittency production problems, i.e., the sun and the wind are resources that cannot be controlled according

J. Bajo et al. (Eds.): PAAMS 2017 Workshops, CCIS 722, pp. 299–306, 2017.
DOI: 10.1007/978-3-319-60285-1_25

the power demand. To fight this, energy storage systems are introduced to store the energy produced by renewables and to be able to deliver the energy according to the instantaneous power demand. An extended review about energy storage systems for mitigating the intermittency energy production from renewables is presented in [1]. Besides these traditional energy storage systems, through the vehicle-to-grid paradigm, the electric vehicle (EV) can also be used as an energy storage system, providing capability to store energy from renewables or to deliver energy to the power grid [2, 3]. This is even more relevant if one takes into account that the EV can operate as distributed energy producer or consumer (prosumer) in different points along the power grid [4]. The contribution of plug-in EVs to smooth the natural intermittency of energy production from renewables and for cost and emission reduction is presented in [5]. For such purpose, smart charging strategies for the EV operation as a contributor to enhance the power grid performance and also to maximize renewables integration into the power grid are proposed in [6]. Energy management considering the EV and renewables integration in a micro-grid scenario is analyzed in [7], where strategies for the EV operation are identified to facilitate the integration of distributed energy resources. The analysis of the EV operation in a micro-grid office building scenario and also considering distributed energy resources is presented in [8].

2 OpenADR

Energy delivery needs a real-time perfect balance between supply and demand. The problems of intermittent production behavior of renewable energy sources and the change in power consumption can be overcome with a high investment in infrastructure or by the implementation of demand side (load) response. Demand Response (DR) is a new paradigm in electricity consumption by end-users where they change their consumption patterns in order to avoid consumption peaks and absorb the renewable production excess [9]. This behavior change by the flexible consumers is promoted by lower electricity use at times of high wholesale market prices or when the system reliability is put at risk.

The fully automated DR illustrated in Fig. 1 can be achieved by the implementation of a standard OpenADR and a Home Energy Management System (HEMS). An HEMS system is responsible for monitoring and managing the operation of in-home appliances, and providing load shifting and shedding according to a specified set of requirements defined by the user and controlled through a central system.

One of the goals of this research is to implement this protocol and a central cloud system to handle renewable production excess in an intelligent way, taking into account intermittent behavior of renewable energy sources, power limitation of the distribution network and energy prices. The EV charging process and the need of enough energy for user's daily mobility process are integrated in this approach.

The OpenADR protocol is based on a communication Internet Protocol (IP) network to handle energy consumption requests based on production availability and is a tool for the integration of renewable energy based on a centralized process that is able to turn on/off appliance. This protocol introduces the concepts of: Virtual End Node (VEN), client energy consumer appliance to turn on/off remote based Demand Request

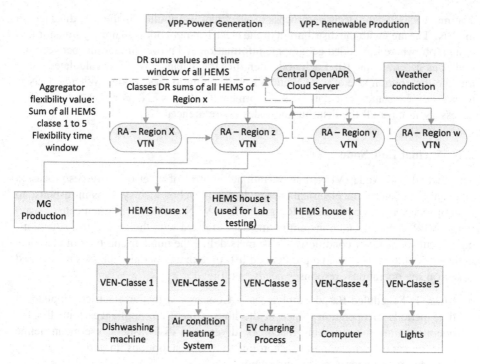

Fig. 1. General overview of the energy market stakeholders and their role on the OpenADR approach.

(DR) events announced by Virtual Top Node (VTN). This VTN performs the role of a Virtual Power Plant (VPP) manager. A VPP consists of an aggregation of Distributed Energy Resources (DERs). The VPP Manager centralizes transitions from VEN with the loaded resources that they interact with and perform decisions about loads based on the distribution distance previously calculated in georeferenced graph. This VPP receives information about the available production resources and based on the demand response tries to fit the resources from the VEN aiming for minimization of power losses and non supplied energy.

2.1   Micro Generation

In the proposed approach, it is also possible to integrate all the local Micro Generation (MG) resources, which can be handled as a VEN with a report service based on a metric device. Taking into account local MG, this VTN can be created at a local substation considering the electrical distribution network (DN) to handle all the energy transactions from all the local MG. A new service to calculate the distribution distance was created. Its output is the distance of a VEN to another energy resource based on a georeferenced graph for the power grid DN. However, the main challenge of this approach is the georeferenced identification of each of these points on the DN. Once this information is collected any geographic database can easily handle the problem.

The main idea for the decision process of electrical distribution is the real distance on the DN. The area with the distribution of the electrical network is manually transformed in a graph, where it is added geographic information and power limitations between the nodes, as described in [10]. Each node identifies the distance, which is calculated using the line distribution size of a VTN and VEN matching to these nodes. When a VEN is registered, a distance calculation is performed to other VEN. For that process it is necessary to have all the distribution nodes georeferenced.

2.2   Virtual End Node

The Virtual End Node (VEN) has operational control of a set of resources/processes and is able to control the electrical energy demand level of such systems in response to a set of received messages (i.e., DR signals). The VEN is able to communicate (2-way) with a VPP receiving and transmitting messages related with the power grid situations, e.g., events or stability conditions. Consumers define the number and type of electrical appliances of the house from a pre-defined list. Five main operation classes are defined based on the operation's responses needs, see Fig. 1:

- Class 1: Scheduled-Based Appliances – Concerns with the electrical appliances time periods of operation. Since in the houses there are appliances with flexible operation time, like washing machines, dryers and dishwashers, users can define their operation time window according to the best options in terms of energy availability and energy cost optimization.
- Class 2: Range Temperature Based Appliances – For appliance with temperature range, like refrigerators, heating systems or air conditioners, for which the users can define the operation ranges, the VPP manager will try to fulfil such range based on energy availability and energy cost optimization.
- Class 3: Battery-Assisted Smart Appliances – The EV charging process can be scheduled and controlled to be adapted according to the energy availability and energy cost optimization, e.g., according to the operation of the other electrical appliances connected to the same electrical installation.
- Class 4: Home electrical appliances with prioritized energy supply (equivalent concept of Quality of Service (QoS) in computer communication [12]), due to the needed of a continuous energy supply when they are turned-on. However, according to the user acceptance they can be turned-off if there is no excess or a need in the distribution to take out this consumption. An example of these appliances could be a music player or a laptop because they have their own battery.
- Class 5: Home electrical appliances that the user do not accept turn-off, but they can take production excess, like the example of lights.

3   Decision System for OpenADR

Figure 1 shows the energy distribution with the associated players and the OpenADR functions. Class operation protocol is performed at the Regional Aggregator (RA) and at a central OpenADR system. The RA controls all the local electrical appliances with

OpenADR interfaces. This RA based on regional flexibility capacity (total power with OpenADR interfaces) exchanges information with a central OpenADR command center. This command center has the mission to divide the renewable production excess among the RAs. This division is based on the load capacity available from each RA and this load capacity changes from day period to day period based on client's performed appliance definition. RA also acts as an adviser for client towards the reduction of the energy invoice by providing suggestions to increase appliance aggregation with OpenADR, increase flexibility times, control heating/cooling systems based on the production availability. Therefore, all of these actions are registered through a local home energy management system, and can be accessed through a mobile device or a web interface. RA aggregates all load requests and shows to a central system its level of demand as a time function. The central system suggestion in a first approach (others could be implemented) to divide renewable production among RAs based on their individual level of demand. If the sum of all RA demand loads is not enough to handle excess energy production, traditional reserves (such as energy storage batteries) should be activated. When the excess of produced energy (offer) is lower than the sum of all loads (demand) a decision rationalizing process is activated. For this we implemented the proportional division among all RAs based on classes priority values. This division can be performed based on several approaches, e.g., queuing theory, market value, among others. Afterwards the RA has to divide the energy by the local electrical appliances. At this point several approaches can be implemented, such as: 1- energy price; 2- priority based on the defined classes; 3- stochastic process and; 4- distributed equal usage based on the created power profile. For example, user A has 20 kW (40% total power available), user B has 10 kW (20% total power available), user C has 15 kW (30% total power available) and user D has 5 kW (10% total power available). For a case of available power of 10 kW, RA gives 4 kW to user A, 2 kW to user B, 3 kW to user C and 1 kW to user D. The next step is performed internally at each house, which is the prioritization in the distribution of available power. Using the example of a user A, with an available power of 4 kW for a total of 20 kW requested, RA follows the diagram represented in Fig. 2, where the first priority is for classes 1 and 3, which are appliances close to the end of their defined time windows. Contrarily,

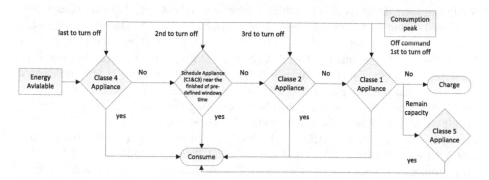

Fig. 2. Prioritization at RA, regarding the distribution of renewable production excess through OpenADR appliances.

if there is a peak of energy consumption (less energy available) it is possible to turn-off appliances in the sequence defined in Fig. 2.

For the same class, the home energy management system turns-off appliances taking into account the power consumption. This approach works based on the energy prices reduction, which changes from operation class to operation class. The price reduction would be achieved by the need for lower reserve levels because demand flexibility was introduced. These reserves (identified as spinning reserves) currently represent around 40% of electricity prices [2].

4   Case Study at the University of Minho

The proposed solution was validated under a supervised laboratorial installation emulating a real residential pilot, considering a set of PV panels, a flexible remotely controlled energy storage system based on EVs, and remotely controllable residential loads (e.g., heating systems, electric boilers, washing machines, lights, etc.). A web/mobile application is used to handle all the information related with the pilot installation: 1- Configure remote OpenADR appliance, e.g., heating systems, lights and other loads; 2- Remote control (e.g., turn-on or turn-off) of appliances such as heating systems; 3- Check energy prices and historical data of consumptions/productions; 4- Check online consumption when appropriate OpenADR interface is available to follow this remotely. In this laboratory test environment, we used also our developed App for Android (operating system) used to track user movements and interact with [11]. So, based on this app it is possible to identify user's returning home and tune starting time of heating or cooling systems. Besides, using real-time visualization it is possible to interact with OpenADR appliances and receive alerts from RA regarding energy prices and turned on/off appliances. The different appliances (PV panels, batteries and electrical appliances) installed in the experimental setup can be monitored in terms of energy transactions and constraints considering the DR flexibility control. As the implemented pilot was supervised in laboratory environment, the technologies were tested in critical situations (e.g., severe delays in communications, communications faults, and failures in appliances). The obtained data from the monitoring system was useful to evaluate the proposed technologies based on the DR flexibility control. Analysing such scenarios, it is possible to define several cases, as following described.

Case 1- Time 17 h, with renewable power available of 5 kW. OpenADR appliance (see Fig. 3) are: washing machine (2 kW) with a window working-time from 14 h to 18 h (class 1), TV plasma 0.3 kW, WC heater 1.2 kW, oil radiator and heater with 2 kW. All of these appliances have a power of 5.5 kW, but our renewable energy source only can produce power of 5 kW. As a consequence our approach consisted in establish a time delay to the starting the of washing machine, because the window working time only finish at 24 h and on class 2 injected less power. Case 2- Time 20 h, start of EV charging process (Class 3 of 3 kW). Together there is a tumble dryer (Class 1 of 3.5 kW), TV Plasma (Class 4 of 0.3 kW) and water heating (Class 2 of 1.5 kW). This represents a total power of 8.3 kW. Taking into account a renewable energy production of 4 kW, in this scenario, the central system decides to give power of the TV plasma and tumble dryer and the remaining 0.7 kW to the water heating. In such

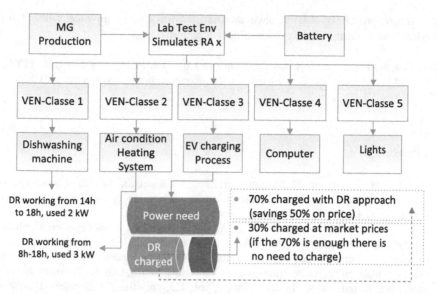

Fig. 3. EV charging process, divided by process priority, a centralization of EV charging profile.

scenario, EV charging process is postponed. Case 3- Time 8 h, with stereo system (Class 4 of 0.06 kW), air condition (Class 2 of 1.8 kW), heating water (Class 2 of 1.5 kW) and EV (Class 4), with an available renewable power of 2.5 kW. In this case, the stereo system works and the remaining power is dived by the two class 2 appliances. EV is in the last charging period and, therefore, the system decides to charge at usual prices avoiding the savings of flexibility charging. An example taking into account laboratory scenario is presented at Fig. 3, where we highlight the EV charging process with a maximization strategy to charge based on DR approach. We simulate also Spinning reserve with a battery introduced and since DR is implemented this battery with 20% of renewable production capacity was able to handle also intermittent behaviour of renewable production and meet the production needs to serve the consumption demand.

5 Conclusions

This work proposes a new decision process and a central approach to handle the Demand Response (DR) concept. Users are invited to participate in such concept by adopting energy consumption flexibility to use electricity at cheaper prices. Along the paper, it is shown the possibility to integrate the proposed decision process with the transactional energy market information system (e.g., OpenADR DR). So, that energy DR transactions can be implemented automatically. As shown in the paper, a small-scale implementation utilizing variable real-time energy demand profiles was considered. If we assume DR market with an average price around 50% of standards prices this approach is able to save around 30% on energy invoice without user behavior change on their energy consumption patterns.

Acknowledgements. This work has been supported by COMPETE: POCI-01-0145-FEDER-007043 and FCT – Fundação para a Ciência e Tecnologia within the Project Scope: UID/CEC/00319/2013.

References

1. Beaudin, M., Zareipour, H., Schellenberglabe, A., Rosehart, W.: Energy storage for mitigating the variability of renewable electricity sources: an updated review. J. Energy Sustain. Dev. **14**(4), 302–314 (2010). Elsevier
2. Yilmaz, M., Krein, P.T.: Review of the impact of vehicle-to-grid technologies on distribution systems and utility interfaces. IEEE Trans. Power Electron. **28**(12), 5673–5689 (2013)
3. Monteiro, V., Ferreira, João C., Afonso, João L.: Operation modes of battery chargers for electric vehicles in the future smart grids. In: Camarinha-Matos, Luis M., Barrento, Nuno S., Mendonça, R. (eds.) DoCEIS 2014. IAICT, vol. 423, pp. 401–408. Springer, Heidelberg (2014). doi:10.1007/978-3-642-54734-8_44
4. Kempton, W., Tomic, J.: Vehicle-to-grid power implementation: from stabilizing the grid to supporting large-scale renewable energy. J. Power Sources **144**, 280–294 (2015). Elsevier
5. Saber, A.Y., Venayagamoorthy, G.K.: Plug-in vehicles and renewable energy sources for cost and emission reductions. IEEE Trans. Ind. Electron. **58**(4), 1229–1238 (2011)
6. Lopes, J.A.P, Soares, F.J., Almeida, P.M., da Silva, M.M.: Smart charging strategies for electric vehicles: enhancing grid performance and maximizing the use of variable renewable energy resources. In: EVS24 International Battery, Hybrid and Fuel Cell Electric Vehicle Symposium, pp. 1–11, May 2009
7. Zhang, M., Chen, J.: The energy management and optimized operation of electric vehicles based on microgrid. IEEE Trans. Power Del. **29**(3), 1427–1435 (2014)
8. Van Roy, J., Leemput, N., Geth, F., Büscher, J., Salenbien, R., Driesen, J.: Electric vehicle charging in an office building microgrid with distributed energy resources. IEEE Trans. Sustain. Energy **5**(4), 1389–1396 (2014)
9. Ferreira, J., Martins, H., Barata, M., Monteiro, V., Afonso, João L.: OpenADR—intelligent electrical energy consumption towards internet-of-things. In: Garrido, P., Soares, F., Moreira, A.P. (eds.) CONTROLO 2016. LNEE, vol. 402, pp. 725–736. Springer, Cham (2017). doi:10.1007/978-3-319-43671-5_61
10. Ferreira, J.C., da Silva, A.R., Monteiro, V., Afonso, J.L.: Collaborative broker for distributed energy resources. In: Madureira, A., Reis, C., Marques, V. (eds.) Computational Intelligence and Decision Making, vol. 61, pp. 365–376. Springer, Dordrecht (2013)
11. Ferreira, J.C., Monteiro, V., Afonso, J.A., Afonso, J.L.: Tracking users mobility patterns towards CO_2 footprint. In: Omatu, S., et al. (eds.) 13th International Conference Distributed Computing and Artificial Intelligence. AISC, vol. 474, pp. 87–96. Springer, Cham (2013)
12. Froehlich, A.: The Basics of QoS, 22 March 2017. http://www.networkcomputing.com/networking/basics-qos/402199215

Distributed Multimodal Journey Planner Based on Mashup of Individual Planners' APIs

Joao C. Ferreira[1,4(✉)], António R. Andrade[3], António Ramos[1],
Ana Lúcia Martins[2], and João Almeida[5]

[1] Information Sciences, Technologies and Architecture Research Center
(ISTAR-IUL), Instituto Universitário de Lisboa (ISCTE-IUL), Lisbon, Portugal
{joao.carlos.ferreira, Antonio_Gabriel_Ramos}@iscte.pt
[2] Business Research Unit (BRU-IUL),
Instituto Universitário de Lisboa (ISCTE-IUL), Lisbon, Portugal
almartins@iscte.pt
[3] IDMEC, Instituto Superior Técnico, Universidade de Lisboa, Lisbon, Portugal
antonio.ramos.andrade@tecnico.ulisboa.pt
[4] Centro ALGORITMI, University of Minho, 4800-058 Guimarães, Portugal
[5] Card4B – Systems S.A., Lisbon - Portugal/MASAI Mobility Community,
Brussels, Belgium
joao.almeida@card4b.pt

Abstract. In this research work we describe the creation of the concept of a
distributed journey planning system that links as many journey planning services as are available in public transportation operators and willing to participate
in one or more networks of journey planners across Europe. This is integrated on
European project MASAI and it is part of a development of mobile solutions
that allows journey plans in Europe based on public transportation availability,
with the possibility of buying tickets in a mobile device with a multi-operator
scenario. A semantic context was created in order to identify which
Application-Programming Interfaces (APIs) from different public transport
operators to use and set start\end trip points.

Keywords: Multi-modal · Journey planner · Ticketing · Personalized
transportation information · Mashup

1 Introduction

Consumers regularly search for, purchase and share travel information online.
According to the Google Travel Study 2014, about 80% of business travellers and 78%
of leisure travellers are using online sources in their travel planning and for their
eventual purchases [1], where 25% of total global travel sales are done online, and this
percentage is rapidly increasing [1]. Air transportation comprises 46% of total online
travel sales, while online travel accommodation sales comprise 23%. The US and
Europe are the regions accounting for most of these sales, while the Asia Pacific region
is expected to double its online travel sales by 2017 [1]. In Europe, online hotel sales
are experiencing a rapid growth. By 2017, Western Europe is expected to reach a share

J. Bajo et al. (Eds.): PAAMS 2017 Workshops, CCIS 722, pp. 307–314, 2017.
DOI: 10.1007/978-3-319-60285-1_26

of 40% of total online travel sales, while Eastern Europe will reach 24%. Online Travel Agents (OTAs) (e.g. Expedia, Priceline and Sabre) are increasingly consolidating the traveller market, leading to stiff competition with direct suppliers. OTAs from emerging markets are expected to expand in advanced markets in the near future [2]. According to the World Travel Monitor, about 70% of international travellers are active social media users [2]. Social media is now influencing the decision making process of approximately 25% of all international trips, with destination choices (about 40%) and accommodation choices (about 30%) being the most common. Nearly 50% of travellers are posting their experiences on review sites (e.g. TripAdvisor) and travel blogs/forums [3]. The trend in sharing travel related reviews and content on social media in recent times is expanding into a second level where the sharing of travel services (e.g. Airbnb, BlaBlaCar and Vayable) merge with active consumers providing apartments, cars, meals and tours. Shared usage platforms are changing the travel economy, giving people new options on where to stay, what to do and how to get around. Adapting to this new reality, by monitoring user-generated content and cooperating with social media, is of great importance for the tourism market and its destination management. Big Data, which is increasingly gathered from cities and public organisation by digital sensing devices and networks, allows Concierge and Service Providers to supply customers with targeted options and personalised offers for a more tailored travel experience. The customer's demand for real-time services is rising with services required to be easily accessible via multiple devices (desktop/tablet, smartphone) with a 24/7 availability. Since poor site experiences often lead to negative impacts on companies and brands, a flexible technological architecture is required to reach consumers on all screens. Concierge and Service Providers need to adopt a holistic approach capable of following customers through all stages of their travel process (dreaming, planning, booking, anticipating, en route, destination) [4].

The creation of seamless travel requires a closer cooperation between large range of industry and policy makers to design services involving integrated ticketing/pricing and infrastructures responding to all travellers' needs. Multi-stakeholders governance models require the alignment in a multi-stakeholder environment (authorities, citizens, and private sector) as well as supported implementation based on a suitable standard that can perform as a major driver of innovation for making travel more comfortable, efficient and sustainable [4].

2   Context of MASAI H2020 Project

Implemented under the EC funded EU HORIZON 2020 Programme, MASAI is primarily supporting the idea of a Smart, Green and Integrated Transport area, addressing fragmentation in Intelligent Transportation Systems (ITS) deployment in Europe creating a digital environment of 'seamless travel'. For detail see [http://masai.solutions]. The vision of MASAI is to satisfy the overall service needs demanded by mobile citizens: a tailor-made aggregation of features - a digital concierge in everyone's pocket. MASAI will achieve this goal by building up a community of stakeholders that contribute continuously toward the development of the core elements of a digital concierge. This allows constant improvements and sustains future technical developments, as illustrated in Fig. 1. The MASAI mission is to empower key stakeholders in the travel and tourism industry (Travellers, Concierges, Service Providers) and to enable a seamless travel experience. This means that MASAI aims to serve: (1) All stages of the travel process, including changes in travellers' mobility patterns; (2) Long-distance travel as well as local travel including all related services (transportation and accommodation); (3) Customers travelling for business as well as for leisure purposes. The MASAI mission is made possible by creating an open ecosystem ("MASAI Mobility Community") characterized by: (1) Its openness for innovations that serves customer needs; (2) Its adaptability and scalability that foster cooperation in a competitive environment; (3) Its potential for direct discovery and connection between all MASAI Community; (4) Stakeholders, while putting travellers in full control of their personal data.

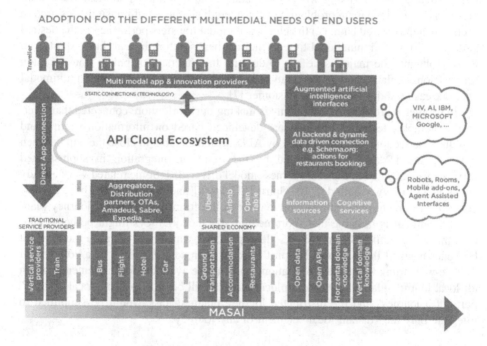

Fig. 1. MASAI project general overview

In this paper, together with the research institutions (ISCTE-IUL and IST), we show how to achieve the point 4 project goal.

The travel and tourism industry is changing due to consumer demands and new possibilities brought advances in technology. This is providing new business opportunities at a fraction of the cost that they involved years ago. The future of travel is based on an open ecosystem providing a seamless multimodal door-to-door travel experience.

3 Multimodal Journey Planners

Taking into account recent advancements of computing, geographic information system (GIS), mobile devices, communication and storage technologies, automatic transit trip planners have been implemented in recent years. Transit trip planners accept the origin, destination and expected departure/arrival time inputted by users and find proper routes using available transit services. Transit trip planners are generally web based. Most of the existing trip planners are based on static schedule data, due to the problem of public transportation data access and integration. However, transit vehicles are often delayed by traffic congestion and accidents, especially transit buses that are often late during the peak hours in metropolitan areas. The trips based on the static schedule data may make planned transfers infeasible if some transit vehicles are late. In the multimodal routing context, many works have studied the multimodal shortest viable path problem [5, 6]. Three main problems are considered: (1) the set of transit modes used to accomplish the desired path; (2) the number of modal transfers performed in the desired path; and (3) the computational time to find the best solution in real time. Apart from these problems, the major issue has to do with the diversity of public transportation information available and its integration among transport providers in a multimodal network easily understood by the customer [7].

In parallel, a growing API economy is making our world more connected than ever. Highly complex technical products are developed based on information sharing and enabling transactions to be processed by APIs, which are able to close the gap between business and IT and are supported by the trend of integration in sophisticated ecosystems - elevated to become business model drivers [8]. Some related work already exists in Delfi [www.delfi.de], EU-Spirit [EU-Spirit] and JourneyWeb [https://www.gov.uk/government/publications/journeyweb] in the form of distributed journey planning systems. It is possible that short/medium distance journeys might be better handled through a Delfi or JourneyWeb style of protocol, whilst long-distance travel might be better handled through an EU-Spirit style of approach. However, if a collation of Europe-wide trunk timetable information can be made available for implementation on all local journey planners, then each local planner will be able to plan "local + trunk" parts of a journey, and the distributed journey planning task would be simplified to integrate only the "distant local" element of any journey.

4 Proposal

This approach is based on other successful approaches of web mashup application development [9]. A mashup process uses content from more than one source to create a single new service displayed in a single graphical interface. One success example of this approach is the Google Maps where there is a combination of different information sources. The term implies easy, fast integration, frequently using open application programming interfaces (open API) and data sources to produce enriched results that were not necessarily the original reason for producing the raw source data. Therefore, this approach could solve the problem of integration of different data schemes of public transportation, but its main contribution is to overcome the problem of public transportation data access. Most of the times public operators do not provide data access.

Our work goal is to use this approach for the multimodal journey planner based on the information integration and manipulation of different journey planners of different operators that can offer services between user's start point A and final point B. The user's requested journey is split into component parts which can be planned by individual local journey planners, in a way that will allow the separate parts of the journey to be linked together into a seamless itinerary. This approach allows an incremental development of journey planning capabilities across Europe as each nation or region creates local journey planning systems that can integrate such a network or networks. It aims to make the user's experience familiar for residents in all countries by enabling existing journey planning systems to seek information about journeys to, from or wholly beyond their own boundaries and to present that information to users, in their own languages and in familiar ways, on the systems that they use for local journey planning.

The journey planning process is based on the following process, as seen in Fig. 2:

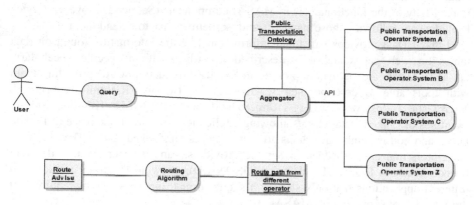

Fig. 2. Proposed system architecture

1. An interface to receive the user's query about transportation needs, by the indication of start and end points of a journey (along with the required time and date of departure or arrival). This can be complemented by a process to resolve any ambiguities in the possible matches;
2. A handle context of local public transportation infrastructure, which is solved by the introduction of Public Transportation Ontology;
3. An interface to different public transportation operators' systems;
4. An aggregator, which based on public transportation space ontology creates the context for multiple operator queries through their available API. The aggregator system sends elements of the journey request to one or more relevant "distant" journey planners and receives a response from each of those planners;
5. An organized output of process 4 to the routing algorithm;
6. The application of routing algorithm and present solution to the user in a map.

5 Aggregation of Journey Planner

MASAI seeks to develop mechanisms that help integrating the Semantic Web concept (https://www.w3.org/standards/semanticweb) when publishing Linked Data that highlights the services provided by a Service Provider. The system follows a flexible structure and a generic vocabulary, able to follow any requirements. MASAI uses the following components: (1) Service Discovery (find appropriates API for the user's query), where the search is based on a set of parameters/attributes, which are concepts related to a descriptor of Linked Data [https://www.w3.org/standards/semanticweb/data]; and (2) Service Provider, for descriptor integration, where Linked Data (descriptors) are embedded at Service Providers' web pages, allowing computers and search engines to understand their content and being able to interact with the services they provide. As an example, it is able to understand the content on web and process as the same content, i.e. as if it was a data table, converting concepts of our daily life as properties in a specific context. From the W3C standard (https://www.w3.org/standards) one of the most relevant areas is the Semantic Web, covering as main areas: (1) Linked Data; (2) Vocabularies/Ontologies; (3) Query; (4) Inference; and (5) Vertical Applications. Many of the functionalities in MASAI components (Service Discovery, Service Provider) are following those standards and, sometimes, try to extend them.

Linked Data provides structured information like the information found on data tables on web pages and it is described according with a specific vocabulary. On MASAI this area is mainly present on Service Providers towards providing them with tools able to describe their services. RDFa [w3.org/TR/xhtml-rdfa-primer/], MicroData [https://www.w3.org/TR/microdata] and JSON-LD [json-ld.org] are examples of Linked Data formats allowing applications to start at one piece of Linked Data, and follow embedded links to other pieces of Linked Data. The designed descriptors that are embedded in Service Providers, can be generated into different formats (such as RDFa, MicroData and JSON-LD), allowing the compatibility with different applications that only support a single format, having solely as requirement the vocabulary supported by MASAI.

The proposed approach allows classifying expressions that are used in a particular application, characterize possible relationships, and define possible constraints based on the use of those same expressions. Their role is to split ambiguities that may exist on specific expressions when used in different data sets. Moreover, the same expression may have different meanings based on the current context. Due to this limitation, they are linked to an Uniform Resource Identifier (URI), which references to the path of a known concept in a specific vocabulary. By the use of vocabulary/ontology modelling tools (e.g. Open Travel Alliance (OTA) [www.opentravel.org/]), or Public Transportation Ontology (PTO) [10], it is possible to extend the current ontology to something able to answer to any requirements wrapping different concepts to a standard vocabulary. With this model, generic descriptors can be generated towards minimizing the replication of the same concept on multiple vocabularies. Some examples, not exclusive, have been considered, towards: (1) using and improving the specific model; and (2) push MASAI to be able to cope with these heterogeneous realities in the MASAI model (i.e. being able to offer mechanisms to provide access to different schemas in the same solution): Schema.org is a generic vocabulary used with many different formats, including RDFa, Microdata and JSON-LD. These vocabularies cover entities, relationships between entities and actions, and can be easily extended through a well-documented extension model. These were created for search engines with the purpose to link contents to structured information, improving the ability of search engines to understand and categorize it, and be more precise on their results. OTA and PTO, despite not being a standard Vocabulary, provide specifications to develop an e-business language intended to encourage development of systems to create new collections of services to better meet the demands and expectations of travellers and the travel industry.

The web is known as a place to share contents, which still does not answer all the requirements. While the initial purpose was to provide information to users, other services were added to provide information to machines, namely the web services [https://www.w3.org/standards/webofservices/], providing a message-based design frequently found on the Web, and developing specialized contents using standardized specifications that other machines can understand. The usual examples are REST or SOAP services that are usually used to provide structured information to objects.

In MASAI, this area is present as a Web Application that offers a Wizard, able to generate descriptors (Linked Data) and specifications able to generate SDKs, where APPs are used to integrate, discover and dynamically interpret services and API's attributes, minimizing the need to develop custom tools to access those same services. Internally, the Wizard is mainly an aggregation of different operations based on the output format (RDFa, MicroData, JSON-LD or APIs.json), supporting mechanisms for publishing at Service Provider's website (crawlable by search engines) or API Publishers (e.g. APIs.io). An example of an external existing concierge could be, for example, SDI4Apps [11], which search POIs over multiple vocabularies in RDFa format, which using MASAI descriptors would not change their behaviour since the format is supported. This standard is present in most components: (1) Service Discovery, are REST services that provide a search engine of Service Providers, discovered in Linked Data that is detected on Service Providers web pages; (2) Service Provider, also has SOAP services that they made available, where is possible to reserve their flights, hotels, REST service available to manage the information of travellers.

6 Discussion and Conclusion

There is a need of standardized API that will make it easier for third parties to develop links with journey planning systems for the use on nomadic devices, on third party web sites or elsewhere. PTO can play an important role in this exchange process.

With the proposed approach, it is possible to incrementally develop network of local journey planners, to provide distributed journey planning across Europe. By adopting this approach, the central overheads are kept to a minimum, whilst an initial network could be operationalized very quick, thereby creating immediate impact and providing the foundations for extension to achieve complete coverage of Europe, as and when more local journey planning systems are available to support this.

This multimodal journey planner provide essential services for mobility process in smart cities, where the sharing of resources is a fundamental approach for savings and fulfil users' requirements.

Acknowledgments. MASAI receives funding from the European Union's H2020 programme under Grant Agreement 636281.

References

1. The 2014 Traveller's Road to Decision. In Google Travel Study. https://storage.googleapis.com/think/docs/2014-travellersroad-to-decision_research_studies.pdf. Accessed 12 Apr 2016
2. The new online travel consumer. Featuring Euromonitor. International and the ETOA. With assistance of Rossini, A., Reed, A., Timmons, J. (eds.) by Euromonitor International. http://www.etoa.org/docs/default-source/presentations/2014-the-new-online-travel-consumer.pdf?sfvrsn=4
3. ITB World Travel Trends Report 2015/2016. Edited by Messe Berlin GmbH. IPK International
4. Connected World. Hyperconnected Travel and Transportation in Action. http://www3.weforum.org/docs/WEF_Connected_World_HyperconnectedTravelAndTransportationInAction_2014.pdf
5. Boulmakoul, A., Laurini, R., Mouncif, H., Taqafi, G.: Path-finding operators for fuzzy multimodal spatial networks and their integration in mobile GIS. In: Proceedings of the 2nd IEEE International Symposium on Signal Processing and Information Technology, Marrakech, Morocco, pp. 51–56, 18–21 December 2012
6. Ziliaskopoulos, A.K., Wardell, W.: An intermodal optimum path algorithm for multimodal networks with dynamic arc travel times and switching tech trends. Eur. J. Oper. Res. **125**(3), 486–502 (2000)
7. Ferreira, J.: Green route planner. In: Grácio, C., Fournier-Prunaret, D., Ueta, T., Nishio, Y. (eds.) Nonlinear Maps and their Applications. Springer Proceedings in Mathematics & Statistics, vol. 57, pp. 59–68. Springer, New York (2014)
8. The fusion of Business and IT. With assistance of Bill Briggs. Deloitte University Press. https://www2.deloitte.com/content/dam/Deloitte/mx/Documents/technology/Tech-Trends-2015-FINAL.pdf
9. Fichter Darlene, What Is a Mashup? http://books.infotoday.com/books/Engard/Engard-Sample-Chapter.pdf
10. Houda, M., Khemaja, M., Oliveira, K., Abed, M.: A public transportation ontology to support user travel planning. In: 2010 Fourth International Conference on Research Challenges in Information Science (RCIS), Nice, France, pp. 127–136 (2010). doi:10.1109/RCIS.2010.5507372
11. http://sdi4apps.eu/spoi/ and http://portal.sdi4apps.eu/semantic-query#

Developing an Individualized Survival Prediction Model for Rectal Cancer

Ana Silva, Tiago Oliveira(✉), Paulo Novais, and José Neves

Algoritmi Centre/Department of Informatics, University of Minho, Braga, Portugal
a55865@alunos.uminho.pt, {toliveira,pjon,jneves}@di.uminho.pt

Abstract. This work presents a survivability prediction model for rectal cancer patients developed through machine learning techniques. The model was based on the most complete worldwide cancer dataset known, the SEER dataset. After preprocessing, the training data consisted of 12,818 records of rectal cancer patients. Six features were extracted from a feature selection process, finding the most relevant characteristics which affect the survivability of rectal cancer. The model constructed with six features was compared with another one with 18 features indicated by a physician. The results show that the performance of the six-feature model is close to that of the model using 18 features, which indicates that the first may be a good compromise between usability and performance.

1 Introduction

The most common cancer of the digestive system is colorectal cancer, also known as bowel cancer, which develops in the cells lining the colon and rectum [18]. About 70% of the colorectal cancer cases occur in the colon and about 30% in the rectum [9]. Although colon and rectal cancers are considered to be very similar pathologies, they have different associated genetic causes and different progressions according to distinct molecular pathways [21]. The work disclosed herein focuses solely on rectal cancer, the anatomic part where material called feces or stool is stored until it is expelled of the body through the anus. Machine learning (ML) methods have been widely applied in cancer research, due to their competence in identifying relevant information from complex datasets. An accurate survivability prediction helps physicians in effective and precise decision-making. Although there are some tools which provide survivability predictions for rectal cancer, none of them apply ML techniques in order to build evolving predictive models. Therefore, and following the previous work developed for colon cancer patients [17], the aims of this work are the following: (i) to make an individualized prediction of the survivability of a rectal cancer patient in each year of the five years following treatment; and (ii) to determine which features are the most important for survivability prediction of rectal cancer patients. The number of features can be crucial when available in a clinical decision support tool, which is the end goal of the work. The number can determine the use or not of a application, taking into account the time to obtain an output (a prediction). The

© Springer International Publishing AG 2017
J. Bajo et al. (Eds.): PAAMS 2017 Workshops, CCIS 722, pp. 315–323, 2017.
DOI: 10.1007/978-3-319-60285-1_27

prediction model was developed using data from the Surveillance, Epidemiology, and End Results (SEER) program [13], the most complete cancer database in the world.

The paper is structured as follows. Section 2 describes related work in rectal cancer survival prediction. Section 3 provides the steps and machine learning methods used to develop the prediction model. The corresponding experimental results are disclosed and discussed in Sect. 4. Finally, Sect. 5 presents the conclusions drawn so far and future work considerations.

2   Related Work

Existing approaches to calculate rectal cancer patients survivability are regression-based. Wang et al. [20] developed nomograms to make an individualized prediction of the conditional survivability for rectal cancer patients. The estimate is valid when calculated after a certain period of time (months) passed since diagnosis and treatment. The model was constructed based on data from 42,830 patients who were diagnosed between 1994–2003, from the SEER database. Conditional survivability prediction is calculated from a Cox proportional hazards model. The primary outcome variable was overall survivability conditional on having survived up to 5 years from diagnosis. Covariates included in the model were age, race, sex/gender and stage. The C-index for the model of this approach was 0.75 and the model is available as a web-based calculator. Valentini et al. [19] developed a tool to predict the probability that a rectal cancer patient will be alive or will have local recurrence or distant metastasis after delivery of long-course radiotherapy, with optional concomitant and/or adjuvant chemotherapy, over a 5-year period after surgery. Based on Cox regression, multivariate nomograms were developed through 2,795 individual patient data collected from five European randomized trials[1], between 1992 to 2003. Selected by training data, the required information for the overall survivability calculator was gender, age at the date of randomization, clinical tumor stage, radiotherapy dose, surgery procedure, adjuvant chemotherapy (yes/no), pathological tumor and nodal stage. The concomitant chemotherapy (yes/no) is used to calculate the local recurrence. However, it must be inserted, even for overall survivability prediction, because it is a field required for the tool. The nomogram for overall survivability had a C-index of 0.70. Another SEER-based approach is the one developed by Bowles et al. [1], also made available in the form of an internet-based individualized conditional survivability calculator. This tool consists of four separate multivariate Cox regression models, taking into account: no radiotherapy, preoperative radiotherapy, postoperative radiotherapy and stage IV patients. These models were created to determine adjusted survival estimates

---

[1] Trial name: European Organisation for Research and Treatment of Cancer, *Fédération Francophone de Cancérologie Digestive*, Working Group of Surgical Oncology/Working Group of Radiation Oncology/Working Group of Medical Oncology of the Germany Cancer Society, Polish and Italian.

(at year 1 through 10) and used to calculate 5-year adjusted conditional survivability. They were constructed using registries of 22,610 patients with rectal adenocarcinoma, who were diagnosed from January 1988 to December 2002. Models
developed for patients who underwent no radiotherapy, preoperative radiotherapy or postoperative radiotherapy, covariates were the same. They included age,
sex/gender, race, tumor grade, surgery type and stage. In the model built for
stage IV patients, i.e., for patients with distant metastasis, the surgery type was
treated as a binary variable in the model (using any radiotherapy or primary
tumor directed surgery as covariates). The measures of performance for this tool
are not available.

The approach developed herein distances itself from already existing works
by treating survival prediction as a classification problem and applying varied
machine learning methods to obtain a qualified model of individualized survival
prediction.

3   Development of the Prediction Model

The rectal cancer survival prediction model should have the capacity to accept
a number of inputs for selected prediction features and, for each of the 5 years
following treatment, produce an output stating whether the patient will survive
that year or not, along with a confidence value for the prediction. Survivability
prediction was approached as a binary classification problem, so that five classification models for each year were developed and were posteriorly combined, in
a programmatic manner. The development of these prediction models involved
the following phases by order of occurrence: preprocessing of SEER data, split
dataset, balancing data, feature selection, modeling, and evaluation. The software chosen to develop the prediction model was RapidMiner, an open source
data mining software. It has a workflow-based interface that offers an intuitive
application programming interface (API).

3.1   Preprocessing, Split Dataset, and Balancing Data

The colorectal cancer data from SEER were collected from 1973 to 2012. It
contained 515,791 registries and 146 attributes, some of them only applicable to
a limited period within the time of data collection. In the Preprocessing phase, it
was defined that the period of interest would be from 2004 onwards, minimizing
the occurrence of missing data due to the applicability of the attributes. Pediatric
patients (age under to 18 years old) were removed. Patients who were alive at the
end of the data collection whose survival time had not yet reached five years (the
maximum period for which the model under development is supposed to predict
survival), and those who passed away of causes other than colon or rectal cancer
were sampled out from the training set as their inclusion was considered to be
unsuited to the problem at hand. Binary classes (*survived* and *not survived*)
were derived for the target labels 1-, 2-, 3-, 4- and 5-year survival. Finally, based
on existing attributes and at the request of a physician who collaborated in this

work, new attributes, such as the number of regional lymph negative nodes, the ratio of positive nodes over the total examined nodes and also patient relapse, were calculated. After the Preprocessing phase, the attributes were reduced to 61, including the new attributes and the target labels and the data was reduced to 12,818 registries. During the Split Dataset phase, the data was separated into five sub-datasets by target label, taking into account the corresponding survivability year. Table 1 shows the class distribution in each sub-dataset.

Observing Table 1 is seen that the classes are not equally represented. Studies [4, 11] show that the problem of using imbalanced datasets is important, from both the algorithmic and performance perspectives. An overview of classification algorithms for the resolution of this kind of problem [7] concluded that hybrid sampling techniques, i.e., combining over-sampling of the minority class with under-sampling of the majority class, can achieve better performances than just oversampling or undersampling. As such, in the Balancing Data phase, hybrid sampling, as described in [7], was applied in order to generate balanced sub-datasets with 12,818 records each.

Table 1. Class distribution for each target label in the sub-datasets.

	Target labels				
	1 Year	2 Year	3 Year	4 Year	5 Year
Not survived	4.03%	5.89%	7.17%	8.08%	8.70%
Survived	87.88%	82.27%	78.41%	75.68%	73.79%

3.2 Feature Selection

For the Feature Selection phase was used the Optimize Selection operator (implementing a deterministic and optimized selection process with decision trees and *forward selection*) [15] of RapidMiner. This phase was essential to discover the most influential features on the survival of rectal cancer patients. The process was applied to each sub-dataset for the target label and the common selected features to all the sub-datasets were used to construct the prediction models. Table 2 shows the selected features and their meaning. The 6 selected features were compared with a set of 18 features indicated by a specialist physician on colorectal cancer. In the subsequent modelling, it was assumed that the features had an equal weight, but further experimentation with biased models is required.

3.3 Modeling and Evaluation

During the Modeling phase, the classification strategy adopted consisted in the application of ensemble methods. In order to boost basic classifiers and improve their performance, the classification schemes used were meta-classifiers. All the classifiers combinations were explored, according to the algorithms and type of

Table 2. Attributes selected in the feature selection process.

Attribute	Description
Age recode with <1 year old	Age groupings based on age at diagnosis (single-year ages) of patients (<1 year, 1–4 years, 5–9 years,..., 85+ years)
CS site-specific factor 1	The interpretation of the highest Carcinoembryonic Antigen (CEA)[a] test results
CS site-specific factor 2	The clinical assessment of regional lymph nodes
Derived AJCC stage group	The grouping of the TNM information combined
Primary site	Identification of the site in which the primary tumor originated
Regional nodes examined	The total number of regional lymph nodes that were removed and examined by the pathologist

[a]CEA is a glycoprotein and is used as a tumor marker. In increased large are associated with adenocarcinoma, especially colorectal cancer.

attributes allowed. The tested meta-classifiers were the same used in the previous work about colon cancer survability prediction [17]: AdaBoost [6], Bagging [3], Bayesian Boosting [15], Stacking [5], and Voting [10].

Since survivability prediction is being handled as a classification problem, a group of basic classifiers were selected to be used in ensembles with the above-described meta-classifiers. The group includes some of the most widely used learners [15] available in RapidMiner, namely the k-NN (Lazy Modeling), the Naive Bayes (Bayesian Modeling), the Decision Tree (Tree Induction), and the Random Forest (Tree Induction). Fourteen classification schemes were constructed for the sets of 6 and 18 attributes and, for 1, 2, 3, 4, and 5 survival years. The combinations of meta-classifiers with basic classifiers were as follows. The Voting model used k-NN, Decision Tree and Random Forest as base learners. The Stacking model used k-NN, Decision Tree, and Random Forest classifiers as base learners, and a Naive Bayes classifier as a Stacking model learner. The AdaBoost, Bagging, and Bayesian Boosting models were combining with each basic classifier. In the evaluation process, 10-fold cross-validation [16] was used to assess the prediction performance of the generated prediction models and avoid overfitting. All classification schemes was evaluated and comparared using the prediction accuracy and the area under the ROC curve (AUC). The accuracy is the percentage of correct responses among the examined cases [2]. The AUC can be interpreted as the percentage of randomly drawn data pairs of individuals that have been accurately classified in the two populations, and it is commonly used as a measure of quality for classification models [2].

4   Experimental Results and Discussion

A vast quantity of results was analyzed. From the results obtained, the top three performing algorithms, for each evaluating method described in Sect. 3, are

Table 3. Survivability percentage accuracy.

Ensemble model	Accuracy									
	1 Year		2 Year		3 Year		4 Year		5 Year	
	18 attributes	6 attributes	18 attributes	6 attributes	18 attributes	6 attributes	18 attributes	6 attributes	18 attributes	6 attributes
Stacking	98.32%	96.45%	98.00%	96.15%	97.72%	95.79%	96.97%	95.05%	96.88%	95.01%
Voting	97.37%	95.97%	97.16%	95.91%	97.20%	95.32%	96.79%	94.63%	96.62%	94.64%
Bayesian boosting with decision tree	97.16%	96.26%	97.08%	96.06%	96.75%	95.19%	96.22%	95.01%	96.42%	94.66%

Table 4. Survivability AUC.

Ensemble model	AUC									
	1 Year		2 Year		3 Year		4 Year		5 Year	
	18 attributes	6 attributes	18 attributes	6 attributes	18 attributes	6 attributes	18 attributes	6 attributes	18 attributes	6 attributes
Stacking	0.988	0.976	0.989	0.981	0.987	0.979	0.984	0.977	0.986	0.977
Voting	0.985	0.975	0.983	0.976	0.983	0.971	0.979	0.969	0.979	0.969
Bagging with decision tree	0.985	0.981	0.974	0.964	0.964	0.955	0.967	0.948	0.962	0.951

present in Tables 3 and 4, for each of the 5 years. For an easier interpretation, the average performances were calculated, allowing a better comparison between algorithms and the selection of the best model. This is shown in Fig. 1a and b for the top three performing algorithms.

Among the 18-attribute models, the stacking algorithm stood out. Among the 6-attribute models, the same has happened. The 18-attribute models had an average accuracy of 97.58%, with values for years 1 to 5 of 98.32%, 98.00%, 97.72%, 96.97% and 96.88%. The average AUC was 0.987, and the remaining values were 0.988, 0.989, 0.987, 0.984 and 0.986 for years 1 to 5. With an average of 95.69% for accuracy and 0.978 for AUC, the 6-attribute stacking models had prediction accuracies for years 1 to 5 of 96.45%, 96.15%, 95.79%, 95.05% and 95.01% (as seen in Table 3), and AUCs of 0.976, 0.981, 0.979, 0.977 and 0.977 (as seen in Table 4). Comparing the results of the 6-attribute stacking models with those of the 18-attribute models, the performances values are close, being slightly better for the 18-attribute models. The gap between accuracy measures are 1.89% and 0.009 for AUC. It is possible to say that the differences are not significant, taking account the contrast of feature numbers. The results show that it is possible to build a model with less than half of the features indicated by the expert physician. Regarding the attributes obtained in the feature selection process, with the exception of the site-specific factors, they were all connected with the features indicated by the specialist physician. The regression based approaches mentioned in Sect. 2 utilized the C-index to evaluate the models. This measure and AUC are considered numerically identical [8]. Since both correspond

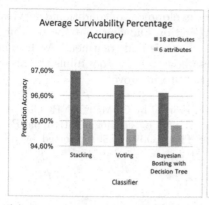

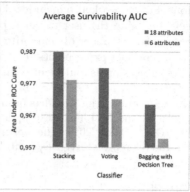

(a) Average survivability percentage   (b) Average survivability AUC.
accuracy.

Fig. 1. Comparison of the 18-attribute models with the 6-attribute models.

to the probability of giving a correct response in a binary prediction problem. As such, the present work represents an improvement and was able to achieve better results. In addition, comparing this approach with the previous work developed for colon cancer [17], results were similar. The third performing algorithm was not the same. However, the best performance scheme also was Stacking. In the colon cancer prediction model, the performance values were slightly better, but not more than 1.13% for accuracy and 0.011 for AUC. The most surprising result of the both approaches are the selected features, which were the same.

5   Conclusions and Future Work

This work involved the application of different meta-classification schemes to construct survivability prediction models for rectal cancer patients. The best performing scheme presented uses a Stacking classification scheme, combining k-NN, Decision Tree, and Random Forest classifiers as base learners and a Naive Bayes classifier as a stacking model learner. The relevant number of features for rectal cancer survivability prediction was found to be 6, the same selected for colon cancer. The set includes: age, CS site-specific factor 1, CS site-specific factor 2, derived AJCC stage group, primary site, and regional nodes examined. Overall, the developed model was able to present a good performance with fewer features than the existing approaches. As future work we intend to construct a mobile application to make both models (colon and rectal cancer prediction models) available to the health care community and to integrate it in settings of ambient assisted living and group decision making [12,14]. In order to have the tool always updated and adapted to new patients, an on-line learning scheme is being prepared. This functionality will allow to dynamically feed new cases to the prediction system and make it change in order to provide better survival predictions. Future work also includes the development of conditional survivability models, enabling the user to get a prediction knowing that the patient has already survived a number of years after diagnosis and treatment. Additionally, we intend to conduct experiments to assess how well the tool fulfils the needs of health care professionals and identify aspects to improve.

Acknowledgements. This work has been supported by COMPETE: POCI-01-0145-FEDER-0070 43 and FCT Fundação para a Ciência e Tecnologia within the Project Scope UID/CEC/ 00319/2013. The work of Tiago Oliveira is supported by a FCT grant with the reference SFRH/BD/85291/ 2012.

References

1. Bowles, T.L., Hu, C.Y., You, N.Y., Skibber, J.M., Rodriguez-Bigas, M.A., Chang, G.J.: An individualized conditional survival calculator for patients with rectal cancer. Dis. Colon Rectum **56**(5), 551–559 (2013)
2. Bradley, A.P.: The use of the area under the ROC curve in the evaluation of machine learning algorithms. Pattern Recogn. **30**(7), 1145–1159 (1997)
3. Breiman, L.: Bagging predictors. Mach. Learn. **24**(2), 123–140 (1996)
4. Chawla, N.V.: Data mining for imbalanced datasets: an overview. In: Maimon, O., Rokach, L. (eds.) Data Mining and Knowledge Discovery Handbook, pp. 853–867. Springer, Heidelberg (2005)
5. Džeroski, S., Ženko, B.: Is combining classifiers with stacking better than selecting the best one? Mach. Learn. **54**(3), 255–273 (2004)
6. Freund, Y., Schapire, R.E.: A decision-theoretic generalization of on-line learning and an application to boosting. J. Comput. Syst. Sci. **55**(1), 119–139 (1997)
7. Ganganwar, V.: An overview of classification algorithms for imbalanced datasets. Int. J. Emerg. Technol. Adv. Eng. **2**(4), 42–47 (2012)
8. Hanley, J.A., McNeil, B.J.: The meaning and use of the area under a receiver operating characteristic (ROC) curve. Radiology **143**(1), 29–36 (1982)
9. U. S. National Institutes of Health, N.C.I.: Seer training modules, colorectal cancer
10. Kittler, J.: Combining classifiers: a theoretical framework. Pattern Anal. Appl. **1**(1), 18–27 (1998)
11. Leon, M., Jalao, E.R.L.: Prediction Model Framework for Imbalanced Datasets, pp. 33–41 (2014)
12. Lima, L., Novais, P., Neves, J., Bulas, C.J., Costa, R.: Group decision making and quality-of-information in e-Health systems. Logic J. IGPL **19**(2), 315–332 (2011)
13. National Cancer Institute: Surveillance, epidemiology and end results program (2015). http://seer.cancer.gov/data/. Accessed 10 Jan 2015
14. Novais, P., Costa, R., Carneiro, D., Neves, J.: Inter-organization cooperation for ambient assisted living. J. Ambient Intell. Smart Environ. **2**(2), 179–195 (2010)
15. RapidMiner: Rapidminer documentation: Operator reference guide (2016). http://docs.rapidminer.com/studio/operators/. Accessed 03 Jan 2016
16. Refaeilzadeh, P., Tang, L., Liu, H.: Cross-validation. In: Liu, L., Özsu, M. (eds.) Encyclopedia of Database Systems, pp. 532–538. Springer, Heidelberg (2009)
17. Silva, A., Oliveira, T., Novais, P., Neves, J., Leão, P.: Developing an individualized survival prediction model for colon cancer. In: Lindgren, H. et al. (eds.) ISAmI 2016, pp. 87–95. Springer International Publishing, Cham (2016). http://dx.doi.org/10.1007/978-3-319-40114-0_10

18. Vachani, C., Prechtel-Dunphy, E.: All about rectal cancer (2015). http://www. oncolink.org/types/article.cfm?aid=108&id=9457&c=703. Accessed 27 Dec 2015
19. Valentini, V., van Stiphout, R.G., Lammering, G., et al.: Nomograms for predicting local recurrence, distant metastases, and overall survival for patients with locally advanced rectal cancer on the basis of European randomized clinical trials. J. Clin. Oncol. **29**(23), 3163–3172 (2011)
20. Wang, S.J., Wissel, A.R., Luh, J.Y., et al.: An interactive tool for individualized estimation of conditional survival in rectal cancer. Ann. Surg. Oncol. **18**(6), 1547– 1552 (2011)
21. Yamauchi, M., Lochhead, P., Morikawa, T., et al.: Colorectal cancer: a tale of two sides or a continuum? Gut **61**(6), 794–797 (2012)

MASGES

Decentralized Surplus Distribution Estimation with Weighted k-Majority Voting Games

Jörg Bremer$^{(\boxtimes)}$ and Sebastian Lehnhoff

University of Oldenburg, 26129 Oldenburg, Germany
{joerg.bremer,sebastian.lehnhoff}@uni-oldenburg.de

Abstract. Future energy grids and associated markets foster dynamic coalition formation in order to allow situational virtual power plant configurations. Collaboratively and distributed, such virtual power plants may take over responsibility on several emerging control tasks within the smart grid as a substitute for no longer available large plants. Temporary teamwork of individually owned and operated distributed energy resources demands for a proper and fair surplus distribution after product delivery. Distributing the surplus merely based on the absolute (load) contribution does not take into account that smaller units maybe provide the means for fine grained control as they are able to modify their load on a smaller scale. Bringing in flexibility, counts for several tasks. Shapley values provide a concept for the decision on how the generated total surplus of an agent coalition should be spread. In this paper, we propose a scheme for efficiently estimating computationally intractable Shapley values in a fully decentralized way. As a scheme to handle a set of different utility evaluation criteria we use weighted k-majority voting games. We demonstrate the applicability of the decentralized estimation by several simulation results in comparison with exact calculations.

Keywords: Shapley value · Surplus distribution · Virtual power plant · Weighted k-majority voting games · Decentralized load planning

1 Introduction

In order to enable the transition of the current central market and network structure of today's electricity grid to a decentralized smart grid, an efficient management of numerous distributed energy resources (DER) will become more and more indispensable.

Virtual power plants (VPP) are a well-known means for aggregating and controlling DER [1]. Integration into current market structures recently led to VPPs that frequently re-configure themselves for a market and product-driven alignment [30]. Based on the size of products from the order book (e.g. traded at a day-ahead market), coalitions of usually small energy resources have to be found that may apply for the product, as single units alone often do not have

© Springer International Publishing AG 2017
J. Bajo et al. (Eds.): PAAMS 2017 Workshops, CCIS 722, pp. 327–339, 2017.
DOI: 10.1007/978-3-319-60285-1_28

sufficient power nor the flexibility to deliver the product. In scenarios with self-dependently operated units that trade their power independently, consequentially self-organizing algorithms are required also for coalition formation to find potential partners specifically for the current product at hand [5].

In general, distributed control schemes based on multi-agent systems are considered advantageous for large-scale problems as expected in future smart grids due to the large number of distributed energy resources that take over control tasks from large-scale central power plants [29,31]. For this reason, each time an active power product is sold on the market, the jointly earned profit after delivery has to be distributed among all participants in a way that satisfies their owners but also reflects the capability of each single unit and considers their values for the VPP coalition in a fair way.

In [7] a decentralized estimation scheme for Shapley values based on ideas from [12] has been introduced for the first time that integrates consideration of individual flexibilities when calculating the utility of a unit. The authors in [7] used the objective function that evaluates the ability of a coalition to fulfil an energy product in predictive scheduling directly to evaluate the utility. In [3] this was relaxed to a weighted majority game taking into account only the amount of delivered energy instead of flexibilities, but with the advantage of extensibility. Additional measures and indicators are integrated and jointly considered for surplus distribution by extending the approach to k-weighted majority games. We will now further develop the extensible but centralized calculation from [3] with a fully decentralized estimation scheme.

The rest of the paper is organized as follows. We start with a brief introduction to predictive scheduling in VPPs and an overview on coalition games for value distribution. After introducing the extension to k-weighted voting games from [3] we further extend this concept to decentralized estimation of surplus distribution schemes based on Shapley values. We conclude with a demonstration of the applicability.

2   Related Work

2.1   Coalitional Games and Value Distribution

A VPP can be seen as a cluster of distributed energy resources (generators as well as controllable consumers) that are connected by communication means for control. From the outside, the VPP cluster behaves like a larger, single power plant. Traditionally, energy management is implemented as centralized control. However, given the increasing share of DER as well as flexible loads in the distribution grid today, the evolution of the classical, rather static (from an architectural point of view) power system to a dynamic, continuously reconfiguring system of individual decision makers, it is unlikely for a centralized control scheme to cope with the rapidly growing problem size. An overview on existing control schemes and a research agenda can e.g. be found in [27,34]. However, fairly distributing jointly earned surplus after product delivery is a rather scarcely scrutinized subject in VPP research.

Grouping agents together so as to form coalitions is a major interaction concept within multi agent systems. The usual intention is that a group of agents might achieve a goal better than a single agent [18, 32]. Often, a group of agents is indispensable, because a single agent alone might not have the capability to achieve the goal. Usually, it is possible to have different groups consisting of a different mixture of agents.

Clearly, each agent (or the associated real world unit) possesses certain traits or benefits that differently contribute to the overall success of the coalition. We will not consider different bargaining power in this paper. In some use cases, the utility of the members of a coalition may be easily quantified. For example, [17] studies several examples from the transport sector with numbers of drivers or trucks and costs expressed in dollar. In the use case studied in this paper, the utility has to be expressed as the contribution that eases a joint planning problem (jointly planning individual electricity generation for gaining a wanted aggregated energy schedule) what has to be expressed in terms of traits and size of individual flexibility in choosing alternative operation modes. The actually chosen schedule is not necessarily proportional to the utility of the unit because the richness of offered opportunities (moreover in terms of having backup capabilities for later re-scheduling) has to be considered; not the taken choice.

Distributing joint cost is a long discussed topic [14]. The division of surplus has use cases and applications in production [14, 37], electricity pricing [21], public goods [9, 25], and other situations modeled by cooperative games. A survey of coalition games applied to several use cases in the smart grid can be found in [36]; e.g. some utility functions (analytically calculable) are given but no profit distribution is discussed.

An early application to power planning has been studied in [41]. They used a bilateral Shapley value approach in a multi-agent system for coalition forming when determining cost distribution among beneficiaries of transmission system expansions. In [8] a payment mechanism for VPPs is proposed based on the accuracy of individually forecasted power supply. Individual utility of the members to the whole coalition is not considered due to the intractability of calculation.

Intractability in general limits applications of exact Shapley values based distribution schemes. Possible approximation schemes are discussed in the next section.

3   Shapley Values

Cooperative game theory is concerned with problems from coalition formation in multi-agent systems and desirable properties of such coalitions [12, 35]. Among others, cooperative game theory offers concepts for fair distribution of jointly earned revenues among all members of a coalition. The Shapley value [38] is such a concept for fair payoff distribution [17]. If cooperative behaviour is enforced by offering better payoff for an agent within coalitions (groups of players), the competition is between coalitions rather than between individual agents. Such game is said to be a coalition game. If the utility may be exchanged between players (for example by side payments) the game is said to have a transferable utility. Let N be a set of n players (agents). A coalition game (N, v) with transferable utility for the set of players N is characterised by a function v that measures the worth $v(S)$ of any non-empty subset $S \subseteq N$. In this sense, $v(S)$ denotes the total jointly earned payoff or benefit of a coalition S, that can be distributed among all members of S. Of course, each member makes an individual contribution that has to be considered when determining individual payoff.

The characteristic function v allows to assess the worth of a coalition in the context of a given scenario but gives no hints on how to share it. Shapley [38] defined a value for games that exhibits certain fairness properties [23]. The Shapley value φ_i that is assigned to player i according to a given characteristic function v in a coalition game (N, v) that determines the gain is defined as

$$\varphi_i(v) = \sum_{S \subseteq N \setminus \{i\}} \frac{|S|!(n - |S| - 1)!}{n!} (v(S \cup \{i\}) - v(S)). \tag{1}$$

The term $v(S \cup \{i\}) - v(S)$ in (1) refers to the marginal contribution of player i to the value of the whole coalition [20].

The marginal contribution defines how much a player i contributes to the overall gain or phrased differently: how important player i is for the coalition. The value assigns a unique distribution of the total generated surplus among all members of a coalition based on the marginal contributions. Shapley values provide a fair distribution scheme [17].

Calculating Shapley values in general is intractable [10, 26] because the calculation is often #p-complete [39]. The complexity depends on the value function v. There are some special cases where computational feasible calculations or at least approximations of Shapley values are known, e.g. supermodular games [20].

Weighted voting games are an example with computationally hard Shapley values [12]. In such games a coalition gets a reward of 1 if the sum of individual weight values assigned to each agent is larger or equal to some given threshold and 0 elsewhere. For a smart grid use case this could translate as follows: if a coalition has to jointly archive at least power q, each generator (or its controlling agent respectively) is assigned a weight of its generation power p_i. A generator coalition is rewarded if $\sum_i p_i \geq q$. An extension to this could demand that the deviation of the joint power to the demanded power is below some given threshold. Another use case would devalue larger deviations from the target schedule and thus continuously evaluate gains by the actually achieved similarity of demanded and achieved schedule. We will stick mainly with this use case.

Several methods have been proposed to approximate Shapley values for coalition games. Mann and Shapley started with proposing a method based on Monte Carlo simulations in [24], but without suggesting how to draw necessary samples of coalitions; a more comprehensive analysis of sampling approaches can be found in [2]. In [33] a multi-linear extension approach with linear time complexity has been proposed, which has to be weakened when improving approximation error [19]; [42] proposed a method based on choosing random permutations from coalitions. We will here adapt an randomized approach from [12] with linear complexity.

4 Weighted k-Majority Voting Games and Utility in Virtual Power Plants

For predictive scheduling, a coalition of energy resources is supposed to operate in a way to jointly produce a desired real power schedule (the energy product) for a given time frame. Usually, time is discretized and the amount of energy in every discrete time period (often 15 min or shorter) is considered. To this end, we have a demanded schedule (real power) for a given future time horizon

$$P = (p_1, p_2, \ldots, p_n) \in \mathbb{R}^d, \tag{2}$$

with p_i denoting mean real power during the i-th time period for d periods. This is the product that the coalition of energy resources is going to deliver according to some market contract. Let $s(i) = (p_{i,1}, p_{i,2} \ldots, p_{i,n}) \in \mathcal{F}_{U_i} \subset \mathbb{R}^d$ denote a schedule of agent i taken from the individual feasible region $\mathcal{F}_{U_i}$ containing all operable schedules for unit U_i. The coalition seeks for a set of schedules $\{s(i)|i \in S\}$ that minimizes

$$\left\| P - \sum_{i \in S} s(i) \right\| \to \min. \tag{3}$$

Phrased informally, each unit from coalition S must choose exactly one schedule from its feasible region of realizable schedules such that all individual schedules jointly resemble product schedule P as close as possible. The individual contribution to the quality of the solution that an agent offers to the coalition is the individual search space and its abilities, not the finally picked schedule. This search space determines the set (size, variability and diversity) of alternative choices from that a planning algorithm might choose. In case of a many-objective version of the above sketched problem, cost indicators for a cost effective choice of alternatives would also be part of the search space. For measuring the worth v_B of a coalition regarding load balancing, we start with the evaluation of product fulfilment for d time intervals and define

$$v_B = \begin{cases} 1 & \text{if } P_i - \epsilon \le \sum_i s(i) \le P_i + \epsilon \ \forall \ 0 < i < d \\ 0 & \text{otherwise} \end{cases}. \tag{4}$$

The deviation from the agreed amount of energy (or mean power equivalently) must not exceed a range of tolerance ϵ. With such definition, weighted voting games can be applied. In a weighted voting game, each player i is assigned a weight w_i; $q \in \mathbb{R}_+$ denotes a quota that the coalition has to achieve in order to win [11,13]. Let $w(S) = \sum_{i \in S} w_i$ for a given coalition S. A weighted voting game $(q, w_1, \ldots, w_n)$ is then a game

$$v(S) = \begin{cases} 1 & \text{if } w(S) \ge q \\ 0 & \text{otherwise} \end{cases}. \tag{5}$$

A generalization extends this idea to the case where coalitions have to reach several quotas with different weight sets at the same time to win [4,13]. For k quota a k-majority voting game $v_1 \wedge \cdots \wedge v_k$ is defined as

$$(v_1 \wedge \cdots \wedge v_k)(S) = \begin{cases} 1 & \text{if } w^t(S) \geq q^t \; \forall \; 1 \leq t \leq k \\ 0 & \text{otherwise} \end{cases} \tag{6}$$

with $w^t(S) = \sum_{i \in S} w_i^t$. The t-th component denotes a single majority game $(q^t, w_1^t, \ldots, w_n^t)$. The coalition is a winning one if it wins every game.

In [3] k-majority voting games have been used for calculating fair surplus distribution in energy coalitions for VPP control. The advantage lies the extendibility. In [3] generated energy, deviation during delivery and production cost have been proposed as criteria for generating the distribution key. So far, a decentralized calculation scheme as usual in decentralized agent control scenarios is missing. Because calculation is intractable, we content ourselves with a decentralized estimation scheme.

Next, we have to define the marginal contribution of a DER for a coalition within the sketched smart grid load balancing scenario. Such a coalition is first and foremost aiming at resembling a given load schedule as close as possible. For this reason, it seems appropriate to choose the metric that measures the distance between achieved load and wanted load as basis for our considerations, because this metric is also used as (at least one) objective during optimization.

Another possible interpretation would be to define an ϵ as a threshold for allowed average load deviation per time period and assign to an agent a marginal value of 1 if he is a swing player, i.e. if the player enables a coalition to fall below the accuracy threshold when joining the coalition; Eq. (4), and 0 elsewise. In this case, the marginal contribution $E\Delta_j^X$ to a coalition of size X can be estimated by [12]: $E\Delta_j^X = (\sqrt{2\pi\nu/X})^{-1} \int_{(q-w_i)/X}^{(q-\epsilon)/X} e^{-X(x-\mu)^2/2\nu} dx$, with quota q that translates to the target load in our use case, a weight w (here: the power contributions of the units) for each player i and μ and ν as mean and variance of the weights. The Shapley value may then be approximated by [12]:

$$\hat{\varphi}_j(v) = \frac{1}{n} \sum_{X=0}^{n-1} E\Delta_j^X \tag{7}$$

In any smart grid scenario with coalitions of agents trying to assemble a profitable product by scheduling their individual loads, the applicability of Eq. (7) depends on whether the agents are swing players (players enabling a gain for a coalition) or not: depending on market and payoff strategy. In any other case, the Monte Carlo approach that averages the mean marginal contribution from a sample of coalitions can be used:

$$\hat{\varphi}_j(v) = \frac{1}{n} \sum_{X=0}^{n-1} v(j, S^X), \tag{8}$$

with S^X denoting a random coalition with size X.

5   Decentralized Shapley Value Estimation

As has been mentioned in Sect. 3, computing Shapley values exactly is computationally hard and therefore intractable for larger coalitions of DER, but [12] proposes a centralized estimation method: instead of calculating all marginal contributions to all possible sub-coalitions for a given player j, draw a random sample of n coalitions with size $1, 2, \ldots, n$. The average of the marginal contributions of Player j in the random sample is taken as an approximation $\hat{\varphi}_j(v)$ for the Shapley value $\varphi_j(v)$. Obviously, this approximation can be achieved with linear time complexity $\mathcal{O}(n)$.

For solving the optimization tasks in our Shapley value estimation, we used the fully decentralized combinatorial optimization heuristics for distributed agents (COHDA). An optimization process is necessary to evaluate the best possible fit to the product schedule. In the following, we will briefly recap the method. An in-depth discussion can for example be found in [16, 30].

An agent in COHDA does not represent a complete solution as it is the case for instance in population-based approaches. Each agent represents a class within a multiple choice knapsack combinatorial problem [22]. Applied to predictive scheduling each class refers to the feasible region in the solution space of the respective energy unit. Each agent chooses schedules as solution candidate only from the set of feasible schedules that belongs to the DER controlled by this agent. Each agent is connected with a rather small subset of other agents from the multi-agent system and may only communicate with agents from this limited neighborhood. The neighborhood (communication network) is defined by a small world graph [40]. As long as this graph is at least simply connected, each agent collects information from the direct neighborhood and as each received message also contains (not necessarily up-to-date) information from the transitive neighborhood, each agent may accumulate information about the choices of other agents and thus gains his own local belief of the aggregated schedule that the other agents are going to operate. With this belief each agent may choose a schedule for the own controlled energy unit in a way that the coalition is put forward best while at the same time own constraints are obeyed and own interests are pursued.

All choices for own schedules are rooted in incomplete knowledge and beliefs in what other agents do; gathered from received messages. The taken choice (together with the basis for decision-making) is communicated to all neighbors and in this way knowledge is successively spread throughout the coalition without any central memory. This process is repeated. Because all spread information about schedule choices is labeled with an age, each agent may decide easily whether the own knowledge repository has to be updated upon message reception. Any update results in recalculating of the own best schedule contribution and spreading it to the direct neighbors. By and by all agents accumulate complete information and as soon as no agent is capable of offering a schedule that results in a better solution, the algorithm converges and terminates. Convergence has been proved in [15].

More formally, each time an agent receives a message, three successive steps are conducted. First, during the perceive phase an agent a_j updates its own working memory κ_j with the received working memory κ_i from agent a_i. From the foreign working memory the objective of the optimization (i.e. the target schedule) is imported (if not already known) as well as the configuration that constitutes the calculation base of neighboring agent a_i. An update is conducted if the received configuration is larger or has achieved a better objective value. In this way, schedules that reflect the so far best choices of other agents and that are not already known in the own working memory are imported from the received memory.

During the following decision phase agent a_j has to decide on the best choice for his own schedule based on the updated belief about the system state γ_k. Index k indicates the age of the system state information. The agent knows which schedules of a subset (or all) of the schedule that other agents are going to operate. Thus, the schedule that fills the gap to the desired target schedule exactly can be easily identified. Due to operational constraints of the controlled DER, this optimal schedule can usually not be operated. In addition, other reasons might render some schedules largely unattractive due to high cost. Because of this reason, each agent is equipped with a so called decoder that automatically maps the identified optimal schedule to a nearby feasible schedule that is operable by the DER and thus feasible. We used a decoder after [16].

This fully decentralized scheme for combinatorial optimization has been extended in [5] to support several interwoven optimization tasks at the same time. The same principle is also used here. Figure 1 shows the basic flow of decentralized surplus distribution estimation.

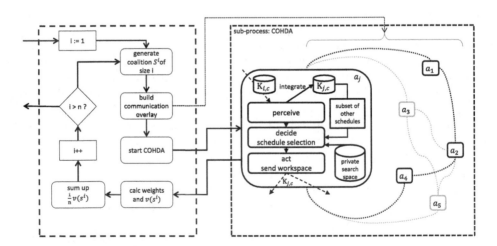

Fig. 1. Flow chart for decentralized Shapley value estimation based on k-vector voting games.

Each agent estimates the Shapley value for its own contribution to the coalition (trust issues are subject to future work). To achieve this, the agents generates a list of random coalitions $S^X \in N\backslash\{i\}$ for all sizes $X \leq |N|$ (see Eq. (8)). For each random coalition in this list, the marginal contribution $v(S^X \cup i - v(S^X))$ of i to the coalition has to be determined and summed up finally to determine the mean contribution. For the calculation of each marginal contribution, two optimization problems have to be solved to take into account the ability to achieve a given power product with a required minimum accuracy; see Eg. (4). For this, a communication network after [40] is established among members from S^X and two separate COHDA processes are started (one with and one without communication link to i) to get the optimization result. In this way, all agents contribute to the calculations of all Shapley values in a fully decentralized manner and no private information has to be revealed.

6   Results

Evaluation was done by simulation with a setup comprising a set of simulated energy resources and a multi-agent system for control. The agent system was implemented after [15]. Each agent is responsible for conducting local decisions and communication with other agents in charge of controlling a small local ensemble of jointly controlled energy resources. As a first model for distributed energy resources we used a model for co-generation plants that has already served in several studies and projects for evaluation, e.g. [6,28]. This model comprises a micro CHP with 4.7 kW of rated electrical power (12.6 kW thermal power) bundled with a thermal buffer store. Constraints restrict power band, buffer charging, gradients, min. on and off times, and satisfaction of thermal demand. Thermal demand is subject to simulated losses of a detached house according to given weather profiles. For each agent the model is individually (randomly) configured with state of charge, weather condition, temperature range, allowed operation gradients, and similar.

Table 1 shows a first result. To get insight into the error induced by Shapley value estimation, several simulations have been conducted with different coalition sizes. The error denotes the mean absolute deviation of the estimated Shapley values from the exact calculated ones in percent. The estimation error degrades with growing coalition sized, obviously because more sub-coalitions are taken into account for estimation. Nevertheless, the number of necessary optimization processes degrades significantly; the evaluation rates denotes the remaining share of optimization processes that have to be solved for estimation compared with exact calculation.

Whereas in Table 1 equal co-generation plants have been considered, Table 2 shows the result for coalitions consisting of different CHP. Table 3 shows the result for the k-majority variant. Here

$$v_F(S) = \begin{cases} 1 & \text{if } \sum_{i \in S} E(\mathcal{F}_{U_i}) \geq e \\ 0 & \text{otherwise} \end{cases} \text{ with } E(j) : j \mapsto \frac{\sum_{\ell=1}^{d} - \sum_k s(j)_\ell^k \cdot \log_2(s(j)_\ell^k)}{d}. \quad (9)$$

Table 1. Estimation error (mean absolute percentage error compared with exact calculation for different coalition (equal CHP) sizes.

Coaltionsize n	Error/%		# Evaluations	Eval. rate
6	9.375×10^{-1}	2.0649×10^{0}	36	9.5238×10^{-2}
10	7.399×10^{-1}	1.3139×10^{0}	100	9.7752×10^{-3}
14	1.4881×10^{-1}	2.9762×10^{-1}	196	8.5454×10^{-4}

Table 2. Estimation error (mean absolute percentage error) compared with exact calculation for different coalition sizes (with differently dimensioned CHP).

Coaltionsize n	Error/%		# Evaluations	Eval. rate
6	1.2083×10^{0}	2.3846×10^{0}	36	9.5238×10^{-2}
14	5.9524×10^{-1}	2.4731×10^{-1}	196	8.5454×10^{-4}

Table 3. Estimation error for the k-majority case with different CHP.

coaltionsize n	Error / %		# Evaluations	Eval. rate
6	3.3717×10^{0}	1.0896×10^{0}	36	9.5238×10^{-2}
10	6.9269×10^{0}	1.2048×10^{0}	100	9.7752×10^{-3}
14	6.4286×10^{-1}	3.3142×10^{-1}	196	8.5454×10^{-4}

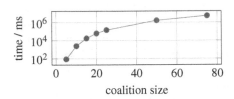

Fig. 2. Computation time for centralized simulation of the agent approach for different coalition sizes.

has been used as a second criterion for surplus distribution. This criterion reflects the flexibility that a candidate brings in for possible re-scheduling operations during product delivery. The flexibility is measured by the entropy of the schedules in the set of feasible schedules of an energy unit.

Comparison with exact calculation is feasible only up to a quite small coalition size. Figure 2 gives an expression on the growth of necessary computation times (all agents simulated on a single computer) for estimating all Shapley values for larger coalition sizes. With today's technology obviously also estimation is limited to coalition sizes with about 50 to 60 members.

7   Conclusion

Having self-organized coalitions of agents from different owners that plan, produce and sell active power products jointly generated by units from different owners, demands for a scheme for fair distribution of jointly gained payoffs. Shapley values are a well-known means of calculating fair shares of payoff for all members of a coalition. Shapley values are an important conceptual basis for gaining unique and fair distribution keys for profit sharing.

In this paper we extended the ideas from [7] for decentralized estimation of Shapley values using the search space as criterion rather than the energy amount that reveals no hints on the ability to further the adaption of a coalition to energy products. Based on the extensibility ideas from [3] by using voting games, we adapted an estimation scheme from [12] to a fully decentralized agent-based system.

In this way, each agent is evaluated according to individual capabilities for easing cost effective overall adaption of the group and not for delivering an assigned schedule that (at least in case of using heuristics) partly relies on random and arbitrariness of the scheduling algorithm. Clearly, the distribution key is only an abstraction that gives hints on how to distribute the surplus of the coalition. Calculating the money value of each agent (or rather of the energy unit the agent is in charge of) has to take into account further considerations of expenses, the course of re-scheduling actions during product delivery, market, and similar.

References

1. Awerbuch, S., Preston, A.M. (eds.): The Virtual Utility: Accounting, Technology & Competitive Aspects of the Emerging Industry Topics in Regulatory Economics and Policy. Topics in Regulatory Economics and Policy, vol. 26. Kluwer Academic Publishers, New York (1997)
2. Bachrach, Y., Markakis, E., Procaccia, A.D., Rosenschein, J.S., Saberi, A.: Approximating power indices. In: Padgham, L., Parkes, D.C., Müller, J.P., Parsons, S. (eds.) AAMAS, vol. 2, pp. 943–950. IFAAMAS (2008)
3. Beer, S.: Dynamic coalition formation in electricity markets. Ph.D. thesis (2017)
4. Bilbao, J., Fernndez, J., Jimnez, N., Lpez, J.: Voting power in the European union enlargement. Eur. J. Oper. Res. **143**(1), 181–196 (2002)
5. Bremer, J., Lehnhoff, S.: Decentralized coalition formation in agent-based smart grid applications. In: Bajo, J., et al. (eds.) PAAMS 2016. CCIS, vol. 616, pp. 343–355. Springer, Cham (2016). doi:10.1007/978-3-319-39387-2_29
6. Bremer, J., Sonnenschein, M.: Constraint-handling for optimization with support vector surrogate models - a novel decoder approach. In: Filipe, J., Fred, A. (eds.) ICAART 2013 - Proceedings of the 5th International Conference on Agents and Artificial Intelligence, vol. 2, pp. 91–105. SciTePress, Barcelona (2013)
7. Bremer, J., Sonnenschein, M.: Estimating shapley values for fair profit distribution in power planning smart grid coalitions. In: Klusch, M., Thimm, M., Paprzycki, M. (eds.) MATES 2013. LNCS (LNAI), vol. 8076, pp. 208–221. Springer, Heidelberg (2013). doi:10.1007/978-3-642-40776-5_19

8. Chalkiadakis, G., Robu, V., Kota, R., Rogers, A., Jennings, N.: Cooperatives of distributed energy resources for efficient virtual power plants. In: The Tenth International Conference on Autonomous Agents and Multiagent Systems (AAMAS-2011), 2–6 May 2011, pp. 787–794. http://eprints.soton.ac.uk/271950/

9. Champsaur, P.: How to share the cost of a public good? Int. J. Game Theory **4**, 113–129 (1975)

10. Deng, X., Papadimitriou, C.H.: On the complexity of cooperative solution concepts. Math. Oper. Res. **19**(2), 257–266 (1994)

11. Elkind, E., Goldberg, L.A., Goldberg, P., Wooldridge, M.: On the dimensionality of voting games. In: In Proceedings of the Twenty Third AAAI Conference on Artificial Intelligence (AAAI-2008), pp. 13–17 (2008)

12. Fatima, S.S., Wooldridge, M., Jennings, N.R.: A linear approximation method for the shapley value. Artif. Intell. **172**(14), 1673–1699 (2008)

13. Fatima, S., Wooldridge, M., Jennings, N.R.: A heuristic approximation method for the banzhaf index for voting games. Multiagent Grid Syst. **8**(3), 257–274 (2012). http://dx.doi.org/10.3233/MGS-2012-0194

14. Friedman, E., Moulin, H.: Three methods to share joint costs or surplus. J. Econ. Theory **87**(2), 275–312 (1999)

15. Hinrichs, C.: Selbstorganisierte Einsatzplanung dezentraler Akteure im smart grid. Ph.D. thesis (2014). http://oops.uni-oldenburg.de/1960/

16. Hinrichs, C., Bremer, J., Sonnenschein, M.: Distributed hybrid constraint handling in large scale virtual power plants. In: IEEE PES Conference on Innovative Smart Grid Technologies Europe (ISGT Europe 2013). IEEE Power & Energy Society (2013)

17. Hsu, M.C., Soo, V.W.: Fairness in Cooperating Multi-agent Systems – Using Profit Sharing as an Example. In: Lukose, D., Shi, Z. (eds.) PRIMA 2005. LNCS, vol. 4078, pp. 153–162. Springer, Heidelberg (2009). doi:10.1007/978-3-642-03339-1_13

18. Kahan, J., Rapoport, A.: Theories of coalition formation. Basic Studies in Human Behavior. L. Erlbaum Associates, London (1984)

19. Leech, D.: Computing power indices for large voting games. Manag. Sci. **49**(6), 831–837 (2003). http://EconPapers.repec.org/RePEc:inm:ormnsc: v:49:y:2003:i:6:p:831-837

20. Liben-Nowell, D., Sharp, A., Wexler, T., Woods, K.: Computing shapley value in supermodular coalitional games. In: Gudmundsson, J., Mestre, J., Viglas, T. (eds.) COCOON 2012. LNCS, vol. 7434, pp. 568–579. Springer, Heidelberg (2012). doi:10. 1007/978-3-642-32241-9_48

21. Lima, J., Pereira, M., Pereira, J.: An integrated framework for cost allocation in a multi-owned transmission-system. IEEE Trans. Power Syst. **10**(2), 971–977 (1995)

22. Lust, T., Teghem, J.: The multiobjective multidimensional knapsack problem: a survey and a new approach. CoRR abs/1007.4063 (2010)

23. Ma, R., Chiu, D., Lui, J., Misra, V., Rubenstein, D.: Internet economics: the use of shapley value for ISP settlement. In: Proceedings of the 2007 ACM CoNEXT Conference, CoNEXT 2007, pp. 6:1–6:12. ACM, New York (2007)

24. Mann, I., Shapley, L.: Values of large games, iv: evaluating the electoral college by montecarlo techniques. Technical report, Santa Monica, CA: RAND Corporation (1960). http://www.rand.org/pubs/research_memoranda/RM2651

25. Mas-Colell, A.: Remarks on the game-theoretic analysis of a simple distribution of surplus problem. Int. J. Game Theory **9**, 125–140 (1980)

26. Matsui, Y., Matsui, T.: NP-completeness for calculating power indices of weighted majority games. Theor. Comput. Sci. **263**(1–2), 306–310 (2001)

27. McArthur, S., Davidson, E., Catterson, V., Dimeas, A., Hatziargyriou, N., Ponci, F., Funabashi, T.: Multi-agent systems for power engineering applications - Part I: concepts, approaches, and technical challenges. IEEE Trans. Power Syst. **22**(4), 1743–1752 (2007)
28. Nieße, A., Sonnenschein, M.: Using grid related cluster schedule resemblance for energy rescheduling - goals and concepts for rescheduling of clusters in decentralized energy systems. In: Donnellan, B., Martins, J.F., Helfert, M., Krempels, K.H. (eds.) SMARTGREENS. pp. 22–31. SciTePress (2013)
29. Nieße, A., Lehnhoff, S., Tröschel, M., Uslar, M., Wissing, C., Appelrath, H.J., Sonnenschein, M.: Market-based self-organized provision of active power and ancillary services: an agent-based approach for smart distribution grids. In: Complexity in Engineering (COMPENG), 2012. pp. 1–5 (June 2012)
30. Nieße, A., Beer, S., Bremer, J., Hinrichs, C., Lünsdorf, O., Sonnenschein, M.: Conjoint dynamic aggregation and scheduling for dynamic virtual power plants. In: Ganzha, M., Maciaszek, L.A., Paprzycki, M. (eds.) Federated Conference on Computer Science and Information Systems - FedCSIS 2014, Warsaw, Poland (9 2014)
31. Nikonowicz, Ł.B., Milewski, J.: Virtual power plants - general review: structure, application and optimization. J. Power Technol. **92**(3), 135 (2012)
32. Osborne, M.J., Rubinstein, A.: A Course in Game Theory, 1st edn. The MIT Press, Cambridge (1994)
33. Owen, G.: Multilinear extension of games. Manag. Sci. **18**(5–Part–2), 64–79 (1972)
34. Ramchurn, S.D., Vytelingum, P., Rogers, A., Jennings, N.R.: Putting the 'smarts' into the smart grid: a grand challenge for artificial intelligence. Commun. ACM **55**(4), 86–97 (2012)
35. Rapoport, A.: N-Person Game Theory: Concepts and Applications. Ann Arbor science library, University of Michigan Press, Michigan (1970)
36. Saad, W., Han, Z., Poor, H.V., Basar, T.: Game theoretic methods for the smart grid. CoRR abs/1202.0452 (2012)
37. Sen, A.K.: Labour allocation in a cooperative enterprise. Rev. Econ. Stud. **33**(4), 361–371 (1966)
38. Shapley, L.S.: A value for n-person games. Contrib. Theory Games **2**, 307–317 (1953)
39. Valiant, L.G.: The complexity of computing the permanent. Theor. Comput. Sci. **8**, 189–201 (1979)
40. Watts, D., Strogatz, S.: Collective dynamics of 'small-world' networks. Nature **393**, 440–442 (1998)
41. Yen, J., Yan, Y.H., Wang, B.J., Sin, P.K.H., Wu, F.F.: Multi-agent coalition formation in power transmission planning. In: Hawaii International Conference on System Sciences, pp. 433–443 (1998)
42. Zlotkin, G., Rosenschein, J.S.: Coalition, cryptography, and stability: mechanisms for coalition formation in task oriented domains. In: Proceedings of the Eleventh National Conference on Artificial Intelligence, pp. 32–437. AAAI Press (1994)

Multi-agent Wholesale Electricity Markets with High Penetrations of Variable Generation: A Case-Study on Multivariate Forecast Bidding Strategies

Hugo Algarvio[1,2](✉), António Couto[2], Fernando Lopes[2], Ana Estanqueiro[2], and João Santana[1]

[1] Instituto Superior Técnico, INESC-ID, Universidade de Lisboa, Lisboa, Portugal
hugo.algarvio@tecnico.ulisboa.pt, jsantana@ist.utl.pt
[2] LNEG−National Research Institute, Est. do Paço do Lumiar 22, Lisboa, Portugal
{antonio.couto,fernando.lopes,ana.estanqueiro}@lneg.pt

Abstract. Electricity markets (EMs) are distributed in nature, complex and evolve continuously. The share of variable generation continue to grow and gain an increasing relevance in EMs. In most of the European countries, the day-ahead market closes at 12 UTC of the day before the day of operation. Consequently, wind power forecasts have to be made 18 to 42 h prior to production, what brings a signicant uncertainty to the process. This article uses an agent-based simulation tool, called MATREM (for Multi-Agent TRading in Electricity Markets), to analyze the potential benefits to the day-ahead market of changing the wind power forecast information, enabling the development of different bidding strategies. Results show that the effect of different bidding strategies on the levelized revenues is higher (when compared with the effect on the day-ahead market prices).

Keywords: Electricity markets · Variable generation · Wind power forecast · Balancing markets · Software agents · Bidding strategies

1 Introduction

Electricity markets (EMs) are distributed in nature, complex and continuously evolving. Three major market models are often distinguished [1,2]: pools, bilateral contracts, and hybrid models. In particular, a pool is a market place where electricity-generating companies submit production bids and corresponding market-prices, and retailers and consumer companies submit consumption bids. A market operator uses a market-clearing system, typically a standard uniform auction, to set market prices.

H. Algarvio and J. Santana—This work was supported by "Fundação para a Ciência e a Tecnologia" with references UID/CEC/50021/2013 and PD/BD/105863/2014.

J. Bajo et al. (Eds.): PAAMS 2017 Workshops, CCIS 722, pp. 340–349, 2017.
DOI: 10.1007/978-3-319-60285-1_29

Multi-agent systems (MAS) represent a relatively new and rapidly expanding area of research and development [3]. Practically speaking, MAS are essentially loosely coupled networks of software agents that interact to solve problems that are beyond the individual capabilities of each agent. Conceptually, a multi-agent approach is an ideal fit to the naturally distributed domain of deregulated electricity markets [4]. Accordingly, an ongoing study at LNEG is looking at using autonomous software agents to help manage the complexity of energy markets, particularly markets with increasing levels of renewable generation (such as wind and photovoltaic solar power). The main aim is to provide an agent-based system to analyze the behavior and outcomes of EMs.

The system, called MATREM (for Multi-Agent TRading in Electricity Markets), supports a power exchange comprising a day-ahead market, an intra-day market, and a real-time market (see, e.g., [5]). The pricing mechanism is founded on the marginal pricing theory—both system marginal pricing and locational marginal pricing are supported. MATREM also supports a derivatives exchange comprising a futures market for trading standardized bilateral contracts. The futures market provides both financial and physical products that span from days to several years and allow market participants to hedge against the financial risk inherent to day-ahead and intra-day prices. Furthermore, MATREM supports a bilateral marketplace for negotiating the details of two types of customized long-term bilateral contracts: forward contracts (see, e.g., [6,7]) and contracts for difference (see, e.g., [8,9]).

Non-dispatchable renewable generation, or variable generation (VG), has several unique characteristics that may influence the schedules and prices of energy markets [10]. In particular, large penetrations of VG may reduce market prices due to their near-zero, zero, or negative-bid costs, increase price volatility (associated with their stochastic behavior), and worsen the capacity utilization of conventional resources. There is, therefore, a need to analyze the potential impacts of VG on energy markets to determine if existing designs are still effective.

This article uses the MATREM system to analyze the potential benefits of changing the wind power forecast information to the simulated day-ahead market. The main aim is: (i) to consider probabilistic techniques enabling the development of different bidding strategies, and (ii) to analyze the impact of the bidding strategies on the day-ahead market prices. The strategies take into account the intrinsic characteristics of the Iberian electricity market (MIBEL).

This paper builds on our previous work in the area of market design and simulation. In particular, it extends the work described in [11,12], where we analyze the impact of both wind forecast errors and high levels of wind generation on the outcomes of the day-ahead market (i.e., the market-clearing prices). The remainder of the paper is structured as follows. Section 2 presents an overview of the day-ahead and real-time markets supported by MATREM. Section 3 describes the different strategies adopted within the scope of this work. Section 4 presents a case study and discusses the results obtained. Finally, Sect. 5 presents some concluding remarks and avenues for future work.

2   Day-Ahead and Balancing Markets

The current version of MATREM supports four key types of agents participating in the simulated markets: generating companies, retailers, aggregators, and consumers. Generating company agents may own a single plant or a portfolio of plants of different technologies. They may sell electrical energy either to the day-ahead market or directly to retailers and large consumers through customized bilateral contracts. Retailer agents buy electricity in the day-ahead market and re-sell it to customers in retail markets (typically, customers that are not allowed, or do not want, to participate in the day-ahead market). Aggregators are entities that support groups of end-use customers in trading electrical energy. Large consumers can take an active role in the market by buying electrical energy in the day-ahead market or alternatively by signing customized bilateral contracts with other market participants (e.g., producers). Small consumers, on the other hand, buy energy from retailers.

The simulated day-ahead market sells energy to retailers (and large consumers) and buys energy from generating companies in advance of time when the energy is produced and consumed. This market clears to meet bid-in load demand for an entire day, one day in advance. A market operator agent ensures a competitive marketplace by running an auction for electricity trades. Under system marginal pricing (SMP), generator companies compete to supply demand by submitting bids in the form of price and quantity pairs. These bids are ranked in increasing order of price, leading to a supply curve. Similarly, retailers and possibly other market participants submit offers to buy certain amounts of energy at specific prices. These purchase offers are ranked in order of decreasing price, leading to a demand curve. The market-clearing price (or system marginal price) is defined by the intersection of the supply curve with the cumulative demand curve. This price is determined on an hourly basis and applied to all generators uniformly, regardless of their bids or location. Generators are instructed to produce the amount of energy corresponding to their accepted bids and buyers are informed of the amount of energy that they are allowed to draw from the system.

All generating companies participate in the simulated day-ahead market under the same rules, whether they are conventional energy source producers or producers who use stochastic sources (such as wind energy). This market is typically the one with the largest trading volume of transactions and normally takes place every day until 12:00 UTC on day d—that is, wind power producers submit offers to the market operator for each hour of the day of operation (d + 1). Due to the stochastic nature of wind power generation, the final energy delivered typically differs from the committed schedule. The differences are counterbalanced in the balancing or reserves market, resulting in imbalances which have to be paid by those who deviate from their original schedule. The imbalances are settled according to either up or down balancing prices (i.e., penalties are paid for both up and down regulation). In practice, producers pay extra money (when upward balancing is needed) or receives less money (when downward balancing is needed).

The revenue (R) of wind power producers is computed as follows:

$$R = \sum_{t=t_{in}+1}^{n} P_t^{bid} C_t^{dayahead} + \begin{cases} \left(P_t - P_t^{bid}\right) C_t^{updeviation}, & \text{for } P_t^{bid} < P_t \\ \left(P_t - P_t^{bid}\right) C_t^{downdeviation}, & \text{for } P_t^{bid} > P_t \end{cases} \quad (1)$$

where:

- t_{in} is the burning period;
- $C_t^{dayahead}$ is the day-ahead price;
- $C_t^{updeviation}$ and $C_t^{downdeviation}$ are the up and down deviation costs, respectively.
- P_t and P_t^{bid} are the observed wind power and the wind power bid, respectively.

3 Strategies, Forecast Method and Representative Days

Taking into account the intrinsic features of the Iberian market (MIBEL), namely the characteristics of the balancing prices formulation, the following three different bidding strategies were developed.

Known Wind Power. The bid is simply set to the historical observed wind power:

$$P_t^{bid} = P_t \quad (2)$$

which is not known at time of bidding. In this case, there will be no costs for up and down regulation. The revenue is the one achieved with a perfect forecast and serves as an upper limit benchmark.

Point Forecast. In this case, the bid is set with the point forecast:

$$P_t^{bid} = \hat{P}_{t|t-k_t} \quad (3)$$

where $\hat{P}_{t|t-k_t}$ is the estimation of the conditional expectation of the wind power, k_t is the time horizon, and t is the time.

Minimizing the Hourly NRMSE (Min. 24h NRMSE). The bid is similar to the point forecast case, but first is determined the optimal quantile that minimizes the wind power forecast (NRMSE) according to the hour of the day:

$$\tau_{h_{opt}} = argmin \sqrt{\frac{\sum_{t=1}^{n} \hat{Q}_h^{p,\tau} - \hat{P}_h}{n}} \quad (4)$$

where $\tau_{h_{opt}}$ is the optimal quantile, $\hat{Q}_h^{p,\tau}$ is the quantile forecasts (or probabilistic forecasts) of the wind power, h is the hour and n the number of records available for each hour.

This strategy is particularly relevant, since the wind power forecast errors usually present diurnal variations (as described by many authors, e.g., [13]), which can be partially explained by the inability of the numerical weather prediction (NWP) models to simulate the stability effects in the lower boundary layer. The forecast methodology used is the K-nearest neighbour method (K-NN) (see, e.g., [12]).

In order to prevent exhaustive simulations for all data available (two years) or to randomly select some days, a methodology to obtain the most common wind power daily patterns was applied. The underlying objective of selecting representative days is to identify the most common wind power daily patterns, and at the same time grouping together days exhibiting similar patterns. The identification of representative days is a widely tool employed to enhance the knowledge of a predetermined parameter allowing to develop decision support systems (e.g., electricity customer classification [14]). In this study, the K-medoids clustering algorithm [15] is used to identify the representative days. The K-medoids technique is a non-hierarchical clustering algorithm for grouping the data in K clusters, where K is previously defined. The suitable number of clusters (in this case the number of representative wind power profiles) was predetermined by calculating the Calinski-Harabasz (CH) criterion [16]. The CH criterion allows to identify the optimal number of clusters by computing the Euclidean distance between the clusters and comparing that with the internal sum of squared errors for each cluster.

4   Case-Study: Multivariate Forecast Bidding Strategies

This case study aims at using the MATREM simulator to analyze the effect of different (wind power) bidding strategies on the market outcomes. The "Point forecast" strategy was used as a baseline strategy, meaning that the results obtained with this strategy were compared with the results of the "Min. 24h NRMSE" and "Known power" strategies. Real supply as well as demand bids from the MIBEL are used in the simulations.

4.1   Wind Power Profiles and Software Agents

The forecast data were available at LNEG for a set of wind parks with a nominal capacity of nearly 250 MW. The forecast methodology is based on a K-nearest neighbor (K-NN) method using the NWP outputs (see [17]). Since the nominal power of the forecast data is less than 10% of the wind power capacity in Portugal (at the end of 2010), an upscaling to 2500 MW was performed in order to verify the effects of changing the bidding strategy in the market.

The software agents represent a system operator, a market operator, 12 supply-side agents (generating companies or producers) and 4 demand-side agents (retailers). Several key features of the supply-side agents are presented in Table 1. Notably, the agent P1 (wind aggregator) represents almost all wind parks in Portugal.

Based on the CH criterion, seven representative days were selected (Fig. 1). The frequency of occurrence of the representative days are depicted in Fig. 2. Due to the interconnection constraints observed in electricity transactions between Portugal and Spain, in the hours that the clearing point results in a violation of those constraints, it was applied a market splitting, and then simulated the day-ahead market for Portugal only.

Table 1. Producer agents

Agent	Country	Type	Maximum capacity (MW)	Marginal cost (€/MWh)
P1	Portugal	Wind	2500	0
P2	Portugal	Renewable mix	2000	0
P3	Portugal	Hydroelectricity	4500	[30; 60]
P4	Portugal	Coal	1800	≈30
P5	Portugal	Combined cycle gas	3000	≈55
P6	Portugal	Fuel oil	2000	≈70
P7	Spain	Renewable mix	30000	0
P3	Spain	Hydroelectricity	16500	[30; 60]
P4	Spain	Coal	10000	≈30
P4	Spain	Nuclear	7500	≈30
P5	Spain	Combined cycle gas	22000	≈55
P6	Spain	Fuel oil	4000	≈70

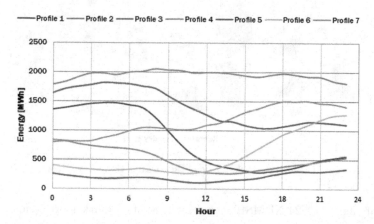

Fig. 1. Wind power profile for the representative days

4.2 Results

The results about the impact of the different wind power bidding strategies on the day-ahead market prices are presented in Fig. 3 (according to the various representative days). On average, the effects of changing the strategy are only slightly significant. These results can be partially explained by the small fraction of wind power used, since it was only considered the changes in the Portuguese wind parks, while in Spain (that also belongs to MIBEL) the installed capacity of wind power was almost eight times above the value observed in Portugal (in 2010). Nevertheless, with the exception of the first representative day, the results

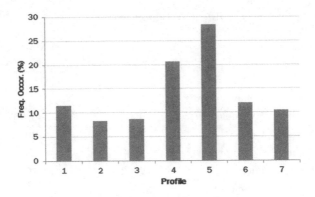

Fig. 2. Frequency of occurrence of the representative days

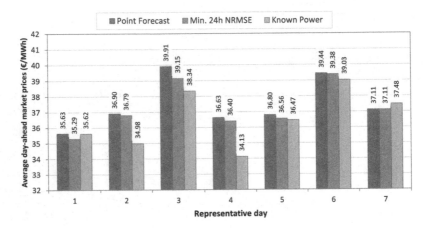

Fig. 3. Average day-ahead market prices (according to each representative day)

show that the "Min. 24 NRMSE" strategy presents a market price closer to the "Know power" strategy.

Figure 4 presents the levelized revenues for the wind power producers taking into account the different bidding strategies. The results suggest that the effect of the different strategies on the levelized revenues is higher (when compared with the effect on the average day-ahead market prices). Moreover, it is possible to conclude that the "Minimizing hourly NRMSE" strategy is slightly better than the "Point forecast"strategy, but far from the "Known power" strategy. This difference occurs due to the minimization of the wind power deviation errors of the "Minimizing hourly NRMSE" strategy (in relation to the "Point forecast" strategy). It should be stressed that the negative levelized revenues observed in the seventh representative day are explained by the high relative deviations to the observed power (and the low observed power). Consequently, and taking into account the penalties, this representative day leads to higher losses.

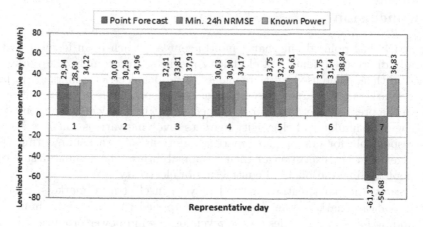

Fig. 4. Levelized revenue per representative days

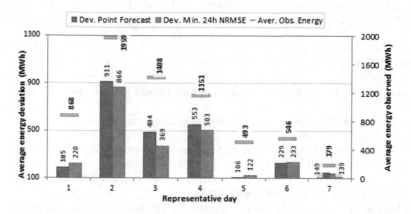

Fig. 5. Average observed energy (green line) and deviations according to each strategy: (i) Point forecast (gray) and (ii) Min. 24h NRMSE (orange) (Color figure online)

Figure 5 presents the average energy deviations between the above strategies and the total wind energy generated. There is a strong relation between the wind power forecast deviations and the levelized revenues. Additionally, it is also possible to observe that, on average: (i) the differences between the revenues obtained with the "Known power" strategy (observed power) and the remaining strategies increase as the wind power forecast deviations also increase, and (ii) the "Min. 24h NRMSE" strategy presents lower deviations when compared with the common "Point forecast" strategy.

These results highlight the need of strategies to improve the forecast, and/or of bidding strategies that lead to reductions in wind power deviations, preventing transactions in the balancing markets (at high costs). Such steps are crucial to increase the economic value of wind power as well as the security of power systems, especially in cases with large-scale integration of wind generation sources.

5   Conclusion

This article has pointed out that a multi-agent approach is an ideal fit to the naturally distributed domain of electricity markets. Accordingly, the work performed in this article used software agents to model electricity markets, in particular, markets with large penetration of non-dispatchable renewable generation (in the present case, wind power). Specifically, this article has presented an overview of a simulator of electricity markets involving various software agents, each responsible for one or more market functions and each interacting with other agents in the execution of their responsibilities. The simulator supports both pool trading and bilateral contracting of electricity.

To study the participation of wind players in electricity markets, particularly day-ahead markets, the simulator was applied to analyze the impact of new bidding forecast strategies on the revenues of wind power producers. It was concluded that the benefits are only slightly significant, and the specific percentage of added market revenue from changing the wind power forecast technique is small for the best bidding strategy—that is, the "Min. 24h NRMSE" strategy.

References

1. Hunt, S., Shuttleworth, G.: Competition and Choice in Electricity. Wiley, Chichester (1996)
2. Shahidehpour, M., Yamin, H., Li, Z.: Market Operations in Electric Power Systems. Wiley, New York (2002)
3. Wooldridge, M.: An Introduction to Multiagent systems. Wiley, Chichester (2009)
4. Lopes, F., Coelho, H.: Multi-agent negotiation in electricity markets. In: Huemer, C., Setzer, T. (eds.) EC-Web 2011. LNBIP, vol. 85, pp. 114–123. Springer, Heidelberg (2011). doi:10.1007/978-3-642-23014-1_10
5. Vidigal, D., Lopes, F., Pronto, A., Santana, J.: Agent-based simulation of wholesale energy markets: a case study on renewable generation. In: Spies, M., Wagner, R., Tjoa, A. (eds.) 26th Database and Expert Systems Applications (DEXA 2015), pp. 81–85. IEEE (2015)
6. Lopes, F., Rodrigues, T., Sousa, J.: Negotiating bilateral contracts in a multi-agent electricity market: a case study. In: Hameurlain, A., Tjoa, A., Wagner, R. (eds.) 23rd Database and Expert Systems Applications (DEXA 2012), pp. 326–330. IEEE (2012)
7. Algarvio, H., Lopes, F., Santana, J.: Bilateral contracting in multi-agent energy markets: forward contracts and risk management. In: Bajo, J., Hallenborg, K., Pawlewski, P., Botti, V., Sánchez-Pi, N., Duque Méndez, N.D., Lopes, F., Julian, V. (eds.) PAAMS 2015. CCIS, vol. 524, pp. 260–269. Springer, Cham (2015). doi:10.1007/978-3-319-19033-4_22
8. Sousa, F., Lopes, F., Santana, J.: Contracts for difference and risk management in multi-agent energy markets. In: Demazeau, Y., Decker, K.S., Bajo Pérez, J., de la Prieta, F. (eds.) PAAMS 2015. LNCS (LNAI), vol. 9086, pp. 155–164. Springer, Cham (2015). doi:10.1007/978-3-319-18944-4_13
9. Sousa, F., Lopes, F., Santana, J.: Multi-agent electricity markets: a case study on contracts for difference. In: Spies, M., Wagner, R., Tjoa, A. (eds.) 26th Database and Expert Systems Applications (DEXA 2015), pp. 88–90. IEEE (2015)

10. Ela, E., Milligan, M., Bloom, A., Botterud, A., Townsend, A., Levin, T.: Evolution of wholesale electricity market design with increasing levels of renewable generation. Report NREL/TP-5D00-61765, Golden, USA, September 2014
11. Algarvio, H., Couto, A., Lopes, F., Estanqueiro, A., Santana, J.: Multi-agent energy markets with high levels of renewable generation: a case-study on forecast uncertainty and market closing time. In: Omatu, S., et al. (eds.) 13th International Conference on Distributed Computing and Artificial Intelligence. AISC, vol. 474, pp. 339–347. Springer International Publishing, Heidelberg (2016)
12. Algarvio, H., Couto, A., Lopes, F., Estanqueiro, A., Holttinen, H., Santana, J.: Agent-based simulation of day-ahead energy markets: impact of forecast uncertainty and market closing time on energy prices. In: Tjoa, A., Vale, Z., Wagner, R. (eds.) 27th Database and Expert Systems Applications (DEXA 2016), pp. 166–170. IEEE (2016)
13. Focken, U., Lange, M.: Physical Approach to Short-Term Wind Power Prediction. Springer, Heidelberg (2005)
14. Ramos, S., Duarte, J., Soares, J., Vale, Z., Duarte, F.: Typical load profiles in the smart grid context a clustering methods comparison. In: IEEE Power and Energy Society General Meeting (IEEE PES GM 2012), USA (2012)
15. Park, H.-S., Jun, C.-H.: A simple and fast algorithm for k-medoids clustering. Expert Syst. Appl. **36**(2–Part 2), 3336–3341 (2009)
16. Calinski, T., Harabasz, J.: A dendrite method for cluster analysis. Commun. Stat. **3**(1), 27 (1974)
17. Couto, A., Rodrigues, L., Costa, P., Silva, J., Estanqueiro, A.: Wind power participation in electricity markets - the role of wind power forecasts. In: 16th IEEE Conference on Environment and Electrical Engineering (2016)

A Linear Programming Model to Simulate the Adaptation of Multi-agent Power Systems to New Sources of Energy

Hugo Algarvio[1,2]($\boxtimes$), Fernando Lopes[2], and João Santana[1]

[1] Instituto Superior Técnico, Universidade de Lisboa, INESC-ID, Lisbon, Portugal
{hugo.algarvio,jsantana}@tecnico.ulisboa.pt
[2] LNEG—National Research Institute, Est. do Paço do Lumiar 22, Lisbon, Portugal
fernando.lopes@lneg.pt

Abstract. Electric power systems (EPSs) are systems composed by several active agents as well as various physical and economical aspects. Electricity markets are systems for effecting the purchase and sale of electricity using supply and demand to set energy prices. This work looks at using software agents to help manage the complexity of power systems. Specifically, this paper presents a linear programming model that accounts for: (i) optimal allocation of thermal generation in EPSs, and (ii) the effect of introducing new generation technology in EPSs. To illustrate the model, the paper presents a case study involving a specific EPS and a simulated day-ahead market. The first part of the case study considers three different types of thermal power plants: coal (base), natural gas (intermediate) and oil fueled (peak). The results indicate a maximal thermal capacity of 21962 MW. The second part considers the addition of renewable generation (8000 MW) to the EPS, composed by three types of sources (wind, photovoltaic and mini-hydro). The results determine a reduction of 2400 MW on the thermal base capacity, and an over-cost between 10% and 17% (in relation to the initial system).

1 Introduction

Electric power systems (EPSs) are systems composed by several active agents, such as producers, retailers, consumers, regulators, system operators and market operators, as well as several physical and economical institutions, such as electricity markets and power grids. Electricity markets (EMs) are systems for effecting the purchase and sale of electricity using supply and demand to set energy prices (see, e.g., [1,2]). Least cost systems are essentially dual-objective systems—they aim at minimizing the long-run costs of EPSs by minimizing the investment costs with power plants, and also the short-run costs by selecting the power plants with the lowest operation cost. The concept of "least-cost system" is associated with a system that optimizes both the long-run (system) design, by selecting specific power plants, and the short-run power plant operation.

H. Algarvio and J. Santana—This work was supported by "Fundação para a Ciência e a Tecnologia" with references UID/CEC/50021/2013 and PD/BD/105863/2014.

© Springer International Publishing AG 2017
J. Bajo et al. (Eds.): PAAMS 2017 Workshops, CCIS 722, pp. 350–360, 2017.
DOI: 10.1007/978-3-319-60285-1_30

Multi-agent systems (MAS) are essentially loosely coupled networks of software agents that interact to solve problems that are beyond the individual capabilities of each agent. Software agents are computer systems capable of autonomous action in order to meet their design objectives [3,4]. Conceptually, a MAS presents itself as a good way to represent distributed domains, such as EPSs, and to simulate the interactions between different entities. Accordingly, this work looks at using software agents to help manage the complexity of power systems, particularly the issues associated with thermal power plant allocation and also variable generation (or renewable generation).

In particular, an ongoing study at LNEG is looking at using autonomous software agents to help manage the complexity of energy markets. The main aim is to provide an agent-based system to analyze the behavior and outcomes of EMs. The system, called MATREM (for Multi-Agent TRading in Electricity Markets), supports a day-ahead market, a shorter-term market known as intraday market, and a real-time market (see, e.g., [5,6]). The pricing mechanism is founded on the marginal pricing theory—both system marginal pricing and locational marginal pricing are supported. The system also supports a bilateral marketplace for negotiating the details of two types of tailored (or customized) long-term bilateral contracts: forward contracts (see, e.g., [7,8]) and contracts for difference (see, e.g., [9,10]). Buyers and sellers are equipped with a negotiation model that handles two-party and multi-issue negotiation [11].

This paper presents a linear programming model for software agents, particularly agents representing power producers. The model incorporates two objective functions and aims at optimizing the allocation of thermal power plants in EPSs. Specifically, the main objective of the model is to obtain the least-cost power system, i.e., the set of power plants (installed capacity by technology) that minimize the annual cost of a particular EPS taking into account the demand. Also, the model analysis the impact of a specific system design in the total cost, the extra cost, and the energy average price.

The paper also describes a case study involving an EPS and three agents with three different types of thermal technologies: coal (base), natural gas (intermediate) and oil fueled (peak). The first part of the case study aims at determining the optimized allocation of thermal technologies. In the second part, we introduce renewable generation to the EPS. This generation is composed by three types of sources (wind, photovoltaic and mini-hydro). The corresponding generators have a feed-in tariff scheme. Their energy have priority and is offered at 0 € in the market. Furthermore, by introducing renewable generation, we aim at analyzing how the system considered in the first part of the case study should be adapted in order to minimize the costs. Another objective is to compare the total costs of the system, before and after considering renewable generation. The remainder of the paper is structured as follows. Section 2 introduces the concept of "least-cost" system. Section 3 presents the linear programming model. Section 4 deals with electricity markets and presents an overview of pools and bilateral contracts. Section 5 presents the case study and discusses the results. Finally, concluding remarks are presented in Sect. 6.

2   Least-Cost System

The main goal of a least-cost system [12] is to supply a required demand of electricity at a minimum cost. So, the operation period of each power technology is optimized. Let $\mathcal{A} = \{a_1, ..., a_i\}$ be the set of power plant agents. To minimize the cost of operating an electric power system, there is a need to consider the variable costs of production, i.e., the marginal costs of the power plants. The lower operating costs should match the lowest cost of the system, i.e., the sum of variable costs and fixed charges. Indeed, with operating dispatchable technologies $1, 2, ..., i, i + 1$, usually characterized by variable costs $c_1 \leq c_2 \leq ... \leq c_i \leq c_{i+1}$, and annual fixed costs $C_1 \geq C_2 \geq ... \geq C_i \geq C_{i+1}$, the most efficient operating situation is achieved if the technology $i + 1$ is presented:

$$h_{i+1} \leq \frac{C_i - C_{i+1}}{c_{i+1} - c_i} \tag{1}$$

where h_{i+1} is the number of hours that the generation technology $i + 1$ should operate in order to optimize the EPS. Technology 1 should be present during the 8760 h of each year, while technology $i+1$ must operate an annually number of hours lower then h_{i+1}.

Most spot markets are based on the theory of partial equilibrium. For illustrative purposes, consider a situation where producers offer their energy at different prices according to the technology, and the demand is perfectly inelastic. This simple situation aims at demonstrating how the market price is calculated (see Fig. 1). The market operator performs the aggregation of the offers of both the producers and the consumers and establishes the supply and demand curves, respectively. The resulting balance of equality between the supply curve and the demand curve leads to the price of the energy (the market price).

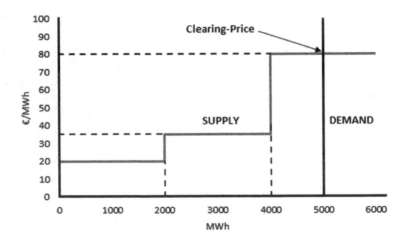

Fig. 1. Clearing price determination for a specific hour

3   Linear Programming Model

This section presents a model to obtain the optimal installed capacity for each different capacity that is presented in a power system, and as a result, the optimal operation time (unit commitment) that minimizes the total cost of the system. The model can also be used to test the introduction of new sources of energy in the power system, in order to analyze how the system can be adapted to these new sources to minimize the cost. We consider a set of K technologies. Each technology $k \in K$ is associated with a specific installed power, $x(k)$, operated at level $y(k,l)$, and at time interval $\tau(l)$. The level of demand is denoted by $d(l)$. The monotonous curve is decomposed into different time slots l, that belong to a set L, i.e., $l \in L$. Figure 2 illustrates the decomposition that corresponds to the discretization of the monotonous curve: the duration τ of time interval (l) and the level of demand $d(l)$ keep the same energy as defined by the actual monotonous curve.

Let the annual cost of the investment, or fixed cost, of technology k, be $I(k)$, and the variable cost of production, which is assumed to be constant, be $c(k)$. The maximum Price-Cap (PC) is the cost of the no supplied energy. In practice, this value may range from 150 to 3000 €/MWh in Europe and from 300 to 3000 \$/MWh in the United states. In the Iberian market, the PC set by the Regulator is 180.3 €/MWh and corresponds to the maximum price bid allowed in this market. Let $z(l)$ be the no supplied power in time interval $\tau(l)$.

Consider now the problem of minimizing the cost of the system operation, $Q(x)$, taking into account the set of available technologies and the corresponding installed power. It is a short-run problem:

$$Q(x) = \min_{y,z} \sum_{l \in L} \left[\sum_{k \in K} c(k)y(k,l) + z(l)PC \right] \qquad (2)$$

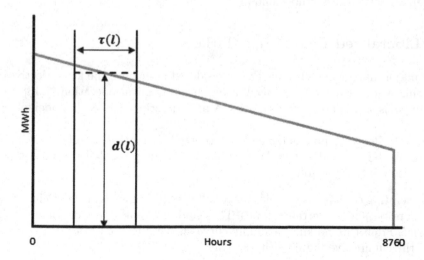

Fig. 2. Monotone curve discretization

subject to:

$$0 \leq x(k) - y(k,l) \qquad\qquad \tau(l)\mu(k,l) \qquad\qquad (3)$$

$$0 \leq \sum_{k \in K} y(k,l) + z(l) - d(l) \qquad\qquad \tau(l)\pi(k,l) \qquad\qquad (4)$$

$$0 \leq y(k,l), \qquad\qquad 0 \leq x(k) \qquad\qquad (5)$$

Note that the dual variables $\mu(k,l)$ and $\pi(k,l)$, associated with the restrictions, are presented on the right-hand of each restriction.

Now, the selection of the investment, technologies and installed power is a long-run issue, which takes into account the minimization of the operation cost, $Q(x)$. This minimization takes place after choosing the set of technologies K and the related installed power.

The problem of minimizing the long-run cost is formulated by the following objective function:

$$F(x,y,z) = \min_{x \geq 0} \left[\sum_{k \in K} I(k)x(k) + Q(x) \right] \qquad\qquad (6)$$

Subject to:

$$0 \leq x(k) - y(k,l) \qquad\qquad \tau(l)\mu(k,l) \qquad\qquad (7)$$

$$0 \leq \sum_{k \in K} y(k,l) + z(l) - d(l) \qquad\qquad \tau(l)\pi(k,l) \qquad\qquad (8)$$

$$0 \leq y(k,l), \qquad\qquad 0 \leq x(k) \qquad\qquad (9)$$

Minimizing the cost of electricity in an EPS is the goal and this approach and could be used is several real systems. To illustrate the applicability of the model, a relevant case-study follows.

4   Liberalized Electricity Markets

Two major market models have been considered to achieve the key objectives of ensuring a secure system and facilitating an economical operation [2,13]: electricity pools and bilateral transactions. A brief description of each model follows.

Electricity Pools. A pool is defined as a centralized marketplace that clears the market for buyers and sellers. While there are many possible variations, a pool operates essentially as follows:

- Generating companies submit bids to sell specific amounts of electricity at certain prices and for certain periods. These bids are ranked in order of increasing price. From this ranking, a supply curve showing the bid price as a function of the cumulative bid quantity is built.

- Similarly, consumers submit offers specifying the quantity and price at which they intend to buy the energy. These offers are ranked in order of decreasing price and a demand curve is established.
- The intersection of the supply and demand curves represents the market equilibrium. All the bids submitted at a price lower than or equal to the market clearing price are accepted and generators are instructed to produce the amount of energy corresponding to their accepted bids. Similarly, all the offers submitted at a price greater than or equal to the market clearing price are accepted and the consumers are informed of the amount of energy that they are allowed to draw from the system.
- The market clearing price represents the price of one additional megawatt-hour (MWh) of energy and is therefore called the system marginal price (SMP). Generators are paid the SMP for every megawatt-hour that they produce, whereas consumers pay the SMP for every MWh that they consume, irrespective of the bids and offers that they submitted.

Since the demand for electricity is highly inelastic, consumers can submit offers to buy energy, or the demand can be set at a value determined by using load forecasting. Now, pool prices exhibit a set of characteristics, notably non-stationary mean and variance, multiple seasonality, calendar effect, high percentage of outliers, and high volatility [14]. They tend to change quickly and variations are usually highly unpredictable. In this way, market participants often enter into bilateral contracts to hedge against pool price volatility.

Bilateral Transactions. A bilateral transaction involves only two parties: a buyer and a seller. Depending on the amount of time available and the quantities to be traded, buyers and sellers will resort to the following forms of bilateral trading [2]: customized long-term contracts, trading "over the counter" and electronic trading.

Standardized bilateral contracts are often negotiated in forward markets. The transactions in a forward market are performed assuming their liquidation, i.e., the seller delivers the product and the buyer pays the product price, in a future date. In addition to forward contracts, other forms of standardized bilateral contracts are often negotiated in derivatives markets, notably futures, options and contracts for differences (CfDs).

5   Case Study

5.1   The Electric Power System and the Simulations

We consider an EPS with three technologies, namely base, intermediate and peak [12], and a day-ahead market involving offers equal to the marginal cost of operation (i.e., producers will bid according to their operation costs and installed capacities). The curve that reflects the variation of consumption, D, of the EPS, according to the number of hours, h, is as follows:

$$D = 22000 - 1.37\,h \tag{10}$$

Table 1. Fixed and variable annual costs

Technology	Annual fixed costs (€/MW/Year)	Variable costs (€/MWh)
Base	240000	20
Intermediate	160000	35
Peak	80000	80

We consider a set $\mathcal{A}_1$ of three different agents: $\mathcal{A}_1 = \{a_1, a_2, a_3\}$. Each agent owns a specific thermal power plant (PP). The parameters that characterize the different technologies are presented in Table 1. The energy not provided is also illustrated in Table 1, which has a marginal cost between 180.3 and 3000 €/MWh. The conditions of consumption and production establish an unequivocally efficient share of the load by technology (see Table 2, below).

Leap years are not considered, and the average length of a non-leap year is equal to $\sum_l \tau(l) = 8760\,$h. The consumption to be satisfied is given by (10). The computational consumption is given by the following expression:

$$d(l) = d(0) - 1.37(2L - 1)\tau(l)/2 \tag{11}$$

where $d(l)$ is the average demand of the EPS in the range L and $d(0) = 22000$ MW is the maximum load of the system.

For the application of the linear programming model, the monotonous curve (11) is discretized into time intervals. To this end, we use time intervals that are integer divisors of 8760 (to obtain an integer number of hours for each interval). The 30 time intervals considered, $\tau(l)$, and their demands, $d(l)$, are as follows:

$$\tau(1) = \tau(2) = ... = \tau(29) = \tau(30) = 292\,h$$
$$d(1) = 21800; d(2) = 21400; ...; d(29) = 10599; d(30) = 10199$$

We consider various scenarios that differ by varying the number of time intervals. Naturally, more time intervals leads to better results. The intention of

Table 2. Simulation results

Technology	LP - part 1		LP - part 2	
	PCs (€/MWh): 180.3	PCs (€/MWh): 3000	PCs (€/MWh): 180.3	PCs (€/MWh): 3000
Base (MW)	14696	14696	12296	12296
Intermediate (MW)	4866	4866	4866	4866
Peak (MW)	1344	2400	1348	2400
Renewable (MW)	0	0	8000	8000
Non installed power (MW)	1089	33	1085	33
Average EM price (€/MWh)	54.58	54.88	47.47	47.77
Annual total cost (€ × 10⁹)	7.470	7.692	8.203	8.351

varying the number of time intervals is to get the best relationship between the error obtained and the time spent in computation.

The case-study involves the following two different parts:

1. Thermal power producers only.
2. The introduction of renewable energy sources (RES) into the EPS over several years, which allows to adjust it (reducing the excess capacity).

Specifically, for the second part of the case study, we consider the introduction of 8000 MW of RES (wind, photovoltaic and mini-hydro) in the EPS, offered at null marginal cost, but with a feed-in tariff of 80 €/MWh. The corresponding annual production is 21 TWh, which represents 15% of the total system consumption. To simplify the analysis, we assume that the RES production follows an uniform distribution throughout the year with an average power of 2400 MW (a power factor of 30%). However, due to the random nature of the intermittent technology, this does not ensure the security of power.

5.2 Results

The results obtained are presented in Table 2. The analysis of the results shows some differences between the technologies, which occur due to the introduction of PCs in the linear programming model. Specifically, the differences occur mainly in the peak technology, since it is the one with the highest marginal cost. Since the PC is the maximum price at which the energy can be traded, the results allow us to conclude that, for a PC equal to either 180.3 €/MWh or 3000 €/MWh, is preferable to avoid the construction of the peak power plants of 1089 MW or 33 MW, respectively (in order to reduce the costs).

Furthermore, by taking into account the case where the PC is equal to 180.3 €/MWh, the main difference in terms of scheduling is that, for the first part of the case study, the base technology with installed capacity of 14696 MW will be enough to feed the load during 3427 h. The situation where the intermediate technology is marginal takes a duration of 3555 h. This technology has an installed capacity of 4866 MW. All the generation technologies are in operation, during the peak period, for 978 h. The marginal technology, in the peak period, has an installed capacity of 1344 MW. And all the required demand is not supplied for 800 h because of the PC. Under these circumstances, we can consider that the EPS is balanced.

In the second part of the case study, with the introduction of 8000 MW of RES, the main differences are a reduction of 2400 MW in the need to consider base PPs, a decrease in the EM marginal price and an increase in the EPS total cost. The difference between the costs, before and after the addition of RES, is called the over-cost. An economic analysis of the results follows.

In the first part of the case study, we can calculate the total annual costs of each technology and also the total cost of the EPS (see Table 3). The producers receive the amounts designated by "Energy Revenues", by trading energy in the market. For the specific market situation under analysis, the total costs of each

Table 3. Total costs and revenues

Technology	Energy revenues ($€ \times 10^9$)	Capacity revenues ($€ \times 10^9$)	Total revenues ($€ \times 10^9$)	Total costs ($€ \times 10^9$)
Base	3.826	1.881	5.940	5.940
Intermediate	0.987	0.565	1.385	1.385
Peak	0.103	0.108	0.368	0.368
TOTAL 1	4.917	2.553	7.470	7.470
Base	3.174	1.574	4.748	4.748
Intermediate	1.002	0.550	1.385	1.385
Peak	0.123	0.108	0.388	0.388
Renewable	1.682	0	1.682	1.682
TOTAL 2	5.981	2.222	8.203	8.203

technology and the total cost of the system are not obtained by considering the market profits only. In fact, if the clearing price of the market equals the marginal cost of the system, then the economic viability of production is not guaranteed. In addition to the marginal cost of the EPS ("Energy Revenues"), all producers operating in the market receive an extra amount, calculated by multiplying the installed capacity by the fixed unit cost of the peak technology ("Capacity Revenues"). Therefore, each technology receives a "Total Revenue" that is equal to the "Total Cost" (see Table 3).

The sum of "Energy Revenues" and "Capacity Revenues" ensures long-term economic viability for all producers. Accordingly, considering the total costs, and calculating the total energy of the system by adding the annual consumption, with value 0.140×10^9 MWh, the average price of the EPS is $54.58 €$/MWh.

Comparing the results of both parts of the case-study, we can conclude that the introduction of RES originates an over-cost of $0.733 \times 10^9 €$/MWh (an increase of almost 10% when compared with the initial system). The percentage of 73% ($0.534 \times 10^9 €$/MWh) of the over-cost results from the high feed-in tariff. The remaining amount (27%) results from the need for reserve energy caused by the penetration of intermittent generation (wind, photovoltaic and mini-hydro).

These results are obtained by considering that the penetration of renewable energy sources increases slightly over the years, allowing to adapt the EPS to these new sources of energy. In a scenario where the renewable energy is abruptly introduced into the EPS, the reserve costs increase, resulting in an increase of $0.576 \times 10^9 €$/MWh in the reserve energy over-cost, and also in a total over-cost of the system of $1.309 \times 10^9 €$/MWh (an increase of 17.5% when compared with the total cost of the initial system).

6   Conclusion

This paper has introduced the concept of "least-cost system", i.e., a system that aims at both minimizing the investment costs with power plants and the short-run costs associated with the participation in energy markets. The paper has also presented a dual objective model—a linear programming model to resolve the problem of obtaining a least-cost system. Furthermore, the paper has presented a case-study to illustrate (and test) the model. The first part of the case study analyzes a system with thermal power plants only. The second part considers the introduction, over time, of a relevant percentage (25%) of renewable generation (with a feed-in tariff scheme) in the power system.

We observed that the introduction of RES causes an over-cost due to the high feed-in tariffs and the required reserve energy, increasing the total cost of the system. Also, the introduction of RES decreases the operation time of PPs and the market-clearing price, decreasing the revenues of PPs. This can result in a decrease in PPs, which can affect the long-term security of EPSs.

Clearly, the linear programming model can dynamically analyze the potential changes that EPSs may suffer due to the introduction of new technologies (e.g., RES). The model can be used to simulate both theoretical and real-life electrical systems. Accordingly, in the future, we intend to use the model to simulate real EPSs and observe how the penetration of RES can affect such systems.

References

1. Stoft, S.: Power Systyem Economis: Designing Markets for Electricity. IEEE Press and Wiley Interscience, Hoboken (2002)
2. Kirschen, D., Strbac, G.: Fundamentals of Power System Economics. Wiley, Chichester (2004)
3. Macal, C., North, M.: Tutorial on agent-based modelling and simulation. J. Simul. **4**, 151–162 (2010)
4. Wooldridge, M.: An Introduction to Multi-agent Systems. Wiley, Chichester (2009)
5. Vidigal, D., Lopes, F., Pronto, A., Santana, J.: Agent-based simulation of wholesale energy markets: a case study on renewable generation. In: Spies, M., Wagner, R., Tjoa, A. (eds.) 26th Database and Expert Systems Applications (DEXA 2015), pp. 81–85. IEEE (2015)
6. Algarvio, H., Couto, A., Lopes, F., Estanqueiro, A., Santana, J.: Multi-agent energy markets with high levels of renewable generation: a case-study on forecast uncertainty and market closing time. In: Omatu, S., et al. (eds.) DCAI 2016. AISC, vol. 474, pp. 339–347. Springer International Publishing, Cham (2016). doi:10.1007/978-3-319-40162-1_37
7. Lopes, F., Rodrigues, T., Sousa, J.: Negotiating bilateral contracts in a multi-agent electricity market: a case study. In: Hameurlain, A., Tjoa, A., Wagner, R. (eds.) 23rd Database and Expert Systems Applications (DEXA 2012), pp. 326–330. IEEE (2012)
8. Algarvio, H., Lopes, F., Santana, J.: Bilateral contracting in multi-agent energy markets: forward contracts and risk management. In: Bajo, J., Hallenborg, K., Pawlewski, P., Botti, V., Sánchez-Pi, N., Duque Méndez, N.D., Lopes, F., Julian, V. (eds.) PAAMS 2015. CCIS, vol. 524, pp. 260–269. Springer, Cham (2015). doi:10.1007/978-3-319-19033-4_22
9. Sousa, F., Lopes, F., Santana, J.: Contracts for difference and risk management in multi-agent energy markets. In: Demazeau, Y., Decker, K.S., Bajo Pérez, J., de la Prieta, F. (eds.) PAAMS 2015. LNCS (LNAI), vol. 9086, pp. 155–164. Springer, Cham (2015). doi:10.1007/978-3-319-18944-4_13

10. Sousa, F., Lopes, F., Santana, J.: Multi-agent electricity markets: a case study on contracts for difference. In: Spies, M., Wagner, R., Tjoa, A. (eds.) 26th Database and Expert Systems Applications (DEXA 2015), pp. 88–90. IEEE (2015)
11. Lopes, F., Coelho, H.: Strategic and tactical behaviour in automated negotiation. Int. J. Artif. Intell. 4(S10), 35–63 (2010)
12. Joskow, P.: Competitive Electricity Markets and Investment in New Generating Capacity. The New Energy Paradigm (2007)
13. Shahidehpour, M., Yamin, H., Li, Z.: Market Operations in Electric Power Systems. Wiley, Chichester (2002)
14. Conejo, A., Carrión, M., Morales, J.: Decision Making Under Uncertainty in Electricity Markets. Springer, New York (2010)

MAS Based Demand Response Application in Port City Using Reefers

Ntountounakis Manolis[1], Ishtiaq Ahmad[2(✉)], Kanellos Fotios[1],
Peter Palensky[3], and Wolfgang Gawlik[4]

[1] School of Production Engineering and Management,
Technical University of Crete, Chania, Greece
[2] AIT, Austrian Institute of Technology, Vienna, Austria
c2ishtiaq@hotmail.com
[3] Delft University of Technology, Delft, Netherlands
[4] Vienna University of Technology, Vienna, Austria

Abstract. Energy system is undergoing remarkable changes due to many factors including increase use of renewables, environmental consideration and technological advancements. This demands for new tools and methods for its efficient and smooth operation. This work proposes distributed demand response application using Multi-Agent System (MAS) for improving voltage in distribution network at port city. Contract-Net-Protocol (CNP) based scheme was used for communication and coordination between agents. A co-simulation framework including power system simulator and agent environment was used to evaluate the proposed MAS based approach. A test network including variable and intermittent renewable generation sources (wind, pv), flexible loads (reefers), non-flexible loads was used to investigate the MAS based approach. Results show that MAS based approach is quite effective for demand response application.

Keywords: Multi-agent systems · Green ports · Demand response · Distributed generation · Reefers

1 Introduction

The port cities face the great challenge to realize the ambitious 20-20-20 agenda for EU countries according to which there should be 20% cut in greenhouse gas emissions (from 1990 levels), 20% of EU energy from renewables and 20% improvement in energy efficiency till 2020. This demands for high energy efficiency and innovation in their energy sector. While energy use in port cities is immense, their energy efficiency is low and renewable energy sources exploitation is still in its infancy. Large port cities constitute an excellent choice to explore the possibilities for large scale implementation of smart energy systems in order to achieve a sustainable future. Many ports have great opportunity of producing power from renewable energy sources. Electricity usage and total cost will rise

© Springer International Publishing AG 2017
J. Bajo et al. (Eds.): PAAMS 2017 Workshops, CCIS 722, pp. 361–370, 2017.
DOI: 10.1007/978-3-319-60285-1_31

significantly in the next decade due to operational, regulatory, and environmental factors [1,2].

In the framework of the European research project "E-harbors" eight partners around the North Sea explored the possibilities for large scale implementation of smart energy networks in their largest port cities with very promising, but empirical results [3]. Similar, results were found by other European research projects, such as "Green Efforts", "EFICONT" and "CLIMEPORT" [4]. Also, new stricter legalization are being adopted globally in the world. Besides, very large ports, such as the port of Rotterdam and the ports of Los Angeles and Long Beach, aim is to apply the new methods and techniques for sustainable power management solutions by adopting rules beyond legalization [5]. A study of the literature concluded that the research in power management in port cities is still at the incunabula. There are only very few elementary research works, with only elementary qualitative results, even though the accessibility to real data from large ports, due to the above mentioned projects.

Emerging electric power system technologies and topologies, such as Microgrid, Smart Grid, Virtual Power Plants, distributed control, Information and Communication Technologies (ICT), are anticipated as crucial in electricity infrastructure in the future [6]. The port energy systems are also changing rapidly and becoming more complex and efficient real-time Power Management Systems are needed [7]. The real-time load management in such systems using a single centralized controller or traditional optimization techniques requires a great amount of computation resources making the application of centralized optimal control systems quite difficult and challenging.

Load management mainly focuses on matching load demand with power production while achieving certain objectives, such as reducing operation cost, ensuring power system stability and reliability etc. In order to develop green ports, power management systems need to be more efficient [8]. Nowadays, a large amount of flexible electric loads are present at large ports e.g. cold stores, cranes, industrial loads etc. Also, electricity cost can be reduced by shifting consumption of ports with installed RES during the sunshine or windy hours, using energy storage. Reefers at ports can be considered as thermostatically control loads which can be utilized for frequency and voltage regulation with proper control mechanism.

This paper focuses on voltage improvement in distribution network by using reefers. Voltage regulation is a well researched problem and there are many equipments and techniques available for improving voltage in a distribution network [9]. Increase use of variable and intermittent generation injection at distribution level is making voltage regulation a challenging task. Some of the equipments used for voltage regulation are; On Load Tap Changers(OLTC), Capacitor Banks, Unified Power Flow Controllers, Static Synchronous Compensator. Grid reinforcement, alternating routing, load balancing, active power curtailment and demand side management techniques are also suggested in literature [10]. As reefers have a potential to serve as a responsive load, it can be used to regulate the voltage by actively modifying the consumption. Demand side management based voltage schemes have been proposed in literature which aim to increase the consumption at the time of higher generation (by DERs i.e. PV, Wind) which reduce the rise in the voltage. Similarly reduction in consumption can result in rise of voltage.

The authors in [11] perform simulations on a real network and claimed that proposed demand side management technique was able to reduce energy loss and significantly improve voltage profile. Similarly, the authors in [12] presented a unified control algorithm to provide ancillary services to the grid by controlling the heterogeneous energy resources such as distributed storage systems and demand-responsive loads. The validation of the proposed algorithm shows that the network voltages are within acceptable limits, while an improvement in the network voltage profiles is also achieved. In another study [13], the authors used Thermostatically Controlled Loads (TCLs) to provide ancillary services for voltage regulation.

In this study, A Multi-Agent System (MAS) based approach is used to control these reefers for eliminating any voltage violation in the network. MAS can be used in both centralized and distributed scheme. In this paper, a central controller communicates with the reefer agents in the network to carry out the control action on the basis of specified criteria. MAS aims to achieve system objectives cooperatively that are difficult to obtain by a single agent or centralized controller. The distributed intelligent control architectures can lead to efficient power management in ports as they ensure unit autonomy and they can handle large data sets. The distributed nature of port power systems and the challenge of solving a highly multi-objective dynamic optimization problem are not addressed by conventional energy management systems, suggest the adoption of a decentralized control structure. With this approach the overall optimization problem is decomposed into smaller sub-problems that individual controllers could solve cooperatively. Each controller manages a single system unit, and groups of controllers report to higher-level coordinators that manage the interaction between the various subsystems. An intelligent agent can be assigned to each controller and all agents together compose MAS.

The paper is arranged as follows; Sect. 1 provides introduction and some literature review on issues in smart power management in large ports -cities and voltage regulation. Section 2 describes the problem statement and basic reefer model. Section 3 gives the Multi-agent system modeling and control algorithm. Co-simulation interface detail is given in Sect. 4. Section 5 presents the test case simulation and results while conclusions are drawn in Sect. 6.

2   Problem Formulation

This section provides the details of voltage management issues in low voltage network and reefer model.

2.1 Voltage Regulation

High penetration of variable and intermittent generation sources (wind and pv) into the low voltage grid tends to raise the voltage level. If there is upper voltage violation, generating units are disconnected from the network. On the other hand, if there is a sudden decrease in power injection voltage decreases rapidly which can also result in low voltage violations. Unlike, high voltage and medium voltage network, x/r ratio in low voltage network is low and voltage variation are more influenced by the change in active power. Distributed generation power curtailment can be used for improving the voltage in the network, however, this scheme is not considered good by the distributed generator owners which are connected at the end of the feeder [14]. In this scenario, load management (change in load consumption) can give an alternative for improving voltage in the network. Flexible loads can be used for this purpose. In this study reefers are used for improving voltage in the network. Reefers can be considered as thermostatically controlled loads which are used for storing and transporting refrigerated goods in a port city. Reefers details are given in the next section.

2.2 Reefers

Reefers rely on external source of power i.e. from electric grid. While transporting, reefers can get power from diesel generators in the cargo. Reefers has the capability of controlling the temperature from -30, $-40\,°C$ upto 30, 40°C. Conventional reefers have peak power power from 10–15 kw while average energy consumption ranges from 3 to $4\,kWh$ [15, 16].

For every reefer and its cargo, there are minimum temperature θ_{min} e.g. $-24\,°C$ and θ_{max} e.g. $-19\,°C$. Let change in temperature is $\Delta\theta$ and given below;
$\Delta\theta = \theta_{max} - \theta_{min} = 5\,°C$.

θ_{min}, θ_{max}, $\Delta\theta$, all depend on the kind of cargo (fruit, vegetables, meat, fish etc.). Reefers work or not work (on - off model). So the consumption is 0 or P_{max}. Typical value of P_{max} is 10–15 KWatt. Let u is state and at $t = 0$, we are at state off (not working) $u = 0$, and temperature is θ_{min}. A basic model is given below;

$$\theta_{current} = \theta_{min} + \lambda_1 * \frac{t}{\Delta\theta} \tag{1}$$

where
λ_1 is a constant for every reefer, but not the same for all the reefers. It depends on the condition of the insulation of the reefer. Typical value for $\lambda_1 = 1°C/hour$. Suppose that at $t = 0$, we are at state on (working), $u = 1$ and temperature is θ_{max}. A basic model for this is given below;

$$\theta_{current} = \theta_{max} - \lambda_2 * \frac{t}{\Delta\theta} \tag{2}$$

where
λ_2 is a constant for every reefer, but not the same for all the reefers. It depends on the condition of the insulation of the reefer. Typical value for $\lambda_2 = 5° C/hour$.

Time flexibility varies with the cargo and the condition of reefers insulation and can vary in practice from 2 h to several hours (about 10 h).

3 Multi-agent System Modeling and Control Algorithm

This section presents agents definition and control algorithm. Two types of agents, ReeferAgent and ControlAgent, were defined and are explained next.

- **Reefer Agent:**
  ReeferAgent corresponds to a reefer in the network. These agents respond on a request for proposal from ControlAgent and communicate its state, available change in active power and duration (time flexibility). Pseudocode for the reefer agent is given in Algorithm 1.
- **Control Agent:**
  ControlAgent initiates a process for removing voltage violation and estimates the desired change in active power for voltage increase or decrease. Pseudocode for ControlAgent is given in Algorithm 2. A RFP message is sent by the Control Agent to reefer agents. All the reefer agents send their information to the controller which include: status, temperature distance and rated power. Control Agent makes a priority list on the basis of temperature distance. Reefers which are close to the switching boundary are given higher priority.

Algorithm 1. Algorithm for each $ReeferAgent \ Rf_j$ of the network

---

Result: Power P
if $(Mode = 1 \ \&\& \ CFP \leftarrow ControlAgent \ )$ **then**
    if $ServiceAvailable$ **then**
        Calculate $temperaturedistence = \theta$, status : u , rated power P ;
        SendProposal $(\theta, u, P) \rightarrow ControlAgent$;
        set $Mode = 2$, waiting for acceptance
    else
        refuse
    end
end
if $Mode = 2$ **then**
    wait for proposal acceptance/rejection;
    if $Acceptance \leftarrow ControlAgent$ **then**
        $Update \ u$;
        $MessageDone \rightarrow ControlAgent$;
        set $Mode = 1$
    else
        set $Mode = 1$
    end
end

Algorithm 2. Algorithm for *ControlAgent* of the network

Result: Status command : u

if $Mode = 1$ then

    $\Delta V_i \leftarrow M_i$, receive change in voltage from network ;

    set $Mode = 0$;

    Call-For-Proposal(*TempratureDistence* , *RatedPower* P $\rightarrow Rf_j$,

        $j = 1, 2, ...m$);

    Receive Proposals (*TempratureDistance, status, RatedPowerP*) $\leftarrow Rf_j$,

        $j = 1, 2, ...m$;

    if *(received all responses)*||*(deadline reached)* then

        $List \leftarrow$ Descend(*tempratuerdistence, RatedPowerP(Rf_j)*),

            $j = 1, 2, ...k$, k =number of proposals received *Accept_proposals* (ΔP_j)

        from Rf_h $h \in List$;

        $MessageDone \leftarrow Rf_h$;

        $SendMessage \rightarrow M_j$;

        set $Mode = 1$;

    end

end

---

4   Co-simulation Framework

Simulations are used for in depth analysis and evaluation of a designed system before its deployment. However, there does not exist any single tool which is capable of simulating systems from different domains. Co-simulation is an effective way to overcome this problem which allows to model each system in a powerful domain specific tool and co-simulate all the tools through proper interfacing [17]. A co-simulation tool developed in [18] was used for simulation and description of the tool is given next.

– **Power System Tool:** Power system was modeled in DigSILENT PowerFactory. It is a powerful tool, capable for modeling and simulation of large and complex power networks with in depth analysis features. It also allows various

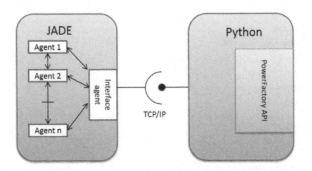

Fig. 1. Co-simulation architecture

option for interfacing with the external tools, some of them are Python API, COM object, DSL etc. and detail is given in [19,20].

- **MAS Tool:** JADE (JAVA Agent DEvelopment framework) was used for Multi-Agent system Modeling. JADE provides distributed environment for agent development and simulation which comply with the FIPA (Foundation of Intelligent Physical Agent) standards [21].
- **Interface Methodology:** Python API for DigSILENT PowerFactory was used for interfacing power factory with JADE. Sockets based communication and data exchange interface between the two tools were developed. In JADE InterfaceAgent was implemented for data exchange with the python through sockets. Figure 1 shows the schematic diagram of co-simulation architecture.

5   Simulation Results and Discussion

A low voltage test network comprising 18 buses for power system was used which includes variable, intermittent generation sources (wind, pv), flexible loads

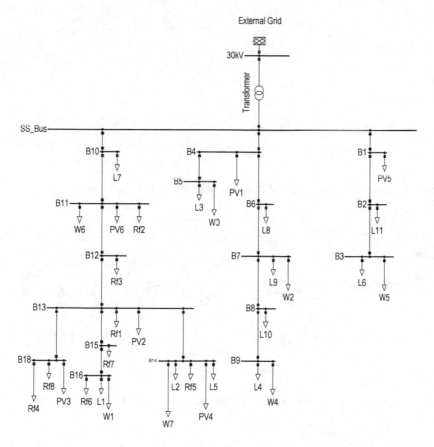

Fig. 2. Test network (W = Wind Generation, PV = PV Generation, Rf = Reefers, L = Loads)

(reefers), non-flexible loads. Figure 2 shows diagram of the test network. One minute load and generation profile for wind and pv were used for simulation. Figure 3 shows the temperature variation and temperature distance from switching boundary. A base case considering only local control of reefers was simulated and compared with the MAS based centralized control. Lower voltage limit was set to 0.95 p.u. After voltage violation at bus 16, control agent, send RFP to all the reefer agents. Reefer agents sends Rated Power, P, temperature distance, and status. Control agent makes a list with respect to temperature distance and sends the on signal to reefer agents which have less distance to the switching boundary. It is assumed that control agent has information of active power injection sensitivities to the bus voltage. Advantage of using temperature distance is that there will be less switching and reefer will be available for longer duration. Figure 4 shows comparison of voltage profile at bus 16 in base case (only local control) and MAS based control. It can be observed that voltage of bus 16 is within allowable limits in MAS based control case.

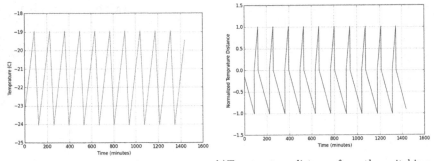

a) Temperature variation of a typical reefer

b) Temperature distance from the switching boundary

Fig. 3. Temperature variation and distance from the switching boundary for a typical reefer

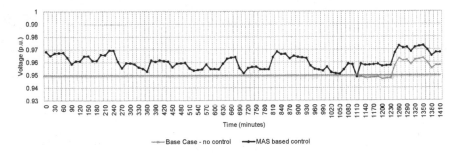

Fig. 4. Voltage profile at bus 16 with base case and MAS based control

6   Conclusion

This paper shows MAS could be an effective solution for demand response application in ports. FIPA-contract-net-protocol was used to devise a plan for agent interaction. A case of voltage regulation for a specific bus (monitoring node) was considered under heavy load conditions and reefers were considered as flexible loads. A co-simulation framework was used to test the proposed approach. Elementary simulation results are encouraging, and show that MAS approach is quite effective for distributed energy management at port cities. Further, energy management tasks such active power management systems can be implemented to lead to greener, sustainable ports. Future work would be to use real data of a port city (electrical network, generation, load, reefers etc.) for evaluation of the proposed approach.

References

1. Doudounakis, M., Kanellos, F.D.: Active power management in green ports. In: European Conference on Shipping, Intermodalism and Ports (ECONSHIP) (2015)
2. Pavlic, B., Cepak, F., Sucic, B., Peckaj, M., Kandus, B.: Sustainable port infrastructure, practical implementation of the green port concept. Therm. Sci. **18**(3), 935–948 (2014)
3. e-harbours project. Municipality of Zaanstad (2016). https://eharbours.eu/
4. Efforts, G.: Green and effective operations at terminals and in ports (2012)
5. Daamen, T.A., Louw, E.: The challenge of the Dutch Port-City interface. Tijdschrift voor economische en sociale geografie **107**(5), 642–651 (2016)
6. Parise, G., Parise, L., Martirano, L., Chavdarian, P.B., Su, C.-L., Ferrante, A.: Wise port and business energy management: port facilities, electrical power distribution. IEEE Trans. Ind. Appl. **52**(1), 18–24 (2016)
7. Acciaro, M., Ghiara, H., Cusano, M.I.: Energy management in seaports: a new role for port authorities. Energy Policy **71**, 4–12 (2014)
8. Tao, L., Guo, D.H., Moser, J., Mueller, D.H.: A roadmap towards smart grid enabled harbour terminals. In: CIRED Workshop - Rome (2014)
9. Hashim, T.T., Mohamed, A., Shareef, H.: A review on voltage control methods for active distribution networks. Prz. Elektrotech **88**, 304–312 (2012)
10. Antoniadou-Plytaria, K.E., Kouveliotis-Lysikatos, I.N., Georgilakis, P.S., Hatziargyriou, N.D.: Distributed and decentralized voltage control of smart distribution networks: models, methods, and future research. IEEE Trans. Smart Grid **PP**(99), 1 (2017)
11. Malik, O., Havel, P.: Active demand-side management system to facilitate integration of res in low-voltage distribution networks. IEEE Trans. Sustain. Energy **5**(2), 673–681 (2014)
12. Christakou, K.: A unified control strategy for active distribution networks via demand response and distributed energy storage systems. Sustain. Energy Grids Netw. **6**, 1–6 (2016). http://www.sciencedirect.com/science/article/pii/S23524677 16000023
13. Bogodorova, T., Vanfretti, L., Turitsyn, K.: Voltage control-based ancillary service using thermostatically controlled loads. In: Power and Energy Society General Meeting (PESGM), pp. 1–5. IEEE (2016)

14. Latif, A., Gawlik, W., Palensky, P.: Quantification and mitigation of unfairness in active power curtailment of rooftop photovoltaic systems using sensitivity based coordinated control. Energies **9**(6), 436 (2016)
15. Verbeeck, J., Kuijper, F.: Application of smart energy networks-part i, summary results of the individual company demand response audits in the port of antwerp, wp. 3.5 report for e-harbours project (2013)
16. Application of Smart Energy Networks Potential flexibility of reefers WP 3.5 Report for E-Harbours Project. e-harbours project (2017). http://eharbours.eu/ wp-content/uploads/WP-3.5-Application-of-Smart-Energy-Networks-Potential-fl exibility-of-reefers.pdf
17. Palensky, P., Widl, E., Elsheikh, A.: Simulating cyber-physical energy systems: challenges, tools and methods. IEEE Trans. Syst. Man Cybern.: Syst. **44**(3), 318– 326 (2014)
18. Ahmad, I., Kazmi, J.H., Shahzad, M., Palensky, P., Gawlik, W.: Co-simulation framework based on power system, AI and communication tools for evaluating smart grid applications. In: 2015 IEEE Innovative Smart Grid Technologies - Asia (ISGT ASIA), pp. 1–6, November 2015
19. Stifter, M., Schwalbe, R., Andrén, F., Strasser, T.: Steady-state co-simulation with powerfactory. In: 2013 Workshop on Modeling and Simulation of Cyber-Physical Energy Systems (MSCPES), pp. 1–6. IEEE (2013)
20. Gonzalez-Longatt, F., Rueda, J.L.: PowerFactory Applications for Power System Analysis. Springer, Heidelberg (2014)
21. FIPA Agent Management Specification. Foundation for Intelligent Physical Agents (FIPA) (2016). http://www.fipa.org/specs/fipa00023/SC00023K.pdf

MASLE

A Model to Aggregate Heterogeneous Learning Objects Repositories

Luiz Henrique Longhi Rossi[(⊠)], Marcos Freitas Nunes,
Paulo Schreiner, and Rosa Maria Vicari

Informatics Institute in Universidade Federal do Rio Grande do Sul,
Porto Alegre, RS 91501-970, Brazil
{lh.rossi,marcos,paulo}@cognitivabrasil.com.br,
rosa@inf.ufrgs.br

Abstract. Technology has increasingly permeated the educational context making the use of learning objects (LOs) very popular. LOs need to be stored and cataloged so they can be located and retrieved in an efficient manner by both students and teachers. Furthermore, the objects collected in different repositories must be examined individually in order to select which ones best match the user's needs. The main goal of this work is to propose a model that, prepared to the Web 3.0, enables LO to be used, reused or adapted from heterogeneous environments. To reach this goal the creation of a LO federation is proposed in order to organize various repositories in a hierarchical system. We describe how these objects can be harvested, indexed and retrieved by users from different standard repositories and how to present them to users in different devices. The system was able to index more than 100 thousand Los.

Keywords: Learning objects · Educational repositories · Educational metadata standards · Multi-agent systems · Federated systems

1 Introduction

The evolution of digital educational systems is notorious and global. There have been neither so many free courses available on the Internet so many students enrolled in undergraduate distance courses. These facts have put educational technologies under the limelight, and making them advance for better use of digital resources for teaching, both in matters of teaching strategies and technologically. The use of Information and Communication Technology is increasingly valued and needed.

LO technology is based on the assumption that it is possible to create components of teaching materials, organize and allow their reuse, saving time and production costs for the purpose of use in distance learning, or even including its use as part of an educational plan in regular classes. According to the IEEE[1], a LO is any content, digital or not (simulation image, movie, etc.) that can be used with an educational purpose and that its context, internally or by association, includes suggestions that can be used.

---

[1] http://ltsc.ieee.org/wg12/files/LOM_1484_12_1_v1_Final_Draft.pdf.

© Springer International Publishing AG 2017
J. Bajo et al. (Eds.): PAAMS 2017 Workshops, CCIS 722, pp. 373–385, 2017.
DOI: 10.1007/978-3-319-60285-1_32

This definition is also adopted in this study, but it is restricted to the case of digital objects. Other concepts underlying this work are presented in the next session.

Differently from other federations like NSDL in the USA, or ARCA in Spain or even the Global, in Brazil we have a greater number of repositories distributed around the country. One institution does not organize those repositories so that the institutions (universities, federal public library, educational foundations, etc.) are free to choose everything about them: there are many different applications, metadata formats, and everything else. So, it is not a simple operation to aggregate them as there is a big challenge about interoperability here, and the approach was centered in scheduled harvesting, translating to a big metadata standard and indexed.

Repositories, generally, are software entities capable of storing and sharing content, more specifically, the LOs repositories that have been developed with a particular purpose. So, to cite the contents here are some of the most important features of the LOs: interoperability, granularity and ease location, but, mainly, allow for an increase of reuse of the material. There are still many challenges, mainly related to ease of location of objects [1] and how can other educators or students adapt the content, or include it in another LO with good granularity, consequently, increasing its reuse [2].

Architecture of the repository, manage both contents and metadata besides providing a basic set of services: store, locate, search and control access to this content [3]. This was one of the subjects most widely investigated for some time in educational technologies. Therefore, work focused on storage and retrieval LOs may be mentioned [4, 5]. More recently, subject has lost its strength against the new advances in other research areas of educational technology, but it has not lost its importance. It can be notice as more recent studies seek new capabilities in repositories through social mining [6] but it has gained strength in relation to pen repositories and their objects, defined as open educational resources [5, 6, 8] and more fundamental issues, such as defense and assessing the quality of LOs and their pedagogical application [9, 10]. Darcy Norman, the creator of the CAREO project, one of the first digital repositories, has already contested the need for institutional repositories in his personal website some time ago in interviews. They are saying that these have now been replaced by other resources, such as YouTube, Flickr, blogs, etc. and that it is no longer necessary a "monolithic institutional repository". What Norman should not have seen in 2007 is that, with the increasing representation of contexts, it is now possible that institutional repositories are no longer monolithic, but continue and evolve comprising the growth of the Internet and sharing their content, making it, therefore a catalyst of diverse content production.

There are also other benefits for the existence of an institution behind a learning material. It is clear that the support of a major university conveys credibility, and it can have influence on the content, with some kind of trusteeship. It has been a time that the death of repositories was decreed, but it is noticeable that what has modified is not the concept of repository, but the adjective given to it: "monolithic". It is among the contributions of this work to increase the flexibility of repositories, as the pattern adopted with the metadata increases its content representation capabilities.

Interoperability is the ability of systems to provide and accept services from others [11]. Nevertheless creating interoperable systems has been a constant and growing challenge for computing and interoperability problems formerly started from the standards of network cabling to the application of systems between different softwares. Even with the creation of widely adopted standards, the emergence of new devices has remained the challenge of generating materials that operate in several of these devices, from TVs to mobile phones [12]. It is important that these materials can run independently of technology platform and that repositories and learning environments are able to lead the student to the most appropriate resources, not only to their study profile, but as sensitive hardware and systems used by it. This feature helps streamline the content and functionality for universality in search, retrieval and access on a global scale. More positive approaches like [13] have never got highly adopted. So, the interoperability in repositories is still a challenge.

2   Methodology

The Internet, since its establishment, has largely increased its number of users, but it probably would not be the same if it were not for the search engines. Through their use, it was possible to identify the most relevant content in every situation, but conversely, educational repositories are still large islands with no communication. The greatest benefit that this work expects to bring is to design a model of integration among educational repositories. Our solution is the implementation of this idea through a centralized portal of information, which contains a search tool. However, in Brazil, the repositories do not follow a pattern or a single implementation in their solutions, so it is necessary to create a system covering all its peculiarities, losing as little as possible information on LOs. To do so, we have created a specific metadata standard for LOs, named OBAA (Agent-based learning objects) [14], which also adds other peculiarities, which will be referred in further sections. OBAA supports also legacy LOs. So, there is a mechanism for translation of existing metadata standards to OBAA. The following sections present: the standard OBAA and how the most common standards in educational repositories can be mapped to OBAA; the project architecture is described and its working system.

2.1   OBAA Standard

The major objective of creating a metadata standard in this work was to establish a specification, which covers technical and functional requirements, as well as the important metadata among many other standards are contemplated in the context of LOs. Another difference is that the OBAA LOs include information, allowing them to be distributed and consumed directly in the Web, mobile devices, and digital TV [14].

The OBAA standard is a LOM extension, i.e. the complete set of OBAA metadata is formed by all categories of LOM, with some more metadata, but complementing the technical and educational categories plus two new ones related to aspects of accessibility and segmentation. The increasing use of the Web platform in the educational environment and the prospect that it extends to the Digital TV and mobile devices has led to a study of the specifications involved in these three platforms (WEB, Digital TV, and mobile devices). The extension also involves the proposal of a new standard for describing LO interoperable.

The metadata specifications internationally recognized for describing educational content IEEE LOM[2] and IMS[3], plus specifications for cataloging multimedia files and TV-Digital, MPEG-7 and SBTVD were taken into account in developing the OBAA standard.

Considering the wide acceptance of the IEEE LOM specification already obtained, and the adequacy of its set of metadata, it was decided to extend it by creating new categories and new elements into existing categories. These elements aim to meet Brazilian needs in terms of technology, education, accessibility and segmentation. Metadata categories OBAA specifications, which differ from the IEEE LOM standard, modified or created, are described in the following sections.

2.1.1   Technical Category

The basis of the category Technical LOM IEEE 1484 standard was maintained, extending mainly to support interoperability platforms. The technical information and requirements for the use of LOs have been defined in this category, with specific media information for each platform (Digital TV, Mobile and Web). Elements were also created to define which services, ontology, content languages and interaction protocols are associated with the object, order to address interoperability issues in Semantic Web [15]. Figure 1 presents OBAA Technical metadata.

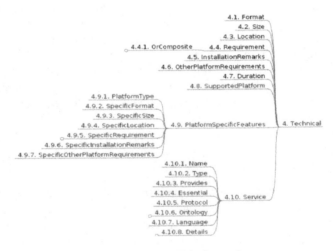

Fig. 1.   OBAA technical metadata

---

[2] https://standards.ieee.org/findstds/standard/1484.12.1-2002.html.

[3] https://www.imsglobal.org/activity/accessibility.

The new elements defined in OBAA for Technical category were:

- *SupportedPlatforms* (4.8): specifies the three basic types of digital platforms for delivery of learning objects: Web, DTV and Mobile;
- *PlatformSpecificFeatures* (4.9): defines the technical information about the media applied to each one of the platforms for which the learning object was developed. If a platform is informed in the item SupportedPlatforms but there is no respective PlatformSpecificFeatures group for it, then the general technical data of the IEEE LOM is also apply to the platform. For each platform represented by this category there should also be specific information about its media;
- *Service* (4.10): They are the set of metadata association responsible for the respective service, and can be expanded for the use of any service provider available. The specification of metadata models proposed access to the service, showing no restrictions on how it can be implemented, giving flexibility so that the necessary services are used, regardless of the technology. The definition of service may be mandatory or optional for the correct execution of the object.

This set of metadata (presented above) that allows any object developed for Semantic Web using artificial agents is able to incorporate all its potential and the metadata representation level fully explore the ability of an agent, for example, in a FIPA platform. Everything that an artificial agent that following the FIPA standard can enter the environment and platform services is included in this set of metadata.

The elements SupportedPlatforms, PlatformSpecificFeatures and Service follow the same definitions and rules of the category 4 of the LO metadata standard. They are applied to each used platform.

2.1.2 Educational Category

The Educational category has also received an extension; hence increasing the amount of items it contains based on the interactionist model, with the premise that the subject knows the world through interaction with objects of knowledge. The following aspects were taken into consideration to achieve this model: organizational, content, methodological and technological. The pedagogical model is composed by a pedagogical architecture and a pedagogical and epistemological conception of the teacher Fig. 2 - Educational Metadata shows educational elements.

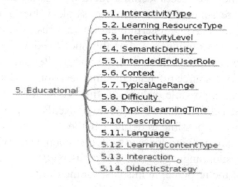

Fig. 2. Educational metadata

The element *LearningContentType* was created to represent this pedagogical model, specifying the content type of the learning object. This content can be classified as factual, concept related, procedural and attitudinal [16]. The interaction between the learning object and the user concerns the behavior of people in relation to other people and systems. It is assumed that a meaningful learning experience can be provided only if the educational solution has been designed as interactive. It is necessary to provide an interface that enables interaction offering learning activities that require student interaction with content, tools and other people. Therefore, the metadata interaction was proposed to define it. So it consists of the sensory mechanism used to transmit information; following the interaction between user and object, mechanisms to inform the co-presence of other users in the environment and the type of relationship between users are necessary to the functioning of the learning object. Reciprocity is a way of relating to others in which all have the same opportunities for participating and interacting in the group. It is hoped that this operation can assist students in cooperative and collaborative learning, where, through exchanges, it is possible to learn and teach. A teaching strategy is defined as a set of actions planned and conducted by the teacher to promote the involvement and commitment of students with a broader set of activities. By specifying the pattern, it is possible to indicate the most appropriate teaching strategy to be adopted in using the learning object, as conceived by the author.

2.1.3   Accessibility Category

The basic elements of this category come from the IMS AccessForAll. The intention here is to store information about student accessibility, defining the settings for users accessing the learning object, allowing its execution in order to meet requirements such as audio for the blind, hearing-impaired subtitle, language and other important specifications seeking inclusion and access to the LO by people with special needs. The requirements for the use of the resources in this metadata category are described by means of specifying if the display and control can be modified at runtime and if there is an equivalent alternative.

Besides that, language references for assessment and reporting, as defined by W3C [17], were included. They are applied to express and compare tests and results, transformability, control, and flexibility of the resources. The ability to point to a resource equivalent to the feature described, or parts of it, was captured. In the same item, it is possible to indicate access learning facilities that are or will be contained in the LO, as one or more support tools. Some possible values for this metadata are: dictionary, calculator, notetaking, peerInteraction, abacus, thesaurus, spellChecker, mindMappingSoftware and outlineTool. For the specification of an alternative visualization, it can be indicated if it will be through audio, alternate text – in the specified language for the primary resource referenced – and description of how colors should be used. Some examples of possible values of this vocabulary are: avoidRed, avoidRedGreen, avoidBlueYellow, avoidOrange, avoidRedBlack, useMaximumContrast and monochrome. It is also possible to define whether the described resource contains graphic and/or visual alternatives for parts of the main text, with an indication of content translated into sign language, or in one of its particular dialects, being faithful to the main contents of the resource. In this case, some examples of possible values are

ASL AmericanBritish-BSL, Brazilian-BRA, Native-GUA Guarani, Spanish-SPA, French-LSF and Japanese-JSL.

2.1.4   Segmentation

Sometimes it is necessary to logical segment an object, allowing its organization in modules or by subject matter. A segment is a continuous fragment of an object. A particular segment may belong to a single program but it can be a member of several groups of segments, characterizing, in this case, a collection of segments that are associated with a particular purpose or due to a common property (see Fig. 3).

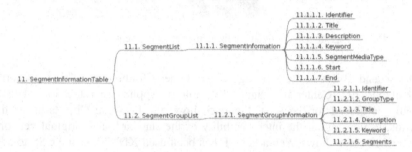

Fig. 3. OBAA segmentation metadata

In order to meet the needs of segmentation, we added an adapted version of TV-Anytime – an European DTV standard to it. Therefore, a new category called SegmentInformation Table was created to support segmentation of learning object and also groups of segments. This category contains identifiers, title, description, keywords, segment type (text document, hypermedia, multimedia file or other) and indicates the beginning and end of the segment in the LO. Internally, each segment is defined by metadata and rules as specified in the standard.

2.2   A Case Study on Interoperable Learning Object

Some objects were adapted as a proof of concept about the interoperability on the OBAA metadata standard. The first learning object adapted is a video that explains the origin of TV, including a little of its history. It explains how the operation of broadcast TV is nowadays, and also provides a broad context of the functioning of this important media to the student. In the original format, this video is in WMV format and 320×240 pixels, in the repository SACCA (Automated System for Cataloging of Audiovisual Content).

SACCA (Automated System for Cataloging of Audiovisual Content) - seeking interoperability, the video was converted to the format H.264/AAC LC and encapsulated in a file ".Mp4". This format allows video play in Ginga-NCL Virtual Set Top Box (for Digital-TV) and on the Web. The video was also converted to the encoding H.263/AAC LC, using file format ".3gp" for execution on mobile devices. Therefore, we have a video in two different formats, allowing the contents to be visualized in the tree environments studied (Web, Digital-TV and mobile). Figure 4 shows the video on the three platforms, even on really small screen cellphone.

Fig. 4. Objeto de aprendizagem "De Onde vem a TV?".

The second object is the learning object "Other Childhoods." This is a learning object of NUTED (Center for Digital Technology Applied to Education), UFRGS, originally developed for the Web. Figure 5 shows the Learning Objects in the three platforms, demonstrating the interoperability of the standard. The original version of this learning object allows Web access. It has been used XDHTML and CSS to adjust the images to view, following the OBAA recommendations for text content.

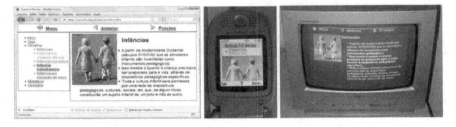

Fig. 5. Objeto de aprendizagem "Outras Infâncias".

2.3 Metadata Translation

Before the growth of the Internet, educational digital content was not designed for their promotion outside the home institution. In that context, compatibility between access devices for both internal and external users to the environment was not necessary. In the 90s this view began to change and began to emerge metadata standards [18], today there are several of them and it has also created the mismatch between educational environments.

The diversity of metadata is a real problem when it comes to education. For this reason, current approaches based on crosswalks as [19] is very useful, however. In this context, the focus of this work is to advance the state of the art seeking to eliminate part of the limitations presented in the current approaches based on crosswalks. The objective of our work is making an important step towards interoperability across heterogeneous environments metadata standards. Until now to translate from one standard to another with the approaches based on crosswalk files one of the patterns must be non-hierarchical. It is based on planar rules, for example, the field "creator" in the CD can be easily mapped to fields "contributor.entity" added the field "contributor. role" = "author" (Table 1).

Table 1. The first cell in DC standard, the second standard in LOM

```
<dc:creator>Ortelius, Abraham</dc:creator>
<lom:contributor>
<lom:entity>Ortelius, Abraham</lom:entity>
<lom:role>author</lom:role>
</lom:contributor>
```

However, it was not possible to migrate with hierarchical standards like LOM and OBAA, making it impossible to use the approach set out in this article.

The extensible Stylesheet Language for Transformation (XSLT) is a global language migration of any XML for any other XML [20] with this ability could design tools with all the diversity that belongs to it, thus be able to add repositories that is in any metadata standard. This way, ISO, W3C, IEEE and other standards can interoperate besides bringing another benefit that is any inconsistencies found in the repository do not need to be replicated on the servers that collects a specific mapping.

Once understood the LOs metadata, a XSLT can be created to each repository in the federated system.

2.4 Service Structure

The tree-based structure shown in Fig. 6 depicts the overall structure envisioned in the project, which consists of several repository federations united by a central node in the top of the hierarchy. This root node is called the confederation. Each one of these federations represents a specific geographical or an institutional region that contains the belonging digital repositories.

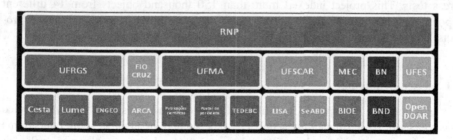

Fig. 6. Tree based infrastructure

Currently there are seven institutions supporting this project, mostly universities. The federated architecture is of great interest for the institutions, as it allows them to provide a single point-of-access for their repositories, in their own web site and with corresponding branding.

2.5   Data Harvesting

The majority of educational repositories today implement an HTTP web service providing its LOs metadata to be collected and this web service is standardized by the Open Archive Initiative (OAI) being called Protocol for Metadata Harvesting[4] (OAI-PMH). As a bot has been daily scheduled, it will harvest all the modifications (creations end exclusions) in every federated repository, then process it translation for further indexing.

3   Results

In order to search for a LO, most users would use a generic search engine such as Google. Despite being very powerful, generic search engines are not the most suitable tools for the task as they index as much data as possible. Therefore, the search results are not restricted to the educational context and might even return inappropriate results. As a matter of fact, in the federated system, each federation is responsible for keeping a minimum level of quality to the LOs and the fact that both, the author and institution of a specific LO, are known lends it a higher credibility.

There are other projects similar to our proposal, though. These projects also aim at aggregating quality to the harvested material. So we can cite the ones below, among others: The ARCA project [21] structures its federation in a different way. Repositories use a custom XML format and the updates use RSS. Another similar project is NSDL [22] that has more in common with the project we are describing here, e.g., they also use OAI-PMH to propagate updates to the federation. An important distinction though, is that NSDL requires that all federations are repositories to implement their specific schema, while we provide online translation capability.

Our system was evaluated in two different aspects, namely user evaluation and service quality. With user evaluation, we are interested in seeing what the users think of the system. In order to do that, we had users in our partner institutions to answer a questionnaire. Service quality was evaluated through a series of response time and stress tests. This project indexed more than 150 thousand objects from 14 different repositories. The use of this system received some visibility from governmental projects like the Brazilian version of one-laptop-per-child and its tablet version.

3.1   User Evaluation

The questionnaire was applied in 3 different locations and dates. The first was applied in a course for basic education teachers (25); the second, in a course about educational laptops, being answered for about 50 teachers and the final questionnaire was applied to post-grad students.

The questions were designed to quantify and describe the characteristics of the portal allowing us to gauge its quality. According to [23], an indicator is an instrument

---

[4] http://www.openarchives.org/OAI/openarchivesprotocol.html.

that puts an unobservable behavior in evidence. The questionnaire is divided in two parts, use and metadata. The experiment was organized as follows:

- A general explanation about LOs and their characteristics is given;
- The users retrieve LOs using each particular repository;
- The users retrieve LOs.

The users select one LO according to their interest and analyze it with the objective of later answering the questionnaire.

About 80% of the interviewed classified the easy-of-use between easy and very easy, and many of the respondents do not have much use of a computer. (The question was: How would you rate the LO search functionality of the system?)

Another question that merits discussion is about the retrieval of a single LO, where the user evaluates not only the interface of the system but the general usability of the system, which also depends heavily on the individual federations and repositories (i.e. good metadata helps a lot). Also, by following the system link, the user is redirected to the repository that contains that object, and not directly to the object itself. Only one user replied 'no' for the question: You find any interesting object?

Other complementary questions were posed, all with the intent of gathering feed-back about the project's interface.

3.2   Partners Evaluation

The questions in this section were posed to our partner institutions. It is crucial to point out that only 4 out of 5 partner institutions to which the questions were applied answered them. The answer for the question: **How hard is to enter the federation?** Was 'easy' among the possibilities very easy, easy, hard, and very hard. Demonstrates how easy it can be to enter in the federation, therefore the work needed is to make the metadata mapping.

The security question (**Have you any security concern?**) came up before an adaptation in the codebase that allows a database to be used in a different machine. The only 'no' answered had that concern.

Data collection in the repositories can be completely automated and collects only metadata. Together with the fact that the updates are done during low traffic hours, it means that the performance impact on the individual repositories is from minimal to non-existent.

3.3   System Evaluation

For the system evaluation, we used the Jmeter1 tool. Each test was run 50 times; data shown refers to the average.

The performance test was carried out on a local network (Ethernet 100 Mbit) in order to avoid external latency influencing the results. Response time for one request is 150 ms. With more simultaneous requests, average response time behaves approxi-mately according to (1) in formula where 'x' is the number of simultaneous requests.

$$\begin{cases} (10,49x + 142,68)\,\text{ms} & 1 \le x \le 8 \\ (27,82x + 32,43)\,\text{ms} & 9 \le x \le 92 \end{cases} \tag{1}$$

The difference between the approximation using the function above and actual response times obtained. Medium absolute error is 10 ms.

The Fig. 7 shows the difference between the approximation using the function above and actual response times obtained. Medium absolute error is 10 ms.

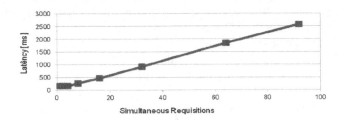

Fig. 7. Graph of error incidence in relation to the parallel requirements. The tests were run on an Intel Xeon E5405 @ 2 GHz QuadCore server, with 4 GB de RAM, a NC105i PCI e Gigabit Server network adapter in a 100 Mb/s Ethernet LAN.

To determine the maximum load the system can handle, we evaluated how many requests the server can answer in parallel (requests sent at the same time), using Jmeter. The test was on the same machine as the System Evaluation tests, and it was also run 50 times. Errors (e.g. Timeout, server did not respond) started to appear at 92 simultaneous requests.

References

1. Nash, S.: Learning objects, learning object repositories, and learning theory: preliminary best practices for online courses. Interdisc. J. E-Learn. Learn. Objects **1**(1), 217–228 (2005)
2. Neven, F., Duval, E.: Reusable learning objects: a survey of LOM-based repositories. In: Proceedings of the Tenth ACM International Conference on Multimedia. ACM (2002)
3. Heery, R., Anderson, S.: Digital Repositories Review (2005)
4. Matkin, G.: Learning Object Repositories: Problems and Promise. The William and Flora Hewlett Foundation, Menlo Park (2002)
5. Dicheva, D., Dichev, C.: Finding open educational resources in computing. In: 2014 IEEE 14th International Conference on ICALT, pp. 22–24. IEEE (2014)
6. Shih, W.-C.: A framework of educational app repositories with recommendation powered by social tag mining. In: 2014 International Conference on Information Science and Applications (ICISA), pp. 1–3. IEEE (2014)
7. Van Acker, F., et al.: The role of knowledge sharing self-efficacy in sharing open educational resources. Comput. Hum. Behav. **39**, 136–144 (2014)
8. Nicholson, D.: LibGuides: Open Educational Resources for Humanities & Social Sciences: Inst'l Repositories/Digital Libraries (2014)

9. Atenas, J., Havemann, L.: Questions of quality in repositories of open educational resources: a literature review. Res. Learn. Technol. **22**, 1–13 (2014)
10. Clements, K., et al.: Why open educational resources repositories fail-review of quality assurance approaches. In: Proceedings of 6th International Conference on Education and New Learning Technologies Barcelona, EDULEARN 2014, Spain, pp. 929–939. IATED (2014). ISBN 978-84-617-0557-3
11. Rezaei, R., Chiew, T.-K., Lee, S.-P.: A review of interoperability assessment models. J. Zhejiang Univ. Sci. C **14**(9), 663–681 (2013)
12. Ashton, K.: That 'internet of things' thing. RFiD J. **22**(7), 97–114 (2009)
13. Warner, S., et al.: Pathways: augmenting interoperability across scholarly repositories. Int. J. Digit. Libr. **7**(1–2), 35–52 (2007)
14. Vicari, R.M., Ribeiro, A., Silva, J.M.C., Santos, E.R., Primo, T., Bez, M.: Brazilian proposal for agent-based learning objects metadata standard - OBAA. In: Sánchez-Alonso, S., Athanasiadis, I.N. (eds.) MTSR 2010. CCIS, vol. 108, pp. 300–311. Springer, Heidelberg (2010). doi:10.1007/978-3-642-16552-8_27
15. Berners-Lee, T., Hendler, J., Lassila, O.: The semantic web. Scientific American 284.5, 28–37 (2001)
16. Wiley, D.: Connecting learning objects to instructional design theory: a definition, a metaphor, and taxonomy (2001). www.reusability.org/read/chapters/wiley.doc
17. W3C: Mobile Web Best Practices 1.0, Basic Guidelines. W3C Recommendation (2008). http://www.w3.org/TR/mobile-bp/. Accessed Feb 2016
18. McClelland, M.: Metadata standards for educational resources. Computer **36**(11), 107–109 (2003)
19. Chan, L.M., Zeng, M.L.: Metadata interoperability and standardization-a study of methodology, part i. D-Lib Mag. **12**(6), 1082–9873 (2006)
20. W3C Standards: XSL Transformations (XSLT). http://www.w3.org/TR/1999/REC-xslt-19991116. Accessed 12 June 2013
21. Moreno, I., Argudo, F.C.: Proyecto Arca, Federación de metadatos sobre contenidos multimedia y retransmisiones programadas. http://arca.rediris.es/
22. Lagoze, C., et al.: Core services in the architecture of the national digital library for science education (NSDL). In: JCDL (2002)
23. Bisquerra, R.J.C., Sarriera, F.: Martínez, "Introdução à estatística: enfoque informático coo pacote estatístico" SPSS. Artmed, Porto Alegre (2004)

Survey of Software Visualization Systems to Teach Message-Passing Concurrency in Secondary School

Cédric Libert[✉] and Wim Vanhoof

University of Namur, Namur, Belgium
cedric.libert@unamur.be

Abstract. In this paper, we compare 27 software visualization systems according to 8 criteria that are important to create an introduction to programming course based upon message passing concurrency.

Keywords: Message passing · Concurrency · Teaching

1 Introduction

In Europe, more and more countries want to teach programming to primary and secondary school students. A 2014 report confirms that 15 European countries either already do or were about to do so [8]. The first programming course is an important issue in the IT curriculum. It is the core of many other IT courses, and it improves essential skills such as problem solving, abstraction and decomposition [3, p. 41].

This preliminary study aims at finding software visualization systems (SVS) to use in an introductory programming course with 16- to 18-year-old students. This course will have new content, concurrent programming, and a corresponding teaching method, the microworld approach. This method consists in integrating a mini programming language into an SVS where agents show the execution of the code and where the teacher can add new programming concepts progressively. To implement this course, we need to find an SVS that fits with concurrency. The experimentation in situ costs a lot of time, so this preliminary work is a first step. Here we intend to justify, in light of the literature, the criteria used to evaluate SVSs.

In Sect. 2, we justify the benefits of a course based on concurrency and an SVS. We present a particularly suitable concurrency model to teach, namely message passing, and show how it helps to improve programming skills and computational thinking. We then define the concept of an SVS and describe the advantages of such systems for teaching. In particular, we talk about one particular kind of system: microworlds. In Sect. 3 we define some criteria for comparing SVSs with each other, build a comparison table of 27 SVSs and use it to categorize and compare existing systems. In the last section we select two good candidates for our course, and we explain why they are close to what we need and how we will manage to make them fulfil our requirements.

© Springer International Publishing AG 2017
J. Bajo et al. (Eds.): PAAMS 2017 Workshops, CCIS 722, pp. 386–397, 2017.
DOI: 10.1007/978-3-319-60285-1_33

2 Why a Concurrency Course with a SVS?

The purpose of our research is to evaluate the efficiency, in terms of the improvement of programming skills and computational thinking, of a first programming course based on message passing. We want this course to use the microworld pedagogical approach [41], based on an SVS. In this section, we justify these choices.

2.1 Advantages of the Message Passing Concurrency Model

Teaching concurrency in an introductory course is usually seen as harder than teaching sequential programming [10,12,48]. But the students live in a concurrent world, so some authors conjecture that this technique may be more intuitive to them [10,12,48], at least with an appropriate teaching method. Furthermore, for some tasks, concurrency allows an easier decomposition into subproblems [48].

The 2013 ACM Computer Science Curricula report [3, p. 44] is in favour of teaching concurrency starting in the first programming course because evolution in three main IT fields (hardware, software and data) requires concurrency. At the hardware level, multicore processors make it possible to physically execute some instructions in parallel and make the most of concurrent programming. In software, reactive user interfaces need concurrency to allow many events to happen and to be dealt with at the same time. Concerning data, thay are so abundant that they need distributed storage and concurrent processing on different computers. Therefore, according to the ACM, teaching needs to support these evolutions, especially with concurrency early in the curriculum.

Message Passing, a Simple Concurrent Paradigm. We present and compare two main concurrency models: message passing and shared-state concurrency. We focus on the former, because the latter, mostly used in imperative and object-oriented languages, has some drawbacks we hope to avoid. Indeed, shared-state concurrency is based on the concepts of threads, interacting by modifying shared variables and protected by some mutual exclusion mechanism to avoid race conditions and data corruption. This way to deal with concurrency is very low-level, which doesn't appear to be efficient in the learning process. This concurrency model seems harder to understand by students [39] than message passing and is considered to be a pessimistic concurrency control, which requires a lot of effort to organize.

Message passing concurrency is a paradigm encompassing the three concepts of higher order functions, threads and ports (unidirectional communicating channels). A program consists in a set of concurrent agents, each one in its own thread. They communicate through the ports with messages containing arbitrarily complex data. They react to messages according to their behaviour, which is a function. Programming in this paradigm consists mostly in defining concurrent agent behaviours and the messages that they send and receive asynchronously.

One of the first languages to exploit this paradigm was Erlang [7]. This language, used in some highly distributed applications such as WhatsApp [14] and some parts of GitHub [31], showed the advantages of message passing concurrency over the shared state concurrency model. The encapsulation of code into isolated but communicating agents avoids programming problems due to shared variables, because each agent is the only one that can modify his own state and, since they are higher level entities, the students do not need to understand how the machine works in order to be able to use them.

Message Passing to Improve Programming Skills. The first programming paradigm taught has a large impact on the mental representation of the learner, and thus on how he will be able to learn programming techniques. Some authors show, for instance, the differences between procedural and object-oriented approaches in tackling a first course. Furthermore, according to White and Sivitanides [52], there may even be interferences between two paradigms. For instance, learning object-oriented after procedural programming seems harder for students than the other way round.

The idea of concurrency in the first programming course dates back to the 90's. Feldman and Bachus show novices can learn concurrency [17]. Lynn Andrea Stein thinks we need to code in a different way, shifting from the "computation as calculation" paradigm, where a program is a function, to the "computation as interaction" metaphor [21], where a program is a community of concurrent agents communicating with each other by exchanging messages. This model also corresponds better with high level systems such as operating systems and the internet [47]. Furthermore, in 1997, Moström and Carr [35] showed on a small sample of 8 novices that the novices found it easier to use concurrent language than sequential language to solve the problems they submitted. This doesn't show that concurrency is easier, because it is hard to generalize from this experiment, but that concurrency, and message passing in particular, may be easy to use, depending on the problem to be solved.

Message Passing to Improve Computational Thinking. According to Wing, computational thinking is a skill involving problem solving, system design and human behaviour understanding [54]. Thus it needs important programming concepts. Computational thinking allows people to answer the questions: how hard is a particular problem to solve? What is the best way to solve it? Furthermore, computational thinking makes it possible to reformulate a hard problem in order to be able to solve it with reduction, composition, etc. It is also an abstraction skill, i.e. the "replacement of a complex and detailed real-world situation [with] an understandable model within which we can solve a problem" [4].

Some researchers [11, 22] and the ISTE (International Society for Technology in Education) [25] formalized computational thinking as the following set of skills: abstracting and generalizing, automating and repeating actions, understanding and using concurrency, decomposing problems, handling conditional structures, using symbols to represent data, processing data in a systematic way, defining algorithms and procedures, knowing the efficiency and the performance constraints of a solution, debugging and systematically detecting errors and executing simulations.

Very few papers describe empirical results about expanding computational thinking in terms of these skills with programming. According to most of them, computational thinking skills do not increase with the ability to program [18, 23,50,51]. But they tend to focus on imperative, object-oriented or event-based (Scratch) paradigms, without really focusing on concurrency. For each of these skills, message passing concurrency should be able to increase computational thinking.

Indeed, message passing concurrency consists in writing automatic procedures to solve problems. It makes it possible to abstract, generalize and automatize. Thus, the concurrency concept makes it possible to get a good idea of parallelism and decomposition into independent subproblems. Message passing makes the data processing and the information representation obvious. And the conditional structures are used very early to define the agent behaviours. Finally, the use of a software visualization system, that fits completely with concurrency, helps to understand performance, simulation and debug.

2.2   Software Visualization Systems and Teaching

A software visualization system is a pedagogical tool whose purpose is to help students in a programming class to learn by addressing their common difficulties [46]. The SVS is supposed to show different programming concepts dynamically by linking code and its execution to visual events. It makes it easier for the students to understand the notional machine, the abstract computer corresponding to the particular paradigm or language they use. It makes it easily to see the step by step execution of the program in order to trace and check the states.

Sorva et al. created a taxonomy of SVSs with three main categories [46]. We propose to extend this taxonomy with the programming game subcategory. We end up with this taxonomy: program animation (textual language generating visual animations), visual programming (visual language, often made of blocks that the student combine to create the program), algorithm visualization systems (algorithms are written as a flowchart) and programming games (subcategory of program animation consisting in making some actors move or act to go through a predefined game).

Advantages of Software Vizualisation Systems. Software visualization systems offer some advantages over textual-only programming languages.

First, the visual nature of these systems makes it easier to understand the programs. Indeed, the human perception requires less translation to represent visual concepts than textual ones [45].

A second advantage is that students feel involved in the system [38], so they tend to assimilate concepts easier. There are some positive experiments with SVSs like App Inventor used by college students [24,44], Scratch [19,32] or Alice [36].

A third advantage is that it makes concurrency and step-by-step debugging easier [37] thanks to the visual support. The former is obviously important for us, and some studies show that such graphic systems tend to encourage the use of concurrency [5] and have been used by professionals in order to more easily implement concurrent and parallel system [56]. The latter, the debugger, is useful for two reasons. Some teachers, such as Cross et al. [16], use the debugger as a teaching tool to show step by step execution of a program to students. But students can also use it to develop some useful skills [15,30], as long as they have good debugging strategies. We also saw that debugging is part of the computational thinking aptitudes described in Sect. 2.1.

Microworld Pedagogical Approach. Programming is hard to teach, because it requires many skills and all relevant concepts are intertwined. Furthermore, students usually see this course as boring and hard, especially when the language is not specifically designed for teaching and when it uses an unnatural syntax. The microworld pedagogical approach, based on SVSs, solves these problems.

A microworld is "a subset of reality or a constructed reality whose structure matches that of a given cognitive mechanism so as to provide an environment where the latter can operate effectively" [41, p. 204]. This improves students' exploration and understanding of new concepts. In a programming course, a microworld is composed of a programming language and an SVS. Both are usually integrated in a unified interface with a script editor and a visualization window.

The main advantage of this kind of environment is that it deals with many pedagogical problems that arise when using a traditional language. Xinogalos [55] and Mciver [33] note some of these problems. First, there are too many instructions in programming languages, compared to microworlds where the vocabulary is more limited and progressively enriched. Second, students tend to focus on syntax of full languages, while microworlds usually offer a simpler syntax. Third, the execution of the program is usually hidden, as opposed to the microworld where agents act according to the script. Usually, students seem to understand programming concepts better with the use of microworlds, according to Xinogalos [55].

3   Comparison of Software Visualization Systems

We now define exactly what visualization system we want. We first define and describe comparison criteria and use them to build a comparison table containing 27 SVSs. We then cluster the table into four categories of systems. We finally select the systems employing concurrency, message passing and microworlds.

3.1   Criteria

In order to select the software visualization system that could help us to build a first programming course based on message passing concurrency, we define some comparison criteria based partially on criteria found in the literature [13,28,29] and on the need we described in Sect. 2.

Extrinsic Criteria. These criteria, such as the release and last update dates, do not concern the nature of the system or the language itself. The release and last update dates are important to us, as we prefer to use a maintained and up-to-date system with modern graphics. We also focus on the license type, because we favour open source software because it does not restrict the installation of software on many computers in a secondary school and at home, and it reduces the cost and is potentially able to be adapted to our needs.

Visual Nature. This criterion constitutes the main advantage of a software visualization system over a textual one for learning, as we saw in Sect. 2.2. We identify categories of visualization environments, and evaluate visual functionalities. The categories of SVSs we identify are adapted from the taxonomy developed by Sorva et al. [46] and were explained in Sect. 2.2.

Languages, Paradigms and Concepts. Each programming visualization system helps to teach a particular language in a particular paradigm defined by a set of concepts. The language used may be an already existing language, like Java or Python, or a language designed for this particular system. Many languages that we encountered in visualization systems are a mix of some of these imperative, object-oriented, event-based, functional and logic paradigms.

Some of these paradigms are not suitable for teaching based on concurrency: imperative and object oriented paradigms, as we saw in Sect. 2.1, seem to be less efficient for teaching concurrency because they usually implement the shared state concurrency model; the event-based paradigm, although conceptually appealing, does not allow asynchronous message delivery in the way described in Sect. 2, and sometimes limits the message structure to something very simple, like a string or an atom.

Despite all of this, we also want to know, independently of the paradigm, whether or not each of these languages is concurrent, because this is the core concept we want to teach.

Debugger. As seen in Sect. 2.2, easy access to a debugger is a double advantage for the teacher demonstrating the execution of the program and for students learning to diagnose programming problems in a visual way. We thus prefer systems that come with a debugger.

3.2 Categories

Table 1, contains the result of applying the defined criteria to 27 software visualization systems. We group them in categories based on two main criteria:

- Do users need to write textual code? This refers to a dichotomy among program animation system, where students need to write code themselves, and visual programming, where they only move code blocks;
- Can users use them to write concurrent programs or only sequential programs? Since we want to teach concurrency, we prefer that they can.

Table 1. A comparison of 27 software visualization systems in four categories: concurrent visual programming (CVP), sequential visual programming (SVP), concurrent program animation (CPA) and sequential program animation (SPA)

Name	Visual Nature	Concurrency	Paradigm	Debugger	Language	License	Creation	Update
App Inventor	visual programming language	yes	Event-based	yes	Blockly	open source	2010	2017
Snap	visual programming language	yes	Event-based, functional	yes	Snap	open source	2011	2015
Starlogo nova	visual programming language	yes	Event-based, object-oriented, agents	yes	Starlogo nova	open source	1996	2014
Kedama	visual programming language	yes	Object-oriented	yes	Squeak/Smalltalk	open source	2005	?
Scratch	visual programming language	yes	Event-based	no	Scratch	open source	2006	2015
Blockly	visual programming language	yes	Imperative	no	Blockly	open source	2012	2017
Alice 3	visual programming language	yes	Object-oriented	no	Java	open source	1998	2016
ToonTalk	visual programming language	yes	Concurrent constraint programming	yes	Toontalk	proprietary	1995	2009
AgentSheets	visual programming language	yes	Active objects	no	Visual AgenTalk	proprietary	1989	2012
Etoys	visual programming language	no	Object-oriented	yes	Squeak/Smalltalk	open source	1996	2012
Amici	visual programming language	no	Imperative	?	Amici	open source	2011	2013
Raptor	algorithm visualization system	no	Imperative	no	pseudocode	proprietary	2015	2016
LARP	algorithm visualization system	no	Imperative	no	pseudocode	proprietary	2004	2008
Robot Code	programming game	yes	Object-oriented	yes	Java	open source	2001	2017
Karel J Robot	program animation system	yes	Object-oriented	yes	Java	open source	2005	2016
Processing	program animation system	yes	Object-oriented	yes	Java	open source	2001	2016
Greenfoot	program animation system	yes	Object-oriented	oui	Java	open source	2004	2015
NetLogo	program animation system	yes	Agent-based	no	Logo + agents	open source	1999	2015
Multilogo	program animation system	yes	Object-oriented and concurrent	?	Logo+LEGO	open source	1990	2007
Microworlds Ex	program animation system	yes	?	?	Microworlds	proprietary	2003	2007
Guido van Robot	program animation system	no	Imperative	yes	Python	open source	2009	2010
Karel++	program animation system	no	Object-oriented	yes	Karel++	open source	1997	1998
Karel the Robot	program animation system	no	Imperative	no	Karel	open source	1981	2000
Löve	program animation system	no	Imperative	no	Lua	open source	2008	2016
Kojo	program animation system	no	Object-oriented, functional	no	Scala	open source	2010	2015
Logo	program animation system	no	Imperative	?	Logo	open source	1967	2002
Jeroo	program animation system	no	Object-oriented	yes	Jeroo (like Java)	proprietary	2004	2014

Sequential (No Concurrency) Program Animation Systems (SPA).
This category gathers some of the oldest systems for teaching programming, like Logo and Karel. These systems aren't up-to-date compared to other categories. Most them are imperative, but some are object-oriented. Kojo [40], although clearly in this category, seems to be an outsider for two reasons. Firstly, although it isn't a visual programming language, the user doesn't have to write all the code himself, because she can click on predefined instructions to add them into the editor. Secondly, since it is based on Scala, it is also a functional language (a rare paradigm in this kind of visual system). Since Scala includes the Akka [9] library for concurrent actors, this system could become very interesting at some point for teaching concurrency if Akka was integrated into Kojo and the graphical interface. But there have been few experiments on the use of Kojo (and, generally, Scala) as a first language. The challenges of this language, as Regnell et al. write [42], are the error messages that are hard to understand and the type system (supposedly harder for slower learner).

Concurrent Program Animation Systems (CPA). Theses systems are mostly based on Java and Logo, and most are object-oriented. One exception is Netlogo [49], where the agent-based paradigm prevails. This language adds concurrency to the old Logo language and has been used to model some complex systems such as patterns emerging in nature [53] or, more lately, street robbery [6]. Unfortunately, there are two drawbacks to this system. First of all, syntax seems a bit hard to learn for novices, because there are many keywords they need to know from the beginning in order to command agents. The second drawback concerns these agents: it seems impossible to define their behaviour, or to define new messages. There are four implemented agent types [1] and they can only react to some predefined "ask" instructions.

Sequential Visual Programming Languages (SVP). This category contains three imperative and one object-oriented language based on Squeak, a SmallTalk dialect. We prefer not to use object-oriented and imperative languages because they make it harder to add a concurrency model based on message passing.

Concurrent Visual Programming Languages (CVP). This category contains the most up-to-date systems and representatives of the most diverse paradigms. Though many of them look interesting, here we focus on the open source systems offering a debugger and implementing an inherently concurrent paradigm. The concurrent constraint programming language **ToonTalk** [26] allows users to handle not only concurrency concepts like actor spawning and termination and sending and receiving messages through unidirectional channels but also constraint/logic programming concepts such as clause, guards and body [27], in a 3D playful city microworld. Some experiments with ToonTalk were conducted with kindergarten children [34] but the author did not mention any statistical result. This language is a good candidate for us, but its target audience, as they mention on their website, is "children", so it might not be suitable for secondary school students. The event-based **App Inventor** for Android [2], unlike ToonTalk, has been successfully used by high school students [24,44] and university students [20]. This language aims at coding Android applications easily. Unfortunately, this language is not really close to the microworld approach we want to use, since it does not imply any agent acting in an environment, but handles sensors and panels of the phone directly. **Star Logo Nova** [43] is similar to NetLogo, but with blocks. Finally, **Snap!** is derived from Scratch, with agents whose behaviour has to be defined according to some event occurring (it has also influenced Scratch, whose procedure blocks derive from Snap!). Scratch was extended by adding higher order functions concept in order to allow students to become more familiar with functional programming. Unfortunately, as in Scratch, the "messages" that agents can send are limited to a simple label, and can only be broadcasted, which seems too limited for what we intend to do. Furthermore, since the reception of a message is an event, the agent stops the task he is currently executing when he receives a new one. There is no "mailbox" that allows agents to receive messages asynchronously.

Conclusion: which SVS to Choose?

In this paper, we conjecture the importance of teaching concurrency properly in order to improve programming skills and computational thinking. We described software visualization systems because the microworld pedagogical approach is convenient to teach concurrency, and because a microworld is an SVS. We finally compared 27 SVSs with respect to six defined criteria and created a table in which we identified four categories, of which the most interesting for our needs seems to be the category of visual programming languages allowing concurrency. This category includes languages whose code is not textual but consists of blocks that the user has to put together to create the program, and where the languages have concurrency concepts. Two SVSs where identified as the best in this category, because they implement interesting paradigms and have a debugger: ToonTalk and Snap!. But are these systems able to address our needs?

Snap! is event-based. This means that its message transfer is not asynchronous. It also does not use a unidirectional channel from one agent to another, but rather a broadcast system. Finally, messages may only contain labels, which is a great limitation because we want to be able to transfer complex data structures between agents in the message passing concurrency model.

ToonTalk seems good with its constraint based concurrency paradigm, including unidirectional channels, complex messages and concurrent actors. But since the target audience is children, secondary students might consider it too childish. So far, no experiment has used this system with teenagers.

The next steps after this preliminary work are to precisely evaluate how difficult it would be to add a proper message passing concurrency model to Snap! and to collect teenage students' perception of ToonTalk. Then we will be able to choose the language that fulfils the requirements of a secondary level introduction to programming course based on message passing concurrency and microworlds.

References

1. Netlogo user manual version 6.0. https://ccl.northwestern.edu/netlogo/docs/
2. Abelson, H.: App inventor for android. Google Research Blog (2009)
3. ACM/IEEE-CS Joint Task Force on Computing Curricula: Computer Science Curricula 2013. Technical report, ACM Press and IEEE Computer Society Press (2013)
4. Aho, A.V., Ullman, J.D.: Foundations of Computer Science, C Edition. Computer Science Press/W. H. Freeman, New York (1992)
5. Aivaloglou, E., Hermans, F.: How kids code and how we know: an exploratory study on the scratch repository. In: Proceedings of the 2016 ACM Conference on International Computing Education Research, ICER 2016, pp. 53–61. ACM (2016)
6. Amrutha, S., Idicula, S.M.: Agent based simulation of street robbery. Department of Computer Science, Royal College of Engineering and Technology Thrissur, India (2014)
7. Armstrong, J.: Programming Erlang: Software for a Concurrent World. Pragmatic Bookshelf, Dallas, Texas - Raleigh, North Carolina (2007)
8. Balanskat, A., Engelhardt, K.: Computing Our Future: Computer Programming and Coding-Priorities, School Curricula and Initiatives Across Europe (2014)
9. Bonér, J., Klang, V., Kuhn, R., et al.: Akka library. http://akka.io
10. Brabrand, C.: Constructive alignment for teaching model-based design for concurrency. In: Jensen, K., Aalst, W.M.P., Billington, J. (eds.) Transactions on Petri Nets and Other Models of Concurrency I. LNCS, vol. 5100, pp. 1–18. Springer, Heidelberg (2008). doi:10.1007/978-3-540-89287-8_1

11. Brennan, K., Resnick, M.: New frameworks for studying and assessing the development of computational thinking. In: Proceedings of the 2012 Annual Meeting of the American Educational Research Association, Vancouver, Canada, pp. 1–25 (2012)
12. Carro, M., Herranz, A., Mariño, J.: A model-driven approach to teaching concurrency. Trans. Comput. Educ. **13**(1), 5:1–5:19 (2013)
13. Castillo-Barrera, F.E., Arjona-Villicana, P.D., Ramirez-Gamez, C.A., Hernandez-Castro, F.E., Sadjadi, S.M.: Turtles, robots, sheep, cats, languages what is next to teach programming? A future developer's crisis? In: Proceedings of the International Conference on Frontiers in Education: Computer Science and Computer EngineeringMTDL, p. 1. The Steering Committee of The World Congress in Computer Science, Computer Engineering and Applied Computing (2013)
14. Chechina, N., Hernandez, M.M., Trinder, P.: A scalable reliable instant messenger using the SD Erlang libraries. In: Proceedings of the 15th International Workshop on Erlang 2016, pp. 33–41. ACM (2016)
15. Chmiel, R., Loui, M.C.: Debugging: from novice to expert. ACM SIGCSE Bull. **36**(1), 17–21 (2004)
16. Cross, J., Hendrix, T.D., Barowski, L.A.: Using the debugger as an integral part of teaching CS1. In: Frontiers in Education, vol. 2, p. F1G. IEEE (2002)
17. Feldman, M.B., Bachus, B.D.: Concurrent programming can be introduced into the lower-level undergraduate curriculum. SIGCSE Bull. **29**(3), 77–79 (1997)
18. Fox, R.W., Farmer, M.E.: The effect of computer programming education on the reasoning skills of high school students. In: Frontiers in Education: Computer Science and Computer Engineering (FECS 2011) (2011)
19. Franklin, D., Conrad, P., Boe, B., Nilsen, K., Hill, C., Len, M., Dreschler, G., Aldana, G., Almeida-Tanaka, P., Kiefer, B., Laird, C., Lopez, F., Pham, C., Suarez, J., Waite, R.: Assessment of computer science learning in a scratch-based outreach program. In: Proceeding of the 44th ACM Technical Symposium on Computer Science Education, SIGCSE 2013, pp. 371–376. ACM (2013)
20. Gestwicki, P., Ahmad, K.: App inventor for android with studio-based learning. J. Comput. Sci. Coll. **27**(1), 55–63 (2011)
21. Goldin, D., Wegner, P.: The interactive nature of computing: refuting the strong church-turing thesis. Mind. Mach. **18**(1), 17–38 (2008)
22. Grover, S., Pea, R.: Computational thinking in K-12: a review of the state of the field. Educ. Res. **42**(1), 38–43 (2013)
23. Gülbahar, Y., Kalelioğlu, F., et al.: The effects of teaching programming via scratch on problem solving skills: a discussion from learners' perspective. Inf. Educ. Int. J. **13**(1), 33–50 (2014)
24. Honig, W.L.: Teaching and assessing programming fundamentals for non majors with visual programming. In: Proceedings of the 18th ACM Conference on Innovation and Technology in Computer Science Education, ITiCSE 2013, pp. 40–45. ACM (2013)
25. ISTE, CSTA: NSF. Computational thinking teacher resources (2011)
26. Kahn, K.: Toontalk TM-an animated programming environment for children. J. Vis. Lang. Comput. **7**(2), 197–217 (1996)
27. Kahn, K.M.: From prolog and Zelta to ToonTalk. In: ICLP, pp. 67–78 (1999)
28. Kiper, J.D., Howard, E., Ames, C.: Criteria for evaluation of visual programming languages. J. Vis. Lang. Comput. **8**(2), 175–192 (1997)
29. Li, F.W., Watson, C.: Game-based concept visualization for learning programming. In: Proceedings of the Third International ACM Workshop on Multimedia Technologies for Distance Learning, MTDL 2011, pp. 37–42. ACM (2011)

30. Lister, R.: Objectives and objective assessment in CS1. In: ACM SIGCSE Bulletin, vol. 33, pp. 292–296. ACM (2001)
31. Lutz, M.J.: The Erlang approach to concurrent system development. In: 2013 IEEE Frontiers in Education Conference, pp. 12–13. IEEE (2013)
32. Maloney, J.H., Peppler, K., Kafai, Y., Resnick, M., Rusk, N.: Programming by choice: urban youth learning programming with scratch. SIGCSE Bull. **40**(1), 367–371 (2008)
33. McIver, L.: The effect of programming language on error rates of novice programmers. In: 12th Annual Workshop of Psychology of Programmers Interest Group (PPIG), pp. 181–192 (2000)
34. Morgado, L., Cruz, M.G.B., Kahn, K.: Working in ToonTalk with 4- and 5-year olds. In: International Association for Development of the Information Society-IADIS International Conference e-Society 2003, p. 988 (2003)
35. Moström, J.E., Carr, D.: Programming paradigms and program comprehension by novices. Luleå tekniska universitet (1997)
36. Mullins, P., Whitfield, D., Conlon, M.: Using Alice 2.0 as a first language. J. Comput. Small Coll. **24**(3), 136–143 (2009)
37. Myers, B.A.: Taxonomies of visual programming and program visualization. J. Vis. Lang. Comput. **1**(1), 97–123 (1990)
38. Naps, T.L.: Jhavé: supporting algorithm visualization. IEEE Comput. Graph. Appl. **25**(5), 49–55 (2005)
39. Ortiz, A.: Teaching concurrency-oriented programming with Erlang. In: Proceedings of the 42nd ACM Technical Symposium on Computer Science Education. pp. 195–200. ACM (2011)
40. Pant, L., Pant, V., Pant, N.: Kojo homepage. http://www.kogics.net/kojo
41. Papert, S.: Computer-based microworlds as incubators for powerful ideas. In: The Computer in the School: Tutor, Tool, Tutee, pp. 203–210. Teachers College Press (1980)
42. Regnell, B., Pant, L., Kogics, D.: Teaching programming to young learners using scala and kojo. In: LTHs Pedagogiska Inspirationskonferens, vol. 8, p. 4 (2014)
43. Resnick, M.: StarLogo: an environment for decentralized modeling and decentralized thinking. In: Conference Companion on Human Factors in Computing Systems, pp. 11–12. ACM (1996)
44. Roy, K.: App inventor for android: report from a summer camp. In: Proceedings of the 43rd ACM Technical Symposium on Computer Science Education, SIGCSE 2012, pp. 283–288. ACM (2012)
45. Smith, D.C.: Pygmalion: a creative programming environment. Technical report, DTIC Document (1975)
46. Sorva, J., Karavirta, V., Malmi, L.: A review of generic program visualization systems for introductory programming education. Trans. Comput. Educ. **13**(4), 15:1–15:64 (2013)
47. Stein, L.A.: Challenging the computational metaphor: implications for how we think. Cybern. Syst. **30**(6), 473–507 (1999)
48. Sutter, H.: The free lunch is over: a fundamental turn toward concurrency in software. Dr. Dobb's J. **30**(3), 202–210 (2005)
49. Tisue, S., Wilensky, U.: NetLogo: design and implementation of a multi-agent modeling environment. In: Proceedings of the Agent 2004 Conference (2004)
50. Unuakhalu, M.F.: Enhancing problem-solving capabilities using object-oriented programming language. J. Educ. Technol. Syst. **37**(2), 121–137 (2008)
51. VanLengen, C., Maddux, C.: Does instruction in computer programming improve problem solving ability? J. IS Educ. **12**, 30–33 (1990)

52. White, G., Sivitanides, M.: Cognitive differences between procedural programming and object oriented programming. Inf. Technol. Manag. **6**(4), 333–350 (2005)
53. Wilensky, U.: Modeling nature's emergent patterns with multi-agent languages. In: Proceedings of EuroLogo, pp. 1–6. Citeseer
54. Wing, J.M.: Computational thinking. Commun. ACM **49**(3), 33–35 (2006)
55. Xinogalos, S.: An evaluation of knowledge transfer from microworld programming to conventional programming. J. Educ. Comput. Res. **47**(3), 251–277 (2012)
56. Zhang, K., Hintz, T., Ma, X.: The role of graphics in parallel program development. J. Vis. Lang. Comput. **10**(3), 215–243 (1999)

Multi-agent Model for Failure Assessment and Diagnosis in Teaching-Learning Processes

Oscar Salazar, Santiago Álvarez, and Demetrio Ovalle^(✉)

Universidad Nacional de Colombia - Sede Medellín, Bogotá, Colombia
{Omsalazaro, Salvarezl, dovalle}@unal.edu.co

Abstract. Currently, there are not effective mechanisms in virtual learning environments, that allow an early detection and diagnosis of learning failures. Incorporating this kind of elements into virtual learning environments could improve learning since the diagnosis provided by the system can design an action plan that contributes to the strengthening of the virtual course topics. The aim of this paper is to present the design and development of a multi-agent model for the assessment and diagnosis of failures which seeks to discover the shortcomings in learning from the virtual assessment process. In addition, the model looks for offering feedback and recommending new educational resources adapted to the learner's profile. Based on the proposed model, a prototype was implemented and validated through a case study. The results obtained allow us to conclude that the students felt accompanied during the assessment process and obtained real-time feedback that identified shortcomings and allowed to recommend educational resources in order to strengthen their learning process.

Keywords: Adaptive virtual courses · E-assessment · Pedagogical multi-agent systems · Ontologies · Learning objects

1 Introduction

The continuous growth of virtual learning environments and the great reception that these are having today, allow a continuous improvement in the teaching-learning processes. This growth demands new e-learning paradigms that allow to work with a large amount of users that these systems currently support. However, the increasing number of users does not allow the development of personalized teaching mechanisms which means that there is a lack concerning the continuous monitoring of students' progress within virtual learning environments [1]. Another great failure in this kind of environments is the lack of personalization of the contents presented to the students, since they do not consider their learning styles.

In addition, there are no effective mechanisms in virtual learning environments for detecting, assessment, and diagnosing learning failures to allow facing. Integrating this kind of elements into virtual learning environments can provide a detailed diagnosis that allows designing an action plan that contribute to the strengthening of the virtual course topics. At the same time, this makes it easier to recommend new educational resources such as learning objects (LO) that helps to face learning shortcomings and improve knowledge acquisition [2]. Failure diagnosis can be described as a process of

© Springer International Publishing AG 2017
J. Bajo et al. (Eds.): PAAMS 2017 Workshops, CCIS 722, pp. 398–408, 2017.
DOI: 10.1007/978-3-319-60285-1_34

observation and monitoring where hypotheses are generated to explain the anomalous functioning of a certain process or system, allowing the generation of repair strategies and actions [3].

The aim of this paper is to present the development of a multi-agent model for the failure assessment and diagnosis of failures in teaching-learning processes, which seeks to discover the shortcomings in students learning from the virtual assessment process. Subsequently, the assessment model seeks to provide feedback and recommendation of new learning resources based on identified shortcomings. The integration of this kind of technology allows an improvement in the monitoring of students learning process and the early detection of failures in order to confront them either by the system or by the teacher from the presentation of assessment reports.

The rest of the paper is organized as follows. Section 2 presents a theoretical framework with the representative concepts of the research area. Later, Sect. 3 offers a literature review on related research papers. Section 4 presents the model proposed and the elements that compose it. The implementation and validation of the model is presented in Sect. 5. Finally, Sect. 6 contains conclusions and points to future research directions.

2   Conceptual Framework

Following are the main concepts and fields related to this research such as Adaptive Virtual Courses, e-assessment, Multi-Agent Systems and ontologies.

The e-assessment term is commonly used to refer to all the activities that teachers carry out to help students in their teaching-learning process and to quantify the corresponding progress of the learning process [1]. Virtual evaluation or e-assessment is an important component of e-learning which provides direction, focus, and orientation to the student while participating in some processes of virtual learning [4]. Using these kinds of automated tools brings speed, availability, consistency, and objectivity at the assessment stage. However, it is important to emphasize that these tools require a careful pedagogical design by the teacher.

Adaptive Virtual Courses (AVC) are educational computing tools capable of guiding students along a particular domain of knowledge for learning purposes. During this process some solving tasks should be performed such as the development of a planning strategy concerning learning activities, adaptation of educational content, and the performance evaluation of students during the development of an online course process [5]. It is important to highlight that the educational resources most currently used in AVC frameworks are the Learning Objects (LO), which are defined as self-described entities using well-defined metadata whose main objective is to allow their storage and retrieval by as many worldwide users as possible [6]. Similarly, the LO metadata reflects the purpose for which the object was created and towards which student population or knowledge domain is focused. In order to standardize LO metadata representation schemas, numerous initiatives have been developed, one of the most recognized is the IEEE-LOM standard, which was used for the development of this research.

Ontologies can be defined as a formal representation of a particular domain using a well-defined methodology that allows the representation of the domain entities and the relationships existing among them [7]. Based on this, it is important to generate a formal representation of the adaptive learning course structure, in order to make inferences and generate recommendations for improving the learning process. On the other hand, there are different languages to represent ontologies, the most used is OWL [8]. The main objective of this language is the automatic processing of information through Web applications, instead of being processed with human intervention as performs on the traditional Web.

Coming from distributed artificial intelligence (IAD), Multi-agent Systems (MAS) are defined as complex systems consisting of autonomous agents which use and process specific knowledge of a specific domain, capable of interacting to perform tasks aimed at achieving a common goal [9, 10]. Another feature of this kind of systems is the highly distributed information acquisition and processing which complements perfectly with ubiquitous computing and mobile devices.

3   Related Works

This section examines some related works concerning the research fields addressed by the present work contrasting advantages and disadvantages of them.

Amelung et al. [1] propose a system for automatically qualifying assessments for computer science teaching. This system offers a service that allows performing automatic tests of programming tasks. The possibility of using the system as a service provides advantages when the system requires to be integrated in a flexible way with various e-learning environments. In addition, the system is able to provide recommendations and feedback from the answers given by the students during the assessment process. This information is stored during the pedagogical assessment design stage made by the teacher.

Scarlat et al. [11] perform the design, development, and validation of an e-assessment system, focusing on the practical issues of formal education in the medical field. This tool uses a case-based assessment and thus it stores, traces, and retrieves the most common cases in the real medical environment, so that students can assess them and generate diagnostic results. By interacting with the system, the student has the ability to visualize the various symptoms of the patients and the issue a diagnosis, which will be compared to the correct answer that has been previously entered by the teacher.

Hajjej et al. [12] address the complex problem of integrating and migration of virtual assessments among different virtual learning platforms. For doing this, authors propose a three-step approach based on a cloud computing service in order to integrate e-assessment functionalities within different LMS using a generalized process of virtual assessment. The first step concerns the development of a generic architecture of the elements that compose a traditional LMS (student, teacher, course administrator, course, content, class, objectives, assessment, etc.). The second step describes a set of assignment rules in order to adapt this generic assessment process to the learning profiles. To ensure greater flexibility in the generic e-assessment process, authors provide a cloud service that defines the allocation rules. Finally, the third step consists in publishing the e-assessment process obtained as a composite service in the cloud that allows flexibility and interoperability for the assessment process of any LMS.

Ahmad and Bokhari [13] propose an e-learning environment based on a multi-agent architecture that considers student characteristics to recommend educational material adapted to their profile, which is designed by a tutor to support the learning process. The main contributions of the system focus on improving the security level and reducing the complexity of the system interaction at the user level. In addition, the system architecture is composed of eight interacting agents to perform: (1) educational resource recommendation tasks, (2) assistance in the design of new materials, (3) student assessment, and (4) course content management.

Salazar et al. [14] present the advantages brought by the integration of ubiquitous computing along with distributed artificial intelligence techniques in order to build an adaptive and personalized context-aware learning system by using mobile devices. Based on this model they propose a multi-agent context-aware u-learning system that offers several functionalities such as context-aware learning planning, personalized course evaluation, selection of learning objects according to student profile, search of learning objects in repository federations, search of thematic learning assistants, and access of current context-aware collaborative learning activities involved. In addition, several context-awareness services are incorporated within the adaptive e-learning system that can be used from mobile devices.

The works previously examined allow to show great improvements within the e-learning field not only from a technological but also conceptual point of view. However, there are still some shortcomings that need to be addressed in order to improve the assessment process within virtual learning environments. These shortcomings concern mainly in the absence of mechanisms that allow feedback and recommendation of new educational resources in virtual assessments, in order to strengthen the learning process. Another notorious failure that generates large dropout rates in the AVC is the lack of accompaniment during the assessment process; this is because the traditional virtual evaluation does not have the ability to find specific learning failures in students in order not only to qualify them but to strengthen them in these gaps. Frequently, learning failures are found in the educational materials proposed in the virtual course or in the way in which they are presented, i.e. among these materials there are no educational resources that properly respond to students' learning styles according to Felder-Silverman classification (active or reflective, sensing or intuitive, visual or verbal and sequential or global) [15].

4 Model Proposed

The model we propose for assessment and failure diagnosis in teaching-learning processes considers two perspectives: the first one allows the structuring and deployment of a specific domain ontology that includes a generic AVC representation structure, as well a user profile representation mechanism. The second perspective regards the conceptualization, analysis, and design of a Multi-Agent model using the phases proposed by the Prometheus methodology [16]. The following describes the development process and the results obtained from each of the mentioned perspectives.

4.1 Knowledge Representation Process

During the knowledge representation process, the domain concepts are initially identified and the properties that define them are then detailed. Figure 1 shows the taxonomy that was obtained as a result which includes the generic structure of the AVC composed by different topics. It is important to highlight that the course topics are deployed by means of LOs. Finally, in order to validate the knowledge obtained by the students through the use of the presented LOs the virtual assessments concerning the course topics are performed.

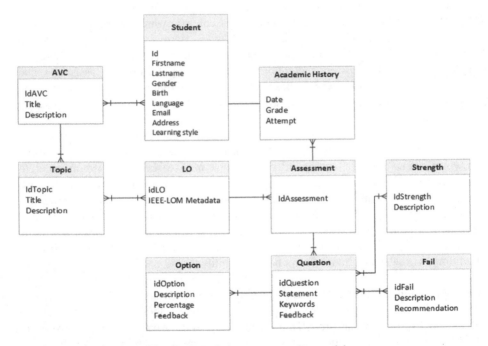

Fig. 1. Knowledge representation model

The assessment concept has several questions associated with it, which in turn have several answers. This allows to have multiple choice questions with single answer and multiple choice questions with multiple answers. It is important to highlight that each question allows the addition of keywords by the teacher during the instructional design phase of the assessments, as well as feedback for both questions and answers. Finally, the teacher has the ability to associate faults and/or strengths to each question, i.e., if a question is correctly answered this will show strengths, otherwise the question will show failures for this specific student. These failures and strengths will allow to generate reports useful for the teacher, so that the teacher can identify in real time which students need to reinforce the course topics and in what punctual concepts require greater feedback. This feature will also make it possible to identify if there are problems in educational resources when the learning failures are generalized.

4.2 Multi-agent Assessment Model Proposed

As previously mentioned the Prometheus methodology was used for the conceptualization, analysis and development phases of the MAS since it allows the development of intelligent systems from a practical, complete, and detailed scheme. In addition, Prometheus offers the necessary tools to define and develop agents based on objectives and plans in order to describe complex, robust and flexible agents at the same time [17]. In this way, the different models proposed by the methodology were developed. Figure 2 presents the system overview involving the actors that interact with the system (teacher and student). In addition, this diagram deploys the interactions among actors and the system using protocols, the information sources of the system (ontology and main database), and the different agent typologies that the system considers. Each of the agents considered for the deployment of the services offered by the MAS are detailed as follows.

- Student agent: is a kind of interface agent that aims to present the information to the student and interact with the internal agents of the system to capture the perceptions (requests) and respond with actions (information). In other words, this agent will be in charge of presenting the assessments, obtain the answers, show the feedbacks and recommendations made by the MAS. Finally, this agent shows the recommended resources in order to strengthen the identified student's learning failures, if exist.
- Teacher agent: similarly, to the student agent this is a kind an interface agent in charge of handling interactions with the teacher. Its main purpose is to assist in the instructional design of the assessments, capturing the information and sending it to the assessment agent for processing. In addition, it has the task of presenting assessment statistics and the summary of the recommendations that were established to address the identified failures considering each of the students.
- Assessment agent: this agent supports several functionalities within the system and thus is responsible for: (1) processing the assessments instructional design and storing them within the ontology, validating inconsistencies at the same time; (2) retrieving the assessments and send them to the student agent when they are requested; (3) processing answers, storing them, and identifying failures, keywords, and feedbacks associated with them; (4) send a report with this information to the student, teacher, statistician and adviser agents. It is important to highlight that the creation of the assessments, the processing of the answers and the detection of failures, are supported by the specific domain ontology, which stores the information and later inferred new knowledge from the application of SWRL rules.
- Recommender agent: is responsible for retrieving the keywords concerning the answers that presented failures for the student and processing them, in order to make recommendations for new educational resources (LOs, assistants, events, etc.). This process is carried out through the integration of the system proposed by Salazar et al. [14].

– Statistical agent: This agent is in charge of processing the assessment information previously stored by assessment agent within the ontology and generating a report from both individually and group perspectives. This report contains information regarding individual scores and group-level averages for assessments and detailed it by question. Also this report includes student-identified failures, the most reiterative failures found within the group, and recommendations made to each student to address such failures.

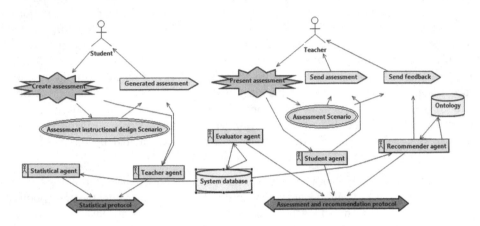

Fig. 2. Assessment multi-agent system overview

5   Model Implementation and Validation

The system was implemented using the JADE Framework [18, 19] which is oriented towards the development of MAS following the standards defined by FIPA (Foundation for Intelligent Agents) which is part of the IEEE. Using this standard gives interoperability to the platform since the same protocols of communication and exchange of messages are used.

The domain ontology development process based on the proposed model was performed through the Protégé framework [20], which allowed us to adequately specify concepts, properties and relationships among them. As a result of this development, an ontology was obtained using OWL language [8] and integrated into the system through the JENA library [21] which is a programmer's API (application programming interface) for Java semantic Web applications.

In order to validate the proposed model, a prototype was implemented and applied to a case study that allowed to demonstrate the behavior of the MAS. In this way, an assessment was developed concerning the course of Artificial Intelligence available at the National University of Colombia - Medellin campus. This course has 32 students, from which a control group (16 students) and an experimental group (16 students) were formed in order to contrast the results obtained at the end. The results obtained from the development of the assessment process are presented as follow.

Figure 3 deploys the assessments instructional design. This interface allows the capture and visualization of fields such as: (1) the name regarding the question; (2) the question statement; (3) each of the possible responses with their percentage and feedback; (4) the keywords concerning the developing question; (5) feedback at the question general level; (6) associated failures regarding the answer and appropriate feedback, and finally (7) strengths that can be evidenced from a correct answer to the question.

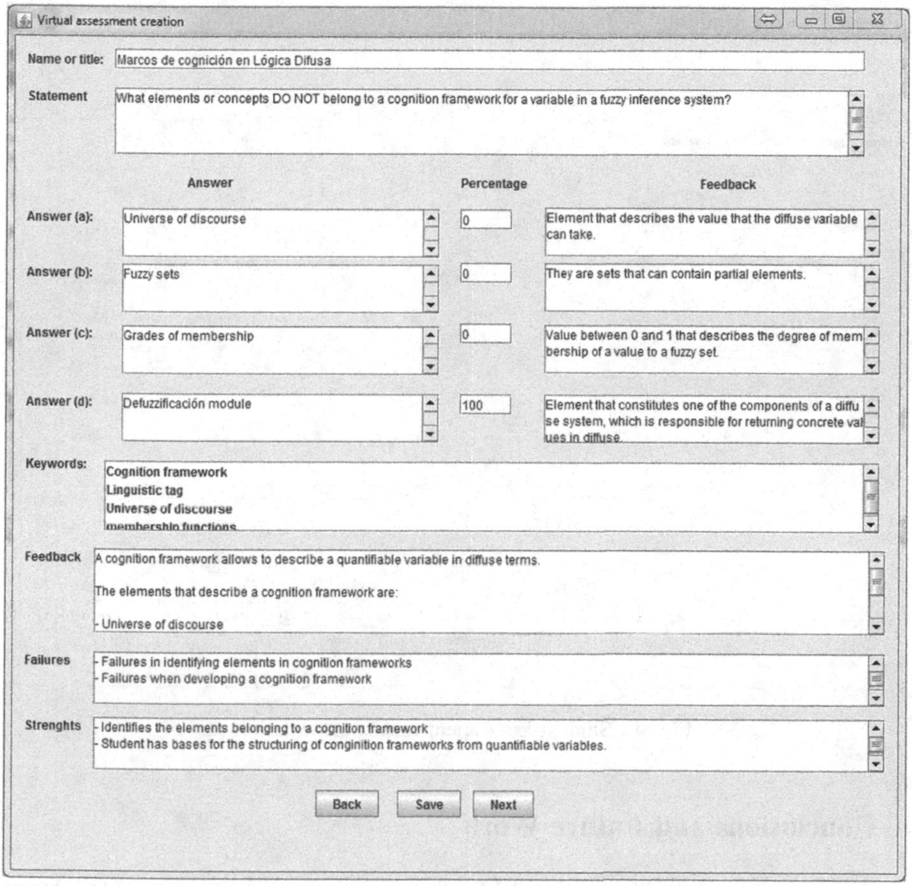

Fig. 3. Assessment instructional design process

Figure 4 presents the interface which deploys the student's assessment results involving: (1) the grade obtained during the assessment test; (2) each of the questions asked; (3) the score obtained by the question performed; (4) the shortcomings or strengths identified from the answers; (5) the feedback from the question asked and corresponded answer delivered; (6) general assessment feedback and finally (7) new recommended resources to address identified shortcomings and strengthen knowledge.

From the deployment of the system it was possible to validate the following scenarios of the proposed case study: (1) the instructional design of the evaluation with all the elements proposed in the model. (2) students performed the assessment by receiving real-time feedback, identifying failures and strengths during the process. (3) The system presented the assessment results to the teacher, grouping the students for failures in order to generate new strategies. It is important to highlight that the case study considered three evaluations, two formative and one summative. The summative evaluation served to contrast the results obtained by the defined groups (control and experimental) and to demonstrate if the identified failures were solved by the resources suggested to the student.

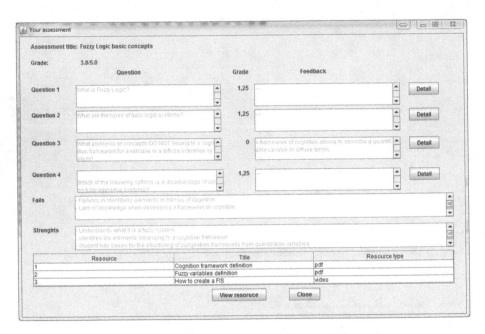

Fig. 4. Student assessment results presentation

6 Conclusions and Future Work

The development of a multi-agent model for the assessment and diagnosis of failures in teaching-learning processes, brought significant contributions into the virtual assessment process; first of all, generated mechanisms allow the detection of failures in real time and then, tools are provided for the strengthening of deficiencies based on new educational resources recommendation. In addition, the model allows the general statistics generation concerning the assessments, the identified failures and the recommended educational resources to face such failures. Another advantage of incorporating the model proposed, is the ability to identify failures involved within LO generated for the topics. The case study allowed performing the model validation when applying within a virtual learning environment; the students' perceptions were very satisfactory because they felt accompanied during the assessment process and they obtained a real time feedback involving the failures identified and recommended resources in order to face them. As a consequence, the model supports the improvement of the learning process. Similarly, the teacher obtained the learning process statistics in real time that allowed him to visualize the deficiencies in some educational resources and to identify the failures from individual and group perspectives, in order to propose new learning activities.

As a future work we attempt to improve the failure process detection by incorporating an automatic mechanism with the ability to analyze the questions in order to find possible failures associated. In addition, in this first approximation, only multiple-choice questions were considered; therefore, a new validation is proposed by using assessments based on essays, games, addition questions, etc. Finally, we would like to extend the model in order to recommend group activities based on the group formation of heterogeneous groups, that is, groups which are formed by students who present strengths and failures in different topics.

Acknowledgments. The research presented in this paper was partially funded by the COL-CIENCIAS project entitled: "RAIM: Implementación de un frame work apoyado en tecnologías móviles y de realidad aumentada para entornos educativos ubicuos, adaptativos, accesibles e interactivos para todos" of the Universidad Nacional de Colombia, with code 1119569-34172. It was also developed with the support of the grant from "Programa Nacional de Formación de Investigadores – COLCIENCIAS".

References

1. Amelung, M., Krieger, K., Rosner, D.: E-assessment as a service. IEEE Trans. Learn. Technol. **4**(2), 162–174 (2011)
2. Mora, N., Caballe, S., Daradoumis, T.: Improving e-assessment in collaborative and social learning settings. In: 2015 International Conference on Intelligent Networking and Collaborative Systems, pp. 288–293 (2015)
3. Feldman, A., Kalech, M., Provan, G.: Exploring the duality in conflict-directed model-based diagnosis. In: AAAI Association for the Advancement of Artificial Intelligence Journal (2012)
4. Thomas, P., Haley, D., deRoeck, A., Petre, M.: E-assessment using latent semantic analysis in the computer science domain: a pilot study, pp. 38–44 (2004)
5. Duque, N.D., Ovalle, D.A.: Artificial intelligence planning techniques for adaptive virtual course construction. DYNA **78**(170), 70–78 (2011)
6. Raju, P., Ahmed, V.: Enabling technologies for developing next-generation learning object repository for construction. Autom. Constr. **22**, 247–257 (2012)
7. Tramullas, J., Sánchez-Casabón, A.-I., Garrido-Picazo, P.: An evaluation based on the digital library user: an experience with greenstone software. Procedia - Soc. Behav. Sci. **73**, 167–174 (2013)
8. Meditskos, G., Bassiliades, N.: A rule-based object-oriented OWL reasoner. IEEE Trans. Knowl. Data Eng. **20**(3), 397–410 (2008)

9. Shoham, Y., Leyton-Brown, K.: Multiagent Systems: Algorithmic, Game-Theoretic, and Logical Foundations. Cambridge University Press, Cambridge (2008)
10. Wooldridge, M.: An Introduction to Multiagent Systems. Wiley, Hoboken (2009)
11. Scarlat, R., Stanescu, L., Popescu, E., Burdescu, D.D.: Case-based medical e-assessment system. In: 2010 10th IEEE International Conference on Advanced Learning Technologies, pp. 158–162 (2010)
12. Hajjej, F., Hlaoui, Y.B., Ben Ayed, L.J.: Personalized and generic E-assessment process based on cloud computing. In: 2015 IEEE 39th Annual Computer Software and Applications Conference, vol. 3, pp. 387–392 (2015)
13. Ahmad, S., Bokhari, M.: A new approach to multi agent based architecture for secure and effective e-learning. Int. J. Comput. Appl. **46**(22), 26–29 (2012)
14. Salazar, O.M., Ovalle, D.A., Duque, N.D.: Adaptive and personalized educational ubiquitous multi-agent system using context-awareness services and mobile devices. In: Zaphiris, P., Ioannou, A. (eds.) LCT 2015. LNCS, vol. 9192, pp. 301–312. Springer, Cham (2015). doi:10.1007/978-3-319-20609-7_29
15. Felder, R., Silverman, L.: Learning styles and teaching styles in engineering education. In: Annual Meeting of the American Institute of Chemical Engineers (1987)
16. Lin, P., Thangarajah, J., Winikoff, M.: The prometheus design tool (PDT) supports the structured design of intelligent agent systems. In: Proceedings of the 23rd National Conference on Artificial Intelligence, vol. 3, pp. 1884–1885 (2008)
17. Carrera, Á., Iglesias, C.A., García-Algarra, J., Kolařík, D.: A real-life application of multi-agent systems for fault diagnosis in the provision of an Internet business service. J. Netw. Comput. Appl. **37**, 146–154 (2014)
18. Bellifemine, F., Poggi, A., Rimassa, G.: JADE – A FIPA-compliant agent framework. In: Proceedings of PAAM (1999)
19. Bordini, R.H., Braubach, L., Dastani, M., El Fallah-Seghrouchni, A., Gomez-Sanz, J.J., Leite, J., Ricci, A.: A survey of programming languages and platforms for multi-agent systems. Informatica (Slovenia) **30**(1), 33–44 (2006)
20. Allen, T.D., Shockley, K.M., Poteat, L.: Protégé anxiety attachment and feedback in mentoring relationships. J. Vocat. Behav. **77**(1), 73–80 (2010)
21. McBride, B.: Jena: a semantic web toolkit. IEEE Internet Comput. **6**(6), 55–59 (2002)

Validation of a Content Recommendation System for Learning Objects, Using Agents that Simulate Disabled People

Paula Rodríguez[2], Luis Londoño[1]([X]), Mauricio Giraldo[2],
Valentina Tabares[1], and Néstor Duque[1]

[1] Universidad Nacional de Colombia Sede Manizales, Manizales, Colombia
{lflondonor,vtabaresm,ndduqueme}@unal.edu.co
[2] Universidad Nacional de Colombia Sede Medellin, Medellin, Colombia
{parodriguezma,maugiraldooca}@unal.edu.co

Abstract. The growth in the number of internet resources with inclusive characteristics suggests the importance of a recommendation system which adapts its suggestions to the disability of a given person. However, performing a validation of whether or not the recommended learning objects are adequate for a given person is difficult, as finding a population of disabled people is an arduous task, as is convincing them to help in the validation process.

This article proposes a model, and the application of a multi-agent system which simulates disabled people, in order to perform the validation. The idea is to create agents with behaviors and characteristics of those with visual and hearing disabilities, and that said agents evaluate the learning objects.

Keywords: Recommendation system · Simulation · Multi-agents system · Learning objects

1 Introduction

Currently, there are a number of repositories for learning objects. These repositories use the following metadata standards: LOM, LOM-ES, SCORM, or Dublin Core [1–3]. However, there are also repositories such as roapRAIM, which adapt the LOM standard in order to consider metadata of accessibility, to make adaptations to learning objects [4]. This is done to have learning objects for people with disabilities. Nevertheless, for a person with disabilities, it is burdensome to find learning objects to which they have access, in accordance with their characteristics. To solve this problem, in this study, a recommendation system is proposed, with a content filter that suggests learning objects to people with visual or hearing disabilities.

This investigation was implemented in a population which does not have an extensive number of disabled people. For this reason, in order to complete the validation of the recommendation system, a multi-agent system was created, where the agents simulate those with visual or hearing disabilities. These agents will receive the learning objects suggested by the recommendation system, and they will evaluate them

J. Bajo et al. (Eds.): PAAMS 2017 Workshops, CCIS 722, pp. 409–419, 2017.
DOI: 10.1007/978-3-319-60285-1_35

in accordance with a number of rules, which come from the characteristics of the agent and of the learning objects.

The remainder of the paper it is organized as follows: Sect. 2 is a revision the main related concepts. Section 3 reviews related work in this area; Sect. 4 describes the proposed model the content-based recommender system. Section 5 explains the model implementation; the results of the proposed model, through a case study it is presented in Sect. 6. Finally, the main conclusions and future research directions, it shows in Sect. 7.

2 Basic Concept

Learning Objects (LO): A learning object is a resource or digital content that facilitates the appropriation of knowledge to the users due to the characteristics and structure of the learning object [7].

Learning Objects Repositories: The repositories are platforms where are store the learning object so that the people can access more easily to the them [8, 9].

Recommendation Systems (RS): RS is defined as a piece of software that facilitates users to discern more relevant and interesting learning information [10]. RS are a tool aims at providing users with useful information results searched and recovered according to their needs, making predictions about matching them to their preferences and delivering those items that could be closer than expected [11]. In the case of educational resources, the system should be able to recommend resources adapted to one or more user's profile characteristics using metadata [12].

Recommender Systems Based on the Content: In this kind of systems, the recommendations are make base on the user's profile created from the content analysis of the LOs that the user has already evaluated in the past. The content-based systems use "item by item" algorithms generated through the association of correlation rules among those items [13].

3 Related Works

In works like [14, 15] shows that recently exist a lot of works in which are used simulators or are created simulations for different goals. This is because in areas like health, made virtual simulations is the bests tool to the medical training, because how it shows in the work [16] where is performed a systematic review of one hundred articles about simulators and it concludes that the 75% of the articles shows the positive effects that had the simulators in the appropriation of knowledge.

In [17] shows the SIMBA simulator (SIMulator for Business Administration), this is a powerful tool to support the decision-making process of business managers and also business education. In this work also it is proposed a reinforcement learning (RL), for the creation of smart agents that can handle virtual companies in SIMBA.

The multi-agents systems are a new technology that right now is having more and more force, for this reason in works like [18] are used a multi-agents system to do the simulation of the behavior of the people in an evacuation after a disaster. This with the objective of capture information to create contingency plans and recommendations for the optimization of the evacuation process.

Another way in which agents can being use is in a recommendation system and in [19–21] shows the use of agents and multi-agents systems for recommendations of learning objects, learning resources and media content is a good strategy.

However, in none of the works founded it is use the multi-agent system to do a simulation for validate a system recommendation which is the purpose in this work.

4   Proposal

In this study, the validation of a recommendation system, based on a content filter for learning objects is proposed. The validation will be made by a multi-agent system, in which simulating agents will have behaviors similar to those of people with disabilities. The model proposed to perform the validation is shown in Fig. 1. This model explains the architecture of the simulation of agents with disabilities, and the interactions between agents.

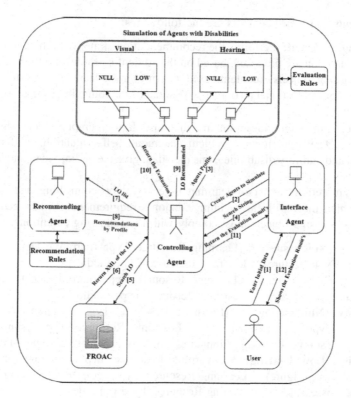

Fig. 1. Multi-agents model

Figure 2 shows an experience model, in which the rules, the way in which agents and the recommendation system work within the system, and the way that the user interacts with the system can be observed.

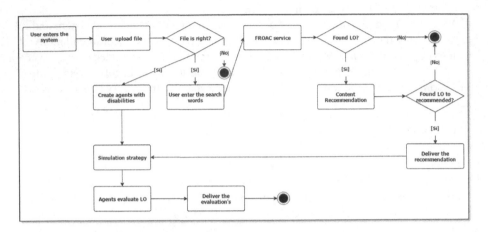

Fig. 2. Experience model of the multi-agent system.

The agents and their behaviors are the followings:

Recommending Agent: Performs the recommendation strategy. In this case, the rules for recommendation are proposed, based on the student's profile, and their relationship with the learning objects' (content-based filtering) metadata. In order to make the recommendation, educational resources with some of the following characteristics were selected:

Exercise, simulation, questionnaire, diagram, figure, graph, index, slide, table, narrative text, test, experiment, problem statement, self-evaluation, conference. To cover visual and auditory disabilities, this metadata give the audio, video and animation resource types.

This agent returns a list of learning objects to the controlling agent, with all resources which meet with the recommendation's requirements. In the recommendation, selected learning objects must comply with the following conditions:

Disability (Null visual) ∧ [Learning Resource Type (narrative text) ∨ Learning Resource Type (lecture) ∨ Learning Resource Type (audio)]

Disability (Low visual) ∧ [Learning Resource Type (narrative text) ∨ Learning Resource Type (lecture) ∨ Learning Resource Type (audio)]

Disability (Nullhearing) ∧ [Learning Resource Type (diagram) ∨ Learning Resource Type (self-assessment) ∨ Learning Resource Type (simulation) ∨ Learning Resource Type (questionnaire) ∨ Learning Resource Type (slide)]

Disability (Low hearing) ∧ [Learning Resource Type (diagram) ∨ Learning Resource Type (figure) ∨ Learning Resource Type (graph) ∨ Learning Resource Type (self-assessment) ∨ Learning Resource Type (table)]

Interface Agent: this agent is responsible of the communication between the multi-agent platform and the user. This agent has an interface where receives the dates enters by the user for do the simulation and search the learning objects. The dates that are necessary for the system operation are name, age and student disability.

Controlling Agent: This agent is responsible for controlling all communications between system agents. Some of the activities carried out by this agent are the creation of those which will simulate people with disabilities, find which learning objects comply with the search string entered by the user, send learning objects found in FROAC (Federation of Repositories of Learning Objects in Colombia) to the recommending agent, receive the list of recommended learning objects, receive and send recommended objects to each of the simulated agents, and send results to the interface agent, so they may be delivered to the user.

Simulated Agent: This agent is created based on the characteristics that the user enters into the system. This agent, following creation, waits for the list of objects which have been recommended for them, and evaluates them, in order to deliver the results of learning object evaluations to the controlling agent.

Evaluation Rules: These rules are being building in base to the rules that were defining in the RAIM project, this rules evaluate the characteristics of the learning objects metadata to adapt these objects to the needs of the users.

> Disability (Null visual) ∧ [audiodescription (yes)] ∧ [Interactivity Level (medium) ∨ Interactivity Level (low) ∨ Interactivity Level (very low)] ∨ [format (audio) ∨ format (video)]
>
> Disability (Low visual) ∧ [audiodescription (yes)] ∧ [Interactivity Level (high) ∨ Interactivity Level (medium) ∨ Interactivity Level (low)] ∨ [format (audio) ∨ format (video)]
>
> Disability (Null hearing) ∧ [HasTextAlternative (yes)] ∧ [Interactivity Level (medium) ∨ Interactivity Level (low) ∨ Interactivity Level (very low)]
>
> Disability (Low hearing) ∧ [HasTextAlternative (yes)] ∧ [Interactivity Level (medium) ∨ Interactivity Level (low) ∨ Interactivity Level (very low)] ∨ [format (text) ∨ format (image) ∨ format (aplication)]

5 Development of the Proposal

The platform developed to the validation of this work, consists in a multi-agent system, which was create in JAVA, using the framework JADE (Java Agent Development Kit), also was used the library swing to build the graphic interface that is used by the agent for the interchange of dates with the user. To solve the need of recuperate learning objects from roapRAIM repository to realize the recommendation and the others process, was use a communication service with the federation FROAC (Federation of Repositories of Learning Objects of Colombia). This service return the xml of the learning objects from roapRAIM that meet the search criteria.

Figure 3, shows a communication diagram that explain how it works the agents.

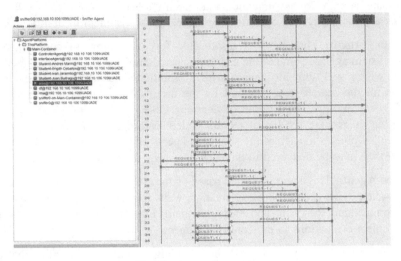

Fig. 3. Agents interactions.

Figure 4, shows the interface of the multi agent system, where the user going to interact and get the results of the simulation.

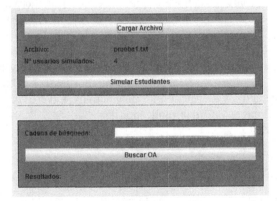

Fig. 4. Interface of multi-agent simulator.

6   Results

To do the validation of the recommendations, two types of tests were generated, in which the user entered a file into the system with the name, age and disability data of the disabled users that are to be simulated, and later, the search string for the learning objects that it wanted to find. In the first test, the entire recommendation process is carried out, and the agents evaluate whether the learning objects are or are not appropriate for them. In the second test, all objects retrieved by the service with FROAC, without the recommendation filter, are delivered. With these results, each of the tests are analyzed to verify whether or not test one's results are more significant than those of test two.

In the Fig. 5, it shows the results that was obtain of multi agent system with the recommender agent.

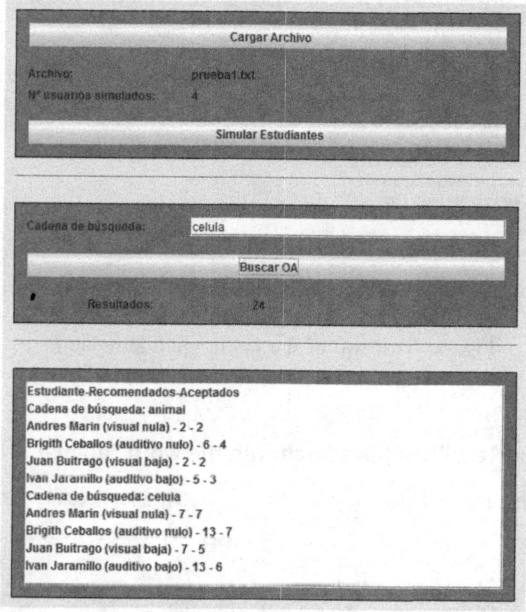

Fig. 5. Test one of the multi-agent simulator.

In the Fig. 6, it shows the results of the multi agent system without the recommender agent.

How it can look, the results in the Figs. 5 and 6 shows that the first search with the search string "animal", are more relevant to the user the learning objects recommended than delivered all the learnings objects, but in the second search with the search string "célula" it can shows that are more relevant delivered all the learnings objects. Then it can get the conclusion that maybe the recommendation can be better if more characteristics are take into account to the recommendations.

In the Figs. 7 and 8 it shows graphically how in general the percentage of acceptance rate of the learning objects are better if it delivered all of them and not only the recommended.

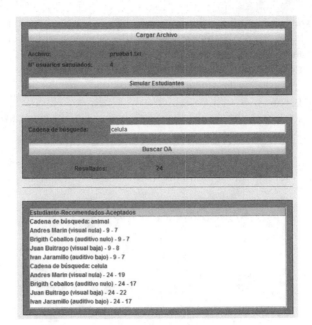

Fig. 6. Test two of the multi-agent simulator.

Results of the search with the word "animal"

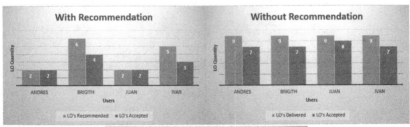

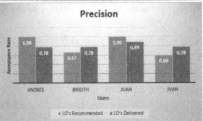

Fig. 7. Test one analysis.

Results of the search with the word "célula"

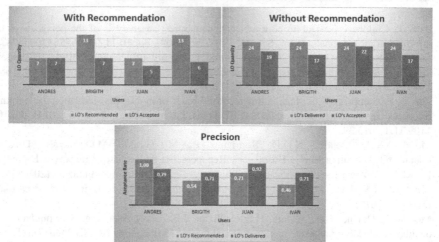

Fig. 8. Test two analysis.

7 Conclusions and Future Work

This investigation shows that it is possible to validate a recommendation system, using agents which simulate disabled people, as the behavior of the agents allow for the characterization of any type of person. For this reason, it is very important to perform a detailed analysis of those behaviors that agents exhibit, since the quality of the multi-agent system depends on said behaviors.

In this article, agents were used to validate a recommendation system. Similarly, this strategy may be used to validate other types of systems or applications. Having accessibility metadata in the learning objects of a repository allows for the adaptation and recommendation of learning objects, in accordance with a user's profile. The model proposed in this study is made up of modules. So that, it allows agents to change their behaviors without affecting the performance of the entire system.

As future work, it is try to simulate agents with different type of disabilities to increase the amount of persons to simulate.

Other future work is do a validation of the recommendation with persons that had visual orhearingdisabilities and compare the results with the results of the simulation, and validate if a simulation had results similar to those of the people.

Acknowledgments. The research presented in this paper was partially funded by the project entitled: "Fortalecimiento de Competencia Digital Basado en Estilos de Aprendizaje: Estrategia Evaluativa para Estudiantes de Primer Semestre" of the Universidad Nacional de Colombia and Universidad de Caldas.

References

1. Park, J., Childress, E.: Dublin core metadata semantics: an analysis of the perspectives of information professionals. J. Inf. Sci. **35**, 727–739 (2009). doi:10.1177/0165551509337871
2. Jadán-Guerrero, J., Guerrero, L.A.: A virtual repository of learning objects to support literacy of SEN children. Revista Iberoamericana de Tecnologias del Aprendizaje **10**, 168–174 (2015). doi:10.1109/RITA.2015.2452712
3. Zervas, P., Sampson, D.G.: Facilitating teachers' reuse of mobile assisted language learning resources using educational metadata. IEEE Trans. Learn. Technol. **7**, 6–16 (2014). doi:10.1109/TLT.2013.39
4. Morales, V.T., Méndez, N.D.D., Rodríguez, P.A.M., Giraldo, M.O., Ovalle, D.A.C.: Plataforma Adaptativa para la Búsqueda y Recuperación de Recursos Educativos Digitales. In: XI Conferencia Latinoamericana de Objetos y Tecnologías de Aprendizaje (2016)
5. Montoya, R.S.: Las autoayudas y los simuladores informáticos en la integración escolar. Dyslexia (2012)
6. Motola, I., Devine, L.A., Chung, H.S., Sullivan, J.E., Barry Issenberg, S.: Simulation in healthcare education: a best evidence practical guide. AMEE guide No. 82. Med. Teach. **35**, e1511–e1530 (2013). doi:10.3109/0142159X.2013.818632
7. Mendez, N.D.D., Carranza, D.O., Cadavid, J.M.: Objetos de Aprendizaje, Repositorios y Federaciones… Conocimento para todos (2014)
8. Guzmán, C.L.: Los Repositorios de Objetos de Aprendizaje como soporte a un entorno e-learning, p. 152 (2005)
9. Fernandez, I.M.S.: Repositorios de objetos de aprendizaje para la enseñanza superior: Dspace. Herramienta telemáticas para la enseñanza universitaria en el espacio europeo de educación superior, p. 18 (2007). doi:http://hdl.handle.net/10201/13419
10. Sikka, R., Dhankhar, A., Rana, C.: A survey paper on e-learning recommender system. Int. J. Comput. Appl. **47**, 27–30 (2012). doi:10.5120/7218-0024
11. Mizhquero, K., Barrera, J.: Análisis, Diseño e Implementación de un Sistema Adaptivo de Recomendación de Información Basado en Mashups. Revista Tecnológica ESPOL-RTE (2009)
12. Li, J.Z.: Quality, evaluation and recommendation for learning object. In: International Conference on Educational and Information Technology, pp. 533–537 (2010)
13. Burke, R.: Hybrid web recommender systems. Adapt. Web **4321**, 377–408 (2007)
14. Holzinger, A., Kickmeier-Rust, M.D., Wassertheurer, S., Hessinger, M.: Learning performance with interactive simulations in medical education: lessons learned from results of learning complex physiological models with the HAEMOdynamics SIMulator. Comput. Educ. **52**, 292–301 (2009). doi:10.1016/j.compedu.2008.08.008. Elsevier Ltd
15. Abboudi, H., Khan, M.S., Aboumarzouk, O., Guru, K.A., Challacombe, B., Dasgupta, P., Ahmed, K.: Current status of validation for robotic surgery simulators a systematic review. BJU Int. **111**, 194–205 (2013). doi:10.1111/j.1464-410X.2012.11270.x
16. Ravert, P.: An integrative review of computer-based simulation in the education process. Comput. Inform. Nurs.: CIN **20**, 203–208 (2002)
17. García, J., Borrajo, F., Fernández, F.: Reinforcement learning for decision-making in a business simulator. Int. J. Inf. Technol. Decis. Making **11**, 935–960 (2012). doi:10.1142/S0219622012500277
18. Bunea, G., Leon, F., Atanasiu, G.M.: Postdisaster evacuation scenarios using multiagent system. J. Comput. Civil Eng. **30**, 05016002 (2016). doi:10.1061/(ASCE)CP.1943-5487.0000575

19. Veloso, B., Malheiro, B., Burguillo, J.C.: A multi-agent brokerage platform for media content recommendation. Int. J. Appl. Math. Comput. Sci. **25**, 513–527 (2015). doi:10.1515/amcs-2015-0038
20. Solís, J., Chacón-Rivas, M., Garita, C.: Agente Híbrido Recomendador de Objetos de Aprendizaje. In: IX Conferencia Latinoamericana de Objetos y Tecnologías de Aprendizaje, pp. 290–301 (2014)
21. Salazar, O.M., Ovalle, D.A., Duque, N.D.: Sistema Multi-Agente para Recomendación de Recursos Educativos utilizando Servicios de Awareness y Dispositivos Móviles, pp. 73–82

Accessibility Evaluation of Learning Object Using Agents

Luis Londoño[1]([⊠]), Valentina Tabares[1], Néstor Duque[1],
and Mauricio Giraldo[2]

[1] Universidad Nacional de Colombia Sede Manizales, Manizales, Colombia
{lflondonor, vtabaresm, ndduqueme}@unal.edu.co
[2] Universidad Nacional de Colombia Sede Medellín, Medellín, Colombia
maugiraldooca@unal.edu.co

Abstract. Learning objects are tools which can help to facilitate a person's learning. However, they are often found in repositories, which commonly have no mechanism to evaluate the accessibility of learning objects. This is a problem, because should a person with a specific condition enter to observe one of these learning objects, it is not guaranteed that said person is able to access the knowledge and contents contained in the object that they have chosen. For this reason, in this article, a solution is proposed: automatic evaluation of the accessibility of learning objects, via a multi-agent system, which will assess the accessibility of learning objects, and make recommendations, in order to improve the object's accessibility.

Keywords: Accessibility · Accessibility evaluation · Learning objects · Agents

1 Introduction

In education, the creation of learning objects is a good alternative to teaching via technological tools [1]. These objects, generally, are stored in repositories, and are available online. However, the accessibility of these objects is unknown, and keeping in mind that currently, internet access is a topic of great importance, thanks to tools, regulations, strategies and internet accessibility standards on an international level [2–9]. This suggests that learning objects should also comply with these internet accessibility guidelines. Learning object repositories are tools that manage educational content [10], for which one must also possess knowledge of which stored resources are and are not accessible. This knowledge would help with the process of personalization, giving users resources which match their characteristics. That said, this article proposes the evaluation of learning object accessibility, using agents. These agents will validate the accessibility of learning object content, and thus, recommend ways for users to make their objects more accessible.

The remainder of the paper it is organized as follows: Sect. 2 is a conceptual revision the main related concepts. Section 3 reviews related work in the area; Sect. 4 describes the proposed model to the accessibility evaluation of learnings objects. Section 5 explains the model implementation; the results of the proposed model,

© Springer International Publishing AG 2017
J. Bajo et al. (Eds.): PAAMS 2017 Workshops, CCIS 722, pp. 420–429, 2017.
DOI: 10.1007/978-3-319-60285-1_36

through a case study it is presented in Sect. 6. Finally, the main conclusions and future research directions it shows in Sect. 7.

2 Basic Concept

To develop the proposal presented in this work in this section some conceptual elements are explain:

Accessibility: accessibility is a characteristic that represents the facility that offer the products or service to a person's regardless of their physical, social, psychological, educative or cultural conditions [11].

Learning Objects (LO): a learning object is a digital resource that have metadata's and characteristics that allow the facility of understand and learn the knowledge that the object content [12]. The learning object had metadata's that explain their characteristics and usually are storage in repositories.

Accessibility Evaluation: the accessibility evaluation is the process where is validate if a content of a resource is or not accessible for persons with or without disabilities [9, 13].

Learning Objects Repositories: the repositories are platforms that storage the learning objects and where the user can search and access to the LO [10].

3 Related Works

In this section, we present some works related to accessible learning objects, the process of evaluating the accessibility of learning objects and the use of agents to solve problems of learning objects.

In works like [11], it exposed the problematic of the accessibility of the educative resources or learning objects, for that reason in this article the authors propose to the accessibility evaluation of the educative resources, using automatic and manual tools to did the validation of the accessibility. So that in the article [12] it is purposed a methodology to create and produce accessible learning objects and in the article [13] it is purposed an educational metadata profile to characterize the educative resources.

Other works like [14], shows the need of mechanism to evaluate learning objects for that reason the authors propose a model to co-create and evaluate inclusive an accessible open educational resources, this model it can use by the teachers to create and evaluate educational resources. The same problem is resolve in the article [15], but in this work the author propose a framework to evaluate the quality of the multimedia learning resources.

Previously in others works of Salazar, Duque y Ovalle use agents to solve a problem with the recommendation of educative resources [16]. Also to solve the same problem with agents, in the works [17, 18], shows different strategies applying agents to recommended educative resources.

Of all articles found, the only where propose an automatically evaluation of the metadata is the article [19], where develop a service to evaluate automatically the metadata of the learning objects. However, any of the works founded apply agents or other technique to do the accessibility evaluation of the metadata learning object. For that reason in this work was used agents because this technique allow advantages like work in parallel, autonomy of the agents, scalability of agent behavior and other characteristics that facilitate the evaluation of the learning object in comparison with other applications.

4   Proposal

This investigation proposes the application of a multi-agent system for the evaluation of learning object accessibility in a repository. To carry out this evaluation, an agent will validate, within the learning object's metadata, those rules which permit the establishment of the level of accessibility of said learning object.

In Fig. 1, details of the functioning of the proposed multi-agent system model may be found. This model was create based on the agents that are necessary to did the

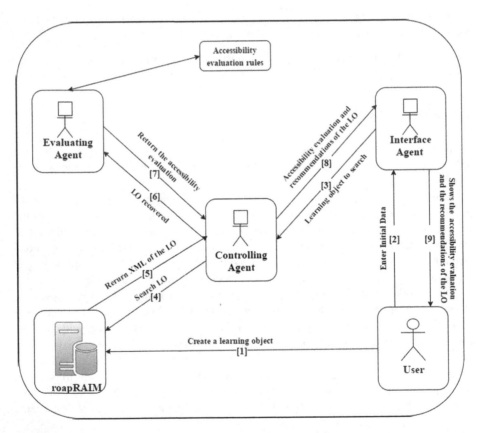

Fig. 1. Multi-agent system model

simulation and the accessibility rules that were defined using some characteristics de other works.

The elements that form part of the proposed multi-agent system model are described in the following paragraph.

User: this will be the creator of the learning object, which will store it in a learning object repository called roapRAIM. Later, it will use the multi-agent system, entering the name and identifier for the learning object to be evaluated.

roapRAIM: this is a repository for learning objects, where the user will store their learning objects. This repository was specifically selected because it offers the possibility of adding specific metadata, which support accessibility level identification. Additionally, it offers a service, which permits the multi-agent system to collect metadata in xml format.

Interface Agent: this agent receive the name and identification data of the learning object, to carry out the accessibility evaluation. It will be further charged with showing the results of the evaluation process, and associated accessibility recommendations.

Controlling Agent: this agent is in charge of receiving data from the Interface Agent, in order to complete the xml query with the LO's (learning object) metadata, via the service offered by the repository. Following obtention of the xml, this will be sent to the evaluating agent for LO evaluation. The results results of said evaluation are sent back, and the Controlling Agent delivers them to the Interface Agent, so that the user can visualize the results.

Evaluating Agent: this agent, upon receiving the LO's xml, as sent by the Controlling Agent, will carry out an analysis of the metadata, in accordance with the following ten rules:

1. If the LO had the metadata <lom:tittle>.
2. If the LO had more than two keywords in the metadata <lom:keywords>.
3. If the LO had the metadata <lom:description>.
4. If the LO had the metadata <lom:language> in the category <lom:general>.
5. If the LO had the metadata <lom:interactivetype>.
6. If the LO had the metadata <lom:learningresourcetype>.
7. If the LO had the metadata <lom:interactivitylevel>.
8. If the LO had the metadata <lom:semanticdensity>.
9. If the LO had the metadata <lom:language> in the category <lom:educational>.
10. If the LO had the metadata <lom:auditory> or <lom:textual> or <lom:visual> or <lom:keyboard> or <lom:mouse> or <lom:voicerecognition> or <lom:audiodescription> or <lom:hearingalternative> or <lom:textualalternative> or <lom:signlanguage> or <lom:subtitles>.

In this first review, each of the rules will have a value of one, because, should a LO comply with each rule; it will have an accessibility level of 10, on a scale of 1–10.

Following the first review, the agent will continue with the second revision, where an analysis to determine which disabled people can access this object will be completed. For this, the agent applies the following rules:

1. [Learning Resource Type (narrative text) ∨ Learning Resource Type (lecture) ∨ Learning Resource Type (audio)], then is accessible to a person with visual null disability.
2. [Learning Resource Type (narrative text) ∨ Learning Resource Type (lecture) ∨ Learning Resource Type (audio)], then is accessible to a person with visual low disability.
3. [Learning Resource Type (diagram) ∨ Learning Resource Type (self-assessment) ∨ Learning Resource Type (simulation) ∨ Learning Resource Type (questionnaire) ∨ Learning Resource Type (slide)], then is accessible to a person with hearing null disability.
4. [Learning Resource Type (diagram) ∨ Learning Resource Type (figure) ∨ Learning Resource Type (graph) ∨ Learning Resource Type (self-assessment) ∨ Learning Resource Type (table)], then is accessible to a person with hearing low disability.
5. If in <lom:voicerecognition> the metadata is yes, then is accesible to a person with motor disability.
6. If in <lom:auditory> or <lom:keyboard> the metadata is yes, then is accesible to person withmotor disability.
7. If in <lom:voicerecognition> or <lom:audiodescription> or <lom:hearingalternative> the metadata is yes, then is accessible to a person with visual disability.
8. If in <lom:textual> or <lom:visual> or <lom:textualalternative> or <lom:signlanguage> or <lom:subtitles> the metadata is yes, then is accesible to a person with hearing disability.

After this second review, the agent will send obtained data to the Controlling Agent, the Controlling Agent will send them to the interface agent, and the user can observe the results of the LO accessibility evaluation.

5   Development of the Proposal

The multi-agent system developed was made using the JAVA language, which permits the use of the JADE (Java Agent Development Kit) framework. Additionally, a swing library was used for the construction of the graphic interface. The user interacts with this part of the system. For the obtention of the xml with learning object metadata, the roapRAIM storage service was used.

The system presented in Fig. 2 is the result of the development of a multi-agent system, based on the proposed model.

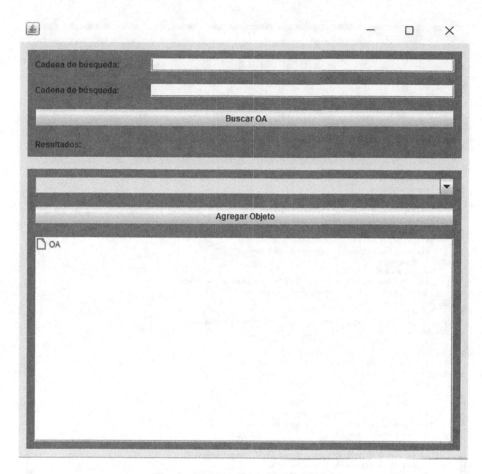

Fig. 2. Multi-agent system interface.

6 Results

In order to complete multi-agent system tests, an evaluation of the accessibility of 5 learning objects was performed, with the following results.

In the Fig. 3, it can show the test that was made, in the test it search learning objects that are related to "*agua*" for that reason in the first field search string "*agua*" was put on. In the second field search string was not put on nothing because that field is to the learning object id but in this test was prefer did the search of all the object that comply with search string and select the learning objects that we want. The results of the search was twelve learning object, which are displayed in a list where is chosen the LO to be evaluated. After that the system apply the rules and delivery the results of the learning object accessibility evaluation.

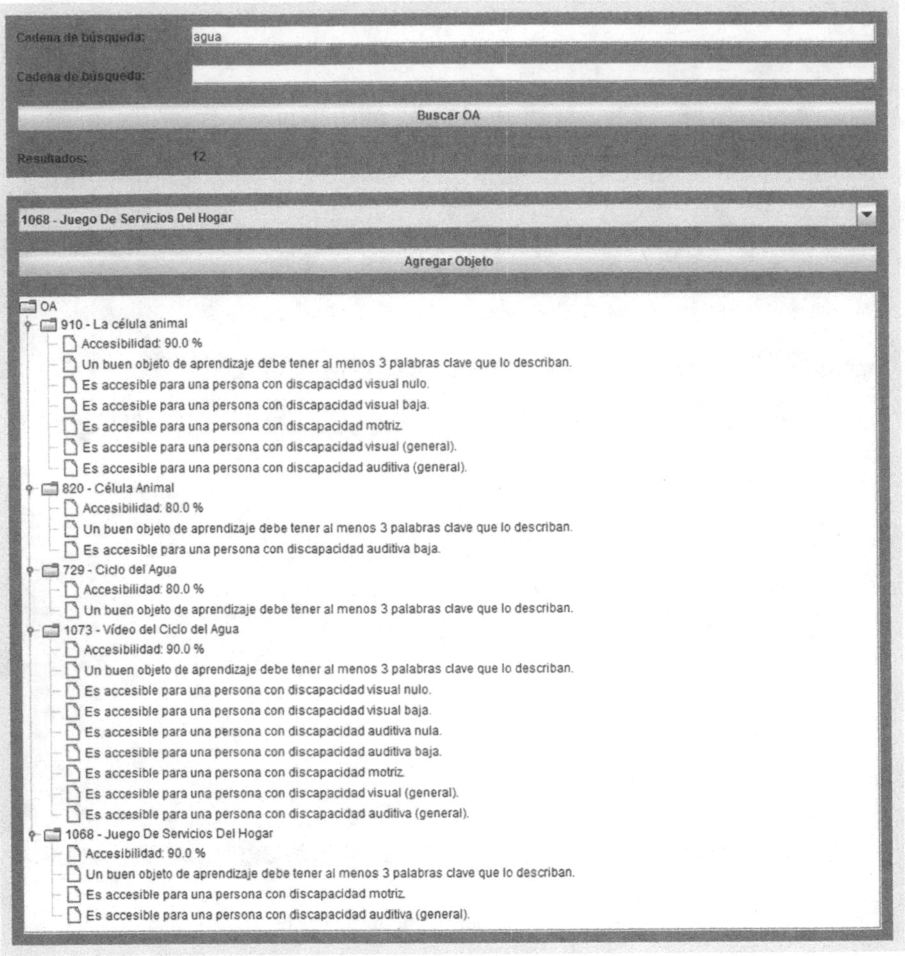

Fig. 3. Test of the multi-agent system

In Fig. 4, it can shows the percentage of the accessibility evaluation of the learning object, where it can perceive that the accessibility average of the five learning objects of roapRAIM is 86% and the accessibility average varies between 80% and 90%.

Figure 5, shows the analysis of the learning object and the users with disabilities that may be can use them. The nomenclature of disabilities is as follows: (0 = any; 1 = Visual-Null; 2 = Visual-Low; 3 = Hearing-Null; 4 = Hearing-Low; 5 = Motor; 6 = Visual-General; 7 = Hearing-General).

The results of this test shows the highest accessibility level of the learning objects evaluated, but also two of the five learning objects evaluated can be access for three type of persons with different disabilities.

The performance of the automatic accessibility evaluation results are good for the accessibility level obtain of the roapRAIM learning objects. These results serves to improve the learning object that don´t comply with a minimum accessibility level and thus ensure that the repository going to have only accessible learning resources.

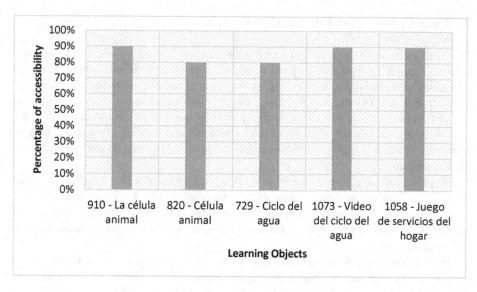

Fig. 4. Results of test of the multi-agent system

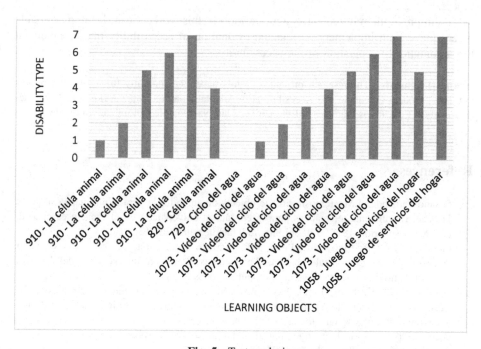

Fig. 5. Test analysis.

7   Conclusions and Future Work

The rules to evaluate the metadata's of the learning objects only work for the learning objects of roapRAIM because they use a metadata standard LOM with other metadata's of accessibility. However, if other repository want to use the multi-agent system purposed in this article, only had to change the accessible evaluation rules in the model and it can do the evaluation of his learning objects below their metadata's standard.

Using agents for the evaluation of learning object accessibility is a good option, as it permits automatic analysis of whether LO contents allow user access, regardless of their condition.

Having accessible learning objects is a very important step for repositories, since they will be able to guarantee that any user can employ their learning objects.

Creating new automatic accessibility evaluation strategies, through the use of agents, is an area which can be further explored, in order to obtain improved accessibility evaluations.

How future work is define more rule to permit the evaluation of more characteristics of the LO that was not considerate in this work. Also do more test with a quantity more bigger of learning objects.

Other future work is create in the multi-agent system a recommender agent that explain to the user the characteristics that had to considered to do an accessible learning object.

To improve the multi-agent system develop in this work, it can develop a module where the system implement the manual evaluation of accessibility that complement the automatically evaluation of the accessibility.

Acknowledgments. The research presented in this paper was partially funded by the project entitled: "Modelo Orientado a la Accesibilidad y Adaptatividad en Repositorios y Federaciones de Recursos Educativos Digitales" of the Universidad Nacional de Colombia, with code 35806.

References

1. Solano Fernandez I.M.: Repositorios de objetos de aprendizaje para la enseñanza superior: Dspace. Herramienta telemáticas para la enseñanza universitaria en el espacio europeo de educación superior, 18 (2007). doi:http://hdl.handle.net/10201/13419
2. Góngora, R.A., Rodríguez, A., León, Y.P., Capote, T.G.: Guía para evaluar Usabilidad, Accesibilidad y Comunicabilidad en Aplicaciones Web con Intervención del Usuario. Revista Antioqueña de las Ciencias Computacionales 2, 59–64 (2013)
3. Santarosa, L.M.C., Conforto, D., Passerino, L.M.: Tecnologías Digitales Accesibles (2011)
4. Persson, H., Åhman, H., Yngling, A.A., Gulliksen, J.: Universal design, inclusive design, accessible design, design for all: different concepts—one goal? On the concept of accessibility—historical, methodological and philosophical aspects. Univers. Access Inf. Soc. **14**, 505–526 (2015). doi:10.1007/s10209-014-0358-z
5. Productivo, Programa. Manual de Accesibilidad Informática (2010)

6. Miñón, R., Moreno, L., Martínez, P., Abascal, J.: An approach to the integration of accessibility requirements into a user interface development method. Sci. Comput. Program. **86**, 58–73 (2014). doi:10.1016/j.scico.2013.04.005. Elsevier B.V.
7. Moreta, C., Baena, R.L.: Pautas, métodos y herramientas de evaluación de accesibilidad web. Universidad de Manizales, Facultad de Ciencias e Ingeniería, pp. 99–115 (2013)
8. Mayor, Universidad. Recursos para fomentar la Accesibilidad Tecnológica en la Comunidad : La tecnología como herramienta de apoyo en la Educación Especial y la Discapacidad, pp. 1–190 (2011)
9. Mascaraque, E.S.: Herramientas para la evaluación de la accesibilidad Web, pp. 245–266 Universidad de Alcalá (2009)
10. López Guzmán, C.: Los Repositorios de Objetos de Aprendizaje como soporte a un entorno e-learning: 152 (2005)
11. Duque, N., Ospina, A., Londoño, L.F., Tabares, V.: Evaluación de Accesibilidad de Recursos Educativos Digitales Multimedia. Revista Ingeniería e Innovación **3**(1), 90–97 (2015)
12. Di Iorio, A., Feliziani, A.A., Mirri, S., Salomoni, P., Vitali, F.: Automatically producing accessible learning objects. Educ. Technol. Soc. **9**, 3–16 (2006)
13. Solomou, G., Pierrakeas, C., Kameas, A.: Characterization of educational resources in e-learning systems using an educational metadata profile. Educ. Technol. Soc. **18**, 246–260 (2015)
14. Avila, C., Baldiris, S., Fabregat, R., Graf, S.: Cocreation and evaluation of inclusive and accessible open educational resources: a mapping toward the IMS caliper. Revista Iberoamericana de Tecnologias del Aprendizaje **11**, 167–176 (2016). doi:10.1109/RITA. 2016.2589578
15. Leacock, T.L., Nesbit, J.C.: A framework for evaluating the quality of multimedia learning resources. Educ. Technol. Soc. **10**, 44–59 (2007). doi:10.1017/CBO9781107415324.004
16. Salazar, O.M., Ovalle, D.A., Duque, N.D.: Sistema Multi-Agente para Recomendación de Recursos Educativos utilizando Servicios de Awareness y Dispositivos Móviles, pp. 73–82
17. Jacqueline, S., Chacón-Rivas, M., Garita, C.: Agente Híbrido Recomendador de Objetos de Aprendizaje. In: IX Conferencia Latinoamericana de Objetos y Tecnologías de Aprendizaje, pp. 290–301 (2014)
18. Veloso, B., Malheiro, B., Burguillo, J.C.: A multi-agent brokerage platform for media content recommendation. Int. J. Appl. Math. Comput. Sci. **25**, 513–527 (2015). doi:10.1515/amos 2015 0038
19. Osorio, Y.A., Trejos, J.S.E., Morales, V.T., Mendez, N.D.D.: Web service to support recovery of learning objects in repositories and federations | Servicio Web para Apoyo a la Recuperación de Objetos de Aprendizaje en Repositorios y Federaciones. In: Proceedings - 2016 11th Latin American Conference on Learning Objects and Technology, LACLO 2016 (2016). doi:10.1109/LACLO.2016.7751796

SCIA

Transport Network Analysis for Smart Open Fleets

Miguel Rebollo, Carlos Carrascosa, and Vicente Julian$^{(\boxtimes)}$

D. Sistemas Informáticos y Computación,
Universitat Politècnica de València, Valencia, Spain
{mrebollo,carrasco,vinglada}@dsic.upv.es

Abstract. Current techniques for intelligent computing based on Multi-Agent Systems and Agreement Technologies can improve the management and control of transport fleets, both for human or goods mobility, in an urban environment. These technologies can offer services to users that are globally optimized and adapted to the changing needs and demands, but also, promoting an efficient use of available resources. In this way it is possible to improve the sustainability of traffic in urban areas, improve energy efficiency and increase the welfare of citizens. To do this it is necessary to provide complex services which offer critical information in order to reason and take decisions. This paper describes the use of complex network analysis as a way to predict the behaviour of the transport network in a city. This service can be used as a way to improve the use of incentives, argumentation or social reputation techniques for the automatic management of urban fleets.

1 Introduction

During last decades, the increase of human mobility and transportation in urban environments presents one of the challenges facing our today's society. It is one of the causes of congestion problems, inefficiencies in logistics and energy use, and air pollution in modern cities. To approach this challenge, innovative solutions for communication networks, information processing, and transport are required in order to assure a more efficient use of resources (vehicles, energy resources, roads, etc.) while also ensuring time flexible mobility solutions for citizens and businesses. The idea of smart cities requires new challenges and claims for new solutions related to traffic and transport. As a direct result, systems that promote the shared use of vehicles have begun to emerge. The main idea behind such systems is to maximize the utilization of vehicles for transportation tasks by reducing the times vehicles are idle. Instead of using private vehicles for a limited number of (private) transportation tasks, vehicles are used by different users, maximizing in this way their utilization. This is the case, for instance, of the bicycle-sharing systems available for shared use to individuals in many cities.

We call this type of solutions "open fleets". Similar to the traditional fleet concept, an open fleet requires a global regulatory entity that manages and coordinates the use of a limited set of resources in order to provide a specific

© Springer International Publishing AG 2017
J. Bajo et al. (Eds.): PAAMS 2017 Workshops, CCIS 722, pp. 433–444, 2017.
DOI: 10.1007/978-3-319-60285-1_37

transportation service. However, open fleets extend the traditional fleet concept towards a new dimension of openness: vehicles may interact with their environment in a Smart city, or join and leave the fleet at any time. Most important, however, the capacity of the global regulatory entity to control the fleet in its entirety may vary considerably. There may be fleets that are totally controllable, and others that allow for very limited control only, as is the case, for instance, in a public bicycle service, where a user will usually decide by himself which bike to take and he will return it at the station he likes to.

The efficiency of an open fleet depends on the use of appropriated coordination and regulation mechanisms that deal with the problem of balancing global and individual objectives. The aim is to maximize the achievement of individual needs and preferences but at the same time assuring an efficient operation with regard to some globally desirable parameters. Regarding the coordination problem of urban fleet, this has traditionally been studied for more closed fleets in different areas, and its impact, especially in the field of emergency services [1]. In recent years research has been extended to the coordination of fleets for vehicles sharing [7].

This work starts from the development of an integrated solution for the management, coordination and regulation of fleets in general, and of open fleets in particular (with different degrees of control capacity of the regulatory entity). The proposed solution, initially described in [2], is based on a set of informatics tools and components that allow the application of different persuasion techniques in order to convince users/driver to act in a specific way, such as incentives, argumentation, social reputation, etc. [3,5,6]. Furthermore, trust and reputation mechanisms may be used to estimate the future behavior of drivers/users based on an analysis of their historic behaviors. Such information may be helpful when deciding on how to persuade a specific person, or when estimating the probability of success of a given assignment and/or deployment solution.

The above commented solution, that was devised in a framework, needs the use of complex services which provide critical information in order to reason and take decisions. In this sense, transport services in a city can be seen as a complex network where nodes represent stations and stops of public transportation systems, and edges connect consecutive stations along a route [8,9]. In the last decade, the area of complex networks has been confirmed as a powerful tool to simplify, analyze and visualize huge amounts of data and discover interactions. Transport networks can be studied adopting this approach to explore their topological characteristics, such as the small-world properties, communities structure, and other statistical properties including static and dynamic aspects of the network. In this sense, we can find previous works as [4,10–12] where the city can be seen as a combination of elements (public transports) interconnected among them showing the relevance of the use of multiplex networks to model transportation network.

Besides the proper information related with the city transport infrastructures, additional information about the citizens' activity can be included. The activity of the people in social networks or phone call logs can be geotagged, analyzed and integrated with the rest of the information as a spatial network. In that way, real-time information about the usage of the resources of the transport network is also available for its analysis. For this reason, the existing framework has been extended with a new module called Transport Network Analysis Module (TNAM), which is the main focus of the work presented in this paper.

The rest of the paper is structured as follows: next section comments the related work; Sect. 2 details not only the framework but the new proposed module and its connections; Sect. 3 explains the new module and the related graphs algorithms used; Sect. 4 discuss about how the new module can be used to improve the services offered by the rest of the framework; and finally, Sect. 5 present some general conclusions.

2 Extended Open Fleet Management Framework

The Framework here presented is an extension of the one presented in [2]. This framework presents a series of services and utilities to be used for open fleet management, and it is shown in Fig. 1. This architecture is divided into three layers. The first one is called "Fleet Operator", and includes the basic components used for global fleet control and monitoring. The second one is called "Fleet Coordination", and it is the heart of the architecture, with all the different perception inputs, task assignments and vehicle deployments that allow such coordination. The upper layer is the one related to the agents associated to the vehicles and public transport stations forming the fleet. These agents provide

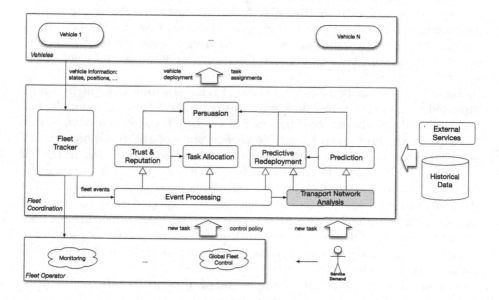

Fig. 1. General architecture for open fleets

information about vehicle status, position, ... and they also receive information to be displayed to the vehicle driver.

In the Fleet Coordination layer, a Fleet Tracker follows the operational states and positions of the vehicles. It informs the Event Processing module about any changes in the fleet that would require an adaptation of the task allocations and/or the deployment of idle vehicles. The Transport Network Analysis module (this is the new addition to the framework and will be detailed in the next section) gives information not only of the different static transport networks with the different stops and routes available for each public transport, but also of the on-line traffic available in such routes. The Event Processing module analyses the incoming events (state changes of vehicles and new task events) and determines whether or not a re-calculation of task assignments and/or deployment of idle vehicles should be done. If necessary, it triggers the execution of the task allocation and predictive redeployment modules. The Task Allocation module, when executed, re-calculates the optimal global assignment of all pending tasks (in the current moment) to vehicles, based on a set of assignment criteria (depending on the application domain). The Predictive Redeployment module, calculates adequate positions for all idle vehicles at the current moment taking into account predictions concerning the appearance of new tasks (based on historical data) and the current state of the fleet.

Prediction is carried out taking into account not only historical data, but also the current state of the transport network (given by the TNAM) and other external sources (e.g. weather forecast, leisure events, etc.). Depending on the application domain, new tasks can be triggered by fleet users (clients) by communicating with the fleet operators or directly with the fleet coordination layer.

In order to deal with the (possible high) autonomy of vehicles, we include persuasion and trust and reputation modules in the architecture. The Persuasion module is in charge of providing actions for inducing agents (vehicles) to carry out the actions that tend to improve the overall performance measure of the system.

Information about previous experience of vehicles within the system can be exploited so as to take better decisions. The Trust and Reputation module is in charge of modeling the expected behavior of agents in the system using feedback provided by the fleet tracker, and the current state of the transport network provided by the TNAM. That information is used at least in two different though related ways: (i) what actions have to be chosen and (ii) how agents can be influenced accordingly. For instance, in a vehicle renting scenario, the information about liability of users to return vehicles at the expected time can be used for estimating the number of available resources, which is important for task allocation decision. Likewise, the information given to a particular user in the course of an explanation or persuasion dialogue can be different depending on his/her expected behavior.

It is important to note that, depending on each particular case, not all modules described in the architecture are necessarily implemented.

As has been commented, next section details the TNAM module and the graph algorithms it is based on.

3   Transport Network Analysis Module (TNAM)

The Transport Network Analysis Module (TNAM) is a component of the framework responsible of the analysis of the transport network of the city, taking into account the physical structure of the different lines and the usage that citizens make of the different media. This module combines techniques of complex network and spatial network analysis, as well as the information available from the activity of the people that can be obtained from social networks, phone call registers and open data portals.

Many approaches consider each transport media as an isolated network, but recent studies have shown that the infrastructures are related and the effects of some events in one of them produce cascades that eventually may affect to other networks. Therefore, to consider the transport network as a multilayer network allows the study of these situations.

A multilayer network is a network of networks in which each layer is a network itself [4]. In the case of transport networks, each layer represents a different transport media. The nodes of the network are stops is a bus or metro line. An edge is created between two nodes if there is a direct connexion between these stops.

But there are transport media in which there is no fixed lines, such as taxi services, bike rental or car sharing services. In those cases, a network have to be generated. The TNAM uses spatial networks techniques to generate a structure that can be integrated in the multilayer network.

Figure 2 shows the multilayer graph of the public transport in the city of Valencia (Spain). Each one of the layers composing such graph represents a different public transport. The Transport Network Analysis module of the proposed architecture makes use of this graph, being able to calculate paths where two or more changes of public transport have to be made (even changing the type of public transport).

Lets consider the bike sharing service of the city of Valencia. Using the position of the stations, a Voronoi diagram is generated (Fig. 3). Each region around a station is defined as the set of points that are closer to this station than to any other. This representation defines a tessellation of the city that allow to identify without ambiguity the position of the bikes. The dual graph that links each vertex of adjacent Voronoi regions is the Delaunay triangulation. When the user rides the bike across the city, the route passes through several Voronoi regions. We can create a path through the stations associated with each one of these regions, which will be a path over the Delaunay triangulation. Therefore, the Dealunay triangulation can be consider the associated network for the bike sharing service.

Once the network has been created, it can be characterized by some structural measures. The distribution of the average degree does not follow a power law

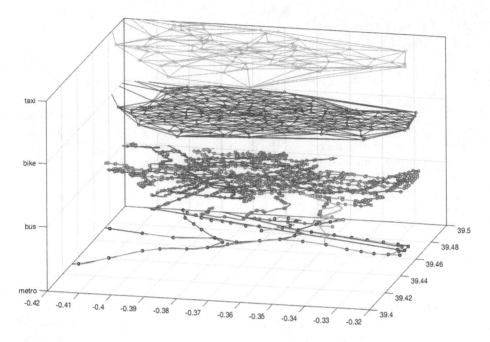

Fig. 2. Multi-layered graph of public transport in the city of Valencia (metro, bus, bikes and taxi, from lower to upper layer).

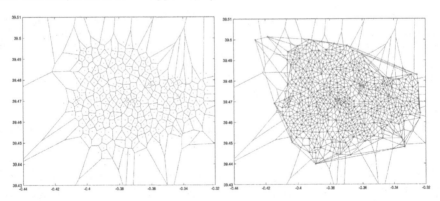

Fig. 3. Map with the stations of the bike sharing service. Voronoi diagram with the area associated to each station and the corresponding network generated from the Delaunay triangulation

distribution, as it can be seen in Fig. 4. Therefore, we can conclude that the structure of the network is not a small-world one. The rest of the characteristics are:

- No. nodes: 275
- No. edges: 810
- average degree: 5.9 ± 0.9

- average shortest path length: 6.6
- network diameter: 13.

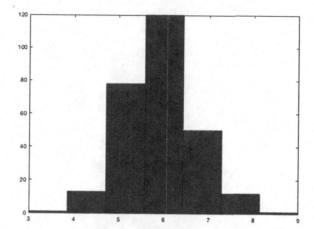

Fig. 4. Degree distribution of the bike sharing network. Clearly it is not a power law distribution, so the network cannot be considered a smal-world network.

Another relevant measure in the network are centrality measures. They determine the relative importance of one station in the network attending to different criteria (see Fig. 5). The degree centrality defines the importance of the nodes according to its degree. The more neighbors one station has, the more important it is in the network. In this case, as the degree distribution follows a Poisson distribution (typical in random networks), there is no specially relevant station. This characteristic makes the network robust and failure tolerant, since the failure in any station barely affects to the rest of the network.

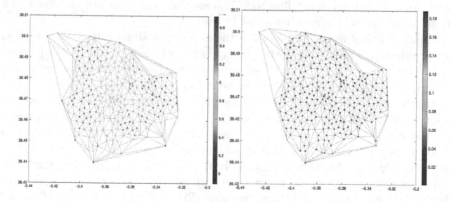

Fig. 5. Centrality measures. Closeness (distance to the rest of the stations) and betweenness (number of shortest paths that pass through the region).

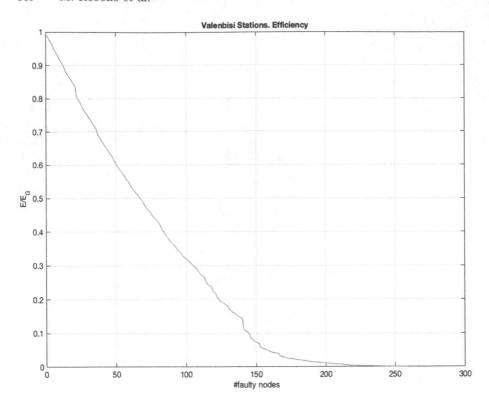

Fig. 6. The efficiency of the network decays linearly when stations fails randomly

A second centrality measure is the closeness. It is defined as the inverse of the sum of the distances to all the rest of the stations. The more central a node is the lower total distance it has from all other nodes. In this case, the nodes in the center of the city typically has a higher closeness value. But we can identify other areas with high centrality too. Travels from this stations minimize the length of the paths to any other point in the city.

Finally, the betweenness quantifies the number of times one station acts as a bridge in the shortest paths between any two stations. As many paths pass by these nodes, the state of the station can affect to the total performance of the network. Besides, these stations use to be critical under failures.

Another measure that can be considered is the efficiency of the network. It measures the global distance among all the nodes. The shorter the paths are and the more connected the network is, the more efficient the network will be. When a station fails, it cannot be used in a path, and the distances in the city will be longer. Eventually, the network can be broken in isolated parts. The efficiency is the proportion between the current network efficiency and the ideal efficiency when all the nodes and paths are available. Figure 6 shows how the efficiency of the bike sharing network decays when stations are eliminated randomly one

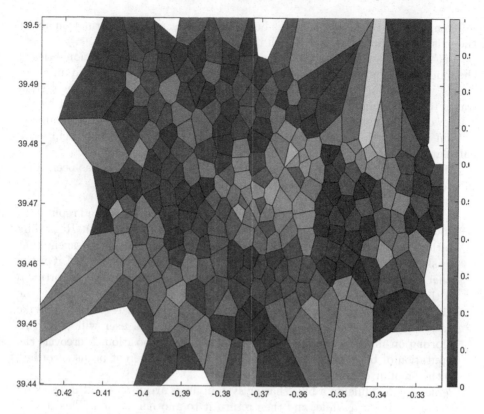

Fig. 7. If the information about the occupation of the stations is included in real time in the Voronoi diagram, a density map of the city can be obtained.

by one. In this case, an empty or full station is considered as a failure in the system, and it even can be studied how these failures propagates along the network generating a cascade of failures in the adjoining stations.

All these measures are structural and they do not change unless new stations are added to the network. But there is additional information about the real usage of the service that can be used to improve the performance of the service. In the case of Valencia, the open data portal provides the occupation of each station in real time. This information can be used to determine which areas are more crowd or even to predict the future behavior of the users. These data can be also added to the TNAM. For example, we add to the Voronoi diagram the occupation of the corresponding station and draw a density map of the city (Fig. 7).

4 Discussion

The new Transport Network Analysis Module is an addition to the existing Open Fleet architecture that allows to manage not only static information about the different public transports networks but also dynamic on-line information about the existing traffic related with such transports.

Let's take a look at how the proposed module improves the functionalities of the modules in charge of offering agreement services. To comment such improvements, we are going to use the following scenario: A user of a bike sharing system wants to go to point B from its current location. The solution provided by the framework may not be the shortest one, because this path could be jammed. It is in this situation where the TNAM, between other things, may help us to calculate this solution.

Moreover, the information provided by the TNAM is used, as has been commented before, in other modules of the framework:

- Trust and Reputation Module: The framework includes a trust and reputation model for all the agents in the system (vehicles and stations). Regarding stations, the trust of an agent depends on the distance from the agent that is asking the information. This distance is provided by the TNAM. On the other hand, reputation of agents modelling stations is inversely proportional to the traffic on such station (also provided by the TNAM). Following the bike sharing transport, when a user asks for information regarding the bike stations in his path from his position to point B, the user will trust this information more as the bike station is closer to his position. Moreover, the reputation of bike stations allow to decide between different paths according to the amount of traffic in such stations.
- Persuasion Module: in a bike-sharing system users arrive at a station, pick up a bike, use it for a while, and then return it to another station. This station is selected by the user. Each station cannot host more bikes than its capacity. This finite capacity usually generates conflicts with users when they try to return a bike and the station is full. In this sense, users can be persuaded by the system using simple incentives users to return to the least loaded station among nearest stations. The TNAM can facilitate the analysis of the nearest stations to the station selected by the user. Moreover, when a user wants to return the bike somewhere, the bike-sharing system indicates to the user which one of the nearest stations has the highest probability to have empty spots.
- Redeployment Module: in order to improve the quality of the service, bikes are usually moved among stations (from stations with a high load to stations with low load). The redeployment module allows to compute the rate at which bikes have to be redistributed by trucks for a given quality of service. The main goal is to minimize the number of redeployments while maintaining the quality of the service. This calculation can be improved with the information provided by the TNAM.
- Predictive Module: To obtain the best quality of service possible, it is not only needed to try to avoid errors as much as possible, but to minimize the effect of such errors if they are produced (trying to avoid the cascade effect). This module is the one in charge of making these two kinds of predictions, using historical data, and the information about the current state of the network

provided by the TNAM. The actions to carry out to avoid these errors include services of the persuasion and redeployment modules.

5   Conclusions

Open urban fleets, like bike or car sharing systems, have proliferated in last years. This kind of fleets offer different advantages like the reduction of the number of vehicles exclusively dedicated to a transportation service and, also, the possibility to adapt, in a flexible way, the size of the fleet to varying service demands. Nevertheless, fleets of this kind require new solution approaches for their management. In this sense, agreement technologies like trust & reputation, persuasion and task allocation can be useful to develop coordination and regulation mechanisms that deal with the problem of balancing global and individual objectives. This paper explores the use of complex network theories through the development of a software module that provides an analysis of the transport network of a city, taking into account the physical structure of the different lines and the usage that citizens make of the different media. This module has been included in an integrated framework which offers a series of services and utilities to be used for open fleet management. The functionalities offered by this new module allow the enhancement of the agreement technologies provided by the framework.

Acknowledgements. This work was supported by the project TIN2015-65515-C4-1-R of the Spanish government.

References

1. Aboueljinane, L., et al.: A review on simulation models applied to emergency medical service operations. Comput. Ind. Eng. **66**(4), 734–750 (2013)
2. Billhardt, H., Fernández, A., Lujak, M., Ossowski, S., Julián, V., Paz, J.F., Hernándoz, J.Z.: Towards smart open dynamic fleets. In: Rovatsos, M., Vouros, G., Julian, V. (eds.) EUMAS/AT -2015. LNCS, vol. 9571, pp. 410–424. Springer, Cham (2016). doi:10.1007/978-3-319-33509-4_32
3. Castelfranchi, C., Falcone, R.: Trust Theory: A Socio-Cognitive and Computational Model. Wiley, New York (2010)
4. Kivelä, M., et al.: Multilayer networks. J. Complex. Netw. **2**(3), 203–271 (2014)
5. Koster, A., Sabater-Mir, J., Schorlemmer, M.: Argumentation and trust. In: Ossowski, S. (ed.) Agreement Technologies, pp. 441–451. Springer, Netherlands (2012)
6. Modgil, S., et al.: The added value of argumentation. In: Ossowski, S. (ed.) Agreement Technologies, pp. 357–403. Springer, Netherlands (2012)
7. Nair, R., et al.: Large-scale vehicle sharing systems: analysis of Vélib. Int. J. Sustain. Transp. **7**, 85–106 (2013)
8. Haznagy, A., Fi, I., London, A., Németh, T.: Complex network analysis of public transportation networks: a comprehensive study. In: Proceedings of 4th Models and Technologies for Intelligent Transportation Systems (MT-ITS) Conference, pp. 371–378 (2015)

9. Zhong, C., et al.: Detecting the dynamics of urban structure through spatial network analysis. Int. J. Geogr. Inf. Sci. **28**(11), 2178–2199 (2014)
10. Tsiotas, D., Polyzos, S.: Decomposing multilayer transportation networks using complex network analysis: a case study for the Greek aviation network. J. Complex Netw. **3**(4), 642–670 (2015)
11. Aleta, A., Meloni, S., Moreno, Y. A multilayer perspective for the analysis of urban transportation systems. arXiv:1607.00072 [physics.soc-ph] (2016)
12. Gallotti, R., Barthelemy, M.: The multilayer temporal network of public transport in Great Britain. Sci. Data **2**, 140056 (2015)

WSNs in FIWARE – Towards the Development of People-Centric Applications

Ngombo Armando[1,2(✉)], Duarte Raposo[1], Marcelo Fernandes[1],
André Rodrigues[1,3], Jorge Sá Silva[1], and Fernando Boavida[1]

[1] Centre for Informatics and Systems of the University of Coimbra (CISUC),
University of Coimbra, 3030-290 Coimbra, Portugal
{narmando, sasilva, boavida}@dei.uc.pt,
{draposo, jmfernandes}@student.dei.uc.pt
[2] Escola Superior Politécnica do Uíge, Universidade Kimpa Vita, Uíge, Angola
[3] ISCAC, Polytechnic Institute of Coimbra, 3040-316 Coimbra, Portugal
andre@iscac.pt

Abstract. Wireless Sensors Networks (WSNs) form the founding block of the Internet of Things (IoT) Sensing Layer. In IoT scenarios, programmers will make the most of IoT if they focus on the development of context-aware applications rather than managing low-level aspects of the network they run on. To this end, providing harmonized data models eases the development of applications. Focusing on crossbow-micaZ sensors, we present an approach to integrate a heterogeneous WSN platform into FIWARE, towards the development of people-centric applications.

Keywords: WSN · FIWARE · micaZ · Heterogeneity · People-IoT interactions · Context-aware application

1 Introduction

IoT is an extension of computer networks and the Internet to connected devices labeled "things" [1]. Currently, there are more than 22 billion connected devices, and this figure should reach over 50 billion by 2020[1]. The exact definition of IoT is still evolving since it was first proposed in 1999 [2]. However, the concept of IoT has rapidly grown to the idea of *Internet of All* where users are humans, machines, and devices, and the network conveys the sensed features of the physical world. In the end, the Internet will provide a larger scale computing system to carry any measurable state of the physical world like emotions, psychological states, physical states, and actions [1]. The neuronal infrastructure enabling both the acquisition and raw processing of the environment's features is called WSN. For this reason, WSNs form the founding block of IoT/ASensing Layer, which the core functions are in fact sense the environment and actuate on it [3].

A typical WSN is a set of wirelessly connected devices called sensor nodes. In general, sensor nodes are micro or nanosystems with power, storage, computational and

---

[1] statista.com, Accessed at December 4th, 2016.

© Springer International Publishing AG 2017
J. Bajo et al. (Eds.): PAAMS 2017 Workshops, CCIS 722, pp. 445–456, 2017.
DOI: 10.1007/978-3-319-60285-1_38

communication limitations. However, some sensor nodes are personal communication devices with augmented hardware capabilities [4]. Sensor nodes form a network that once deployed commence sensing the environment and report its features to a central node called sink. The sink aggregates the values communicated by the sensor nodes and forwards the packets to a management station. Once in management station, the sensor data is processed to produce information about the state of the target environment [5]. WSNs have application in both monitoring and tracking activities [6–9].

The natural heterogeneity of hardware, software, and protocols technologies under is a critical factor toenhance both resilience and lifetime of WSNs [3, 10]. To this end, heterogeneity must be driven by common specifications so that sensor nodes will be one computing platform at the disposal of smart applications developers. Indeed, there is a diversity of solutions for designing and implementing a WSN which is not always easy for stakeholders to choose and integrate them. These equations become more complexin cases users are not in touch but need each other to mount a virtual common infrastructure [3, 11]. Among the specifications providing standardized API (Application Programming Interface) and harmonized data models there is a European solution labeled FIWARE.

Our work aims at presenting the integration of WSNs in FIWARE, towards the development of people-centric, smart applications. The rest of the article is organized as follows. In next section, an in-depth presentation of FIWARE will be done. In Sect. 3 we will discuss the main object of this work, which is the integration of a heterogeneous WSN platform WSN in FIWARE, towards the development of people-centric, smart applications. We will conclude our work in Sect. 4, by tackling some open issues and challenges.

2   The FIWARE Platform

FIWARE or FI-Ware (where *FI* stands for Future Internet, and the prefix *Ware* stands as analogy referring to a kind of software) is a European set of specifications to provide APIs that ease the development of Smart Applications in multiple vertical sectors. FIWARE is open, public and royalty-free[2].

2.1   Background

The FIWARE project started in 2011 within the Seventh Framework Programme (FP7) of the European Commission as part the Future Internet Public-Private Partnership Programme (FI-PPP). On the one hand, the primary goal of FI-PPP wasto advance a process for a harmonized European technology platforms and their implementation. On the other hand, the aim was to provide integration and harmonization of relevant policies frameworks. The process was divided into three phases. The first phase (from May 2011 to April 2014) was aimed at creating the technological core called FIWARE, while the second phase (from April 2013 to March 2015) was mainly aimed at the

---

[2] fiware.org, accessed on 12/12/2016.

implementation of FIWARE nodes. Finally, the last phase covered from September 2014 to September 2016 and aimed primarily at creating a sustainable ecosystem for Small Medium Enterprises, through the selection of sixteen business accelerators[3]. The ecosystem of developers and entrepreneurs met for the first time at in Malaga, from 13th to 15th December 2016. This meeting was the first in a series of six-monthly events that will be organized by the FIWARE Foundation to surround all those who work to promote the adoption of the technology.

2.2 Architecture

FIWARE is based on a library of components called Generic Enablers (GEs) that are meant to implement APIs. GEs offer reusable and commonly shared functions "as a Service". Through APIs, GEs allow developers to put into effect functionalities making programming much easier by combining them. GEs are classified into seven technical chapters[4], namely:

- *Cloud Hosting.* A set of components to provide computation, storage and network resources on top of which services are provisioned and managed.
- *Data/Context Management.* A set of components to facilitate the access, gathering, processing, publication and analysis of context information at large scale. The enablers here also transform the data into valuable knowledge available to applications.
- *Architecture of Applications/Services Ecosystem and Delivery Framework.* A set of enablers to co-create, publish, cross-sell and consume applications or services, addressing all business aspects.)
- *Interface to Networks and Devices.* A set of components to make the most of the network infrastructure capabilities, building communication-efficient distributed applications, exploiting advanced network capabilities and easily managing robotic devices.)
- *Security.* A set of components to provide mechanisms to make delivery and usage of services trustworthy by meeting security and privacy requirements.
- *Internet of Things Services Enablement.* A set of components to leverage the ubiquity of different devices, making connected things available, searchable, accessible, and usable.
- *Advanced Web-based User Interface.* A set of components to facilitate the use of 3D and Augmented Reality capabilities in web-based user interfaces.

Based on the FIWARE for developers[5] and [12], in Fig. 1 we display an instantiation of FIWARE architecture[6] tailored to approach a generic IoT platform.

---

[3] https://www.fi-ppp.eu, accessed on 12/12/2016.

[4] https://catalogue.fiware.org/, accessed on March 18th, 2017.

[5] https://www.fiware.org/2015/03/27/build-your-own-iot-platform-with-fiware-enablers/, accessed on December 17th, 2016.

[6] https://forge.fiware.org/plugins/mediawiki/wiki/fiware/index.php/FIWARE_Architecture_R3, accessed on December 17th, 2016.

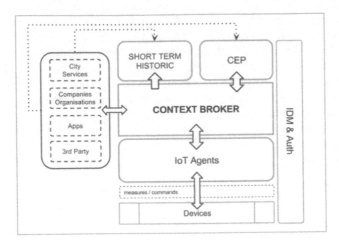

Fig. 1. The FIWARE IoT platform. (https://www.fiware.org/tag/iot/, accessed on March 20th, 2017)

City services/companies & organizations/Apps/3rd Parties are stakeholders that consume, transform and provide an end-utility to the data collected by the Devices.

The Devices refer mainly to the GE Chapter of *Interface to Networks and Devices*. They represent the network of sensors and actuators. Devices are context producers as they provide data to attributes and upload attributes for the entities. Here, a context producers are seen in a broad context where data can be collected through stationary sensors, mobile sensors, personal communication sensors, participatory sensing and Open Data Management Platform like CKAN (Comprehensive Knowledge Archive Network). Among the technical chapters, CKAN refers to *Data/Context Management*.

The IoT Agents refer to the GE Chapter of *Internet of Things Services Enablement*. They are the platform backend to manage Devices. That is, IoT Agents are gateways for the devices to communicate with the rest of the components in FIWARE. Further, IoT Agents act as translators between the communication protocols used by devices, and both a common language and data model across the FIWARE platform called NGSI (for Next Generation Service Interfaces).

The Context broker refers to the GE Chapter of *Data/Context Management*. It is the core and control piece of the platform, in charge of providing virtual representations of devices by developing a data/context scenario.

The Short Term Historic refers to the GE Chapter of *Cloud Hosting*. It is a database to manage the on-the-fly information and quick computational operations by third applications. These operations are performed using a time series database without an intermediate step to process the whole set of data to obtain the desired information. For instance, calculate the minimum, maximum, mean, bias or deviation of a set of data.

The CEP (Complex Event Processing) refers to the GE Chapter of *Data/Context Management*. It is intended to analyze and react to events, generating an immediate response and triggering actions due to changing conditions. It makes possible instant response or reaction to a series of events occurring within a time window (SMS delivery and electronic mail notifications). CEP can be considered as the way to create new data from the arriving data.

Both *IdM* (The Identity Manager) & *Auth* (for authentication) are related to the mechanisms that enable privacy, security, and dependability in delivering services. Security is specified to be a transversal chapter to other chapters. IdM and Auth refer to the GE Chapter of *Security* in charge of carrying the information about users, roles, profiles, sending and validating tokens, and authentication mechanisms. Enablers to identity management and access control policies are complemented by two other elements which are: A Policy Enforcement Point (PEP) and PAP/PDP (for Policy Administration Point/Policy Decision Point).

Some FIWARE-based applications can be found in [13, 14]. In the next Section, we presentan approach to integrate a heterogeneous WSN platform in FIWARE, towards the development of people-centric smart applications.

3 The Integration of WSNs in FIWARE

3.1 The SOCIALITE Project

SOCIALITE[7] (for Social-Oriented Internet of Things Architecture, Solutions, and Environment) is an ongoing project within the Centre for Informatics and Systems of the University of Coimbra (CISUC). The main objectives of the project are:

- Define a first generic version of an IoT people-centric architecture by developing and exploring a generic Cyber-Physical System/IoT architecture that can be used to support both, People2People interaction and People2Thing interaction.
- Explore the developed middleware and services in people-centric context, with the aim of demonstrating their use in enhancing the autonomy and quality of life of citizens, by identifying the needs and means towards general monitoring, and interaction with several user types.

Among the groups involved in SOCIALITE, the Laboratory of Communications and Telematics (LCT) is responsible for the design and the implementation of the network infrastructure on top of which, people-centric applications will be developed. Concerning the developed middleware in people-centric context, the LCT chose to align its solution to FIWARE specifications. To this end, the group has been developing a pilot scenario to infer the academic success of the students by monitoring their lifestyle. The application to be developed is called *ISABELA (for Iot Student Advisor & BEst Lifestyle Analyzer)*. Since the LCT group works on the infrastructure to feed the database, the data processing, Machine Learning and Artificial Intelligence is out of the scope of this paper.

Based on FIWARE generic platform, the tailored IoT scenario developed by LCT is depicted in Fig. 2.

---

[7] https://www.cisuc.uc.pt/projects/show/215.

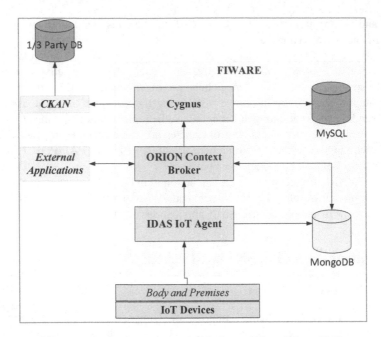

Fig. 2. ISABELA IoT scenario platform. (adapted from [15])

In FIWARE, the context information is represented by values assigned to attributes that characterize entities in the application. Hence, for this pilot entities have been created to describe the student's lifestyle environment. Some of the entities are a Student, its Rooms, the premises and entertainment facilities they use. Based on the inputs uploaded by sensors, through Machine Learning and Artificial Intelligence algorithms, it would be possible to infer the conditions that characterize the academic success of the students.

Even though the aim is to deploy sensors in the student's environments, the current state of the pilot scenario is only performed in a testbed. We already provide real-time sensed data from both mobile and stationary sensors, integrated by the FIWARE runtime. All sensed data are stored in a MySQL and "CKAN"[8] databases. These data are exploited to feed the primary version of ISABELA application allowing to simulate some aspects of the student's environments. The setup for the current version of the application can download here (link). The values displayed in the current version of the application correspond to those uploaded by the remote sensors placed in the testbed i.e. in LCT Laboratory. In the following Subsection, we will describe the general architecture of the project and will better understand the limitations on the current version to analyze one's Lifestyle.

---

[8] http://socialiteckan.dei.uc.pt/dataset/socialite.

3.1.1   General Network Architecture

The physical architecture of the network for the pilot integrated heterogeneous devices for data acquisition. As illustrated in Fig. 3, the sensor devices are mainly divided into two groups. The first group is set by mobile devices to ensure the student activities monitoring. The mobile devices are also used for the IoT-Student interaction through the smart application interface. The mobile devices form a mobile WSN composed by smartphones accoupled to Motorola Moto 360 smartwatches. This WSN is deployed to enable the acquisition of the student's activities e.g.: heart rate, communications counts, steps and location. Both smartphone and smartwatch run in Android environment. Hence, the applications in this WSN are developed in Android Studio IDE and uploaded to the watch via the smartphone. The immobile devices are intended to ensure the monitoring of the premises where students are supposed to develop some activities or rest such as classrooms or their personal rooms. Hence, the immobile devices forma stationary WSN currently composed by Arduino Uno sensor nodes and soon micaZ sensor nodes will integrate the stationary WSN. The Arduino's set uses a Raspberry Pi as gateway to the Internet and enables to acquire the temperature, the humidity and the noise level of the premises. However, additional data can be acquired depending on the nature of the transductors connected to the Arduino sensor node. The libraries on the Arduino are developed in C language while the requests in the Raspberry Pi were are made using command lines in Python. In Arduino, the application can be developed using other programming languages such as Java and C. Even though micaZ nodes offer expansion for a myriad of sensing activities[9], here itis only intended to the acquisition of both temperature and luminosity.

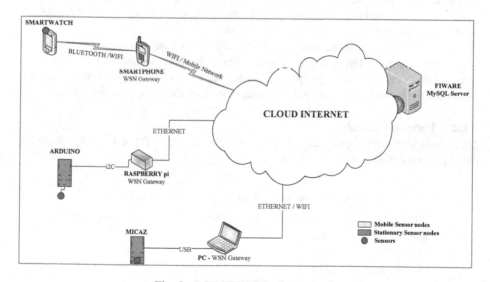

Fig. 3. LCT FIWARE pilot network

---

[9] http://www.cmt-gmbh.de/Produkte/WirelessSensorNetworks/MPR2400.html.

The dataset from the current testbed can be accessed at http://socialiteckan.dei.uc. pt/dataset/socialite (The *student resources* in the page correspond to data uploaded by mobile sensors).

The development environment of micaZ nodes is nesC-TinyOS and in the next subsection, we will be focusing its integration in the FIWARE within the scope of SOCIALITE project. The general integration of the three WSN in FIWARE towards the development of *ISABELA* is to be done according to the following steps [15]:

1. Creation IoT entities using Orion Context Broker;
2. Creation and registration of IoT devices in IDAS;
3. Sending of sensor data using the UltraLightIoT Agent;
4. Storage Persistent Data in a MySQL Database using Cygnus.

The broker enables to contextualize the information so that applications can interact with "things" instead of sensors. IDAS is the module in charge of handling all IoT devices, and Ultralight2.0 is the protocol used to provide IoT-Agents. To implement the communication client–server, HTTP (HyperText Transfer Protocol) and RESTful APIs are used for requests. It means, REST (Representational State Transfer) architectural style operations are adopted to reach resources (entities and attributes). JSON (JavaScript Object Notation) representation is the adopted format for the Payload. The on-the-fly data is stored in MongoDB database while Persistent data storage is done in a MySQL database through Cygnus Container. MongoDB is a snapshot database for the case of an interruption/DOS happens to Orion Context broker. The technical step-by-step guidelines can be found in [15], and all details concerning the API structures, experiments, and hands-on work can be found in fiware.org developers guide. As a case study, we will focus on the integration of micaZ in the FIWARE by describing a simple setup to upload sensor data.

In the next subsection, we will present the step-by-step guide to create an entity and send data directly to Orion context broker. Since the aim is only an introduction to some tools to enable the integration of WSNs built in micaZ, we will not tackle the creation of subscription to external description neither the store persistent data.

3.1.2   Focus on micaZ

The technical specification of micaZ sensor boardis shown in Table 1 and the setup for our case study is illustrated in Fig. 4.

Table 1. Specifications of the MicaZ - MPR2400 [16]

MCU	Atmega 128L - Up to 16MIPS Throughput at 16 MHz
RAM	4 KB
EPROM	4 KB
Flash memory	128 KB
Radio module	CC2420–2.4 to 2.48 GHz IEEE 802.15.4, AES-128
Transmission rate	250 Kbps
Extensions	Analog I, Digital I/0, I2C, SPI, UART

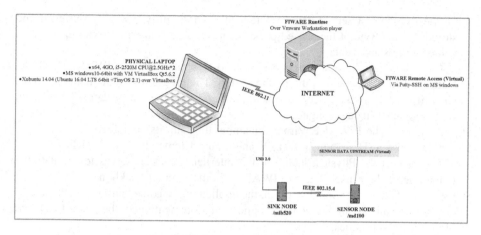

Fig. 4. The case study setup overview

In the Laptop, we installed a turnkey Xubuntu OS via VM VirtualBox™. The turnkey solution includes a Linux Ubuntu distribution and the package TinyOS, libraries, and nesC compiler. We used a second Virtual Machine player (VMware Workstation 12™) for the FIWARE runtime machine. Given some technical issues, we had to install and run the Java playground in the OS of the Physical laptop (MS Windows™). Besides having knowledge of programming languages used in the case study, the training in [15] is a prerequisite to succeed the next instructions.

The hands-on work to integrate MicaZ in FIWARE is done as follows:

Step 1 - In TinyOS, write a sensing application, then couple the MicaZ hardware to the mda100 sensor board and the mib520 programming board. Finally, connect the whole set to a USB port of the Physical laptop and install the application in the sensor node using the command ~/Oscilloscope$ *SENSORBOARD = basicsb make micaZinstall,1 mib510,/dev/ttyUSB0*. Remark the specification of the sensor board at the beginning of the installation command. This is due to TinyOS protocol regarding the compilation of programs that run on the sensor nodes. As sensing application, we used the generic *Oscilloscope* program from TinyOS libraries (~apps/Oscilloscope). Disconnect the sensor node from the programming board and connect the Sink node.

Step 2 - Staying in TinyOS, write the dispatcher program, then connect the Sink node to the mib510 board. Finally, install the dispatcher in the Sink node using the command *make micaZ install,0 mib510,/dev/ttyUSB0*. Do not disconnect the whole set (sink and programming board) from the Laptop. Remark that we changed the TOS_ID_NODE (node identification number) to 0. By convention, the number 0 is reserved to identify the Sink node in a WSN. As dispatcher program, we used the generic *BaseStation* program from TinyOS libraries (~apps/BaseStation).

Step 3 - In TinyOS, write a program to fetch sensor data from the dispatcher and store it in a text file. We used a modified *seriallisten* program from TinyOS libraries (~support/sdk/c/sf). By default, *seriallisten* enables to displays the results on the terminal screen. We edited the *seriallisten.c* file and inserted a function to store on-the-fly, the last sensor data in a text file. To simplify, we only retrieved and stored the last Byte of the sensed packets. In our case study, this Byte represents a value of the sensor data.

Step 4 - Write a middleware program to upload to sensor data to FIWARE database, from the text file created in the previous step. The program should enable to create an entity, create a service, register the device and send the sensor data. Our solution was developed in Java language.

Step 5 - Launch the FIWARE Virtual Machine, then run its containers.

Step 6 - Open a SSH session in puTTY and connect remotely to FIWARE.

Step 7 - Connect the Physical laptop to the Internet. This step serves to simulate the uploading of the sensor data to FIWARE via the Internet backbone.

Step 8 - Start the sensor node. It will run the application to collect and report the sensor data to the Sink. Using the generic application aforementioned, the green LED start blinking in both nodes.

Step 9 - Return to TinyOS and run the program to fetch sensor data from the dispatcher. Stop the application after retrieving at least one packet. If using the example in step 3, open a Terminal and run the modified *seriallisten* program with the command $\sim$ ...c/sf\$.*/seriallisten/dev/ttyUSB1 micaZ*. Remark that now we use the USB Port number 1. In fact, there are two ports associated with the mib520 programming board namely: port USB0 for configuration of the sensor nodes, e.g. to install applications in the nodes and port USB1 for the Application layer for instance to retrieve data from the sensor nodes [16].

Step 10 - Run the middleware program. In our case, the IDE is installed in MS Windows environment and the text file produced by *seriallisten* is a shared file to both MS Windows and Ubuntu over VM. If both the entity and its last attribute value have been uploaded to Orion context broker with success, a HTTP code is received in the IDE workstation added to the sensor value. Typical a 201 means the request has been fulfilled and the entity was created. A 20xcode is a standard response for successful request. For our case study, we will assume that any other code translates an unsuccessful request.

Step 11 - Ultimately, return to the SSH session and verify the existence of the entity created with the value uploaded.

The setup is subject to several optimizations in both hardware and software environment. For the former, the Physical laptop can be replaced by a smaller computing system like Arduino, to make the setting more practical in deployment scenario. For the latter, one Virtual Machine is enough to run all the virtual systems in the Physical laptop. Moreover, the WSN runtime can be simplified by developing both the retrieving and the middleware program in only one language (Java or C). Indeed, both languages enable to develop the mechanism to fetch the sensor data from the dispatcher, then format it before uploading dynamically to the FIWARE.

4   Conclusion

Technological heterogeneity in WSNs enlarges the robustness for data acquisition and provision towards IoT applications. Dealing with diversity in both hardware and software solutions, as well as guaranteeing their transparency for the development of people-centric smart applications is a permanent issue. Smart applications are context-aware applications. To this end, FIWARE offers powerful tools for having standardized API and harmonized data models for the development of applications, allowing People-IoT interactions. One of the main challenges of FIWARE is its consolidation as the open-source standard for IoT-enabled applications. Providing easy interoperability APIs to other IoT architectures such as OpenIoT, CitySDK, and IES Cities [17], may be an important step towards an international reference standard. On top of the services provided by WSNs and FIWARE, the SOCIALITE project aims at developing a people-centric, context-aware, cognitive framework that will ease the development of applications and, at the same time, bridge the gap between technology and its users.

The SOCIALITE Project began in July 2016 and is planned to end by 2019. The current paper focus on a technical aspect about how FIWARE can be leveraged to integrate an old sensor technology in a larger IoT computing system, towards the development a people-centric application. In future papers, more details describing the integration of all sensors deployed in the project will be done, as well as the evolution of functions in the smart application *ISABELA*.

Acknowledgments. The work presented in this paper was partly carried out in the scope of the SOCIALITE Project (PTDC/EEI-SCR/2072/2014), co-financed by COMPETE 2020, Portugal 2020 - Operational Program for Competitiveness and Internationalization (POCI), European Union's ERDF (European Regional Development Fund), and the Portuguese Foundation for Science and Technology (FCT).

References

1. Nunes, D., Zhang, P., Silva, J.: A survey on human-in-the-loop applications towards an internet of all. IEEE Commun. Surv. Tutorials **17**(2), 1 (2015)
2. Li, S., Da Xu, L., Zhao, S.: The internet of things: a survey. Inf. Syst. Front. **17**(2), 243–259 (2015)
3. Oteafy, S.M.A., Hassanein, H.: Resilient IoT architectures over dynamic sensor networks with adaptive components. IEEE Internet Things J. **1**(5), 1 (2016)
4. Savithri, G., Sujathamma, P., Padmavati, S., Visvavidyalayam, M.: Android in WSN applications – a survey. Int. J. Emerg. Technol. Comput. Appl. Sci. (IJETCAS) **1961**, 329–333 (2013)
5. Su, W., Sankarasubramaniam, Y., Cayirci, E., Akyildiz, I.F.: Wireless sensor networks: a survey. Int. J. Adv. Res. Comput. Sci. Softw. Eng. **38**, 393–422 (2002)
6. Wu, D., Yang, B., Wang, H., Wu, D., Wang, R.: An energy-efficient data forwarding strategy for heterogeneous WBANs. IEEE Access **4**, 1 (2016)

7. Rawidean, M., Kassim, M., Harun, A.N.: Applications of WSN in agricultural environment monitoring systems (2016)
8. O'donovan, T., et al.: The GINSENG system for wireless monitoring and control: design and deployment experiences. ACM Trans. Sens. Netw. **10**(1), 4 (2013)
9. Hussain, M.A., Khan, P., kyung Sup, K.: WSN research activities for military application. In: 11th International Conference on Advanced Communication Technology, vol. 1, pp. 271–274 (2009)
10. Giorgetti, A., et al.: A robust wireless sensor network for landslide risk analysis: system design, deployment, and field testing. IEEE Sens. J. **16**(16), 6374–6386 (2016)
11. Figueira, A., Nunes, D., Barbosa, R., Reis, A., Aguiar, H., Sinche, S., Rodrigues, A., Pereira, V., Dias, H., Herrera, C., Raposo, D.: WeDoCare: a humanitarian people-centric cyber-physical system for the benefit of refugees. In: IEEE Global Humanitarian Technology Conference (GHTC) (2016)
12. Nájera, K.: Arquitectura básica para FIWARE. In: Mooc INFOTEC (2016). https://www.youtube.com/watch?v=j1XCjgeAW2c&t=62s. Accessed 12 Dec 2016
13. Fazio, M., Celesti, A., Marquez, F.G., Glikson, A., Villari, M.: Exploiting the FIWARE cloud platform to develop a remote patient monitoring system. In: Proceedings of IEEE Symposium Computers Communications, vol. 2016, pp. 264–270 (2016)
14. Ramparany, F., Marquez, F.G., Soriano, J., Elsaleh, T.: Handling smart environment devices, data and services at the semantic level with the FI-WARE core platform. In: Proceedings of 2014 IEEE International Conference Big Data, IEEE Big Data 2014, pp. 14–20 (2015)
15. Raposo, D.: Fiware basic operations. LCTSens, DEI-Universidade de Coimbra, Coimbra (2016)
16. Boavida, F., Silva, J.S., Silva, R.M.: Redes de Sensores Sem Fios, 1st ed. Lisboa (2016). ISBN: 978-972-722-830-0
17. Sooriyabandara, M., Vatsikas, S., Kalogridis, G., Lewis, T.: The experience of using the IES cities citizen-centric IoT platform. IEEE Commun. Mag. Manuscr. **55**, 40–47 (2016)

Toward Smart Island Simulation Application
A Case Study of Reunion Island

Tahina Ralitera$^{(\boxtimes)}$ and Rémy Courdier

Laboratoire d'Informatique et de Mathématiques,
University of Reunion Island, Saint-Denis, France
{tahina.ralitera,remy.courdier}@univ-reunion.fr

Abstract. Simulation models are often used by policy makers as decision support tools for smart city design and planning. However, many of them are designed to be suitable for a particular kind of territory with the corresponding characteristics; especially for city contexts. Therefore, limitations could appear when transferring such simulation models to island contexts. Indeed, because of their relative geographical and socio-cultural differences, cities and islands could react differently to the same changes. That could generate useful insights for the discussion of transferability of smart city solutions from cities to islands. In this paper, we demonstrate how an agent based simulation model for island context related projects can be designed from enrichment of an existing simulation model that was previously applied to cities only. Experiments are made based on the Repast Simphony simulation platform. Thereby, after application to the particular case of Reunion Island, we present a more generic simulation model that could be easily applied to both cities and islands.

Keywords: Multi-agent simulation · Smart island · Model re use · Software refinement

1 Introduction

Cities and islands are currently facing to the increase of the urbanization followed by the growth of economic and environmental crises that put pressures on their structure and the management of their resources. Thus, combining competitiveness and sustainable development becomes a challenge. Consequently, searching for technical solutions for those problems becomes a priority. Therefore, the development of the ICTs seems to be an interesting track leading to the growing popularity of the concept of smart cities since this last decades [8]. [10] defines a smart city as a "place and territorial context where use of planned and wise of the human and natural resources, properly managed and integrated through the various ICT technologies already available, allows for the creation of an ecosystem that can be used of resources and to provide integrated and more intelligent systems". However, because of their remoteness, their isolation and other specific geographical constraints, islands are subject to additional difficulties such

© Springer International Publishing AG 2017
J. Bajo et al. (Eds.): PAAMS 2017 Workshops, CCIS 722, pp. 457–469, 2017.
DOI: 10.1007/978-3-319-60285-1_39

as multiple challenges in managing energy, resources or transport. These difficulties differentiate them from cities and have led to thinking about "smart islands". Currently, to our knowledge, if lots of research are done for smart city design and planning, the concept of smart island is subject to few studies. Moreover, most of the time, simulation models are applied to cities [2,6,7,15]. However, because of their relative differences islands and cities could react in different ways to the same changes. Consequently, it could be also interesting to have a re-usable simulation model that could be easily applied to islands. To address this, the idea is to enrich an existing smart city simulation model in order to make it transferable to an island context. For that, experiments are made on an existing Agent-Based Simulation Model previously applied to city systems. Application is done in the particular case of Reunion Island and using the Repast Simphony [14] simulation platform. That generates useful insights for the discussion of transferability of smart city solutions from a city to an island. This paper is structured as follows Sect. 2 describes the simulation model, Sect. 3 gives an overview of agent based simulations of electrical vehicle mobility flow as stated in the literature and a comparison between urban and insular systems. Section 4 describes the experiments done on Reunion Island. Finally, Sect. 5 reflects the approach and discusses the contributions.

2   The SmartCityModel

The SmartCityModel is an agent based simulation model, build upon the Repast Simphony Agent-based Modelling and Simulation platform [14] which is free and open source. The model was previously applied to different use case in different cities. For example, it was used in London for simulating the interactions between land use, transport and electric vehicle charging demand [6], for simulating residential electricity and heat demand [4], or for estimating plug-in electric vehicle demand flexibility [5]. It was also used for modelling water and sanitation infrastructure use in Ghana [16]. The approach used is an activity-based approach, which means that travel comes from the demand for personal activities such as work, shopping or leisure that individuals need or wish to perform [13].

The use case described in this paper is for application in the area of electric transport and is about simulation of Plug-in Electric Vehicle (PEV) flows. For illustration, experiments are conducted on Reunion Island.

Agent Model: In this use case, agents are PEV owners. They take travel and charging decisions depending on their perceptions and memories. They also have the capacity to adapt to a particular situation such as reduction in the charging tariff.

- Agent goal:
  The agent should be able to achieve all his activities (shopping, work, leisures, etc.). That requires that optimization of all of his displacements, using his electric vehicle and the charging stations at its disposal.

– Agent resources:
  The agent owns an electric vehicle with an average power consumption and
  an electric charge capacity.
– Agent activity profile:
  In the model, the activity profile AP_i for each group i of PEV owners is
  defined with a list of 4-tuples:
  $AP_i = (ACT_j, MDT_j, SD_j, PD_j)$ [5]
  Where ACT_j represents the activity j, MDT_j the mean departure time, SD_j
  the standard deviation, and PD_j the probability of departure for the activity j.

Environment Modelling Elements: The model environment is defined using
GIS representation (shape files). 2 kinds of entities are used: buildings and roads.

– Buildings are polygon entities. They could represent a particular area on the
  real map such as individual buildings, towns, districts or countries, depending
  on the level of details and the chosen scale. Activity areas are inside the
  buildings, represented by points with specific geographical coordinates. They
  can be classified into 4 types:

  • Residential areas
  • Working areas
  • Commercial areas
  • Leisure areas

  Charging stations are also contained inside of buildings and are represented
  by point entities.
– Roads are polyline entities. They correspond to the road network followed by
  the agents when they move from one place (activity area) to another.

Inputs and Outputs: The simulation model takes, as input, GIS and statistical data. GIS data in the shape file format (SHP) are used not only to define
the environment (buildings and roads) but also have attributes that contain statistical data such as population density per commune, type of roads, etc. Those
attributes and other statistical data that are entered in global variables are used
in the simulation model. For example to generate random activity area locations.

Metrics, such as electricity consumption and charging station usage profiles
are generated in the output of the simulation. They are stored in .csv files and
could be used for further studies, using post-processing software.

In this use case of the SmartCityModel, the objective of the multi-agent
system is to be able to provide an electrical charging station infrastructure that
best supports the agents' level of activity. Results can be used to propose a
geolocalized charging station infrastructure.

3   Related Work

3.1   Agent Based Simulation Models

In the literature, transport mobility are simulated using different approaches
such as trip-based approach, tour-based approach and activity-based approach,

the approach used in the SmartCityModel. It means that travel results from the demand for personal activities such as work, shopping, or leisure that individuals need or wish to perform [13]. In the example, the SmartCityModel [5] (see Sect. 2) is used for application in the area of electric transport. It simulates Plug-in Electric Vehicle (PEV) transport and its impact on the electricity consumption depending on the agents activity schedule. Other works can be found in the literature [15], however, none, not even the SmartCityModel take into account particular parameters that could be very important for some kind of strong constraints territories such as oceanic islands. Example of usually neglected parameters but that could affect the power consumption in great constraints territories are road slopes [12] and transport behaviours such as vehicle speed or use of comfort items [3,9]. Consequently, such simulation models may not be relevant when they are directly transferred in contexts where these missing parameters are important (territory with big hills or mountainous for example). It is therefore interesting to explore how these features could be added to an existing approach.

3.2 Urban and Insular Contexts

Currently, there is no universal definition of what a smart city and a smart island are. A smart city is defined by [10] as a "place and territorial context, where use of planned and wise of the human and natural resources, properly managed and integrated through the various ICT technologies already available, allows for the creation of an ecosystem that can be used of resources and to provide integrated and more intelligent systems". This definition may be ambiguous according to the territorial context considered. We classify these contexts into 2 types: urban and insular contexts.

Urban Context: According to [17] an urban area is defined as an area that contains one or several of the following features: local municipality, large population, high population density and economic activity which does not mainly depend on primary resources exploitation. The topic is well defined at a national level but not in international. This raises important issues in the comparison of urban zones located in different countries, as diverging city definitions might create misleading results. On the other hand, administrative definitions of cities boundaries are not covering the entire real city. However, the major part of the data are based on those definitions as they are provided by the local government. Consequently, using another boundary such as the urban agglomeration or the hinterland, could induce complexity in the research of geographic limits and data collection. Moreover, using data collected based on different boundaries for each sector (for example a specific boundary for energy, another boundary for heath data, another for governance, etc.) could question the relevance of the simulation results.

Consequently, all those limitations could introduce ambiguity in the previous definition of the smart city. Ambiguity that can be avoided in the case of insular contexts.

Table 1. Key structural differences between islands and cities.

	Islands	Cities	Consequences
Physical boundaries	Set by geography, constant	Many possibilities, Time-dependant	Geographic limit and data collection is easier for island contexts
Geographical constraints	Often strong in oceanic island	Often small or null	Islands are ideal candidate for tests under real-life conditions
In/out flows	Easy to evaluate	Hard to determine	Islands are easier to define and to study as a system

Insular Context: Insular systems can be defined as systems that have more or less marked spatial boundaries and that identify, at least in theory, a set of elements from diverse origin that participate in the same territorial dynamics. They are therefore favorable to the study of the functioning and the viability of systems [11]. An interesting example is the island system. First of all, island has boundaries that are already set by geographic constraints (the sea) and which do not vary through the time. Consequently, this removes ambiguity resulting from the differences in territorial boundaries considered by the actors in various fields in term of data collection. Second, unless they have a direct link with the mainland, most of the time, the in and out flows are easily traceable for islands as they usually occur by plane or by boat. Thus, the input and output points are easily identifiable: ports or aerodromes. This considerably reduces the number of actors that are implied in the flow management. Finally, the usual classification of islands is relatively clear (ocean and continental) and do not depend on the local government. That removes the ambiguity in term of comparison of different islands systems and allows the use of real data instead of estimates and statistical data as input of the simulation model. Apart from these facts, islands could contain cities and towns so the previous considerations about urban system characterization are also valid for islands having high population levels and urban centres.

Island and urban systems present very different structural features. Because of their relative differences, the two systems could react in very different ways to the same changes. Table 1 summarizes the comparison of the two systems.

Indeed, it is easier to define and to break down islands into elementary units. Moreover, because of their fixed boundaries and their more common structure, it seems to be easier to define and to study them as a system. So, they could be considered as ideal candidates for tests under real-life conditions.

Therefore, if we consider the previous definition of a smart city and the particular characteristics of urban and insular system. We could define a smart island as a smart city that fulfil the following the 3 criteria:

- Boundaries are fixed and are the same for all key fields,
- In and out flow can be determined,
- The size is less than or equal to large cities.

4   Experiments on Reunion Island

Experiments are done following 2 steps. The first is a theoretical analysis of the geographical and socio-cultural particularities of Reunion Island and the second is about experiments by simulation. They are done following the three steps experiment process used in [7]:

- Experimentation specification (scenario definition and setup),
- Simulation execution,
- Result analysis and visualisation.

That allows to take into account all the aspects of the simulation model, going from the initialisation of the simulation, its parameterization, to the results interpretation. These aspects seem to be important to consider because they are all linked, contribute to the generic nature and the relevance of the simulation model.

4.1   Reunion Island

Reunion Island is a French island of $2,512\,km^2$ and populated by 843,529 inhabitant in 2015. Situated in the south hemisphere, next to Madagascar and Mauritius in the Indian Ocean, it has a tropical climate.

As can bee seen in Fig. 1, in opposite to cities that could have moving boundaries Reunion Island's boundary is constant and delimited by the sea. As a completely remote island, all the flows that come from and to it are easier to define. The center of the island which is a national park has a very high elevation. The relief is very contrasted with an altitude variation from 0 to 3070.50 m (the Piton des Neiges). Consequently, physical characteristics represent a constraint to population housing and mobility, which are thereby concentrated in the coastal areas. The temperature also varies according to the localisation. Indeed, it is lower in mountainous areas and higher in the coastal ones. The average precipitation is around 10 000 mm per year. Consequently, there is an important use of comfort items such as air conditioning, heating and wipers that could affect the vehicle energy consumption.

To sum up, the non-exhaustive list of parameters that seem to be important to consider when transferring the SmartCityModel in Reunion Island context, can be classified in 3 types:

- Geographical parameters linked to the relief such as slope,
- Socio-cultural parameters such as population density, population geographical distribution and speed,
- Climate related parameters such as the use of comfort items and the temperature variation.

These parameters could greatly affect the electric vehicle consumption [3,9,12].

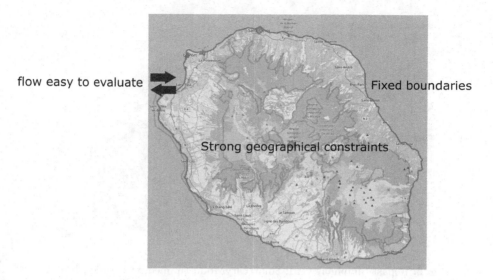

flow easy to evaluate

Fixed boundaries

Strong geographical constraints

Fig. 1. Reunion Island map

4.2   Experimentations

To implement a Reunion Island case, primary changes are done in the level of the shape files (the map) and the statistical data used.

Figure 2 shows the Repast Simphony GUI with the Reunion Island map.

Limitations appear after first experiments. Same limitations that could also appear when conducting experiments in other simulation models and in similar territories such as oceanic islands or territories with high geographical constraints. Improvements are therefore done, following the 3 steps cited in Sect. 4:

Simulation Initialization: Simulation users could benefit from simulated territory that could be defined through easily interchangeable maps. No flexibility was given at this level in the SmartCityModel. Therefore a generic process for manipulating customizable maps was introduced, with a process that check and validate maps properties. That allow to ensure compliance with the model criteria used by the model and to avoid errors during the simulation run. Examples of criteria are activity zone localization that have to be accessible from the road network, the necessity of including of specific attributes relative to specific variables in the program, the entire road network that must be joined together (there cannot be any disconnected road), two crossed roads that should break at the intersection, etc.

Simulation Core: Statistic data are used in the simulation model. That could lead to non realistic behaviours. For example, during experiments in Reunion island, unrealistic population distribution was detected due to the use of statistics that lead to the definition of the agent location based on the density per

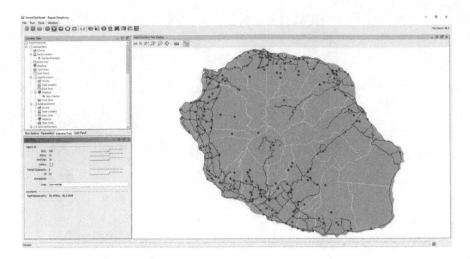

Fig. 2. Repast Simphony GUI: SmartCityModel applied on Reunion Island

town. Consequently, large numbers of agents were located in the center of the island which in reality is a very sparsely populated area (Fig. 3) but part of a very populated town. To overcome these limitations the simulation model is enriched by the use of maps with geolocalized activity zones. On the other hand essential parameters that could influence the energy consumption such as geographical and socio-cultural parameters (road slope, speed, etc.) are neglected. Improvements are made to better take into account these aspects.

Simulation Results: Instead of dealing with raw data that need additional post-processing, simulation users could benefit from automatic data post-processing for analysis and visualization. Thus, a library is developed and allows to link the simulation output with a web geobrowser for spatialized visualisation of the simulation results.

4.3   Example of Implementation

Implementations are made on the same 3 previous levels:

Initialisation of the Simulation: It involves the implementation of 3 new features:

- a feature that allow to define the scenario parameters using an independent .csv file that is completed in advance,
- a feature that set up the display automatically,
- a test feature that check wrong files, variable formats and missing attributes, in order to avoid errors that could appear during the simulation run.

Simulation Core:

- Improvements in the algorithm: In order to have a more realistic geographical population distribution, a buffer zone is added around the road network. It allows to locate agents and their activities nearby roads (See Fig. 4). Consequently, it reflects the reality in the island where population and their activities are concentrated in the coastal areas and nearby roads. Moreover, it does not have any negative effects on the simulation for cities because in opposite to Reunion Island, where most of the roads covers only the coastal area, in most of cities, the road network covers roughly the territory so the addition of buffer did not bring many changes.

  The following pseudo-code shows how the buffer zone is used to generate a random location nearby a road:

```
set BUFFER_DISTANCE to buffer radius
Initialise nearestRoad to null
    while nearestRoad==null do
        set coords = random coordinate inside
        a building
        set nearestRoad = the road where the distance from coords is equal to BUFFER_DISTANCE
    end do
return coords;
```

  Then, a new feature is created for more precision and to give an alternative for the use of statistical data. It consists of defining the activity area locations from shape files (one shape file per set of activity zones). Generated locations correspond to the precise location of the activity zones in the real world. According to the available data, the method used is chosen automatically at the initialisation of the simulation step.

- Improvements in the simulation setting: A list of parameters that could affect the relevance of the simulation results was given in Sect. 4.1. So, the simulation model should take those parameters into account. This is a part that is still in progress, but currently the consideration of the speed variation is already implemented. For that, a new attribute is added in the road shape files. This new attribute takes the value of "majorRoad" if the road is a major road. Then a speed advantage is assigned for car drivers when driving on a major road.

```
set MAJOR_ROAD_ADVANTAGE to speed advantage
for all roads do
    Initialise the road speed to 1
    If the road is a major road then
        set the road speed advantage to MAJOR_ROAD_ADVANTAGE
    end if
end do
```

Visualisation of the Simulation Results: The simulation model could benefit from linking with post-processing tools. That will allow automated treatment and a more adequate visual exploitation of simulation results. As shown by [1,7],

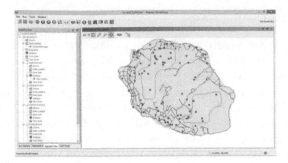

Fig. 3. Population distribution, before adding buffer.

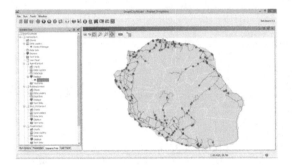

Fig. 4. Population distribution, after adding buffer.

an example of interesting functionality is a spatialized display of the simulation metrics in an earth browser such as Google Earth. That could be more convenient for domain expert validation as it gives the possibility to replay a previous simulation run. The advantages over a video recording is that it allows inspection capabilities, inclusion of web applications animation and layering with other spatial data sets. Therefore, a library which records the simulation and its metrics and exports it to KML format is developed. It allow to incorporate data in displays using an interactive geobrowser. This export function can be used to create a web interface showing the output of a simulation run and the variation in the time of the metrics across different parts of the simulated area. An example of display is shown on Fig. 5.

4.4   Results

As shown in Fig. 6, in its new process, the 3 parts (scenario definition, simulation execution, result analysis and visualisation) of the SmartCityModel becomes separated into 3 connected blocks. In this way, the initialisation process become simpler as the user only need to fill the .csv file, and in case of new territory, to add the map in a new folder. Display is set up automatically so no need to be familiar with Repast Simphony and changing the simulated territory is easier.

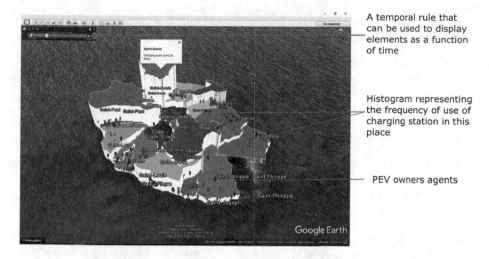

A temporal rule that can be used to display elements as a function of time

Histogram representing the frequency of use of charging station in this place

PEV owners agents

Fig. 5. An example of results display on Google Earth for Reunion Island case.

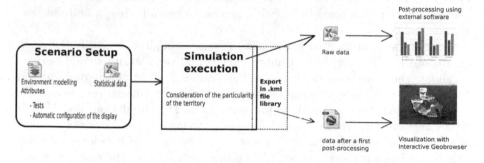

Fig. 6. SmartCityModel 3 steps process, after improvements.

Moreover, the results can be displayed in a 3 dimensions map, in this way, visualization is better and there is an automatic first results post processing.

5 Conclusion and Further Work

The work presented in this paper demonstrates how an agent based simulation model of the mobility flow in island could be implemented from enrichment of an existing agent based simulation model previously applied to cities. Implementation is done based on 3 criteria that we think distinguish smart islands:

– Fixed boundaries,
– In and out flow precisely determinable,
– Size less than or equal to large cities size.

Criteria that make the islands ideal candidates for tests under real-life conditions. Application is done Reunion Island, an island system which compared to cities has a very different geographical and socio-cultural structures. The experimentations is divided in 2 parts:

- A theoretical analysis that allows to define a non-exhaustive list of essential parameters that should be considered in the simulation models, parameters that have influence in the electric vehicle energy consumption.
- Experimentations by simulation.

    Improvements are done on 3 levels:

- The scenario definition and setup;
- The simulation execution;
- The result analysis and visualisation.

    The results show that making experiments on islands could generate useful insight that can help in improving the transferability of such city simulation models from a city to an island or a similar territory with strong constraints. Comparative studies between island and city systems have led to a definition of smart island based on the 3 previous criteria. Thus, we define a smart island as a smart city that has fixed boundaries, precisely determinable in and out flow and size less than or equal to large city's size.

    Most of the implemented features are generic enough to be easily reused in other contexts. However, further improvements and verifications should be done to validate the simulation model. Especially, missing essential geographical and socio-cultural parameters should be implemented in the simulation core.

    For example, taking the slope into account in the simulation model could affect the agent route choice. Indeed, for energy saving and vehicle power reasons, an agent might prefer a road with a less steep slope even if it is longer instead a short one but with steep slopes. This could contribute to the emergence of a collective phenomenon that lead to the concentration of the traffic on coastal roads, where slopes are lower. A reality in the Island. Moreover, improvements relatives to oceanic islands could be also relevant and applicable for cities with big hills or even mountains such as Rio de Janeiro of Lisbon. That shows that oceanic islands could be ideal candidates for tests before implementation in cities.

    Therefore, we think that future work will be focused on 3 points. First work will be about the implementation of the neglected geographical and socio-cultural parameters. Then, validation will be done by experiments on other urban and island systems. Finally, we will proceed to the verification of the simulation results by domain experts.

References

1. Augusseau, X., et al.: Simulation cartographique au service de l'innovation collective. In: SAGEO 2013, Brest, France, 16 p., September 2013. http://hal.cirad.fr/cirad-00850243
2. Badariotti, D., Weber, C.: La mobilité résidentielle en ville. modélisation par automates cellulaires et système multi-agents à bogota. L'espace géographique **31**(2), 97–108 (2002)
3. Bingham, C., Walsh, C., Carroll, S.: Impact of driving characteristics on electric vehicle energy consumption and range. Intell. Transp. Syst. IET **6**(1), 29–35 (2012)
4. Bustos-Turu, G., van Dam, K.H., Acha, S., Markides, C.N., Shah, N.: Simulating residential electricity and heat demand in urban areas using an agent-based modelling approach. In: 2016 IEEE International Energy Conference (ENERGYCON), pp. 1–6. IEEE (2016)
5. Bustos-Turu, G., van Dam, K.H., Acha, S., Shah, N.: Estimating plug-in electric vehicle demand flexibility through an agent-based simulation model. In: 2014 IEEE PES Innovative Smart Grid Technologies Conference Europe (ISGT-Europe), pp. 1–6. IEEE (2014)
6. Bustos-Turu, G., Van Dam, K., Acha, S., Shah, N.: Integrated planning of distribution networks: interactions between land use, transport and electric vehicle charging demand. In: 23rd International Conference on Electricity Distribution, Lyon, France (2015)
7. Čertický, M., Jakob, M., Píbil, R.: Analyzing on-demand mobility services by agent-based simulation. J. Ubiquit. Syst. Pervasive Netw. **6**(1), 17–26 (2015)
8. Dijkstra, L., Garcilazo, E., McCann, P.: The economic performance of European cities and city regions: myths and realities. Eur. Plan. Stud. **21**(3), 334–354 (2013). http://dx.doi.org/10.1080/09654313.2012.716245
9. Karabasoglu, O., Michalek, J.: Influence of driving patterns on life cycle cost and emissions of hybrid and plug-in electric vehicle powertrains. Energy Policy **60**, 445–461 (2013)
10. Longo, M., Roscia, M., Lazaroiu, G.C.: Innovating multi-agent systems applied to smart city. Res. J. Appl. Sci. Eng. Technol. **7**(20), 4296–4302 (2014)
11. Magnan, A.: Systèmes insulaires, représentations pyramidales et soutenabilité: approche comparative océan indien/petites antilles. Les Cahiers d'Outre-Mer. Revue de géographie de Bordeaux **62**(248), 529–548 (2009)
12. Maia, R., Silva, M., Araújo, R., Nunes, U.: Electric vehicle simulator for energy consumption studies in electric mobility systems. In: 2011 IEEE Forum on Integrated and Sustainable Transportation System (FISTS), pp. 227–232. IEEE (2011)
13. McNally, M.G., Rindt, C.R.: The activity-based approach. In: Handbook of Transport Modelling, pp. 55–73. Emerald, September 2007
14. North, M.J., Collier, N.T., Ozik, J., Tatara, E.R., Macal, C.M., Bragen, M., Sydelko, P.: Complex adaptive systems modeling with repast Simphony. Complex Adapt. Syst. Model. **1**(1), 3 (2013)
15. Sweda, T., Klabjan, D.: An agent-based decision support system for electric vehicle charging infrastructure deployment. In: 2011 IEEE Vehicle Power and Propulsion Conference, pp. 1–5, September 2011
16. Trust, T.E.S.: resilience.io (2016). http://resilience.io/. Accessed 23 Jan 2017
17. Unicef, et al.: The state of the world's children 2012: children in an urban world. Technical report, eSocialSciences (2012)

Intelligent Transport System Through the Recognition of Elements in the Environment

Pablo Martín-Martín[1], Alfonso González-Briones[2($\boxtimes$)],
Gabriel Villarrubia[2], and Juan F. De Paz[2]

[1] University of Salamanca, Salamanca, Spain
pmartinm@usal.es
[2] BISITE Research Group, University of Salamanca,
Edificio I+D+i, 37007 Salamanca, Spain
{alfonsogb,gvg,fcofds}@usal.es

Abstract. Autonomous vehicles are becoming one of the developmental elements, not only for the transport of people but also in the field of data collection and monitoring, control of external elements or supervision and security. Their advantage is the ability to access dangerous areas which often cannot be accessed by humans. It is necessary that the vehicle recognizes its surrounding and reacts in an adequate way. In this work a study was carried out of the main techniques of artificial vision, machine learning and supervised learning applied in vehicles so they recognize the road and do not leave it. This work presents the viability of the different machine learning techniques for their application in the problem of autonomous driving. For this, an automobile robotic prototype has been constructed and an algorithm has been developed based on the Artificial Neural Network (ANN) algorithm and a user application which allows to carry out all integrated analysis and observe in real-time the vehicle's view and the processing of the different snapshots. We have also demonstrated that the application of the stated algorithm, diverse processing techniques and artificial vision was sufficient, so that our robot could drive with precision and keep on the track of a road in a controlled environment.

Keywords: Autonomous driving · Robotics · Principal component analysis · Artificial neural networks · Machine learning

1 Introduction

According to the statistics published by the European Commission [1], deaths caused by traffic accidents have increased for the first time in this century.

In 2015 an average of 51.5 deaths per one million inhabitants had been recorded, this mortality rate has been similar in the last two years. This however, is still a significant reduction of 8% in 2012 and 2013 [1]. Some of the factors that usually cause road accidents are; the loss of reflexes and lack of attention [2], the loss of eyesight in the elderly as observed in a study carried out by Owsley et al. in [3]. Other accidents occur due to the lack of knowledge on road safety, which leads to uncertainties while

© Springer International Publishing AG 2017
J. Bajo et al. (Eds.): PAAMS 2017 Workshops, CCIS 722, pp. 470–480, 2017.
DOI: 10.1007/978-3-319-60285-1_40

driving, especially on turns and at intersections, not knowing whose priority it is, is a frequent cause of accidents [4]. These are some of the factors that intervene in safe vehicle driving, which, we are now intending to eliminate through the incorporation of artificial intelligence techniques or even creating entirely intelligent vehicles. For this reason, this work proposes the construction of a robot which behaves like an autonomous vehicle and allows to evaluate the application of various machine learning techniques used in autonomous driving, where the car does no go out of the road track, recognizes its environment and responds to it.

In the field of autonomous vehicle development, research has been carried out on the different techniques, from techniques such as ultrasounds [6], sonar [7, 8] and lasers with artificial vision techniques [9] to artificial intelligence techniques such as fuzzy control systems [10] or neural networks. Pomerleaus was one of the first researchers who applied neural network techniques to autonomous vehicles in the ALVINN project [11, 12], in these works a neural network was used called single hidden layer backpropagation network which had the capability of learning, within a time of under 5 min, to autonomously control the Navlab by watching the reactions of a human driver. Neural networks have also been used in the recognition of traffic signs [13]. Foedisch et al. developed an adaptive application based on neural networks for road detection in real-time, for autonomous driving. One of the novelties of this work was system training while it was functioning. One of the studies in which they start to employ multilayer perceptrons is that carried out by Shinzato and Wolff [15] in which parts of the area were identified, ones that could be travelled by and others which should be avoided.

This paper therefore explores the feasibility of different machine learning techniques and their effectiveness when these techniques are combined and applied to the problem of autonomous driving within roads. The study of these techniques requires the construction of a robot that behaves like a vehicle according to the applied algorithms. During the construction of the robot various, appropriate configurations have also been analyzed for better results.

The remainder of the paper is organized as follows: Sect. 2 the proposal, Sect. 3 shows the results and finally Sect. 4 presents conclusions and future work.

2 Proposed Prototype

This section describes the different proposals for steering systems, image snapshots, controllers and learning techniques that should be considered in the development of autonomous vehicles.

2.1 Rotation System

The output of the learning algorithm that gives autonomy to our robot is the knowledge, at all times, of the direction in which it must turn so that it does not go out of its track. Therefore, three rotation systems have been proposed, the advantages and disadvantages of each one have been carefully considered and analyzed:

Three Direction Steering System with Direct Current (DC) Motor
There are only 3 possible directions (left, right, center) in which the car can move. Although the use of an excessive number of states as outputs for an Artificial Neural Network may be counterproductive (for example, when obtaining a set of representative samples for each of the states), the opposite case is equally inappropriate as it would not grant the required system precision.

Differential Wheeled Steering System
This system is a common approach in the construction of robotic vehicles. The speed of each wheel is controlled by Pulse-Width Modulation (PWM) pulses that are sent from the Raspberry PI to the general Purpose Input/Output (GPIO) pins corresponding to each of the motors, in this way it is possible to consider all possible degrees of rotation, varying the speed difference between each one of the wheels.

Steering System with Servo Motor
Servomotors, unlike standard DC motors, have the capability to position themselves in any position within their operating range (usually 180°) and to remain stable (to a greater or lesser extent) in that position. These servos operate via PWM signals. This type of signals of specified duration are sent at regular intervals to the servo. Depending on the duration of the signal (pulse width), the servo will be positioned in one place or another. According to the values of pulse width, we consider as many degrees of rotation as we deem convenient, making this system the most suitable option for our prototype.

The only difficulty of this system is the jitter that can be generated when using PMW via software with the Raspberry PI. In order for the servo to remain steady in the same position, the interval between each signal must be constant. Raspbian is not a suitable Operating System for real-time tasks and therefore this problem can be presented.

2.2 Dimensionality Reduction

One of the most crucial steps is to deal with the problem of dimensional reduction, since each snapshot has a resolution of 80×60 pixels (minimum possible resolution of Raspberry Pi Camera). This implies a total of 4800 dimensions. Feeding the original image with all these components to our learning algorithms has a very high computational cost.

Apart from this, a high dimensionality in the input data, requires an even larger number of samples in our database, that is, given a fixed number of samples, the predictive capacity of our learning algorithm decreases as dimensionality increases. This aspect is known as the Hughes phenomenon. Given our image as a vector of 4800 features, we can define a dimensional reduction function as follows:

$$f : R^{4800} - - - - \to R^k$$

with $0 < K < 4800$

The value of K should not be arbitrary, but should be done on the basis of what is known as the percentage of variance maintained. That is, the percentage of information we maintain from the original image for a given value of K. This percentage varies depending on the learning problem that we are facing, with the most common values being in the range of 99% to 90% of maintained variance. To reduce dimensionality, the following algorithms will be used:

- Principal Component Analysis (PCA) - is a dimensional reduction algorithm that works on the basis of high dimension registers which are generally composed of correlated variables; therefore, the relevant information is concentrated only in a small set of dimensions. These dimensions are known as Principal Components and they contain the maximum variance of data [16]. This algorithm is used in the majority of works that deal with the topic of artificial vision techniques, which reduce dimensionality, as occurs in systems of facial recognition [17].
- Independent Component Analysis (ICA) - This algorithm, like PCA, tries to find a new basis on which to represent the data, however, the objective pursued is very different [18]. It looks for linear projections that are as statistically independent as possible, this does not necessarily include orthogonal projections. Although the PCA algorithm tries to find vectors (eigenvectors) that maximize the variance of the data, ICA tries to find statistically independent components, which is considered a higher order criterion, much more restrictive than the variance [19].
- Linear Discriminant Analysis (LDA) - One of the problems posed by PCA is that subtracting the main components of greater variance does not ensure that we maintain all the possible classes present in the data set. The labeling of the data is not taken into account in the execution of the algorithm. LDA solves this problem by performing a dimensional reduction which includes data labeling; it looks for combinations of characteristics that allow to separate the elements of different classes, placing elements of the same class as close as possible to each other and separating those of different classes. It is, therefore, unlike the other methods of dimensional reduction analyzed, a supervised learning method. For this reason, we can use this algorithm as both dimensional reduction method and linear learning algorithm.

2.3 Classifiers

Once the database and the techniques of light normalization and dimensional reduction have been applied, our model is trained (multilayer perceptron) using machine learning algorithms. Also, to compare results and to determine which of the two algorithms is more effective in the problem of autonomous navigation, the Support Vector Machine (SVM) has been implemented from the scikit-learn library on Python.

3 Case Study

This section explains why the rotation system, the motor controller and the snapshot system have been chosen for the construction of the robot and the results of the autonomous navigation tests.

3.1 Rotation System Selection

The three-way rotary drive system with a DC motor results in extreme behavior, making it unsuitable for training a learning algorithm. The tests performed have been unsatisfactory, although the neural network learns correctly to differentiate between the states of a complete turn to the left and a complete turn to the right, the biggest problems occur when it is necessary to keep the car in a straight line. The final result is a navigation with excessively abrupt and constant turns that entail difficulties in following the road correctly for all the degrees of curve.

The wheel rotation system with the independent motors has been discarded since it is necessary to have two exactly equal motors for each of the wheels, in practice, the result is that it is impossible for the vehicle to move forward in a completely straight line in the open loop. Therefore, some type of a closed system is required, such as a PID control through the use of *encoders* in the wheels to fulfill this goal. Another problem presented by this model is that the use of the unreliable caster wheel, which causes all sorts of movements and unwanted turns, on some terrain types.

Using the Rotation System with the servomotor, when implementing PMW through the software offered by the RPI.GPIO library, jitter has been noted, however, it has not been in sufficient to affect navigation adversely, in any of the cases.

3.2 Motor Controller

The Tamiya radio-controlled car has a 12 V electric motor for the front-wheel drive. Due to the need to control the speed of the motor using PWM, in addition to the direction of rotation with the Raspberry Pi we need to rely on an engine controller that uses an electronic circuit known as H-Bridge, enabling the voltage to be applied across a load in any direction. This is what allows a DC motor to move in both directions.

We have also tested the L293D driver (Texas Instruments), a circuit that can control two motors at the same time. However, it is an old controller and has a very high voltage drop. In the first tests performed, it was used to control small 6 V motors, however, losses of between two and three volts were detected, reducing the power of the motor by almost a half.

In order to alleviate these problems, the TB6612FNG Toshiba model has been used, which has an almost negligible potential drop. This controller can also sustain up to two motors at a time, but in our case, we will only use the pins needed for one, since we control the servo directly from the Raspberry PI.

3.3 Snapshots

The snapshots are made in real time using the Raspberry PI Camera because, apart from offering direct connection, it also offers numerous libraries. One of the disadvantage is that the camera has to be connected via a 15 cm Flex cable, limiting greatly the position of the camera. Also, the camera is very delicate, having little resistance to static electricity; it can be disabled accidentally if handled in excess.

3.4   Final Prototype

For the construction of the vehicle, we have reused the chassis of a Tamiya radio controlled car. This car comes with a built-in servomotor for the front-wheel drive system. This servomotor is not suitable for our needs since it lacks internal circuitry (calculations are performed on the R/C plate of the car), so it has been replaced by an HD-3001HB servo. The Raspberry PI controller has been used, although Arduino has native PWM hardware support for the control of motors and servomotors, the PWM software support is offered by the RPI.GPIO library.

Characteristics and components of the prototype:

- Raspberry Pi 2 Model B +
- Hobby Servo model 3001 BH
- 9.6 V electric motor
- Toshiba TB6612FNG Engine Driver
- Raspberry Pi Camera v2 8 Mpx
- Power Bank Aukey 1000 mh for Raspberry PI
- External battery of 4.8 V for the servo
- External 9.6 V battery for motor

Below is the complete diagram of all the components (Fig. 1):

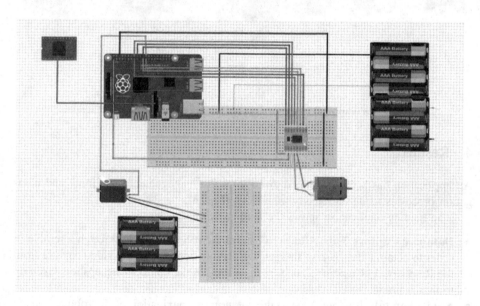

Fig. 1. Diagram of all the connected components to the Raspberry PI 2

3.5   Creation of the Database

We have opted to obtain the database for training by steering the vehicle using a remote control and storing in the memory the snapshots taken at regular intervals which correspond to the direction of the rotation read from the Bluetooth Xbox 360 Controller. A number of random circuits have been constructed with different straight and curved roads trying to obtain enough samples for each of the degrees of rotation established for our servo. Characteristics of stored data:

- **Images**: Input images with 80×60 pixel resolution (minimum resolution supported by the Raspberry Pi camera v2) have been captured, converted to grayscale.
- **Direction of rotation**: Each image is stored next to the degree of rotation of the corresponding servo at the time of capture. They have taken into account a maximum of twenty degrees of rotation for the training. This number can be further reduced to find the optimal number of inputs to the training algorithms.
- **Number of samples**: Considering that the aim is to have a representative number of samples for each of the degrees of rotation (taking into account the number of maximum degrees of rotation), a total of 2000 snapshots have been taken, out of which between 50–70% of them have been retained for training. The rest have been split to create cross-validation sets and tests.

The diagram below represents the process flow (Fig. 2):

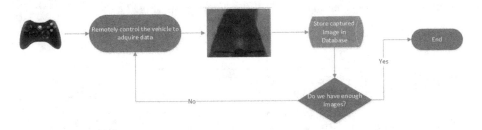

Fig. 2. Workflow of the process of obtaining the database of images

4   Results

An application has been developed that allows the management of training and navigation processes using an already trained set (Fig. 3).

The training application shows the configuration options:

- **Database Capture Tab**: Allows to control the robotic vehicle through a remote in order to obtain a database of images. Displaying continually the video capture from the Raspberry Pi Camera v2, on screen, as well as the number of snapshots taken up to that moment.
- **Navigation tab**: It allows to start the autonomous navigation of the robotic vehicle by means of a classifier previously trained, showing at any moment by screen the video capture coming from the Raspberry Pi Camera v2.
- **Dimensional reduction tab**: Allows to apply different techniques of dimensional reduction on a database for later use in training, monitoring the process through a progress bar and textual messages.

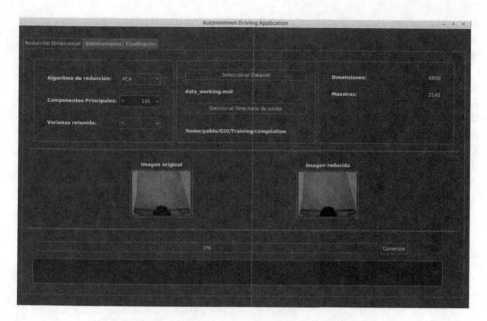

Fig. 3. Autonomous driving application main screen

- **Training tab**: Enables machine learning techniques to be applied in the training of a classifier and its subsequent use in the test or navigation screen.
- **Test tab**: Allows to test a previously trained classifier on the images uploaded by the user, providing information of various kinds.

In order to use the identification or test tabs we must first apply one of the three dimensional reduction techniques (PCA, ICA, LDA) based on the data we just uploaded, selecting the number of the main components that we want to keep in the process. The "Retained Variance" option is only available for use with PCA, allowing us to adjust the number of main components after the reduction based on that criterion.

Several combinations have been tested with the dimensional reduction and training algorithms analyzed in the previous section. The aforementioned database of 2000 manually taken images was used.

This database has been divided using a standard convention:

- 70% of images for training
- 15% of images for cross-validation
- 15% for tests.

Each image is labeled with the corresponding degree of rotation of the servo for that image. A total of 22 degrees of rotation has been chosen, with 0 being the maximum degree of rotation to the left and 21 the maximum degree of rotation to the right.

A dimensional reduction algorithm has been combined with a training algorithm. For each case the operation has been repeated ten times and the mean has been obtained. When reading the percentages of success, it must be taken into account that the output of the training algorithms follows a Gaussian distribution. This means that if the correct output of an image is 10, the most likely results should be approximately in the range [8, 12].

For this reason, success rates can be misleading. It is possible that the learning algorithm has a success rate of only 55% in the test set. Although the failures will be located in the vast majority of cases in the values closer to the Gaussian bell, however, this does not mean that the robot will not follow the path correctly. It is also possible that the database used is not large enough to present a sufficient number of representative samples for each of the possible degrees of rotation of the servo. For this reason the algorithm lacks the necessary information to differentiate between, for example, A 14 and a 15 or between a 4 and a 5.

The following table shows a summary of the results of each of the combinations used (Table 1).

Table 1. Summary of results obtained from the algorithms

Algorithms	Hit rate (%)	Parameters
ANN & PCA	55.7	$K = 135$ $\alpha = 0.01$ $iterations = 500$
ANN & ICA	56.7	$K = 135$ $\alpha = 0.01$ $iterations = 500$
ANN & LDA	90.6	$K = 14$ $\alpha = 5$ $iterations = 5$
SVM & PCA	62.3	$K = 135$ $C = 10000$ $iterations = 1000$ $kernel = rbf$
SVM & ICA	66.3	$K = 135$ $C = 10000$ $iterations = 1000$ $kernel = rbf$
SVM & LDA	98.2	$K = 14$ $C = 1$ $iterations = 100$ $kernel = rbf$
LDA & PCA	65.6	$K = 135$
LDA & ICA	66.7	$K = 135$
LDA & LDA	99.4	$K = 14$

5 Conclusions and Future Work

From the results shown and the tests carried out with the vehicle, we can reach to the conclusion that all the machine learning techniques can successfully equip the vehicle with autonomous navigation by the means of a road in a controlled environment. The best results are obtained through dimensional reduction applied with LDA, obtaining the best results for all learning algorithms (98–99% accuracy). In the group of non-linear learning algorithms, SVM is superior to ANN in all tests performed. From the tests carried out with the vehicle we conclude that a number of degrees of rotation smaller than the one used is sufficient to follow the road correctly, since none of the learning techniques applied had captured information of all the possible degrees.

The results and conclusions obtained, encourage us to work on new improvements in the future. The performance of the machine learning techniques analyzed in this project could be compared with artificial vision techniques and their performance in the problem addressed; edge detection. In the future, we could also include the detection of other elements in the environment, such as signals, vehicles, etc., using sensors and other traditional artificial vision techniques and machine learning techniques such as DNN.

Acknowledgements. This work has been supported by project MOVIURBAN: Máquina social para la gestión sostenible de ciudades inteligentes: movilidad urbana, datos abiertos, sensores móviles. SA070U 16. Project co-financed with Junta Castilla y León, Consejería de Educación and FEDER funds.

The research of Alfonso González-Briones has been co-financed by the European Social Fund (Operational Programme 2014–2020 for Castilla y León, EDU/128/2015 BOCYL).

References

1. Road Safety: new statistics call for fresh efforts to save lives on EU roads (2016). http://europa.eu/rapid/press-release_IP-16-863_en.htm
2. Trick, L.M., Enns, J.T., Mills, J., Vavrik, J.: Paying attention behind the wheel: a framework for studying the role of attention in driving. Theoret. Issues Ergon. Sci. 5(5), 385–424 (2004)
3. Owsley, C., Ball, K., McGwin Jr., G., Sloane, M.E., Roenker, D.L., White, M.F., Overley, E.T.: Visual processing impairment and risk of motor vehicle crash among older adults. JAMA 279(14), 1083–1088 (1998)
4. Choi, E.H.: Crash factors in intersection-related crashes: an on-scene perspective (No. HS-811 366) (2010)
5. Wöhler, C., Anlauf, J.K.: Real-time object recognition on image sequences with the adaptable time delay neural network algorithm—applications for autonomous vehicles. Image Vis. Comput. 19(9), 593–618 (2001)
6. Figueroa, F., Mahajan, A.: A robust navigation system for autonomous vehicles using ultrasonics. Control Eng. Pract. 2(1), 49–59 (1994)
7. Cao, Y., Stuart, D., Ren, W., Meng, Z.: Distributed containment control for multiple autonomous vehicles with double-integrator dynamics: algorithms and experiments. IEEE Trans. Control Syst. Technol. 19(4), 929–938 (2011)

8. Newman, P.M., Leonard, J.J., Rikoski, R.J.: Towards constant-time SLAM on an autonomous underwater vehicle using synthetic aperture sonar. In: Dario, P., Chatila, R. (eds.) Robotics Research, pp. 409–420. Springer, Heidelberg (2005)
9. Subramanian, V., Burks, T.F., Arroyo, A.A.: Development of machine vision and laser radar based autonomous vehicle guidance systems for citrus grove navigation. Comput. Electron. Agric. **53**(2), 130–143 (2006)
10. Sugeno, M.A., Nishida, M.: Fuzzy control of model car. Fuzzy Sets Syst. **16**(2), 103–113 (1985)
11. Pomerleau, D.A.: ALVINN, an autonomous land vehicle in a neural network (No. AIP-77). Carnegie Mellon University, Computer Science Department (1989)
12. Pomerleau, D.A.: Efficient training of artificial neural networks for autonomous navigation. Neural Comput. **3**(1), 88–97 (1991)
13. Srinivasan, D., Choy, M.C., Cheu, R.L.: Neural networks for real-time traffic signal control. IEEE Trans. Intell. Transp. Syst. **7**(3), 261–272 (2006)
14. Foedisch, M., Takeuchi, A.: Adaptive real-time road detection using neural networks. In: 2004 Proceedings of the 7th International IEEE Conference on Intelligent Transportation Systems, pp. 167–172. IEEE, October 2004
15. Shinzato, P.Y., Wolf, D.F.: A road following approach using artificial neural networks combinations. J. Intell. Rob. Syst. **62**(3), 527–546 (2011)
16. Yang, J., Zhang, D., Frangi, A.F., Yang, J.Y.: Two-dimensional PCA: a new approach to appearance-based face representation and recognition. IEEE Trans. Pattern Anal. Mach. Intell. **26**(1), 131–137 (2004)
17. Briones, A.G., Rodríguez, J.M.C., de Paz Santana, J.F.: Sistema de predicción de edad en rostros. Avances en Informática y Automática, 125
18. Yang, J., Yang, J.Y.: Why can LDA be performed in PCA transformed space? Pattern Recogn. **36**(2), 563–566 (2003)
19. CS229 Lecture notes: Independent Components Analysis (2017). http://cs229.stanford.edu/notes/cs229-notes11.pdf. Accessed 16 Mar 2017

A Serious Game to Reduce Consumption in Smart Buildings

Oscar García[2], Pablo Chamoso[1], Javier Prieto[1], Sara Rodríguez[1(✉)],
and Fernando de la Prieta[1]

[1] Computer and Automation Department,
University of Salamanca, Salamanca, Spain
{chamoso,javierp,srg,fer}@usal.es
[2] R+D Department, Nebusens, S.L. Villamayor, Salamanca, Spain
ogargar@gmail.com

Abstract. The research described in this paper presents a social system where intelligent management helps control energy consumption in buildings. In this work we used the CAFCLA framework, which makes it possible to combine various technologies that simplify the creation of context-awareness and social computing systems. The created system is capable of influencing user behavior in a way that favors the efficient management of energy resources in the workplace. This is achieved by merging a number of techniques; Wireless Sensor Networks and Real-Time Locating Systems, along with the use of Collaborative Learning and Virtual Organizations of Agents. These artificial intelligence (AI) techniques provide a great potential for the development of serious games that foster the acquisition of good energy saving habits among workers and users in public buildings.

Keywords: Intelligent systems · Virtual organizations · Distributed systems · Context-awareness · Serious games · Smart cities · Smart buildings · Energy efficiency · Social computing

1 Introduction

The idea of a Smart City is an increasingly common concept nowadays and it is addressed in many technological projects. The balance between the environment and the natural resources is key for these paradigms, their objective being, to reach a level of comfort for citizens and institutions, based on sustainable development. In this respect, achieving better energy efficiency is paramount, not only for the reduction of energy costs, but also to foster environmental and economic sustainability.

Unlike in the past, today many works focus on the measurement of energy consumption in buildings and households, these projects attempt to develop advanced hardware and control systems, these solutions have been proven to be technologically available and sustainable [7]. In this regard, one of the biggest challenges is controlling energy consumption in public spaces and workplaces [28]. However, energy waste in these areas is elevated due to a number of reasons. Old buildings usually lack systems that could aid the efficient use of energy, also it is difficult to model the comfort level of

© Springer International Publishing AG 2017
J. Bajo et al. (Eds.): PAAMS 2017 Workshops, CCIS 722, pp. 481–493, 2017.
DOI: 10.1007/978-3-319-60285-1_41

users because of the disparity of needs among them [29], and another big factor is the users' carelessness with the energy resources, since in public buildings they are not responsible for the energy costs directly. The goal of serious games is to change user behavior through educating users, motivating them and encouraging participation. At present, the creation of an effective serious game is still a challenge, in this work we decide to make use of Context-aware Learning, which provides the environmental characteristics of the place in which the game is taking place, which provides real-time data through Real-Time Locating Systems (RTLS) and Wireless Sensor Networks (WSN) [6].

The work presented in this paper is focused on new ways of triggering behavioral change in users with the aim of improving energy efficiency. Specifically, this paper presents a serious game that aid behavioral change in users in a public building, creating more energy saving habits. The technical and social features of the game are developed by means of the CAFCLA (Context-Aware Framework for Collaborative Learning Applications) framework [26]. A social computing perspective has been adapted for the design of the framework and for this social and contextual information is used. Contextual information is gathered by the WSNs, providing access to data on energy consumption, the presence of users in rooms and the use of electronic devices. Furthermore, the RTLS determines the behavioral habits followed by users and provides guidelines on how to improve these habits in their workplace. A VO (Virtual Organization) supports the framework, providing intelligence to the game and the learning process [33] by managing the process of the game, updating contextual information, monitoring users' actions and providing players with information. The use of these technologies within the paradigm of social computing has generated an innovative game by customizing it for each user and offering the possibility of inter-action among them; working together to achieve a common goal. The article is structured as follows: the background Sect. 2 reviews the current state of the art presented in projects and research conducted in the field of smart cities and energy control. Section 3 describes the created system, its operation and details of the techniques used. Finally, in Sect. 4 results and conclusions drawn from this work are presented.

2 Background

The concept of smart cities, smart buildings, or smart homes [1] itself is still an emerging idea in our society. Building a "smart" city is currently one of the most popular objectives in research, often approached as a strategy of mitigating the problems caused by rapid urban growth. The lack of resources, pollution, traffic congestion and deteriorating infrastructure are some of the many challenges faced by the increasingly large urban communities [10]. One of the many definitions of Smart Cities is: *"The use of smart computing technologies to make city services more intelligent, interconnected and efficient - which includes administration, education, health care, public safety, real estate, transportation and utilities."* [34]. It seems clear that the purpose of these is sustainable economic development, based on new technologies (ICT) to provide better quality of life and wise management of natural resources through the engagement of all citizens. Today, more and more cities around the world, including Spain, are committed to the development of pilot projects related to this movement. Some of the examples in Spain are, SmartSantander[1]: for now the city has a great display of parking sensors that indicate free parking spaces to drivers. They also have a local Wi-Fi network which can be accessed in the entire city, and augmented reality applications that boost tourism. Málaga Smart City[2]: the goal of this projects it to save energy by micro power management: the storage of energy in batteries for use in buildings, street lighting and electrical transport, promoting the use of electric cars, etc. Smart City Valladolid-Palencia[3]: is concerned with the two cities, where the problem of transport between them is considered. It has a smart meter network, which integrates electric cars, energy efficiency in buildings and traffic organization, etc.

In this section we briefly describe the main goals of this project and the techniques that were involved in this research; serious games, WSN, Context-aware Learning and Social Computing. Firstly, we will discuss the necessity of behavioral change as a basis for efficient energy management.

Buildings are responsible for the largest share of European final energy consumption and they present the greatest potential for reducing our energy spending. Buildings are long-term assets expected to remain useful for 50 or even more years and 75–90% of those standing today are expected to remain in use in 2050 [14]. Energy efficiency investments in public buildings are unique in that the public owner can perceive both the energy savings, productivity and value improvements, as well as the public benefits of re-employment rise, reduction of emissions and improvements on public accounts. Recently, various energy policies concerning the efficient use of energy have been implemented [14]. For these initiatives to be effective, many require a direct change in the behavior of users and energy saving habits. In this sense, many studies are inclined to give more importance to changing user habits than to the technical implementation itself [12].

Therefore, it is necessary to model the behavior of users to determine how they do things. The design of models that promote the user behavioral change differs depending on whether it is for domestic or non-domestic users. While home users have a direct responsibility for the energy costs, the policies implemented in the non-domestic sector are made at the organizational level, lacking a direct relationship with the behavior, habits and benefits for users or workers. For this reason, motivating users to save energy in public buildings is a hard task that requires the use of attractive tools which support and assert the acquisition of these habits [14].

Research on energy efficiency has recently produced ast literature on the topic. However, due to the direct relationship between users and their energy expenses at home, most research addresses the domestic area [17]. Among the proposed solutions within households are those based on providing feedback to users on their consumption by using smart meters or displays reporting energy use in real time [2], and some

---

[1] http://www.smartsantander.eu/.

[2] http://www.lacatedralonline.es/innova/system/Document/attachments/12351/original/IDCCiudadesinteligentes.pdf.

[3] http://www.valladolidadelante.es/lang/modulo/?refbol=adelante-futuro&refsec=smart-city-vyp&idarticulo=79302.

proposals extrapolate the solutions used in homes to offices [4]. However, promoting behavioral change in users requires their awareness of the benefits of saving energy, as well as the efficient use of the most frequently used resources, such as MELs (Miscellaneous Electric Loads, including PC, scanners, printers, etc.), which consume more than 25% of energy in offices [5].

Serious games are presented in this work as an alternative technique that has the optimal characteristics which enable it to trigger behavioral change in users for more energy efficient behavior in the public sector and in the working environment. They have been used in different areas to promote this change [1]. Serious games are a broad trend in which traditional mechanisms of games are used in multiple environments such as public policies, business management, healthcare, or energy saving [7]. The objective of these games goes beyond entertainment, paying special attention to the educational purpose, allowing users to acquire skills through play-based activities by using their inherent playfulness and interactive characteristics. They also make it easier to motivate, train and engage participants who improve their habits through the acquisition of new knowledge and skills.

Various approaches to serious games in the energy sector are being piloted or commercially deployed, each adopting differing gamification techniques and having different key objectives. A common factor is their use of granular and real-time energy data, which allows them to provide instantaneous feedback. The use of serious games in office environments is rarely used and are mostly based on making users aware of energy consumption and promoting energy savings.

Despite the multiple solutions and researches that have been analyzed, the use of supporting technologies is not fully. One of the main weaknesses is the underuse of Wireless Sensor Networks when designing and deploying serious games for energy efficiency. Although some technologies, mostly smart meters, are used to obtain power consumption, WSNs offer a great potential of collecting parameters that affect the behavior of users during the game and create richer activities. Thus, the contextual information provided by the sensors becomes a great source of information that helps monitor and customize the game, giving feedback and encouraging awareness among users. Dey in 2001 refers context to "any information that can be used to characterize the situation of an entity" while "an entity is a person, place, or object that is considered relevant to the interaction between a user and an application, including the user and applications themselves" [3]. Context-aware Learning arises from the inclusion of context-awareness in the learning process [32]. Thus, the educational process takes advantage of the flexibility provided by the use of real-time environmental information within the process. Moreover, the use of technologies that obtain contextual information, such as WSNs and RTLSs enriches the learning process [25].

Furthermore, serious games benefit when contextual and location data is included in their design and development, as multiple lines of research have proven [8]. This gives us an idea of the potential that contextual information offers in the design of games, whose objective is that the participants acquire habits which enable them to make use of the energy in a more efficient way. However, many games developed for the encouragement of efficient energy use do not consider the use of sensor networks and real-time location of users to enrich the learning process.

From a novel viewpoint, sensor networks help obtain an accurate "energy picture" of the environment in which the game is played [22]. Likewise, sensors act automatically on the environment once the parameters of user behavior are determined. In addition, the ability to locate users in real time enables the game to launch challenges that promote and enhance both energy saving and the acquisition of good habits. Otherwise, the use of intelligent management techniques is not taken into account in the researches; these techniques improve the game and trigger behavioral change through prediction, adaptation and anticipation of users' actions [11]. Finally, the behavioral change pretended with the solutions mentioned above is not addressed from the point of view of social computing.

Regarding behavioral change for energy efficiency, there are a number of proposals that address the problem by using serious games through social networks [9]. However, human-machine interactions are not deeply addressed in these solutions leaving aside, for example, contextual information that may be useful in the field on which we are focused. In addition, none of the proposals have a complete view as to social computing, they do not offer functional infrastructures that would allow to integrate different technologies, communication protocols or diverse ways of encouraging social relations based on the needs that arise in the game. Our work presents a framework based on social computing and context-awareness that allows the creation of learning scenarios, such as serious games, which encourage a change in users' behavior in public buildings, to actions which are more energy efficient.

Recent trends have led to the social computing paradigm for designing social systems that have helped us build such sociotechnical tools. Thus, it is possible to design tools where humans and machines collaborate to resolve social problems. These tools have a high level of complexity and require the use of artificial intelligence to manage artificial societies, but provide the necessary capacities for effective collaboration between humans and machines [23]. Agent technology, which makes it possible to form dynamic virtual organizations of agents, is particularly well suited to act as a support for the development of these open systems [13, 18, 30]. Modelling an open multi-agent organization makes it possible to describe structural compositions and functional behavior, and it can incorporate normative regulations for controlling agent behavior, the dynamic entry/exit of components and the dynamic formation of agent groups [21].

3 Proposed System

This section describes the proposed system, which aims to deploy a serious game in a public building, encouraging users to use energy resources more efficiently, by changing their behaviors and habits. The system integrates WSNs and RTLSs in order to manage the relations among humans and between humans and material resources. The work depicted here uses the CAFCLA (Context-Aware Framework for Collaborative Learning Activities) [26] framework, designed by the BISITE research group and focused on collaborative learning through the use of contextual information. The aim of CAFCLA is the mixing of several technological resources to simplify the development and design of learning actions based on social computing and contextual information.

The users of CAFCLA have at their disposals numerous which simplify social inter-actions and contextual information. Moreover, this mixing not only makes it easier to design learning activities, but also decreases the development time enabling the game to start faster.

CAFCLA has been used for collaborative learning activities that use contextual information in museums [27], gardens [26] and other educational settings [25]. In the present work, CAFCLA is used in a non-academic environment with a specific pur-pose: to educate, raise awareness and trigger behavioral change for the efficient use of energy in public buildings. To this end, a serious game has been designed and developed, with the aim of making users aware of their energy use so that they naturally acquire good habits and change their actions to those that benefit energy saving. The game developed under CAFCLA has been aimed at the users of the research laboratory to test whether the game succeeded at reducing energy consump-tion and acquiring good energy habits. By means of a WSN the use of lighting is monitored, the energy consumption at the work site of each user (whether they turn off or suspend their computer), their location is also monitored continuously (and even if users use the elevator or the stairs to get into the lab). All these data will help verify whether users meet certain energy efficiency targets and good habits. Depending on their performance, users are either rewarded or penalized with virtual coins.

The game designed using CAFCLA requires the integration of different physical devices and technologies. CAFCLA has been designed as a layer architecture. Each layer includes a set of technologies that fulfil the requirements of the game. These devices and technologies will support data collection, communication, contextualiza-tion of the environment even facilitate the development of the application used by the users.

(1) Physical Layer. At the lowest level of the CAFCLA layers is the physical layer, which includes all devices that will be used by the framework. An important part of this layer is the infrastructure necessary to collect all the contextual information. More specifically temperature on/off, luminosity sensors and consumption sensors are inte-grated into plugs that monitor the power consumption of each job site. Location beacons are also used to obtain the position of users and each of them will wear an identification tag. Tablets, laptops and smartphones have been integrated into CAF-CLA. Through these devices users access and use the game interface. Furthermore, communication between devices requires some physical infrastructure. In this case, Internet access points via Wi-Fi and Ethernet, as well as data collectors and hubs that send, via Internet, the data collected by sensors and the RTLS. In addition, the system requires a server to store data and run the application. All these technologies are integrated by CAFCLA transparently to users, making an appropriate use of each depending on the needs raised by the game at any time of its performance.

(2) Communication Layer. In order to send and receive information between different physical devices, CAFCLA integrates different communication protocols. In this case of use, the framework integrates the following wireless communication protocols: Wi-Fi, ZigBee and 4G/3G/GPRS. On the one hand, Wi-Fi and 4G/3G/GPRS protocols are mostly used to transmit data to players or for the communication between mobile devices. On the other hand, ZigBee is the protocol used by the WSN that transmits the

data from any sensor (including RTLS detection of tags by beacons) to the collectors and hubs that forward it to the server.

(3) Context-awareness Layer. Within the game designed using CAFCLA, contextual information plays a key role. Through this information we find out about energy consumption, which resources are being used and whether this use is being done efficiently is known at all times. This information allows players to better understand the challenges they face and, through incentives generated by the rules, they can make more efficient use of energy resources they have in their work environment. In turn, the behavioral change of players occurs transparently through the acquisition of good energy habits and awareness of not wasting energy unnecessarily. To develop effectively the features explained above, CAFCLA has carried out the integration of a WSN and RTLS platform. This technology allows to know at all times, on the one hand, the physical quantities that permit the system to determine the contextual status of the environment (temperature and luminosity sensors), instant and historical energy consumption of each job site (electricity consumption sensors), the status of lighting and, on the other hand, the location of the participants of the game. Thus, the system is able to determine the number of people in the rooms, use of the elevator or if they are at their work site. The platform selected to deploy the wireless sensor network is n-Core [24], which allows integration of all the sensors used in this case of use. The n-Core platform uses the ZigBee communication protocol (IEEE 802.15.4), which enables communication of the sensors (n-Core Sirius RadIon along with IOn-E devices, shown on Fig. 1) with the other devices of the system in a very simple way: the sensor data are sent through the ZigBee network to data collectors which, in turn, send the information collected by these to the server hosting the database through the Wi-Fi protocol. All the data collected and stored and the states generated are used for the development of the game. The n-Core platform also facilitates the deployment of the indoor location system that allows locate each user in real time. In this case, CAFCLA integrates n-Core Polaris [24], which is also based on the ZigBee wireless communication protocol that allows to determine the position of users up to one meter accuracy. To carry out the location, n-Core requires the deployment of a set of beacons that collect the signal sent by tags (n-Core Sirius Quantum devices, see Fig. 1) that are worn by the players. That signal, and its associated data, is sent to the server that implements the location engine that calculates the position of each player. Players wear a n-Core Sirius Quantum tag responsible for sending that signal and provided with an accelerometer that determines whether the user is moving. The beacons (n-Core Sirius RadIOn devices) forward these data to the server in the same way that the sensor data are sent, through Wi-Fi data collectors. n-Core allows the deployment of the wireless sensor network and the location system using the same platform and physical infrastructure. Thus, the sensors integrated in the ZigBee network can act themselves as beacons for the location system, reducing costs and energy consumption. Furthermore, both systems share data collectors for forwarding data to the server. For the game, the location system can distinguish several areas where players can be found: personal job sites, meeting rooms, elevators and stairs, in order to define the context in which each player is at a given time towards the development of the game. As we can see in Fig. 2, during the design of the game different points that measure temperature and luminosity have

been defined, consumption sensors have been placed at each position, on/off sensors which determine the state of the lighting and HVAC (Heating, ventilation and air conditioning) system have been placed and the different areas where the game is taking place have been defined (two meeting rooms, working area, 2nd and ground floor stairs and 2nd and ground floor lifts).

Fig. 1. n-Core Sirius RadIOn device, n-Core Sirius Quantu, device, n-Core Sirius Ion-E device

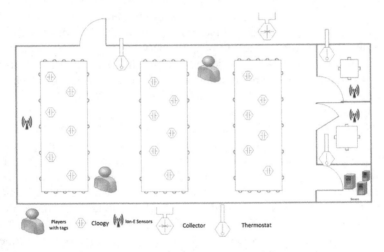

Fig. 2. Distribution of sensors in the laboratory.

(4) <u>Management Layer</u>. This layer integrates the social machine which is in charge of context-awareness and operation of the communication layers in a distributed, effective and predictable way. One of the biggest challenges that the development of Social Computing systems has to face is the communication and coordination between the participating entities, whether human or machine [31]. To address this challenge, current trends recommend the use of Virtual Organizations (VO), that can be defined as a set of individuals and institutions that are needed to coordinate and manage, across institutional boundaries, services and resources [16]. This work considers that a VO is an open system composed of heterogeneous entities that collaborate with each other and whose different forms and functions are required in order to define the behavior of each one. Moreover, VO agents (VOs) technology has facilitated the resolution of challenges related to autonomy, training, collaboration or management of communication between

groups [15] because it allows the creation of dynamic agent organizations, especially useful for the development of the game presented here. Its use favors the description of functional behaviors such as schedules, tasks or services and describe logical structures and interactions, relationships or roles. The main purpose of the management layer is to implement the social machine using VOs. Those VOs will support the context-aware game. The proposed architecture includes different organizations:

- Data Gathering Organization: This organization is responsible of the data that the system has available come from different sources that require a thorough control. The data available to the system come from different sources that require a thorough control. This organization is responsible for managing these heterogeneous sources, such as sensor networks, the location system or even information published or consulted, among others.
- Data Management Organization. This organization is responsible of maintaining the integrity of data during the game. It makes the decision of what data should be developed and stored at all times. The game performance depends on data availability, so this issue is determined during the process. It is related with the Data gathering organization, that gathers new information, and the Game organization that makes the decision of what information has to be stored or requests a concrete data. This VO also classifies the information to be delivered, depending on the context and social information that surrounds the player at a particular time while developing the game.
- Context-aware Organization. This organization manages the information collected by the sensor network. It needs to be coordinated with the Data management organization in order to keep updated the information from any physical service implemented by the sensor network.
- Game Organization. The whole activity is under the control of this organization (management and coordination). All the information from the social machine (players, contextual data, information, etc.) is received and managed by this organization. It finally decides what information is provided to the player according to the stage in which the game is.

Social Machine Organization. This organization is responsible for performing analyses that extract socially relevant information related to the interaction of different agents. Player agents: grouped in organizations, they store all the information related to the game process. This organization enables the player-player interaction and player-machine interaction. Configuration agent: this agent creates, modifies and monitors the development of the game and establishes the social rules of the social machine organization. Collaborative agent: grouped in organizations, this agent monitors the process of the communication with the Context organization and the Activity organization.

- Challenges and Recommendations Organization. This organization produces engaging personalized actions for the players to meet the objectives set in the Activity organization.

(5) Application Layer. The top layer in CAFCLA schema is the application layer. This supports the game development and provides the interface for players and game

organizers, as well as for other components that are part of it, such as the configuration of different devices. To determine the features that this layer may have, as well as for the integration of the necessary technologies, it has been considered a social and serious games approach. Thus, firstly the game is defined and designed using CAFCLA and then technologies that support it are chosen. In this case, a specific game where players will be rewarded or penalized depending on their energy use at work. The scenario in which the game takes place is one of the working laboratories of the BISITE research group in the R&D&I building at the University of Salamanca. This lab has 18 workstations in a common working area and two separate meeting rooms. It is located on the second floor of the building, which can be accessed by a lift or the stairs. Through the various technologies implemented by CAFCLA contextual information of the working environment are controlled at all times, as well as the position of each of the participants. Contextual information is given by the following parameters: temperature and luminosity of each of the zones (working area and meeting rooms), status (on/off) of lighting and measurement of electrical consumption of each work site and the position of each of the people working in the laboratory. All workers are involved in the game (18 in total) whose main objective is to get virtual coins through energy efficient behaviors. To encourage participants, 250 virtual coins permits players to grab a coffee or a soft drink for free. Actions that helped to win or lose virtual coins are as follows:

- The use of light in the meeting room: if one or more users are in the meeting room they should not use artificial light if natural lighting is greater than 200 lx, each of the users gets 10 virtual coins. Otherwise, he/she is penalized.
- The use of the HVAC system in the meeting room: if users do not make use of the HVAC system to change temperature in the room if it is above 18°C in winter or below 25°C in summer, each of them will be rewarded with 10 virtual coins. Otherwise, he/she is penalized.
- Use of the elevator and stairs: every time a player goes up or down the stairs he/she will be rewarded with 10 virtual coins. The use of the lift is penalized.
- If the last user leaving the laboratory turns off lights and HVAC system, he or she receives 10 virtual coins.

Energy consumption: all player whose consumption of electricity during the day is below the average of the previous day, they will receive 10 virtual coins.

A Cloogy[4] power plug was installed at each workstation, a total of 18, to check the progress of energy saving. All sensors were part of the ZigBee network in which real time power consumption data for each position was transmitted. The plug has ZigBee communication capabilities and contains an electrical consumption sensor, with an accuracy of $\pm 1\%$ ± 0.5 W. With intervals of 15 min, consumption data was sent to the server. This data is brought together by a crawler integrated within the agents of the Data Gathering Organization from the web page on which the consumption is published. The players could check their consumption history, as well as their electricity consumption throughout the day, and its 466 comparison to the consumption of other

---

[4] http://www.cloogy.com/media/30958/brochura_cloogy_residential_en.pdf.

users; these acted as an encouraging factor, since the results of others incited competition in energy savings. Moreover, with these data is possible to establish which users were above and below the average consumption each day. It was intended that users were aware, for example, of the times they should turn off or suspend their computers if they were not going to be used for long periods of times.

To encourage a more moderate use of HVCA and lighting systems, four IOn-E devices were deployed along the same wireless sensor network (see Fig. 1). Two of these devices collected data in the shared work environment and one was located in each of the two meeting rooms. Furthermore, users could check the lighting and temperature on demand, they had knowledge of the data collected by these sensors and so could evaluate whether the use of artificial lighting or HVAC systems was necessary or not. The 18 BISITE research group employees in the laboratory participated during 30 days. The data obtained from the desktop monitoring showed that the average total consumption per day of all the users in their workplaces was 2.875 kWh, and the hourly energy consumption per player in his workplace was 0.1597 kWh. These results establish that there has been savings between 6.6% and of 6.9% with respect to the measurements made before the game.

4 Conclusions and Future Work

This paper presents a serious game based on the social computing paradigm that integrates advanced technologies through the framework CAFCLA, including WSN and RTLS. This integration enables to resolve the human-machine interaction and context-awareness issues so that users acquire energy saving habits in public buildings. The use of wireless WSN and RTLS displays a great potential for the development of systems that promote behavioral change in users' energy consumption habits. In this case, players are informed at all times on the energy consumed at their work site. In this way, they are motivated and can interact with others to reduce their energy consumption a, the system will also provide real-time recommendations to users on how they can improve savings and acquire good habits. CAFCLA has added value in comparison to other solutions as the integration of multiple technologies and communication protocols can substantially improve context-awareness, covering a larger number of potential cases of use to be implemented.

Future work includes developing an experimentation stage at the BISITE Research laboratory in order to test the system, observe the changes in the users' behaviors and measure the derived reduction in power consumption, in comparison to other systems.

Acknowledgements. This work was supported by the Spanish Ministry, Ministerio de Economía y Competitividad and FEDER funds. Project. SURF: Intelligent System for integrated and sustainable management of urban fleets TIN2015-65515-C4-3-R.

References

1. Salah, A.A., Lepri, B., Pentland, A.S., Canny, J.: Understanding and changing behavior [Guest editors' introduction]. IEEE Pervasive Comput. **12**(3), 18–20 (2013). doi:10.1109/MPRV.2013.59
2. Ingle, A., Moezzi, M., Lutzenhiser, L., Diamond, R.: Better home energy audit modelling: incorporating inhabitant behaviours. Build. Res. Inf. **42**(4), 409–421 (2014). doi:10.1080/09613218.2014.890776
3. Dey, A.K.: Understanding and using context. Pers. Ubiquit. Comput. **5**(1), 4–7 (2001). doi:10.1007/s007790170019
4. Kamilaris, A., Kalluri, B., Kondepudi, S., Wai, T.K.: A literature survey on measuring energy usage for miscellaneous electric loads in offices and commercial buildings. Renew. Sustain. Energy Rev. **34**, 536–550 (2014). doi:10.1016/j.rser.2014.03.037
5. Kamilaris, A., Neovino, J., Kondepudi, S., Kalluri, B.: A case study on the individual energy use of personal computers in an office setting and assessment of various feedback types toward energy savings. Energy Build. **104**, 73–86 (2015). doi:10.1016/j.enbuild.2015.07.010
6. ACM. Aware automated analysis and annotation of social human–agent interactions. ACM Trans. Interact. Intell. Syst. (TiiS), **5**(2), 1–33 (2015). doi:10.1145/2764921
7. Orland, B., Ram, N., Lang, D., Houser, K., Kling, N., Coccia, M.: Saving energy in an office environment: a serious game intervention. Energy Build. **74**, 43–52 (2014). doi:10.1016/j.enbuild.2014.01.036
8. Lu, C., Chang, M., Huang, E., Ching-Wen, C.: Context-aware mobile role playing game for learning - a case of Canada and Taiwan. J. Educ. Technol. Soc. **17**(2), 101 (2014). ISSN: 11763647
9. Zato, C., de Paz, J.F., de Luis, A., Bajo, J., Corchado, J.M.: Model for assigning roles automatically in egovernment virtual organizations. Expert Syst. Appl. **39**(12), 10389–10401 (2012). doi:10.1016/j.eswa.2012.01.185
10. Chourabi, H., Nam, T., Walker, S., Gil-Garcia, J.R., Mellouli, S., Nahon, K., Pardo, T.A., Scholl, H.J.: Understanding smart cities: an integrative framework. In: 2012 45th Hawaii International Conference on System Sciences, pp. 2289–2297 (2012)
11. Traynor, D., Xie, E., Curran, K.: Context-awareness in ambient intelligence. Int. J. Ambient Comput. Intell. **2**(1), 13–23 (2010). doi:10.4018/978-1-466-0038-6.ch002
12. Shove, E.: Converging conventions of comfort, cleanliness and convenience. J. Consum. Policy **26**(4), 395–418 (2003). doi:10.1023/A:1026362829781
13. Val, E.D., Criado, N., Rebollo, M., Argente, E., Julian, V.: Service-oriented framework for virtual organizations. In: International Conference on Artificial Intelligence (ICAI), vol. 1, pp. 108–114
14. EEFIG. Energy Efficiency – the first fuel for the EU Economy. How to drive new finance for energy efficiency investments. EEFIG Final Report (2015). https://ec.europa.eu/energy/sites/ener/files/documents/Final%20Report%20EEFIG%20v%209.1%2024022015%20clean%20FINAL%20sent.pdf. Accessed 13 June 2016. ISBN: 978-84-606-6087-3
15. Villarrubia, G., De Paz, J.F., Bajo, J., Corchado, J.M.: Ambient agents: embedded agents for remote control and monitoring using the PANGEA platform. Sensors **14**(8), 13955–13979 (2014). doi:10.3390/s140813955
16. Foster, I., Kesselman, C., Tuecke, S.: The anatomy of the grid: enabling scalable virtual organizations. Int. J. High Perform. Comput. Appl. **15**(3), 200–222 (2011). doi:10.1177/109434200101500302

17. Vassileva, I., Campillo, J.: Increasing energy efficiency in low-income households through targeting awareness and behavioral change. Renew. Energy **67**, 59–63 (2014). doi:10.1016/j. renene.2013.11.046
18. De Paz, J.F., Bajo, J., López, V.F., Corchado, J.M.: Intelligent biomedic organizations: an intelligent dynamic architecture for KDD. Inf. Sci. **224**, 49–61 (2013). doi:10.1016/j.ins. 2012.10.031
19. Gómez-Romero, J., Serrano, M.A., Patricio, M.A., García, J., Molina, J.M.: Context-based scene recognition from visual data in smart homes: an information fusion approach. ACM/Springer J. Pers. Ubiquit. Comput. **16**(7), 835–857 (2012). Special Issue on Sensor-driven Computing and Applications for Ambient Intelligence
20. Dermibas, M.: Wireless sensor networks for monitoring of large public buildings. Comput. Netw. **46**, 605–634 (2005)
21. Salas, M.I.P., Martins, E.: Security testing methodology for vulnerabilities detection of XSS in web services and WS-security. Electron. Notes Theoret. Comput. Sci. **302**(25), 133–154 (2014). doi:10.1016/j.entcs.2014.01.024
22. Moreno, M., Úbeda, B., Skarmeta, A., Zamora, M.: How can we tackle energy efficiency in IoT based smart buildings? Sensors **14**(6), 9582–9614 (2014). doi:10.3390/s140609582
23. Shadbolt, N.: Knowledge acquisition and the rise of social machines. Int. J. Hum Comput Stud. **71**(2), 200–205 (2013). doi:10.1016/j.ijhcs.2012.10.008
24. Nebusens. n-Core®: A Faster and Easier Way to Create Wireless Sensor Networks. http:// www.nebusens.com/en/products/n-core. Accessed 18 June 2016
25. García, Ó., Tapia, D.I., Alonso, R.S., Rodríguez, S., Corchado, J.M.: Ambient intelligence and collaborative e-learning: a new definition model. J. Ambient Intell. Humaniz. Comput. **3** (3), 239–247 (2011). doi:10.1007/s12652-011-0050-6
26. García, Ó., Alonso, R.S., Tapia, D.I., Corchado, J.M.: CAFCLA, a framework to design, develop and deploy AmI-based collaborative learning applications. In: Curran, K. (ed.) Recent Advances in Ambient Intelligence and Context-Aware Computing, 1st edn., pp. 187–209. IGI Global, Hersey (2014). doi:10.4018/978-1-4666-7284-0.ch012
27. García, Ó., Alonso, R.S., Guevara, F., Sancho, D., Sánchez, M., Bajo, J.: ARTIZT: applying ambient intelligence to a museum guide scenario. In: Ambient Intelligence-Software and Applications, 2nd International Symposium on Ambient Intelligence (ISAmI 2011), pp. 173–180 (2011). doi:10.1007/978-3-642-19937-0_22
28. Masoso, O.T., Grobler, L.J.: The dark side of occupants' behaviour on building energy use. Energy Build. **42**(2), 173–177 (2010). doi:10.1016/j.enbuild.2009.08.009
29. Shaikh, P.H., Nor, N.B.M., Nallagownden, P., Elamvazuthi, I., Ibrahim, T.A.: Review on optimized control systems for building energy and comfort management of smart sustainable buildings. Renew. Sustain. Energy Rev. **34**, 409–429 (2014). doi:10.1016/j.rser.2014.03.027
30. Heras, S., De la Prieta, F., Julian, V., Rodríguez, S., Botti, V., Bajo, J.: Agreement technologies and their use in cloud computing environments. Prog. Artif. Intell. **1**(4), 277–290 (2012)
31. Rodríguez, S., Julián, V., Bajo, J., Carrascosa, J., Botti, V., Corchado, J.M.: Agent-based virtual organization architecture. Eng. Appl. Artif. Intell. **24**(5), 895–910 (2003). doi:10. 1016/j.engappai.2011.02.003
32. Laine, T.H., Joy, M.S.: Survey on context-aware pervasive learning environments. Int. J. Interact. Mob. Technol. **3**(1), 70–76 (2009). doi:10.3991/ijim.v3i1.680
33. Chou, T.L., Chanlin, L.J.: Location-based learning through augmented reality. J. Educ. Comput. Res. **51**(3), 355–368 (2014). doi:10.2190/EC.51.3.e
34. Washburn, D., Sindhu, U., Balaouras, S., Dines, R.A., Hayes, N., Nelson, L.E.: Helping CIOs understand "Smart City" initiatives. Growth **17** (2009). http://c3328005.r5.cf0. rackcdn.com/73efa931-0fac-4e28-ae77-8e58ebf74aa6.pdf

Author Index

Printed in the United States
By Bookmasters